American Foreign Relations

American Foreign Relations: A New Diplomatic History is a compelling narrative history of American foreign policy from the early settlement of North America to the present. In addition to economic and strategic motives, Walter L. Hixson integrates key cultural factors—including race, gender, and religion—into the story of American foreign policy. He demonstrates how these factors played a vital role in shaping the actions of the United States in world affairs. Beginning with the history of warfare and diplomacy between indigenous peoples and Europeans before the establishment of the United States, this book shows the formative influence of settler colonialism on the country's later foreign policy and the growth of American empire.

Clearly written and comprehensive, the book features:

- Extensive illustrations, with over 100 images and maps
- Primary documents in each chapter, showcasing the perspectives of historical actors
- "Interpreting the Past" features that explore how historians' understanding of events has changed over time
- Selected bibliographies of key resources for further research in each chapter

In one concise volume, *American Foreign Relations* covers the full sweep of American foreign policy from the colonial period to the present day. It is an essential introduction for anyone seeking to understand the history of America's role in the world.

Walter L. Hixson is Distinguished Professor of History at the University of Akron. His previous books include *American Settler Colonialism: A History*, *The Myth of American Diplomacy: National Identity and US Foreign Policy*, and *Parting the Curtain: Propaganda, Culture, and the Cold War, 1945–1961*.

To K. L. H.

American Foreign Relations

A New Diplomatic History

Walter L. Hixson

NEW YORK AND LONDON

First published 2016
by Routledge
711 Third Avenue, New York, NY 10017

and by Routledge
2 Park Square, Milton Park, Abingdon, Oxon OX14 4RN

Routledge is an imprint of the Taylor & Francis Group, an informa business

Library of Congress Cataloging-in-Publication Data
Hixson, Walter L.
   American foreign relations : a new diplomatic history / Walter L. Hixson.
      pages cm
   Includes index.
   1. United States—Foreign relations.   I. Title.
   E183.7.H594 2015
   327.73—dc23
   2015012652

ISBN: 978-0-415-84105-4 (hbk)
ISBN: 978-0-415-84106-1 (pbk)
ISBN: 978-0-203-76668-2 (ebk)

Typeset in Baskerville
by Apex CoVantage, LLC

Printed and bound in the United States of America by
Edwards Brothers Malloy on sustainably sourced paper

Contents

Illustrations

Preface

This text surveys the history of American foreign relations (variously referenced as foreign policy, diplomacy, and world affairs). A couple of features distinguish this textbook from others on the same subject (hence the subtitle, a "new" diplomatic history). An entire chapter (Chapter 1) analyzes the centuries of diplomatic history *prior* to the creation of the United States. The long history of warfare, diplomacy, and settler colonization of land inhabited by indigenous people had both immediate and long-term consequences for American foreign relations, yet diplomacy between and among Euro-Americans and Indians receives relatively little attention in other diplomatic history texts.

Further distinguishing this text from others is the emphasis on cultural factors, especially race, religion, and gender, in explaining the history of American foreign relations. Created and shared in common, culture influences how people perceive and understand history as well as contemporary issues. Racial mores, gender roles, and religious convictions thus influence the way people shape, understand, and respond to foreign policy issues. Perceptions of civilization and savagery, heathenism and godliness, masculinity and weakness, for example, influence the course of history, including diplomatic history. The widespread cultural conviction that the United States was an exceptional nation destined to lead the world also powerfully influenced US foreign policy.

The text does not impose a thoroughgoing cultural interpretation on the reader nor does it obscure more traditional explanatory themes. Cultural factors are integrated into the narrative but economic and strategic motives, perceptions of national interests, realism and idealism, and soft power all remain central to the history of American foreign policy and receive most of the attention in the pages that follow.

Throughout the text certain names, terms, and events, especially those pertaining to foreign countries, appear in **boldface** to underscore their importance. The ability to define and explain the significance of the highlighted terms will help the reader to gain a comprehensive understanding of the history of US foreign policy (thus instructors may wish to employ the terms in student exams). The reader should assume, however, that all US presidents, their advisers, and other key American figures, though not highlighted, are nonetheless essential to understanding US foreign relations.

Each chapter begins with an "Overview," a brief summation of the contents and analytic framework to follow. Each chapter also contains two select primary source documents under the heading "In Their Words" to provide the reader with the perspective of historical actors during the time in question. Given the limited number of these entries, students are strongly encouraged to consult additional primary sources on the history of American diplomacy. An excellent source is the multi-volume *Foreign Relations of the United States*, which can be accessed online (https://history.state.gov/historicaldocuments/about-frus), but there are many other possible primary sources and collections available for consultation.

Each chapter includes a boxed insert called "Interpreting the Past," which analyzes how historians have interpreted particular issues and events and sometimes how those interpretations have changed over time. Students should also consult the Select Bibliography of 15 books, which appears at the end of each chapter (with the exception of Chapter 16) and helps to inform it. By no means a comprehensive list, the bibliographies only hint at the wealth of historical works available on the topics covered in the text. For additional sources and up to date scholarship, a good source is the journal *Diplomatic History* as well as the online review and discussion site H-Diplo (https://networks.h-net.org/h-diplo). Though it may seem an old-fashioned method, a survey of the shelves in the university or public library might also prove fruitful.

Language and terminology present challenges but they also offer insights for students and scholars. I use the term "Indian," actually a misnomer, because "Native American" and other terms are equally problematic. "American" is also problematic, in that all residents of the Western Hemisphere, not only the residents of the United States, can lay claim to be "Americans." Nonetheless, I use the term American synonymously with the United States for the sake of convention and clarity. Periodically throughout the text terms appear inside quotation marks to underscore how words have been used for specific purposes and often to convey power relationships.

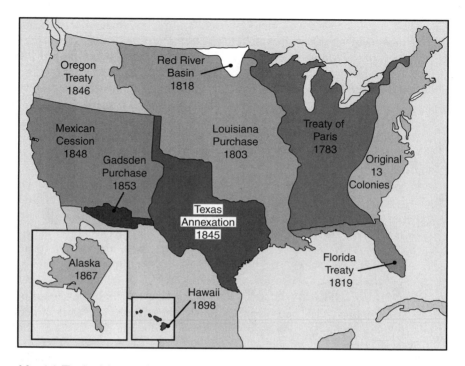

Map 1.1 Territorial expansion of the United States, 1776–1898.

1   The First Foreign Policy

Euro-American Relations with
Indigenous People, 1492–1800

Overview

American foreign policy found its roots in European settler colonization of
the North American continent. A settler-driven "foreign policy" of westward
expansion onto lands inhabited by indigenous people culminated in the American Revolution. Although Indians proved to be willing partners in trade and
diplomacy, they did not relinquish their homelands and hunting grounds without a fight. Often indiscriminate violence on the part of both Indians and settlers thus pervaded the settler colonial era.

Following the American Revolution the United States pursued a diplomatic
strategy of removing Indians by means of formal legal treaties. However, most
of these accords were fraudulent and backed by both settler and regular army
violence. By 1800 settler colonization had established an enduring framework
for an aggressively expansionist American foreign policy.

Settler Colonization

Centuries before anyone had imagined a new country called the United States,
European settlers flocked to North American shores. While economic motives—
the desire for trade and land to build homes, farms, and communities—underlay
colonization, racial and religious perceptions served as justification for the settler expansion. The vast majority of Euro-American settlers viewed traditional
hunting-based, indigenous societies that had lived in North America for thousands of years as inferior to settler society. Categories of racial classification
created distinctions and hierarchies among "races" of people, as opposed to
viewing all of humanity as equivalent regardless of the color of their skin or their
way of life. Colonists often avowed that their settlement of the "New World"
enjoyed Divine sanction, or the blessings of God, while many perceived Indians as "heathen" and "savage" people. Belief in racial superiority thus worked
hand in hand with faith in religious destiny and economic motives to fuel settler
colonization. Masculinity also played a role, as settlers strove to build strong
communities while displaying strength and power over their adversaries. Settlers
often feminized both their indigenous and European rivals as weak and inferior.

Interpreting the Past

The Framework of Settler Colonialism

In recent years scholars have employed a new framework, settler colonialism, to explain the growth and emergence of the British and other colonies, as well as the United States. Settler colonialism refers to a history in which settlers drove indigenous populations from the land in order to construct their own ethnic and religious national communities. Masses of settlers arrived and created new societies, typically emboldened by faith that they were chosen peoples and racially superior to the indigenous population. Settler colonial societies include Argentina, Australia, Brazil, Canada, Israel, New Zealand, South Africa, and the United States.

Under settler colonialism the migrants typically pushed indigenous populations beyond an ever-expanding frontier of settlement. Settlers thus presented indigenous people with "facts on the ground." When they encountered resistance from the indigenous population, settlers engaged in violence including massacres to achieve their aim of taking control of new lands. Settlers wished less to exploit the indigenous population for economic gain or to govern them (as under conventional colonialism), but rather to remove them entirely from the land. Settler colonies created their very identities by forcing indigenous people from the land while at the same time resisting the authority of the "mother" country. Few countries offer a better example of this historical process than the United States.

European settlement created an entirely new world for indigenous peoples as well as for Europeans. For the Indians the encounter brought new technologies and desirable trade goods but at the same time introduced disease, disruption, enslavement, indiscriminate killing, and loss of ancestral homelands. The indigenous way of life rooted in reciprocal relations with the natural, spiritual, and human worlds had been irrevocably changed by the encounter. Whereas Indians viewed nature as there to be exploited in balance, establishing community or moving from place to place as needed for fishing, hunting, planting, and gathering, Europeans established boundaries and sought to *possess* geographic spaces.

The changes brought by the Europeans were not, however, simply imposed on Indians, who often recognized what was happening, adapted, and seized the opportunities available to them. The Europeans brought a burgeoning global marketplace with them, giving rise to the fur, deerskin, and other trade markets. Indians wanted and often needed to access the new technologies and trade goods introduced by Europeans, especially guns and ammunition, but also tools, metals, cloth, and alcohol. They took part in the market-driven economy, contributing to extremes and imbalances if the market so demanded in order to get the things they needed or desired. For example, Indians willingly participated in the fur trade, which spurred near extermination of the beaver for the making of felt hats to sell in Europe and global markets.

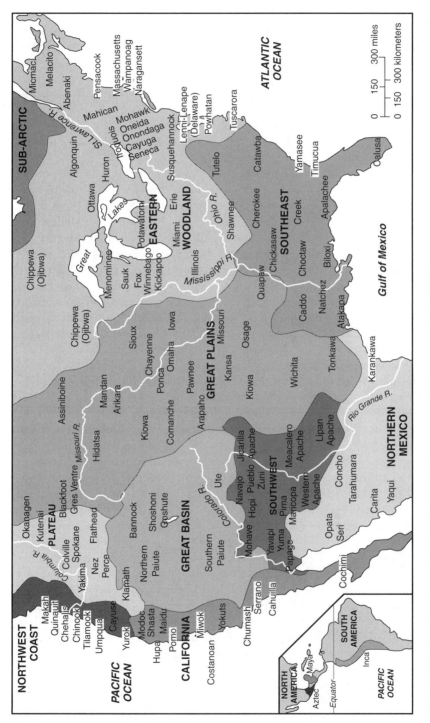

Map 1.2 The first Americans: location of major Indian groups and culture areas in the 1600s.

From tenuous beginnings (merely surviving the trans-Atlantic voyage and then finding food to eat were challenge enough), over time the Euro-American newcomers forged viable economies and communities. They often achieved these goals with the cooperation of indigenous people, who exploited the presence of the Europeans for their own economic needs and security ends. Indigenous North Americans defied the stereotype that lumped them all together as "Indians." In actuality they lived in distinct bands or tribes while viewing other natives as separate and often rival peoples. Most indigenous bands had powerful chieftainships and warrior cultures and had engaged in trade and warfare for centuries before the Europeans arrived.

Indian interactions with Europeans varied widely depending on the peoples involved, the time, and the place. England (Great Britain after 1707) became the dominant settler colonial society but other Europeans, notably France and Spain, had long and consequential histories of interactions with indigenous people. Spain, which had taken the lead in the "discovery" of the Americas by securing the services of the Italian sailor Christopher Columbus in 1492, sought riches for the Crown and the expansion of Christendom. Conditioned by centuries of conflict with "infidels" on the Iberian Peninsula, the Spanish viewed Indians as heathens and conducted several brutal campaigns of plunder and destruction against them. Over time Spain focused its North American colonizing efforts around the *presidio*, or fortress, and the mission, wherein priests sought with only limited success to convert indigenous people to Catholicism.

While the Spanish *presidio* and mission spread across the South and Southwest, from Florida to California, the French migrated from a base in modern-day Quebec down through the Great Lakes and into the Mississippi Valley. Whereas the British colonies—the future United States—drove Indians off the land to make way for settlers, the "interior French" lived among the Indians. The French traded and conducted diplomacy with Indians. French men often intermarried with indigenous women. Intermarriage, trade, and diplomacy allowed for long periods of peaceful relations between Europeans and Indians. Over time, as Frenchmen as well as Spaniards had children with Indian women, communities of mixed ethnicity evolved across North America in defiance of rigid racial classifications.

British Settler Colonialism

Much more inclined than the French and the Spanish to bring their wives and families overseas, the British became the dominant settler society of North America. With less intermarriage, the British were more inclined to adopt racial classifications and hierarchies and to view Indians as "other" and lesser people. Beginning in the sixteenth century the Protestant Reformation distinguished the British colonies from Catholic France and Spain. Thus the family, private property, Protestantism, and legal structures anchored British settlement in North America, as in other British colonies.

The English and other European settlers conducted a robust trade and entered into diplomatic alliances with the eastern Indian tribes. Some of the colonists sought to convert and "save" the heathen Indians. Over time, however, as endless streams of settlers flocked across the sea in search of land and opportunity, British settlers drove Indians from their ancestral homelands to make way for farms and communities. Encroachment on Indian land accelerated as the balance of numbers tilted in favor of the colonists. Racial classifications, the promotion of civilization over savagery, and faith in providential destiny served to justify English colonization and Indian removal.

From the outset of English colonization in Virginia, beginning with the Jamestown settlement in 1607, conflict erupted between settlers and Indians. Violence was nothing new to Indians but the scope and intensity of the colonial violence was unprecedented. Both the English and the indigenous Powhatan confederacy embarked on wars of extermination. Ultimately the continuing waves of settlers, who created a viable economy rooted in the cultivation of tobacco, enabled the Virginians to prevail.

Later in the century, **Bacon's Rebellion** (1676) showed that Virginia settlers would take land from Indians regardless of whether they had approval from the Crown or local authorities. Upon their arrival later in the seventeenth century, newcomers like Nathaniel Bacon, son of a well-heeled English family, found that the prime agricultural land had already been taken. At the same time Virginia and Crown authorities sought to control settlement on the colony's western frontier. Bacon and his followers, some elites and others a hardened lot of former indentured servants, rejected limitations on settlement of land held by Indians, whom Bacon described with such terms as "delinquents" and "barbarous outlaws." The settlers defied the governor and seized control of Indian lands through military aggression to make way for new settlements. Bacon's Rebellion against Crown authority enflamed Virginia, culminating in the burning of Jamestown before being subdued (Bacon died during the conflict, probably from dysentery).

As in the Chesapeake region, New England settlers carried on trade and alliances with Indians but ultimately the dominant foreign policy was to remove them from the land. In 1637 the righteousness of the Puritan settlers in Massachusetts prompted them to launch a holy war against the Pequot Indians. Viewing themselves as providentially destined and the Pequot as the devil's minions, the Puritans carried out an exterminatory campaign, killing men, women, and children and razing entire villages. In a struggle pitting the forces of good against satanic evil, no amount of indiscriminate killing would be considered too great. "Sometimes the scripture declareth that women and children must perish with their parents," Captain John Underhill explained. "We had sufficient light from the Word of God for our proceedings."

As would occur throughout the long history of North American Indian removal, other tribes, in this case the Massachusetts and Narragansett, allied with the settlers against the Pequot, their traditional indigenous rivals. Even as they endeavored to wipe out the Pequot the Puritans conducted trade as well as alliances with Indians. They also created "praying towns" in which they strove to convert them to Christianity. However, as settlers continued to arrive in waves the demands for Indian land proved paramount.

PHILLIP alias METACOMET of Pokanoket.
Engraved from the original as Published by Church.

Figure 1.1 Metacomet ("King Philip"), chief of the Wampanoag.

Source: Library of Congress, Prints and Photographs Division, LC-USZ62-96234.

In 1675 the so-called **King Philip's War** erupted over settler encroachments, erosion of the Indian way of life, and unequal treatment of Indians (including capital punishment) under the English justice system. Joined by the powerful Narragansett and other tribes, the Wampanoag under the *sachem* (chief) Metacomet, also known as King Philip, led the resistance in what the New Englanders at the time called the Narragansett War. Metacomet explained that the Europeans were overrunning fields and hunting grounds, breaking agreements, killing Indians, and seeking to "drive us and our children from the graves of our fathers . . . and enslave our women and children." Now the spirits of those ancestors "cry out to us for revenge."

In Their Words

"Edward Randolph's Report on King Philip's War, 1675"

Various are the reports and conjectures of the causes of the present Indian warre. Some impute it to an imprudent zeal in the magistrates of Boston to christianize those heathen before they were civilized and enjoining them the strict observation of their laws . . . The people, on the other side, for lucre and gain, entice and provoke the Indians to the breach thereof, especially to drunkenness, to which those people are so generally addicted that they will strip themselves to their skin to have their fill of rum and brandy . . .

Some believe there have been vagrant and jesuitical priests, who have made it their business, for some years past, to . . . exasperate the Indians against the English and to bring them into a confederacy, and that they were promised supplies from France and other parts to extirpate the English nation out of the continent of America . . .

But the government of the Massachusetts . . . [has] contributed much to their misfortunes, for they first taught the Indians the use of arms, and admitted them to be present at all their musters and trainings, and shewed them how to handle, mend and fix their muskets, and have been furnished with all sorts of arms by permission of the government.

A vicious war ensued in which both sides engaged in indiscriminate slaughter and mutilation of the dead. The settlers adapted to the North American "frontier" by adopting the Indian style of irregular warfare, previously viewed as savage and dishonorable, as they now attacked by surprise, carried out hit and run assaults, and offered bounties for Indian scalps. Indiscriminate warfare, ranging, and scalp hunting became integral to the long history of North American settler colonialism. Race, religion, and gender fueled the conflict, as the settlers believed they were a superior race destined to inherit the land. Both "white" and "red" men depicted the war as a struggle for one group of men to gain mastery over the other, thus reinforcing masculinity.

New England communities mobilized—men, women, and children—in the campaign against the "savages." Warfare reinforced masculinity while at the same time altering women's roles as the New England settlers fought for their lives. Both Indians and settler males referred to warfare as a quest to determine which one would "master" the other, hence what was at stake was their very manhood. In the struggle for survival, New England women assumed unprecedented direct as well as supporting roles in the traditionally male realm of warfare. The settlers ultimately prevailed in King Philip's War but not before hundreds of people had died and many towns were destroyed. Many New Englanders now viewed all Indians as a "brutish enemy" that should justifiably be driven from the land if not exterminated.

King Philip's War devastated the indigenous tribes of southern New England. Metacomet, described as a "great, naked, dirty beast," was hunted down, executed, his body drawn and quartered, and his severed head hung from a pole for decades. His child and wife were sold into slavery along with scores of other Indians.

Indian Slavery

Beginning in the sixteenth century, indigenous people assumed a key role in the evolution of the **Indian slave trade**, which is often overshadowed by the better-known history of African slavery. The trade in captive Indians was widespread and destroyed many tribes while giving rise to other new and powerful confederations. Indians carried out slaving raids and warfare against other indigenous bands as part of the European-introduced market system. Slaves were captured and traded to Europeans, who exploited them for labor and sex. In return Indians procured European products, especially firearms and gunpowder but also tools, metals, cloth, and alcohol. As the slave trade spread from the Southeast across the continent, many tribes faced a stark choice: either to play an active role in the slave trade or to become slaves themselves.

Indian slavery combined with the spread of European diseases crippled many indigenous communities and left them vulnerable to being overrun by the ever-increasing number of settlers. Millions of Indians died from diseases such as smallpox, cholera, and measles to which they had acquired no immunity. Europeans often interpreted the large number of Indians dying from disease as evidence of God's plan to have them displace the native peoples, increasingly viewed as a "dying race."

In the early eighteenth century the Indian slave trade came to an end. The Carolina colony, founded in 1670, had been at the epicenter of the Indian slave trade, but the practice died out after the Yamassee War (1715–17), which had been destructive for the Carolinians as well as Indians. South Carolina remained the center of slavery, but from this point forward the North American settler colonial economy became increasingly dependent on Africans and Afro-Caribbean peoples rather than Indians for servile labor.

The wars of Indian slavery had destroyed many Indian peoples yet new Indian confederacies emerged—the Cherokee, Choctaw, Creeks, and Iroquois among them—and would remain powerful players in North American warfare and diplomacy for more than a century. With the end of the Indian slave trade a period of relative peace and cooperative trade prevailed between

Euro-Americans and indigenous people. Rather than trafficking in human beings Indians exchanged furs and deerskins for European trade products.

Diplomacy Between Indians and Europeans

Indians and Europeans engaged in diplomacy to facilitate trade and in an effort to keep the peace. Relations were often strained over settler expansion and other issues, yet intermediaries labored to forge understanding and head off outbreaks of violence. Some of the intermediaries or go-betweens were persons of mixed parentage who knew Indian as well as European languages and cultural practices. Such knowledge was crucial because Indians and Euro-Americans approached diplomacy in sharply different ways.

Among the many differences in their approaches to diplomacy Europeans emphasized written treaties and the authority of law. For Euro-Americans the primary goals of diplomacy were to gain control of land for speculators and settlers and to secure alliances in time of war. Indians viewed diplomacy more broadly, as a means to establish mutual respect and kinship ties that would enable relations to go forward. Indians thus emphasized the process and rituals of diplomacy whereas the Euro-Americans emphasized the outcome of negotiations. Indians, with their cultures rooted in oral traditions rather than writing, often were not fully aware of the terms and significance of the written accords. Symbols and gestures meant more to them than words. Mutual smoking of the *calumet*, for example, which took the newly formed kinship ties and understandings to the spirits in the sky by means of the smoke, was highly significant to Indians, but sometimes considered a waste of time by Europeans.

While Euro-Americans were often anxious to come to terms, Indians typically were in no hurry to conclude an accord. Euro-Americans considered the negotiations to be over once a treaty had been signed whereas to Indians the signatures might appear as merely a ritual valued by the other side, but not something to bring an end to the negotiations as a whole. Often tired and hungry by the time they arrived at the council fires, Indians preferred to eat, drink, and get acquainted for a few days rather than rush into an accord. Gift giving was a crucial component of Indian diplomacy. Indians frequently demanded gifts as a precondition for negotiations and often based their judgment of the Euro-Americans on the quality and extent of their gift giving. The Euro-Americans learned to capitalize on Indian fatigue, hunger, and desire for alcohol, as well as the allure of guns, ammunition, and trade goods, to secure the kind of agreements they wanted.

Although double-dealing and misunderstanding frequently undermined relations, Indians as well as Euro-Americans often secured alliances, material gains, political leverage, and advantage against their enemies through diplomacy. On several occasions Europeans escorted Indian chieftains to Europe, where they were treated with respect by royal courts. Trade and diplomacy enabled relatively peaceful relations between Europeans and Indians until the continuing settler influx steadily undermined Indian landholding. Indigenous people were willing to try negotiations but when talks failed they were also willing to take up the hatchet to preserve their homelands.

Figure 1.2 "The Captivity of Mrs. Rowlandson."
Source: Library of Congress, Prints and Photographs Division, LC-USZ62-113682.

Violent Indian resistance traumatized settlers, inflamed public opinion, and led to campaigns of dispossession backed by indiscriminate violence. The colonial press routinely referenced Indian resistance as "murder" and "massacre" perpetrated by "barbarians" and "savages" against innocent "white" men, women, and children. Graphic narratives recounted Indian captivity, torture, scalping, and mutilation of settler victims. In a famous account the settler Mary Rowlandson described an attack on her home in 1675 by the "bloody heathen" who killed men, women, and children, including shooting to death the baby she held in her arms before taking her captive. Her account circulated throughout the colonies reinforcing notions of helpless women and maidens confronting violent assaults on their families including the specter of sexual assault, the proverbial "fate worse than death" at the hands of the savages. These **captivity narratives** obscured that to Indians taking captives was a normal accompaniment to warfare. Indians took captives to adopt and replace those who had died of disease or warfare, thus to "cover the dead." Indians also exchanged captives through diplomacy to facilitate bringing an end to conflict.

Settlers homed in on Indian violence, invariably affixed with the label of savagery, which overshadowed a long history of trade, diplomacy, and accommodation. Children learned "to hate an Indian, because he always hears him spoken of as an enemy," explained the settler James Hall. "From the cradle, he listens continually to horrid tales of savage violence, and becomes familiar with narratives of aboriginal cunning and ferocity." Another settler avowed, "The tortures which they exercise on the bodies of their prisoners justify extermination."

As the explosive growth of settler colonialism shifted the balance of power from the indigenous people to the settlers, the pace of Indian removal accelerated. By mid-century the non-Indian population was 1.2 million, quadruple the number on the continent in 1700. The colonizers pursued dispossession by treaty, by force, or simply by settlers squatting on the land, which they quickly dotted with cabins, farms, and communities. Even when colonial officials strove to rein in settlement, squatters and speculators showed contempt for their directives and disregard for Indian claims to the land. Some of the European migrants, notably the Scots-Irish, brought entrenched traditions of conflict and resistance to British authority to the colonies. Landing predominantly on the southeast coast they migrated into the interior and would allow neither Indians nor colonial authorities to impede their squatting and land seizures.

The rapidly growing settler population encroached on Indian land, confronting the indigenous people with a choice of violent resistance or retreat. Many Indians began to see that the only chance for the survival of their way of life lay in exploiting the rivalries among the European powers as they fought for control of the continent. Indians recognized that their military prowess and intimate knowledge of the land could prove pivotal as the Europeans battled for supremacy in North American colonization.

The Great War for Empire

By 1700 the British had established profitable colonies along the eastern seaboard but still had to contend with France and Spain for power in North America. As the European rivalries heated up, Indians took part in the conflict to enhance their access to European goods and trade, to undermine their own indigenous rivals, display their manhood, and, above all, to attempt to preserve their lands. A series of imperial wars pitted the English, allied with the powerful Iroquois Confederation based in the Finger Lakes region of New York, against the French and their Indian allies on the Midwest borderlands. After a series of off and on conflicts from the late 1600s to mid-century, the **French and Indian War** (1754–63) proved decisive.

Indians, as the name of the war suggests, played a crucial role in the power struggle between the British and the French in North America. The war broke out in the Pennsylvania woodlands, expanded throughout North America and the Caribbean, and coincided with the Seven Years War (1756–63) in Europe. Control of the Ohio Valley and the American West was the ultimate prize of the "Great War for Empire," as the French and Indian War has been called. Europeans knew little about the Far West of the continent, but presumed there might be an uninterrupted water route to the Pacific as well as untold riches, including perhaps great deposits of gold and silver. British, French, and Spanish officials feared that if one took control of this vast area, the others would suffer the consequences. None of the European powers accorded legitimacy to any "aboriginal" claim of the vast western lands.

In the early stages of the French and Indian War the British suffered a series of devastating defeats, as they badly underestimated indigenous warriors and failed to adapt military strategy and tactics to the frontier environment. The imperious British commander, General Edward Braddock, summarily dismissed an offer

DEFEAT OF GENERAL BRADDOCK, IN THE FRENCH AND INDIAN WAR, IN VIRGINIA, IN 1755.

Figure 1.3 In July 1755 indigenous Americans allied with the French carried out a devastating surprise attack east of modern-day Pittsburgh, Pennsylvania. The attackers routed British forces, killed General Edward Braddock, and ignited the French and Indian War.

Source: Library of Congress, Prints and Photographs Division, LC-USZ62-1473.

of alliance from the Delaware Indians, who sought to preserve their lands in return. "No savage shall inherit the land," Braddock contemptuously declared before marching his Red Coats in traditional style toward the confluence of rivers where the French were fortifying a new outpost, Fort Duquesne.

On July 9, 1755, the French and their Indian allies attacked by surprise and routed Braddock's approaching army, killing him and more than 450 troops and support personnel in the **Battle of the Monongahela**. French and Indian losses were minimal by comparison. With the war now raging, the Delaware, Mingo, Ottawa, Potawatomi, Shawnee, and other tribes attacked across the Pennsylvania backcountry, killing settlers indiscriminately and driving them from the land.

In August 1757, after the outnumbered British accepted a French offer of surrender at Lake George, New York, Indians allied with the French carried out the **Fort William Henry Massacre** of 185 men and women. The tribes also took some 300–500 captives. The massacre as well as the captive taking violated the terms the French had promised to the British. In response to the Fort William Henry Massacre the British colonies offered scalp bounties enabling the indiscriminate killing of Indians. To the tribes, killing and taking trophies and captives was their just reward for the crucial help they provided to the French, evidence of their accomplishments as warriors and men, and essential to the survival of many bands, whose numbers had been ravaged by disease.

The colonists would long remember the Indian assaults, and would later avenge them, but the British also belatedly realized the importance of securing

MONTCALM TRYING TO STOP THE MASSACRE.

Figure 1.4 General Montcalm tries unsuccessfully to restrain his Indians allies as they attack British captives who had peacefully surrendered to the French commander in 1757. The massacre at Fort William Henry outraged British-American colonists, who proceeded to carry out massacres of their own.

Source: Library of Congress, Prints and Photographs Division, LC-USZ62-120704.

Indian allies against their European rivals. Future American rebels Benjamin Franklin and George Washington (who had narrowly survived Braddock's folly) advised the British that Indians were masters of irregular warfare and could provide crucial battlefield intelligence as well. In 1758, following tense negotiations, the British, the settlers, and representatives of 13 tribes came to terms in the **Treaty of Easton**. In return for allying against the French, the Indians won concessions on hunting grounds and a British promise to halt settlement onto Indian lands west of the Appalachians. The treaty held that the Indian lands "shall remain your absolute property."

The alliance with the Indians and the leadership of William Pitt ultimately paved the way to a British victory in the French and Indian War. At the **Treaty of Paris** in 1763 the French, now utterly defeated, surrendered their claim to North America. The Indians had cooperated in the war in the expectation that in return the British would reward them with trade and gifts and keep their promise to respect indigenous lands and access to hunting grounds. The tribes of the Great Lakes region were accustomed to trade, gift exchange, and cultural interaction with the French, but now found the British less giving and less respectful of them. During the course of the war the British had erected a chain of forts in the Upper Great Lakes region and thus felt secure enough to cut off trade with the Indians in weapons and powder, further alienating the tribes.

Although some middlemen, colonial elites, and British officials understood the need for diplomacy, British Indian policy was inconsistent and fragmented between the various colonies. Many settlers and squatters nurtured racial hatred of Indians and had no intention of respecting their claims to the land. Fraudulent land deals, alcohol peddling, violence, and sexual assault against Indian women were common events. Moreover, the new British commander, **Jeffrey Amherst**, expressed contempt for Indians and little respect for land claims, diplomacy, trade, and the giving of gifts to savages. He believed instead that Indians needed to be "convinced of our superiority."

With the defeat of the French, indigenous people no longer had two great powers to play off against one another through diplomacy. Instead they confronted a teeming settler colonial society that viewed them as inferior and with no legitimate claim to the land that they had lived and hunted upon for centuries. Once again, however, the British dramatically underestimated the tribes, which now put aside their own differences to take up the hatchet against the settlers, speculators, and British regulars. Amherst declared Indians lacked the "capacity of attempting anything serious" and if they tried he meant to "punish the delinquents with entire destruction, which I am firmly resolved on whenever any of them give me cause."

In the spring of 1763 the tribes proved Amherst wrong, as the Chippewa, Delaware, Huron, Ottawa, Seneca, and Shawnee led by a warrior named Pontiac assaulted forts and settlements throughout the borderlands, killing indiscriminately and sending the Redcoats and settlers into a panicked retreat. Dubbed **Pontiac's Rebellion**, the uprising stunned the British high command and prompted Amherst to authorize biological warfare in the form of sending blankets infected with smallpox into Indian country. He called openly for an unlimited war to "extirpate this execrable race . . . I wish to hear of no prisoners."

The Indians were too numerous, united, and adept at borderland warfare to be defeated much less wiped out, hence the British recalled Amherst and turned once again to diplomacy with the tribes. In so doing they unwittingly set the stage for the American Revolution and the loss of all they had gained in the French and Indian War. The Crown issued the **Royal Proclamation of 1763**, drawing a line prohibiting trans-Appalachian land grants or purchases and requiring a permit for colonists who wished to conduct trade on the western side of the mountains. Moreover, the Proclamation outlawed private sales by Indians to settlers or speculators, decreeing that only the Crown was authorized to make land purchases.

Indebted as a result of the all out war effort against the French, and chastened by Pontiac's uprising, the British sought to regulate western expansion to avoid Indian conflict as they recovered from the war. Economic recovery required new revenue streams, to which the British asked the colonials to contribute by paying a series of newly decreed duties and taxes. The colonists resisted the taxes while speculators and settlers defied the Proclamation Line. Their resistance ultimately culminated in a full-blown colonial rebellion and the **American Revolution**.

As the rebellion unfolded in the 1760s settlers continued to stream into the western and southern borderlands in defiance of British authority. Many of these settlers had lost family and friends to Indian raids and otherwise displayed racial contempt for people they considered heathen savages who were unfit to hold the land. More and more the settlers identified themselves as "white" people destined to inhabit the spaces claimed by an inferior race. Ironically, at this same time many Indians, inspired by the Delaware prophet Neolin, began to see themselves no longer as separate tribes but as a united "red" people. Neolin and other Indian leaders called for resistance not only against seizures of Indian land but also against adoption of the white man's way of life.

Settlers often made little distinction between Indians and many called for driving out or killing any and all of them. As the English trader, go between, and land speculator George Croghan observed, settlers "thought it a meritorious act to kill Heathens whenever they were found." In late 1763 and early 1764, a Pennsylvania mob known as the Paxton Boys determined to exterminate a "nest of perfidious enemies," seized 14 Indians from protective custody in Lancaster, and killed and mutilated them. Declaring that all Indians were "enemies, rebels, and traitors," the Pennsylvania governor made the colony a free fire zone, thereby authorizing settlers "to embrace all opportunities of pursuing, taking, killing, or destroying" Indians. The practice of offering bounties to scalp hunters whose targets included Indian women and children proliferated.

The momentum of violent Indian removal and resistance to British authority came from the bottom up and from the top down—from common people as well as colonial elites. As the balance of forces continued to shift in favor of the Euro-Americans, diplomacy and trade took a backseat to Indian removal. Land speculators joined the settlers in advocating the removal of Indians and defiance of British decrees limiting expansion. Future leaders of the American Revolution—Patrick Henry, Thomas Jefferson, and George Washington among them—were deeply involved in land speculation.

In addition to the elite land speculators more than 50,000 settlers lived on the trans-Appalachian borderlands on the eve of the American Revolution, beyond the reach of colonial authorities. British officials described these settlers and squatters as "low" and "the very dregs of the people." They acknowledged, however, that they were "too numerous, too lawless and licentious ever to be restrained."

Desperate to maintain their control of the land and of their North American colonies, the British turned to their longtime Indian allies, the Six Nations of the **Iroquois Confederation**. The Iroquois had a long tradition, rooted in the competition for control of the fur trade, of mounting attacks on other tribes living beyond their base in New York. The Iroquois also proved amenable to entering into a cynical diplomatic agreement at the expense of other Indians. In 1768 the Iroquois received silver and trade goods in return for signing off on the **Treaty of Fort Stanwix**. The treaty opened new lands to settlers and speculators in the Ohio country and in Kentucky. It was one of the more corrupt in a long history of fraudulent Indian treaties. Under this treaty the Iroquois sold thousands of acres of land far from their homes and long used by other tribes.

In Their Words

The Mingo Indian leader Logan made this statement, known as "Logan's Lament,"
in the wake of Dunmore's War in the Ohio Country in 1774

I appeal to any white man to say, if ever he entered Logan's cabin hungry, and he gave him not meat; if ever he came cold and naked, and he clothed him not. During the course of the last long and bloody war, Logan remained idle in his cabin, an advocate for peace. Such was my love for the whites, that my countrymen pointed as they passed, and said, Logan is the friend of white men. I had even thought to have lived with you, but for the injuries of one man. Col. Cresap, the last spring, in cold blood, and unprovoked, murdered all the relations of Logan, not sparing even my women and children. There runs not a drop of my blood in the veins of any living creature. This called on me for revenge. I have sought it: I have killed many: I have fully glutted my vengeance. For my country, I rejoice at the beams of peace. But do not harbour a thought that mine is the joy of fear. Logan never felt fear. He will not turn on his heel to save his life. Who is there to mourn for Logan? Not one.

The fraudulent treaty intensified the conflict between settlers backed by speculators and Indians, leading to open warfare in the Ohio Valley. As the governor of Virginia overturned royal decrees against speculation in Indian lands, the Shawnee and other tribes mounted a violent resistance. More and more settlers killed Indians regardless of whether they were hostile. In an incident in 1774, drunken settlers killed several Indians including the pregnant sister of the Mingo chief Logan, who prior to this had advocated tolerance and accommodation between Indians and settlers. Bound to seek blood revenge in the time honored Indian tradition, Logan killed a like number of settlers and then called for a return to toleration. The Virginia settlers and speculators, however, seized the opportunity to destroy entire Indian towns and villages to facilitate the seizure and sale of their lands.

Indians and the American Revolution

The emphasis on "taxation without representation" as the cause of the American Revolution often obscures the extent to which an expansionist foreign policy against Indian peoples fueled the revolt. Determined to claim and settle western lands, the American revolutionaries would not be deterred by British colonial policies or Indian resistance. North American Indians played a major role in the **Revolutionary War** (1775–83) as they fought and entered into alliances to preserve their homelands and cultures. While most histories of the Revolutionary War focus on relations with Europe and the politics and warfare along the Atlantic seaboard, the western borderlands were the scene of intense fighting between settlers, soldiers, and Indians.

British efforts to limit and control western expansion, as well as the Crown's alliances with the Iroquois and other tribes, angered the newly proclaimed Americans. The **Declaration of Independence** (1776) excoriated King George III for unleashing "on the inhabitants of our frontiers, the merciless Indian savages, whose known rule of warfare is undistinguished destruction of all ages, sexes, and conditions." By blaming the British for inciting Indians on their "frontier," Americans depicted Indians as mercenaries rather than people fighting to preserve their homelands and way of life. The phrase "merciless Indian savages," however, accurately reflected widely held racial stereotypes of indigenous people.

Hardly an ignorant savage, the Mohawk Indian **Joseph Brant** (Thayenda-negea) was a multi-lingual graduate of the future Dartmouth College, a member of the Anglican Church, a wealthy, cultured, landowning elite. Brant led

Figure 1.5 The Mohawk chieftain Joseph Brant (Thayendanegea) led the Iroquois Confederation in alliance with the British against the French, the Americans, and other tribes.

Source: Library of Congress, Prints and Photographs Division, LC-USZ62-45500.

the Iroquois Confederation (his Mohawks were one of the now six nations in the confederacy) into a Revolutionary War alliance with the British out of his conviction that if the Americans were victorious they would not rest until Indians had been driven from the land. The British and their Indian allies took the fight to vulnerable western settlements as a means of punishing the rebels and forcing them to divert resources to the borderlands. In July 1778 in the Wyoming Valley of Pennsylvania, the Iroquois Confederation joined British forces in a massacre of settlers centered on the township of Wilkes-Barre, which had been named after rebellious Whigs in the British parliament and had become an American rebel stronghold. In the wave of murder, torture, scalping, and mutilation that followed the British and their Indian allies killed 227 while taking only 5 prisoners.

Resolved to exact revenge, General Washington sent an invasion force against backcountry loyalists and into the heart of the Iroquois homelands in the Finger Lakes region. The assault, General John Sullivan reported to Washington in 1779, achieved "total ruin of the Indian settlement, and the destruction of their crops, which were designed for the support of those inhuman barbarians, while they were desolating the American frontiers." The Iroquois, left to starve and freeze in winter, ever after dubbed Washington "the Town Destroyer."

Fighting raged in the Ohio Valley, where settlers had constructed forts or "stations" as a means of survival against Indian assaults. Zealous young warriors wanted to fight to the death against the invaders of their homelands and hunting grounds but some Indian elders tried to seek accommodation with the never-ending stream of settlers. One such leader, the Shawnee chief Cornstalk, embarked on a peace mission in 1777, but a settler mob executed and mutilated Cornstalk and his son. At the same time settlers in and around Fort Pitt killed innocent Delaware and Seneca Indians.

Colonel George Rogers Clark launched a raid into southern Ohio and Indiana replete with indiscriminate killing of Indian women and children. In February 1779, Clark sought to make an impression on British territorial Governor Henry Hamilton, notorious among the Americans as the "hair-buyer" for his incitement of the Indian tribes. Clark summarily executed an Ottawa Indian outside the gates of the British fort. Clark told Hamilton that as to the Indians "for his part he would never spare man, woman or child of them."

A growing number of American settlers could perceive Indians only as "merciless savages" in need of extermination. "On this side of the mountain," one American acknowledged, "the country talks of nothing but killing Indians and taking possession of their lands." The worst atrocity occurred at **Gnadenhutten**, a Moravian Christian mission in eastern Ohio. In the late winter of 1782, a group of militiamen from Virginia and Pennsylvania entered Gnadenhutten. Although the Indians at Gnadenhutten were peaceful converts to Christianity, the militiamen took a vote and decided to kill them all. On March 8 and 9 the Americans executed and scalped 96 Indians at Gnadenhutten, including 39 children. Many Americans condemned the atrocity and an investigation ensued, but no one was punished for killing Indians. A cycle of indiscriminate killing and blood revenge followed in the wake of Gnadenhutten. After an Indian coalition defeated a settler invasion force in north-central Ohio, the Delaware and their allies slaughtered captives and stripped, mutilated, and slowly burned at the stake the US commander, William Crawford.

The Revolutionary War provided an opportunity for Carolinians, Georgians, and Virginians to attack the Cherokee, one of the powerful tribes that arose in the aftermath of the Indian slave trade. Eager to lash out at the Indians and seize their land, American rebels called for "the first warfare of our young republic" to be a campaign in which the "awe and dread of the power of the white people" would be driven into "the breast of the Indians." Jefferson, who had coined the phrase "merciless Indian savages" in the Declaration, called for the Cherokee to "be driven beyond the Mississippi." The Cherokee warrior Dragging Canoe envisioned a fight to the death, as it "seemed to be the intention of the white people to destroy us from being a people." Backed by the British the Cherokee waged an indiscriminate conflict with the settlers throughout the Revolutionary War. In 1785, two years after the British recognized American independence, the Cherokee signed a treaty at Hopewell, SC moving them deeper into the Appalachian hills (where they remain to this day).

Bitter fighting between Indians and Americans continued even after the British surrender at Yorktown in 1781. The summer of the following year an Indian coalition, joined by some 50 Loyalists, defeated the Americans at the Battle of Blue Licks in northern Kentucky. Victories on the battlefield notwithstanding, the British abandoned their Indian allies under the terms of the **Treaty of Paris** (1783). By recognizing American boundaries to the Mississippi River (excluding Canada and Spanish Florida), the British left the tribes alone to face the growing hordes of American settlers. The Creek leader Alexander McGillivray declared that the British "most shamefully deserted" their Indian allies, as the Americans laid claim to the entire "frontier."

The British withdrawal undermined the ability of Indians to play off one European power against another. The triumph of the United States in the Revolutionary War thus left North American Indian tribes to confront an increasingly unified people who believed it was the white man's providential destiny to take sole possession of the continent. The Americans would accept nothing less than removal of Indians from all but a few pockets of the land east of the Mississippi River.

To the newly independent Americans racial perceptions, religious convictions, and national aspirations justified Indian removal. The Americans viewed themselves as a nation chosen by Providence to expand republicanism and lead the world toward liberation from monarchy and aristocracy. The United States was a sovereign nation-state and as such had a right to settle in defined spaces, whereas Indians were viewed as primitive hunter-gatherers, children of the forest, warlike and uncivilized heathens, members of a "vanishing race." For centuries settlers had attributed the devastating impact of disease on Indians to a higher plan from God to displace the savages. Having defeated the British and laid claim to all the land east of the Mississippi, the Americans descended on their new frontier with renewed determination to drive out the Indians. "The Indian will ever retreat as our settlements advance upon them," Washington declared in 1783. "The gradual extension of our settlements will certainly cause the savage as the wolf to retire; both being beasts of prey though they differ in shape."

The foreign policy of western expansion and Indian removal was believed to be vital to the security of the new republic. As a surveyor and western land speculator, Washington like Jefferson and other early national leaders understood the importance of seizing Indian land in order to cultivate the support of settlers and to put the new nation on more sound financial footing. Even though it had survived the struggle against the British, the United States remained surrounded by enemies and plagued by a sizable debt accrued in the Revolutionary War. Only by occupying and converting Indian land into private property could the Americans generate the revenues needed to retire the war debt, address the claims of war veterans, and appease land speculators. Moreover, by seizing Indian land, the United States could better secure its borders against the lurking world powers of Spain, ensconced in the South and eager to foment settler rebellion there, and the British who continued to occupy forts in the northwest until the mid-1790s. The United States sought to gain control of the fluid and expanding borderlands, to build trading posts and fortifications to secure settlement and preclude alliances between Indians and foreign governments.

The United States claimed that indigenous people had lost all rights to lands east of the Mississippi because some of the tribes had sided with the British during the Revolutionary War. In the Commerce Clause of the **US Constitution** (1787) Congress assumed the power to "regulate Commerce with foreign nations, and among the several States, and with the Indian tribes." As uncivilized natives, Indians could not be perceived as "foreign nations" yet the foundational legal document did require the United States to conduct diplomacy with them. In 1790 the Federal Intercourse Act provided the national government the exclusive right to extinguish Indian title, regulate trade, and negotiate treaties.

US diplomacy with Indians emphasized coerced treaties as the primary means of taking Indian land while providing a veneer of legality. In the 1780s a series of treaties forced on the various tribes resulted in massive forfeiture of lands with little or no compensation. Even the once-powerful Iroquois were now considered a "subdued people" with no right to the lands they had occupied for centuries. As General Philip Schuyler told the Six Nations in 1783, "We are now masters and can dispose of the lands as we think proper or more convenient to ourselves." New York forced upon the Iroquois vast land cessions for a fraction of their value. The Iroquois resisted vigorously, as they sought to preserve a tenuous hold on their land through negotiations, by proposing leases instead of land sales, and offering direct payments to Americans to stay out of Indian land. They also sought to preserve their own legal system and cultural practices rather than be subjected to those of New York.

To the West, the **Northwest Ordinance** (1787) passed by the Confederation government laid the groundwork for dispossession of indigenous people in the Northwest (today's Midwest). The ordinance facilitated the incorporation of vast tracts of land comprising the future states of Illinois, Indiana, Michigan, Ohio, and Wisconsin. The ordinance solemnly promised, "The utmost good faith shall always be observed towards the Indians." The ordinance claimed that Indian "lands and property shall never be taken from them without their consent; and, in their property, rights, and liberty, they shall never be invaded or disturbed, unless in just and lawful wars authorized by Congress." The Americans pledged to prevent "wrongs being done to them, and preserving peace and friendship with them."

Many Americans sincerely called for more fairness in dealing with the tribes yet when push came to shove settlers nearly always received the backing of all levels of government in their drive to dispossess Indians of their land. Jefferson, who crafted the original Northwest Ordinance (1784), often voiced his respect for Indians, yet he like Washington personally invested in western expansion and would go on to build the nation's most powerful political party behind a constituency of western settlers who were determined to seize Indian land for farms and slave plantations. Jefferson perceived Indians as "children" whose lives, liberty, and pursuit of happiness ultimately did not extend to stewardship of the land.

Like many others Jefferson advised Indians to remove voluntarily to lands further west or face the wrath of the settlers. As Timothy Pickering, the Indian commissioner for the United States, observed. "It is in the highest degree mortifying to find that the bulk of the frontier inhabitants consider the killing of Indians in time of peace to be no crime." The "frontier miscreants," he added, were "far more savage and revengeful than the Indians." As Secretary of War Henry Knox averred in 1787, "The Whites and Savages" could never be "good neighbors." "With minds previously inflamed the slightest offense occasions death—revenge follows which knows no bounds. The flames of a merciless war are thus lighted up which involve the innocent and helpless with the guilty."

Indian Removal from the Ohio Valley

Indians on the newly acquired US borderlands were thus given a stark choice in the years after the Revolution: vacate the land voluntarily or face indiscriminate violence. However sympathetic many federal leaders were over the plight of the Indians, the government invariably sided with the "white" settlers over the "red" savages whenever warfare erupted. General Arthur St. Clair, the governor of the Northwest Territory, acknowledged, "Though we hear much of the injuries and depredations that are committed by the Indians upon the whites, there is too much reason to believe that at least equal if not greater injuries are done to the Indians by the frontier settlers of which we hear very little." Nonetheless, St. Clair referred to the Indians as "indolent, dirty, inanimate creatures" and would mount what proved to be a disastrous assault against them.

Ethnic violence raged south of the Ohio River as settlers and Indians conducted brutal campaigns of irregular warfare. Indians killed some 300 Kentuckians from 1783 to 1787 but the latter would not be outdone. Irregular and scorched earth warfare proved decisive in cleansing the future Bluegrass state, as Kentuckians burned Indian villages and cornfields with devastating effect. Indians responded to settler colonial expansion with more concerted efforts to craft pan-Indian alliances. Charismatic leaders who had proven themselves during the Revolutionary War—Blue Jacket of the Shawnee, the Iroquois leader Brant, the Miami chief Little Turtle, and McGillivray of the Creeks,—forged alliances for homeland defense. Other Indian tribes joined the resistance, including the Kickapoo, Mascouten, Mingo, Munsee, Ojibwa (Chippewa), Ottawa, Piankashaw, Potawatomi, Sauk, and Wea.

The Indian coalition mounted a determined resistance in the Ohio country and won a series of stunning albeit short-term victories. In 1790, the Shawnee under Blue Jacket, joined by the Miami under Little Turtle, decisively repulsed a foolhardy, traditional, European-style US military assault near the (modern-day) Indiana–Ohio border. With the Kentucky militia forced into a desperate retreat, St. Clair mobilized an armed force for "vengeance" and "utter destruction" of the Shawnee and Miami, but the Americans instead suffered a humiliating and total defeat in the **Battle of the Wabash**. On November 4, 1791, the Americans—disorganized, poorly equipped, absent effective scouts, and blundering headlong into battle much as Braddock had done in 1755—suffered a total rout in which some 650 were killed, including 69 of 124 commissioned officers, and 270 wounded, the casualties including scores of women and children. The victorious tribes stuffed the mouths of the dead with dirt to mock their lust for Indian land. Only 21 warriors had been killed and 40 wounded in the slaughter on the Wabash River. With two and a half times the number dead as George A. Custer's command would suffer at Little Big Horn in 1876, it was the worst defeat the army ever suffered in battle with Indians, yet few Americans would remember the battle in the future.

The Indian confederates celebrated their decisive victory, but were under no illusions about their future prospects in view of the relentless settler colonial advance. "The pale faces come from where the sun rises, and they are many," Little Turtle lamented. "They are like the leaves of the trees. When the frost comes they fall and are blown away. But when the sunshine comes again they come back more plentiful than ever before."

The United States mobilized for violent retribution under the command of General Anthony Wayne, who declared his eagerness to lay siege to the "haughty and insidious enemy." Provided with a large federal appropriation, Wayne mobilized an infantry of 2,200 men backed by 1,500 Kentucky volunteers eager for revenge. Choctaw and Chickasaw mercenary "scouts" came up from the South to assist the US assault on the northern tribes. Irregular forces were offered bounties for as many scalps as they could deliver. Wayne's careful planning, mobilization, and construction of new fortifications led to a decisive victory. Wayne unleashed his rangers on Indian villages and cornfields throughout the Miami and Maumee River Valleys, with the campaign culminating in the **Battle of**

WAYNE'S DEFEAT OF THE INDIANS.

Figure 1.6 In the wake of a series of defeats at the hands of indigenous forces in the Ohio country, the United States rallied behind General "Mad" Anthony Wayne, who defeated the Indian coalition in 1794 at the Battle of Fallen Timbers near modern-day Toledo, Ohio.

Source: Library of Congress, Prints and Photographs Division, LC-USZ62-110274.

Fallen Timbers (1794) near modern-day Toledo, Ohio. Blue Jacket surrendered the upper Ohio country to Wayne in return for bribes, a commission in the US Army, and ample supplies of liquor. Representatives of the Delaware, Miami, Piankashaw, Shawnee, and Wea also signed off on the loss of their homelands following elaborate surrender ceremonies. With the Indians defeated, the settler population of Ohio rocketed from 5,000 in 1796 to 230,000 by 1810.

By the time of the American Revolution a foreign policy of settler colonial expansion had been firmly established. The Americans streaming into the borderlands, joined by land speculators and the ruling elite in both the local and national governments, would take the land from the indigenous inhabitants by treaty if possible, by exterminatory violence if necessary. Indians could remove voluntarily but if they stayed and fought for their homelands the Americans branded them savages and unleashed indiscriminate warfare against them. By the time of the American Revolution the trade, diplomacy, and alliances that had prevailed in earlier periods of colonial history gave way to a determined campaign of removing Indians from the American frontier.

Select Bibliography

Hixson, Walter L. *American Settler Colonialism: A History*. New York: Palgrave Macmillan, 2013.

Starkey, Armstrong. *European and Native American Warfare*. Norman: University of Oklahoma Press, 1998.

Taylor, Alan. *American Colonies: The Settling of North America*. New York: Penguin, 2001.

Gallay, Alan. *The Indian Slave Trade: The Rise of the English Empire in the American South, 1670–1717*. New Haven, CT: Yale University Press, 2002.

Elliott, John H. *Empires of the Atlantic World: Britain and Spain in America, 1492–1830*. New Haven, CT: Yale University Press, 2006.

Mancall, Peter C. and Merrell, James H. eds. *American Encounters: Natives and Newcomers from European Contact to Indian Removal, 1500–1850*. New York: Routledge, 2000.

White, Richard. *The Middle Ground: Indians, Empires, and Republics in the Great Lakes Region, 1650–1815*. London: Cambridge University Press, 1991.

Mapp, Paul W. *The Elusive West and the Contest for Empire, 1713–1763*. Chapel Hill: University of North Carolina Press, 2011.

Richter, Daniel. *Facing East from Indian Country: A Native History of Early America*. Cambridge, MA: Harvard University Press, 2001.

Cave, Alfred. *The Pequot War*. Amherst: University of Massachusetts Press, 1996.

Mandell, Daniel. *King Philip's War: Colonial Expansion, Native Resistance, and the End of Indian Sovereignty*. Baltimore, MD: Johns Hopkins University Press, 2010.

Calloway, Colin G. *New Worlds for All: Indians, Europeans, and the Remaking of Early America*. Baltimore, MD: Johns Hopkins University Press, 1997.

Cohen, Eliot A. *Conquered into Liberty: Two Centuries of Battles along the Great Warpath that Made the American Way of War*. New York: Free Press, 2011.

Silver, Peter. *Our Savage Neighbors: How Indian War Transformed Early America*. New York: W.W. Norton, 2008.

Banner, Stuart. *How the Indians Lost Their Land: Law and Power on the Frontier*. Cambridge, MA: Harvard University Press, 2005.

2 The Diplomacy of the New Republic

Overview

Interactions with indigenous people left a deep imprint on American identity and foreign policy, but so did relations with Europeans. Americans fought against the dominant European power, Great Britain, and allied with France and other European states in order to gain their independence. The United States pursued trade and commerce with Europeans even as they idealistically pursued a "new diplomacy" of delimiting formal diplomatic ties with the "Old World" regimes. The new nation demanded recognition and respect from Europeans yet at the same time wanted to drive them out of the Americas. As they cultivated a new national identity, Americans viewed themselves as an exceptional people, a rising empire, and a model for the rest of the world to emulate.

Revolutionary Diplomacy

In 1775 it was a loose grouping of disparate colonies rather than a united nation that went into revolt against Great Britain. Nation building was a gradual process, one that the "Americans" had not desired or envisioned until the colonial rebellion unfolded. Benjamin Franklin, the Philadelphia printer and inventor and often considered the first American diplomat, had called for greater unity among the British colonies as early as 1754. At the **Albany Conference** in New York, Franklin advocated creation of a formal union of the colonies in order to better work together to defeat the French and their Indian allies, but the plan had been rejected. Twenty-two years later, in the wake of the revolt against the Proclamation Line (1763), the Stamp Act (1765), and the Declaratory Act (1766)—in which the Crown claimed the prerogative to implement any measure it saw fit to govern the wayward colonies—the Americans coalesced in revolt against George III.

The **Declaration of Independence** (1776) was a foreign policy statement as well as a powerful articulation of natural rights philosophy—the notion that "all men are created equal" and had the "inalienable rights" to "life, liberty, and the pursuit of happiness." The declaration was thus a multi-purpose document designed to pull the disparate states together in common cause, to

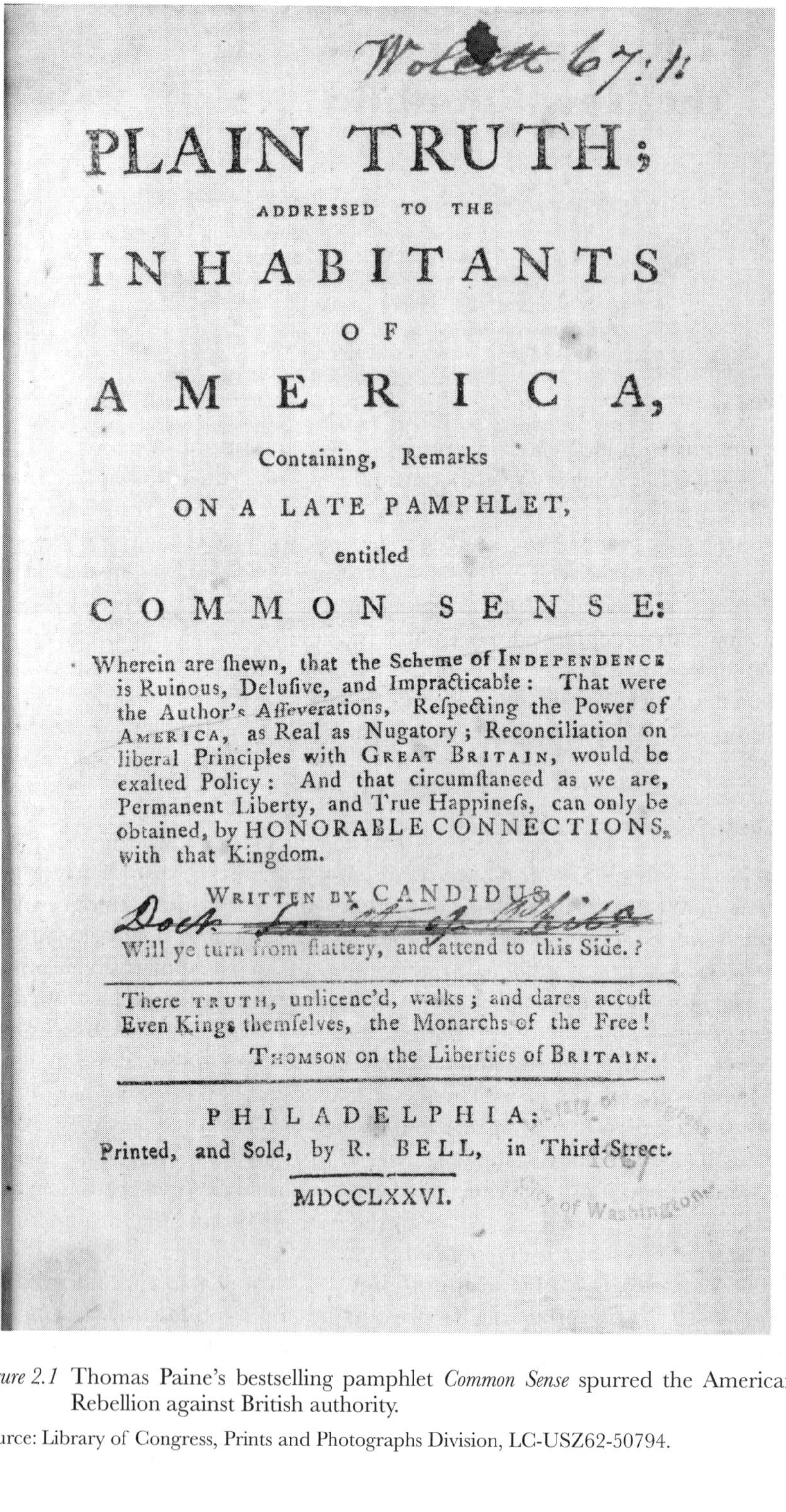

Wolcott 67:1.

PLAIN TRUTH;

ADDRESSED TO THE

INHABITANTS

OF

AMERICA,

Containing, Remarks

ON A LATE PAMPHLET,

entitled

COMMON SENSE:

Wherein are ſhewn, that the Scheme of INDEPENDENCE is Ruinous, Deluſive, and Impracticable: That were the Author's Aſſeverations, Reſpecting the Power of AMERICA, as Real as Nugatory; Reconciliation on liberal Principles with GREAT BRITAIN, would be exalted Policy: And that circumſtanced as we are, Permanent Liberty, and True Happineſs, can only be obtained, by HONORABLE CONNECTIONS, with that Kingdom.

WRITTEN BY CANDIDUS.

Doct.

Will ye turn from flattery, and attend to this Side.?

There TRUTH, unlicenc'd, walks; and dares accoſt
Even Kings themſelves, the Monarchs of the Free!

THOMSON on the Liberties of BRITAIN.

PHILADELPHIA:
Printed, and Sold, by R. BELL, in Third-Street.

MDCCLXXVI.

Figure 2.1 Thomas Paine's bestselling pamphlet *Common Sense* spurred the American Rebellion against British authority.

Source: Library of Congress, Prints and Photographs Division, LC-USZ62-50794.

advance the natural rights philosophy, but also to justify the rebellion in the eyes of Europeans and others around the world. Rebellion against monarchy and aristocracy was considered radical in the eighteenth century, hence the Americans felt the need to justify the revolt by setting forth a list of grievances against King George III. Thomas Jefferson and his colleagues sought to affirm for Americans that their cause was just and to convince as many Europeans as possible—especially Great Britain's rivals—the rebellion was legitimate and could succeed.

The radical British Enlightenment thinker Thomas Paine, newly arrived in the American colonies, pursued the same agenda in his powerful revolutionary tract **Common Sense** (1776). Paine brilliantly combined natural rights philosophy with arguments justifying rebellion against the "royal brute" of England. Like the Declaration of Independence, *Common Sense* depicted the American revolt as a transcendent event. "The cause of America is in great measure the cause of all mankind," he declared. In the pamphlet, which circulated rapidly throughout the colonies, Paine depicted the revolt as a natural rather than a radical step. After all, where in the natural world did an island govern a continent? Paine reassured Americans, many of whom worried that the rebellion would leave the states isolated and economically weakened, that Europeans were equally dependent on American resources. "Our plan is commerce," he advised, and the economy would prosper "as long as eating is the custom of Europe."

While Paine, Jefferson, and other architects of rebellion cultivated foreign support, they wanted no formal diplomatic connections with the Old World of Europe. Influenced by the Enlightenment philosophers, the US Revolutionary elite associated classical diplomacy—characterized by treaties, alliances, and Machiavellian *realpolitik*—as a source of perpetual conflict. Classical diplomacy, Jefferson averred, was "the pest of peace . . . the workshop in which nearly all the wars of Europe are manufactured." In the new "age of reason" modern states should conduct free trade uninhibited by alliances, secret agreements, and the endless conflict that they spawned. Amity, commerce, and the pursuit of natural rights would anchor the new diplomacy and, he maintained, obviate the need for war.

In the first formal statement of American diplomacy, the **Model Treaty** (1776) crafted primarily by the Boston attorney John Adams, the United States proclaimed a desire for free and reciprocal trade with any and all nations but formal political connections with none. The Model Treaty reflected the American determination to break free of the economic and commercial restrictions imposed under British authority, a crucial cause of the colonial rebellion. The idealistic quest to enjoy the fruits of trade and commerce while otherwise eschewing diplomatic ties would prove overly optimistic, especially with the United States fighting for its new life in the Revolutionary War. In addition to issuing the Declaration of Independence and the Model Treaty, the Continental Congress crafted the Articles of Confederation, a loose grouping of the states with no chief executive or power to tax. In 1781 the Confederation

Congress created a new **Department of Foreign Affairs** directed by Robert Livingston of New York.

Armed with only limited federal powers, the Americans embarked on a war against the most powerful nation and empire in the world. Few European observers thought they could prevail, especially as the British occupied New York, blockaded the coastlines, and began to implement a strategy of cutting off and isolating New England, long the center of the rebellion. The British meant to destroy the rebellion in the North while bolstering the support of loyalists in the southern colonies. The southern planters depended on Britain for marketing of their agricultural products and at the same time many feared the potential implications of the notion that "all men are created equal" for the future of slavery, the foundation of their economy and social relations.

On the day after Christmas in 1776 the American military commander George Washington won a boldly calculated and much needed surprise victory at Trenton, New Jersey. He then kept the desperately under-supplied Continental Army from unraveling over the course of a bitterly cold winter at their Valley Forge, Pennsylvania, encampment. In October 1777 the Americans won the pivotal **Battle of Saratoga** when British General John Burgoyne—unprepared to fight an unconventional war on the American

Figure 2.2 Perhaps the most important battle in American history came early on, in October 1777, at Saratoga, New York. The Americans forced the surrender of the overconfident British General John Burgoyne, providing a much-needed boost of confidence as well as foreign support for the upstart United States.

Source: Library of Congress, Prints and Photographs Division, LC-USZC4-2912.

borderlands—found his force of some 6,000 men trapped and defeated in upstate New York. Burgoyne surrendered, delivering to the Americans a resounding victory. One American soldier declared, "It was a glorious sight to see the haughty Britons march out and surrender their arms to an army which but a little before they despised and called poltroons [cowards]." The Battle of Saratoga not only affirmed American manhood, it convinced many Americans that they could win the struggle for independence. Just as importantly, the victory convinced many Europeans—and especially the longtime British rival, France—that the American rebels could prevail in battle.

Franklin exploited the dramatic battlefield triumph to convince the French to come in on the American side and gain revenge for their abject defeat in the French and Indian War that ended in 1763. Franklin's brilliance extended to public relations, as he donned a fur cap to appeal to the French aristocracy's fascination with the American frontier. The witty Philadelphian, famous for his myriad writings and inventions, charmed the well-connected French aristocracy at Parisian balls and fetes. Franklin's mission in Paris was disorganized, infiltrated by British spies, and he spent much of his time conducting personal business deals, but in the end the French succumbed to the temptation to strike back at their inveterate British rivals.

In entering into the **French Alliance** (1778) Americans as much as admitted that the Model Treaty had been idealistic and that they had no choice but to engage in classical diplomacy with Old World nations in order to secure their independence. Under the terms of the alliance, France formally recognized American independence while the United States pledged to fight with France in the event it went to war with Great Britain. The United States and France agreed on various territorial provisions and extended an open invitation to other nations to join their anti-British coalition. In 1779 Spain entered the war on the side of the United States and France, providing the Americans with both the diplomatic and financial support of another European power. As expected the British, livid over the French intervention in the colonial rebellion, declared war on France and then on Spain. When Holland joined in the anti-British coalition, the American Revolutionary War, like the French and Indian War, had become an international conflict. All of this worked crucially in the Americans' favor, as the British were now spread thin as they confronted multiple enemies on multiple fronts, from the Caribbean to the Mediterranean Sea.

The United States did not defeat Great Britain militarily as much as it avoided being defeated. The rebels exploited British over-extension, diplomatic isolation, and the costs and sacrifices that would be required to continue the fight to maintain the colonies. In 1781 the United States, aided by crucial funding from France, won a decisive campaign at the **Battle of Yorktown** in Virginia. British General Charles Cornwallis found his 8,000-man army trapped in a land–sea pincer and forced to surrender. The defeat wrecked Britain's stronghold in the South and prompted many observers back home to call for an end to the war with the Americans in order to focus on battling the French, the Spanish, and the Dutch in Europe and the Caribbean.

Franklin, joined by Adams and John Jay, negotiated settlement terms bringing an end to the Revolutionary War with the **Treaty of Paris** (1783). The terms they secured exceeded any rational expectations that might have been held in 1776. Most importantly Britain recognized American independence to the Mississippi River, thus granting the US claim to millions of acres and several future states—areas that comprised the homelands of indigenous tribes. Not for the first or last time, the Europeans and the Americans excluded the "savages" from the diplomatic summit. The British rejected Franklin's demands for a US takeover of Quebec and signed separate agreements with France, Spain, and Holland involving Caribbean and Mediterranean possessions. Spain received Florida with an undefined and soon to be contested northern boundary with the new United States. The Americans pledged to resolve debts with British creditors and to "earnestly recommend" that the individual states restore property confiscated from North Americans who had remained loyal to Britain. The British pledged to withdraw from their forts in the Great Lakes "with all convenient speed."

The Confederation Congress ratified the treaty in 1784, but it gradually became evident to American elites that their loose grouping of states was ill-equipped to respond to both domestic and foreign challenges. On the domestic side, Shay's Rebellion (1786), an economic revolt led by an officer veteran of the Revolutionary War, and other social and economic conflicts directly challenged the central government, still hampered by the absence of authority to raise revenue through taxation. It remained to be determined, the Virginian James Madison warned, "whether prosperity and tranquility or confusion and disunion" would prevail within the new republic.

On the international front, despite the Treaty of Paris many Europeans did not expect the fledgling United States to remain united, given the wide disparities of geography, culture, and economy among them. "Mutual antipathies and clashing interests," declared an English diplomat, meant that only "writers of romance" could expect the states to remain united. As the United States failed to resolve its debts or to return confiscated properties to most loyalists, the British made no effort to vacate the northwestern forts. Spain showed little respect for American independence, as it controlled traffic down the Mississippi River to New Orleans, a crucial outlet for western trade, and threatened to woo the affected states out of the union and into a rival political formation.

Foreign policy concerns were thus a driving force behind the decision to "form a more perfect union" through the drafting of the **Constitution of the United States**. The nation's elite leaders concluded that the United States would never get the respect of foreign powers unless it established a stronger central government. Convening in Philadelphia, they drafted the new Constitution that included a powerful chief executive, a bicameral legislature with the power to tax, and a federal judiciary. In 1787 the federalists narrowly won approval of the document by means of state ratifying conventions.

American Exceptionalism

The tumult of the American Revolution, followed by the crafting of a new Constitution, created a powerful nationalist consciousness that would strongly influence the nation's outlook and foreign policy long into the future. Scholars have described nations as "imagined communities," explaining that they are created culturally through a blending of history, philosophy, mythology, religious faith, racial hierarchy, and gender norms. Nations thrive when a sufficient number of people, though unknown to one another and ranging over a broad geographic space, share the same sense of community rooted in common ideas and perceptions. Enlightenment philosophy, scientific discoveries, and advancing technologies, notably the printing press, enabled wide circulation of knowledge and ideas, paving the way for modern nationalist sentiment to cohere.

The act of separating from Europe underscored the uniqueness of the United States, cementing a new national consciousness that had been evolving on North American shores over the centuries of colonization. Even before they conceived of themselves as a distinct national community of "Americans," the people living in the British colonies had begun to evolve customs, religious practices, modes of dress, housing, material culture, economy, their own vernacular, and other aspects of life that distinguished them from Europeans. Thus Adams would later aver that the American Revolution had already taken hold "in the minds and the hearts of the people" well before the actual uprising against British authority.

In Their Words

John Winthrop's "City upon a Hill," 1630

The Lord will be our God, and delight to dwell among us, as his oune people, and will command a blessing upon us in all our wayes. Soe that wee shall see much more of his wisdome, power, goodness and truthe, than formerly wee have been acquainted with. Wee shall finde that the God of Israell is among us, when ten of us shall be able to resist a thousand of our enemies; when hee shall make us a prayse and glory that men shall say of succeeding plantations, "the Lord make it like that of New England." For wee must consider that wee shall be as a citty upon a hill. The eies of all people are upon us. Soe that if wee shall deale falsely with our God in this worke wee have undertaken, and soe cause him to withdrawe his present help from us, wee shall be made a story and a by-word through the world. Wee shall open the mouthes of enemies to speake evill of the ways of God, and all professors for God's sake. Wee shall shame the faces of many of God's worthy servants, and cause theire prayers to be turned into curses upon us till wee be consumed out of the good land whither wee are a goeing.

The new American nation cultivated a powerful sense of what has been termed American exceptionalism. By overthrowing centuries of monarchy in favor of a republic, by achieving the first successful nationalist anti-colonial revolt—against the most powerful empire in the world no less—Americans had every reason to view themselves as special and uniquely progressive people. These secular achievements blended with a deep-seated religiosity to fuel the notion that the nation was destined to lead and was meant to serve as a model for all of humanity. In the decades leading to the American Revolution a "great awakening," a highly emotional and uniquely American form of Protestantism featuring hellfire sermons, confessions of sin, and pleas for salvation had swept across the British colonies.

The intense religiosity of the Great Awakening carried over into the American Revolution, which thus was not merely a political but also a profoundly spiritual event ordained by God. From common people, to the pulpit, to the founding fathers, references linking the nation with the will of God were widespread. As one minister proclaimed on the eve of the Revolution, "If God be with us, who can be against us?" Even the deist Jefferson and the leading scientific rationalist Franklin shared the sense of American providential destiny and mission to lead the world. "Our cause is the cause of all mankind, and we are fighting for their liberty in defending our own," Franklin explained. "It is a glorious task assigned us by Providence." A decade before the outbreak of fighting at Lexington and Concord, Adams declared, "I always consider the settlement of America with reverence and wonder, as the opening of a grand scheme and design of Providence for the illumination and emancipation of the slavish part of mankind all over the earth."

The ebullient nationalism of the American Revolution harkened back to the Puritan mission. In 1630 the Puritan leader John Winthrop called on his followers in the Massachusetts Bay Colony to erect a biblical "city on a hill," a New Israel that would serve as a model for all to emulate. Invocations of this providentially sanctioned exceptionalist vision became a *sine qua non* of American cultural and political identity. Ordinary Americans, politicians, and virtually every US president into the twenty-first century offered ritual references to the United States as a "city on a hill," a "shining beacon to the world," or some variation of the chosen nation narrative.

Although the Americans formally separated Church and state in the First Amendment of the Constitution, there was no doubting that the new republic was a Protestant Christian nation. Thus above the pyramid on the great seal of the United States are the words, in Latin, "God has favored our undertaking." Washington established a pattern that would be repeated throughout US history by offering in the first inaugural address "fervent supplications" to the "Almighty Being," as it appeared that "every step by which we have advanced to the character of an independent nation seems to have been distinguished by some token of providential agency."

Interpreting the Past

The radicalism of the American Revolution

The American Revolution was a transcendent international event that affected not only the United States, but also Europe and other parts of the globe. The American Revolution was not, however, without its contradictions and scholars have long debated the extent to which the Revolution represented radical or truly "revolutionary" change. On the one hand, the American rebels threw off aristocracy and monarchy, which had dominated European society for centuries, and at the same time offered new dignity to the average man (but not women, as patriarchy—male domination of society—remained unchallenged). The American example helped inspire the even more radical French Revolution (1789) and also established a precedent with the first successful anti-colonial nationalist revolt, providing a model that would be emulated by scores of new nations in later years.

On the other side it can be argued that Americans fought mainly to preserve their rights as Englishmen more than to blaze a new revolutionary path. While the assertion that "all men are created equal" was indeed radical and inspirational, Americans did not immediately follow through on this pledge. The new United States continued to remove Indians from the land and sanctioned slavery in the Constitution. Despite rejecting the authority of the king the United States created a powerful chief executive, especially as pertained to foreign affairs, and for generations maintained class distinctions, with almost all states initially requiring ownership of property as a condition of voting rights. The American Revolution thus embodied both progressive and conservative features—much like the US foreign policy that flowed from it.

The powerful drives of nationalism, mission, and providential destiny fueled American exceptionalism, establishing it as a driving force behind the nation's foreign policy. Despite such potent nationalist aspirations, in the early national period Americans were of necessity far more concerned with preserving their unity and international security than in redeeming all of mankind. Political, economic, racial, and cultural disputes and divisions plagued the new republic. Hostile forces encircled the United States—Britain controlled Canada and remained ensconced in the northwest forts; Spain established a buffer in the South and Southwest; and "merciless Indian savages" fought to defend their homelands, which the United States claimed as its own "frontier."

In the Shadow of the French Revolution

The Americans had scarcely ratified the Constitution and ensconced the hero Washington in the presidency as commander in chief when the **French Revolution**

(1789) brought a sea change in world politics and diplomacy. Inspired in part by the American Revolution, the French revolutionaries went further, attempting a full-scale social revolution challenging all class distinctions. The French shocked the world by executing the king and queen along with myriad other perceived counter-revolutionaries by means of the guillotine. Some American elites, notably Jefferson and Madison, the principal architect of the Constitution, welcomed the French Revolution as it furthered the cause of republican government. As to the violence, Jefferson allowed, "The tree of liberty must be refreshed from time to time with the blood of patriots and tyrants." The excesses of the French revolt appalled Washington and his chief confidant Alexander Hamilton, the secretary of the treasury. The New Yorker Hamilton advocated putting aside the acrimony of the Revolutionary War in deference to reestablishing close economic and security ties with the "mother" country Great Britain.

The French Revolution as well as disagreements over domestic policy—and especially disputation over the extent of the powers that inhered in the new Constitution—sharply divided Washington's Cabinet and the new US government. At the end of 1793 Jefferson resigned as secretary of state and together with Madison began to form a rival political party to challenge the authority of the Federalists. Earlier that year Washington had issued a **Neutrality Proclamation** in response to the renewal of war between France and Britain. To Jefferson and Madison neutrality was tantamount to supporting monarchy over republicanism. They feared that the Federalists, and Hamilton especially, meant to undermine all that they had fought for in the American Revolution. For their part, Washington, Hamilton, and other Federalists became alarmed by the rabble-rousing activities of **Edmund-Charles Genêt**, the ambassador dispatched by the French revolutionary government to generate popular support for the cause in America. While Federalists feared that mob rule would migrate from France to America, the emergent Jeffersonian Democratic-Republicans expressed greater faith in the wisdom of the people.

Both Federalists and Democratic-Republicans viewed the United States as a rising empire destined to expand and assume its inevitable place as a leading nation in the world. They diverged, however, on political ideology, economic philosophy, and the advocacy of the "old" and "new" diplomacy. While Federalists predominated in New England and the eastern seaboard, the agriculturally based Jeffersonians championed small farmers and western settlers. Federalists wanted slavery gradually to fade away whereas Southerners defended the plantation system. The settlers also demanded support from the new government against Indians and Europeans on the borderlands. In 1786 the hostile reactions of settlers and their political backers shot down the **Jay–Gardoqui Treaty**, which would have guaranteed Spanish control of navigation of the Mississippi River. Western settlers threatened to join Spain or create a new political entity if the US government would not back their settlements and trade routes.

Foreign policy issues thus played a central role in the emergence of the US political party system, something that had not been envisioned by the founders of the new republic. The Federalists, the more urban and elite-centered political party, pursued a strengthened central government to retire the debt and put the nation on a sound financial footing. Preferring British commerce to French radicalism, the Federalists tended to embrace traditional diplomacy and *realpolitik* but were most concerned about creating viable economic and political structures conducive to establish the United States as a reliable trade partner. More idealistic and optimistic about the French Revolution and the new diplomacy, the Democratic-Republicans endorsed only limited decentralized government and opposed large financial institutions as well as broad executive power.

While Jefferson and Hamilton compromised in 1790 on retiring the debt and creating a new national bank, foreign policy issues remained bitterly divisive. The highly controversial **Jay Treaty** (1795) between the United States and Great Britain deepened the divisions between the Federalists and the Democratic-Republicans thereby cementing the rival two-party political system. Jay, appointed as a special envoy by Washington and closely advised by his fellow New Yorker Hamilton, sought to normalize relations in order to pursue the Federalist aims of broadening commercial ties with the British. Under the Jay Treaty, the British belatedly assented to withdraw from Detroit and the other northwestern forts, as mandated under the 1783 Treaty of Paris, and granted the United States most favored nation trade status. Jefferson and his followers, suspecting a plot to side with Britain and monarchy, nearly defeated the treaty, which the Senate approved by precisely the required two-thirds vote (20–10).

Ironically, despite the opposition of the Jeffersonians, the Jay Treaty ultimately served the interests of their settler constituency and of westward expansion because of the impact it had on Spain. The Spanish feared in the wake of Jay's Treaty that the British and the Americans might ally against them on the North American borderlands. As a result they became more flexible about the issue of navigation on the Mississippi. In 1795 the **Treaty of San Lorenzo** (also known as Pinckney's Treaty) clarified the US–Spanish western boundary and, crucially, provided the United States with navigation rights on the Mississippi and the right of deposit in New Orleans.

Contentiousness over these foreign policy issues, along with the continuing debate over strict and loose construction of the powers inherent in the Constitution, laid the groundwork for the first contested US presidential election in 1796. Jefferson lost the campaign to the Federalist Vice President Adams, who immediately confronted an angry French response to Washington's neutrality policy. As he stepped down the venerable Washington, deeply disturbed by the political divide within the new republic, left the nation with two significant precedents. Washington established the two-term presidential tradition, which would prevail until 1940, and also the tradition of delivering a **farewell address**. Washington took the occasion to warn against the dangers of "permanent alliances," a clear allusion to the Revolutionary War pact with France.

Revolutionary France viewed Washington's supposed neutrality as in reality pro-British and a violation of the French Alliance, which technically remained in effect. In retaliation the French essentially declared war on American shipping, attacking US vessels on the high seas and precipitating what is known as the **Quasi War**. Somewhat analogous to the cold war that would emerge a century and half later, the Quasi War was a period of intense hostility that stopped short of open or declared warfare. Caught between the "High Federalists" led by Hamilton (whom he loathed) and the Democratic-Republicans, whom he thought too radical, President Adams strove to protect US interests while avoiding all-out war with France. War nearly erupted in 1797–98 over the so-called **XYZ Affair**, in which agents of the French foreign ministry (who initially remained anonymous and were identified only by the last three letters of the alphabet) treated US diplomats contemptuously, including demanding a bribe before granting them an audience.

The Quasi War deeply divided the nation, undermined civil liberties, and left important legacies. In 1798 Adams and the Federalists enacted a series of laws targeting recently arrived immigrants, who were perceived as infected with radical French revolutionary sentiment (and thus likely to support the Democratic-Republican opposition). The **Alien and Sedition Acts** encompassed deportations of "dangerous" radicals, lengthening of the period of naturalization before granting citizenship, and curbs on speech critical of the government. Bitterly condemning the repressive legislation, Jefferson and his followers sponsored the Kentucky and Virginia Resolutions in which those states declared that they would not be bound to obey laws they viewed as unconstitutional. These precedents of curbs on civil liberties in wartime and assertions of states' rights would resurface repeatedly in American history and with profound consequences.

Presiding over a deeply divided nation, Adams doggedly pursued a diplomatic settlement, to which France eventually acceded. The **Treaty of Mortefontaine** (also known as the Convention of 1800) brought an end to the Quasi War and terminated the French Alliance. The turmoil of the Quasi War and popular resistance to the Alien and Sedition Acts undermined Adams politically, paving the way for the first electoral defeat of a sitting president. With Jefferson again at the head of the ballot, the Democratic-Republicans triumphed in the election of 1800. Jefferson immodestly called his victory "the Revolution of 1800" but he appealed for unity in his inaugural address by emphasizing, "We are all federalists, we are all republicans."

Windfall in the West

Despite the treaty with France, war remained a real possibility, with the aggressive dictator **Napoleon Bonaparte** apparently seeking to restore French influence in the Caribbean and North America. As Jefferson came into office in 1801 France secured a treaty with Spain taking possession of the sprawling Louisiana Territory. Referring to the event as the "Mississippi Crisis," Americans feared that France would seize control of riverine traffic and woo settlers away from the United States. No longer a Francophile now that the French Revolution had devolved into a military dictatorship, Jefferson lamented that the United States might be left with no choice other than to "marry ourselves to the British fleet and nation."

Seeking to avoid war, Jefferson tried diplomacy—and hit the proverbial jackpot. The president dispatched veteran diplomats James Monroe and Livingston to offer to purchase the "island" of New Orleans from France. The Americans did not contemplate a larger sale of North American geography hence they were stunned when the French offered to sell not merely New Orleans, but the entire Louisiana Territory.

Figure 2.3 Thomas Jefferson was the principal author of the Declaration of Independence, minister to France, the first secretary of state, and a keen architect of American expansion. As president his purchase of the vast Louisiana Territory from France in 1803 was a monumental step toward the realization of American continental "destiny."

Source: Library of Congress, Prints and Photographs Division, LC-DIG-det-4a26387.

Jefferson's subsequent decision making on the Louisiana Purchase reflects his blending of idealism and realism. The Virginian had deep concerns about the constitutionality of such a sale and the rise of federal over state power that it entailed and which he opposed in theory (though less so now that he was the president). Moreover, many expressed uncertainty about the prospect of incorporating a massive polyglot territory full of Creoles, Frenchmen, Hispanics, and Indians. Yet these concerns were swept aside by an offer that for the imperially minded Americans was too good to refuse. The Louisiana Purchase affirmed Jefferson's vision of an expanding republic whose agricultural production would anchor overseas commerce and preclude the need for engaging in "Old World" diplomacy. Of course, it was precisely such diplomacy he now embraced in accepting the French offer, which the US Senate readily approved and the House of Representatives voted to fund.

It would be difficult to exaggerate the significance of the **Louisiana Purchase** (1803), not just in terms of foreign policy but also for the very identity of the young republic. From a group of once fledgling colonies the United States was now poised to emerge as a great continental and, ultimately, world power. At the stroke of a pen the young nation more than doubled in size, taking in 828,000 square miles in the heart of the continent, an area larger than all of Western Europe, and at a sale price of less than 3 cents an acre, or some 15 million dollars. To many Americans the Louisiana Purchase affirmed the nation's providential destiny to inherit the entire continent and become the leading nation in the world.

In the Louisiana Purchase the United States was the beneficiary of both great and small power politics. In terms of the great powers Napoleon had set his course on another war with Britain and domination of Europe. The decision to abandon the effort to rebuild the French Empire in the "New World" stemmed from small power politics, namely the defeat France suffered at the hands of a slave revolt on the Caribbean island of Saint-Dominigue. Thousands of French troops died in the fighting and from yellow fever in a futile effort to maintain the slave colony against the insurrection led by **Toussaint Louverture**. The Adams administration had backed the Louverturian regime with arms, amity, and investments during the Quasi War.

US support for Louverture contributed to the French defeat, paving the way for Napoleon's decision to abandon the Americas, selling the vast Louisiana Territory to the United States in the process. The French captured Louverture, who soon died in prison, but ultimately they had been forced out of Saint-Dominigue in defeat. Jefferson refused to recognize the new Caribbean republic, which adopted the pre-Columbian Arawak name **Haiti** and replaced Saint-Dominigue in 1804. Strongly entrenched perceptions of superior and inferior races precluded recognition of a black republic. Jefferson condemned the slave uprising, which he feared would spread to the American South.

While the United States had decided at the constitutional convention gradually to phase out the international slave trade, that decision paradoxically solidified the domestic institution of slavery. The Constitution ensconced slavery with the three-fifths compromise after having excluded it in theory from the Northwest Territories (many slave-owners took their chattel into the territories regardless). In 1790 in return for acceding to Hamilton's economic plans Jefferson and Madison secured an area around the Potomac River in slave-holding Virginia for the location of the new federal capital. As the Haitians proclaimed their independence, slave laborers constructed the Capitol building in the new Federal City. Rather than fading away slavery was more deeply ensconced than ever as a result of the ongoing settler colonization of the South, the Louisiana Purchase, and pro-slavery presidents controlling the White House for 40 of the first 48 years of the new nation's existence.

In addition to race, religion and manliness remained cornerstones of American identity and foreign relations. Whiteness, Protestantism, and a determination to stand up to and prevail over its perceived enemies thus undergirded American foreign policy. As highly educated men steeped in the histories of ancient Greece and Rome, the founding fathers often referred to the United States as a budding empire. Hamilton had referred to the United States as "Hercules in the cradle," thus envisioning a future colossus of unbounded power. Typically, however, it was Jefferson who coined the decisive terminology. Rather than becoming another in a series of Old World empires, the sage of Monitcello asserted that the United States would be a new empire, an **"empire of liberty."**

A proud and manly empire would not suffer idly affronts to its honor and dignity, especially from dark-skinned, non-Christian peoples, as the United States demonstrated in response to the **Barbary pirates** on the western coast of North Africa. The rulers of Algiers, Morocco, Tripoli, and Tunis had long preyed upon foreign shipping in the Mediterranean, including US merchant vessels, seizing cargo, taking prisoners, and demanding ransoms. Determined to show that the United States was not impotently in the grasp of pacifist "Quaker principles," Jefferson sent the Marines, joined by a large contingent of irregular forces, to strike back on the shores of Tripoli. The assault culminated with a dramatic draping of the American flag on the walls of the port city of Derna, giving rise to the martial Marine Corps hymn. The mission secured the release of US captives, though the United States still had to pay a $60,000 ransom. Americans expressed pride in having "spread the American eagle in Africa."

Manliness, race, and religion surfaced prominently in this conflict, as Americans were determined to stand up to the pirates, who were depicted as a lower race of Africans adhering to a "fanatic" religion of Islam. Across the young nation in sermons, political declarations, and travel accounts Americans denounced "Oriental despotism" while excoriating the Prophet Mohammed and the Muslim faith. Like many European Christians, Americans thus exalted their religion, culture, government, and political thought by condemning the "merciless Mahometans" of the Islamic world.

The War of 1812

In the everyday life of the early nineteenth century affronts to a man's honor led to fighting and brawling for lower classes of men, whereas dueling provided the means by which the upper class could respond to challenges to individual manhood. In 1803 the most famous "affair of honor" ended in the death of the Revolutionary hero and architect of the American economy, Hamilton, shot dead just outside New York City by his longtime political rival Aaron Burr, the vice president of the United States. Just as challenges to an individual's honor demanded a manly response so did challenges to the nation.

Britain and France continued to show little respect for the upstart American republic, especially on the high seas where both powers attacked US shipping in the midst of the **Napoleonic Wars** (1803–15). The United States demanded respect for free trade and neutral rights and ultimately proved willing to go to war over the issue. With a smaller population than France and determined to maintain its advantage at sea, Britain placed a premium on naval manpower, hence British sea captains regularly assaulted US vessels in order to impress sailors into the British Navy. Moreover, **impressment** was a means by which the British showed their contempt for American independence and the continuing desire of many Britons to re-colonize the upstart United States. In these de-masculinizing assaults the British ran roughshod over US neutral rights, as they whipped and hanged alleged deserters while impressing able-bodied men into the Royal Navy. The ***Chesapeake–Leopard* Affair** of 1807 was a particularly galling incident, as the British warship *Leopard*, lurking just a few miles off the coast of Norfolk, Virginia, assaulted the US frigate *Chesapeake* and impressed crew members.

The ongoing campaign of humiliation directly impinged on manliness and national honor, yet Jefferson was reluctant to go to war. War with Great Britain, unlike the limited strike against the Barbary pirates, was likely to prove a long and expensive proposition. Jefferson and other classical republican theorists associated war with entrenched executive power and higher taxes to fund a large standing army, all of which reminded them of British Red Coats and royal tyranny. The radical republican Paine had argued that creating a standing army as opposed to local militias would promote chauvinism and war because the state "will have no excuse for its enormous revenue and taxation, except it can prove that, somewhere or another, it has enemies." Thus war represented "the art of conquering at home," an opportunity for the "predatory classes" to prey on the "productive classes."

Unlike some future American presidents Jefferson thus viewed war as a last resort, hence the Virginian tried diplomacy, including what would later be termed economic sanctions. Interim diplomatic agreements quickly broke down, as neither Britain nor France would sacrifice military advantage out of concern for US neutral rights. In 1807 Jefferson took a drastic step, instituting the **Embargo**, cutting off trade with the European powers in the misguided hope that they were so dependent on the US market that they would respect American neutral rights. The Embargo failed to sway the Europeans, but it did cripple US shipping and commerce, especially in Federalist-dominated New England where Jefferson was already unpopular.

Victorious over the Federalists in the presidential campaign of 1808, Madison inherited the simmering conflict over impressment and Indian assaults against the expanding settlements. As diplomatic efforts failed and the Embargo undermined the economy Madison eventually decided on war as the only remaining option. He also established an important precedent on how to go about it: through a presidential address asking the Congress to declare war, as stipulated in the US Constitution. With Federalists opposed and many Republicans reluctant as well, the declaration of war against Britain encountered opposition before passing the House 79–49 and the Senate 19–13.

While France had also routinely violated US neutral rights at sea, popular outrage focused on the British bully, especially in the new Western states and territories where "John Bull" had long been blamed for inciting Indians against American settlers. As the population continued to rise in the West, an influential group of senators known as the **War Hawks** took control of the key Senate Foreign Relations Committee, blamed Britain rather than settler expansion for conflict with Indians, and called for a manly response. The charismatic Kentucky Senator Henry Clay decried the "shameful degradation" at the hands of Indians and the British. "Americans of the present day will prove to the enemy and to the World," declared South Carolina's John C. Calhoun, "that we have not only inherited the liberty which our fathers gave us, but also the will and power to maintain it." Citing British incitement of "the ruthless savage to tomahawk our women and children," Senator Felix Grundy of Tennessee vowed, "We shall drive the British from our Continent."

Once again the United States went to war with the most powerful nation in the world, a war that nearly proved disastrous and might well have been avoided. On the eve of war the British withdrew the orders-in-council that targeted US shipping. However, by the time news of that decision in London reached American ports the war had already begun. As **John Quincy Adams** later wrote of the War of 1812, "Its principal cause and justification was removed at precisely the moment when it occurred."

The United States went to war ill-prepared both militarily and strategically and suffered a series of defeats at the hands of Britons, Canadians, and Indians. As a cardinal tenet of the American imperial vision, it had long been expected that Canada would be incorporated within the "empire of liberty." Thus at the outset of the War of 1812 the Americans attacked Canada, as they had at the outset of the Revolutionary War, and once again the invasion force was repulsed. Many of the Canadian settlers were British loyalists who had removed north as a result of their opposition to the American Revolution. The US attackers included Irish immigrants, who relished an opportunity to strike back at Britons for their suppression of an Irish rebellion against royal authority in 1798. In the end the failed American attempt to take Canada served only to strengthen an emerging Canadian national identity, which would eventually lead to the rise of an independent nation north of the US border.

The Americans suffered another blow with the loss of Fort Michilimackinac, a key strategic point at the confluence of Lakes Michigan and Huron. Even worse, US forces ignominiously surrendered Detroit when British General Isaac Brock threatened to unleash "the numerous body of Indians who have attached themselves to my troops" and who would be "beyond control the moment the contest commences." With Napoleon's abdication in April 1814 and Britain assured of victory in Europe, the United States suffered another humiliation that summer when British forces conducted a punitive expedition into Washington, sacked the city, and burned the presidential mansion. The assault forced James and Dolley Madison to flee into the countryside with a portrait of George Washington and a few other priceless possessions in tow. Before setting the executive mansion aflame the British invaders, delighted to find the table set and fresh meat on the spit, sat down for a sumptuous meal accompanied by the president's favorite wines.

As in the Revolutionary War the United States won some key victories, however, most significantly Oliver Hazard Perry's triumph in the **Battle of Lake Erie** in September 1813. The naval victory enabled the United States to recapture Detroit, win the Battle of the Thames River, and mount a punitive expedition culminating in the burning of York (modern-day Toronto), which the British then avenged with the sacking of Washington. Yet the British were

Figure 2.4 Commander Oliver Hazard Perry's victory on Lake Erie in September 1813 was the turning point in the War of 1812. The United States entered the conflict unprepared, but escaped with its independence intact and patriotic spirit on the rise.

Source: Library of Congress, Prints and Photographs Division, LC-DIG-det-4a26407.

exhausted from the Napoleonic Wars and as in the Revolutionary War preoccupied with wider domestic and imperial concerns, hence they once again struck a peace accord with the United States. The **Treaty of Ghent** (1814) essentially brought an end to the war on the basis of the prewar status quo. Britain refused formally to renounce impressment but with the Napoleonic wars ending there would be no need for attacks on US shipping and seizure of sailors.

On January 8, 1815, before word of the treaty reached US shores, the former Tennessee militia leader, now Major General Andrew Jackson obliterated British invaders in the **Battle of New Orleans**. This lopsided triumph—the British suffered more than 2,000 casualties to about 70 for the US forces—had profound repercussions. The culminating victory enabled Americans to bask in a glow of triumph in what had been overall a middling and nearly disastrous war effort. Perhaps even more significant, the battle elevated Jackson to national prominence. He thus became the nation's most popular military and political hero since the venerable Washington.

While Jackson became a rising and ultimately unstoppable political force, the Federalists were destroyed as a viable political party. Most Federalists opposed the war from beginning to end. In December 1814 the Federalists convened the **Hartford Convention** in Connecticut in which they decried the "rule of Virginia" embodied in the presidents Washington, Jefferson, and Madison and called for changes in the "national compact," including reconsideration of the pro-slavery Constitution. The meeting proved poorly timed. The following month, in the wake of the ringing US victory in New Orleans, most Americans viewed the Hartford Convention an unpatriotic if not treasonous act in the midst of a foreign war.

The dissolution of the Federalists made the United States in effect a one-party state, which in turn further ensconced slavery as the foundation of the expanding southern economy, linked as it was with northern shipping and other industries. Despite the end of the international slave trade in 1808, the number of slaves doubled between 1800 and 1820 and continued to increase thereafter. In addition to sowing the seeds of civil war the expansion of slavery had foreign policy implications, singling out the United States in a world in which otherwise slavery was discredited and rapidly diminishing. At the time, however, the demand for southern cotton made slavery a profitable and expanding institution in the United States. Although subject to downturns such as the Panic of 1819, overall the US economy flourished after the War of 1812. A Market Revolution, fueled by landed expansion, increased internal trade and production, and a highly motivated immigrant workforce drove the dynamic economy of the new republic.

Although innocuously dubbed the War of 1812, the second power struggle with Britain thus had been both consequential and bitterly divisive. More than a fight between Britain and the United States, the war took on the character of a civil war, as Americans, Englishmen, Indians, and Irish not only fought each other but also carried on battles within their own ranks. In the end, however, though Americans remained divided on many issues, the permanence of the United States, which had been doubted by many, was now assured, at least until the Civil War more than two generations hence.

In September 1814, in the midst of the defense of Fort McHenry during the Battle of Baltimore, **Francis Scott Key** immortalized the nation's destiny to endure, that through the "perilous fight" the Stars and Stripes yet waved "o'er the land of the free and the home of the brave." The nation adopted Key's inspirational poem as its national anthem. At war's end editorial writers proudly proclaimed America's arrival "in the first rank of nations" after a "triumph of virtue over vice, of republican men and republican principles over the advocates and doctrines of Tyranny." Victory elevated the nation to, as Clay put it, "a proud and lofty station among the first nations of the world."

The preservation of American independence in a second war with Great Britain thus reinvigorated American exceptionalism, including the strong sense of providential destiny. Commemorations repeatedly invoked America's destiny for greatness "under God." "No nation, save Israel of old," exalted one writer, "hath experienced such great salvations" of liberty and national vindication. In 1815 a Methodist preacher from Brooklyn echoed popular sentiment when he declared, "It appears evident that God has been on our side."

While the war advanced US nationhood, it had profoundly negative consequences for indigenous people. As in the Revolutionary War Indians played a major role in the War of 1812. They won most battles in which they fought yet in the end the tribes were once again abandoned by their European allies and left squarely in the path of steamrolling American settler colonization.

After being driven out of the Ohio Valley in the 1790s, Indians mobilized resistance in the Indiana Territory behind the leadership of two charismatic Shawnee brothers, **Tecumseh** and **Tenskwatawa**. The latter, like many Indians, had fallen into drunkenness and despair before undergoing a personal spiritual revival and regaining sobriety. Soon known as The Prophet, Tenskwatawa preached that the whites and their ways were evil and the path to salvation lay in a return to Indian ways of living, dressing, speaking, worshipping, and consuming. The brothers and their followers asserted that if Indians united and rid themselves of the contamination of pale face culture, they could endure as independent peoples. Tenskwatawa gave Indians hope, spurred cultural renewal, and cleared the way for his brother to mobilize violent resistance.

In Their Words

Note delivered by Tecumseh to William Henry Harrison in Council at Vincennes, August 12, 1810

I am a Shawnee. My forefathers were warriors. Their son is a warrior. From them I take only my existence; from my tribe I take nothing. I am the maker of my own fortune; and oh! that I could make of my own fortune; and oh! that I could make that of my red people, and of my country, as great as the conceptions of my mind, when I think of the Spirit that rules the universe. I would not then come to Governor Harrison to ask him to tear the treaty and to obliterate the landmark; but I would say to him: "Sir, you have liberty to return to your own country."

The being within, communing with past ages, tells me that once, nor until lately, there was no white man on this continent; that it then all belonged to red men, children of the same parents, placed on it by the Great Spirit that made them, to keep it, to traverse it, to enjoy its productions, and to fill it with the same race, once a happy race, since made miserable by the white people, who are never contented but always encroaching. The way, and the only way, to check and to stop this evil, is for all the red men to unite in claiming a common and equal right in the land, as it was at first, and should be yet; for it never was divided, but belongs to all for the use of each. For no part has a right to sell, even to each other, much less to strangers—those who want all, and will not do with less.

Despite his contempt for the Americans, who had killed his father and two brothers and driven him from his burning village as a boy, Tecumseh gave diplomacy a try in talks with **William Henry Harrison**, governor of the Indiana Territory. An aggressive proponent of dispossessing Indians, Harrison had orchestrated fraudulent land sales on both sides of the Wabash River. When Harrison proved uncompromising, Tecumseh responded, "You have taken our lands from us and I do not see how we can remain at peace with you if you continue to do so." President Madison, he added, could "sit still in his town, and drink his wine, while you and I will have to fight it out."

While Tecumseh traveled south to organize pan-Indian resistance, Harrison set out with 1,200 soldiers to destroy Tenskwatawa's base at Prophetstown. On November 7, 1811, the Indians attacked Harrison's approaching forces along Tippecanoe Creek. The unprepared Americans suffered heavier casualties than the outnumbered Indians, who eventually had to call off the attack as ammunition ran low. They burned Prophetstown behind their retreat. The War Hawks welcomed conflict with Indians as they sought to seize Indian land for sale and settlement. The Americans knew that if they could drive the British from the continent, Indians and their lands would be left vulnerable to settler occupation and takeover.

Brutal violence between Americans and Indians replete with atrocities on both sides raged throughout the War of 1812. In January 1813, a group of Indians, having swilled a case of whiskey, slaughtered 30 to 40 Americans in southeastern Michigan following the **Battle of River Raisin**, the largest battle of the War of 1812 and a defeat for the United States. The American press was aflame with stories of the "savage" Indian killing and mutilation, but paid little attention to US scorched earth tactics across Indian country.

Figure 2.5 Indians fought both for and against the United States in the War of 1812. The print (circa 1860) depicts the Shawnee leader Tecumseh, who in 1813 died in the Battle of the Thames, saving the life of one of his brethren. Despite the efforts of Tecumseh and his brother, Tenskwatawa (The Prophet) more Shawnee actually fought with than against the United States in the conflict.

Source: Library of Congress, Prints and Photographs Division, LC-USZ62-46488.

As Britain began to scale back its war effort in the wake of the Battle of Lake Erie, the Red Coats once again abandoned their Indian allies. Tecumseh, who had been the architect of the British–Indian victory at Detroit, now expressed his contempt. The British, he declared, were "like a fat animal that carries its tail upon its back," but when frightened "drops its tail between its legs and runs off." With the news that on October 5, 1813, Tecumseh had been found dead and mutilated after the Battle of the Thames, the Indian resistance was now without its charismatic leader as well as the British ally. As in the Revolutionary War, the Treaty of Ghent excluded Indians from any involvement in the white man's diplomacy. First the British gave away Indian land in the Paris Treaty of 1783, then Napoleon sold off Indian homelands in the Louisiana Purchase, and now the British had left the Indians at the mercy of the Americans once again. The United States would not fulfill its pledge in Article IX of the Treaty of Ghent to make peace with the Indians and "forthwith to restore to such tribes or nations, respectively, all the possessions, rights, and privileges which they may have enjoyed or been entitled to" before the war broke out.

Not all Indians opposed the United States, however. Many Indians allied with the Americans in the War of 1812 in hopes of integrating into US society. The fate of the Shawnee offers a revealing example. More Shawnee actually fought with the United States than against it in the Battle of the Thames yet Americans did not reward these Indians with acceptance into their culture and society. Throughout the nineteenth century most "white" Americans viewed "red" and "black" people as well as Asians as racially inferior. With news of the River Raisin Massacre, settlers burned, plundered, and killed Shawnees regardless of whether they were allies or enemies. In the two decades following the War of 1812, the United States forced most Shawnee to yield their lands and become refugees west of the Mississippi River. In 1824, citing drunkenness and occasional violent clashes between whites and "roving Indians," the Ohio governor pronounced the remaining Shawnee "morally depraved" and thus subject to removal.

As settlers flooded into the territories after the War of 1812, Indian removal or ethnic cleansing soon followed. As they entered the federal union, Kentucky (1792), Tennessee (1796), Ohio (1803), Indiana (1816), Illinois (1818), Michigan (1837), Iowa (1846), and Wisconsin (1848) simultaneously drove out not only Indians but also "half-breeds." As Americans stepped up the march to achieve their "manifest destiny" in the years after the War of 1812, the dreams of Tenskwatawa and Tecumseh to save their homelands and way of life had turned to ashes.

Select Bibliography

Dull, Jonathan R. *A Diplomatic History of the American Revolution*. New Haven, CT: Yale University Press, 1985.

Bloch, Ruth H. *Visionary Republic: Millennial Themes in American Thought, 1756–1800*. New York: Cambridge University Press, 1985.

Perkins, Bradford. *The Cambridge History of American Foreign Relations, Volume I: The Creation of a Republican Empire, 1776–1865*. New York: Cambridge University Press, 1993.

Gould, Eliga. *Among the Powers of the Earth: The American Revolution and the Making of a New World Empire*. Cambridge, MA: Harvard University Press, 2012.

Marks, Frederick III, *Independence on Trial: Foreign Affairs and the Making of the Constitution*. Wilmington, DE: Scholarly Resources, 1986.

Harper, John L. *American Machiavelli: Alexander Hamilton and the Origins of US Foreign Policy*. Cambridge: Cambridge University Press, 2004.

Johnson, Ronald A. *Diplomacy in Black and White: John Adams, Touissaint Louverture, and Their Atlantic World Alliance*. Athens: University of Georgia Press, 2014.

Cogliano, Francis D. *Emperor of Liberty: Thomas Jefferson's Foreign Policy*. New Haven, CT: Yale University Press, 2014.

Kastor, Peter J. *The Nation's Crucible: The Louisiana Purchase and the Creation of America*. New Haven, CT: Yale University Press, 2004.

Aron, Stephen. *How the West Was Lost: The Transformation of Kentucky from Daniel Boone to Henry Clay*. Baltimore, MD: Johns Hopkins University Press, 1996.

Stagg, J. C. A., *The War of 1812: Conflict for a Continent*. Cambridge: Cambridge University Press, 2012.

Wood, Gordon S. *The Radicalism of the American Revolution*. New York: Knopf, 1992.

Dowd, Gregory Evans. *A Spirited Resistance: The North American Indian Struggle for Unity, 1745–1815*. Baltimore, MD: Johns Hopkins University Press, 1992.

Taylor, Alan. *The Civil War of 1812: American Citizens, British Subjects, Irish Rebels, and Indian Allies*. New York: Alfred A. Knopf, 2010.

Waldstreicher, David. *In the Midst of Perpetual Fetes: The Making of American Nationalism, 1776–1820*. Chapel Hill: University of North Carolina Press, 1997.

3 Manifest Destiny

Overview

The years between the War of 1812 and the Mexican War (1846–48) marked the high tide of Manifest Destiny. Eager to incorporate new lands for settlers and market-driven development, the United States expanded and solidified its control of the Southeast before focusing its attention on the Southwest and especially California. Ongoing campaigns of Indian removal and a war of annexation targeting newly independent Mexico enabled the United States to achieve what many believed was its providential destiny to take command of much of the North American continent. Settler colonial expansion, bolstered by faith in American exceptionalism, continued to drive US foreign relations in this era.

Taking Florida

Although Americans typically think of Jamestown, Virginia, founded in 1607, as the first North American colony it was actually St. Augustine, established by Spain on the Atlantic coast of "La Florida" in 1565. In 1763 Spain lost Florida in the French and Indian War, but got it back from Britain under the Treaty of Paris 20 years later. Thereafter as US traders and settlers filtered into the Southeast tensions mounted between and among the United States, Spain, and the myriad indigenous tribes of the region. Particularly in the wake of the Louisiana Purchase, many US leaders sought to bring the divided Florida territory into the Union.

In 1810 the United States annexed West Florida by proclamation. President James Madison and Secretary of State James Monroe set their sights on East Florida and dispatched General George Mathews to reconnoiter the area and consider the prospects of US annexation. Mathews went beyond his vague instructions, colluding with various settlers and adventurers to seize Amelia Island and proclaim East Florida part of the United States. However, with the nation on the verge of war with Britain, Madison and Monroe backed off, repudiated Mathews, and focused their attention on the war to the north with Britain and the Indians.

Americans made little effort to mask their expansionist ambitions. As the leading "War Hawk" Henry Clay put it in 1810, the United States ultimately would consist of "not only the old thirteen colonies, but the entire country west of the

Mississippi [and] East Florida." Spain, which for centuries fought with indigenous tribes for control of Florida, now allied with the Indians against the American threat. The Spanish also allied with runaway slaves, called "maroons" by American slaveholders and described as "the vilest species" of people on earth. Settlers damned the Spanish for encouraging Indian attacks on their farms and plantations and for arming and incorporating blacks into militias. As long as Spain held East Florida the region could serve as a haven for hostile Indians and runaway slaves, neither of which the United States would tolerate over the long term.

Negro Abraham.

Figure 3.1 Runaway slaves, called "maroons" by the Americans, allied with the Seminole Indians in Florida and together became formidable opponents of the United States. Abraham, the runaway slave pictured above, acted as an interpreter for the Seminole.

Source: Library of Congress, Prints and Photographs Division, LC-USZ62-75977.

Before he became the hero of the Battle of New Orleans, Andrew Jackson first rose to national prominence by defeating a faction of the Creek (Muskogee) Indians in the **Battle of Horseshoe Bend** on the Tallapoosa River in central Alabama. On March 27, 1814, Jackson led a 2,500-man force of Tennessee militia and Indian allies against the Red Stick faction of the Creek Indians, whose resistance had been inspired in part by Tecumseh. Jackson's forces slaughtered more than 800 Red Sticks (cutting off the tips of their noses to get an accurate count)—557 in the battle and some 300 more who plunged into the river and tried unsuccessfully to swim to safety. In the Treaty of Fort Jackson, signed on August 9, 1814, the US war with the Creeks formally ended with a massive annexation of more than half of all Creek land. A large faction of acculturated Creeks had sided with the United States against the Red Sticks, as civil war roiled the Creek nation. As with its Indian allies in previous wars the United States refused to reward the wartime alliance by allowing the Upper Creeks to keep their land, which instead went over to settlers and land speculators.

The triumph in New Orleans and news of the Treaty of Ghent ended the War of 1812, thus relieving the United States of the British threat and prompting renewed efforts to seize control of the Southeast. In the wake of Horseshoe Bend, the United States constructed Fort Gadsden and other military posts and laid siege to the so-called "Negro Fort" where blacks and Indians were holding out along the Apalachicola River. On July 27, 1816, a red-hot cannonball fired from a US gunboat hit the magazine at the fort, blowing it to pieces and killing scores of people (the precise number is disputed). "The great Ruler of the Universe must have used us as instruments in chastising the blood-thirsty and murderous wretches that defended the fort," a brigadier general declared.

In his characteristic aggressive style, General Jackson would not be deterred from the quest to "liberate" all of Florida. On April 6, 1818, amid the so-called **First Seminole War** Jackson razed several Indian villages, seized Fort Marks from the Spanish, and hanged two British subjects in the process. The British expressed outrage, but realistic observers in both London and Madrid perceived that the United States inevitably would incorporate the southeastern portion of the continent. In 1819 Spain acquiesced, as Secretary of State John Quincy Adams negotiated the **Transcontinental Treaty** (also known as the Adams–Onís Treaty). Spain turned East Florida over to the United States and established agreed upon boundaries pertaining to Texas and the Southwest. Perhaps most significantly, as the name "transcontinental" implies, Spain became the first nation to recognize US boundaries extending to the Pacific Ocean. The United States was well on the way to achieving its "destiny" to extend its power from "sea to sea."

The Monroe Doctrine

In the years following the War of 1812 Britain and the United States began to forge closer ties, a "**rapprochement**" (bettering of relations) rooted in the Jay

JOHN QUINCY ADAMS
6^(th) PRESIDENT OF THE UNITED STATES.

Published by G. ENDICOTT, 5? Broadway
NEW YORK.

Figure 3.2 Considered by many the greatest diplomat in American history, John Quincy Adams served as minister to Britain, secretary of state, and became the sixth president of the United States. He negotiated the Transcontinental Treaty, taking US borders to the Pacific, and was the architect of the Monroe Doctrine.

Source: Library of Congress, Prints and Photographs Division, LC-USZ62-94849.

Treaty (1795). However, it would require more than a century for the Anglo-American rapprochement to fully flower. Americans resented (and perhaps envied) British power as well as the seeming arrogance of "John Bull," yet at the same time the British Empire offered a reliable market for American farmers, especially cotton growers, as well as manufacturers. Despite simmering resentments, Britons and Americans viewed themselves as something of a common people with supposedly shared racial characteristics (a mythical "Anglo-Saxon" heritage), and imperial destinies to rule over lesser peoples. In 1817 the British and Americans signed the **Rush–Bagot Treaty**, an agreement on limitation of naval armaments on the Great Lakes.

In 1823 the British proposed issuing a joint statement with the United States against the reassertion of Spanish power in Latin America. The British diplomatic initiative came in response to a series of revolts against Portuguese and Spanish imperial rule throughout Latin America. As a result of the revolts only Cuba and Puerto Rico would remain under Spanish rule. As the Latin American revolutions unfolded British Foreign Secretary George Canning approached the United States about the prospect of a joint statement against any future European colonization (or re-colonization) in the Americas. Some members of Monroe's Cabinet, notably Secretary of War John C. Calhoun endorsed Canning's proposal, but Adams distrusted the British, who held onto various spheres of influence in Lain America. Moreover, Adams wanted to strike an independent course for US foreign policy. Why should the United States come in merely "as a cockboat in the wake of a British man-of-war?" he queried.

Monroe saw the logic of this proposal, hence the United States issued a unilateral rather than a bilateral declaration pronouncing that North and South America "are henceforth not to be considered as subjects for colonization by any European powers." At the same time the United States pledged its commitment to non-intervention in European affairs, which it lacked the power to accomplish in any case. While Europeans scoffed at the presumptuous pronouncement, Americans greeted the declaration, made by Monroe in his annual message to Congress on December 2, 1823, with widespread approval.

The **Monroe Doctrine**, as it became known in later years, emphasized sharp distinctions between the "Old" and "New" Worlds while asserting US leadership of the latter. The statement thus powerfully reinforced American exceptionalism. It also shrewdly combined an anti-imperial message—non-colonization of other peoples—with a subtle assertion of power, namely that the United Sates rather than Europeans would supervise the course of events in the Western Hemisphere. The Monroe Doctrine was purely a declaration—it called for no direct action—but it was an important example of a robust US nationalism, one opposed to European intervention in the Americas without renouncing its own prerogatives. Finally, the Monroe Doctrine spurred national unity that had been tested by divisions spawned by the Panic of 1819 as well as a crisis of the Union over the expansion of slavery narrowly averted by the Missouri Compromise (1820).

The US leaders did not consult any Latin American before issuing the doctrine nor did they consider the racially inferior and Catholic states capable of self-government. Well aware of these attitudes, the Latin American states led by Colombia, Mexico, and Peru only belatedly and grudgingly invited the United States to attend the first **Congress of Panama** in 1826. Adams emphasized non-colonization and economic ties in an effort to shore up relations, but observant Latin Americans could anticipate eventual US expansion into Texas, Cuba, and beyond.

The Indian Removal Act

Settler colonization—the determination to expand to create new economic opportunities for a chosen people—remained a driving force behind US foreign relations on the North American continent. While many Americans empathized with Indians over the erosion of their homelands and cultures, others had bitter memories of the "savages" who had allied with the nation's adversaries, Britain and Spain, and waged war on settler communities as well as the battlefield. Most Americans agreed with Calhoun, who observed that victory over Britain in the War of 1812 had brought an "important change." Bereft of their British ally Indians now could be dictated to rather than negotiated with by the United States. As Calhoun put it, "Our views of their interest, and not their own, ought to govern them."

Following his election in 1828, President Jackson orchestrated the most sweeping Indian Removal campaign in American history. An unapologetic slaveholder and Tennessee plantation owner, Jackson had both allied with and fought against Indians. Ultimately, however, he viewed them as a menace "constantly infesting our frontier." Writing to William Henry Harrison after the Battle of Tippecanoe in 1811, Jackson declared, "The blood of our murdered countrymen must be avenged . . . That banditti must be swept from the face of the earth." Indian removal from the Southeast was Jackson's top priority as president and, as was characteristic of him, nothing would stand in his way. He and his avid supporters especially in the southeastern states overcame Indian resistance, political rivals, humanitarian reformers, and even the Supreme Court.

The **Indian Removal Act** (IRA) of 1830 proposed that "such tribes or nations of Indians *as may choose*" relinquish their land in return for "districts" west of the Mississippi River. Few, least of all the indigenous people, were fooled by the illusion of choice in the legislation, as it became clear that Indians were being forced from their homes and lands. Under the IRA the United States pledged to "forever secure and guarantee to them, and their heirs or successors, the country so exchanged with them," but this promise would also come up empty. Jackson better captured the actual spirit of the law, explaining that progress required "the *extinction* of one generation to make room for another"; to replace "a country covered with forests and ranged by a few thousand savages [with] our own extensive Republic, studded with cities, towns, and prosperous farms."

In Their Words

"Against the Forcible Removal of the Indians without the Limits of the United States," Memorial of the Ladies of Steubenville, Ohio, February 15, 1830

To the Honorable Senate and House of Representatives of the United States,

The present crisis in the affairs of the Indian nations calls loudly on all who can feel for the woes of humanity, to solicit, with earnestness, your honorable body to bestow on this subject, involving, as it does, the prosperity and happiness of more than fifty thousand of our fellow Christians, the immediate consideration demanded by its interesting nature and pressing importance. It is readily acknowledged, that the wise and venerated founders of our country's free institutions have committed the powers of Government to those whom nature and reason declare the best fitted to exercise them; and your memorialists would sincerely deprecate any presumptuous interference on the part of their own sex with the ordinary political affairs of the country, as wholly unbecoming the character of the American females. Even in private life, we may not presume to direct the general conduct, or control the acts of those who stand in the near and guardian relations of husbands and brothers; yet all admit that there are times when duty and affection call on us to advise and persuade, as well as to cheer or console . . . When injury and oppression threaten to crush a hapless people within our borders, we, the feeblest of the feeble, appeal with confidence to those who should be representatives of national virtues as they are the depositaries of national powers, and implore them to succor the weak and unfortunate. In despite of the undoubted national right which the Indians have to the land of their forefathers, and in the face of solemn treaties, pledging the faith of the nation for their secure possession of those lands, it is intended, we are told, to force them from their native soil, to compel them to seek new homes in a distant and dreary wilderness. To you, then, as the constitutional protectors of the Indians within our territory, and as the peculiar guardians of our national character, and our counter's welfare, we solemnly and honestly appeal, to save this remnant of a much injured people from annihilation, to shield our country from the curses denounced on the cruel and ungrateful, and to shelter the American character from lasting dishonor. And your petitioners will ever pray.

Indian removal was hotly contested in Congress not least because it targeted the "five civilized tribes" of the Southeast who had done the most to acculturate to the American way of life. Thousands of Cherokee, Chickasaw, Choctaw, Creeks, and Seminole Indians spoke English, lived and dressed like Americans, had adopted white gender roles (men farming and women holding down the domestic sphere), and many even owned slaves. Some Americans who "thought it had been right to supplant the savage hunter with the civilized farmer" questioned whether it was right to "remove the Indian farmer so the white farmer could enjoy his country." The opponents of the removal campaign came overwhelmingly from north of the Mason–Dixon line and many linked the defense of Indians with their growing opposition to slavery as well as what they perceived as overweening southern political influence over the nation. A group of activist women mounted a massive anti-removal petition campaign that went before the Congress. Many of the opponents of Indian Removal and of slavery were Protestant reformers who pointed out that many Indians had acculturated and converted to Christianity. Protestant missionaries, aided by the federal

Civilization Act of 1819, had long been streaming into Indian country to save souls, a project that gained momentum with the spread of the Second Great Awakening religious revival of the 1820s to 1840s.

Hostile to northern interference with Indian removal as well as with slave owning, Jackson and his southern constituents in Alabama, Georgia, and Mississippi were determined to prevail. The invention of the cotton gin and the profitability of cotton on the international market reinforced the desire to seize Indian land for new farms and slave plantations for white settlers. Moreover, gold had been discovered on Cherokee land in 1829. In the final analysis, as one Georgia politician put it, Indians were "useless and burdensome" and a "race not admitted to be equal."

The IRA passed by a narrow margin—101–97 in the House and 28–19 in the US Senate. After bludgeoning the Choctaw into signing the **Treaty of Dancing Rabbit Creek** in 1830, the United States seized control of 11 million acres and forcibly removed some 12,500–14,000 Choctaw from Mississippi to the Indian Territory of Oklahoma. Plagued by the disorganization, unscrupulousness, and insufficient funding that characterized the entire removal program, as many as a third of the Choctaw died along the way or shortly after arrival in the Oklahoma Territory. Cholera and other diseases ravaged their ranks.

The pattern of coerced treaties followed by forced marches that proved lethal to the Indians thus had been set. Americans next drove the Chickasaw from their homes in Mississippi. From 500 to 800 of the 4,000 of them died en route to the west. The Creeks mounted a violent resistance in the "Creek War" of 1836 but they could not overcome the settlers backed by the state and federal governments. Alabama militia and federal forces captured some 2,500 Creeks, put them in chains, and crowded them onto barges for the trip down the Alabama River and over some 800 miles of land for the three-month journey to Oklahoma. A total of nearly 20,000 Creeks were removed, including "the friendly disposed part of them" who had fought with Jackson against their Red Stick rivals. During the removal of 1834–37, some 3,500 Creeks died en route or shortly after arrival in Oklahoma.

No tribe had done more to "Americanize" than the Cherokee, who also proved to be a most formidable political opponent of the removal campaign. A large number of Cherokee were Christians and mixed bloods (partly "white") and hundreds had fought with the United States in various conflicts. The tribe held 15 million acres with abundant farms and livestock and worked by hundreds of slaves. The Cherokee nation had a written constitution with three branches of government and had established its own police forces.

The Cherokee resisted tenaciously, as they editorialized, lobbied, protested, and ultimately argued their case before the Supreme Court. In his March 18, 1831, decision on *Cherokee Nation v. Georgia*, Chief Justice **John Marshall** rejected the Cherokee claim to be a foreign people, declaring instead that they were a "domestic dependent nation." When a tiny minority of Cherokee succumbed to the state and federal pressure and signed the **Treaty of New Echota** in 1835, the vast majority of Cherokee denounced them as traitors

Figure 3.3 John Ross, a wealthy, bilingual mixed-blood, was chief of the Cherokee nation for decades, both before and after removal to Oklahoma, which he had vigorously contested.

Source: Library of Congress, Prints and Photographs Division, LC-USZC4-3156.

and eventually assassinated several as collaborationists. In the infamous "trail of tears" a minimum of 4,000 and possibly as many as 8,000 of some 18,000 Cherokee who were removed died in the stockades or en route. Along the way the Indians were robbed, cheated by contractors, and left to freeze and starve before trailing wolf packs.

While the Cherokee put up the best legal fight, the Seminole exploited geography and their alliance with runaway slaves to mount the strongest and most prolonged military resistance in the entire history of American settler colonialism. The so-called **Second Seminole War** lasted from 1835 to 1842 and was followed by a third Seminole War in 1856 that lasted another two and a half years. On December 28, 1835, the Seminole and their black allies defeated a US assault force under Major Francis L. Dade, who died in the battle that Americans labeled a "massacre." On Christmas Eve of 1837, a combined force of 380–480 under Colonel Zachary Taylor lost a battle on the shores of Lake Okeechobee, though Taylor claimed victory nonetheless. Livid over the Indians' ongoing resistance, Jackson now in retirement blamed "damned cowards" for the "disgraceful" war effort. Demanding a more manly national response, the old general insisted that "with fifty women" he could "whip every Indian that ever crossed the Suwannee" River.

The United States eventually put in camps and then removed some 3,000 Seminole, but about 1,500 Americans and an unknown number of African-Americans and Indians died in the process. Just as a community of Cherokee held out in the mountains of North Carolina, a band of Seminole remained in Florida and successfully resisted removal yet again in the Third Seminole War. In fact both tribes remain ensconced in their respective enclaves to this day.

In the wake of the IRA, massive waves of immigration swallowed up Indian communities and hunting grounds all across the eastern approaches to the Mississippi River. In Illinois, for example, land sales accelerated from less than 100,000 acres a year in 1829 to 2 million acres in 1836. Wisconsin grew from 11,000 inhabitants in 1836 to more than 300,000 by 1850. As Americans built their farms and communities, indigenous people were forced to become refugees in the "Indian country" west of the Mississippi.

Indian resistance to US settler colonization proved futile. Indians could win battles but not the war, as evidenced by the **Black Hawk War**. Black Hawk's tribe, the Sac, along with the Foxes, Winnebago, and other bands had lost land to the United States through coerced and fraudulent treaties throughout the early nineteenth century. The United States quelled an "uprising" by the Winnebago in 1827 and used the occasion to seize additional Indian land. Black Hawk and

Figure 3.4 The "Battle" of Bad Axe in 1832 in modern-day Wisconsin was actually a slaughter of Sac and Fox Indians.

Source: Library of Congress, Prints and Photographs Division, LC-USZ62-90.

the Sac did not seek conflict with the United States but fighting erupted when the Indians went in search of hunting grounds on the eastern side of the Mississippi.

Once fighting began in 1832 Black Hawk orchestrated an effective resistance, holding off a much larger force in the Battle of Wisconsin Heights. The Americans responded with a large federal force and hundreds of volunteers to slaughter some 500 Indians in what was called the **Battle of Bad Axe**. Invoking predominant racial and religious mores, a settler observed that the "Ruler of the Universe" had overseen the victory over "the savage enemy and the common enemy of the country." Potawatomi and Winnebago bands allied with the United States in the Black Hawk War but their hopes that the military assistance would enable them to keep their own lands proved unfounded.

Solidifying National Identity

With the passing of the Revolutionary generation Americans began to establish lasting traditions reinforcing American exceptionalism rooted in a distinctive national identity. Following Washington's death in 1799 Mason ("Parson") Weems exalted the heroic Revolutionary leader and first president with a glowing biography. Franklin, who died in 1790, was also sanctified in American history and memory. On July 4, 1826, as the nation celebrated the Jubilee of

THE DECLARATION OF INDEPENDENCE.
JULY 4ʰ 1776.

Figure 3.5 Beginning in the 1830s the wide circulation of this painting celebrating the signing of the Declaration of Independence reflected growing national pride and patriotism in the United States. July 4 began to be celebrated nationally following the coincidental deaths of revolutionary heroes John Adams and Thomas Jefferson on July 4, 1826.

Source: Library of Congress, Prints and Photographs Division, LC-USZC2-2244.

Independence on the fiftieth anniversary of the Declaration, Jefferson and John Adams, longtime political rivals who had reconciled and developed friendship and correspondence, both died. Many Americans viewed the coincidence of the deaths on July 4 as divinely inspired. From that point forward, the Fourth of July became a prominent national holiday celebrated by nearly all Americans.

The United States distinguished itself from Britain and the rest of Europe not merely with celebrations and assertions such as the Monroe Doctrine, but also with a distinctive culture. Americans dressed differently, spoke their own version of English, drank coffee rather than tea, and celebrated their democracy in contrast to the reinforcement of monarchy and aristocracy in Europe following the Napoleonic Wars. Suffrage for white males had been broadened under Jackson giving rise to the era of the "common man." Political participation, turnout of eligible voters, and pride in the political system reached their peak at this point in American history.

Pride and patriotism characterized the United States. The second war with Britain, the ouster of Spain, and Indian Removal were triumphs of masculine power and rugged individualism in a nation that had "tamed the frontier." Despite the serious economic recessions of 1819 and 1837, overall the economy grew rapidly. The nation became better integrated as a result of the Transportation Revolution, a rapid proliferation of new roads, canals, steamboats, and railroads. The United States remained a magnet for immigrants, a land of opportunity. However, extremes of wealth and poverty prevailed and periods of boom and bust characterized the nation's political economy.

The United States was a "white man's country" in which other races and notably African-Americans, Hispanics, and Indians were considered inferior and thus subjugated. Indians were removed; Hispanics became second-class citizens; and slavery rather than withering away as many of the Founding Fathers anticipated had been reinforced by the expansion of "King Cotton" in the Deep South. Ominously, many slaveholders unapologetically defended slavery as, in Calhoun's words, a "positive good" rather than viewing it as a necessary evil that eventually would wither and die.

Americans were also exceptionally religious. From the 1820s to the 1840s the Second Great Awakening burned over the nation. Emotional sermons and prolonged camp meetings reignited the fires of sin and individual salvation. The emotional Protestant revival reinforced the widespread belief in American providential destiny. As the Reverend Lyman Beecher declaimed, "This nation, in the Providence of God, is destined to lead the way in the moral and political emancipation of the world."

In 1831 a young visiting French scholar, **Alexis de Tocqueville**, proved a shrewd observer of America's democratic society and the nation's powerful sense of exceptionalism. On religion Tocqueville observed that the formal separation of Church and state ironically "increased its real strength," as Christianity was "an established and irresistible fact which no one seeks to attack or defend." Though Americans had freedom of speech and the press they nonetheless tended to embrace a sameness of outlook, a "tyranny of the majority" in which "common opinion" had "become a sort of religion, with the majority

Figure 3.6 The famous painting "American Progress," though released in 1873, came to signify "Manifest Destiny," a widespread faith in the nation's providential destiny to inherit the North American continent.

Source: Library of Congress, Prints and Photographs Division, LC-DIG-ppmsca-09855.

as its prophet." Finally, Americans, having been "constantly told that they are the only religious, enlightened, and free people" had cultivated "an immensely high opinion of themselves and are not far from believing that they form a species apart from the rest of the human race." Fascinated by the evolution of America's unique democratic society, Tocqueville published his two-volume *Democracy in America* in 1835 and 1840, which has since been considered indispensible for understanding antebellum society and US national identity.

These American characteristics—pride and patriotism, the drive for economic opportunity, exaltation of whiteness, faith that they enjoyed a special blessing from God, and a manly confidence of victory in the event of war—lay behind the emergence of an aggressively expansionist foreign policy. Americans called it **Manifest Destiny**.

Interpreting the Past

The Mexican War

Historical research has illuminated previously unexplored aspects of the so-called Mexican War. By viewing the conflict exclusively within an American context, generations of scholars paid little attention to either the Mexican perspective or the crucial role Indians played. From the Mexican perspective, Hispanic residents of the northern borderlands had conflicting loyalties between incoming American settlers, with which they had many financial ties, and the distant government in Mexico City, which failed to protect them from Indian attacks. In the final analysis, the "North American invasion" proved to be a devastating loss for Mexico with enduring geographic consequences and repercussions.

Indian tribes were crucial, though long overlooked, participants in the "Mexican" War. As a result of their attacks on Hispanic residents throughout Mexico's northern borderlands, the Comanche, Kiowa, and other tribes left Mexico's northern frontier weakened and vulnerable to a US invasion. Indians thus played a critical role in a conflict typically depicted as involving only the United States and Mexico. Perceiving Mexico as vulnerable because of the preexisting conflict with Indians, President James K. Polk and his advisers decided to go to war to oust Hispanics as well as indigenous people, neither of which they considered legitimate claimants to the "American frontier."

The War with Mexico

The term "**Mexican War**" (1846–48) misleads as much as it informs as a label for the conflict in which the United States seized control of Texas, the sprawling territory of New Mexico, and, most significantly, California. In actuality Mexico, which gained its independence from Spain in 1821, never had control of these vast regions. Beginning in the late sixteenth century, Spain had tried, but failed to establish colonial authority through the Catholic Church backed by a string of fortresses from Texas to northern California. Although some Indians converted to Christianity, neither Spain nor Mexico came close to establishing authority over the wide variety of tribes who populated the vast region.

By the time of the war with the United States division and disunity plagued newly independent Mexico, especially on its northern borderlands. Indian tribes, notably the powerful Comanche but also the Apache, Kiowa, Navaho, Ute, and other bands spread death, enslavement, and depredation through raids across Mexico's northern frontier. The Spanish residents of these regions—*Californios*, *Neuvomexicanos*, and *Tejanos*—had no reason to be loyal to a distant and elite dominated government in Mexico City that failed to protect them from the marauding bands. Meanwhile, Americans had begun to filter into the region, especially after the opening of the Santa Fe Trail in 1821.

Keenly aware of Mexico's inability to control its northern frontiers, the United States would take advantage of Mexico's weakness and incorporate the contested borderlands into the expanding federal union. Like the Indians, the Mexicans found themselves squarely in the path of a crusading nation determined to extend its settler colonization across the continent. As with the history of Indian tribes, the United States would willingly go to war in order to achieve its expansionist ambitions.

While dispute over the status of Texas provided the immediate cause of the war, California was the ultimate prize. By taking control of the west coast, the United States would become a Pacific power and thus a future world power. In the end the United States would seize more than half of Mexico's territory, incorporating Texas, the Southwest, and California. With the addition of the Oregon Territory the United States laid claim to much of the continent from the Rio Grande to the 49th parallel. All of this territory remained occupied by hundreds of thousands of non-Americans in scores of Indian tribes as well as Hispanic residents and various hybrid ethnicities.

Beginning in the 1820s Mexico authorized US settler expansion into Texas, in large part to check the power of the predatory Indian tribes. Mexico formally required the migrants to become citizens, speak Spanish, and convert to the Catholic Church, but these requirements could not be enforced. Americans, primarily from the southern states, soon outnumbered the *Tejanos* and in time would take control of the territory and establish it as a slaveholding republic.

The Texans' declaration of independence in 1836 brought an immediate military response from Mexico, including massacres of Texas-Americans at the Spanish missions Alamo and Goliad. The Texans rallied and on April 21 their forces led by Sam Houston surprised the army of **Antonio Lopez de Santa Anna** at San Jacinto and won the decisive "battle" for Texas's independence. Exacting their revenge for Goliad and the Alamo, the Texans slaughtered 630 Mexicans to only nine deaths of their own. Santa Anna preserved his own life by signing off on Texas's independence, a pledge he renounced upon his return to Mexico City.

The southern states especially identified with the Texans and favored inclusion of Texas in the Union as a slave state. In 1837 the United States formally recognized the independent **Lone Star Republic** after Mexico rejected a US offer to purchase Texas. Hostilities between the Texans and Mexicans continued, including a bloody battle in 1842 for control of San Antonio.

In 1844 the election to the presidency of James K. Polk, Jackson's protégé from Tennessee, became the catalyst of the Mexican War. Like Jackson in the case of Indian Removal, Polk would allow nothing to stand in the way of US annexation not only of Mexico but also of California and the Southwest. In February 1845 the US Congress annexed Texas by joint resolution. Upon its acceptance later that year Texas formally entered the Union as the twenty-eighth state.

In Their Words

John O'Sullivan, "Annexation," United States Magazine and Democratic Review *(July–August 1845)*

It is now time for the opposition to the Annexation of Texas to cease . . . It is time for the common duty of Patriotism to the Country to succeed—or if this claim will not be recognized, it is at least time for common sense to acquiesce with decent grace in the inevitable and the irrevocable . . . Texas is now ours . . . Other nations have undertaken to intrude themselves into it, between us and the proper parties to the case, in a spirit of hostile interference against us, for the avowed object of thwarting our policy and hampering our power, limiting our greatness and checking the fulfillment of our manifest destiny to overspread the continent allotted by Providence for the free development of our yearly multiplying millions . . .

The independence of Texas was complete and absolute. It was independence not only in fact, but of right. No obligation of duty towards Mexico tended in the least degree to restrain our right to effect the desired recovery of the fair province once our own—whatever motives of policy might have prompted a more deferential consideration of her feelings and her pride, as involved in the question . . . The singular result has been produced, that while our neighbor has, in truth, no real right to blame or complain—when all the wrong is on her side, and there has been on ours a degree of delay and forbearance, in deference to her pretensions, which is to be paralleled by few precedents in the history of other nations . . .

California [will] fall away from the loose adhesion which, in such a country as Mexico, holds a remote province in a slight equivocal kind of dependence on the metropolis. Imbecile and distracted, Mexico never can exert any real governmental authority over such a country . . . The Anglo-Saxon foot is already on its borders. Already the advance guard of the irresistible army of Anglo-Saxon emigration has begun to pour down upon it, armed with the plough and the rifle, and marking its trail with schools and colleges, courts and representative halls, mills and meeting-houses . . . and American millions—destined to gather beneath the flutter of the stripes and stars, in the fast hastening year of the Lord 1845!

Americans seized upon a term popularized by a New York journalist in 1845, asserting continental expansion was the nation's "manifest destiny." Manifest Destiny was an amalgam of nationalism, crusading Protestantism, and material self-interest. Calling on the United States to go beyond Texas to incorporate California and the Southwest, Sullivan described annexation of new territories as the "fulfillment of our manifest destiny to overspread the continent allotted by Providence for the free development of our yearly multiplying millions." Sullivan, editor of the *Democratic Review*, thus popularized the term "manifest destiny," which apparently had been coined by one of his staff writers, Jane McManus Cazneau, a fervid expansionist later dubbed the "mistress of manifest destiny."

As a chosen nation on a mission to take control of the continent, Americans could justify expansion onto lands held by inferior and polyglot races of Hispanics and Indians. "Exterminating" Mexico's "weaker blood . . . we regard with as much certainty as we do the final extinction of the Indian races, to

JAMES K. POLK.

PRESIDENT ELECT OF THE UNITED STATES.

Figure 3.7 President James K. Polk, elected in 1844, was an aggressive expansionist in the mold of his fellow Tennessean Andrew Jackson. Polk successfully spurred a war of US expansion with Mexico and blustered for US possession of all of the Oregon Territory before accepting a negotiated settlement with Great Britain in 1846.

Source: Library of Congress, Prints and Photographs Division, LC-USZC4-6089.

which the mass of the Mexican population seem very little superior," the Reverend H. W. Bellows averred in the midst of the war. Strongly anti-Catholic rhetoric, which had gained strength in the 1840s in response to the unsettling waves of Irish immigration, was now applied to the Mexicans. Proponents of war criticized Mexican men as weak whereas the "pretty *señoritas*" were desirable and well suited to become "wives and mothers of a better race." The most popular song of the day, "Yankee Doodle Dandy," reinforced manliness and depicted the Mexican War, like the Revolutionary War, as a fight for liberty and nationhood.

On the eve of the Mexican War the United States nearly provoked a third war with Great Britain. Conflict was averted when Polk backed down from an unrealistic claim to the 54° line of latitude in the disputed Oregon Territory. The Tennessean had nearly shattered the budding rapprochement with the "mother" country, which had gained momentum with the signing of the **Webster–Ashburton Treaty** in 1842. Under that accord the United States and Britain had settled border disputes between Maine and New Brunswick, affirmed the 49th parallel as the border along Lake Superior, and agreed on shared usage of the Great Lakes. By that time American settlers had begun streaming up the Oregon Trail to the Northwest, where the boundary with Britain had not been settled. As the British outfitted the Royal Navy for war, Polk took the advice to abandon the reckless claim of "54–40° or fight" and settled at the 49th parallel in keeping with precedent. The **Oregon Treaty** (1846) established the boundary and the road to a full Anglo-American rapprochement continued, though many bumps still lay ahead.

Polk had not given up on expansive claims to disputed borders. While he compromised with the fellow Protestant and "Anglo-Saxon" British, the president confronted the "mongrel" Catholic Mexicans with the demand for a new US border at the Rio Grande rather than the Nueces River border of Texas that the Mexicans had previously acknowledged. War could be averted only if Mexico accepted not only the unprecedented new border with Texas but also the loss of California and New Mexico. The vast terrain of New Mexico encompassed not only the modern-day Southwest (west Texas and the states of Arizona and New Mexico) but also nearly all of contemporary Nevada and Utah and stretched east as far as Nebraska. In June 1845, Polk sent General Taylor to the banks of the Rio Grande in a deliberate effort to provoke war with Mexico. Lieutenant Ulysses S. Grant acknowledged, "We were sent to provoke a fight but it was essential that Mexico should commence it." He later called the conflict he helped to spur a "wicked war" and regretted that he "had not the moral courage to resign."

On April 25, 1846, the war began when Mexicans clashed with a US patrol in the disputed territory, killing 11 dragoons and giving Polk the pretext he sought for war. The legislation he sent to Congress did not ask for a declaration but rather declared that a state of war already existed "by act of Mexico." Polk thus misrepresented the conflict, declaring that the Mexicans had "shed American blood on American soil." In truth, Mexico had refrained from going to war over the loss of Texas and never encroached on US soil. Determined to carry out Manifest Destiny by aggression, the US Congress reflected popular sentiment as it voted 174–14 in the House and 40–2 in the Senate to wage war.

Mexico was no match for the United States in the war. The United States possessed three times the population of Mexico, had 50 years more development as an independent nation, and enjoyed the backing of a zealous public fired by Manifest Destiny. The United States did not have a large army but one that had grown increasingly professional since the establishment of the US military academy in **West Point** in 1802. More important, legions of volunteers including many seasoned Indian fighters would turn out for the conflict. By contrast, the Mexican Army, like the economy and society of the young republic, was in disarray. Given these realities Mexico would have been wise to sell California and at least part of New Mexico to the United States, yet Mexico too had its nationalist pride and religious zealotry. With greater commitment to diplomacy, the Mexican War might have been averted.

Despite the appeals from Mexico City to defend the Catholic faith and the homeland, many if not most *Californios*, *Neuvomexicanos*, and *Tejanos* were inclined to side with the Americans. The Mexican government thus dramatically underestimated the disillusionment of people who lived far from the center and had received no protection over the years from Indian raids. The United States was poised to exploit these cleavages but instead the chauvinism and indiscriminate violence of the US war effort quickly alienated the vast majority of Mexicans.

US volunteers, outnumbering Army regulars by almost two to one, streamed into Texas and became the vanguard of Manifest Destiny. Americans remained leery of standing armies long associated with British Red Coats and tyranny. Moreover, mainstream Americans had little respect for the Army regulars, many of which were immigrants and Catholics. By contrast the public perceived the 59,000 volunteers as more authentic American "citizen soldiers" and bulwarks of republicanism. Polk distrusted the regular Army while exalting volunteers as "free citizens, who are ever ready to take up arms in the service of their country when an emergency requires it."

The volunteers, who came from all over the country though mostly from the South, quickly proved undisciplined and indiscriminate in their application of violence. In May 1846, as General Taylor's forces defeated the Mexican Army in a bloody fight at the northeastern city of Matamoros, packs of volunteers descended on the city to engage in drunken brawls, violent assaults, theft, rape, desecration of churches, and other crimes. Taylor condemned the violent disorder, perceiving that it would undermine the war effort by alienating Hispanics who otherwise might have given the US occupation a chance to succeed. "Were it possible to rouse the Mexican people to resistance, no more effectual plan could be devised than the very one pursued by some of our volunteer regiments," Taylor lamented. "There is scarcely a form of crime that has not been reported to me as committed by them."

With the Army unable to control the masses of untrained US volunteers, the war in northern Mexico devolved into a bitter and prolonged guerrilla conflict. Undisciplined and poorly led, the volunteers "act[ed] more like a body

Figure 3.8 General Zachary ("Old Rough and Ready") Taylor was a hero of the
Mexican War, which propelled him to a short-lived presidency in the election
of 1848. During the war Taylor deplored the behavior of US volunteers who
waged indiscriminate warfare alienating Hispanics who might otherwise have
supported the United States.

Source: Library of Congress, Prints and Photographs Division, LC-USZ62-38086.

of hostile Indians than of civilized whites," declared Army regular George
Meade, the future hero of Gettysburg. "They rob and steal cattle and corn of
the poor farmers" and commit violent crimes "for no other object than their
own amusement." As Taylor's Army moved from Matamoros into the interior, the Mexican Army put up strong resistance before surrendering Monterey.
Beginning in September 1846, the occupation of Monterey would last two

years, the longest of any Mexican city, and was atrocity filled. Taylor established no security patrols hence the populace was subjected to the "beastly depravity and gross outrages of the volunteers," a disgusted Lieutenant Daniel H. Hill observed.

In February 1847 Americans cheered the triumph, made possible by superior US artillery, in the **Battle of Angostura** (also known as the Battle of Buena Vista), the last regular armed confrontation in northern Mexico and one of the bloodiest fights in US history up to the time. The Mexicans fought tenaciously, killing 270 and wounding some 400 others in Taylor's Army, while 591 of its own men were killed and more than 1,000 wounded. The region thereafter became a theater of guerrilla attacks followed by a US scorched-earth response. The US volunteers, especially those from Texas who well remembered the Alamo and Goliad, remained indiscriminate and undisciplined. "The mounted men from Texas have scarcely made one expedition without unwarrantably killing a Mexican," Taylor charged.

Disaffection from the distant government in Mexico City combined with extensive trade ties with the Americans on the Santa Fe Trail inclined many *Neuvomexicanos* to support the United States at the outset of the war. In the summer of 1846 General Stephen Watts Kearney marched the Army into Santa Fe and pledged to improve the condition of life for the residents, who had been plagued by the marauding Indian tribes. Despite his best intentions Kearney angered *Neuvomexicanos* by putting in charge a group of US merchants who reaped the profits from sales of stock and supplies to the newly arrived army. Meanwhile, Apache, Comanche, Kiowa, Navaho, and Ute, continued to exploit the disarray brought on by the war to attack farms and communities. In January 1847, the impoverished Pueblo Indians and Hispanics lashed out against the US occupiers and Mexican collaborationists. In Taos, long the center of American trade and settlement, an angry mob broke into the home of Governor Charles Bent to murder and decapitate him as his wife and children fled through a hole in the wall of their adobe abode.

In California as in New Mexico the US invaders alienated the Hispanic population otherwise predisposed to favor them over the distant and incompetent Mexican government. In June 1846 John C. Frémont, accompanied by the famous scout Kit Carson and a motley crew of mountain men and adventurers, proclaimed the "**Bear Flag Revolt**." After landing at Monterey the US Navy Commodore Robert F. Stockton alienated the *Californios* through racism and arbitrary imprisonment of prominent Hispanic leaders. By the time Kearney arrived from New Mexico, California like northern Mexico had become inflamed with guerrilla resistance.

By 1847 the United States had seized California, New Mexico, and Texas, but the war would not end until Mexico formally turned over sovereignty. When Mexico refused to accommodate the Americans, Polk authorized an invasion of Central Mexico. General Winfield Scott had been appalled by the atrocities committed by the US volunteers, declaring it had been "unchristian

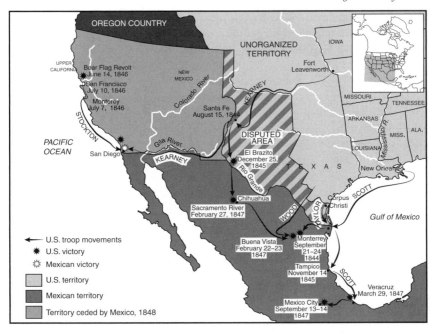

Map 3.1 The Mexican War, 1846–48.

and cruel to let loose upon any people—even savages—such unbridled persons." While attempting without much success to clamp down on the volunteers, Scott bombarded Vera Cruz, destroying much of the port city and killing hundreds of people. "My heart bled for the inhabitants," Captain Robert E. Lee told his wife. The Mexicans surrendered the city but irregular warfare continued, prompting Scott to authorize summary executions and collective punishment of civilians.

In September 1847 Scott's forces took Mexico City in a blood-drenched fight. With Manifest Destiny sentiment at its apogee, most US citizens appeared to favor seizing control of the entire country. As the Americans approached the fabled halls of Montezuma, the **"All-Mexico" Movement** gained momentum. "Your ancestors, when they landed at Plymouth" dealt with the Indians by "cheating them out of their land," Sam Houston declaimed at an All-Mexico rally. "Now the Mexicans are no better than the Indians, and I see no reason why we should not go in the same course now and take their land." Absorbing and democratizing Mexico was work "worthy of a great people," the *New York Herald* averred.

Despite the ebullient rhetoric the occupation had already begun to wear on the United States, which could not have pacified "All Mexico." A tortuous path to a diplomatic settlement ensued. Polk, Scott, and State Department diplomat Nicholas Trist were bitterly divided over war aims and terms of a settlement while the Mexican government was in total disarray. On February 2, 1848, months of haggling and conflict culminated in the signing of the **Treaty of Guadalupe Hidalgo**, bringing an end to the Mexican War. The United States incorporated Texas to the Rio Grande, as well as the vast reaches of New Mexico, and California. Washington paid Mexico $15 million in return and pledged to respect the rights of newly incorporated peoples and to protect them from Indian depredations. The treaty provided the Hispanic residents of the Southwest the right to become US citizens, but for generations they would be relegated to second-class citizenship encompassing segregation, "greaser laws," and various other varieties of discrimination. The Senate ratified the Treaty of Guadalupe Hidalgo by a vote of 38–14.

Some Americans opposed and criticized the Mexican War and tried to call attention to the atrocities, but in the end Manifest Destiny sentiment overwhelmed these critics. Philosopher **Henry David Thoreau** withheld a tax payment, passed a night in jail, and later wrote "Resistance to Civil Government," an essay justifying "civil disobedience" in response to war, slavery, and injustice. Thoreau's essay inspired similar protests generations later, for example by Martin Luther King, Jr. and opponents of the Vietnam War (Chapter 12). Many Whigs and New Englanders blamed the Mexican War on Polk and southern slaveholders, yet throughout the conflict the president received the funding and support he needed from Congress. Most Americans thus rallied behind the flag, condemned war protesters, celebrated martial glory, and proved indifferent to US atrocities against Hispanics.

"Young America"

A series of republican uprisings in Europe coincided with Manifest Destiny and thus reinforced the belief that the "young" United States was a model for reform of the Old World. In the **Young America** Movement political, literary, and cultural figures celebrated the nation's anti-aristocratic, republican traditions as representative of the wave of the future. Americans were in a "lather of excitement," as they anticipated a "holy millennium of liberty," the poet Walt Whitman observed. These sentiments first surfaced in the 1820s, as Americans perceived the Latin American revolts against Spanish and Portuguese rule as evidence of the expansion of liberty in the American image.

From 1821–32 Americans closely followed developments in the **Greek War of Independence**, which they viewed as another step in the march of Christianity and democracy with the United States serving as the model for the world. In no position to join Britain, France, and Russia in backing the ultimately successful struggle for Greek independence, Americans nonetheless followed the events closely and identified strongly with the predominantly Christian Greeks against their perceived Muslim oppressors. As in the Barbary Wars in the first decade of the century, the Greek independence struggle prompted Americans to venerate Christianity while condemning the Islamic faith of the Ottoman Empire. After suffering "a bitter and unending persecution of their religion" under the Ottomans, Senator Daniel Webster declaimed before Congress, the Christian Greeks had achieved liberation from the "religious and civil code . . . fixed in the Koran."

The Young America Movement reached its peak in the context of a series of revolutionary uprisings in Europe in 1848. The French ousted Louis Philippe, the last French monarch, inaugurating the Second Republic. The events in France destabilized the Habsburg Empire in East-Central Europe and ignited an independence movement in Hungary. Americans identified with the Hungarian freedom fighters, but as in France where an authoritarian regime under Louis Napoleon came to power the Hungarian liberal movement succumbed to counter-revolutionary forces backed by Russia.

The United States did not have the power or the inclination to intervene in Europe, but the uprisings nonetheless reinforced American exceptionalism. Through their enthusiastic reception of the Hungarian freedom fighter **Louis Kossuth** during his eight-month tour of the United States in 1851–52, the Americans were celebrating their own republican traditions and powerful sense of providential destiny and mission. "We Americans are the chosen people, the Israel of our time," Herman Melville wrote in 1850. "We bear the ark of the liberties of the world."

The Filibuster Movement

For all the excitement about being the exemplar of liberty the United States was still a slaveholding republic, a contradiction that precipitated a growing sectional crisis and ultimately the Civil War. Opposition to the *expansion* of slavery (more than to the *immorality* of it) animated American politics in the wake of the Mexican War. Initially celebrated as a dramatic triumph of continental expansion, the new territories taken from Mexico became instead a source of irreconcilable political conflict. The sectional crisis put the brakes on state-sponsored US expansion but did not stop individual crusaders, known as **filibusters**, from stepping into the breach.

Filibusterism—the word derived from French and Spanish versions of the Dutch term "freebooter"—encompassed an array of irregular armies acting independently of the US government. Typically led by a charismatic individual, filibusters attempted to take over other countries and bring them into the American "empire of liberty." Racial superiority and manly aggression—taking foreign lands through militant assertions of power regardless of an absence of state support—characterized the antebellum filibuster movement. Despite their repeated failures, filibusters received enthusiastic public support because they reflected mainstream Manifest Destiny sentiment.

The Mexican War followed by the California gold rush spurred the filibuster movement. The war glorified aggression against peoples deemed racially and politically inferior, while the gold rush brought thousands of young men streaming to California, only to find the readily available gold had been quickly panned out. Many of them joined filibustering expeditions. Some of the

ONE OF THE PEOPLE'S SAINTS
for the Calendar of Liberty
1852.

"*Fight for us*"

Figure 3.9 Americans identified with the Hungarian revolt of 1848 led by Louis Kossuth
(at the center of the artist's rendering above) against Austria, depicted as a
monster. The monster represents monarchy and Roman Catholic papal
authority while Kossuth represents liberty, truth, and eloquence and enjoys
the support of other nations including the United States whose flag appears
on the left.

Source: Library of Congress, Prints and Photographs Division, LC-USZ62-89603.

filibuster efforts centered on Baja, or Lower California, which many Americans thought should have been annexed along with Upper California during the Mexican War. All of these efforts failed, including one in which a former California state senator, Henry Alexander Crabb, was captured, decapitated, and his head put on display in a jar of mescal in the Mexican village of Caborca.

The most charismatic and famous filibusterer **William Walker** also tried to take Baja, as well as the Mexican state of Sonora. The Tennessean recruited financial backers and a band of irregulars and set off for the Baja Peninsula. Walker and his men killed several Mexicans, fashioned a crude flag in an effort to emulate California's Bear Flag Revolt, and proclaimed the new "Republic of Lower California" in 1853. The New Orleans *Daily Creole* declared Walker would bring "Anglo-American institutions" to the "feeble descendants of the once haughty and powerful Spaniard." However, the small invasion force lacked basic necessities such as food, water, and medicine. Walker left Baja, crossing the Sea of Cortez to proclaim a new Republic of Sonora in 1854. The Mexicans drove out the invaders, who were arrested by US authorities upon their return to San Diego for violating the **Neutrality Law of 1818**, which forbade such acts as piracy or attacks on countries with which the United States was at peace. Filibusterism was popular, however, and after only eight minutes of deliberation a jury found Walker not guilty.

While Walker shifted his focus to Central America, other filibusterers and mainstream politicians focused their attention on Cuba, which had long been considered a future candidate for statehood. John Quincy Adams once predicted that Cuba would fall like an apple from a tree out the Spanish orbit into the American lap. But for the crisis over slavery—Cuba, rich in sugar-cane, would have been a slave state—the United States probably would have annexed the island. In 1851 the filibusterer Narciso Lopez, a Venezuelan by birth, landed a small army in an effort to claim Cuba for the United States. Spanish officials captured and executed Lopez by means of the *garotte* (slow strangulation). Manifest Destiny enthusiasts mourned the demise of Lopez through pronouncements, paintings, songs, and poetry decrying the evil Spanish Dons ("Ten thousand soldiers in a moment rise, To drive the harlot Spain from her Cuban prize").

US diplomats posted in Europe reflected the filibustering spirit by laboring to "detach" Cuba from Spain. Meeting secretly in the Belgian city of Ostend in 1854, the pro-slavery diplomats crafted a document, dubbed the **Ostend Manifesto** and soon leaked to the public, asserting in the spirit of the Mexican War that if Spain refused to sell Cuba the United States would be "justified in wresting" the island from Spain's possession. Amid the bitter sectional crisis over Kansas and Nebraska, however, the anti-slavery northern press denounced the "buccaneering document," which fueled opposition to the southern "Slave Power" in US politics. Cuba remained the focus of slaveholder and expansionist desires nonetheless. A popular toast held, "Cuba, we'll buy or fight but to our shore we'll lash her, if Spain won't sell we'll turn in and thrash her!" The New York-based *Democratic Review* joined the slaveholding South in advocating the manly conquest of a feminized Cuba, whose "rosy, sugared lips" revealed that "she is of age—take her, Uncle Sam!"

While many Americans lusted after Cuba, others focused on Central America and the construction of an isthmian canal to speed transportation and progress. The State Department negotiated the **Bidlack–Mallarino Treaty** (1846) with New Granada (later Colombia), which provided the United States with access to a canal zone in the province of Panama, which was not yet an independent nation. A New York company built a railroad across the Panamanian isthmus, uprooting farms and communities and raising tensions. In 1856 a drunk American filibusterer refused to pay for a piece of fruit at a market, initiating a riot that resulted in the deaths of 17 people, mostly Americans. The United States landed troops—the first of 13 US occupations of Panama between 1856 and 1903—to establish order after the riot, which a US investigator blamed on the "colored population" of Panama. The United States exacted more than $400,000 in damages from the government in New Granada and left a legacy of bitterness in the province of Panama.

Nicaragua was also a site of US intervention as well as the potential construction of an isthmian canal. In 1850 the United States and Britain concluded successful negotiations in an effort to ward off conflict over rights to build the canal. Under the **Clayton–Bulwer Treaty**, the United States and Britain agreed that neither would seek to fortify or gain exclusive rights should a canal be built in Nicaragua. The treaty was another important step in the budding Anglo-American rapprochement, but as events transpired an isthmian canal was still more than half a century away from construction and would be built in Panama rather than Nicaragua (see Chapter 5).

Unfortunately for the Nicaraguans, Walker had set his sights on their country for his next filibustering expedition. Many Nicaraguans initially welcomed Walker and his invasion force in hopes that they would undermine the power of the Conservative elites in the impoverished and bitterly divided nation. The opposition Liberals hoped to work with the Americans to overthrow the Conservatives to facilitate construction of the canal and promote economic progress for the country. The same goals prompted Nicaraguans to sign a contract with Cornelius Vanderbilt's transit company, which required it to establish agricultural colonies along the transit route. The Nicaraguans badly misjudged the Americans, especially Walker.

In 1855 Walker and his irregular forces won a quick victory over the Conservatives, thus briefly solidifying Walker's reputation as a conquering hero. Americans back home hailed the triumph of Manifest Destiny, prompting some 10,000 additional settlers and adventurers to flock to Nicaragua. Nicaraguans of all factions soon discovered that rather than developing the country Walker moved to siphon off the best land for the US migrants. As the dark-skinned Nicaraguans were "mongrels" and members an "amalgamated race," Walker decided to reintroduce slavery, which had been outlawed in the country for a generation. After a fraudulent election in 1856, in which Walker proclaimed himself the new president of Nicaragua, other Central Americans led by Costa

Figure 3.10 William Walker was a popular leader of the American filibuster movement despite his failed efforts to seize portions of Mexico and annex Nicaragua to the United States. In 1860 Walker was executed by firing squad in Honduras.

Ricans rallied to drive Walker and his band into the sea. As they departed Walker and his fanatic followers killed hundreds if not thousands, raped women, looted, and gratuitously put the historic city of Grenada to the torch.

None of these activities prevented Walker from being celebrated in the United States. The administration of Democrat Franklin Pierce had even briefly recognized his claim to represent the legitimate government of Nicaragua. Nothing if not determined, Walker returned three times to Central America until his capture by the British Navy, which turned him over to Honduran authorities. On September 12, 1860, a Honduran firing squad summarily executed Walker. Filibusterism was over; civil tumult lay just ahead.

Select Bibliography

Stephanson, Anders. *Manifest Destiny: American Expansionism and the Empire of Right.* New York: Hill and Wang, 1995.

Cusick, James G. *The Other War of 1812: The Patriot War and the American Invasion of Spanish East Florida.* Gainesville: University Press of Florida, 2003.

Sexton, Jay. *The Monroe Doctrine: Empire and Nation in Nineteenth-Century America.* New York: Hill and Wang, 2011.

Burstein, Andrew. *The Passions of Andrew Jackson.* New York: Vintage Books, 2003.

Wallace, Anthony F. C. *The Long, Bitter Trail: Andrew Jackson and the Indians.* New York: Hill and Wang, 1993.

Perdue, Theda and Green, Michael D. *The Cherokee Nation and the Trail of Tears.* New York: Penguin Books, 2007.

Jung, Patrick J. *The Black Hawk War of 1832.* Norman: University of Oklahoma Press, 2007.

Missall, John and Missall, Mary Lou. *The Seminole Wars: America's Longest Indian Conflict.* Gainesville: University Press of Florida, 2004.

Hämäläinen, Peka. *The Comanche Empire.* New Haven, CT: Yale University Press, 2008.

DeLay, Brian. *War of a Thousand Deserts: Indian Raids and the U.S.-Mexican War.* New Haven, CT: Yale University Press, 2008.

Clary, David. *Eagles and Empire: The United States, Mexico, and the Struggle for a Continent.* New York: Bantam Dell, 2009.

Greenberg, Amy S. *A Wicked War: Polk, Clay, Lincoln, and the U.S. Invasion of Mexico.* New York: Knopf, 2012.

Roberts, Timothy M. *Distant Revolutions: 1848 and the Challenge to American Exceptionalism.* Charlottesville: University of Virginia Press, 2009.

Robinson, Cecil, ed. *The View from Chapultepec: Mexican Writers on the Mexican-American War.* Tucson: University of Arizona Press, 1989.

Weeks, William Earl. *The New Cambridge History of American Foreign Relations, Volume I: Dimensions of the Early American Empire, 1754–1865.* Cambridge: Cambridge University Press, 2013.

4 Preserving the Union, Taking the West

Overview

The Civil War placed a monumental roadblock in the path of empire. It would take decades for the nation to fully recover and rebuild consensus for foreign policy expansion. Diplomacy was thus halting and uneven in the post-bellum years. Yet despite lingering sectional divisions through the remainder of the nineteenth century, the United States purchased Alaska, asserted its influence in Latin America, advanced the Anglo-American rapprochement despite episodic but often serious tensions with Great Britain, and conducted a massive campaign of Western Indian removal culminating in an internal colonialism. By the end of the nineteenth century the United States was an emerging global power.

Civil War Diplomacy

The Civil War was a crisis for the Union and thus for American foreign relations. "United" States diplomacy ceased to exist on April 12, 1861. For the next four Aprils the Union and Confederacy competed in diplomacy as well as warfare. Abraham Lincoln, the Republican president whose election in 1860 sparked southern secession, viewed the Confederacy as illegitimate. He declared that the Union would be hostile to any country that might afford legitimacy to the "rebels." Like Lincoln, Secretary of State William Seward meant to preserve the Union at all costs and went so far as to recommend starting a war with either France or Spain to rally nationalistic sentiment and thus head off the internecine conflict. Lincoln rejected this unrealistic advice, which nevertheless reflected Seward's understanding that foreign wars can function to promote domestic unity. In this case, however, it was too late to avert the already long-deferred Civil War.

Lincoln and Seward focused on preventing foreign nations, especially Europeans and even more specially Great Britain, from aiding or recognizing the Confederate States of America (CSA), which had been proclaimed in February 1861. Naturally the CSA pursued precisely the opposite course in its diplomacy. If successful in securing recognition from Britain, France, and other

Figure 4.1 Secretary of State William Seward's ambitions for US expansionism knew
few bounds, but lingering sectional divisions limited his ability to carry out
his vision.

Source: Library of Congress, Prints and Photographs Division, LC-DIG-cwpb-04948.

world powers, the CSA could then negotiate alliances, secure loans to finance
the war, and above all garner international legitimacy. These eventualities
would go a long way toward securing the Confederate goal of independence.

Following the outbreak of fighting at Fort Sumter off the coast of South
Carolina on April 12, Lincoln instituted the **Union blockade** of southern
ports. The Union Navy was inadequate to enforce the blockade over the vast

coastline surrounding the Confederacy yet the blockade was an important assertion of the North's determination to contain and ultimately rein in the rebel states. Led by Great Britain, several European nations responded to the blockade—considered an act of war under international law—with **neutrality declarations**. The declarations angered the Union because neutrality recognized the existence of war between two belligerent states whereas the United States insisted that the conflict was an internal rebellion rather than a war.

In contrast to the War of 1812 in which the United States championed neutral rights, the Union warned foreign nations that free trade and political ties with the Confederacy would not be tolerated. Lincoln and Seward sent Charles F. Adams, son and grandson of the two former presidents, as the US minister to London. Adams warned the British that any move to "fraternize with our domestic enemy" could result in a US declaration of war. Such an eventuality would have been a bonanza for the Confederacy and nearly came to pass as a result of a serious clash at sea between the Union and Britain.

On November 8, 1861, as part of a US naval campaign to enforce the blockade by stopping and searching ships, the *San Jacinto* boarded the British mail packet, *Trent*, which was bound from Cuba to Britain. On board the Americans found two high level CSA diplomats, James Mason and John Slidell, who were bound for England and France to lobby the two leading European powers to grant formal diplomatic recognition to the Confederacy. Although they had acknowledged a state of belligerency the European nations had maintained diplomatic relations with the Union and not with the CSA. Mason and Slidell did not get the chance to make their case in 1861, as the Navy commander removed them from the *Trent* before allowing it to resume course to England.

The British, already irritated by other incidents including previous interruption of their mails at sea, responded sharply to the ***Trent* Affair**. They condemned the removal of the CSA envoys from the British ship as a violation of neutral rights, demanded their immediate release, and an apology from the Union. Adams urged Lincoln and Seward to meet these demands to avoid a serious breach in relations and a possible war with Great Britain in the midst of the Civil War in which the United States was already floundering after defeat in the Battle of Bull Run. In late December 1861 Seward wrote a formal diplomatic note conceding that the Navy had lacked the authorization for the summary seizure of the two diplomats, who were then released. This concession satisfied the British thus resolving the diplomatic dispute.

As the northern war effort continued to go badly the British frequently angered the Union with various statements and actions. In October 1862 the British Liberal politician and future prime minister William Gladstone declared in a public speech that the Confederates had "made a nation," adding "We may anticipate with certainty the success of the Southern States so far as regards their separation from the North." British ship builders also built warships, disguised as merchant vessels, to circumvent British neutrality laws, which produced a belligerent response from the United States and years later

Figure 4.2 The US naval vessel *San Jacinto* overtakes the British mail packet *Trent* in 1861. The US seizure of the British ship and the removal of Confederate envoys James Mason and John Slidell nearly brought a rupture in relations with Great Britain, which could have changed the course of the American Civil War.

Source: Library of Congress, Prints and Photographs Division, LC-USZ62-108243.

demands for restitution of damages. Diplomatic indignation cut both ways, however, as the British sharply protested the conscription or imprisonment for draft resistance of British nationals living in the United States. Overall some 189,000 British and Irish men fought in the Union Army.

While the Union struggled to mobilize for war the CSA's victory under General Robert E. Lee at Second Bull Run prompted a British offer of **mediation** in August 1862. The British and other European statesmen argued that the war was becoming a major bloodletting that was disrupting global commerce and ought therefore to be brought to a humane end through mediation. Livid over the diplomatic intrusion, Seward responded with another of his repeated threats to declare war on Britain or any other power that enabled the Confederate rebellion. The British did not want war with the Union, as it would threaten Canada and force them to devote considerable financing and resources to yet another North American conflict, one that their national interests did not require.

With the Union effort in disarray in the early phases of the Civil War the CSA sought to exploit British and French dependence on southern cotton

Figure 4.3 Confederate diplomacy invested heavily in the belief that dependence on southern cotton to fuel British textile mills would compel London to recognize the Confederacy, but "King Cotton" diplomacy proved a panacea. The bales shown here derived from slave labor in Greenwood, Mississippi.

Source: Library of Congress, Prints and Photographs Division, LC-USZ62-36638.

to compel diplomatic recognition and assistance. Exulting, "Cotton is King!" southern politicians and CSA leaders confidently asserted that the European states one by one would recognize the Confederacy under the threat of southern planters withholding the cotton crop from British and French textile mills. The British textile industry especially had become dependent on the pure, cheap, and abundant cotton supplied by the southern plantations. According to one estimate nearly one-fifth of the British population depended on the southern cotton mills for economic sustenance.

The CSA exaggerated the power of **King Cotton diplomacy**, which failed to deliver the desired result. The British and French, who were also dependent on American cotton, resented southern efforts to extort international support. The curbs on cotton exports forced layoffs and closure of some mills, but the British tapped other sources, notably Egyptian cotton, to keep some mills running. The European states and Britain especially had more to gain, despite the importance of cotton, through trans-Atlantic trade with the Union, hence it was never in their national interest to recognize the Confederacy and go to war with the North.

The blood-drenched **Battle of Antietam** on September 17, 1862, proved to be the turning point in the Civil War and in the failure of southern efforts to gain diplomatic recognition. Still the bloodiest day in American history, with more than 3,600 men killed and more than 17,000 injured, the battle revived the Union war effort even though the epic struggle along Antietam Creek in Sharpsburg, Maryland, had ended in a draw. Lincoln claimed victory but moreover the president seized the moment to issue the historic **Emancipation Proclamation** announcing that as of the New Year all slaves in the rebel states would be considered free. From that point forward the Civil War took on the character of a campaign against slavery rather than merely to save the federal union.

With the war emerging as a moral crusade the European states, especially Britain, would not recognize the CSA and thereby intervene on the wrong side of history. By 1862 the American Civil War was the most captivating event in the world and observers frequently commented on its transcendent importance. The German radical theorist of communism, **Karl Marx**, called the American internecine conflict the "first grand war of contemporaneous history" in which the "highest form of popular self-government till now realized is giving battle to the meanest and most shameless form of man's enslaving recorded in the annals of history." European conservatives and aristocrats, however, welcomed the anticipated breakup of the American experiment in democracy, which they opposed as a threat to their domination of their own societies. Whatever the viewpoint, all over the world and especially in Europe, from taverns and dinner parties to meeting halls, people discussed *la question américaine*, as the French called the Civil War, and speculated on its outcome and implications.

France was second only to Britain as the focal point of both Blue and Gray diplomacy. At the helm of the second empire was **Louis Napoleon**

(Napoleon III), the nephew of Bonaparte, who dreamed of restoring the grandeur of France. The Confederacy offered Napoleon an incentive of unlimited cotton and free trade in return for flaunting the Union blockade. The dictator instead sought to take advantage of the American infighting to rebuild the French Empire in Mexico and the Caribbean. Spain, too, sought to capitalize on the Civil War to reassert its colonial authority in Latin America. In 1861, much to Seward's chagrin, Britain and Spain joined France in an occupation of the Mexican port city of Vera Cruz in response to Mexico's inability to pay its debts to European governments.

Napoleon's ambitions went beyond debt collection, however, as he landed thousands of French troops the next year and anointed the Austrian Prince **Maximilian** to sit on the throne as a French puppet emperor in Mexico. Seward warned the French that once the Confederacy had been tamed the United States would go to war to oust them from Mexico. Direct US intervention proved unnecessary, however, as widespread Mexican guerrilla resistance, a looming French war with Prussia, and the fall of the Confederacy undermined Napoleon's reckless adventure. In 1866, as battle tested US troops amassed on the Rio Grande the French withdrew. The following year the Mexicans executed Maximilian by firing squad. Despite its preoccupation with the Civil War the United States had invoked the Monroe Doctrine, smuggled arms to the Mexican resistance, and largely weathered the French and Spanish threat to its claim to the right to oversee events in Latin America.

Interpreting the Past

The Uncivil War

In recent years scholars, carefully analyzing census and other data, have increased the estimated number of dead in the American Civil War from the previously agreed upon figure of some 620,000 to 750,000. The high casualty figures showed that Americans engaged in indiscriminate warfare not only against foreigners but against one another as well. Historians are thus beginning to explore more fully the continuities and similarities between conflicts normally considered separately such as the Mexican and Civil Wars, the Indian Wars, and diplomatic history.

In 1862, when the Confederacy approved the **Partisan Ranger Act**, Union generals pronounced the authorization for irregular forces as a dishonorable and inexcusable resort to guerrilla warfare for which the South deserved indiscriminate retribution. Thereafter, in every belligerent state, but most notoriously in Missouri and Texas, sniping, hit and run assaults, summary executions, massacres, and collective punishment (for example burning an entire town if perpetrators of an ambush could not be identified), all flourished. In late 1864 General William T. Sherman's famous (or infamous in the South) "March to Sea," in which he blazed a deliberately destructive scorched-earth path through Georgia and South Carolina, was not anomalous but rather reflected an already established pattern of punitive warfare in which both sides engaged. With such intense hatreds engendered, it would take generations for the United States to reunite and recover from what Lincoln aptly termed "this terrible war."

In 1863 crucial victories in Vicksburg and Gettysburg turned the Civil War toward the eventual Union triumph ending with Lee's surrender in April 1865. Outnumbered and economically overmatched even while clinging to slavery, the South could have survived only by securing international support, as the United States itself had done in its infancy through alliance with France in the Revolutionary War. Ineffectual southern diplomacy but moreover the immorality of slavery doomed the CSA, which nonetheless put up a long guerrilla resistance that made the Civil War still by far the most violent conflict for Americans in their history.

Caught in the Middle: Indians and the Civil War

Despite having been removed to the supposedly independent "Indian country," indigenous people could not escape the torment of the Civil War. The conflict among the whites offered some western tribes such as the Comanche an opportunity to exploit the war to expand their raids into Texas and the Southwest, but for most Indians "the war between the two fires" proved highly destructive. Some 20,000 Indians fought in the Civil War, mostly but not exclusively on the Union side. For some Indians participation offered an outlet for their masculine warrior drives while others hoped simply to improve their lives through military service.

The Civil War badly divided and severely damaged the southeastern tribes who had been forcibly relocated west into the Indian Country. They lost farms, homes, schools, and churches as the internecine conflict raged throughout Indian country (centered in modern-day Oklahoma). Thousands of Indians became refugees. Unionist forces raided Indian country from Kansas to the north while Southerners entered from the south and east. More importantly, however, the tribes divided against each other and amongst themselves as they joined in the conflict. While most Cherokee sided with the Union, the tribe was badly divided. The Choctaw and the Chickasaw sided with the South, while the Seminole and the Creeks like the Cherokee were divided in their loyalties.

The Union triumph left in its wake a strengthened US military while spurring industrialization, homesteading, and railroad development, all of which would be mobilized to undermine Indian cultures. After the Civil War the United States cited partial indigenous support for the Confederacy as a pretext for taking additional land away from Indians.

Pursuing Monroe's Legacy

With the Civil War over, and the French driven out of Mexico, the United States moved haltingly to shore up the Monroe Doctrine. Seward, who remained secretary of state under Andrew Johnson after the assassination of Lincoln in April 1865, viewed the Civil War as a tragic diversion from the US destiny to expand and become a world power. Nothing if not ambitious, Seward sought "possession of the American continent" (including Alaska and Canada) and "control of the world."

Memories of the antebellum efforts to expand slavery, including filibusterism, and the struggle over Reconstruction undermined Seward's ambitious agenda. In 1869 the Senate rejected a treaty Seward negotiated with Colombia to build an isthmian canal. Seward negotiated the purchase of the Virgin Islands from Denmark to enhance US economic and strategic interests in the Caribbean, but Congress turned down the ill-timed treaty after an earthquake rattled the islands. Congress also rejected a reciprocity treaty with the Pacific island of Hawai'i, but in 1867 did approve Seward's purchase of Brooks Island, later renamed **Midway Island** (as it lay roughly midway between California and East Asia), which would become a pivotal US naval base.

Seward's most significant achievement was the **Alaska Purchase** in 1867. Most Americans knew nothing about "Russian America"; Seward himself knew very little. Americans did not know or care about the indigenous people—among them Aleutian islanders, the Haida and Tlingit on the southeast coast, and the Inupiat and Yup'ik along the Arctic coast. As with American Indians, the Alaska natives were viewed as backward and inferior races whose land might be rightfully taken over by an advanced race of whites. As with treaties and purchases with Britain, France, and Spain in early American history, a European power (in this case Russia) sold off land already occupied by indigenous people.

Russian claims to "Alaska" (an Aleut word meaning "great land") dated to the eighteenth century. Tsar Peter the Great financed the Danish navigator Vitus Bering's explorations ranging from the Arctic to the Oregon coast. The fur trade rather than permanent settlement anchored Russian America. By the mid-nineteenth century the fur trade had ebbed and Britain had decisively defeated Russia in the Crimean War (1853–56). With only a few hundred

Figure 4.4 Seeking to improve relations with the United States in the years following its
defeat by Britain in the Crimean War, Russia agreed to sell the massive but
little known land of Alaska to the Americans. Baron Eduard Stoeckl (above),
the Russian minister to the United States, negotiated the sale in a late-night
meeting with Secretary of State William Seward.

Source: Library of Congress, Prints and Photographs Division, LC-DIG-cwpbh-02873.

trappers living in Alaska, the Russians could not hold the land from either the
British or the Americans. Seward seized the opportunity to negotiate the purchase in a late-night meeting with the Russian minister to Washington Eduard
Stoeckl. For $7.2 million, less than 2 cents an acre, the United States claimed
possession of more than 591,000 square miles.

In Their Words

Years after the event Frederick Seward recounted how his father consummated the Alaska Purchase with Russian Foreign Minister Eduard Stoeckl

On the evening of Friday, March 29th, Seward was playing whist in his parlor with some of his family, when the Russian Minister was announced. "I have a dispatch, Mr. Seward, from my government, by cable. The Emperor gives his consent to the cession. Tomorrow, if you like, I will come to the Department and we can enter upon the treaty."

Seward, with a smile of satisfaction pushed away the whist table, saying: "Why wait till tomorrow, Mr. Stoeckl? Let us make the treaty tonight."

"But your Department is closed. You have no clerks, and my secretaries are scattered about the town," said Stoeckl.

"Never mind that," responded Seward. "If you can muster your legation together before midnight, you will find me awaiting you at the Department, which will be open and ready for business."

. . . The debate [that] followed in the Senate was animated and earnest, but in the end the treaty was confirmed. But the purchase was not consummated without a storm of raillery in conversation and ridicule in the press. Russian America was declared to be, "a barren, worthless, God-forsaken region, whose only products were ice bergs and polar bears." It was said that the ground was frozen six feet deep and the streams were glaciers. "Walrussia" was suggested as a name for it, if it deserved to have any . . . It was "Seward's Folly" . . .

It was a surprise to the Eastern public, when they were informed, a few years since, that the neglected territory was already paying into the national treasury more than it had cost, and that its productions and revenue were yearly increasing. Within another decade, the explorers, miners and prospectors began to report their discoveries of gold, silver, copper and coal in apparently inexhaustible supply. Alaska commenced repaying its cost price over and over again, each year—so that now, in return for our seven millions, we are likely to have seventy times seven.

. . . During the last year of Seward's life [1872] he was [asked], "Governor Seward, which of your public acts do you think will live longest in the memory of the American People?" Seward replied, "the purchase of Alaska. But," he added, "it will take another generation to find it out."

Source: Seward, Frederick William. "Alaska." Circa 1907. Department of Rare Books, Special Collections and Preservation, University of Rochester River Campus Libraries.

Despite references to "Seward's Icebox" and "Walrussia," public opinion backed the Alaska Purchase, which the Senate approved by a vote of 37–2. However, when word leaked after the Senate action that Stoeckl had distributed some $200,000 to various congressmen to "publicize" the value of Alaska, the scandal left a bad taste and undermined future expansionist gambits. Charles Sumner, chairman of the Senate Foreign Relations Committee (SFRC), had not needed persuasion. He supported the Alaska Purchase to outflank the British and eventually drive them out of Canada. Seward and other US expansionists shared this goal and viewed British possession of Canada as a violation of the Monroe Doctrine. Seward coveted Greenland and Iceland as well.

The United States failed to take over Canada, which entered into dominion status linking the various provinces in 1867. Domestic issues—economic, ideological, and political—underlay the **Dominion of Canada** (1867), but so did concern about the threat of US expansionism. The Americans had invaded Canada twice in their previous history and did little to hide their view that it ought to be incorporated into the Union. As Canada's first prime minister John MacDonald explained in 1870, "The United States government is resolved to do all it can, short of war, to get possession of our western country, and we must take immediate action and vigorous steps to counteract them." In addition, anti-British, Irish-American Fenians had carried out periodic cross-border raids targeting British Canadians.

Blocked by Britain and Canada to the north, the Civil War hero turned president Ulysses S. Grant sought to annex the Caribbean island of Santo Domingo, which Spain had briefly occupied during the Civil War in "violation" of the Monroe Doctrine. Grant's aide Orville Babcock helped negotiate the purchase from the island's dictator and orchestrated a plebiscite in which it was claimed that the islanders had approved the US takeover. The dubious nature of the plebiscite as well as Babcock's own personal financial investments and land holdings on the island soon became known, about the same time that Stoeckl's Alaska handouts became public knowledge. Moreover, Santo Domingo unlike Alaska was a Caribbean island redolent with the history of slavery.

Grant envisioned Santo Domingo as a site to colonize American blacks, which remained the preferred solution over assimilating them into the United States. Throughout the Civil War the Lincoln administration had pursued colonization projects including negotiations with the British and Dutch governments over potential sites in the Caribbean, South America, and West Africa. Despite Grant's motive of colonization, many Americans feared the proposed annexation of Santo Domingo ultimately would result in black in-migration. Journalist E. L. Godkin, founder of the liberal journal *The Nation*, sharply opposed annexing Santo Domingo and its 200,000 "ignorant Catholic-Spanish negroes." Sumner turned against annexation, enraging Grant, who eventually had the Massachusetts senator removed from the SFRC. By that time, however, the treaty had been rejected and the Grant administration plagued by a series of scandals.

Some Americans flirted with the idea of incorporating Haiti, which shared the Caribbean island with Santo Domingo, but the proposal went nowhere. In 1889 Frederick Douglass, who had been the most prominent African-American in the United States since the antebellum era, became the US ambassador to

Haiti. However, just two years later, when Douglass failed to secure Haitian approval for the lease of a harbor to the United States, critics demanded that a "vigorous, aggressive white man" be sent in his place. Douglass was recalled.

The United States paid keen attention to events on the dominant Caribbean island of Cuba, which remained under Spanish control in yet another "violation" of the Monroe Doctrine. Memories of the Ostend Manifesto (1854), filibuster invasions, and phobias of racial amalgamation with the dark-skinned, Catholicized Cubans dampened annexation sentiment in the post-bellum era, yet the United States wanted Spain ousted nonetheless. The Cubans themselves launched an anti-Spanish revolt in 1868 but the rebel movement lapsed after a decade without succeeding in driving the Spaniards out.

The United States nearly got caught up in the Spanish–Cuban conflict as a result of the 1873 ***Virginius* affair**. A former Confederate ship, *Virginius* had been outfitted by American mercenaries coming to the aid of the Cuban rebels. Spain captured the ship and summarily executed 53 irregulars of various nationalities, including the US captain, precipitating calls for war back in the States. Spain issued an apology, paid an indemnity, and the crisis passed. The ouster of the Spanish from Cuba was another quarter century from fruition.

Following the French departure from Mexico the United States moved in, not with troops but with capital and political influence. As the United States

Figure 4.5 The American survivors of the *Virginius* crew depicted arriving back in New York in 1874. The *Virginius* incident spurred resentment of Spanish control of Cuba in "violation" of the Monroe Doctrine.

Source: Library of Congress, Prints and Photographs Division, LC-USZ62-121645.

industrialized in the years following the Civil War, American investors homed in on opportunities south of the border. US diplomats and financial elites collaborated with the Mexican dictator **Porfirio Díaz**, who seized power in 1876 and opened Mexico to US economic exploitation. American investors tapped Mexico's natural resources, including timber and oil, built railroads, and by 1910 owned 43 percent of Mexican property. In the late 1880s Secretary of State Thomas Bayard outlined a strategy to "saturate" the Mexicans with US influence in order to "control their political action."

Moving away from the bilateral Clayton–Bulwer agreement with Britain and toward unilateral construction of an isthmian canal, the United States intervened in the Colombian province of Panama and signed another canal treaty with Nicaragua. "Either an American canal or no canal must be our motto," declared President Rutherford B. Hayes, who dispatched US warships to Panama in 1880. Four years later the US Senate again rejected, but by only a few votes, a treaty negotiated with Nicaragua giving the United States exclusive rights to build a canal. As with political change in Cuba, realization of plans for an isthmian canal awaited a future generation.

US statesmen attempted to bolster the Monroe Doctrine and check British and other foreign influence by acting as mediators and promoting pan-Americanism. Secretary of State James G. Blaine sought to mediate the Pacific War, which broke out in 1879 between Chile and Peru over territorial disputes and control of profitable guano deposits. During a second stint as secretary of state in 1889 Blaine presided over the first **Pan-American Conference**, which produced an arbitration convention to help settle disputes but achieved few other tangible results. Anti-Yankee sentiment flared throughout Latin America. In 1891 a barroom brawl in Santiago, Chile, ended with the death of 2 US sailors and injuries to 17 others. A war scare petered out with a belated Chilean apology for the American casualties suffered in the tavern fight.

Tugging the Lion's Tail

Great Britain remained the *bête noir* of post-Civil War American diplomacy, as memories of British dalliances with the Confederacy were vivid. The Alaska Purchase and the Dominion of Canada incited Anglo-American tensions, but the most divisive issue in the post-bellum years pertained to the *Alabama Claims*. The *Alabama* was a raiding vessel built in British shipyards and then armed by the Confederacy and used to assault Union shipping during the Civil War. In the two years before it was finally sunk the *Alabama* traveled 75,000 miles and took 64 prizes. The British argued that they had committed no violation of neutrality, as the ship had not been armed when sold, but Seward, Sumner, and other Americans were not appeased. In one of his many orations before the Senate Sumner made an inflated claim for indirect damages while privately averring that Britain should turn over Canada and/

or its possessions in the Caribbean as compensation for the damage done to the Union.

Grant's capable secretary of state Hamilton Fish agreed to arbitration of the *Alabama* Claims, which were resolved by the **Washington Treaty** of 1871. The arbitrators awarded the United States $15.5 million for the *Alabama* Claims, a fraction of what Seward and Sumner had demanded, with the British officially admitting of no responsibility. The Washington Treaty also established arbitration to settle an Anglo-American-Canadian dispute in the Puget Sound area, under which the United States took possession of the San Juan Islands. The Americans also received fishing privileges off Canadian shores in return for $5.5 million.

The Washington Treaty put the **Anglo-American rapprochement**, which had been severely tested during the Civil War, back on course. Disputes over fishing rights and other maritime issues, as well jockeying for rights to build the isthmian canal, continued to arise, however, and the United States remained sensitive about British possessions and political influence in the Caribbean and Latin America. Just as in later generations politicians would condemn their opponents for being "soft" on communism or terrorism, political figures hastened to show a manly toughness by standing up to John Bull.

The **Sackville-West Affair** in the midst of the 1888 presidential campaign underscores the US proclivity for tugging on the tail of the British lion to score points in American politics. Lionel Sackville-West, the British minister to the United States, fell into a trap set by a Republican from California who wrote to him describing himself merely as a former Englishman asking which presidential candidate would be preferred in British counsels. Sackville-West urged a vote for the Democrat Grover Cleveland. The California letter writer, a partisan of Republican Benjamin Harrison, promptly publicized the correspondence, thus tarring Cleveland with the appearance of being pro-British. Political pressure compelled Cleveland to demand Sackville-West's recall for interfering in American politics, an action that soured Anglo-American relations. Cleveland lost the 1888 election in the Electoral College despite winning the popular vote.

Another test of the Anglo-American rapprochement came in the context of a boundary dispute between Venezuela and British Guiana in 1895. Washington backed Venezuela and Secretary of State Richard Olney sent London a 12,000-word document dubbed "**Olney's 20-inch gun**," a rousing reiteration of the Monroe Doctrine. "Today the United States is practically sovereign on this continent, and its fiat is law upon the subjects to which it confines its interposition," Olney declared. After the lofty rhetoric was scaled back the British accepted the US call for arbitration, which later came out in Britain's favor. Although the British rejected Olney's language, the willingness to follow the US lead in resolving the crisis showed that as the new century approached the Monroe Doctrine was in the midst of transition from rhetoric to realization.

Figure 4.6 In 1895 Secretary of State Richard Olney fired his "20-inch gun," an aggressive diplomatic note to Great Britain over a disputed boundary between Venezuela and British Guiana. The British ignored the note but could not long ignore mounting US assertiveness in the Western Hemisphere.

Source: Library of Congress, Prints and Photographs Division, LC-DIG-ggbain-05196.

Indian Removal from the American West

Although many Americans sympathized with indigenous people, settler colonization continued relentlessly to displace them. As the nation industrialized, bankers, railroad builders, farmers, ranchers, miners, missionaries, and immigrants flocked into the far western "frontier." When Indians resisted being removed from their homes and deprived of their hunting grounds, American settlers and the Army forced them out, destroyed their crops and villages, took away their children, and killed thousands. By the end of the century Amerindians were relegated to an **internal colonialism** that proved destructive of their cultures and way of life.

Under the Indian Removal Act of 1830, the United States had pledged to "forever secure and guarantee" the new Indian country. In 1834 congressional legislation formally created a huge swath of the continent stretching from Oklahoma across the Great Plains to modern-day Montana. In urging Indians to exchange their land east of the Mississippi, Lewis Cass, the Michigan Democrat who served as Andrew Jackson's secretary of war, offered the "solemn promise" that the new lands would be "reserved for the red people; it will be yours as long as the sun shines and the rain falls." Such pledges proved meaningless. Instead Indian land and hunting grounds rapidly disappeared as settlers built towns, ranchers carved out farms, miners constructed camps, the Army built forts, capitalists built railroads, and hunters slaughtered bison.

Western Indian removal began in the antebellum era as the overland trails, the Mexican War, and the gold rush sent settlers streaming across the continent. The population of the American West soared from about 1 million in 1815 to 15 million by 1860. Most Americans viewed Indians as a pre-modern obstruction to commercial expansion and Manifest Destiny hence the tribes had either to be removed from the desired land or face extermination. Before federal Indian agents could negotiate treaties, which Congress often declined to ratify in any case, American settlers and territorial governments often took the "Indian problem" into their own hands. From Missouri and Nebraska, to Texas, across the Upper Plains and into the Great Basin, and in Arizona, California, and the Oregon Territory, Americans perpetrated myriad massacres as they drove indigenous people off of land claimed by settlers. Many Americans openly advocated genocide.

The Army condemned massacres and often tried to protect Indians, yet its leaders shared the settlers' contempt for the tribes and the desire to remove or eliminate them. The Army went on the offensive in the post-Civil War West in a campaign to force Indians onto reservations and to kill resisters. The extreme pressures brought on by US internal colonialism divided Indians within their own tribes, often generationally as young warriors waged violent resistance against the settlers while older leaders futilely strove for accommodation.

Reformers mostly in the East viewed Indian removal as inevitable and appropriate but argued that the savages should be educated, taught to farm, and graced with Christianity. However, even these reforms destroyed Indian communities and cultures by denying them religious freedom, undermining traditional gender roles, and perhaps most egregious by removing children from their families. In an effort to accommodate the humanitarian reform movement, President Grant announced a new "**Peace Policy**" toward Indians. Grant named his wartime aide Ely Parker, a Seneca, as the first indigenous commissioner of Indian affairs. He also appointed pacifist Quakers to head Indian agencies across the country.

In 1871 Congress terminated treaty making with Indians, who henceforth would be approached exclusively as a subjugated minority population. The "Peace Policy" required Indians to abandon their homelands and hunting grounds and to relocate onto reservations. Grant warned, "Those who do not accept this policy will find the new administration ready for a sharp and severe war policy." As thousands of Indians would resist the destruction of their way of life, the "Peace Policy" in actuality assured continuation of the violent removal program.

The US foreign policy of Indian removal carried across the Plains and into the Rocky Mountains. Younger warriors such as the Cheyenne "dog soldiers" were eager to prove their manhood by standing up to the whites. They continued raiding and fighting, infuriating settlers and the Army with their resistance and often-deadly assaults replete with mutilation. Cheyenne elders such as the chief **Black Kettle**, seeing that resistance to the vast hordes of settlers ultimately would prove futile, sought accommodation. In 1864 Black Kettle successfully negotiated an accord in which he and some 600 Cheyenne followers were allowed to make winter encampment along Sand Creek, an isolated spot on the eastern Colorado plains.

Belying their pledge of safety, Colorado's territorial governor John Evans and John Chivington, a Methodist minister and the head of the Colorado militia, perpetrated a massacre of the unsuspecting Indians at their winter encampment. At sunrise on November 29, 1864, Chivington and a force of 700 volunteers, backed by 4 howitzers, slaughtered some 150 Indians, looting and burning their lodges before withdrawing. Reformers, the Army, and federal investigators condemned the **Sand Creek Massacre**, but Evans and the Colorado settlers defended the assault. "The benefit to Colorado of that massacre, as they call it, was very great for it ridded the plains of the Indians," Evans declared. The *Rocky Mountain News* praised "the brilliant feats of arms in Indian warfare."

Outrage over the Sand Creek Massacre spurred the US Congress to create the Indian Peace Commission in 1867. The federal government also ratified treaties that were signed that same year at Medicine Lodge Creek in Kansas. The Apache, Arapaho, Cheyenne, Comanche, and Kiowa received cash payments and pledges of food, clothing, tools, schools for their children, and other services in return for relocating onto reservations from which they would be allowed to go on buffalo hunts south of the Arkansas River. The United States did not, however, provide the promised provisions nor did it uphold its pledge to keep intruders off the designated Indian land. Neither did all of the tribes cease their raiding and resistance, hence the peace effort collapsed almost immediately.

As diplomacy failed the Civil War heroes Generals Sherman and Philip Sheridan went on the offensive. Under their direction on November 26, 1868, Lieutenant Colonel George A. Custer of the Seventh Cavalry led another attack on the Cheyenne. The Americans and their Osage scouts killed more than 100 Indians encamped along the Washita River in today's western

Figure 4.7 The 1878 engraving above depicts "the noble red man" caught between the competing US bureaucracies of the Interior and War Departments. General Philip Sheridan represents the War Department, but lurking behind him is the ironically named General William Tecumseh Sherman, who proved as relentless in pursuit of Indians as he had of Confederates.

Source: Library of Congress, Prints and Photographs Division, LC-USZ62-55403.

Oklahoma, burning the camp and killing some 700 ponies and horses in order to deprive the Indians of food in the winter and mobility in the spring. Among the Indians killed was Black Kettle, who had survived the Sand Creek Massacre. Custer ordered a timely retreat before Indians downstream could respond to the attack, thus leaving behind a column of men who would be killed and mutilated.

Indiscriminate killing and removal devastated the Indians of California. As a result of the gold rush, settlers flowed into California before the federal government had time to negotiate treaties with the far western tribes. The "white" population of California catapulted from 92,000 in 1851 to 380,000 by 1860. As settlers poured into the Golden State they perpetrated massacres and openly advocated genocide. Most of the killing was unprovoked and indiscriminate. In 1851 the first civilian governor of California, Peter Burnett, sanctioned "a war of extermination . . . until the Indian race becomes extinct." An Army major acknowledged that the settlers had carried out a "relentless war of extermination . . . They have ruthlessly massacred men, women, and children."

An Indian population estimated at about 300,000 in 1769 when the Spanish built their first missions on the Pacific coast had been halved by the time of the 1849 gold rush. Over the next decade, it plummeted another 80 percent, to around 30,000 Indians, as a result of murder, disease, famine, and declining birth rates. By 1900 only about 15,000 Indians remained in California.

As in California, violence between and among Indian tribes and Hispanic settlers long preceded the arrival of the Americans in the Great Basin, the vast region between the Rockies and the Sierra Mountains. The Spanish and the Mexicans clashed with the powerful Ute Indians and all parties traded captives taken from other Indian tribes. The establishment of mining districts in Montana and Nevada brought hordes of settlers and herds of cattle that drained and polluted water sources. Indians lashed out at settlers, often killing them indiscriminately. In the **Ward Massacre** of 1854, for example, a Shoshone band killed and mutilated 19 emigrants from Missouri near Fort Boise. Anxious emigrants, in fear of "wild" Indians, also attacked and killed indiscriminately. On January 29, 1863, the Army perpetrated the **Bear River Massacre** near the Utah–Idaho border. Colonel Patrick E. Connor issued orders to "destroy every male Indian whom you encounter" and to "immediately hang them, and leave their bodies thus exposed as an example of what evil-doers may expect." The attackers went out of control, killed hundreds of Shoshone, raped women, and slaughtered babies. Like Evans in Colorado, Utah Governor James Doty declared the massacre was salutary because "it struck terror into the heart" of the Shoshone, who "now acknowledge the Americans are the masters of this country." The Cayuse and Nez Perce tribes had joined the Army in a federal campaign to hunt down Shoshone.

The Ute also allied with the Americans against other tribes, but this collaboration could not head off their own eventual dispossession. The Ute sought to preserve their autonomy by aiding first the Hispanics and then the Americans at the expense of the Paiutes, Shoshone, and other weaker tribes. The

US takeover of New Mexico and California undermined the Ute by shutting down markets for their ruthless slave raids and trade. The Utes clashed with the Mormons whose settlements dramatically impacted lands, streams, and hunting grounds undermining indigenous subsistence patterns. The Ute leader **Ouray** carried out a deft diplomacy, as he conducted negotiations in New York, Boston, and Washington that preserved Ute lands for as long as possible. Ultimately, however, the treaties he signed proved ineffectual and the Ute were driven off the vast majority of their lands.

Like the "five civilized tribes" of the antebellum Southeast, the Navaho living in the southwestern United States had long done what Americans said they wanted of Indians: they had become effective farmers and herders. Nonetheless, from 1864–68 the Army, assisted by the Hopi, Ute, and Zuni, drove the Navaho out of the Arizona Territory. The legendary trapper Kit Carson led a scorched-earth assault on homes and fields. The campaign culminated in the "**Long Walk**," a death march in which some 8,000–9,000 poorly provisioned Navaho were forced on a trek to the barren land of the Bosque Redondo

Figure 4.8 The US Army, directed by the legendary scout Kit Carson, drove the Navaho from northeast Arizona on a forced march to the New Mexico badlands. In 1868 through deft diplomacy the Navaho secured the right to return to their homeland at Canyon de Chelly (above), where they remain today.

Source: Library of Congress, Prints and Photographs Division, LC-DIG-det-4a24910.

in eastern New Mexico. Thousands of Navaho died yet the tribe persisted, resisted, and in 1868 exploited the "Peace Policy" to negotiate a treaty that allowed them to return to their homeland at Canyon de Chelly in northeastern Arizona, where the Navaho remain today.

The Apache, Comanche, and Kiowa, were less fortunate. In the mid-1870s, a series of clashes known as the **Red River Wars** culminated in the ethnic cleansing of Texas. Sheridan encouraged mass slaughter of the buffalo, the lifeblood of the Plains tribes, noting in 1875 that by "destroying the Indians' commissary" the buffalo hunters "have done more in the last two years to settle the vexed Indian question than the regular army has done in the past thirty years." The Comanche and other tribes also bore responsibility for the decline of the buffalo, however, as they had slaughtered vast numbers of bison for subsistence and for trade.

Although the Apache would become the stock villains of Hollywood Westerns, Americans had allied with them during the Mexican War. Alliance with the United States failed to preserve their homelands and way of life, as settlers began to kill Apache indiscriminately in the Arizona Territory. At dawn on April 30, 1871, more than 100 Mexicans and Papago Indians along with a few whites—but all under the direction of the leaders of the Arizona territory— killed and mutilated at least 108 Apache camped along a stream on a refuge in the Aravaipa Canyon some 60 miles northeast of Tucson. The Army condemned the **Camp Grant Massacre** as "but another massacre, in cold blood, of inoffensive and peaceful Indians who were living on the reservation under the protection of the Government." The overwhelming majority of Arizona settlers approved of the mass killings, however, and a jury took only 19 minutes to exonerate the perpetrators. Moreover, the Army assisted in ridding the Arizona Territory of Indians. The Army reported killing 29 Apache in 1865, 154 in 1866, 172 in 1867, and 129 in 1868.

In the Northwest, most of the thousands of settlers who arrived on the Oregon Trail lumped Indians together as a "doomed race" with no legitimate claim to lands and hunting grounds. "We came not to establish trade with the Indians," a settler acknowledged, "but to take and settle the country exclusively for ourselves." Settlers followed by the Army conducted indiscriminate campaigns against the Cayuse, Klamath, and other Oregon tribes. In 1855 Oregon's first territorial governor **Isaac Stevens**, a zealous proponent of Manifest Destiny and railroad development, forced the indigenous tribes to sign over their land in treaties or face "extermination." Stevens informed a Yakima chief in 1855, "If you do not accept the terms offered, you will walk in blood knee deep." Stevens simultaneously served as governor, head of the Pacific Railroad Survey, and although he had no expertise on indigenous people he also landed the key position of superintendent of Indian affairs for the territory.

US relations with the Nez Perce had been amicable since 1805 when the explorers Meriwether Lewis and William Clark spent a month resting with the tribe. In 1858 the discovery of gold brought miners flooding onto Nez Perce land and found the Americans declining to enforce the restrictions against white settlement. The **Nez Perce War**, one of the most famous and roman-ticized of Indian resistances in the history of American settler colonialism, broke out in 1877. Once fighting began the Nez Perce under Chief Joseph took flight and repeatedly outmaneuvered their Army pursuers. Aided by Cheyenne and Sioux scouts, General Nelson Miles finally tracked down the Nez Perce before they could reach the Canadian border. Like the Navaho, Chief Joseph never gave up on returning to his homeland. Taking advantage of his fame and claiming to have converted to Christianity, Joseph in 1885 negotiated the return of his people from Kansas to a reservation in Idaho.

The Great Sioux Wars

The tribes, collectively known as the Sioux, put up a formidable resistance against American expansion into the upper Plains. In the antebellum era the Santee Sioux under chief Little Crow lost their land and way of life to a flood of Minnesota settlers. In August 1862, over Little Crow's opposition, the Santee Sioux launched a bloody surprise assault slaughtering mostly German immigrant families in what became the largest Indian massacre of settlers in American history. Before the Army could rein in the rampage, 400–600 set-tlers and some 140 soldiers had been killed in the outbreak of the **Dakota War**. In response settlers and the Army ranged and killed Sioux throughout the region while sentencing 303 Indians to death, a number reduced to 38 after a review by President Lincoln. On the day after Christmas in 1862, the Army hanged the Indians, including Little Crow, in the largest mass execution in US history.

Sioux bands to the west flourished, often at the expense of other tribes that they ruthlessly attacked, including the Crow, Kiowa, and Pawnee. By the 1840s, American settlers on the Oregon Trail complained of aggressive Sioux bands demanding tolls for passing through the territory. The Sioux proved willing to conduct diplomacy, however, and entered into negotiations with the United States. In the subsequent **Fort Laramie Treaty** of 1851 several tribes prom-ised safety to migrants in return for payments and land guarantees.

The United States soon violated the treaty provisions as settlers, squatters, miners, speculators, railroad builders, and the Army descended on the upper Plains. In August 1854, a Sioux band killed 30 men at a trading post near Fort Laramie, sparking the **First Sioux War**. The war ended the next year in the slaughter of at least 86 Sioux, more than half of them women and children, at Blue Water Creek near the Platte River in contemporary Nebraska. In 1866, as the Army surrounded the Sioux with forts, Captain William Fetterman led a force of 80 men out of Fort Phil Kearney in the Powder River country and directly into a trap set by the young militant Oglala Sioux Crazy Horse. The Indians proceeded to kill and mutilate the entire US force in the **Fetterman Massacre**. Disgusted by eastern reformers, Sherman demanded waging war with "vindictive earnestness against the Sioux, even to their extermination, men, women, and children."

Confronted with a possible genocide, the Oglala under Red Cloud called for a diplomatic solution. In April 1868, with the "Peace Policy" forces mobilizing in Washington, the United States agreed to a second Fort Laramie Treaty under which it guaranteed the Sioux that they could keep in perpetuity the western half of the present-day state of South Dakota, including the sacred **Black Hills**, as the Great Sioux Reservation. The Indians would also be allowed to roam and hunt in "un-ceded Indian territory" in the Powder River region further to the west, which was to be closed to Americans. Ongoing settler expansion, the discovery of gold in the Black Hills, and the US desire to construct the Northern Pacific Railroad across the Sioux lands quickly doomed this accord. As the United States reneged on its treaty obligations, Sheridan in 1874 dispatched Custer with a huge expeditionary force to confirm the existence of the gold and consider a site for another fort.

Assisting Custer were the Crow Indians, inveterate enemies of the Sioux and well known for their warrior societies. This service would help the Crow hang onto a reservation in the eastern Montana flatlands, though the Army did remove them from their homelands in the mountain valleys of western Montana. Some of the Crows tried to warn Custer about the trap that awaited him, but Custer was certain that Indians lacked the discipline and cohesion

Figure 4.9 General Custer's Death Struggle. In 1876 a coalition of Sioux, Cheyenne, and
Arapaho warriors crushed the US Cavalry forces led by General George
Armstrong Custer at the Battle of the Greasy Grass (Little Big Horn). The
defeat stunned Americans in the midst of the nation's centennial celebration.

Source: Library of Congress, Prints and Photographs Division, LC-DIG-pga-04166.

needed to field a large army in battle. On June 25, 1876, a coalition of Lakota Sioux, Northern Cheyenne, and Arapaho warriors defied these stereotypes and overwhelmed the Seventh Cavalry in the **Battle of the Greasy Grass** (the Americans called the creek the Little Bighorn). The Indians wounded 55 and killed 268, including Custer, leaving behind their scalped and mutilated bodies.

The victory at the Greasy Grass was short-lived, as General Miles adopted a successful strategy of relentless pursuit that eventually wore down the Sioux. In subsequent years many of the Sioux adapted to life on the reservation and pursued education and acculturation to white society. In the late 1880s, as American settlers and ranchers seized additional reservation land amid the "Great Dakota Boom," the Sioux responded with the spiritually inspired **Ghost Dance**. Familiar to other tribes as well, the Ghost Dance envisioned the revival of the Sioux culture, prosperity, and way of life. Although peaceful, the revival of Indian spirituality and cultural autonomy created anxiety among the Americans, prompting Miles to summon additional forces to the reservation.

In Their Words

In the 1930s Flying Hawk, Oglala Sioux warrior and historian, recounted the Wounded Knee Massacre he had witnessed in December 1890

This was the last big trouble with the Indians and soldiers and was in the winter in 1890. When the Indians would not come in from the Bad Lands, they got a big army together with plenty of clothing and supplies and camp-and-wagon equipment for a big campaign; they had enough soldiers to make a round-up of all the Indians they called hostiles. The Government army, after many fights and loss of lives, succeeded in driving these starving Indians, with their families of women and gaunt-faced children, into a trap, where they could be forced to surrender their arms. This was on Wounded Knee creek, northeast of Pine Ridge, and here the Indians were surrounded by the soldiers, who had Hotchkiss machine guns along with them. There were about four thousand Indians in this big camp, and the soldiers had the machine guns pointed at them from all around the village as the soldiers formed a ring about the tepees so that Indians could not escape. The Indians were hungry and weak and they suffered from lack of clothing and furs because the whites had driven away all the game. When the soldiers had them all surrounded and they had their tepees set up, the officers sent troopers to each of them to search for guns and take them from the owners . . .

It was an ugly business, and brutal; they treated the Indians like they would torment a wolf with one foot in a strong trap; they could do this because the Indians were now in the white man's trap,—and they were helpless. Then a shot was heard from among the Indian tepees. An Indian was blamed; the excitement began; soldiers ran to their stations;

officers gave orders to open fire with the machine guns into the crowds of innocent men, women and children . . . A terrible blizzard raged for two days covering the bodies with Nature's great white blanket; some lay in piles of four or five; others in twos or threes or singly, where they fell until the storm subsided. When a trench had been dug of sufficient length and depth to contain the frozen corpses, they were collected and piled, like cord-wood, in one vast icy tomb. While separating several stiffened forms which had fallen in a heap, two of them proved to be women, and hugged closely to their breasts were infant babes still alive after lying in the storm for two days in 20° below zero weather. I was there and saw the trouble,—but after the shooting was over; it was all bad.

Source: McCreight, M. I. Chief Flying Hawk's Tales: The True Story of Custer's Last Fight. New York: Alliance Press, 1936.

On December 15, 1890, after the largest US military force sent anywhere since the Civil War arrived on the Pine Ridge reservation, tensions escalated with the murder of the revered chief Sitting Bull along with one of his sons. On December 29, with the soldiers in the midst of taking weapons from the Indians, a rifle was accidentally fired skyward, precipitating the **Wounded Knee Massacre**. The soldiers began firing indiscriminately, as five-barrel Hotchkiss guns mowed down Indian men, women, and children. Some 150 Indians died in the initial outburst and another 100 or so were hunted down and killed in the next few days. "There can be no question," an investigator determined, "that the pursuit was simply a massacre, where fleeing women, with infants in their arms, were shot down after resistance had ceased." No one knows the precise death toll, as the Indian men, women, and children were buried in a mass grave. Twenty-five troopers died, mostly from friendly fire in the initial outburst. Although episodic conflict continued into the next century, the American Indian wars were coming to an end.

Internal Colonialism

American foreign relations with Indians shifted gradually from military conquest to internal colonization. Reformers, many motivated by their Protestant faith, frequently lamented the "passing" of the Indian and the cruel treatment to which indigenous people were being subjected. Helen Hunt Jackson emphasized the broken treaties and broken promises toward Indian peoples amounting to a "century of dishonor," as she entitled her 1881 bestseller. The widespread corruption and inefficiency in the government's administration of Indian affairs prompted a congressional investigation, which concluded that the Indian Bureau functioned as "simply a license to cheat and swindle the Indian in the name of the United States." Congress had been complicit in the destruction of Indian cultures by refusing to approve treaties or to enforce those that were approved and more generally by disdaining the tribes as savages in the path of progress.

Missionaries often took the lead in efforts to Christianize and acculturate Indians. Established in 1810, the American Board of Commissioners for Foreign Missions promoted Christianizing and civilizing efforts. In 1819 Congress had passed the Indian Civilization Act to promote Indian education to help prevent their "decline and final extinction" while "introducing among them the habits and arts and civilization." From 1837 to 1893, the Presbyterian Church's Board of Foreign Missions sent more than 450 missionaries to live among 19 tribes.

As in Australia and other settler colonial societies, the United States forcibly removed Indian children from their homes and communities and placed them in reeducation camps. Like massacres and warfare, removal of children from their "heathen parents" undermined Indian cultures and their way of life. Many, like President Hayes, justified the program by asserting, "The children being removed from the idle and corrupting habits of savage homes are more easily led to adopt the customs of civilized life." The federal government sometimes withheld rations and promised payments to force compliance with the child removal program.

In 1879, the effort to educate a new generation of Indians centered on the prototype "school for savages" opened in an abandoned Army barracks in Carlisle, Pennsylvania. Under the motto, "Tradition is the Enemy of Progress," the **Carlisle Indian Industrial School** strove to "kill the Indian, save the man"

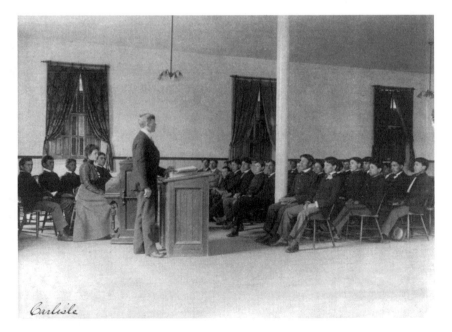

Figure 4.10 Native American men are shown attending a chapel service at the Carlisle (PA) Indian Industrial School. More Indian youths died than graduated at the "school for savages" from its opening in 1879 to closure in 1918.

Source: Library of Congress, Prints and Photographs Division, LC-USZ62-55419.

through forced acculturation. Directed by an Army disciplinarian, Richard Henry Pratt, and backed by the national organization "Friends of the Indian," Carlisle provided English-only instruction and forbade any use of indigenous languages. Indian youth, often sick and terrified from their ordeal of capture, transport, and separation from their families, were given new names, had their hair cut, were dressed in military style clothing, and compelled to abandon their cultural and religious practices and to adopt Christianity. In its first 24 years, 158 students graduated from Carlisle while 186 died at the school, mostly of disease, by the time of its closure in 1918.

In 1887 Congress passed the centerpiece of the drive for Indian assimilation, the **General Allotment Act** or Dawes Act, which subdivided reservation land into 160-acre individual plots while freeing up "surplus" land for sale to settlers by the US government. The "humanitarian" shift from removal to assimilation thus opened additional land for settlers and speculators while attempting to eradicate the Indian way of life. Americans sought to transform Indian gender relations by making men into farmers, women into domestics, and removing Indian children from the family altogether. Theodore Roosevelt accurately described allotment as "a mighty pulverizing engine to break up the tribal mass."

Under the Dawes Act, which prevailed from 1887 to 1934, American Indians lost 86 million of the 138 million acres they possessed in 1887. Thousands of Indians assumed US citizenship under the legislation when they qualified for an individual allotment. After centuries of Indian removal, the Dawes Act allowed Indians to have their own land—but only after they severed relationships with their tribes and thus became more like Americans.

Select Bibliography

LaFeber, Walter. *The Cambridge History of American Foreign Relations, Vol. II: The Search for American Opportunity, 1865–1913*. Cambridge: Cambridge University Press, 1993.

Jones, Howard. *Blue and Gray Diplomacy: A History of Union and Confederate Foreign Relations*. Chapel Hill: University of North Carolina Press, 2010.

Hauptman, Laurence M. *Between Two Fires: American Indians in the Civil War*. New York: The Free Press, 1995.

Myers, Philip. *Caution and Cooperation: The American Civil War in British-American Relations*. Kent, OH: Kent State University Press, 2008.

Holbo, Paul S. *Tarnished Expansion: The Alaska Scandal, the Press, and Congress, 1867–1871*. Knoxville: University of Tennessee Press, 1983.

Hixson, Walter L. *American Settler Colonialism: A History*. New York: Palgrave Macmillan, 2013.

Sutherland, Daniel E. *Savage Conflict: The Decisive Role of Guerrillas in the American Civil War*. Chapel Hill: University of North Carolina Press, 2009.

Blum, Edward J. *Re-forging the White Republic: Race, Religion, and American Nationalism, 1865–1898*. Baton Rouge: Louisiana State University Press, 2005.

Schoultz, Lars. *Beneath the United States: A History of U.S. Policy Toward Latin America*. Cambridge, MA: Harvard University Press, 1998.

Unrau, William E. *The Rise and Fall of Indian Country, 1825–1855*. Lawrence: University Press of Kansas, 2007.

Wooster, Robert. *The Military and United States Indian Policy, 1865–1903*. New Haven, CT: Yale University Press, 1995.

Reyhner, Jon and Eder, Jeanne. *American Indian Education: A History*. Norman: University of Oklahoma Press, 2004.

Donovan, James. *A Terrible Glory: Custer and the Little Big Horn—The Last Great Battle of the American West*. New York: Back Bay Books, 2008.

Ostler, Jeffrey. *The Plains Sioux and U.S. Colonialism from Lewis and Clark to Wounded Knee*. New York: Cambridge University Press, 2004.

West, Elliott. *The Contested Plains: Indians, Goldseekers, and the Rush to Colorado*. Lawrence: University Press of Kansas, 1998.

5 Caribbean Empire

Overview

In just two generations the United States transitioned from a nation on the brink of dissolution into a rising global empire. In 1898 the United States entered into and triumphed in a foreign war, taking new colonial possessions and becoming an international imperial power in the process. While expanding across the Pacific the United States simultaneously instituted colonial rule in the Caribbean Basin and Central America. Combining gunboat diplomacy with economic and political influence, the United States built the Panama Canal, reinforced the Monroe Doctrine, turned the Caribbean Sea into an American lake, and intervened militarily in revolutionary Mexico.

Causes of the "Spanish–American" War

The North's victory in the Civil War ensured the perpetuation of the federal Union, but the conflict left Americans badly divided. An assertive foreign policy required consensus, but national unity was slow to evolve amid the lingering sectional division and dynamic change of the Industrial Era. The postwar Reconstruction Era spurred enduring resentment on both sides of the Mason–Dixon Line, and ultimately proved a failure. The United States industrialized in the post-bellum era—a crucial prerequisite to its rise to world power—as heavy Union wartime investment spurred the dominant railroad industry, iron and steel production, banking and finance, and the rise of big business. The incorporation of America enriched elites but left farmers, workers, the middle class, and the poor frustrated, especially as two severe depressions collapsed the economy in the 1870s and again in the 1890s. Reforms aimed at reining in trusts, bossism, and political corruption proved ineffectual and late nineteenth-century presidents offered little leadership. Immigrants continued to pour into the country and into the industrial workforce, overcrowding the burgeoning cities, where they were not always welcomed. Preoccupied with these dramatic changes on the home front, the United States was not poised to assert itself overseas until the late 1890s.

The so-called **Spanish–American War** of 1898 actually involved more than two countries. The conflict ought more accurately, albeit cumbersomely, to be called the Spanish–American–Cuban–Puerto Rico–Hawai'i–Guam–Filipino War, as it dramatically affected these and other countries as well. The war unfolded in the context of a new international "age of imperialism," but also reflected domestic drives. Economic and cultural factors thus conjoined with geopolitical considerations culminating in war and the establishment of an overseas US colonial empire.

Considering the long American history of settler colonialism and aggressive expansion, the war of 1898 appears to reflect continuity rather than discontinuity with the prior history of US diplomacy. On the other hand the new possessions lying outside the continent presented different, albeit not entirely unrelated challenges than the removal and subjugation of American Indian tribes or internal colonization of blacks and Hispanics. US colonialism and imperialism shared much in common with other "white" Western nations, which exerted their influence over darker-skinned peoples across the vast, non-industrial regions of Asia, Africa, and Latin America. In the century following the Napoleonic wars, direct European control expanded from 35 percent to 85 percent of the earth's landed space. The industrial revolution laid the foundation for global colonialism, as the new era of steel, oil, and modern finance capitalism drove the quest for natural resources, markets, and coaling stations for naval and merchant ships and offered sites for spreading Christianity and garnering international prestige. The United States took part in this scramble for colonies in the last half of the nineteenth century and came away with new Pacific and Caribbean possessions.

During the 1890s the most devastating depression up to that time in American history heightened the focus on economic issues and geopolitical competition. Many US businessmen and politicians believed that increased exports and foreign commerce were needed to revive a flagging American economy, which had produced high unemployment and labor strife. War and empire thus flowed from a growing alliance between industrial capitalism and the nation's expansionist foreign policy. The United States joined other nations in competition for natural resources and exports as well as for the ports and coaling stations needed to transport them. The administration of William McKinley—sometimes described as the first "modern" president—was keenly aware of all of these factors, as the Republican Party had been closely allied with the new urban–industrial complex of late nineteenth-century America.

Race, religion, and gender also influenced the new American colonial empire. By establishing its control of the Caribbean Basin and asserting itself as a power in Asia and the Pacific, the United States joined other colonial powers in exercising authority over weaker nations deemed racially inferior. Although slavery ended with the Civil War, the repression of African-Americans, the passage of "greaser laws" regulating Hispanics, and the subjugation of Indians reinforced white supremacy, a racism that carried over into the nation's foreign policy. Rather than bring the dark-skinned, Spanish-speaking Caribbean islanders into the Union, the United States sought to stabilize their populations and integrate them economically as "unincorporated territories."

108 *Caribbean Empire*

Interpreting the Past

Gender and the Spanish–American War

Many factors can be cited in explaining the causes of the Spanish–American War. In addition to economic motives and other more familiar arguments, in recent years some scholars have emphasized gender. Proponents of the war perceived the United States as having passed through adolescence and at last arrived at the time to "put aside childish things and assume the functions of manhood." The outspoken imperialist Senator Albert Beveridge called for a war that would provide "millions of young Americans with a virile manhood." Theodore Roosevelt, assistant secretary of the Navy, gloried in the "strenuous life" and perceived the nation in its "lusty youth," primed to exert its power. He later described war as "a great thing" because it "brought us a higher manhood." Asserting "Idleness and luxury have made men flabby," the journal *North American Review* avowed, "A great war might help them to pull themselves together."

The emphasis on exerting masculine strength to defend national honor placed intense pressure on President McKinley to choose war over diplomacy with Spain. When McKinley kept diplomatic lines open after the explosion of the battleship *Maine*, including the possibility of peaceful mediation, critics questioned his manhood. The *New York Journal* looked for "any signs, however faint, of manhood in the White House." Roosevelt privately declared that McKinley had "no more backbone than a chocolate éclair." Charging McKinley with pursuing a "weak, ineffectual, pusillanimous policy," the *Chicago Tribune* declared, "The people want no disgraceful negotiations with Spain." Newspapers and congressmen received thousands of letters from belligerent citizens impatient to assert American military might over the haughty Spaniards. "I wish to God we had a [sic] Andy Jackson" in the White House, one of them fumed.

An officer in the Civil War as a young man, McKinley already had been bolstering US military preparedness and was not simply goaded into war. Although the pressure on McKinley to prove his manhood did not "cause" the war with Spain, it did narrow the president's options and thus factored into his decision to ask Congress for a declaration of war.

Religion also undergirded the turn of the century imperial thrust. A Third Great Awakening of evangelical Protestantism followed the Civil War, affirming the widespread view that the United States was a chosen nation, destined by God to expand and exert its influence. During the Civil War Congress voted to imprint the motto "In God We Trust" on the nation's coins; "God bless America" became a common invocation in prayer; and the "Battle Hymn of

Figure 5.1 In 1913 former Union and Confederate soldiers met at Gettysburg on the fiftieth anniversary of the epic Civil War battle. The Gettysburg reunion reflected the resurgence of national patriotism as bitter memories of the civil tumult faded.

Source: Library of Congress, Prints and Photographs Division, LC-DIG-ggbain-13834.

the Republic" ("Glory, Glory Hallelujah") reinforced faith in the nation's martial destiny. Some Americans cast a critical light on the Caribbean and Philippine islanders because they had embraced Spanish Catholicism.

Patriotism flourished in the last two decades of the nineteenth century and peaked with the outbreak of war. In the decades following the Civil War the public venerated the American Flag and celebrated new national holidays. The American Flag Association and other groups promoted the Stars and Stripes, as did new laws requiring flying of the flag on warships, at military installations, in classrooms and outside of schools and public buildings, while criminalizing any misuse or abuse of "Old Glory." Reverence of the flag as well as public singing of the "Star-Spangled Banner" helped to heal sectional divisions, a process that culminated at Gettysburg in 1913 as 53,000 aged Confederate and Union veterans met at the epic battlefield site in common commemoration. The new national holidays of Thanksgiving and Memorial Day, both originating in the Civil War, also became forces of national unity. In sum, the post-Civil War revival of patriotism helped bridge the sectional divide, provided recently arrived immigrants with ways to demonstrate their loyalty, and generally promoted unity amid the rapid changes of the industrial era. The rebuilding of national unity left the United States poised to resume the course of imperial expansion, which had been derailed by the Civil War and its aftermath.

The United States capitalized on the collapse of Spanish authority following decades of Cuban resistance to assert control over the largest Caribbean island. Spain had ruled by the sword in Cuba, as it regularly quashed revolts, including a decade-long uprising from 1868–78. By the late 1890s, with the Cubans again on the rise, Spain responded with a re-concentration, a brutal counterinsurgency program against the rural population led by General Valeriano "Butcher" Weyler. Cuba suffered mightily, as war and disease killed as many as 170,000 Cubans, as much as one-tenth of the island's population. Spain lost a few thousand men in combat but many thousands more to disease, notably yellow fever.

By 1898 both Spain and the Cuban resistance had been weakened, making the island ripe for the American taking. Increasingly literate and informed by a proliferating penny press, Americans could read daily news stories of Spanish atrocities on the island located only 90 miles off the Florida coast and long coveted by the United States. In the mid-1890s the United States began offering covert aid to the Cuban rebels.

On February 15, 1898, the mysterious destruction of the battleship **Maine** in Havana harbor killed some 270 Americans and accelerated the conflict with Spain. Relations had deteriorated sharply the previous week when the US press published the **De Lôme Letter**, a private correspondence of the Spanish ambassador to the United States that was leaked. De Lôme described McKinley as a "weak . . . would-be politician." Anti-Spanish sentiment accelerated

Figure 5.2 The battleship *Maine* before its destruction in Havana Harbor on February 15, 1898.

Source: Library of Congress, Prints and Photographs Division, LC-USZC2-4584.

over the insult to the president as well as the destruction of the *Maine*, which most Americans assumed had been a deliberate act of Spain. Increasingly few considered the possibility that the explosion stemmed from the ship's bituminous coal bins, a not uncommon catastrophe at that time. The precise cause of the *Maine* explosion, whether a bomb or an internal mishap, has never been conclusively determined.

Figure 5.3 President William McKinley in a full-length portrait in June 1898 only weeks after he quieted critics of his "backbone" by asking for and receiving a congressional declaration of war against Spain.

Source: Library of Congress, Prints and Photographs Division, LC-USZ62-5627.

The insulting De Lôme Letter and the destruction of the *Maine*, both heavily publicized, produced a steady drumbeat for war. Demanding a manly response to Spanish insults and the explosion of the *Maine*, "Jingoes" (a British euphemism to avoid blasphemous utterance of "Jesus") demanded war as the only viable means to defend the nation's honor. Spain was the weaker nation and also lacked any significant allies in the coming conflict with the Americans. The Spanish Navy was in decline whereas the United States had constructed a modern new fleet by 1898. In an effort to avert the conflict, Spanish officials agreed to end the brutal re-concentration policy and declare an armistice with the Cuban rebels. It was too late, however, as nothing less than humiliating withdrawal and capitulation, and probably not even that would appease the United States.

As the slogan "Remember the *Maine*, to hell with Spain" reverberated across the nation, the United States declared war against Spain. On April 19 the House of Representatives voted overwhelmingly for war (311–6) but the Senate was divided on the joint resolution, which passed 42–35, foreshadowing the subsequent anti-imperialist movement. Patriotic unity prevailed after the vote was tallied, as Congress stood as one amid the patriotic bunting and sang the "Battle Hymn of the Republic."

The margin in the Senate would have been even narrower, and the resolution might have failed, without an amendment by Senator Henry Teller of Colorado in which the United States renounced any plans to annex Cuba. By pledging that Cuba would be liberated and turned over to "its people," the **Teller Amendment** won over senators who insisted they wanted to help the Cubans but not to engage in an American imperialism by taking over the island. Many of them declared they wanted to head off any prospect of incorporating the racially mixed Cubans under the American Flag.

Figure 5.4 Admiral George Dewey hovers over Manila Bay in an artist's rendering of the exhilarating US conquest of the Spanish fleet on May 1, 1898.

Source: Library of Congress, Prints and Photographs Division, LC-USZ62-36338.

As with the outbreak of most US wars, the public responded enthusiastically to the declaration. Volunteers, as in previous wars, flocked by the hundreds of thousands to join the ranks of fighting men. "It was the apotheosis of patriotism," Secretary of War Russell Alger declared. Communities across the nation prayed, rang church bells, paraded the American Flag, and proudly packed their young men off to war. When they received the stunning news that a US naval force under Admiral **George Dewey** had destroyed the Spanish fleet in Manila Bay on May 1 it electrified the nation. Some 100,000 citizens poured into New York's Madison Square for a spontaneous celebration of the nation's arrival as a global power. Similar celebrations erupted in other communities across the country.

In June the US Navy seized Guantánamo Bay, Cuba, as the base for naval operations in the Caribbean Sea. The next month the United States defeated the Spanish fleet in the Battle of Santiago de Cuba, the largest naval battle of the Spanish–American War. In July the Americans won key battles at El Caney and San Juan Hill outside of Santiago de Cuba, where Roosevelt and his volunteer contingent of Rough Riders earned distinction. Mindful of his budding political career, Roosevelt energetically publicized his personal heroism and the role of the volunteer units. His and other accounts often skimmed over the role of Regular Army units as well as the contributions of African-American troops, generically known as "buffalo soldiers." Some 15,000 Regular Army troops took part in the battle for the high ground around Santiago, Cuba, on July 1, including some 2,000 black soldiers. The more than 200 soldiers killed included 30 black troops.

Also often overlooked was the crucial role of the Cuban rebel forces, led by General **Calixto García** and comprising combat forces, scouts, guides, and interpreters. Like Filipinos, the Cubans at first welcomed US intervention but most Americans did not reciprocate. "Both officers and privates have the most lively contempt for the Cubans," noted war correspondent Stephen Crane. One American officer dismissed the Cuban insurgents as "degenerates, absolutely devoid of honor or gratitude." The Americans denied the Cubans a more active role in liberating Santiago, claiming that they would plunder and pillage the city, prompting García to respond bitterly, "We are not savages who ignore the principles of civilized warfare." Despite US denigration of the Cuban role in the war, the defeated General Weyler declared that without the Cubans "the Americans would not have been able to effect their landing, attack the city of Santiago de Cuba with success, and secure its surrender." The Cubans thus provided crucial intelligence and guerrilla resistance but could not have won the war without the infusion of American troops and firepower.

In Their Words

Cuban General Calixto García sent the following letter to General William R. Shatter on July 17, 1898

Sir:

On May 12 the government of the Republic of Cuba ordered me, as commander of the Cuban army in the east to cooperate with the American army following the plans and obeying the orders of its commander. I have done my best, sir, to fulfill the wishes of my government, and I have been until now one of your most faithful subordinates, honoring myself in carrying out your orders as far as my powers have allowed me to do it.

The city of Santiago surrendered to the American army, and news of that important event was given to me by persons entirely foreign to your staff. I have not been honored with a single word from yourself informing me about the negotiations for peace or the terms of the capitulation by the Spaniards. The important ceremony of the surrender of the Spanish army and the taking possession of the city by yourself took place later on, and I only knew of both events by public reports.

I was neither honored, sir, with a kind word from you inviting me or any officer of my staff to represent the Cuban army on that memorable occasion. Finally, I know that you have left in power in Santiago the same Spanish authorities that for three years I have fought as enemies of the independence of Cuba. I beg to say that these authorities have never been elected at Santiago by the residents of the city; but were appointed by royal decrees of the Queen of Spain.

I would agree, sir, that the army under your command should have taken possession of the city, the garrison and the forts. I would give my warm cooperation to any measure you may have deemed best under American military law to hold the city for your army and to preserve public order until the time comes to fulfill the solemn pledge of the people of the United States to establish in Cuba a free and independent government. But when the question arises of appointing authorities in Santiago de Cuba under the special circumstances of our thirty years strife against Spanish rule, I cannot see but with the deepest regret that such authorities are not elected by the Cuban people, but are the same ones selected by the Queen of Spain, and hence are ministers appointed to defend Spanish sovereignty against the Cubans.

A rumor, too absurd to be believed, General, describes the reason of your measure and of the orders forbidding my army to enter Santiago for fear of massacres and revenge against the Spaniards. Allow me, sir, to protest against even the shadow of such an idea. We are not savages ignoring the rules of civilized warfare. We are a poor, ragged army as ragged and poor as was the army of your forefathers in their noble war for independence, but like the heroes of Saratoga and Yorktown, we respect our cause too deeply to disgrace it with barbarism and cowardice.

In view of all these reasons, I sincerely regret being unable to fulfill any longer the orders of my government, and, therefore, I have tendered today to the commander-in-chief of the Cuban army, Maj. Gen. Máximo Gómez, my resignation as commander of this section of our army.

I am respectfully yours,

Calixto García

In August the US forces began their withdrawal from Cuba, having won the conflict despite inept military preparation, planning, and execution. Unprepared for a foreign war, the government had supplied troops with woolen uniforms to fight a conflict in the tropical heat. The Regular Army and volunteers suffered from a lack of adequate food, potable water, medicine, and other supplies. Two days after his victory at San Juan Hill, Roosevelt implored Washington to send food and ammunition. On July 7 the Rough Rider declared that "the mismanagement has been beyond belief" and the inept war effort "has brought us to the very verge of disaster." In 1969 two government historians, one an army officer, assessed the war effort as "incompetent" and "unbecoming a nation on the eve of becoming a world power." But Spain, accustomed to fending off the Cuban guerrillas, had been ill-prepared for a conventional assault, equally badly supplied, and in the end easily defeated.

Under the terms of the Treaty of Paris (1898) Spain turned over Cuba, Puerto Rico, Guam, and the Philippine islands of Southeast Asia in return for a US payment of $20 million. As in the long history of Indian treaties, the "subject peoples" were excluded from the negotiations that determined their fate. The American public reveled in victory in what diplomat John Hay termed a "**splendid little war**." The wartime triumph offered catharsis from the long shadow cast by the sectional crisis, the rapid changes of the industrial era, and the depression and divisions that had plagued the nation in the 1890s. Fewer than 400 Americans had died on the battlefield, though nearly 3,000 others died from other causes, the vast majority from tropical disease.

The triumph over an "Old World" European power spurred patriotic fervor and revived American exceptionalism after decades marked by internal division and dramatic change. Americans put aside their sectional differences to rally around the flag in war against a Catholic nation that was in "violation" of the Monroe Doctrine through its occupation of Cuba and Puerto Rico. The quick and decisive victory over Spain, in both the Caribbean and across the Pacific, allowed Americans to celebrate their nation's arrival as a world power.

Establishing Colonial Rule

Tensions escalated as the Cubans discerned that the United States was taking full credit for the victory and had no intention of withdrawing to allow for completion of the nationalist revolution and the emergence of an independent Cuba. Economic and strategic considerations underlay McKinley's announcement, "Until there is complete tranquility in [Cuba] and a stable government inaugurated, military occupation will be continued." The United States established coaling stations and the base at Guantánamo Bay as linchpins of its emerging Caribbean Empire. Meanwhile US investors already had millions of dollars at stake in Cuban sugar and railroads with additional investment in the works. In sum, the McKinley administration deemed Cuba too valuable to give up and too backward and racially inferior to grant independence.

Figure 5.5 Corporate attorney and Secretary of War Elihu Root orchestrated US neo-colonialism in Cuba under the Platt Amendment (1901), which authorized US military intervention on the island whenever it was deemed necessary.

Source: Library of Congress, Prints and Photographs Division, LC-USZ62-72828.

The task of finding a legal sanction for the occupation of Cuba fell to Elihu Root, a corporate attorney and the US secretary of war. In 1901 Root's handiwork became embodied in the **Platt Amendment**, a rider attached to a military appropriations bill sponsored by Senator Orville Platt of Connecticut. A deacon and Bible school teacher in the Congregational Church, Platt averred that "in the Providence of God the time has come when the institutions of the English-speaking peoples" should take control of the world. Platt thus proved receptive to Root's suggestions of a framework for US occupation and rule over newly "liberated" Cuba.

The Platt Amendment granted Cuba only nominal independence, while providing the United States with the "right to intervene" at its discretion "for the protection of life, property, and individual liberty." The United States also secured coaling stations, permanent bases for occupation forces and provisions against Cuban alliances with other foreign powers. As General Leonard Wood wrote privately to Roosevelt, "There is, of course, little or no independence left in Cuba under the Platt Amendment." Under a 1903 lease agreement the United States established the naval base at Guantánamo Bay, which it retains to this day over Cuban objections.

The US establishment of colonial rule in the Caribbean proved far less controversial—and less violent—than the subsequent war in the Philippines (see Chapter 6). Even so-called anti-imperialists, who sharply opposed the US annexation of the Philippines, embraced the cause of Caribbean Empire. They praised the Platt Amendment, as one put it, as "eminently wise and satisfactory." Many opponents of Philippine annexation viewed the Caribbean Basin differently because of its proximity. The leaders of the opposition Democratic Party, former President Grover Cleveland, and presidential candidate William Jennings Bryan, endorsed the Platt Amendment. As with Indians and Negroes, Americans viewed the Cubans as inferior to whites and unfit for self-government. Platt explained that as the Cubans "are like children," Americans had to "be in a position to straighten out things" by maintaining the occupation.

The Cuban people, who had fought for decades against Spanish colonialism, bitterly opposed the Platt Amendment and the barely disguised US colonial rule that it enabled. "None of us thought that [US intervention] would be followed by a military occupation of the country by our allies, who treat us as people incapable of acting by ourselves, and who have reduced us to obedience," the Cuban leader Máximo Gómez declared. "This cannot be our ultimate fate after years of struggle." Cuban resistance had smoothed the path for US intervention, but the Americans had aborted the nationalist revolution, which would not come until 1959.

Not unlike the pattern of negotiating treaties with Indians, the United States compelled Cuba to ratify the Platt Amendment in order to provide legal standing and a veneer of consent for US authority. The Americans made it clear the military occupation would not end until Cuba endorsed the *plattista*, including the US right to intervene whenever it saw fit. When the Cubans refused Root charged they were being "ungrateful and unreasonable" and threatened that in the future Washington "will not quite be so altruistic and sentimental" in its dealings with the islanders. In the end, the titular Cuban leadership had no choice but to accede to the demand to incorporate the provision in the new constitution.

Crime and disorder plagued the Cuban countryside, compelling the US occupation authorities to take action in order to establish their credibility to rule. General Wood, who relished his "absolute" authority over the island, directed indigenous Cuban security forces to address the growing problem of rural banditry and lawlessness. His goal was to "let the Cubans kill their own rats." However, much of the rural population shielded the bandits, thus showing their contempt for the US-backed police forces, which they viewed as tools of the colonial occupation. Frustrated by the continuing banditry and disorder, which if left unchecked he feared might lead to a wider guerrilla war, Wood authorized summary executions of suspected criminals. He ordered "the brigands be brought in dead or alive, preferably dead."

While the United States thus instituted repression to bolster colonial rule, Wood also oversaw a variety of reforms. The occupation authorities instituted sanitary and health reform, including efforts to eradicate yellow fever, as well as internal improvements. Reforms benefited the occupation, for example by protecting the colonizing forces from disease, promoting economic development and profits, and providing justification of imperial rule on the basis of advancing progress in backward societies. At the same time the US occupation mirrored colonial rule by Europeans over countries throughout the world, combining economic exploitation, repression of resistance, with limited reforms and internal improvements.

In 1902 the United States withdrew occupation forces only after establishing its ultimate authority and instituting white rule over the island. Mirroring domestic racial perceptions Americans had been wary of the "Negro hordes," thus they worked closely with light-skinned Cuban elites by offering rewards and opportunities in return for their collaboration. Cuba remained politically and social unstable under colonial rule, prompting the return of US military occupation forces from 1906–09, again in 1912, and from 1917–22.

By establishing a "protectorate" over Cuba, the United States secured its investment in the sugar industry, which increased sixfold from 1902–24. As was typical under colonialism, the island became dependent on the US market for the sale of its primary export crop. The dominance of the sugar industry resulted in the consolidation of land in fewer and fewer hands, as many small farmers lost their land to the big sugar plantations. The export-based economy thus rewarded US investors and a relatively few Cuban elites while doing little to create economic opportunity or improve the plight of the average Cuban. Cuba thus remained wracked by both rural and urban poverty, devastated by decades of warfare, its economy stagnant.

While largely overshadowed by events in Cuba and the Philippines, Puerto Rico became an American colony as a result of the Spanish–American War. As in Cuba, Puerto Rican resistance forces joined the Americans in fighting the

Spanish on the ground while the US Navy attacked Spanish ships in Guánica Bay. General Nelson Miles, a hero of the Indian wars, led the fight against Spain and became military governor of Puerto Rico after Spain capitulated. The United States did not seek to annex the racially mixed island, much less offer statehood, yet Puerto Rico, more compact and modernized than Cuba, proved relatively easy to occupy and control.

Americans depicted the Puerto Ricans as "pathetic and childlike" and, like the Cubans, in need of paternal supervision. As with Cuba, the occupiers established a coaling station on the island and integrated sugar cane production into the American market. The United States implemented a variety of reforms, including education and disease control. The Americans sent 60 Puerto Rican youths to the Carlisle Industrial School in Pennsylvania, which had been established to bring civilization to Indian children, but most escaped and only 7 graduated from the school.

Puerto Ricans received neither US citizenship nor self-determination. In 1900 the **Foraker Act**, narrowly passed by Congress, designated Puerto Rico an "unincorporated territory," neither a state nor an autonomous country. In an appeal for Catholic support the United States guaranteed Puerto Ricans religious freedom. Otherwise, Congress was (and remains today) empowered to govern Puerto Rico as it saw fit. Colonialism spurred the rise of a Puerto Rican nationalist movement, which would become more assertive in time.

In US society both critics and supporters questioned the constitutionality of the newly acquired colonial empire. From 1901–10, in the landmark **Insular Cases** the US Supreme Court provided a legal stamp of approval. The high court upheld the constitutionality of colonialism by ruling that territories such as Guam and Puerto Rico did not have to be accorded full citizenship rights as long as their citizens had certain fundamental rights, such as freedom of religion. By means such as the Platt and Foraker Amendments, bolstered by the Insular Cases, the United States had provided legal sanction for its new colonial empire.

Roosevelt Takes the Reins

Another important consequence of the Spanish–American War was to increase the power and prestige of the presidency. McKinley separated himself from the series of middling presidents who as a result of incompetence, corruption, and domestic divisions had done little to distinguish the office since the Lincoln administration. McKinley, having from the outset aligned his administration with corporate America, realized that taking charge of foreign policy would complete the package of the modern presidency. While an assassin's bullets deprived McKinley of seeing the transition through, Roosevelt seized the opportunity when he assumed the presidency in September 1901.

Roosevelt reveled in the presidency, which provided as he put it a "bully pulpit" to advocate both domestic and foreign policies. As a war hero and outspoken imperialist, Roosevelt left no doubt that he sought to vault the United

Figure 5.6 Few men could command an audience like Theodore Roosevelt, war hero, secretary of the Navy, vice president, president from 1901–09, and tireless advocate of an aggressive US rise to global power.

Source: Library of Congress, Prints and Photographs Division, LC-DIG-ppmsca-36653.

States into the first rank of nations. A New Yorker from an aristocratic family, Roosevelt exalted the responsibilities of "civilization." He believed that white, Christian, and modern nations—predominantly the United States and the west European countries—not only had the right but the duty to shepherd darker-skinned, backward peoples toward progress and enlightenment. He believed that empire and colonialism were the natural order of things and not something to apologize for or weakly shy away from in an unmanly avoidance of responsibility.

As the United States shored up colonial rule in the new possessions, Roosevelt turned his attention to achieving the decades-long quest to build and fortify an isthmian canal. Befitting its rise to world power, the United States sought to construct the canal unilaterally. Going it alone would require Great Britain's acquiescence to revocation of the Clayton–Bulwer Treaty (1850), which called for bilateral construction of a canal. By the twentieth century the **Anglo-American rapprochement**, which had evolved haltingly throughout the nineteenth century, had achieved new levels of understanding. While the British undertook the "white man's burden" of colonialism in India, South Africa, and Malaya, among other places, the United States had done the same across the Pacific and in the Caribbean Basin.

Despite some lingering tensions the two "Anglo-Saxon" powers shared an affinity of race and worldview. "The downfall of the British Empire I should regard as a calamity to the race and especially to this country," Roosevelt declared in 1899. The British offered no opposition to the US war with Spain while the United States reciprocated over the British Raj in India and the Boer War in South Africa. "It is in the interest of civilization," Roosevelt explained, "that the English speaking race should be dominant in South Africa, exactly as it is [that the United States] should be dominant in the Western Hemisphere."

Lingering tensions remained over Canada, especially in the wake of Secretary of State Richard Olney's assertion in 1895 that the United States was "practically sovereign on this continent." In 1897–98 a **US–Canadian boundary dispute** erupted amid the Klondike gold rush in the Yukon Territory near the border with Alaska. In 1903 the dispute was resolved by arbitration, with the British member of the six-man arbitration panel siding with the US position. Canadians remained wary and resented US condescension. Senator Henry Cabot Lodge, a member of the arbitration panel, referred to Canadians as a "collection of bumptious provincials" while Roosevelt declared that his nation "regards the Canadian with the good-natured condescension always felt by the free man for the man who is not free."

The Anglo-American rapprochement took a giant step forward with the **Hay–Pauncefote Treaty** of 1901. Under the treaty the United States and Britain abrogated the Clayton–Bulwer Treaty, thus giving the United States the right to unilaterally build, control, and fortify an isthmian canal. In November 1901 the US Senate, having rejected a previous version that lacked the provision to fortify the canal, quickly approved the second Hay–Pauncefote Treaty.

Roosevelt wasted little time in seeking to build the canal in the Colombian province of Panama rather than the other potential site, Nicaragua. In 1902, under the **Hay–Herran Treaty**, the United States agreed to pay Colombia $10 million plus $250,000 annually for construction of a six-mile wide canal zone. However, when the Colombian Senate unanimously rejected the treaty, Roosevelt denounced the "contemptible little creatures" and covertly authorized a bloodless coup by Panamanian elites, many of whom had long advocated independence from Colombia. Wall Street got in on the act, as New York financiers, keenly interested in the canal project, funded the well-timed payoffs in gold to members of the Colombian armed forces. The US Navy arrived on familiar shores, having intervened repeatedly in Panama since the mid-nineteenth century, to oversee the secession of Panama from Colombia.

In Their Words

From a letter of protest by José Marroquín, President of Colombia. "The Rights of Colombia—A Protest and Appeal," November 28, 1903

The Government of the United States is treating Colombia in a manner that seems dishonorable to all the people of that country. American Secretary of State Hay has astonished the world by finding a right to exclude the troops of Colombia from the Isthmus of Panama.

The United States violated international law by recognizing the independence of Panama only days after the revolution and before the nation
of Colombia had a chance to put down the insurrection. Colombia did
not recognize the southern states which seceded during the American
Civil War—why should the United States recognize the seceding states
of Panama?

How are you to escape the condemnation of history? Never has any
nation dealt with a weak one in a way that seemed dishonorable to any
considerable part of its own people but that history has affirmed the
judgment of the protesting minority.

Ignoring Colombian protests, the subsequent treaty provided the United
States with "all the rights, power and authority" within a 10-mile wide canal
zone bisecting the isthmus, as well as the right to intervene in Panama "at its
discretion." Panama received the $10 million, annual rent, and nominal inde-
pendent status yet no Panamanian, or even a Latin American signed the canal
treaty. As with the Cubans, Puerto Ricans, and Indian tribes, the Panamanians were excluded from the diplomacy that determined the future direction of
their suddenly independent isthmus. Instead in 1903 the United States negotiated the **Hay–Bunau-Varilla Treaty** with a Frenchman, Philippe Bunau-
Varilla, whose company held the rights to build a canal in Panama.

Anti-imperialists condemned Roosevelt's "rough-riding assault on another
republic," but the president blasted both the Colombians and his domestic
critics. In December 1903 the *New York Times* labeled the Canal Zone "stolen
property" and blamed the machinations of "a group of canal promoters and
speculators and lobbyists" for the coup in Panama. Roosevelt dismissed and
de-masculinized his home front critics as a "small body of shrill eunuchs." In
February 1904 the Senate supported the popular president ratifying the Hay–
Bunau-Varilla Treaty by a vote of 66–14.

Further ensconcing authority over foreign policy in the White House—a
hallmark of twentieth century diplomacy—Roosevelt averred years later, "I
took Panama and let Congress debate." At the time Roosevelt remained silent
about the US machinations and kept the focus on the Colombians, who had
"misgoverned and misruled." Completed in 1914, the **Panama Canal** was a
spectacular feat of modern engineering, transportation, and commerce—but
also a potent symbol of US intervention in Latin America.

The coup in Panama and the subsequent **Roosevelt Corollary** (1905) to
the Monroe Doctrine completed the conversion of the Caribbean Sea into an
American lake in the years following the Spanish–American War. In the corollary Roosevelt fended off the threat of European intervention in the Dominican Republic (known in earlier years as Santo Domingo), which had failed to
pay its debts to foreign bankers. In 1902–03 the British, French, and Germans
had used gunboats to force Venezuela to keep up its debt service and Roosevelt

Figure 5.7 President Roosevelt draws a picture for Congress of Uncle Sam digging the Panama Canal. Years later the Rough Rider president acknowledged, "I took Panama and let Congress debate."

Source: Library of Congress, Prints and Photographs Division, LC-DIG-ppmsca-37843.

came under pressure to prevent the same thing from happening in 1904 in the Dominican Republic. Accordingly the president responded by siding with the Europeans while at the same time arranging to keep their gunboats out of the region, as per the Monroe Doctrine. Under the new corollary Roosevelt announced that the United States would intervene on behalf of the Europeans, serving their financial interests while deterring them from direct intervention in the hemisphere. Using the language of masculinity and modernity, Roosevelt pledged that the United States would intervene on behalf of all "civilized" nations to correct "chronic wrongdoing" or "impotence" on the part of "backward" nations.

The new Caribbean Empire reflected the influence of the **Progressive Era** in the first two decades of the twentieth century. Just as the nation implemented an array of pragmatic reforms to improve society on the local, state, and national levels, Progressive foreign relations would seek to establish order,

Figure 5.8 William Howard Taft as governor-general of the Philippines. He succeeded Roosevelt as president (1909–13) and attempted to implement indirect control of the nation's new colonial empire through a policy of "dollar diplomacy."

Source: Library of Congress, Prints and Photographs Division, LC-DIG-ds-04253.

stability, and market relations with the non-white and non-industrialized world, especially in the American "backyard." Through both diplomacy and non-governmental economic, social, and cultural initiatives the United States would carry out its mission to uplift other peoples (the "white man's burden") while at the same time promoting free trade and US economic expansion. Now that the continental "frontier" had been settled the world lay before the Americans to expand their values as well as their export markets. They would not necessarily seek direct intervention if these aims could be accomplished by indirect economic and cultural means, but as events from Panama to the Philippines showed the United States would use gunboats and Marines when deemed necessary.

Under a framework known as "**dollar diplomacy**," pursued by Roosevelt's successor William Howard Taft, the United States emphasized economic influence—substituting "dollars for bullets"—in an effort to avoid direct intervention. Latin Americans and anti-imperialists opposed blatant gunboat diplomacy, but expressed less opposition to informal empire. Under this neo-colonial framework, the United States would use its economic clout to bolster "protectorates" and "dependencies" to control trade and police the hemisphere. Growing US economic and political oversight would crowd out European influence in the Americas. Direct intervention remained an option, as the United States would, as Roosevelt once put it, "speak softly" but it would also "carry a big stick."

Dollar diplomacy ultimately failed, as colonialism heightened insecurity rather than order and stability in the region, thus prompting direct US intervention. From 1898 to 1920 US military forces landed on the shores of Caribbean countries for policing missions on at least 20 occasions. In 1909 Taft and his secretary of state, Philander C. Knox, a wealthy corporate attorney from Pennsylvania with little experience in foreign affairs, sent warships and 400 Marines into Nicaragua in support of a faction aligned against the dictator **José Zelaya**. The Nicaraguan ruler dreamed of uniting all of Central America under his authority. The United States had been bolstering neighboring El Salvador, which Zelaya was also attempting to control. After US Marines landed on Nicaragua's east coast to back the rebel faction, Zelaya's troops captured and executed two American mercenaries caught laying a dynamite charge. The United States responded by forcing Zelaya into exile in Spain. In 1912, amid popular protests against Zelaya's US-backed successor in Nicaragua, Taft and Knox again sent in the Marines, this time a sizable force of 2,600. They stayed until 1925 to police the Nicaraguans, described as a "most worthless, useless lot of vermin" by one Marine officer.

In addition to military forces, investors led by a small group of "banana men" also descended upon the Central America states in a successful quest to reap profit from the abundant yellow fruit. US mining, railroads, shipping, and banking investments flourished in Central America, but there was no business on the isthmus like the banana business. By 1910 in Honduras, the quintessential "banana republic," US companies controlled 80 percent of the banana plantations. Banana men and other mainland investors established enclaves throughout the isthmus and cultivated the support of elites who sought to profit from the US presence and promote development of their countries. However, few profits from banana sales trickled down to the deeply impoverished peasantry. Led by the Boston-based **United Fruit Company**, and backed by episodic US military landings, the banana companies kept the populace compliant and stifled reforms that might threaten their interests. Taft defended the "relationship of guardian and ward," which "indicates progress in civilization."

As the Progressive Era gained momentum in the United States, critics sometimes condemned dollar diplomacy as well as sending in the Marines. Many Progressives, while implementing a wide range of domestic reforms, also sought to redeem the world. Following the lead of John Bassett Moore, an international lawyer, peace Progressives held congresses with representatives of other nations as part of a growing twentieth century transnational movement promoting peace and the rule of law in world affairs. The industrialist turned philanthropist Andrew Carnegie won broad international support promoting the concept of a league of nations. Carnegie and other peace Progressives endorsed **The Hague Conventions** of 1899 and 1907 in which the nations meeting in the Netherlands endorsed arbitration, established laws of war, and initiated a world court of justice. Peace internationalists received support from church organizations, overwhelmingly Protestant, as they sought to build a world order rooted in consultation, arbitration, adjudication, and avoidance of war. Such groups as the American Peace Society, the Carnegie Endowment for International Peace, and the League to Enforce Peace reflected mainstream Progressive values. Prominent political figures such as Root, Taft, and Woodrow Wilson endorsed the movement to establish a framework of international law.

The moralistic dimension of progressivism attracted Wilson, who showed however that it could be mobilized for intervention as well as for peace activism. Formerly president of Princeton University, governor of New Jersey, and a pious minister's son, Wilson won the presidency over the split Republican Party in the election of 1912. Although he had criticized intervention and dollar diplomacy, Wilson would intervene more forcefully and more widely than either Roosevelt or Taft. In so doing Wilson followed Roosevelt's lead increasing unilateral executive power over foreign relations.

Intervention in Mexico

Wilson confronted instability in Mexico where President **Porfirio Díaz** had ruled since 1876 and enabled deep-seated US economic penetration of the country. The United States controlled 75 percent of Mexico's mines and 50 percent of its oil fields. Popular resentment of the dictatorship as well as American economic domination produced frequent clashes including one in Cananea in the northern province of Sonora in 1906. There, Mexican workers along with thousands of Chinese laborers were paid less than their American co-workers. The Mexicans and Chinese, who were also forced to work in dangerous conditions in the US-owned mines, decided to go on strike. US owners responded by summoning a posse of Arizona rangers to cross the border and put down the labor action, prompting a clash in which 23 people died.

By 1910 Mexico's rural and urban poor, led by a variety of inspirational rebels, engaged in an uprising against foreign and domestic elite domination of the Mexican economy. The next year the nearly octogenarian Díaz was finally toppled and forced into foreign exile. Ensuing free elections brought to power Francisco Madero, who proved ineffective. In 1913 troops loyal to General Victoriano Huerta assassinated Madero, as Mexico devolved deeper into civil tumult.

The US ambassador to Mexico, Henry Lane Wilson (no relation to the president) had been complicit in the army plot against Madero because US property and lives were at stake as the **Mexican Revolution** unfolded. Property was seized and scores of Americans out of the 50,000 or so who lived in the country had been killed in various clashes. The newly inaugurated President Wilson rejected the advice of the ambassador and others to recognize Huerta in hopes the Army could bring stability to Mexico. Characteristically, Woodrow Wilson declared he would "never recognize a government of butchers." The devout Presbyterian and former professor Wilson believed he could forge a "covenant" between the United States and Mexico and thereby "teach the Latin American Republics to elect good men." These convictions propelled a direct intervention in Mexico, one that Taft had avoided.

Wilson's interference stirred anti-American sentiment in Mexico, helping further to ensconce Huerta in a struggle against Constitutionalists headed by Venustiano Carranza. At this point the American response to the otherwise innocuous **Tampico Incident** prompted a direct American military intervention in Mexico. On April 9, 1914, as a US Navy whaleboat was refueling at Tampico on Mexico's Atlantic coast, a Mexican patrol arrested and jailed the small crew. Superiors quickly recognized the error, apologized, and freed the sailors who returned to their boat in less than an hour. The incident might have ended there but Admiral Henry T. Mayo, commander of the naval squadron, demanded a written apology. Moreover he demanded that the Mexican Army "hoist the American flag on a prominent position on shore and salute it with twenty-one guns." Huerta offered to sack the arresting officer and send a written apology, but no self-respecting Mexican nationalist could fire a salute to the American Flag flying on Mexican shores.

Wilson, with backing from Congress and the public, ordered the Atlantic fleet to blockade Mexican ports until the salute to Old Glory was fired. It never was. On April 20 Wilson authorized several hundred US Marines to go ashore at Mexico's principal port of Vera Cruz to prevent unloading a shipload of arms to Huerta from a German manufacturer. Fighting erupted in which 80 Americans died and more than 300 Mexicans became casualties. All sides in Mexico's internal struggle condemned the **Vera Cruz intervention**, forcing Wilson to accept mediation from Argentina, Brazil, and Chile. While the talks presided over by the South Americans went nowhere the US solidified

Figure 5.9 General John "Black Jack" Pershing, shown here surveying the landscape outside his tent during the US punitive expedition into Mexico in 1916, proved unable to track down the elusive Francisco "Pancho" Villa.

Source: Library of Congress, Prints and Photographs Division, LC-USZ62-89218.

its occupation. The Americans instituted municipal and much-needed sanitary reforms, including medical screening of prostitutes whose services the US sailors frequently solicited. As in Cuba, the municipal reforms won over few Mexicans amid the pervasive opposition to the foreign military intervention.

In July 1914 the Constitutionalists overthrew Huerta, who followed Díaz into exile, prompting a reluctant decision by Wilson to recognize the new Carranza government. Wilson's decision angered the rebel leader in northern Mexico, **Francisco "Pancho" Villa**, who branded Carranza an American puppet. In the opening months of 1916 Villa's men began killing Americans and carried out a shocking cross-border raid into Columbus, New Mexico. Villa's forces rampaged through the town and then rode off unmolested. With Congress and the public aflame over the incident, Wilson ordered Army General John "Black Jack" Pershing, commanding a force of 6,000 troops, to march into Mexico in pursuit of Villa, whose popularity soared as a result.

Pershing's troops never found Villa but found plenty of trouble in a country long resentful of US invasions and in the throes of revolution. In the spring of 1916 several of Pershing's forces died in clashes with Mexican troops and public mobs, yet the US forces killed more than they lost. Caught up in another no-win situation in Mexico, Wilson accepted Carranza's offer to release captured US soldiers and open talks. In September the talks began in Atlantic City but quickly stalemated. The United States demanded the right to intervene in Mexico to protect its citizens and property, a proposal Carranza summarily rejected. In 1917 Mexico's new constitution further aggravated the situation. It included **Article 27**, which asserted Mexico's right to control sub-surface minerals and resources, including oil, as well as the right to expropriate foreign holdings, all of which constituted a direct threat to the extensive US economic interests. Mexico held the upper hand in the conflict, as the US interventions had been ineffective. Moreover the United States turned its attention from south of the Rio Grande to the other side of the Atlantic and the carnage that had begun to unfold on the battlefields of Europe.

Occupying Haiti

Before it became preoccupied with World War I, the United States dispatched thousands of Marines for a 20-year **occupation of Haiti** (1915–34). In the previous century the United States had engaged in at least eight incidents of gunboat diplomacy in Haiti, spread its economic influence, and contemplated establishing a US naval base there. Confronted with economic and political instability in Haiti, Wilson's secretary of state, the supposed anti-imperialist William Jennings Bryan, struggled to grasp the concept of black people speaking French.

When war broke out in Europe Wilson feared that Haiti, wracked by poverty, indebtedness, and political conflict, could become vulnerable to Germany or France. The French were the original colonizers and remained influential in Haiti. In 1915 the assassination of the Haitian president provided an opportunity for US intervention, ostensibly to prevent "anarchy," but in reality to protect US economic interests and reinforce the Monroe Doctrine.

Under the **Haitian-American Treaty** of 1915, the United States took over Haitian finances and secured the right to intervene whenever it wished. Washington established a puppet government in Port-au-Prince, seized the customhouses, supervised financial institutions, instituted forced labor, built new roads, wharves, and schools, and encouraged various social reforms. When the puppet ruler attempted to promulgate a new constitution allowing foreign land ownership, the legislature rejected this plan and began to discuss a constitution limiting foreign influence. The US-sponsored regime responded by dissolving the legislature.

The United States supervised a new Haitian security force, which engaged in extreme racial violence. Occupation policies of racial segregation, press censorship, and forced labor spurred a peasant rebellion in 1919. The US Marines conducted an ongoing guerrilla war with rural insurgents, dubbed Cacos, and killed some 11,500 Haitians over the length of the occupation. Although US soldiers tended to view Haitians as inferior to the Negroes at home, as in past wars they often linked the domestic and foreign racial violence. One soldier, for example, delighted in "steadying down on my job of popping at black heads much as those behind the 'hit the nigger and get a cigar' games at American amusement parks." Though rarely acknowledged, rapes of Haitian women occurred frequently.

Beginning in 1920 both the US military and the US Senate investigated the atrocities but took no action. Amid the tumultuous aftermath of US intervention in World War I neither the press nor the public paid much attention to Haiti. Journalist Oswald Garrison Villard pointed out that reporters rarely "take the trouble to examine into the facts" of the occupation, adding that with respect to foreign affairs "a watchful, well-informed, intelligent, and independent press was . . . sorely lacking."

In 1916 the United States also carried out a military occupation on the neighboring island of the Dominican Republic, where dollar diplomacy had failed to produce stability. When the Dominican president refused to follow American orders the US Marines deposed him and established martial law. US forces proceeded to disarm Dominicans and launched a counterinsurgency campaign to hunt down bandits in the Dominican hills. The American occupiers built a road across the island and created the *Guardia Nacional Dominicana*, comprised mostly of uneducated and desperately poor men, where the future Dominican dictator, **Rafael Trujillo**, got his start. As in Haiti the US occupation benefited only a minority of elites while the majority of the population remained impoverished.

The war in Europe spurred concern about the security of the entire Caribbean Basin, including the small islands comprising the Danish West Indies. Although Denmark remained neutral in the European war there was the possibility that the German government could attack and annex Denmark and at the same time take over its Caribbean possessions. In 1867 Seward had arranged to buy the Danish isles, but the Senate had rejected the treaty. This time the Senate approved. In 1917 the Danish West Indies, renamed the **US Virgin Islands** (comprising St. Croix, St. John, St. Thomas) were turned over to the United States, which paid Denmark $25 million in gold coins.

Concerned about American racial policies, the Danes had called for a plebiscite to get the approval of the predominantly black islanders before the sale could become final. The Danes also sought guarantees that the islanders would receive US citizenship, but Secretary of State Robert Lansing flatly rejected these provisions and threatened that if Denmark refused to sell the United States might occupy the islands, justifying the action by invoking the Monroe Doctrine. Denmark acquiesced and the US Navy took over administration of the islands. In 1920 the United States decreed that Virgin Islanders had "American nationality" but not the "political status of citizens."

Digesting the New Empire

Not all Americans were comfortable with intervention and colonialism in the Caribbean Basin. Many Progressives and some journalists condemned gunboat diplomacy and the violent occupation regimes. These critics did not win the debate, however, as the public backed military intervention in response to perceived affronts to national honor, as in the Spanish–American War and the Mexican interventions. For most Americans faith in racial superiority, providential destiny, and masculine power joined with economic and strategic drives in generating consensus behind US foreign policy.

From 1876 to 1916 a series of international exhibitions attended by millions of Americans reinforced empire, colonialism, and the requirements of advancing civilization over primitivism. Emphasizing race, religion, gender, and Social Darwinism, the exhibits affirmed that the stronger, white, Anglo-Saxon, Protestant nations were more advanced than primitive nations and therefore had responsibility to take control and shepherd them toward civilization and progress. The exhibitions echoed the terminology and frameworks that McKinley, Roosevelt, and European imperialists had used to justify colonial rule. The racial justifications for imperialism abroad reinforced internal colonial rule over Indians, "greaser laws" against Hispanics, and the Jim Crow system of segregation and ritual lynching of blacks on the home front.

The exhibitions presented colonial empire as a logical extension of the American frontier. At the World's Columbian Exposition, held in Chicago's neoclassical White City in 1893, the historian Frederick Jackson Turner propounded the "**frontier thesis**." He explained that after "crossing a continent, winning a wilderness," the nation's continental frontier was now closed, ending an era in American history and raising the question of where it might expand in the future. By this time William "Buffalo Bill" Cody had captivated audiences for years with his Wild West Show, a spectacle about the "gradual civilization of a vast continent," once a "Primeval Forest, peopled by the Indian and Wild Beasts only." Like the Wild West show, the White City displayed Indians as defeated savages in full, feathered regalia who had given way to civilization and progress.

In 1901 the Pan-American Exposition in Buffalo followed an explicit plan "to justify, by means of the most available object lessons we can produce, the acquisition of new territory." The Louisiana Purchase Exhibition in St. Louis in 1904 and other fairs before World War I contrasted "barbaric tribes" with the advance of Western civilization. The Darkest Africa display at Buffalo represented Africans, some of whom were played by African-Americans, in a similar fashion. An Old Spain display described Mexicans as having "no ingenuity" and "absolutely lacking in mechanical skill."

In addition to the exhibitions and comparable museum exhibits, in an increasingly literate US society, newspapers, magazines, dime novels, and travel and missionary accounts all perpetuated the advance of civilization over primitivism. Wild West literature, popularized by Owen Wister's *The Virginian* (1902) linked "taming the frontier" with advancing civilization over backward peoples in Africa, Asia, and Latin America. The unique combination of savagery and civilization drove the popularity of Edgar Rice Burroughs's fictional *Tarzan*, published in 1911. Although raised among the apes as a baby, Tarzan was a

Figure 5.10 Filipino men, dressed in loincloths, dancing, and beating drums, at the Louisiana Purchase Exposition in 1904. Such displays served to justify colonialism by reinforcing the primitivism of native peoples.

Source: Library of Congress, Prints and Photographs Division, LC-USZ62-132396.

displaced aristocrat by birth, a white man who thus became through Darwinian "natural selection" the "king of the jungle."

In exalting whiteness, civilization, progress, muscular Christianity, and the inevitable march of manly empire, these novels, exhibitions, and other sources of popular culture affirmed the nation's imperial foreign policy for the millions of citizens. Perceiving themselves as citizens of an exceptional nation, most Americans embraced the national mission to promote civilization and progress on the world stage.

Select Bibliography

LaFeber, Walter. *The Cambridge History of American Foreign Relations, Vol. II: The Search for American Opportunity, 1865–1913*. Cambridge: Cambridge University Press, 1993.

Schoultz, Lars. *Beneath the United States: A History of U.S. Policy Toward Latin America*. Cambridge, MA: Harvard University Press, 1998.

Hannigan, Robert E. *The New World Power: American Foreign Policy, 1898–1917*. Philadelphia: University of Pennsylvania Press, 2002.

Love, Eric T. L. *Race over Empire: Racism and U.S. Imperialism, 1865–1900*. Chapel Hill: University of North Carolina Press, 2004.

Langley, Lester D. and Schoonover, Thomas. *The Banana Men: American Mercenaries and Entrepreneurs in Central America, 1880–1930*. Lexington: University Press of Kentucky, 1995.

Bouvier, Virginia M., ed. *Whose America? The War of 1898 and the Battles to Define the Nation*. Westport, CT: Praeger, 2001.

Tone, John Lawrence. *War and Genocide in Cuba, 1895–1898*. Chapel Hill: University of North Carolina Press, 2006.

Hoganson, Kristin L. *Fighting for American Manhood: How Gender Politics Provoked the Spanish-American and Philippine-American Wars*. New Haven, CT: Yale University Press, 1998.

Perez, Louis A., Jr. *The War of 1898: The United States and Cuba in History and Historiography*. Chapel Hill: University of North Carolina Press, 1998.

Bederman, Gail. *Manliness and Civilization: A Cultural History of Gender and Race in the United States 1880–1917*. Chicago: University of Chicago Press, 1995.

Beale, Howard. *Theodore Roosevelt and the Rise of America to World Power*. Baltimore, MD: Johns Hopkins University Press, 1984; 1956.

Rosenberg, Emily S. *Financial Missionaries to the World: The Politics and Culture of Dollar Diplomacy, 1900–1930*. Cambridge, MA: Harvard University Press, 1999.

Benbow, Mark. *Leading Them to the Promised Land: Woodrow Wilson, Covenant Theology, and the Mexican Revolution, 1913–1915*. Kent, OH: Kent State University Press, 2010.

Renda, Mary E. *Taking Haiti: Military Occupation and the Culture of U.S. Imperialism, 1915–1940*. Chapel Hill: University of North Carolina Press, 2001.

Rydell, Robert W. *All the World's a Fair: Visions of Empire at American International Expositions, 1876–1916*. Chicago: University of Chicago Press, 1984.

6 Becoming a Pacific Power

Overview

American expansion across the Pacific Ocean in the second half of the nineteenth century paved the way for the nation's rise to world power in the twentieth. While the United States took only baby steps in Africa and the Middle East during this period, Americans joined with western European states forcefully asserting their interests in China, Japan, and Korea.

In contrast with Alaska, which the United States secured virtually overnight in 1867, the American takeover of the Hawaiian Islands was gradual and took decades to achieve. Alaska and Hawai'i, complemented by Midway and Wake Island, as well as Guam and Samoa, facilitated US expansion across the Pacific. After the Spanish–American War (1898), the United States capped its rise as a Pacific and world power by subduing the Philippines through a lethal campaign of counterinsurgency warfare.

Early Connections with Africa and the Middle East

Slavery and its legacies forged the early American connections with Africa. By the nineteenth century, as slavery became an increasingly divisive domestic political issue, some Americans envisioned re-colonization of blacks to Africa or the Caribbean as a solution. Beginning in the late eighteenth century free blacks from Britain and Canada, under the sponsorship of British philanthropists and joined by escaped slaves from the United States, migrated to Sierra Leone on the west coast of Africa. US Republican Timothy Pickering of Massachusetts was among many Americans who viewed such colonization efforts as the best means to "remove a population that we could well spare," as he put it in 1814.

In 1817 the Kentuckian Henry Clay took the lead in creation of the **American Colonization Society** whose purpose was to promote compulsory removal of blacks, thus preserving the perceived US identity as a white man's republic. The tiny new country of Liberia directly south of Sierra Leone became the site of colonization of American blacks. In February 1862 the United States accorded Liberia formal diplomatic recognition as a new nation. By that time, however, the Civil War was already escalating, as colonization schemes could not head off the sectional conflict.

In the ensuing decades colonization to Liberia was limited, in part because free blacks and their Republican backers in the North opposed it. These reformers rejected colonization as a white supremacist scheme whereas they labored for racial equality in America. In all more than 1,000 African-Americans migrated to Liberia, not because they identified with Africa as their homeland, but rather to escape racial oppression in the post-Reconstruction South. On the other hand, many of the migrants found conditions in Liberia equally challenging for economic and cultural reasons. Colonization was never adequately funded nor embraced by Congress as a "solution" to the American race problem. By the mid-1890s, with Booker T. Washington urging African-Americans to accept racial inequality in deference to the pursuit of job training, the colonization movement faded away.

Some Americans took an interest in Africa for potential economic opportunities, particularly in the wake of the severe recession of the 1870s. In 1878 the quest for new markets for US exports prompted a remarkable two-year naval expedition authorized by Secretary of State William Evarts. Navy Admiral **Robert Shufeldt** headed the expedition by the *Ticonderoga*, which traversed the west coast of Africa before continuing to the Middle East, India, Southeast Asia, Japan, and China. As instructed, Shufeldt successfully negotiated a settlement over a contested boundary between Sierra Leone and Liberia. After exploring inland up a series of African rivers Shufeldt rounded the Cape of Good Hope and landed at Madagascar, the large island off the southeastern coast of the African continent. Shufeldt reported that Africa was potentially the "great commercial prize of the world," but also that the United States was well behind the European nations in what became known as the "**scramble for Africa**." The State Department hoped to gain a foothold in the Congo trade by supporting the murderous regime of Belgium's King Leopold. Negative publicity, led by the African-American leader George Washington Williams, called into question public support for Leopold's bloody reign.

Shufeldt sailed next to the Middle East, once again noting that the British and the French were well ahead of the Americans. Following his tour of the Middle East the admiral recommended establishment of relations with Persia (modern-day Iran). As a result the United States opened a legation there in 1883. The State Department had cultivated little formal connection with the Middle East since the Barbary Wars early in the century but traders and travelers had filtered through the region. As with the European colonialists Americans displayed racial and religious prejudices toward Arabs and Muslims. By 1840 more American tourists had traveled to Egypt than citizens of any other country except Britain.

In the post-Civil War years US entrepreneurs conducted a profitable trade with the Ottoman Empire, including massive quantities of Turkish opium. Christians flocked to the region to visit the biblical holy land and to save souls. Americans returned home with commodities such as carpets, colorful décor, and often clichéd artistic renderings of harem scenes, desert oases, flying carpets, and the like. Pejorative terms such as "Turk" and "Mohammedanism" were often employed to contrast Middle Eastern cultures with the more civilized, modern, and Christian culture of the West. Rarely reluctant to give voice to the racial stereotypes common to the era, Theodore Roosevelt declared it was "impossible to expect moral, intellectual and material well being where Mohammedanism is supreme." Extensive and formal ties with the Middle East would not be forthcoming until the twentieth century.

Across the Pacific

The United States made much greater progress in expansion across the Pacific and into Asia than into Africa. Westerners had been captivated by the allure of the Orient since the thirteenth century travels of the Venetian merchant Marco Polo. The desire to become a Pacific power had been one of the prime motivations for Manifest Destiny expansion into California during the Mexican War. In the years following the Civil War, as the United States recovered, industrialized, and emerged as a world power, expansion across the Pacific became a driving force in US foreign policy.

Even before the takeover of California, the United States began to follow in the British wake into the fabled China market. After British gunboats forced open Chinese ports to foreigners in the First Opium War (1839–42), the United States negotiated the **Treaty of Wanghia**, signed on the island of Macau in 1844. Under its terms the United States received most favored nation (MFN) trade status—meaning that no other nation would have better terms of trade; and extraterritoriality—meaning that foreigners were subject to their own legal, judicial, and financial rules while being exempt from those of the home country. The Americans thus adopted the imperial model set forth by the British, French, Portuguese, and other European states.

As the United States industrialized after the Civil War, capitalists sought cheap Chinese "coolie" labor, especially for the dangerous work in mining and railroad construction in the western states and territories. Under the **Burlingame Treaty** (1868) Secretary of State Seward and Anson Burlingame, the US minister to China's Qing dynasty, recognized China's territorial integrity after the Second Opium War with Britain in return for more trading privileges as well as the importation of cheap Chinese labor. Within a generation, however, after much of the hard labor had been completed, Americans heaped racial prejudice on the Chinese. Mirroring the white supremacist violence of the South, Westerners expressed a feral hatred of the "rat-eating Chinaman" and proceeded to drive them out of towns and communities, seizing their property and beating and killing scores. The campaign against the "yellow peril" culminated in 1882 with passage by Congress of the **Chinese Exclusion Act**, shutting off all Chinese emigration into the United States.

Like China, Japan tried but ultimately failed to prevent Westerners from establishing trading privileges and treaty rights in the country. Viewing free trade as an inherent right in the modern world, the United States and other Western powers strove to open closed Japanese ports. In the summer of 1853 President Millard Fillmore, encouraged by American traders, whalers, and missionaries, ordered the Navy's East India Fleet under **Commodore Matthew Perry** to sail uninvited into Japanese waters to demand the opening of trade. Perry marched ashore in Edo, as Tokyo was then called, and presented an array of impressive gifts including a telegraph machine, daguerreotype, clocks, pistols, and topped them off with cases of whiskey. Impressed by the technology but alarmed by the effrontery of the Western "barbarians" in their steaming black ships, the Japanese refused to come to terms for weeks.

Perry's Christian benevolence inspired him to offer "the gospel of God to the heathens" but he also threatened war if the "weak and semi-barbarous" Japanese refused to open their ports to trade. Returning in February 1854 with an impressive force of eight warships Perry marched 500 troops ashore while the band blared the "Star-Spangled Banner." He bluntly informed Japanese officials that the United States had conquered Mexico in war and "circumstances may lead your country into a similar plight." The Japanese agreed to open two treaty ports and grant MFN trade status, but rejected the US demand to open a coaling station. They also pledged to safeguard shipwrecked US sailors, who had sometimes disappeared after landing on Japanese shores.

The **Treaty of Kanagawa** (1854), signed by the ruling Shogun, set forth these provisions thus culminating the "opening" of Japan. The British, French, and Russians followed the US lead in exacting treaty rights from Japan. A

Figure 6.1 An artist's rendering of Commodore Matthew C. Perry being received into Yokohama following the forced "opening" of Japan to the United States in 1854.

Source: Library of Congress, Prints and Photographs Division, LC-USZC4-3379.

follow-up treaty with the United States in 1858 established concessions with minimal taxation and provided extraterritoriality for foreigners. Many Japanese condemned the "unequal treaties," which became a source of domestic division and simmering resentment of the Western powers.

In 1863 conflict over trade and treaty rights between Japan and the Western powers including the United States provoked the **Shimonoseki War**. In an effort to drive out the foreigners Japanese forces attacked American, French, British, and Dutch targets, eventually burning the US legation in Tokyo. The US warship *Wyoming* sank two Japanese vessels while suffering 14 casualties in response to the attack, but with the Civil War raging at home the United States was content to let the Europeans take the lead. In a culminating battle in 1864 the Americans played only a token role in a British-led assault that pummeled the Japanese anti-foreign faction into submission. Robert Pruyn, the US minister to Japan, played a lead role in negotiating a ceasefire and exacting a sizable indemnity.

Japan was now open and modernizing, but resentment of Western gunboat diplomacy would not be forgotten. The Japanese resolved never again to be humiliated by the more powerful Western intruders. The US-led opening sparked political tumult leading to the Meiji Restoration (1868), ending Japan's isolation and putting it on a path of modernity and industrialization enabling the country to compete with the Western powers.

An American effort to open Korean ports to Western trade sparked a major conflict in 1866. The *General Sherman*, an armed merchant ship named for the Union Civil War hero, sailed into Korean waters and upriver to Pyongyang, where a bloody clash ensued. The US warship fired into crowds but the Koreans fought back with fireboats. Unable to put out the flames a couple of Americans and their mostly Chinese crew jumped into the river before being killed by the angry Koreans. The incident confirmed for Koreans the need to remain isolated from the West, but the United States and European powers were equally determined to gain access to Asian ports.

In 1871 the United States took the lead in the effort to force open the **"hermit kingdom"** of Korea. A force of more than 600 men invaded on attack boats backed by two warships from the Asiatic Squadron. A major fight ensued—the largest battle involving American troops between the Civil War and the war with Spain in 1898—though it is little known in the United States. Hundreds of American invaders and tenacious Korean resistance fighters died in what the *New York Herald* dubbed the "Little War with the Heathen." More than a decade later, in 1882, Shufeldt negotiated the first US treaty with Korea, which granted trading privileges, MFN status, and extraterritoriality. Shufeldt negotiated the treaty with Chinese officials claiming to speak for Korea, which by this time had become a pawn in the East Asian power struggle.

By the time the United States forced its way into Korea, Asian-Pacific expansion was all the rage. Businessmen, aided by the State Department, sought commercial opportunities extending to the China market; Protestant missionaries sought to save souls, especially in China; and proponents of the US emergence

Figure 6.2 In 1890 Alfred Thayer Mahan, president of the Naval War College, fueled US naval and Pacific expansion with the publication of *The Influence of Sea Power Upon History*.

Source: Library of Congress, Prints and Photographs Division, LC-DIG-ggbain-17956.

as a powerful and manly nation called for a naval buildup to facilitate imperial competition across the Pacific. By the 1890s the naval theorist Alfred Thayer Mahan, author of *The Influence of Sea Power Upon History*, had won over key politicians, notably Senator Henry Cabot Lodge of Massachusetts, and the up and coming New York patrician Roosevelt. In 1887 Roosevelt, serving as a visiting lecturer at the newly created Naval War College, embraced Mahan's theories on the critical importance of sea power. A US naval buildup began in the 1880s and accelerated the next decade when Congress approved construction of big battleships to complement the fleet of smaller cruisers.

Improving the capabilities of the Navy became more urgent in 1889, as the United States clashed with Britain and Germany over control of the Pacific islands of **Samoa**, especially valued for the harbor at Pago Pago. The United States sought to establish coaling stations for refueling on trans-Pacific voyages. In 1872, five years after taking possession of Brooks Island (Midway), the Navy secured an agreement with the Samoans for a coaling station at Pago Pago, but the US Senate rejected it amid the era of scandals and lingering domestic divisions. In 1878 the United States was back, negotiating an MFN agreement as well as a veiled pledge to back the Samoans in the event of conflict with another power.

A war scare materialized in the contest for Samoa, a grouping of 14 islands strategically located in the South Pacific along trade routes to Australia and New Zealand. However, a hurricane struck in the midst of the escalating imperial conflict, devastating the islands and paving the way for a diplomatic settlement in which the United States, Britain, and Germany partitioned Samoa. The United States took the major prize, the harbor at Pago Pago, an important milestone in the eventual US takeover of the islands.

US Expansion in Hawai'i

The emergence of the United States in the latter half of the nineteenth century as an Asia-Pacific power pivoted on the purchase of Alaska and the creeping annexation of the Hawaiian Islands. Expansion into the two future states laid a foundation for the subsequent imperial thrust into the Philippines and other commercial, strategic, and cultural outposts in East Asia and the Pacific. The takeover of Alaska, Hawai'i, and the other island possessions deepened American connections with China, Japan, Korea, Russia, and Southeast Asia, with profound implications for future US foreign policy.

Once again the United States followed in the British wake to Hawai'i, but it was the Americans who established permanent settlements on the islands and gradually took them over. In January 1778, in the midst of his third Pacific voyage, the British sea captain **James Cook** landed at Waimea Harbor, Kauai, and promptly named the island chain after the 4th Earl of Sandwich, a backer of his voyages. The islanders initially celebrated the arrival of Cook and his crew but the sailors wore out their welcome after a return voyage in 1779. On Sunday, February 14, 1779, Cook led a punitive force with the intent to punish the Hawaiian king personally for the theft of a small boat. Defenders of the monarch intercepted the force and stabbed and bludgeoned Cook to death in a fight just offshore. The British sailors retaliated by killing scores of Hawaiian men, women, and children before departing the islands. Following another clash a decade later, the British-American trader Simon Metcalfe killed more than a hundred Hawaiians, firing upon them with his ship's cannon in what is known as the Olowalu Massacre on Maui.

In the ensuing years British, Spanish, French, Russian, and American sailors, traders, and missionaries landed on the Sandwich Islands to trade or obtain provisions during Pacific voyages. The Westerners traded guns, ammunition, nails, cloth, trinkets, and grog to the Hawaiians for water, food, vegetables, firewood, and sex. Many visitors chose to stay on the island paradise, which quickly became renowned for its beauty and agreeable weather. Beginning in the 1820s, American settlers and missionaries—mostly from New England— began to assert themselves and eventually to take over the islands.

In Their Words

The Rev. Josiah Strong, Our Country (1885)

It seems to me that God, with infinite wisdom and skill, is training the Anglo-Saxon race for an hour sure to come in the world's future. Heretofore there has always been in the history of the world a comparatively unoccupied land westward, into which the crowded countries of the East have poured their surplus populations. But the widening waves of migration, which millenniums ago rolled east and west from the valley of the Euphrates, meet today on our Pacific coast. There are no more new worlds. The unoccupied arable lands of the earth are limited, and will soon be taken. The time is coming when the pressure of population on the means of subsistence will be felt here as it is now felt in Europe and Asia. Then will the world enter upon a new stage of its history—the final competition of races, for which the Anglo-Saxon is being schooled. Long before the thousand millions are here, the mighty centrifugal tendency, inherent in this stock and strengthened in the United States, will assert itself. Then this race of unequaled energy, with all the majesty of numbers and the might of wealth behind it—the representative, let us hope, of the largest liberty, the purest Christianity, the highest civilization— having developed peculiarly aggressive traits calculated to impress its institutions upon mankind, will spread itself over the earth.

Protestant missionaries played an important role in US expansion across the Pacific, and perhaps nowhere more than in Hawai'i. Established in 1816 at Williams College, the Foreign Mission School trained missionaries for service in Hawai'i and also brought Hawaiians back to the college in far western Massachusetts for religious study. Fired by the Second Great Awakening and the antebellum reform movements in the United States, missionaries flocked to Hawai'i. By mid-century more than 20 percent of Hawaiians had converted to Protestantism.

Hawaiian elites tried to avoid being colonized while at the same time taking advantage of what the Westerners had to offer. The Hawaiian monarch, **Kamehameha I**, traded with the *haole* (whites) for guns and other technologies that helped him defeat his domestic opponents in a violent struggle to unite the Hawaiian Islands under his rule in 1795. The king subsequently employed carpenters and other skilled Europeans to bolster his power, giving many of them land to live upon and to farm in return. Kamehameha I and other Hawaiians, much like the American Indians, had no concept of private property or individual appropriation of land in perpetuity. When Kamehameha gave the Europeans land in trade or in exchange for services, he meant that they could *use* it, not that they could *own* it. From the outset, however, the Westerners pressed for conversion to a system of fee simple individual land ownership.

As increasing numbers of missionaries and settlers arrived in Hawai'i in the nineteenth century, the Hawaiian monarchs acquiesced to new laws and religious conversion while attempting to fend off outright colonization. Hawaiian elites learned English, adopted Western modes of dress, and often allied with the missionaries rather than traders, who might exploit them, and sailors, prone to drunkenness and violence. From the missionaries they could learn English and Western ways. Adaptation may have been the Hawaiians' only hope but in the end this strategy too failed to ward off colonization and ultimately the annexation of the islands by the United States.

Racial mores played an important role in the US takeover of Hawai'i and Pacific expansion generally. Even as they sought to civilize and Christianize Hawaiians the Americans viewed them, like the Hispanics, Indians, and Negroes back home, as inferior peoples who justifiably could be ruled by a superior race. One settler from a missionary family averred, "The negro and the Polynesian have many striking similarities," and both required education and salvation.

In a process that unfolded across the latter half of the nineteenth century, American ideas, institutions, and law gradually took hold in Hawai'i. "The idea that this floating, restless, moneymaking, go-ahead white population can be governed by natives only, is out of the question," the missionary Richard Armstrong declared in 1847. "The time has gone by for the native rulers to have the management of affairs, though the business may be done in their name."

During the 1840s Americans outnumbered and outmaneuvered other Western powers as well as the monarchy to assert their control over the Hawaiian Islands—the name they popularized to displace Cook's Sandwich Islands. As with treaties made with the Indians, the Americans dispossessed the Hawaiians by legal means. In 1848, the same year the United States took control of Texas, New Mexico, and California by treaty, the **Great Mahele** or land division began to convert the ancient Hawaiian land tenure system to individual ownership in fee simple. The Western businessmen and the predominantly New England Protestants sought to enhance land values and attract investors and settlers through the new land laws. Well-meaning but no less ethnocentric US missionaries had ensured that under the Mahele the common people of Hawai'i could retain ownership of land plots by filing claims, but many did not understand this provision and were soon dispossessed of what little land they held.

In addition to establishing Western legal and economic structures, the settlers sought to infuse their morality over the islands. As with the campaign for Indian assimilation, the settlers implanted Western gender roles and the nuclear family. While plantation owners employed a predominately male labor force, missionaries insisted that Hawaiian women define themselves as wives and mothers anchoring the domestic sphere. While women were relieved of hard work in the sugar fields, they were required to comply with Western norms pertaining to clothing, cleanliness, eating habits, sexual restraint, and other cultural practices. The missionaries sometimes judged Hawaiian men and women harshly, one referencing them as "ignorant and lazy," lacking "everything like modesty," and "in great need of improvement."

Annexation

As the Americans took charge of the land and the people of Hawai'i, massive profits began to roll in from the burgeoning sugar industry. Beginning in 1875 the elimination of trade barriers through reciprocity agreements enabled the planters to sell their product duty free to a tariff-protected US market. The planters imported cheap Asian labor, initially mostly from China but also from Japan, Korea, and the Philippine Islands. Five dominant firms, held or managed by a tight-knit group of elite, intermarried families, controlled the sugar industry and much of the islands' economy. By 1911, journalist Ray Stannard Baker declared Hawai'i was not merely a tropical paradise but also "a paradise of modern industrial combination. In no part of the United States is a single industry so predominant as the sugar industry in Hawai'i."

While the planters exploited cheap labor for massive profits from Hawaiian sugar cane, expansionists and naval enthusiasts coveted Hawai'i for strategic reasons. Hawai'i had featured prominently in Seward's targeted expansion but he ultimately had to settle for the purchase of Alaska and the Midway Islands, located some 1,300 miles northwest of Honolulu. Senator and Secretary of State James G. Blaine perceived "the Hawaiian islands as the key to the dominion of the American Pacific." Lodge, Mahan, Roosevelt, and other architects of US expansion shared the vision that Hawai'i—including control of the coveted port at Pearl Harbor—was essential to the rise of the United States as an Asia-Pacific power. Hawai'i and other islands provided the coaling stations and trans-Pacific trade centers that were crucial to expansion and trade with China.

With backing in Washington, the Americans who had taken control of the land and established highly profitable sugar and fruit plantations, set their sights on terminating the monarchy and seizing direct political control of the islands. By the late nineteenth century, extrapolations from the evolutionary theories of Charles Darwin emphasized "natural selection" and "survival of the fittest" species to justify a wave of overseas Western colonialism and imperialism. The Western powers engaged in a "scramble" for Pacific outposts that mirrored the scramble for Africa. Europeans as well as Americans undertook the "white man's burden" of spreading civilization by force over "primitive" peoples perceived as unable to keep pace with the modern world.

As strategic ambitions and economic self-interest aligned, the American elite led by Lorrin Thurston and Sanford Dole formed the **Hawaiian League**, a shadow organization that plotted an outright takeover of the islands during a meeting in Dole's home. Thurston and Dole were prominent men from well-established missionary families; both were attorneys and both had been elected to the Hawaiian legislature. After overthrowing the monarchy, the *haole* elite would have complete control of the islands and could orchestrate their eventual annexation by the United States.

In July 1887 the Americans forced King Kalakaua to sign what Hawaiians would later dub the "**Bayonet Constitution**" in which the monarch turned over executive powers to the oligarchy of planters and businessmen. Mirroring the spread of Jim Crow segregation of African-Americans on the mainland, the new constitution disenfranchised Hawaiians and the Asian immigrant workforce. The United States also claimed an "exclusive right" to build and maintain a coaling station at Pearl Harbor in conjunction with a renewed reciprocity treaty. Hawaiians had vigorously opposed and successfully fought off previous American efforts to take control of the coveted harbor. As Hawaiians protested in the streets, the elite-controlled militia reined them in with bayonets in place.

As they strove to contain Hawaiian resistance the planter elite moved to terminate the monarchy and to annex Hawai'i to the United States. In 1889 Blaine appointed John Stevens, a close associate from their native Maine and an avowed annexationist, as US minister to Hawai'i. In January 1893 Stevens launched a coup, reporting back to Washington, "The Hawaiian pear is now fully ripe, and this is the golden hour for the United States to pluck it." US marines landed, ostensibly to protect property, as Stevens declared Hawai'i a protectorate under the benevolent guidance of the United States.

In Their Words

Queen Liliuokalani Protests, January 17, 1893

I Liliuokalani, by the Grace of God and under the Constitution of the Hawaiian Kingdom, do hereby solemnly protest against any and all acts done against myself and the Constitutional Government of the Hawaiian Kingdom by certain persons claiming to have established a Provisional Government of and for this Kingdom.

> That I yield to the superior force of the United States of America whose Minister Plenipotentiary, His Excellency John L. Stevens, has caused United States troops to be landed at Honolulu and declared that he would support the Provisional Government.
>
> Now to avoid any collision of armed forces, and perhaps the loss of life, I do this under protest and impelled by said force yield my authority until such time as the Government of the United States shall, upon facts being presented to it, undo the action of its representatives and reinstate me in the authority which I claim as the Constitutional Sovereign of the Hawaiian Islands.

As they attempted to overthrow the monarchy the Americans condemned **Queen Liliuokalani**, who had ascended to the throne, as both a woman and a representative of a backward race. Resisting the US effort to drive her from power, Liliuokalani attempted to work through the political system to promulgate a new constitution affirming the monarchy. She proved so persistent that the Americans seized land held by the monarchy, placed Liliuokalani under house arrest, and put her on trial in 1895. Arriving back in Maine, Stevens proudly averred that the "semi-barbaric monarchy" had been brought under US control.

Just as many Americans condemned mistreatment of African-Americans and Indians at home, the takeover of Hawai'i had been too blatant for many to stomach. The Hawaiian coup became a hot political issue as President Grover Cleveland, a Democrat, condemned US imperialism and rejected the treaty of annexation submitted by his Republican predecessor. "The provisional government owes its existence to an armed invasion by the United States," Cleveland flatly declared, although he made no effort to restore the Hawaiian monarchy. Anti-imperialism had little staying power in the United States, however, and soon gave way to celebration of the nation's rising power in the world.

On the deliberately chosen date of July 4, 1894, the planter elite proclaimed the existence of the new Republic of Hawai'i. The United States proffered immediate diplomatic recognition, with Great Britain and most European countries following suit. Thousands of Hawaiians protested the hoisting of the American Flag outside the Iolani Palace and continued to sign petitions against the dissolution of the monarchy. The planter elite, joined by the strategists of Pacific expansion, called for outright annexation of Hawai'i "in the interests of the white race," as Roosevelt put it. "If I had my way we would annex those islands tomorrow," he declared in 1897.

Roosevelt got his wish the next year. Amid the excitement of the Spanish–American War, the United States annexed Hawai'i by joint resolution of Congress. This action required only a simple majority rather than the constitutionally mandated two-thirds needed in the Senate for approval of treaties. "We need Hawai'i just as much and a good deal more than we did California," proclaimed Cleveland's successor, the Republican President William McKinley. "It is manifest destiny."

Unlike other colonies taken from Spain, which would be brought under indirect US control, the annexation of Hawai'i made it, as one congressman put it, a "true American colony." Proponents argued that as a result of the success of the missionaries and the planters in spreading Christianity, the English language, and American ways, Hawai'i was more suited for annexation than the other more "primitive" and racially suspect possessions. Although indigenous Hawaiians were incapable of governing themselves, they were not "savages" but rather "barbarians of a milder and more progressive type," Lodge assured his colleagues. The Massachusetts senator pointed out that physically the Hawaiians had features "resembling the Europeans" and were "olive" in color rather than "yellow like the Malay nor red like the American Indian." Blending perceptions of race and gender, Lodge described the Hawaiian woman as a "dazzling vision of sparkling eyes, pearly teeth, bright flowers, and bare legs . . . her voluptuous bust rounding in graceful curves."

Dispossessed and rendered second-class citizens, Hawaiians were gradually outnumbered by Asian laborers imported by the planter elite. A census conducted in 1872 found the islands comprised of 86 percent Hawaiians and another 4 to 5 percent of mixed-Hawaiians. By 1890, however, as a result of the rapid influx of Asian laborers and settlers, Hawaiians comprised only 38 percent of the population, with part-Hawaiians comprising another 7 percent. The number of American settlers steadily increased yet they comprised a mere 2 percent of the population even as they dominated the islands politically and economically.

Counterinsurgency War in the Philippines

In addition to the takeover of Hawai'i, the Spanish–American War of 1898 facilitated US annexation of the Philippine Islands. Unlike Alaska, Hawai'i, and the Caribbean, securing the Philippines required a bloody counterinsurgency war, the first of a series of such conflicts that the United States would fight in Asia.

When the United States declared war against Spain in April 1898, Americans anticipated their soldiers fighting in Cuba, but most did not know that Spain also possessed the Philippines. Few Americans knew where the islands were located. Advocates of Pacific expansion, however, were keenly aware of the strategic significance of the Southeast Asian archipelago. Weeks before war had been declared Roosevelt, who had become assistant secretary of the Navy, ordered Admiral George Dewey to steam toward the Philippines. On May 1, 1898, Dewey led the Pacific Squadron into Manila Bay, where it crushed the decaying Spanish fleet in a swift and decisive naval battle. Dewey declared that "the hand of God" had been evident in a triumph in which not a single American sailor died. The reality was more mundane: knowing they were outclassed by the US invasion force the Spanish put up only a token resistance to assuage their honor before surrendering.

After landing in Manila the American forces allied with the Philippine rebels, who were well on their way before the Americans arrived to drive out the Spanish colonialists. Led by José Rizal, a martyred national hero, the Philippines had begun to evolve a national consciousness. US officials assured **Emilio Aguinaldo**, a Filipino elite and leader of the anti-Spanish rebels, that the United States came as a liberator and had no intention of colonizing the islands. Calling the United States an "honorable friend," Aguinaldo declared the Philippines independent and set about drafting a constitution. Six months later, in December 1898, the United States, having defeated Spain on every front, took the Spanish surrender in the **Treaty of Paris**. Under terms of the treaty the United States paid Spain $20 million for the turnover of the Philippines. Spain also turned over Guam, an island some 1,500 miles east of the Philippines and another important coaling station that would facilitate US trans-Pacific expansion.

McKinley ultimately made the decision to annex the Philippine archipelago rather than allow the islands to achieve independence. A champion of business, rising corporate power, and overseas trade, McKinley pointed out that the Philippines offered "commercial opportunities to which American statesmanship cannot be indifferent." Deeming the islanders unfit for self-government, McKinley declared that the United States would pursue a policy of "benevolent assimilation." The US-occupiers hoisted the American Flag in Manila and laid claim to the archipelago. Like American Indians, Cubans, Puerto Ricans, and Hawaiians, the Filipinos had been the objects of Western diplomacy and were excluded from decision making.

In addition to race, religion played an important role in McKinley's decision making and in public support for the US mission to take over the islands. "In the providence of God, who works in mysterious ways," McKinley declaimed, "this great archipelago was put into our lap." McKinley told a group of Methodist ministers that he had prayed for guidance before making the decision that the United States should annex the Philippines in order to "uplift and civilize them and Christianize them." (Spain had already Christianized the Filipinos, who were overwhelmingly Catholic.)

McKinley's decision to annex the islands ignited a military conflict in Manila and a major debate in the United States. Between the signing of the Treaty of Paris in December 1898 and its narrow ratification on February 6, 1899, Congress debated the implications of the nation's emerging overseas empire. Few disagreed that the United States, as a white, Protestant nation and an emerging great power, had a mission to shepherd backward, racially inferior people toward freedom and progress. Yet many congressmen expressed concern about US intervention in the faraway and little known Philippines and by the decision formally to take on colonies. These representatives and their public followers perceived intervention in the Philippines as a European-style departure from traditional American diplomacy.

Six months after Dewey's triumph in Manila Bay, the **Anti-Imperialist League**, chartered in Boston, denounced the extension of sovereignty over "foreign territory, without the free consent of the people thereof . . . in violation of constitutional principles, and fraught with moral and physical evils to our people." The league featured such luminaries as Cleveland, former Interior secretary Carl Schurz, industrialist Andrew Carnegie, diplomat Charles Francis Adams, Stanford president David Starr Jordan, and the labor leader Samuel Gompers. The League condemned "the subjugation of any people" as "criminal aggression," adding, "We regret that it is necessary in the land of Washington and Lincoln to reaffirm that all men of whatever race or color are entitled to life, liberty, and the pursuit of happiness."

The leading imperialists argued, in contrast, that "benevolent assimilation" of the Philippines was consistent with the nation's history of subduing and civilizing the Indian tribes. Calling attention to the various ethnic groups in the Philippines—Malays, Moros, and Tagalogs, for example—US "experts" described the islands as inhabited by an "aggregate of tribes" rather than being a country suited for national independence. The term "tribes" resonated with the recent US history of warfare and internal colonization of Indians. These arguments ultimately proved convincing, as most Americans accepted that "wild" Indians had needed to be tamed on the "frontier." If the Filipinos like the Indians were backward peoples, then it made sense to most Americans that they should be brought under the control of a superior and chosen race.

If subjugation of the Philippines was a crime, as anti-imperialists charged, "then our whole past record of expansion is a crime," Lodge declared. The outspoken imperialist Senator Albert Beveridge explained that the United States had long "governed the Indian without his consent. And if you deny it to the Indian at home how are you to grant it to the Malay abroad?" Former Senator Henry Dawes drew on his reputation for expertise on assimilation to advise that the history of Indian relations should guide the nation's "experience with other alien races whose future has been put in our keeping."

Roosevelt, the Rough Rider hero of the battle of Cuba's San Juan Hill, commanded broad public support for his imperialist position. Not only a war hero, Roosevelt also resonated authority as the author of the four-volume history *The Winning of the West*, published from 1889 to 1896. The account emphasized savage Indian violence and atrocities in defiance of America's civilizing mission. The settlers "had justice on their side. This great continent could not have been kept as nothing but a game preserve for squalid savages," Roosevelt explained in the first volume. The Seminole, he now explained, "rebelled and waged war exactly as some of the Tagals have rebelled and waged war in the Philippines . . . we are making no new departure." For the United States the conflicts were "precisely parallel between the Philippines and the Apaches and Sioux." Other imperialists cited the colonization of Hawai'i as reason for optimism in taking civilization to the Philippines. "The example of Hawai'i gives great encouragement to the philanthropist and the Christian who may look hopefully to the future," as Senator John T. Morgan put it.

By adding the Philippines to the growing US Pacific Empire the United States could compete with Europeans economically and position itself to broaden trade with China and Japan. With memories still fresh of the severe depression of the mid-1890s, some businessmen, investors, and politicians argued that exports and increased foreign trade held the key to avoiding a future economic debacle. American exceptionalism remained central to perceptions and the rhetoric of empire, as myriad politicians and public figures argued it was the nation's duty and providential destiny to expand its influence worldwide.

Race, religious faith, and the desire for the United States to assert itself as a manly empire repeatedly surfaced as justification for the imperial venture. Most congressmen and much of the press and public joined McKinley in justifying the intervention as a Christian mission. Roosevelt was the most forceful of many proponents who argued that it would be weak and unmanly for the United States to depart the islands and leave the backward Filipinos unable to govern themselves and vulnerable to intervention by Britain, Germany, or another great power. The racial inferiority of the Philippine "natives" and "tribes" was virtually unquestioned. Scores of American newspaper editorial cartoons depicted McKinley or Uncle Sam attempting to tame caricatured natives wearing grass skirts, with bones through their noses, spears at their side. Nearly always darkened in skin color, the Filipinos were viewed in the same context as African-Americans and Indians, inferior races unready for civilization.

On February 4, 1899, in the midst of the congressional debate, a firefight erupted outside Manila and quickly escalated into a full-scale war. The American public blamed the savage and backward Filipinos for the outbreak of violence. The *New York Times* declared that the Filipinos' "insane attack . . . upon their liberators" was sufficient evidence of "their incapacity for self-government." The Philippine resistance aided the imperialist quest to achieve the required two-thirds Senate approval of the Paris Treaty. On February 6, two days after the outbreak of fighting, the Senate ratified the treaty with Spain including handing over the Philippines, by a vote of 57–27, narrowly achieving the required two-thirds margin.

Once fighting broke out, the press, the public, and the US military were enthusiastic about going to war to combat the "Philippine Insurrection." On February 5 the United States prevailed after fighting in and around Manila in the largest and bloodiest battle of the entire **Philippine War** waged over a 16-mile front. The Americans went on to capture several cities, including the revolutionary capital of Malolos to the north of Manila, which they subjected to a punishing naval bombardment with much destruction and a high rate of civilian casualties.

As in future conflicts the outbreak of fighting left anti-imperialists vulnerable to charges that the anti-war position undermined American troops on the field of battle. In the presidential election of 1900 Democrat William Jennings Bryan made anti-imperialism a centerpiece of his campaign. Bryan declared that the "war of conquest would leave its legacy of perpetual hatred, for it was God Himself placed in every human heart the love of liberty. He never made a race of people so low in the scale of civilization or intelligence that it would welcome a foreign master." Bryan condemned the effort to "imitate European empires," adding that an "imperial policy" would lead to future wars of conquest and "rapid growth of our military establishment." Mirroring the result of the 1896 campaign, McKinley defeated Bryan in a decisive repudiation of the anti-imperialist position.

Guerrilla Resistance and Indiscriminate Warfare

With the United States committed to war the Filipinos understood they would be unable to confront the better-trained and equipped American forces head on. In November 1899 Aguinaldo called on the Philippine people to wage a war of guerrilla resistance. Driven into the countryside, the Filipinos adopted tactics of sniping, stabbings with their *bolos* (long knives easily hidden in clothing), ambush and hit and run assaults, and sabotage of roads and telegraph lines. The rebels could move seamlessly in and among the populace, which largely supported them but whose loyalty could otherwise be demanded at penalty of death. The United States thus faced the daunting prospect of subduing irregular forces through the length (more than 1,100 miles) and breadth (more than 700 miles) of the archipelago.

The United States fought the resistance forces militarily while at the same time attempting to win over the population with reforms and assistance. Citing the "barbarous savagery" of the Filipino rebels, the Americans waged indiscriminate warfare even as they developed plans for the "benevolent assimilation" of the natives. Often-indiscriminate violence and massive destruction resulted from the difficulty of identifying rebels from within the general population of Filipinos. In response, the Army took the approach, as General Elwell S. Otis, military governor of the Philippines, acknowledged, that "every Filipino was really an insurgent." The lack of discrimination led to "the oppression of thousands of innocent natives," Otis admitted. As the Union had done during the Civil War, the Americans denied irregular forces protection under the international laws of war. Torture, collective punishment (destroying an entire village or town, for example), and indiscriminate killing followed. As US forces patrolled the cities and set out into the "boondocks" (*bunduk*, in Tagalog, for mountains), only those Filipinos who displayed "strict obedience" to US authority could hope to be safe.

As in other colonial wars waged by Europeans—from the Belgian Congo to the Australian outback—racist perceptions of the colonized people enabled violent oppression. US forces adopted language familiar on the home front, as they routinely referred to the Filipinos as "niggers." The islands would not be pacified, a soldier from Kansas explained, "until the niggers are killed off like the Indians." It was merely "sport to hunt the black devils," soldiers acknowledged.

Almost 90 percent of generals and many other officers were veterans of the Indian wars and thus experienced in campaigns focused on "extirpation of guerrilla bands." Many officers had little interest in disciplining soldiers in a race war against "treacherous and cowardly" rebels who, like Indians, engaged in sniping and hit and run attacks. In addition to indiscriminate killing, Americans made arbitrary arrests, deported and tortured prisoners, often by means of the suffocating water cure. As in the Indian wars, US forces targeted food supplies, crops, and farm animals in order to deprive the guerrillas of sustenance.

Lacking a large enough army to accomplish the mission, the United States as in previous wars relied on volunteer units, which proved to be generally well trained and effective. However, volunteers sometimes fired their weapons indiscriminately, ransacked and plundered homes and offices, and raped Filipino women. The US volunteers sometimes did "things too scandalous to write," as Major Matthew A. Batson put it. During the capture of San Fernando, north of Manila, in the spring of 1899, as Batson informed his wife, the volunteers ransacked churches, private houses, and wantonly destroyed furniture. "We come as a Christian people to relieve them from the Spanish yoke and bear ourselves like barbarians," Batson pointed out. "Why, if I was a Filipino I would fight as long as I had a breath left."

Warfare, famine, and disease took a massive toll on the civilian population of the Philippines. Estimates vary widely, from 300,000 to 800,000 Filipinos killed, overwhelmingly from famine and disease rather than direct conflict. The US forces moved south from their base in Luzon to occupy Cebu, a mountainous island in the center of the archipelago. From 1898 to 1906 some 100,000 of the approximately 600,000 island residents died from warfare, famine, and disease. The destruction of houses, farms, and food supplies forced the population into concentration camps, where disease, especially cholera, spread rapidly.

Filipino resistance fighters struck back at the Americans when opportunities arose. In September 1901 at **Balangiga** on the island of Samar, villagers orchestrated a surprise attack with their *bolos*, slaughtering 48 unsuspecting American soldiers at an early Sunday morning breakfast. US forces avenged the attack with indiscriminate campaigns not only on Samar but also throughout the Philippine archipelago. General Jacob H. Smith, a veteran of the Indian wars including Wounded Knee, issued an infamous order to convert Samar into a biblical "howling wilderness," as he authorized the killing of any Filipino aged 10 or above. "I want no prisoners," Smith declared. "I wish you to kill and burn, the more you kill and burn the better you will please me." The troops followed their orders, as they razed the town and killed indiscriminately. As a result of the blatant violations of the rules of war, Smith was brought before a court martial and convicted but merely admonished and retired.

Frustrated by stubborn guerrilla resistance, General J. Franklin Bell conducted a brutalizing campaign in the province of Batangas on Luzon. "Civilization demands that the defeated side, in the name of humanity, should surrender and accept the result," he declared. When the rebels refused to submit, Bell's forces conducted summary executions, liberally employed the water cure (near drowning of the prisoner), and wantonly destroyed Filipino

Figure 6.3 US soldiers wading into battle during the "Philippine Insurrection."
Source: Library of Congress, Prints and Photographs Division, LC-USZ61-958.

property. US confiscations of food stores "made it difficult for the people to obtain rice," Bell acknowledged, hence many were starving. Disease took the heaviest toll on the people of Batangas as a result of their close confinement in detention camps. The Army's scorched-earth policy encompassed burning homes and rice stores, destroying or capturing livestock, and killing or driving the peasantry into the fortified encampments.

The Army censored battlefield news but reports of atrocities filtered across the Pacific nonetheless. Forced by public pressure to investigate Bell's indiscriminate campaign, Lodge closed to the public the hearings of his Committee on Insular Affairs. Bell escaped public censure and went on to become Army chief of staff.

While most Filipinos supported independence, the islanders had never been fully united and some were willing collaborators with the Americans. As in other colonial wars, the United States organized auxiliaries in the pacification effort, just as they had used indigenous allies in the Indian wars and created militias in Cuba, Haiti, and the Dominican Republic. The Macabebes, an ethnic group from the province of Pampanga and historic enemies of other Filipino ethnic groups, were ripe for recruitment and proved highly effective in their campaigns. On October 29, 1899, Batson gleefully reported, "With my battalion of Macabebe Scouts I am spreading terror among the *Insurrectos*." The Americans recruited other indigenous forces as well. By 1901, 50 "Native

Scout" companies of 50 men each had been organized. Thousands of other Filipinos served in paramilitary units, militia, police, and as guides and scouts.

Gradually worn down by the US forces, Filipinos began to defect, notably insurgent leaders and the economic and political elites of Philippine society. In March 1901, the revolutionary forces suffered a crippling blow with the capture of Aguinaldo. The rebel leader capitulated to US rule, prompting defections by other insurgent leaders. Sporadic resistance continued, however, even after the last of the revolutionary leaders surrendered in June 1902.

After 1902 continuing resistance centered on **Muslim Mindanao**, the second largest island, located in the far south of the Philippine archipelago. The Christian Americans distinguished the "Moros," as the Spanish had dubbed the various ethnic groups who had converted to Islam, from the Catholic Filipinos. The "Moro problem," as one US official put it, "was not only a question of governing uncivilized tribes but of controlling the dominant Mohammedan element." In 1899 the United States in a strategic move signed an agreement recognizing the Muslim faith and allowing the sultan to rule "Moroland." At the time Mindanao was not a high priority in the US pacification campaign and the agreement pleased the sultan, who sought the US alliance to better combat the opposition Christian Filipinos to the north.

Despite the interim agreement with the sultan, the Americans viewed Muslims as religious fanatics who would have to be pacified. As the United States collaborated with Catholic elites after the collapse of the resistance in 1902, the Muslims in Mindanao violently opposed being subjugated to the northern, non-Muslim Filipinos. In the end, "Force seems to be the only method of reaching them," Secretary of War William Howard Taft avowed. The United States thus launched a series of brutal military campaigns throughout "Moroland."

General Leonard Wood, a fellow Rough Rider hero and close confidant of Roosevelt, viewed the Muslims as "religious and moral degenerates" and proceeded to launch a campaign of extreme violence. In March 1906 Wood unleashed a three-day artillery assault against some 1,000 "Moro malcontents" who had taken refuge in Bud Dajo, an extinct volcano. Hundreds of non-resistant men, women, and children died in the attack. An Army major acknowledged that the people on Dajo were refugees who had "had no intention of fighting—ran up there only in fright." Indiscriminate campaigns against Muslims and peasant rebels in the southern islands continued for years, culminating in June 1913 with the slaughter of more than 300 Muslims at Bud Bagsak.

Pacification Through Reform

US counterinsurgency strategy in the Philippines combined warfare with efforts to discourage resistance and win over the populace through reform. From the outset McKinley had framed the US intervention as a campaign of "benevolent assimilation" in which the United States would "win the confidence, respect and affection of the inhabitants." The Army thus focused not only on warfare but also established municipal government, schools, hospitals, and police forces. The United States devoted substantial energies and resources to road building, sewer construction, food distribution, literacy programs, disease control, and municipal, legal, economic, educational, and judicial reform.

The reform and infrastructure programs were coercive rather than collaborative and sought not only to uplift the Filipinos, but also to reinforce and legitimate the occupation and the broader counterinsurgency campaign. The civilizing projects reinforced the perception of Filipinos as childlike primitives unable to care for themselves. Disease control isolated the Americans from contact with the contaminated natives, who were also subjected to medical experimentation. Roads and other infrastructure improvements served the occupation while social and educational reform was conducted on American terms often with disdain for local traditions.

The McKinley administration created the **Philippine Commission** to effect the transition from military rule to civil government. In 1900, the second Philippine Commission directed by Taft engaged Filipinos in civic action programs promoting trade, reconstruction, and municipal services. Many of these apparent collaborators continued covert support for the guerrillas while taking part in the Commission's efforts to remake Philippine society.

Figure 6.4 The United States sought to reform Philippine society while militarily defeating the revolutionaries. The Americans built schools, hospitals, and collaborated with Filipino elites to create new frameworks for governing civil society. Here an American teacher is shown with his class at a girls' school on Luzon.

Source: Library of Congress, Prints and Photographs Division, LC-USZ62-103380.

US reform efforts won increasing numbers of converts as the guerrilla effort waned and the civilian population suffered the effects of the counterinsurgency campaign. While the Americans had the power and resources to offer Filipinos a variety of inducements, the guerrillas had little to offer beyond the diminishing hope of independence. The Americans thus combined the allure of safety and some new opportunities with the palpable threat of confinement, disease, death, and destruction.

US counterinsurgency efforts exploited and expanded divisions in Philippine society to foster collaboration with elites while forestalling the drive for independence. By empowering a Christian Filipino elite, including priests and members of the Catholic hierarchy, the United States cultivated alliances in order to quell the revolution and establish a framework for colonial rule. The Americans promoted distinctions among the islanders based on racial classifications, which functioned as something of a "divide and conquer" strategy by promoting expectations and hierarchies of race and religion. By separating out Muslims and minority groups, the Americans and Filipino elites established a foundation for postwar collaboration.

Elite Filipinos and members of security forces thus made the transition in American eyes from "treacherous savages" to "little brown brothers" and partners against an internal opposition. Muslims, lower-ranked ethnic groups, reformers, and revolutionaries were isolated, policed, incarcerated, and killed as deemed necessary to reinforce the new order. The US occupiers worked with a newly organized constabulary to implement surveillance, covert operations, and often-brutal suppression of free speech, political activism, and reform. Corruption and police repression outlived the US occupation and continued to characterize Philippine society into the twenty-first century. Moreover the Philippines served as an imperial laboratory, as the techniques of repression pioneered there would be applied in other US imperial settings and against radicals and reformers on the home front as well.

Volatile Diplomacy in East Asia

By colonizing the Philippines and establishing a major naval base at **Subic Bay**, the United States culminated its rise as a Pacific power. Critical to Asian-Pacific geopolitics was the fate of China, which remained deeply divided and vulnerable to foreign influence as well as domestic warlords. Anti-foreign sentiment, which had grown steadily in China since the First Opium War (1839–42), erupted sensationally in the **Boxer Rebellion** of 1900. The rebellion, named for a secret society of pugilists, targeted Chinese Christians, missionaries, and foreign influence generally. Urged on by the empress of the declining Manchu dynasty, masses of Chinese took to the streets, especially in Peking (Beijing), to attack and kill foreigners and besiege the foreign embassies. The United States sent more than 2,000 troops as it joined Britain, France, Italy, Japan, and Russia in putting down the "rebellion." The foreign powers exacted indemnities for damages, with the United States later donating much of its share to fund education of Chinese students.

Interpreting the Past

The Open Door Notes

The Open Door Notes issued in 1899 and 1900 by Secretary of State John Hay have long commanded the attention of diplomatic historians. Some early post-World War II "realist" scholars derided the diplomatic notes outlining US policy toward China as examples of foreign policy idealism reflecting a preoccupation with "legalistic-moralistic" frameworks. They pointed out that the United States did not have the military power or overseas influence to enforce the diplomatic missives, which called for free trade and opposed spheres of influence (a "closed door") that would undermine the "territorial integrity" of China. Therefore, they argued, the diplomatic notes served little purpose.

Most scholars, however, have viewed the Open Door Notes as consequential. They argue that the notes enabled the United States to assert itself as a rising world power while striking an anti-imperialist image that placed other nations, primarily Europeans, under pressure to show some restraint in China. Other scholars have gone further, arguing that the Open Door Notes are paradigmatic of the driving force behind US foreign policy, namely a quest to keep foreign markets open to bolster free trade and US economic supremacy. The Open Door Notes harken back to the Model Treaty (1776) and forward to US efforts to promote modernization and liberal capitalism in the post-World War II period. The Open Door Notes thus reflected economic drives behind US foreign policy while at the same time affirming American exceptionalism, with the United States prescribing international norms for other nations of the world to follow.

Domestic unrest and the vulnerability of China to foreign influence prompted the United States to issue the **Open Door Notes** in 1899 and 1900. In the first note Secretary of State John Hay called for all of the foreign powers in China to allow free trade and equal opportunity rather than sealing off individual spheres of influence. The second note, issued as a warning against foreign takeovers in the wake of the Boxer uprising, emphasized the need to maintain China's "territorial and administrative integrity." The Open Door Notes were non-binding and the United States lacked the power to back them up, but they were largely adhered to by the European powers.

The Open Door Notes were addressed primarily albeit indirectly to Japan as well as the European powers. By the early twentieth century Japan was no longer weak and vulnerable but rather a rising power in its own right. Patterning itself on the Western nations, Japan had modernized and industrialized in the late nineteenth century. Roosevelt, who had replaced McKinley, assassinated in Buffalo, New York, in September 1901, was a shrewd observer of world affairs. He recognized the potential Japanese threat to the US possession of the

Philippines, especially after Japan followed up a defeat of China in war in 1895 with an even more impressive triumph in the **Russo-Japanese War** in 1905.

The victory by the supposedly inferior "Asiatic" Japanese over the supposedly racially superior Caucasian Russians shocked Western public opinion, but Roosevelt exploited the opportunity to advance US influence worldwide. Asserting the United States as the primary mediator of the conflict, Roosevelt sponsored the **Portsmouth Conference** in New Hampshire, which brought an end to the Russo-Japanese War. For his efforts Roosevelt won the Nobel Peace Prize in 1906, which further enhanced US global prestige. Much of the Japanese public, however, opposed the Portsmouth Treaty, which denied Japan sole possession of Sakhalin Island and indemnities it had demanded from the defeated Russians.

With many Japanese already resenting the United States over the outcome of the Portsmouth Conference, relations worsened as a result of US racism directed at Japanese immigrants especially in California. Tensions mounted as the San Francisco Board of Education passed a segregation order barring children of Japanese descent from attending schools with white American children. Japan bitterly resented growing demands in the United States for national exclusionary legislation reminiscent of the Chinese Exclusion Act of 1882. As

Figure 6.5 The Great White Fleet, having just been reviewed by President Theodore Roosevelt, departs in December 1907 from Hampton Roads, Virginia, for its show of force across the Pacific.

Source: Library of Congress, Prints and Photographs Division, LC-DIG-det-4a15934.

a result of these tensions Roosevelt negotiated the **Gentlemen's Agreement** (1907) in which the Japanese ceased issuing their citizens passports to immigrate to the United States. This action obviated the need for restrictive legislation in the United States.

Roosevelt continued to engage Japan diplomatically, but made a show of force as well. From 1907–09 Roosevelt sent the **Great White Fleet**—16 battleships in four squadrons, all painted white—on an around-the-world tour. In October 1908 the fleet steamed into Tokyo Bay where the Japanese offered a ceremonial welcome replete with a choir of schoolchildren singing "Hail Columbia" and the "Star-Spangled Banner." Roosevelt had made his point about growing US naval power and the Japanese had responded in a friendly manner.

The reception of the Great White Fleet cleared the way for the **Root–Takahira Agreement** (1908) in which the two powers acknowledged the other's spheres of influence at the expense of weaker Asian peoples. Japan acknowledged US possession of Hawai'i and the Philippines as well as the Open Door in China. The agreement calmed tensions, securing US influence in the Asia-Pacific region, but the accord also acknowledged Japan's special position in Manchuria, the resource-rich region of northern China that Japan meant to exploit economically. Further, the agreement sanctioned Japanese annexation of Korea.

The United States and Japan thus achieved a *modus vivendi* through great power diplomacy, yet tensions remained and would explode in the future. The Root–Takahira Agreement also reveals the limitation of the "Open Door" diplomacy. While the United States had less than a decade earlier exalted free trade and the Open Door in China, the pact with Japan ensured that doors remained closed in Hawai'i, the Philippines, and Korea, while green-lighting Japanese expansion into Manchuria.

The outbreak of World War I centered attention on Europe rather than Asia, though as the name suggests the war carried global implications. By the time the world war began the United States had succeeded in consolidating its new colonial empire by employing differentiated strategies adjusted to the divergent regions of the world. In the Pacific region, Wake Island, Samoa, and Guam had been incorporated primarily as strategic outposts and coaling stations whereas Alaska and Hawai'i were put on the path to statehood. In the Caribbean Basin, Cuba, Puerto Rico, the Panama Canal, and the Roosevelt Corollary facilitated strategic and economic linkages and reinforced the Monroe Doctrine.

In all of the new possessions the Americans instituted direct colonial or indirect neo-colonial rule that precluded the pursuit of self-determination by the subject peoples. At the same time, in both its new colonies and spheres of influence, the United States introduced a variety of reforms from health and sanitation to education and transportation. These reforms, however, directly benefited the occupiers and a minority of elite collaborators and failed to uplift or win over the majority populations. US imperialism, whether through economic takeovers, gunboat diplomacy, or resort to war ultimately fostered instability rather than long-term stability and thus required perpetual monitoring and policing of the new empire.

The US emergence at the turn of the century as a transnational imperial state laid the foundation for twentieth century interventions and modernization efforts, with implications for the home front as well. Though pioneered in the Philippines and the Caribbean, some of the policing techniques of surveillance, covert operations, and suppression of alleged radicals carried over into the United States and were applied during the post-World War I Red Scare (next chapter). Efforts to crack down on the opium trade in the Philippines spurred the first national efforts to rein in and regulate narcotics on the mainland. In these and many other ways foreign policies migrated back to the home front, reshaping the identity of the colonizer as well as the colonized.

Select Bibliography

Cumings, Bruce. *Dominion from Sea to Sea: American Ascendancy and Pacific Power*. New Haven, CT: Yale University Press, 2009.

Hixson, Walter L. *American Settler Colonialism: A History*. New York: Palgrave Macmillan, 2013.

Schueller, Malini Johar. *U.S. Orientalisms: Race, Nation, and Gender in Literature, 1790–1890*. Ann Arbor: University of Michigan Press, 1998.

Osorio, Jonathan K. *Dismembering Lahui: A History of the Hawaiian Nation to 1887*. Honolulu: University of Hawaii Press, 2002.

Parker, Linda S. *Native American Estate: The Struggle over Indian and Hawaiian Lands*. Honolulu: University of Hawaii Press, 1989.

Merry, Sally E. *Colonizing Hawai'i: The Cultural Power of Law*. Princeton, NJ: Princeton University Press, 2000.

Grimshaw, Patricia. *Path of Duty: American Missionary Wives in Nineteenth Century Hawai'i*. Honolulu: University of Hawaii Press, 1989.

Kramer, Paul A. *The Blood of Government: Race, Empire, the United States, and the Philippines*. Chapel Hill: University of North Carolina Press, 2006.

McCoy, Alfred W. and Scarano, Francis A., eds., *Colonial Crucible: Empire in the Making of the Modern American State*. Madison: University of Wisconsin Press, 2009.

Harris, Susan. *God's Arbiters: Americans in the Philippines, 1898–1902*. New York: Oxford University Press, 2011.

May, Glenn A. *Battle for Batangas: A Philippine Province at War*. New Haven, CT: Yale University Press, 1991.

Majeras, Resil B. *The War Against the Americans: Resistance and Collaboration in Cebu, 1899–1906*. Manila: Ateneo de Manila University Press, 1999.

Shaw, Angel V. and Francia, Luis H. *The Philippine-American War and the Aftermath of the Imperial Dream, 1899–1999*. New York: New York University Press, 2002.

Thompson, Lanny. *Imperial Archipelago: Representation and Rule in the Insular Territories Under U.S. Dominion after 1898*. Honolulu: University of Hawaii Press, 2010.

Iriye, Akira. *Pacific Estrangement: Japanese and American Expansion, 1879–1911*. Cambridge, MA: Harvard University Press, 1972.

7 War and Disillusion

Overview

In the Great War (World War I) Europeans employed the advanced technology of modern warfare to kill one another in new ways and in previously unimaginable numbers. After avoiding direct involvement for nearly three years, the United States intervened and helped bring the war to an end. Intervention in World War I strained and divided American society, sowing disillusionment following the collapse of President Woodrow Wilson's wartime diplomacy. Nonetheless, the United States emerged from the war with the world's strongest economy and unprecedented global influence.

Despite rejecting the League of Nations the United States remained engaged internationally following the war. During the 1920s US diplomacy focused on efforts to stabilize postwar Europe while containing communism, which had taken hold in Russia in 1917. By decade's end, the onset of the Great Depression shattered visions of a new era of global economic growth and international stability.

The Great War

When war erupted in Europe in August 1914, few Americans could conceive of direct US intervention. In his farewell address in 1796, President George Washington had warned against alliances with European nations. The Monroe Doctrine (1823) perceived Europe and the Americas as separate spheres, politically as well as geographically. While never isolated from Europe—a crucial trading partner, source of immigration, and site of extensive cultural exchange—the United States had adhered to the tradition of avoiding direct involvement in European affairs. Thus it was natural that the United States would respond to the outbreak of the European war with a **neutrality declaration**.

While the United States remained neutral most Americans came to sympathize with the **Triple Entente** (Britain, France, and Russia) over the **Central Powers** (Germany, Austria-Hungary, Bulgaria, and the Ottoman Empire). By this time the Anglo-American rapprochement had come full circle and Britain was the country favored by most Americans. President Wilson, his adviser

Colonel Edward House, Secretary of State (after May 1915) Robert Lansing, former President Theodore Roosevelt, and Senator Henry Cabot Lodge were all ardent Anglophiles. However, German, Central-European, and many Irish immigrants to the United States sympathized with the Central Powers.

For nearly three years the United States formally remained neutral while at the same time insisting on maintaining rights to free trade and freedom of the seas. The United States protested violations of neutral rights and negotiated with the belligerents in an attempt to uphold its rights while remaining out of the war. US neutrality proved highly problematic from the outset. The demand that its neutral rights be respected ran headlong into British efforts to control the seas—London instituted a European naval blockade in March 1915—as well as German efforts to combat the blockade by attacking ships in the war zone around the British Isles. Moreover American trade and loans, which were used to secure supplies and to finance the war effort, went overwhelmingly to the Triple Entente. The United States reacted more forcefully to violations of its neutral rights by the Central Powers than it did to the British blockade and other restrictions imposed by the Triple Entente. Thus even as the United States formally pursued a diplomacy of neutrality and exercised its right to free trade and freedom of the seas, it tilted increasingly in favor of the Entente powers.

The growing German reliance on submarine warfare to combat the British advantage at sea aroused indignation and heightened US sympathies for the Triple Entente. The *Unterseeboot* or "U-boat" was not illegal under international law yet the rules of engagement surrounding its usage were disputed. Although many viewed the underwater attacks by an unseen enemy as disturbing and dishonorable, the U-boat was crucial to German efforts to combat otherwise superior British sea power.

Tension with the Central Powers spiked in May 1915 when 128 Americans were among the 1,198 dead when a German U-boat sank the British luxury liner **Lusitania**. The German government had issued warnings including advertisements in US newspapers that freighters and passenger ships traveling in "waters adjacent to the British isles" might be attacked. Anti-German sentiment soared in the United States as a result of the high death toll, including the American victims, and controversy over the usage of the U-boat. Little noted at the time the *Lusitania*'s secret cargo included munitions and other war-related goods en route from New York to the British port of Liverpool.

Expressing his moral outrage over the sinking of the luxury liner Wilson issued a strongly worded note of condemnation to Berlin. Wilson and his first secretary of state, the longtime Democratic stalwart William Jennings Bryan, shared in common a powerful sense of Protestant morality. However, the Midwesterner Bryan opposed favoritism toward the British, which was most strongly expressed on the US eastern seaboard. Bryan resigned over Wilson's adoption of a harder line toward German violations of neutral rights in the wake of the *Lusitania* incident. Thus not all Americans were outraged by the German U-boats, one of which crossed the Atlantic and in July 1916 docked in

Figure 7.1 On May 7, 1915, the sinking of the British luxury liner *Lusitania* off the coast of Ireland by a torpedo launched from a German U-boat aroused indignation. The United States remained neutral for two more years but in the wake of the sinking of the cruise ship most Americans sympathized with the Entente powers.

Source: Library of Congress, Prints and Photographs Division, LC-USZC4-13285.

Baltimore. The U-boat commander took the occasion to visit Washington's historic home in Mt. Vernon, Virginia, before returning to the vessel and resuming his mission. Britain expressed indignation over the US policy of neutral ports and the friendly greeting accorded the German commander.

Berlin's pledge in the wake of the *Lusitania* incident to halt attacks on passenger ships without first issuing warnings enabled perpetuation of US neutrality. While opposition to direct US involvement in the Great War remained strong, interventionist sentiment began to grow and a national debate gained momentum and intensity. Interventionists promoted a national **preparedness movement** to lay the groundwork for eventual US involvement in the war. The movement featured speeches, parades, rallies, and film depictions of spike-helmeted German "Huns" invading a US city. In 1916 hundreds of thousands of Americans marched for preparedness in demonstrations in all major cities while others championed universal military training, a step toward the coming national draft. Recognizing that it was a short step from preparedness to direct intervention, a wide array of peace activists, internationalists, and feminists countered the interventionists with **anti-war demonstrations**. The American Union Against Militarism worked closely with the Women's Peace Party, the American Church Union, and other anti-war groups. Socialists and staunch Progressives accused capitalist elites of marching toward war to reap greater profits. The preparedness movement provided a mere cover for "the commercial, industrial, and imperialistic schemes of the great financial masters of this country," the Progressive Senator Robert Lafollette charged.

Wilson and most Americans remained wedded to neutrality in 1916, the year in which the president was reelected behind the slogan, "He kept us out of the war." In January 1917 Wilson's position shifted, however, as the German government broke off discussions with the United States and announced it would renew unrestricted submarine warfare. In a fatally flawed decision the German high command, increasingly dominated by General Erich Ludendorff, pursued a plan to drive Britain out of the war in order to gain favorable terms from France and the other Allied powers, thus ending the war on Berlin's terms. This decision would instead lead to US intervention and Germany suffering far worse terms at the end of the war than it otherwise might have received.

In February 1917 publication of the **Zimmermann Telegram** aroused a groundswell of pro-war sentiment in the United States. Considering the possibility of US entry into the war, Germany secretly (or so it thought) reached out to Mexico on the heels of the US intervention there (Chapter 5) about the possibility of an alliance. This information, contained in a telegram from the German foreign minister Arthur Zimmermann and sent to the German embassy in Mexico City, was intercepted and deciphered by British intelligence, which turned it over to the United States. The action was typical of the British, who directed a steady stream of propaganda to the United States, much of it false but in this case the telegrammed German offer was genuine. Publication of the note, including the hint that Germany might support Mexico in recovery of territory taken in the Mexican War (1846–48), angered Americans and turned many firmly against the Central Powers.

Interventionists led by Roosevelt were apoplectic, as they bitterly condemned Wilson for clinging to unmanly US neutrality. Roosevelt gloried in war but, ironically, some people otherwise morally opposed to war also now advocated US intervention. They argued that the bloodletting in Europe, which had exceeded almost all worst-case scenarios, cried out for humanitarian intervention to bring it to an end. In addition to the U-boat, the frightening weapons of modern war included for the first time the airplane, tanks, machine guns, and poison gas. Ultimately some 10 to 13 million young men died—2,000 a day at one point in 1916—in the trenches of Verdun, the Somme, at Gallipoli, and across the Eastern Front as well. By the spring of 1917 Wilson and much of the public had come to the conclusion that the United States should intervene to bring an end to the war.

The European war had spurred the US economy, lifting the nation out of a serious recession in 1914, but Wilson and his chief advisers feared that Germany might use the advantages of unrestricted submarine warfare to win the war and shut off the European economy to US trade and investment. By this time US financial elites, dominated by the incomparably powerful **House of Morgan**, had loaned Britain and France more than $2 billion. Should they lose the war the massive loans could not be repaid, with interest, as they presumably would be otherwise. John P. Morgan, whose banking house had more wealth and power than most governments and served as the de facto US central bank, had a clear financial interest in promoting victory by the Triple Entente. Despite the growth in the economy, gold had drained out of the country and the US and other stock markets had shut down amid the tumult of war. In sum, either a German victory or a prolonged conflict threatened US financial stability.

By the spring of 1917 a critical mass of Americans concluded that the nation's providential mission to redeem the world might require intervention in the war. Many agreed with Roosevelt and other interventionists that direct US involvement would vault the nation into a position of global leadership. As a moral Christian nation, millions believed, America should not remain aloof from the most destructive conflict in history. Millions more, however, remained opposed to intervention in a distant war in which the United States had not been attacked.

Events in revolutionary Russia removed a stumbling block in the path of US intervention in the world war. In February 1917 a provisional government overthrew the tsarist monarchy, thus transforming Russia into a "fit partner" in war against the Central Powers. Before the takeover by the new liberal government, the tsar's autocratic and increasingly irrational regime would have made a mockery of efforts to justify intervention as being on the side of progress. The **February Revolution** convinced Wilson that if the war could be brought to an end a more democratic world would emerge from the ashes.

On April 2, in an eloquent address to the nation, Wilson called on the United States to enter the war to make the world "safe for democracy." Invoking American exceptionalism, the president suggested that intervention would lead to nothing less than a globe transformed in America's image. He insisted, however, that the United States would enter the war only as an "associated" rather than a formally Allied power in an effort to preserve US autonomy and to ease concerns about foreign alliances. By the time Wilson went before Congress, most of the public was ready for war. The Senate voted 82–6 in favor of the declaration; the tally was 373–50 in the House of Representatives.

Most Progressives joined labor leaders, African-Americans, and women's rights advocates in support of intervention. They included the philosopher John Dewey, journalist Walter Lippmann, labor leader Samuel Gompers, the African-American intellectual W. E. B. Du Bois, feminist Carrie Chatman Catt, and millions of others who embraced the war as a crusade to make the world safe for democracy. Du Bois, Catt, and others concluded that intervention would create jobs and advance the causes of racial and gender equality. American socialists and some Progressives including Lafollette maintained their opposition to the war.

Race, religion, and gender mores remained important factors underlying US foreign relations. The Christian and millennial traditions fueled the drive toward intervention. Clergymen described the war as "a crusade, the greatest in history—the holiest." The nation's most popular evangelist, Billy Sunday, declared that "the fight between America and Germany" paralleled that of "Hell against Heaven." The war provided an opportunity for American Jews and Catholics to gain a greater measure of inclusiveness in American society by joining majority Protestants in expressing their righteousness in behalf of inter- vention. The Young Men's Christian Association (YMCA), National Catholic Council, and Jewish Welfare Board reflected the broad based religious support for the war. Many US Jews embraced the war in support of the historic British **Balfour Declaration** (1917), which promised to support creation of a Zion- ist homeland for Jews in the biblical holy land. In June 1918 the deeply reverent Wilson declared that the United States was "an instrument in the hands of God to see that liberty is made secure for mankind."

American racial motivations and justifications paralleled those of religion. As white Anglo-Saxon peoples the United States and Britain needed to exer- cise world leadership, and this required the defeat of Germany in the heart of Europe. Wilson concurred with Roosevelt and other interventionists that the war was undermining "Western civilization." Underscoring US racial anxiet- ies, in 1916 the eugenicist Madison Grant published *The Passing of the Great Race*, which argued that with the waning of "white civilization" world leadership might be lost to the yellow and black hordes of Asia and Africa.

Interventionists viewed war as a means to assert the masculine strength of both the individual and the nation. They condemned opposition to war as weak and feminine. In January 1917, when Wilson called for the war to be brought to an end on the basis of "peace without victory," Roosevelt derided the notion as "national emasculation." Recalling the "splendid little war" with Spain, he and other interventionists perceived war as a tonic for the complacency of a society increasingly preoccupied with commercialism and consumerism, with drink, dances, movies, bicycle rides, and other carefree entertainments that failed to inculcate a strenuous masculinity in young men. The Germans, a "pack of hungry, wolfish Huns" who had been responsible for the "rape" of Belgium, needed to be confronted and defeated by a superior race of men.

Interventionists condemned peace organizations and pacifism, which they equated with weakness and impotence. "No nation ever amounted to anything if its population was composed of pacifists and poltroons, if its sons did not have the fighting edge," Roosevelt declared. Although more idealistic and mor- alistic than Roosevelt, Wilson also advocated intervention in masculine terms. In remarks before the Pittsburgh YMCA as early as 1914, he expressed "an exquisite combination of contempt and hate" for "the moral coward." The president concluded, "Be militant!"

The emphasis on masculinity brought criticism of female reformers and continuing opposition to woman's suffrage. The press condemned the peace activism of social worker Jane Addams, who had been famous for decades for her tireless efforts to aid the poor and immigrants in settlement houses. Mili- tarists worried that the country might become "a nation of Jane Addamses." One newspaper dismissed Addams and Congresswoman Jeanette Rankin as "a couple of foolish virgins" as a result of their opposition to the war. A judge sentenced the socialist activist Kate Richards O'Hare to five years in prison for declaring that the nation treated women like "brood sows" to bear children to be sent off to war and "made into fertilizer." Thrown in jail in 1917 for demanding suffrage instead of war, Alice Paul went on a hunger strike, was force fed, and moved to a psychiatric ward and solitary confinement before being released after seven months of imprisonment.

Interventionists thus marginalized domestic opposition as the United States entered the Great War, which it would impact dramatically. As Americans mobilized for war another stunning development unfolded in Russia. In October 1917 the **Bolshevik Revolution** ousted the liberal government and brought communists to power under the leadership of **Vladimir I. Lenin**. His call for "peace, bread, and land" struck a chord in Russia, devastated by the war and famine, and led to the **Treaty of Brest-Litovsk** in March 1918 under which Russia pulled out of the conflict, thus relieving Germany and its allies of pressure on the Eastern Front. The Germans won a major battle against Italian forces and were closing in on Paris. These developments along with unrestricted submarine warfare raised the possibility of a German victory until US intervention changed the course of the war.

"Over There"

Unlike all the other belligerents, weakened by three years of brutal conflict, the United States had profited from trade and loans and was well positioned economically to make a military difference in Europe. Perhaps the greatest impact the Americans made "over there," as the popular song put it, was psychological. The arrival of masses of fresh US troops dramatically boosted Allied morale and undermined that of the Central Powers. US Navy destroyers and submarine chasers made an immediate military impact, attacking German vessels, sowing mines at sea, blockading the German coast, and generally countering the renewed German U-boat offensive. In September 1918 the **American Expeditionary Force (AEF)** under General John J. Pershing hammered into German forces on the battlefield at St. Mihiel, France. In the skies above the battlefield William Mitchell—considered the "father" of the US Air Force—led a successful Allied assault on German positions. Next, more than a million men from the AEF carried out the massive **Meuse-Argonne Offensive** across the Western Front.

Anxious to get the young Americans into battle albeit in units separate from the European Allies, Pershing launched reckless assaults that took a high toll of US casualties. Failing to learn from his allies, well schooled in the bitter lessons of trench warfare, Pershing underestimated the carnage that came from attacking German artillery and machine gun nests over open ground. His "open war" strategy ill fitted the Meuse-Argonne region of dense forests and rugged outcroppings, which protected defensive fortifications in place since 1914. Despite the heavy toll in casualties the Americans had shown the Germans that

Figure 7.2 Sergeant Alvin York, flanked by members of Congress, became the most celebrated American hero of World War I. A farm boy from Tennessee, York and his comrades fought their way from behind enemy lines during the Meuse-Argonne Offensive, capturing 132 prisoners in the process.

Source: Library of Congress, Prints and Photographs Division, LC-DIG-hec-12126.

they could not win the war. While neither defeated nor occupied, Germany was weakened, moreover the allied Austro-Hungarian and Ottoman Empires were disintegrating. On November 11 the Great War finally came to an end with the Armistice based on terms set down by the American president.

In Their Words

President Wilson's Fourteen Points

I. Open covenants of peace, openly arrived at, after which there shall be no private international understandings of any kind but diplomacy shall proceed always frankly and in the public view.

II. Absolute freedom of navigation upon the seas, outside territorial waters, alike in peace and in war, except as the seas may be closed in whole or in part by international action for the enforcement of international covenants.

III. The removal, so far as possible, of all economic barriers and the establishment of an equality of trade conditions among all the nations consenting to the peace and associating themselves for its maintenance.

IV. Adequate guarantees given and taken that national armaments will be reduced to the lowest point consistent with domestic safety.

V. A free, open-minded, and absolutely impartial adjustment of all colonial claims, based upon a strict observance of the principle that in determining all such questions of sovereignty the interests of the populations concerned must have equal weight with the equitable claims of the government whose title is to be determined.

VI. The evacuation of all Russian territory and such a settlement of all questions affecting Russia as will secure the best and freest cooperation of the other nations of the world in obtaining for her an unhampered and unembarrassed opportunity for the independent determination of her own political development and national policy and assure her of a sincere welcome into the society of free nations under institutions of her own choosing; and, more than a welcome, assistance also of every kind that she may need and may herself desire. The treatment accorded Russia by her sister nations in the months to come will be the acid test of their good will, of their comprehension of her needs as distinguished from their own interests, and of their intelligent and unselfish sympathy.

VII. Belgium, the whole world will agree, must be evacuated and restored, without any attempt to limit the sovereignty which she enjoys in common with all other free nations. No other single act will serve as this will serve to restore confidence among the nations in the laws which they have themselves set and determined for the government of their relations with one another. Without this healing act the whole structure and validity of international law is forever impaired.

VIII. All French territory should be freed and the invaded portions restored, and the wrong done to France by Prussia in 1871 in the matter of Alsace-Lorraine, which has unsettled the peace of the world for nearly fifty years, should be righted, in order that peace may once more be made secure in the interest of all.

IX. A readjustment of the frontiers of Italy should be effected along clearly recognizable lines of nationality.

X. The peoples of Austria-Hungary, whose place among the nations we wish to see safeguarded and assured, should be accorded the freest opportunity to autonomous development.

XI. Rumania, Serbia, and Montenegro should be evacuated; occupied territories restored; Serbia accorded free and secure access to the sea; and the relations of the several Balkan states to one another determined by friendly counsel along historically established lines of allegiance and nationality; and international guarantees of the political and economic independence and territorial integrity of the several Balkan states should be entered into.

XII. The Turkish portion of the present Ottoman Empire should be assured a secure sovereignty, but the other nationalities which are now under Turkish rule should be assured an undoubted security of life and an absolutely unmolested opportunity of autonomous development, and the Dardanelles should be permanently opened as a free passage to the ships and commerce of all nations under international guarantees.

XIII. An independent Polish state should be erected which should include the territories inhabited by indisputably Polish populations, which should be assured a free and secure access to the sea, and whose political and economic independence and territorial integrity should be guaranteed by international covenant.

XIV. A general association of nations must be formed under specific covenants for the purpose of affording mutual guarantees of political independence and territorial integrity to great and small states alike.

In regard to these essential rectifications of wrong and assertions of right we feel ourselves to be intimate partners of all the governments and peoples associated together against the Imperialists. We cannot be separated in interest or divided in purpose. We stand together until the end.

For such arrangements and covenants we are willing to fight and to continue to fight until they are achieved; but only because we wish the right to prevail and desire a just and stable peace such as can be secured only by removing the chief provocations to war, which this program does remove. We have no jealousy of German greatness, and there is nothing in this program that impairs it. We grudge her no achievement or distinction of learning or of pacific enterprise such as have made her record very bright and very enviable. We do not wish to injure her or to block in any way her legitimate influence or power. We do not wish to fight her either with arms or with hostile arrangements of trade if she is willing to associate herself with us and the other peace-loving nations of the world in covenants of justice and law and fair dealing. We wish her only to accept a place of equality among the peoples of the world—the new world in which we now live—instead of a place of mastery.

The Central Powers sued for peace on the basis of President Wilson's historic **Fourteen Points**. Announced in a speech in January 1918, the Fourteen Points contained some specific war aims but mainly comprised general principles including free trade, freedom of the seas, and national self-determination. The crucial Fourteenth Point called for a new **League of Nations** to create a basis for a durable peace in line with Wilson's dream of rendering World War I a "war to end all wars." The Fourteen Points marked the apogee of efforts by Wilson and the transnational movement of peace Progressives to establish a progressive **New Diplomacy** to replace one rooted in national self-interest, conflict, alliances, and war. Wilson and the peace Progressives would find, however, that implementation of the New Diplomacy was far more challenging than an eloquent expression of them.

The War at Home

Americans celebrated the Armistice and the apparent triumph of their idealistic values overseas, yet disillusionment lay ahead. The public welcomed home the "doughboys" (because they were "molded" into warriors), but minus the 53,000 US troops who died in combat. More than 60,000 others succumbed to non-battlefield fatalities including a devastating epidemic of the influenza virus. The soldiers found the country to which they returned had been changed profoundly by the war. Ironically, in World War I Americans triumphed abroad but turned against each other on the home front.

Once the decision had been made to intervene, Wilson and other opinion leaders launched a propaganda campaign and demanded that all Americans support the war effort. The campaign of preparedness became one of persuasion and then of compulsion and retribution. In June 1917, only a year after his "He kept us out of war" reelection campaign, Wilson declared, "Woe be to the man or group of men that seems to stand in our way." Following the congressional vote for intervention, diplomat Elihu Root averred, "We must have no criticism now."

From 1917 to 1919 the **Committee on Public Information** (CPI) marshaled support for the war. "What we had to have was no mere surface unity," explained the Progressive journalist George Creel, appointed by Wilson to head the CPI. Creel mobilized the public information campaign behind "a passionate belief in the justice of America's cause that should weld the people of the United States into one white-hot mass." The CPI distributed millions of posters, pamphlets, press releases, exhibitions, and advertisements. It prepared succinct public addresses delivered by a trained force of some seventy-five thousand **Four-Minute Men**. Sticking to their abbreviated script emphasizing patriotic conformity, the pro-war men addressed millions of Americans in homes, schools, churches, clubs, and union halls.

US intervention in the war prompted the first compulsory military service since the Civil War. The **Selective Service Act** of May 1917 enabled the nation within a year to send more than 2 million men overseas despite widespread resistance on the home front. As had occurred in the Civil War, many Americans opposed mandatory military service as an infringement on their freedom or because they simply did not want to risk their lives for a war in faraway Europe. Draft riots erupted including the "green corn rebellion" in Oklahoma in which three people died and scores were imprisoned. The US government launched a nationwide campaign against "slackers," but many young men successfully avoided conscription while others dutifully shipped out overseas.

Intervention in the European war exacerbated profound domestic divisions over race, ethnicity, gender, and class. The war fostered anxieties about and among more than 4.5 million immigrants from Germany and the Austro-Hungarian Empire residing in the United States. Wilson condemned "hyphenate Americans" and he and others demanded "100 Percent Americanism."

Figure 7.3 Persuasion and propaganda became an important tool of the US government to generate support for World War I. The Committee on Pubic Information mobilized the Four-Minute Men, who promoted the war effort in US communities nationwide.

Source: Library of Congress, Prints and Photographs Division, LC-USZC4-10662.

The CPI's anti-German propaganda featured the renaming of German foods (the hamburger briefly became a "liberty sandwich"), the banning of Beethoven's music, burning German books, prohibiting teaching of the language, and assaulting and on occasion murdering insufficiently patriotic German-Americans. Newspapers whipped up anti-German sentiment, including the myth that "the Huns" were collecting dead bodies from the battlefield and shipping them by rail to factories to boil into soap and other products.

The war created opportunities for immigrants, African-Americans, and women to show their patriotic *bona fides*, but it could also spur a backlash against them. Movies and posters targeted black audiences urging their patriotic support for the war effort, often with images of Abraham Lincoln paired with well-known African-Americans. Some 367,000 black men entered the armed forces in segregated units and overwhelmingly in menial, non-combat positions. More than double that number migrated into new residences and new jobs on the home front, which had opened up as a result of the spike in demand for laborers in war industries.

The **Great Migration** of African-Americans from the South into northern and western cities succeeded economically but failed socially. Unlike newly migrated white workers, the arrival of new black workers and neighbors aroused explosive racial anxieties and violence. **Wartime race riots** killed scores of people, the vast majority black, in Chicago, Houston, St. Louis, Tulsa, and other cities. While the National Association for the Advancement of Colored People, the Urban League, and other organizations called for a government response, the Wilson administration proved indifferent. Du Bois, who supported the war and had called on African-Americans to "close ranks shoulder to shoulder with our fellow white citizens," was left deeply disillusioned. He concluded that his country was "yet a shameful land" on matters of race.

Native Americans responded to the war in a variety of ways ranging from using it to assert their independence to using it to better assimilate. Several Indian tribes unilaterally declared war on Germany as a means of reasserting their claim to be independent nations. Motivated by their strong warrior traditions, some Indian men volunteered while others were conscripted or forced to register for the draft, even those that were not US citizens. In all some 12,000 Indians fought in the war mostly in the Army. Unlike African-Americans, Indians were not placed in segregated units. Wartime service by indigenous people contributed to the decision to grant all Indians US citizenship under the postwar 1924 immigration law.

The war to make the world safe for democracy finally brought democracy to women at home, thanks largely to the persistence of Addams, Catt, Paul, and other suffragists, more than 200 of whom had been arrested for wartime protests. Women already voted in 17 states, and their labor was crucial to the war effort. "For every fighter a woman worker," urged one mobilization poster. Publications, notably the *Ladies Home Journal*, advised women on ways to anchor the home front by being thrifty housewives and volunteering their time in war-related initiatives. Gender was often linked with religion, as when

Figure 7.4 Suffragists picketing the White House in January 1917. The need for women's
support and the quest for unity on the home front during World War I created
a climate culminating in the long struggle for voting rights for women in the
Nineteenth Amendment to the US Constitution.

Source: Library of Congress, Prints and Photographs Division, LC-USZ6-994.

a minister advised that through "approval, encouragement, smile and practical
aid of woman . . . man comes nearest to that real heroic warrior who will wield
the sword of the Lord." Thousands of female laborers, though often plagued
by discrimination and sexual harassment, worked in war industries, hospitals,
and offices in support of the war effort. Long opposed to woman's suffrage,
Wilson finally relented and in January 1918, endorsed the Susan B. Anthony
amendment, which Congress eventually approved and the states ratified as the
Nineteenth Amendment in 1920.

Intervention in the war fostered rapid conversion to war production and
massive federal spending, creating millions of new jobs and record profits for business and industry. Training, equipping, and transporting overseas
some 2 million men spurred unprecedented collusion between government
and the private sector. Under the Wall Street financier Bernard Baruch, the
War Industries Board (WIB) set high prices to encourage production and
rewarded the largest firms, thus promoting centralization of industry. Profits

soared in the arms, shipbuilding, chemical, and other war industries. Justice Department antitrust activities virtually ceased, as the Webb–Pomerene Act of 1917 specifically exempted exporters from antitrust laws. With the emphasis on rapid wartime production over all else, conflicts of interest, profiteering, and malfeasance proliferated.

The war thus brought an end to the Progressive Era, as the Wilson administration now promoted corporate profits rather than checks on wealth and power. The WIB represented the growing corporate influence that populists and the more radical Progressives had sought to curtail. Moreover, US intervention in World War I gave birth to the modern **military–industrial complex** that would fully flower in the second half of the century. Militarization of the economy began with the National Defense Act of 1914 and evolved swiftly in the wake of direct intervention.

The war shattered the vision once held by Wilson and other Progressives of unions and industry working arm in arm. Although the war brought near full employment and rising wages, inflation and awareness of windfall corporate profits spurred unprecedented labor unrest and more than 3,000 strikes annually from 1914–20. The Wilson administration used every means at its disposal to combat work stoppages—anti-labor propaganda, revocation of mail permits, injunctions, indictments, infiltration, arrests, warrantless searches, phone taps, vigilante assaults, and strikebreakers. Police and state militia repression of a national steel strike delivered a blow to labor everywhere, as workers from other industries fell in line. Amid the largest coal strike in US history, the government issued a back-to-work order described by the union leader Gompers, who had supported the war, as "so autocratic as to stagger the human mind."

Work stoppages combined with the anxieties fostered by the Bolshevik Revolution sparked the **Red Scare**, which undermined free speech and civil liberties. Congress passed the Espionage Act of 1917 and the Sedition Act of 1918, laws that enabled prosecutions of workers, immigrants, and alleged radicals. The first act provided a wide berth to interpretations as to actions considered treasonous or disruptive of the military effort and also allowed revocation of mailing privileges. The Sedition Act outlawed comments deemed disloyal or subversive even if delivered in private, as well as expressions of contempt or scorn for the government. Only the Armistice in November 1918 prevented a flood of repressive prosecutions. Similar assaults on free speech had occurred during the Quasi War and the Civil War but on a smaller scale.

Under Attorney General A. Mitchell Palmer, the Justice Department ordered raids in 33 cities and 22 states. Infiltration, surveillance, and covert operations techniques, pioneered in the colonial Philippines and the Caribbean, were now applied on the home front. Wartime surveillance and repression targeted workers, immigrants, and radicals but also African-Americans, Jews, women, and noncompliant Progressives. In January 1920 the **Palmer raids** hauled in more than 4,000 suspected radicals, with widespread public support. The *Washington Post* editorialized against "hairsplitting over infringement of liberty" in deference to ridding the country of radical influence. Although the Palmer raids emanated from Washington, state and local governments exceeded the federal government in the purge of radicals. Some 3,000 alleged radicals were deported after the Palmer raids and local prosecutions.

The Failed Peace

As Americans divided on the home front Wilson clashed with the leaders of the victorious Allied nations at the peace conference at the Palace of Versailles outside of Paris. The "**Big Four**"—Wilson and Prime Ministers David Lloyd George of Britain, Georges Clemenceau of France, and Vittorio Orlando of Italy—faced myriad contentious issues in attempting to arrive at a comprehensive peace settlement. The goal of achieving a lasting peace was complicated if not doomed from the start by the decision to exclude both Germany and Russia, now the pariah nations of Europe. The Allies blamed Germany alone for the war and sought to isolate and undermine the communist regime in Russia.

With US intervention having provided the turning point in the war, American prestige in the world vaulted to unprecedented heights. Upon his arrival on the continent Wilson was greeted as a virtual saint by much of the European

Figure 7.5 The Big Four (left to right) Lloyd George (Great Britain), Vittorio Orlando (Italy), Georges Clemenceau (France), and Woodrow Wilson (United States) outside the peace conference in Paris.

Source: Library of Congress, Prints and Photographs Division, LC-DIG-ggbain-29038.

public, grateful as they were for the bloodletting having been brought to an end. The Allied leaders, however, resented Wilson's popularity and his idealistic commitment to New Diplomacy. Clemenceau disliked Wilson's missionary style as well as his faith that he had divine backing. The crusty French leader observed that humanity had broken each of the Ten Commandments and was likely to do the same with Wilson's Fourteen Points.

Lloyd George was anxious about the transition under way in the wake of World War I in which the United States was beginning to displace Great Britain as the leading power in the world. The dollar was beginning to outshine the British pound sterling and New York was in the process of replacing London as the financial center of the world. Moreover, Lloyd George viewed Wilson's emphasis on self-determination as a mortal threat to Britain's worldwide colonial empire. Orlando was in the weakest position at the conference but was no less determined to secure Italy's frontiers and to increase its influence in the Mediterranean and Adriatic Seas.

Wilson and the Allies concurred on the desire to contain and ultimately destroy the Bolshevik regime in Russia but they diverged on Germany. The three European prime ministers wanted to saddle Germany with war guilt and exact reparations to help rebuild from the destruction caused by the Central Powers. Wilson had emphasized a non-vindictive approach to the settlement as the best means to establish peace. Wilson would be proven wiser on this point, but he lost the diplomatic debate at Versailles. The Allied leaders believed that the United States, as a faraway "associated power," did not appreciate the damage caused by Germany, which deserved to be severely punished. The Allies thus saddled Berlin with both war guilt and a devastating bill for reparations that sowed the seeds for German *revanchism* and a second war in Europe a generation later.

The decisions of the Big Four had global implications in the wake of the collapse of three empires—the Ottoman, Austro-Hungarian, and Russian—and the worldwide appeal of the US-led call for self-determination. New states would arise in Europe while the war gave birth to the modern "Middle East," beginning with the rise of an independent Turkey achieved through massive violence against Ottoman Greeks and Armenians in a war lasting from 1919–23. In Asia, Africa, and Latin America, millions of people responded enthusiastically to the rhetoric of self-determination yet the victors, especially Britain and France, meant to retain their territorial empires.

Much to Wilson's consternation, it became known that during the war the Allies, including Japan, had signed **secret treaties** dividing up the possessions of the Central Powers amongst themselves. Russia had been in on the duplicity before the seizure of power by the Bolsheviks, who embarrassed the Allies by publishing the secret accords. Self-determination did lead to the creation of new states in Europe, including Poland, Czechoslovakia, Hungary, and Yugoslavia, but the Allies also seized possessions of their former enemies. In the Asia-Pacific region Japan took control of German possessions, notably China's Shantung Peninsula. Allied capitulation to the Japanese sphere of influence ignited the May Fourth Movement of nationalist protest in China while at the same time sparking the rise of Chinese communism.

Wilson protested territorial aggrandizement in violation of the Fourteen Points but he again compromised—not least because the Europeans pointed out that the United States too possessed colonies in the Caribbean and Pacific regions and had no plans to grant them self-determination. The compromise framework was the **mandate system** under which colonies were to be shepherded toward independence. Three classes of mandates were established under the neo-colonial framework, which determined the fate of millions of people in the Middle East, Africa, and the Asia-Pacific region without their consent. The mandate system allowed the Allies to control the subject peoples, deemed racially inferior and unprepared for national independence, while holding out the promise of eventual self-determination. Bitterly disappointed by the Allies' failure to live up to the lofty rhetoric of self-determination, many leaders of what would later be called the Third World turned to revolutionary ideologies including communism.

Wilson was willing to compromise more than he wished because the president exalted the new **League of Nations**, the Fourteenth Point, above all else. Wilson came to believe the future League would have the potential to cure all ills and provide a lasting legacy for his campaign to make the world "safe for democracy." The League, he declared, was inspired "by the hand of God" and represented "the only hope for mankind." As throughout American history, as "we dreamed at our birth, America shall in truth show the way."

Having struggled with the Allies abroad Wilson re-crossed the Atlantic to face a bitter political fight at home. The president's missionary style blinded him to devastating political realities that would prove the undoing of his handiwork in Europe. After appealing during the mid-term elections of 1918 for the voters to provide him with a Democratic majority, the president further fueled partisanship by excluding prominent Republicans from his entourage at Versailles. In the 1918 mid-term elections the public turned against the president, electing Republican majorities to both houses of Congress. In the Senate, Wilson's inveterate political rival, Lodge, presided over the crucial SFRC through which the Treaty of Versailles had to pass.

The Republicans, joined by some Democrats, opposed the treaty for a variety of reasons, some substantive and others purely political. The most contentious issue proved to be **Article X** of the Covenant of the League of Nations (Wilson had insisted on the use of the term "covenant" because of its linkage with the Old Testament). Article X called for collective security as a means of deterring future aggression and war. Under collective security the threat of other nations allying against it would in theory deter a nation from embarking on a course of aggression and war. Article X raised many questions, however, including whether the Untied States would be forced to go to war by the international agreement, thus trumping the congressional prerogative to declare war. Critics also pointed out that other nations might band against US military interventions in the Caribbean and other venues. They thus argued that the collective security provisions of the League of Nations threatened the Monroe Doctrine.

These and other points of disagreement produced an inconclusive debate in the Senate that carried through 1919 and into 1920. Wilson refused to compromise, pointing out that he had entered into an agreement with the Europeans, and could hardly change it now, but the Senate was no less determined to exercise its constitutional prerogative to approve or reject foreign treaties. Lodge eventually offered to support the treaty with certain "reservations," which entailed amending specific portions of it, but Wilson refused to bargain over the treaty.

Figure 7.6 President Wilson at his desk with his wife, Edith Bolling Galt Wilson, in 1920. After suffering a series of debilitating strokes, the president became increasingly dependent on his wife, who as legend had it became "the first woman to run the country."

Source: Library of Congress, Prints and Photographs Division, LC-USZ62-62850.

Declaring that he would go over the heads of the senators and directly to the people, Wilson in September 1919 embarked on a 22-day, 8,000-mile, nationwide tour to rally support for the treaty. On September 25 the president, who had suffered a series of minor strokes over the years, collapsed at Pueblo, Colorado, suffering from a more serious stroke that debilitated him for the remainder of his presidency. Wilson's health was broken and so was his New Diplomacy. The Senate rejected the Treaty of Versailles and over the next few years entered into separate agreements formally ending the state of war with Germany and the Central Powers.

Despite the Senate rejection of the League of Nations and the Treaty of Versailles US diplomacy in the Great War made a lasting impact. The world war had been brought to an end on terms set forth by the American president, thus elevating the United States in international affairs. Even though Wilson's New Diplomacy had been rejected at home, it would continue to resonate in future generations. Collective security, free trade, self-determination, and a world organization of states to establish and enforce international law gradually became cornerstones of diplomacy into the twenty-first century.

The Great War brought unprecedented destruction but also unprecedented levels of humanitarian assistance in which the United States took the lead. Groups such as the YMCA, the American Friends Service Committee, the Knights of Columbus, the Salvation Army, and above all the **American Red Cross** raised money and mobilized volunteers for relief, medical care, and other forms of humanitarian assistance. The Red Cross, founded in 1881 by the legendary Civil War nurse Clara Barton, raised millions of dollars to assist injured and impoverished war victims. Following the Armistice the American Relief Administration, headed by Herbert Hoover, distributed hundreds of millions of dollars in food and other assistance to millions of Europeans in more than 20 countries culminating in 1923 in a massive famine relief program in Russia.

Interwar Diplomacy

Contrary to legend the United States did not become "isolationist" after the Great War. The nation and its leaders repudiated the crusading Wilsonian style of internationalism, but not the desire to be a world power. The United States would remain engaged in Asia, Europe, and Latin America. Despite its rejection of membership in the League of Nations, US economic and cultural influence remained extensive. US foreign policy was less grandiose in the wake of World War I, to be sure, but hardly isolationist.

The wartime campaigns for "100 Percent Americanism" and against "hyphenate-Americans" carried over into the postwar era as the United States enacted the most restrictive immigration legislation in its history, the **National Origins Act** (1924). The legislation cut off Asian immigration (excepting Filipinos), severely curtailed immigrants from eastern and southeastern Europe, and established the Border Patrol while nonetheless enabling the entry of low-paid migrant farm workers from Mexico, many of whom never left. The Ku Klux Klan enjoyed a revival and Americans displayed suspicion and hostility to foreigners in other ways such as the conviction and execution in 1927 for bank robbery and murder, on dubious evidence, of the Italian-American anarchists Nicola Sacco and Bartolomeo Vanzetti.

Anti-foreign sentiment was only one factor in the complex and often contradictory diplomacy of the 1920s. The European conflict, along with the death of popular militants such as Theodore Roosevelt, had dampened enthusiasm for foreign adventurism and the supposedly "splendid" conquests of war. Bitter memoirs, journalistic accounts, war stories, histories, literature, films, and speakers condemned the senseless violence of the Great War and the inequities of the Treaty of Versailles. The **Women's International League for Peace and Freedom** (WILPF), depicted as subversive during the Red Scare, revived in the 1920s under the tireless leadership of its national secretary, Dorothy Detzer. WILPF, the American Friends Service Committee, the Carnegie Endowment for International Peace, the National Council for Prevention of War, and myriad church and pacifist groups lobbied in the wake of the shockingly destructive Great War for disarmament, arbitration, and other efforts to prevent a future conflict.

Peace Progressives were not anti-foreign isolationists but rather internationalists in pursuit of disarmament and strengthened global institutions of international justice consistent with their values. One peace activist warned against "too much isolationism" and "not enough of an appreciation of the necessity of international cooperation, if peace is to be attained and maintained . . . The issue we face is not 'neutrality' or war. The third course is 'cooperation for peace.'" Internationalists advocating peace and disarmament had taken part in the congresses at The Hague in 1899 and 1907, which created the Permanent Court of International Justice, or **World Court**. Peace internationalists in Congress variously condemned the flawed terms of the Treaty of Versailles, non-recognition of the Bolshevik regime in Russia, and ongoing US imperialism in Latin America and the Caribbean. Many of the congressional peace internationalists urged joining the World Court and at least informal participation in the League of Nations.

Critics from the American Legion, Daughters of the American Revolution, and the Hearst press, among others, often condemned peace internationalists, who also tended to embrace reforms on the home front such as economic justice, women's rights, and racial equality. Critics labeled peace internationalists variously as head-in-the-sand isolationists, "pinks," "parlor Bolsheviks," and unmanly pacifists. As one activist acknowledged, "The peace movement needs in it more men who chew tobacco."

Charles Evans Hughes, secretary of state under Republican President Warren G. Harding, elected in 1920, responded skillfully to the peace internationalists and postwar disillusionment as well. A former New York governor, associate justice of the Supreme Court, and presidential candidate in 1916, Hughes restored competence and prestige to American diplomacy. With peace activists

Figure 7.7 Secretary of State Charles Evans Hughes signing the treaties culminating
in the Conference on Limitation of Armaments (Washington Conference),
February 5, 1922. Hughes presided over the disarmament conference, a
triumph of postwar diplomacy.

Source: Library of Congress, Prints and Photographs Division, LC-USZ6-1755.

and people all over the world sickened by the unexpected level of violence in
the world war, Hughes took the lead as the United States played host to a major
disarmament conference. Senators and opinion leaders that opposed Wilson
and the commitments entailed in League membership now rallied behind
Hughes's internationalism.

The **Washington Conference** (1921–22) over which Hughes presided was
highly productive. The Five-Power Treaty, signed by the United States, Great
Britain, Japan, France, and Italy, established ratios based on overall tonnage
thereby containing a burgeoning naval arms race. The Four-Power Treaty, also
agreed to in Washington, subsumed an alliance between Japan and Britain
within a larger framework that also brought in the United States and France.
The four signatories pledged to respect each other's possessions and spheres
of influence. The third major agreement was the Nine-Power Treaty in which
Belgium, China, the Netherlands, and Portugal joined the signatories of the
Five-Power Treaty in affirming the second Open Door Note to respect China's "territorial integrity." Japan released its leasehold on the Shantung Peninsula but remained committed to having a special position in Manchuria, the
resource-rich northern region of China.

Hughes's shrewd diplomacy calmed international waters, pleased peace Progressives, and set the tone for post-Wilsonian internationalism. The United States had assumed world leadership in sponsoring peace and disarmament while maintaining a sizable army and navy that could be mobilized for intervention. Japan had been brought into the international system and given the respect it craved from the Western nations, though resentments over racist immigration restrictions remained palpable. Peace internationalists had played an important role in the pursuit of arms control and continued to do so. Detzer pressured Herbert Hoover to achieve broader agreements on naval arms control, forcing the president to appoint the first woman ever to represent the United States at a major diplomatic conference, Mary Wolley, a member of the US delegation to arms talks in Geneva in 1932.

Between the two global wars American technological, institutional, and cultural influence—referenced years later as "**soft power**"—radiated around the globe. The United States frequently led the way in forging international connections between scientific organizations, the arts, museums, intellectuals, and student exchange programs. The United States had impressed by acquiring electricity, telephones, automobiles, and other technological innovations faster than most countries. US prestige soared in the postwar era whereas Europe's declined in the wake of the unprecedented bloodletting of the Great War.

By the mid-1920s Hollywood produced the majority of movies shown in European theaters and came to dominate the global industry. American jazz was all the rage in the cafes and clubs in London, Paris, and other capitals. In 1927 thousands of Frenchmen poured into Le Bourget Field to greet the American Charles Lindbergh on his solo flight from New York to Paris, an international *cause célèbre*. "Culture follows money," proclaimed the novelist F. Scott Fitzgerald, part of an American renaissance in literature, which enjoyed wide European readership. "We will be the Romans in the next generation."

During the 1920s the business of America was business, as President Calvin Coolidge put it, and the products from US factories and assembly lines circulated worldwide. American internationalists believed that economic supremacy would enable the United States to wield global influence without the costs and conflicts of grandiose Wilsonian intervention. "There is no country where the power of the dollar has not reached," a *New York Times* reporter pointed out. Every country in the world has to "take the United States into consideration . . . Isolation is a myth."

The booming US economy proved decisive in stabilizing postwar Europe. From 1921–26 US industrial production shot up 38 percent, exports soared, and the United States entered into what many considered a "new era" of perpetual economic growth and prosperity. In 1923 Americans stepped in when the deeply flawed economic agreements set down at Versailles broke down. The French had occupied the industrial Ruhr region of Germany and taken over the German coal and steel industries in order to force the Weimar Republic to keep up its reparations payments. Under the **Dawes Plan**, orchestrated by Hughes and other administration officials in conjunction with Chicago banker Charles Dawes, US financial elites worked with their counterparts in London to arrange loans enabling the Weimar government to resume debt payments. With the implementation of the Dawes Plan the United States led the way in stabilizing the European economy. The French and Belgians withdrew from German territory and in the "spirit of Locarno" in 1925 the Europeans signed an agreement accepting the prevailing boundaries of the respective states.

Despite its non-membership in the League of Nations, and refusal to join the World Court, the United States had nonetheless played a critical role in disarmament, European economic stabilization, and seemingly in helping to establish a foundation for a lasting peace in the wake of World War I. Peace internationalists throughout the world continued to advocate the New Diplomacy, bringing an end to war and making the world safe for democracy. In 1928 the United States under Secretary of State Frank Kellogg converted a French request for a bilateral security treaty into a universal declaration against war. The **Kellogg–Briand Pact**, signed by 33 nations, condemned "recourse to war for the solution of international controversies" which would instead be solved by "pacific means."

American diplomacy became more professional under the **Rogers Act** (1924), which created the professional Foreign Service. Through teaching of language skills and other training the Foreign Service developed a core of diplomats who would serve for generations. However, consistent with the prejudices of the time, the early Foreign Service admitted only male, Protestant elites, thus excluding women, blacks, Hispanics, Catholics, and Jews throughout the interwar period. Also during the 1920s the Council on Foreign Relations, based in New York, emerged as an establishment forum on world affairs.

Interpreting the Past

US intervention in the Russian Civil War

From 1918–20 the United States intervened militarily in the Russian Civil War, sending some 14,000 troops (175 of whom died on Russian soil) into Russia's far north and into Siberia in its far east. Historians have identified the primary motivations for the **Russian Intervention**: notably American anti-communism; support of Britain and France, both of which also intervened in an effort to reopen the eastern front in the latter stages of the war; coming to the aid of a Czechoslovakian military contingent that had become trapped in Russia during the war; and positioning the United States to keep an eye on Japan, which had also intervened in Siberia but in far greater numbers.

After first reacting cautiously to the Bolshevik Revolution, Wilson ultimately authorized an undeclared secret war in Russia, bypassing Congress and the public in the process. The United States and Russia's former allies in the war aided reactionary forces in the Russian Civil War, which pitted the Bolsheviks (the Reds) against an uncoordinated array of foes (the Whites), ranging from socialists to brutal tsarist militarists, notably Admiral Alexander Kolchak. Foreign assistance to Kolchak backfired, leading to more support for the Bolsheviks, who controlled Moscow and St. Petersburg and had backing in other cities and the countryside based on Lenin's popular pledge of "peace, bread, and land." The various factions in the Civil War carried out summary executions (including the Bolshevik execution of the royal family in 1918) and engaged in indiscriminate killing. By 1922 the Bolsheviks had prevailed and all the allies had pulled out. The US–Allied intervention was thus wholly ineffectual and served mainly to provide the victorious Bolsheviks ever after with a popular domestic propaganda theme emphasizing the efforts of Western nations to strangle the revolution in its infancy.

The professional diplomats were staunchly anti-communist and thus hostile to the **Union of Soviet Socialist Republics** (USSR), in which the Bolsheviks under Lenin had united Russia, Ukraine, and several other states ranging from the Baltic Sea to Central Asia. Some American socialists, peace internationalists, and feminists, the latter citing the Bolsheviks' support for woman suffrage and equality, supported the regime and were vilified accordingly in the Red Scare. Wilson feared that African-Americans would engage in "conveying Bolshevism to America," while Hoover suspected Jews lay behind "Communist outbreaks."

Wilson doubtless spoke for the majority of Americans in describing Bolshevism as "the negation of everything American." Communist ideology viewed capitalism as a predatory system that was bound to collapse under the iron laws of history. Lenin theorized that imperialism had caused the world war and was the last gasp stage of capitalism. The Marxist ideology not only vilified capitalism, it foreordained its destruction and in 1919 created a radical international organization, the Comintern, to push the process along. In addition to fomenting revolution against capitalism, the "godless Communists" called for the abolition of religion. Marx explained that people turned to religion as a result of their exploitation within capitalist society, hence religion constituted "the opium of the people." Communists including the Bolsheviks equally disdained Western precepts of liberal pluralism, notably electoral politics and a free press.

The devastated condition of Europe after years of brutal warfare heightened fears of the spread of the Bolshevik contagion. At Versailles the Allies created the new states of Poland, Czechoslovakia, Hungary, and Yugoslavia in part to serve as a *cordon sanitaire* isolating the Bolshevik regime. Ultimately, however, the Western nations did not merely wish to contain the communist regime, they wished to destroy it. The new US Foreign Service diplomats were trained that the Soviet Union was a "pariah regime" bent on world conquest and unworthy of being engaged diplomatically.

New Deal Diplomacy

Anti-communism conjoined with economic stabilization, naval arms limitation, trade, and cultural expansion anchored US foreign policy during the 1920s. In the fall of 1929 the financial collapse and the ensuing and seemingly insoluble **Great Depression** changed everything. The Crash brought declining production, loss of earnings, mass unemployment, bank failures, falling exports, trade disputes and protectionism, and ultimately the rise of fascism, imperial rivalry, and a second world war. The US Gross National Product (GNP) fell from $98.4 billion in 1929 to almost half as much within three years. Nearly 15 million people lost their jobs. The first of many low points came in 1929 in a clash between the US government and the "**Bonus Army**" of World War I veterans. The veterans who had fallen on hard times set up camps in Washington's Anacostia Flats, insisting they would not leave until they received early payment of their service bonus. In late July the same army in which the veterans had once served employed bayonets and tanks to drive them out of their makeshift camp, and burn it to the ground.

Despite the limited efforts of Herbert Hoover, elected overwhelmingly in 1928, the United States failed to pull out of the Depression, which radiated across the globe. In 1932 former New York Governor Franklin D. Roosevelt, a Democrat and distant cousin of Theodore Roosevelt, defeated Hoover in a landslide and launched a "**New Deal**" program of domestic reform. Roosevelt's program emphasized relief, reform, and recovery and a willingness to use federal initiatives to achieve those aims. The Roosevelt administration marked some success at relief and reform but failed to achieve recovery, as the Depression continued throughout the 1930s.

As with his domestic program, Roosevelt's foreign policy emphasized change, beginning with economic policy. Roosevelt sent his Secretary of State Cordell Hull to the **London Economic Conference**, which convened in 1933 in an effort to stabilize world currencies and exchange rates. The issue ultimately facing the United States was whether to pursue economic nationalism or internationalism under which the value of the dollar would be tied to the fluctuating price of gold on the global financial market. Despite the Depression the United States still had the world's strongest economy, hence the decision was a crucial one. Roosevelt decided that adherence to the gold standard, allowing the value of the dollar to fluctuate, could exacerbate economic instability on the home front. He chose economic nationalism, de-linking the dollar from gold and in effect torpedoing the London Conference, which ended without agreement. While the United States focused on efforts to promote domestic recovery, the global depression continued, heightening international instability and conflict.

The "Good Neighbor" Policy

Another aspect of New Deal diplomacy, with its emphasis on breaking with policies of the past, was the announcement of a new **Good Neighbor**

Figure 7.8 In 1932 World War I veterans descended upon the Capitol to demand early payment of their military service bonus in the midst of the Great Depression. The Hoover administration eventually summoned the US Army to drive the "Bonus Army" veterans out of the nation's capital.

Source: Library of Congress, Prints and Photographs Division, LC-DIG-hec-36872.

Policy. The United States was hardly "isolationist" toward the Caribbean and Latin America, as it supervised and occupied hemispheric protectorates in Cuba, Haiti, Puerto Rico, and Panama and had various levels of control over the economies of the Dominican Republic, Nicaragua, and the West African nation of Liberia. Under the **Jones Act** in 1917, the United States granted citizenship to Puerto Ricans while their island remained a colony with no prospect of self-determination. In the ensuing decades the United States suppressed the Puerto Rican nationalist movement, jailing and sometimes killing in clashes with police its proponents. In 1932 the United States extended full citizenship to all residents born in the US Virgin Islands. Four years later Congress provided the islanders with a greater measure of self-government, but the Virgin Islands remained colonies and would not have an elected governor until 1970.

At the end of World War I, prolonged military occupation of Haiti and Santo Domingo had generated opposition, especially through Progressive magazines such as the *Nation* and the *New Republic.* Congressional hearings on the Haitian occupation publicized incidents of murder, torture, and rape. Many Progressives who had endorsed supervision over various "backward" and "dependent" states before the war now condemned such action as imperialistic. Dollar diplomacy increasingly fell into disrepute as anti-imperialists in both the United States and in borrowing countries condemned the colonial framework.

Domestic opposition, Latin American resistance, and the onset of the Depression ushered in the Good Neighbor Policy. At the Havana Conference of 1928, the Latin delegates resolved, "No state has a right to intervene in the affairs of another." Peace internationalists took up their cause, prompting first Hoover and then Roosevelt to sign on. In 1928 the **Clark Memorandum**, drafted by a State Department diplomat and jurist, concluded that the Monroe Doctrine did not sanction US military intervention in Latin America. In 1933 Secretary Hull, attending the seventh international conference of American states in Uruguay, endorsed the non-intervention policy. The next year the United States abrogated the Platt Amendment and the right to US intervention in Cuba, but retained the naval base at Guantánamo. The same year the United States ended the long Haitian occupation. The United States also negotiated a series of reciprocal trade agreements with Latin American states.

In Their Words

President Franklin D. Roosevelt Discusses the Good Neighbor Policy in Chautauqua, New York, August 14, 1936

In the whole of the western hemisphere our good neighbor policy has produced results that are especially heartening. The noblest monument to peace and to neighborly economic and social friendship in all the world is not a monument in bronze or stone, but the boundary which unites the United States and Canada—3,000 miles of friendship with no barbed wire, no gun or soldier, and no passport on the whole frontier. Mutual trust made that frontier—to extend the same sort of mutual trust throughout the Americas was our aim.

The American Republics to the south of us have been ready always to cooperate with the United States on a basis of equality and mutual respect, but before we inaugurated the good neighbor policy there was among them resentment and fear, because certain administrations in Washington had slighted their national pride and their sovereign rights.

In pursuance of the good neighbor policy, and because in my younger days I had learned many lessons in the hard school of experience, I stated that the United States was opposed definitely to armed intervention . . . Throughout the Americas the spirit of the good neighbor is a practical and living fact. The twenty-one American Republics are not only living together in friendship and in peace; they are united in the determination so to remain . . .

We can keep out of war if those who watch and decide have a sufficiently detailed understanding of international affairs to make certain that the small decisions of each day do not lead toward war and if, at the same time, they possess the courage to say "no" to those who selfishly or unwisely would let us go to war.

Of all the nations of the world today we are in many ways most singularly blessed. Our closest neighbors are good neighbors. If there are remoter nations that wish us not good but ill, they know that we are strong; they know that we can and will defend ourselves and defend our neighborhood. We seek to dominate no other nation. We ask no territorial expansion. We oppose imperialism. We desire reduction in world armaments.

We believe in democracy; we believe in freedom; we believe in peace. We offer to every nation of the world the handclasp of the good neighbor. Let those who wish our friendship look us in the eye and take our hand.

Being a "good neighbor" did not mean the United States would cease to exert economic and political controls over Central America and the Caribbean states. The Roosevelt administration, no less than its Republican predecessors, continued the policy of indirect intervention in Latin America. Relations with Mexico fluctuated but were mostly embittered over resentment of past US military interventions and competition for control of Mexico's natural resources. Americans still tended to view the Mexicans as backward and racially inferior, hence the United States should have the right as a more advanced nation to maintain its access to Mexican land and resources. The essential problem, Ambassador James Sheffield explained, was Mexico's "Latin-Indian mind, filled with hatred of the United States."

Relations improved after Coolidge appointed Dwight Morrow as ambassador in 1927, but the battle over resources and fear of Bolshevism continued to raise tensions. The United States viewed Mexican efforts to gain control of their resources as communist-inspired. Coolidge insisted on the "undeniable fact that the Mexican government today is a Bolshevist government." While many Mexican intellectuals had been influenced by Lenin's critique of imperialism, Soviet foreign policy proved heavy-handed in Mexico, which broke off relations with the USSR in the late twenties. By that time J. Edgar Hoover, head of the Justice Department's Bureau of Investigation (precursor to the Federal Bureau of Investigation (FBI), had infiltrated Mexico with propaganda and forged documents purporting to show Russian plans to instigate a communist revolt in Mexico.

Good neighbor sentiment was in short supply in 1938, as Mexican President Lázaro Cárdenas defied the United States by turning away from an earlier agreement and seizing additional property claimed by Americans. Next Cárdenas nationalized the $400 million oil industry, which prompted Hull to call for a showdown with "these communists down there." The United States cut off all loans and economic aid for five years. By 1939, however, the desire for hemispheric solidarity against Nazi Germany overwhelmed all other considerations and the parties reached an understanding, including provisions to compensate the US oil companies.

The Central American and Caribbean nations, much weaker than Mexico, remained under various levels of US control. The State Department, backed by creditors, investors, and corporations, avoided direct intervention while still exerting influence, typically by bolstering friendly dictators. Although it withdrew the Marines, the United States kept a tight rein on Haitian finances, helped crush a peasant rebellion, and facilitated the rise of the postwar dictatorships of François "Papa Doc" Duvalier and his son, Jean-Claude "Baby Doc." In the adjacent Dominican Republic, occupied by US Marines from 1916–24, a dictatorship under **Rafael Trujillo** received US support by adhering to the dictates of dollar diplomacy. Americans trained the constabulary and looked the other way as Trujillo's troops slaughtered as many as 25,000 Haitian migrants looking for work in the Dominican sugar fields. Washington maintained financial supervision until World War II.

In the Central American republics the United States bolstered a system of elite control in which a tiny minority of the population collaborated in return for wealth and power while the bulk of the population remained desperately poor. The United States backed corrupt and repressive dictatorships, which in return for personal wealth and power kept their countries in line with Yankee economic and defense policies. Because of these inequities rebellion and political instability were endemic.

In Nicaragua in 1926, political instability and fear of Bolshevism had prompted the United States to send Marines back into the country after having ended a 15-year occupation the previous year. US military pilots took commissions from the Nicaraguan government in order to kill hundreds of alleged rebels in bombing and strafing raids, the first use of airpower in Central America. The charismatic rebel leader **Augusto César Sandino** defied the United States, as thousands of US Marines proved unable to hunt him down or stop his raids. Journalist Carleton Beals did find Sandino and published several

Figure 7.9 US Marines scoured the countryside in pursuit of rebel leader Augusto César Sandino during a prolonged US intervention in Nicaragua beginning in 1926. In 1934 the US-backed Nicaraguan National Guard assassinated Sandino and took control of the Central American nation.

Source: Library of Congress, Prints and Photographs Division, LC-USZ62-71946.

articles based on an interview. Secretary of State Henry Stimson denounced the "revolutionist propaganda [which] had quite seriously warped the accuracy of American news." The State Department closely monitored Beals's journalism, referred to him as an "alleged American citizen," intercepted his mail, and started a file on him headed "Anti-American Activities."

Peace internationalists led once again by Detzer at the helm of WILPF joined Beals in condemning the Nicaraguan occupation, which Stimson concluded had to be brought to an end. In 1931 Stimson announced the withdrawal, citing the deaths of several Marines, the expense of the occupation in the midst of the Depression, and the embarrassing parallels being drawn with Japanese aggression in Manchuria. With the foreign intervention at an end, Sandino declared an end to his rebellion and paraded triumphantly into Managua, where he and his followers received amnesty. However, in February 1934 the US-trained Guardia Nacional under **Anastasio Somoza** arrested Sandino as he left a dinner party with the president, took him to a Managua airfield, and executed him. Many of his followers met the same fate.

Somoza spoke English, had lived in the United States, was an avid baseball fan, and opened up his country to US investment and control. The United States thus supported the Somoza family dictatorship as a good neighbor and a model for all of Central America. He and his two sons ruled and plundered the country for the next 43 years.

The United States orchestrated a similar outcome in El Salvador, where the charismatic nationalist **Augustín Farabundo Martí**, a young intellectual more radical than Sandino, sought to liberate all of Central America by means of socialist revolution. After the State Department warned of a "serious situation in Salvador resulting from the Communistic outbreak," the United States commended the Salvadorean oligarchy, which killed the so-called bolshevist Martí and slaughtered perhaps 30,000 of his followers in 1932. The bloodbath created stability and won prompt US recognition of the military regime that had carried it out. Under American supervision, the coffee oligarchy continued to displace peasants from the land in order to expand its plantations.

In Guatemala, the dictator Jorge Ubico caved in to pressure and agreed to conduct trade on US terms, including abrogating an MFN agreement with Great Britain. Honduras remained a US-controlled "banana republic," as exports dominated the economies of all the Central American countries. Northern markets and US corporations had the power to make or break the small exporting states. In Costa Rica, for example, in 1929 coffee and bananas represented $17 million of the $18 million total export revenues.

Despite its abrogation of the Platt Amendment the United States remained committed to control of Cuba's political economy. The Americans long backed the dictatorship of Gerardo Machado, a former cattle rustler, until the Depression brought a collapse in sugar prices, undermining Machado's authority. Roosevelt backed the diplomat Sumner Welles's decision to oust Machado, who left the island for good. Livid over continued instability in Cuba, Welles on at least two occasions specifically requested a landing by US Marines, but Roosevelt refused to authorize rupture of the Good Neighbor pledge.

The United States denied recognition to Ramón Grau San Martín, a surgeon and anatomy professor at the University of Havana. His array of domestic reforms including woman's suffrage, rights for labor, and hostility to foreign ownership appeared to US leaders as a threat to take Cuba down a socialistic path. The United States thus allied with **Fulgencio Batista**, the head of the Cuban armed forces. Beals reported that the United States now backed "an illegal government which looked legal," reflecting an "interventionist attitude not one whit different" from that which existed before the Good Neighbor Policy. Batista soon assumed direct authority over Cuba, which he ruled for more than two decades. The United States thus fought off the threat of revolution or reform and tightened its control over Cuba.

By the onset of World War II, the United States exercised considerable economic and political control over Latin America while refraining from direct military intervention. The renunciation of force paid off, as the Latin American states overwhelmingly rallied behind the United States following the outbreak of World War II. At the same time, through its collusion with local strongmen—dubbed "the good neighbor of tyrants" by the Peruvian leader Haya de la Torre—the United States kept most Latin American nations in debt, dependent on northern markets, and limited in their economic diversification and trade with European nations.

Select Bibliography

Doenecke, Justus. *Nothing Less than War: A New History of America's Entry into World War I.* Lexington: University of Kentucky Press, 2011.

Zieger, Robert H. *America's Great War: World War I and the American Experience.* New York: Rowan & Littlefield, 2000.

Kennedy, David M. *Over Here: The First World War and American Society.* New York: Oxford University Press, 1980.

Dawley, Alan. *Changing the World: American Progressives in War and Revolution.* Princeton, NJ: Princeton University Press, 2003.

Manela, Erez. *The Wilsonian Moment: Self-Determination and the International Origins of Anti-Colonial Nationalism.* New York: Oxford University Press, 2007.

Iriye, Akira. *The Cambridge History of American Foreign Relations, Vol. III: The Globalizing of America, 1913–1945.* Cambridge: Cambridge University Press, 1993.

Gregory, James N. *The Southern Diaspora: How the Great Migration of Black and White Southerners Transformed America.* Chapel Hill: University of North Carolina Press, 2005.

Irwin, Julia. *Making the World Safe: The American Red Cross and a Nation's Humanitarian Awakening.* New York: Oxford University Press, 2013.

Costigliola, Frank. *Awkward Dominion: American Political, Economic and Cultural Relations with Europe, 1919 to 1933.* Ithaca, NY: Cornell University Press, 1984.

Preston, Andrew. *Sword of the Spirit, Shield of Faith: Religion in American War and Diplomacy.* New York: Knopf, 2012.

Gardner, Lloyd C. *Safe for Democracy: The Anglo-American Response to Revolution, 1913–1923.* New York: Oxford University Press, 1984.

Foglesong, David. *America's Secret War against Bolshevism: US Intervention in the Russian Civil War, 1917–1920.* Chapel Hill: University of North Carolina Press, 1995.

Spenser, Daniella. *Impossible Triangle: Mexico, Soviet Russia, and the United States in the 1920s.* Durham, NC: Duke University Press, 1999.

Johnson, Robert D. *The Peace Progressives and American Foreign Relations.* Cambridge, MA: Harvard University Press, 1995.

Gellman, Irwin F. *Good Neighbor Diplomacy: United States Policies in Latin America, 1933–1945.* Baltimore, MD: Johns Hopkins University Press, 1979.

8 The Diplomacy of World War II

Overview

When a second war in a generation erupted in Europe in 1939 the United States once again adopted a policy of neutrality. Once again, that neutrality did not endure. And once again the United States sided with Britain, France, the USSR, and other allies against Germany. Even more than World War I, World War II was a truly global conflict, one the United States did not formally enter until December 8, 1941, following the Japanese attack on the US colony of Hawai'i. The United States then waged, and won, an incomparably destructive two-front war in Europe and Asia, emerging as indisputably the preeminent power in the world. The war, however, also sowed the seeds of the ensuing cold war with the Soviet Union and the world communist movement.

The Rise of Fascism

The National Socialist (Nazi) dictator **Adolf Hitler** assumed power in 1933, the same year Franklin Roosevelt became president of the United States. Armed with a fanatical ideology, Hitler capitalized on popular resentment of the punitive peace heaped upon Germany following the Great War. He denounced the League of Nations, from which Germany withdrew, and launched a massive military buildup. Preoccupied with the ongoing Depression, neither the United States nor the European states grasped the extent of Hitler's expansionist ambitions, the virulence of Nazi racism and anti-Semitism, and ultimately the Führer's lust for war.

Nazism was part of a broader movement of European **fascism** emerging in the 1920s and especially in the Depression-era 1930s. The characteristics of fascism included: extreme authoritarianism typically headed by a single dictator; racial and cultural chauvinism backed by mass demonstrations emphasizing the power and glory of the nation; the repression and often killing of domestic political opponents; collusion between business, government, and the armed forces in the context of military buildup; and foreign aggression. In the mid-1920s, well before Hitler's Nazi regime replaced the Weimar Republic, **Benito Mussolini** dismissed all pretenses of democracy in Italy and established himself as "Il Duce" (the leader) of a fascist state. In 1935–36 Mussolini's regime invaded and militarily occupied Ethiopia in northeast Africa.

Overwhelmed by the Depression at home, the United States played only an indirect role in European affairs. Roosevelt, well traveled during his aristocratic upbringing, was an internationalist but the domestic New Deal clearly took priority in 1933, as his decision to withdraw from the London Economic Conference in favor of implementing a domestic recovery program had shown. With memories of World War I still vivid, beginning in 1935 Congress passed a series of neutrality acts intended to keep the United States from being pulled into a foreign war. At the same time Hitler skillfully exploited both at home and abroad the harsh peace terms forced on Germany in the Great War to suggest the Third Reich was merely reasserting Germany's rightful place in the heart of Europe.

The rise of fascism did not impede US trade and financial connections with both Italy and Germany. American firms loaned Mussolini's regime more than $460 million while direct investments in Italy accounted for another $121 million. In 1933 Roosevelt declared he was "deeply impressed by what [Mussolini] has accomplished" and said, "I am keeping in fairly close touch with

Figure 8.1 Adolf Hitler and Nazi filmmaker Leni Riefenstahl revel with country women in native costume at a Nazi rally in Nuremburg in 1934. Hitler's fiery speeches and Riefenstahl's powerful imagery helped construct a popular fascist warfare state in Germany.

Source: Library of Congress, Prints and Photographs Division, LC-USZ62-71875.

that admirable Italian gentleman." The United States later condemned Italian intervention in Ethiopia, but the aggression did not cause a break in relations. Similarly, although many Americans expressed contempt for Nazism, the United States conducted a robust trade with Germany carried out by such firms as DuPont, IBM, Standard Oil, and Union Carbide, among others. These corporations, backed by Roosevelt, ignored a State Department protest that the Nazis employed the capital provided by US corporations "for the maintenance of the German industrial program and . . . for German rearmament" designed to facilitate "aggressive measures."

US neutrality facilitated the triumph of fascism in Spain under General **Francisco Franco**. In July 1936 the Spanish fascists under Franco refused to abide by the electoral victory of the leftist Popular Front and struck against it. The US response to the Spanish Civil War was a strengthening of the neutrality law in 1937, forbidding the sale of weaponry to either side. While neither the United States nor western European nations came to the aid of the loyalist government, Hitler and Mussolini aided Franco's forces. American

Figure 8.2 Dorothy Detzer (far left), executive director of the Women's International League for Peace and Freedom, exercised as powerful an influence over US foreign policy during the interwar period as any woman and most men. Here she is shown with a WILPF delegation leaving the White House after a meeting with President Roosevelt.

Source: Library of Congress, Prints and Photographs Division, LC-DIG-hec-33887.

liberals and leftists, some journeying to Spain to fight for the loyalists in the volunteer **Abraham Lincoln Brigade**, protested the actual non-neutrality of Washington's policy. The peace progressive **Dorothy Detzer** demanded justification for an arms embargo that was being enforced against the Spanish Republic but not applied to "all the secondary supplying countries." Senator Gerald Nye introduced a joint resolution calling for repeal of the embargo, which benefited Spanish fascism. Strongly opposed by Roosevelt, Nye's resolution died in committee.

American diplomats preferred Franco's regime, which triumphed over the loyalists in 1939, to a left-wing or socialist regime. The State Department feared the spread of "Bolshevist influences" or Spain falling into "the coils of the communistic serpent." When the Soviet Union sent aid and war material to the loyalists to counter German and Italian support for Franco, it heightened US concerns about the spread of Bolshevism. The loyalist takeover and occupation by armed workers of the holdings of the Spanish subsidiary of International Telephone and Telegraph exacerbated these fears. Preferring the Spanish right to the left, the United States recognized Franco's regime on April 1, 1939, three days after it took power in Madrid.

Roosevelt was not as virulently anti-communist as the State Department and he typically paid little attention the advice of professional diplomats in any case. In 1933, as part of his New Deal agenda of change amid the Depression, Roosevelt ended the US policy of non-recognition of the Soviet regime, a policy that had been in place since the Bolshevik Revolution in 1917. There was little outcry over **recognition of the Soviet Union**, though Roosevelt shrewdly made the announcement simultaneous with the more sensational news of the end of Prohibition. Trade and cultural ties with the USSR had increased in the 1920s and some Americans had even flirted in the midst of the Depression with an attraction to Soviet state planning in the form of five-year plans. Sinclair Oil, mining corporations, and tractor making factories launched by Henry Ford were among the US investors in the USSR.

The United States opened an embassy in Moscow in 1933, but little diplomacy was attempted or accomplished with the regime of **Joseph Stalin**. The Soviet dictator had seized full power in 1929 and orchestrated a brutal collectivization of agriculture and industry, with Soviet authorities killing and imprisoning anyone who stood in their way. Stalin also liquidated his political opposition, including many heroes of the Bolshevik Revolution, by means of sensational show trials followed by forced confessions and summary executions. Most Americans knew little about events in Europe, the USSR, or the rest of the world, as they remained preoccupied with the devastating Depression on the home front. The State Department diplomats, especially those posted in Moscow, detested the Soviet regime, but Roosevelt paid them little attention.

By the late 1930s foreign affairs could no longer take a back seat to the domestic economy. The New Deal reform era was over and both Asia and Europe were convulsed by conflict that clearly threatened wider wars. In Europe the scope of the belligerence and brutality of the Nazi regime had become increasingly apparent. In 1936, after building up an unrivaled war machine, Hitler remilitarized the Rhineland in blatant violation of the Versailles agreement. In November 1938, the virulence of Nazi anti-Semitism played out through direct attacks on Jewish homes and businesses on *Kristallnacht* ("Crystal Night"). Prejudice against Jews, who were identified as a separate "race" of people under the 1924 US immigration law, was not uncommon throughout the world, but the depth of Nazi malevolence was only beginning to be understood. Roosevelt responded by withdrawing American diplomats from Berlin and sponsoring the adoption by the US and Latin American states of a resolution condemning Nazi race doctrines.

In September 1938 British Prime Minister Neville Chamberlain tried to come to terms with Nazism by adopting a policy of **appeasement** at the **Munich Conference**. By this time the Nazis had annexed Austria and laid claim to the Sudetenland of Czechoslovakia, yet Hitler insisted that he only sought to incorporate German-speaking peoples under the Third Reich. When Hitler pledged at Munich that he intended no further aggression Chamberlain announced that the conference had achieved "peace for our time." Roosevelt, the French, and other European nations backed the appeasement policy in hopes of avoiding another European war. In so doing they continued to underestimate the depth of Hitler's resentment of Germany's humiliation in World War I, in which he had served, and his desire to exact violent retribution.

At Munich Hitler spoke the language of peace and security, but the Nazis were on a course of war. Appeasement was in the end a failed policy yet with Hitler no form of diplomacy short of war could deter his plan to march to the east in order to seize "living space" (*lebensraum*) from the lesser peoples (*untermenschen*) of Slavic Europe. In this vision the Nazi dictator and key advisers such as Heinrich Himmler drew inspiration from the history of American expansion into the West at the expense of the "Red Indians."

In March 1939 the Nazis annexed the rest of Czechoslovakia in blatant violation of the Munich agreement, prompting an immediate British and French declaration that any further aggression would mean war. The only potential means of containing Nazism, as the subsequent war would prove, was an alliance with the Soviet Union. However, the Western countries including the United States had long considered communism worse than fascism, thus they summarily rejected the prospect of allying with Stalin's regime. The Soviet dictator understood Hitler better than did the Western leaders. Stalin and his foreign minister Maxim Litvinov repeatedly called for collective security against the Nazis. In 1935 the Comintern, the communist international organization, authorized a new **popular front** strategy allowing for coalitions and alliances with non-communist countries as a means of combating the rise of fascist regimes. The USSR had put the strategy into effect in the Spanish Civil War but Soviet aid alone was not enough to defeat Franco.

With the West having rejected the Soviet offers of collective security against fascism, Stalin reversed course and entered into a cynical agreement with Hitler. The 1939 non-aggression pact, or **Nazi-Soviet Pact**, enabled Hitler to

Figure 8.3 Vyacheslav Molotov, foreign minister of the Soviet Union, signs the Nazi-
Soviet Pact of 1939, which facilitated the outbreak of World War II. The
Soviet leader Joseph Stalin (second from right) and German foreign minister
Joachim von Ribbentrop (center) look on.

Source: Library of Congress, Prints and Photographs Division, LC-USZ62-43787.

start World War II. Now united in aggression, Germany and the USSR partitioned Poland while Stalin secured German approval for reincorporation of
the Baltic States—Estonia, Latvia, and Lithuania—which had been part of the
tsarist empire. The Nazi-Soviet Pact enabled Hitler to continue his aggressive
course in Poland, which brought on the declaration of war by Britain and
France in September 1939. The USSR invaded Finland, which put up a stout
resistance before succumbing to occupation in 1940.

Whether or not a major war would erupt in Western Europe remained
uncertain, with some skeptics calling the conflict between Germany and Britain and France a "phony war." Beginning in April 1940 the Germans made
a bitter mockery of such skepticism with their ***blitzkrieg*** or lightning war
attacks on Scandinavia, France, and the Low Countries. By June 1940 the
Nazis had conquered most of Western Europe. In July the Nazis unleashed
their Air Force on the British Isles.

Americans overwhelmingly sympathized with the victims of German
aggression but were reluctant to enter into another European war. They had
bitter memories of World War I, which had failed to make the world "safe
for democracy" and in the end had left the nation deeply divided. Noninterventionists and peace internationalists emphasized the wartime secret treaties,
the hypocrisies of Wilsonian self-determination, and postwar disillusion and

Figure 8.4 Republican Senators William Borah of Idaho (left) and Gerald Nye of North Dakota, shown here in 1937, sharply opposed US intervention in another European war. From 1934–36 Nye led a Senate Select Committee investigation of war profiteering flowing from the nexus between government, bankers, and arms merchants during World War I.

Source: Library of Congress, Prints and Photographs Division, LC-DIG-hec-22663.

the Red Scare to warn against intervention in another European war. Moreover, much of the public believed that intervention in the Great War had been driven by propaganda that covered up the selfish interests of bankers and munitions makers. Such views were especially powerful during the Depression years, as many blamed bankers and speculators for the Crash while Roosevelt denounced "economic royalists."

Especially influential in mobilizing anti-war sentiment was the Senate **Nye Committee**, which investigated the interconnections between war, banking, and industry during World War I. After holding highly publicized hearings from 1934–36, the Senate Select Committee chaired by Nye of North Dakota concluded that the war had been accompanied by price fixing, corruption, collusion, and windfall profiteering by banks and arms manufacturers, dubbed the "merchants of death" in a popular book on the subject. WILPF, which under Detzer's leadership grew from nine branches and 2,000 members in 1921 to 120 branches and 13,000 members in 1937, played a key role in mobilizing support and publicity for the Nye Committee. Detzer testified in the hearings declaring that "the munitions industry should be nationalized" in order to remove the profit motive from warfare.

Through its massive investigation the Nye Committee revealed no conspiracy as such yet verified "some of the very worst suspicions" about what in later years would be called the "**military–industrial complex**." The Committee documented the existence of "an unhealthy alliance" between munitions makers and the government, forming "a self-interested political power which operates in the name of patriotism and satisfies interests which are, in large part, purely selfish." Munitions makers, financiers, and government officials variously "evaded or ignored laws . . . relied on bribery . . . perpetuated war scares" and engaged in "shameless profiteering." The findings created a climate conducive to passage of the neutrality laws and a determination by many Americans to stay out of another European war.

By 1939 Roosevelt focused as intently on foreign affairs as he had on domestic policy at the outset of his presidency. After centering his annual message on foreign policy, Roosevelt launched dramatic increases in defense spending including a major rearmament program. Following the outbreak of war the United States amended the neutrality policy to allow "cash and carry" under which belligerents could purchase arms as long as they paid cash and shipped them on non-US vessels. The United States began selling military aircraft to Britain and France. Unlike President Wilson, who in the years before US intervention had called on Americans to be "neutral in thought as well as deed," Roosevelt declared in a fireside chat in 1939, "This nation will remain a neutral nation, but I cannot ask that every American remain neutral in thought as well. Even a neutral cannot be asked to close his mind or his conscience."

By the summer of 1940 the German *blitzkrieg* and the **Battle of Britain** had begun to erode anti-war sentiment. Striving to keep the United States out of the war, Hitler declared, "The Germans have nothing against the Americans and the Americans have nothing against the Germans." Roosevelt and many others feared, however, that if the Nazis controlled Europe they would then move in on Latin America, cutting off the United States economically, leaving it politically and militarily isolated and vulnerable to attack. Roosevelt and others warned with scant evidence that the Nazis possessed elaborate plans for invasions and takeovers in Latin America. Roosevelt invoked the Monroe Doctrine's "no-transfer" clause (of any American state to a European power), winning the approval of the Latin American states at the **Havana Conference**, attended by Secretary of State Cordell Hull, in the summer of 1940.

Vividly reported on radio through daily eyewitness accounts, the "Blitz," the German bombing of Britain, elicited widespread sympathy for the fellow "Anglo-Saxon" and Protestant British, America's closest ally and trans-Atlantic trade partner. The new British wartime leader, **Winston Churchill**, whose mother was American, rallied British resistance while appealing to the United States for help. Roosevelt responded by selling Britain war materiel and negotiating the **destroyers for bases deal** in which the United States received 99-year leases for naval and air bases in seven British possessions in the Americas, from Newfoundland to Trinidad, with Bermuda in between, in return for supplying Britain with 50 naval destroyers. Roosevelt unilaterally extended the Monroe Doctrine to Greenland and Iceland, states more European than American. The United States landed troops on Iceland in the first military expedition outside the Western Hemisphere since World War I, while extending the "neutrality zone" a thousand miles from US shores. "The people seem to regard Iceland as an island off the coast of Maine," the noninterventionist senator Robert Taft complained. Accelerating the trend of growing executive power over foreign affairs, Roosevelt insisted that these acts of "hemispheric defense" did not require congressional approval.

As Roosevelt moved the country closer to war, he received support from the interventionist **Committee to Defend America by Aiding the Allies**. Backed by some 300 local chapters, the Committee sponsored rallies and speakers and distributed such films as *It Could Happen Here*, which depicted a German invasion of the United States. The pro-British Century Group lobbied tirelessly for aid to Britain and for the United States to fulfill its destiny as a world power by taking a role in the war.

Noninterventionist sentiment remained strong, however, hence a "**great debate**" took place from 1939–41 over the US role in the European war. In September 1940 anti-interventionists formed the **America First Committee (AFC)**, headquartered in Chicago but with offices sprouting across the country. Most AFC members concurred with Nye, who accused Roosevelt of steering the country "straight into a war of European power politics." Roosevelt denied the charge, declaring during his campaign for an unprecedented third term, "Your president says this country is not going to war." After winning the 1940 election Roosevelt, recalling the mistakes of Wilson, who had alienated the opposition party in wartime, added two prominent interventionist Republicans to his administration, including former Secretary of State Henry Stimson.

Both sides in the debate over intervention generally agreed that the United States, as an exceptional and providentially chosen nation, ultimately should lead the world. Noninterventionists argued, however, that US leadership could be provided by example rather than direct involvement in war. By remaining disengaged from the European war, they reasoned, the United States could pursue its mission to provide the world with a model of democratic government. Noninterventionists thus invoked Washington's Farewell Address warning to avoid "permanent alliances" as well as John Quincy Adams's Fourth of July (1821), which had warned against going in search of "monsters to destroy."

Interventionists rejected the notion that the United States could be economically viable with a mere "continentalist" foreign policy centered on Western Hemisphere trade and defense. "We would never be satisfied to be bottled up in the American continent," the diplomat William Phillips declared. If the economy remained stagnant or deteriorated because of Nazi domination of European markets, interventionists argued, capitalism could give way to a regimented economic order at home. They feared the result would be "the

Figure 8.5 By far the most popular speaker for the anti-interventionist AFC was the famed aviator Charles Lindbergh, the first man to fly a solo aircraft from New York to Paris in 1927. The aviation pioneer and other America First advocates, shown here in a rally in New York City in April 1941, declared that the Nazis did not pose a direct threat to the United States.

Source: Library of Congress, Prints and Photographs Division, LC-USZ62-132621.

probability of ultimate Bolshevism" or "social revolution." Military production would not be sufficient to meet the Nazi threat "until we got into the war ourselves," Stimson observed.

The "great debate" peaked with the battle over the Lend-Lease Act, which interventionists numbered **House Resolution 1776**, thereby suggesting that its approval would be an act of patriotism, its disapproval perfidy. Appealing to the nation's heritage in a fireside chat on December 29, Roosevelt declared, "Never before since Jamestown and Plymouth Rock has our American civilization been in such danger as now." Calling on the public to display "the same spirit of patriotism and sacrifice as we would show were we at war," the president called on the nation to serve as the "great arsenal of democracy." The fireside chat reached 76 percent of the public, either directly or indirectly, and met an overwhelmingly favorable response. "Mr. Roosevelt has brought the country along step by step in a masterly way," the banker Thomas Lamont observed.

The AFC opposed lend-lease aid to the Allies hence a bitter debate ensued. The aviation hero Charles Lindbergh testified before Congress that the United States was under no direct threat to its security from the German Air Force. Roosevelt's defenders dismissed Lindbergh's arguments, charging he was a Nazi sympathizer. The noninterventionist Senator **Burton Wheeler**, a Democrat from Montana declared that lend-lease, like a New Deal crop destruction program, would "plow under every fourth American boy." Although Roosevelt called Wheeler's comment the most "dastardly, unpatriotic thing that has ever been said," many people expressed concern about the potential loss of American life in another war. Memories of the slaughter and devastating trench warfare of World War I remained vivid. "We cannot re-conquer a continent without wholesale death," advised the *New York Times* military correspondent Hanson Baldwin, a Navy veteran. Some noninterventionists predicted as many as a million American casualties in the European war.

With Roosevelt emphasizing that the United States would act only indirectly, as the "great arsenal" rather than a direct belligerent, lend-lease passed the House 265–165 and the Senate 60–31. The president signed it into law in March 1941. A renewed Nazi *blitzkrieg* in April aided the cause of the interventionists. The Nazis overwhelmed Greece and Yugoslavia in a matter of days while they continued to rain bombs on London, striking the House of Commons. Newspapers published maps of Europe darkened by fresh waves of Nazi conquest.

On June 22 a stunning development, the Nazi invasion of the Soviet Union, changed the nature of the debate and the course of the war. Hitler and the Nazis had long targeted communists as their ultimate enemies and dreamed of constructing a thousand-year Reich by exploiting the people and natural resources of Slavic Europe. Hence Hitler launched **Operation Barbarossa**, the greatest land invasion in history, and tore through Soviet territory in the first months of the attack. The *Wehrmacht* bogged down after the fall of Kiev however, as despite massive losses the Soviets continually rebuilt defensive lines and fought tenaciously. By late July the Nazis had failed to take Leningrad or Moscow, and the *New York Times* described German losses as "staggering."

Many American observers delighted in this turn of events in the European war. The Nazi assault on Russia was "the best thing that could have happened," the prominent diplomat Joseph Grew declared. "Dog, eat dog. Let the Nazis and the communists so weaken each other that the democracies will soon gain the upper hand or at least will be released from their dire peril." The *Luftwaffe* had also suffered great losses during the Blitz and failed to break British morale, prompting Hitler to cancel Sea Lion, a planned cross-Channel invasion of the British Isles. Interventionists could no longer plausibly emphasize any immediate Nazi threat to the Americas. Moreover, Barbarossa reduced the chances that an incident would bring the nation into the war, as Hitler meant to avoid war with the United States until victory over the USSR was assured. In June 1941 the Führer ordered, "Every incident involving the USA is to be avoided."

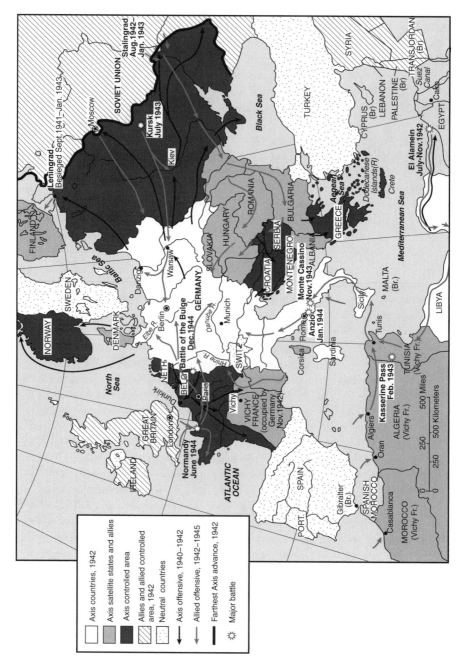

Map 8.1 World War II in Europe.

Despite having opened a two-front war, a German victory still appeared possible and Churchill was no less insistent that the United States should intervene to assure British security. In August at the Atlantic Conference, a historic meeting aboard ship off the Newfoundland coast, Roosevelt and Churchill collaborated, sang hymns in a somber Sunday morning religious service at sea, and formed an enduring bond that would carry them through the war together. They signed the **Atlantic Charter**, reminiscent of Wilson's Fourteen Points, which denounced aggression and territorial aggrandizement and called for disarmament of aggressor nations. The Charter also advocated free trade, freedom of the seas, and global cooperation to improve economic and social conditions throughout the world. The Atlantic Charter would become the basis of the Allied war effort but it had even more enduring significance, as it provided a foundational blueprint for postwar aspirations of freedom and self-determination.

In Their Words

President Roosevelt's fireside chat in the wake of the Greer *incident,*
September 11, 1941

My fellow Americans:

The Navy Department of the United States has reported to me that on the morning of September fourth the United States destroyer GREER, proceeding in full daylight towards Iceland, had reached a point southeast of Greenland. She was carrying American mail to Iceland. She was flying the American flag. Her identity as an American ship was unmistakable.

She was then and there attacked by a submarine. Germany admits that it was a German submarine. The submarine deliberately fired a torpedo at the GREER, followed later by another torpedo attack. In spite of what Hitler's propaganda bureau has invented, and in spite of what any American obstructionist organization may prefer to believe, I tell you the blunt fact that the German submarine fired first upon this American destroyer without warning, and with deliberate design to sink her.

Our destroyer, at the time, was in waters which the Government of the United States had declared to be waters of self-defense—surrounding outposts of American protection in the Atlantic . . . This was piracy—piracy legally and morally. It was not the first nor the last act of piracy which the Nazi Government has committed against the American flag in this war. For attack has followed attack . . . The important truth is that these acts of international lawlessness are a manifestation of a design (which)—a design that has been made clear to the American people for a long time. It is the Nazi design to abolish the freedom of the seas, and to acquire absolute control and domination of these seas for themselves . . . It is time for all Americans, Americans of all the Americas to stop being deluded by the romantic notion that the Americas can go on living happily and peacefully in a Nazi-dominated world.

Generation after generation, America has battled for the general policy of the freedom of the seas . . . Hitler has begun his campaign to control the seas by ruthless force and by wiping out every vestige of international law, (and) every vestige of humanity . . . No tender whisperings of appeasers that Hitler is not interested in the Western Hemisphere, no soporific lullabies that a wide ocean protects us from him—can long have any effect on the hard-headed, far-sighted and realistic American people . . . The Nazi danger to our Western world has long ceased to be a mere possibility. The danger is here now—not only from a military enemy but from an enemy of all law, all liberty, all morality, all religion . . .

We have sought no shooting war with Hitler. We do not seek it now. But neither do we want peace so much, that we are willing to pay for it by permitting him to attack our naval and merchant ships while they are on legitimate business . . . But when you see a rattlesnake poised to strike, you do not wait until he has struck before you crush him.

These Nazi submarines and raiders are the rattlesnakes of the Atlantic. They are a menace to the free pathways of the high seas. They are a challenge to our own sovereignty. They hammer at our most precious rights when they attack ships of the American flag—symbols of our independence, our freedom, our very life . . .

But let this warning be clear. From now on, if German or Italian vessels of war enter the waters, the protection of which is necessary for American defense, they do so at their own peril . . . The sole responsibility rests upon Germany. There will be no shooting unless Germany continues to seek it . . .

The American people have faced other grave crises in their history— with American courage, (and) with American resolution. They will do no less today . . . And with that inner strength that comes to a free people conscious of their duty, (and) conscious of the righteousness of what they do, they will—with Divine help and guidance—stand their ground against this latest assault upon their democracy, their sovereignty, and their freedom.

At this point, although Roosevelt had refrained from asking Congress for a declaration of war, the United States had essentially entered into an alliance with Great Britain. Churchill reported to his cabinet that Roosevelt had promised that "he would wage war, but not declare it, and that he would become more and more provocative. If the Germans did not like it, they could attack American forces." Without informing the public Roosevelt ordered US naval vessels to escort British convoys and if necessary to attack German submarines. Roosevelt had indicated that "everything was to be done to force an 'incident.'"

The first incident came on September 4, when the US warship *Greer* fired on a Nazi submarine it had stalked. Roosevelt misrepresented the incident to a Navy Day audience, declaring, "We have wished to avoid shooting. But the shooting has started. And history has recorded who fired the first shot."

The Path to Pearl Harbor

Events in the Pacific and not the Atlantic ultimately brought the United States into World War II. The US-Japanese conflict that erupted in open warfare on December 7, 1941, had deep roots. Since the late nineteenth century Japan had resented **Western colonialism** and the racism and exploitation of Asian labor and natural resources that facilitated it. The United States aroused resentment through segregation policies targeting Japanese and Asian American children in Californian schools during the early part of the twentieth century and by shutting off Japanese immigration under the 1924 law. By World War I Japan was an industrialized, imperial nation that had defeated both China and Russia at war and incorporated Korea as a colony. With its own natural resources limited, Japan coveted the resource-rich region of Manchuria in northern China. In 1915 Japan forced a weakened China to acquiesce to the **Twenty-One Demands**, an imperial blueprint designed to convert China into a Japanese sphere of influence while driving out the Western powers.

Japan proved willing to engage in diplomacy after World War I, as it signed the naval arms limitations in the Washington Treaty, withdrew from China's Shantung Peninsula, and acceded to the Open Door without however giving up its designs on Manchuria. The Washington accord on battleship tonnage, however, angered increasingly dominant Japanese militarists who remained opposed even after adjustments in Japan's favor at a follow-up naval conference in London in 1930. The next year Japan created a pretext and invaded Manchuria, which it renamed **Manchukuo** and sought to sever the region from China. By this time the Army and Navy, backed by **Emperor Hirohito**, dominated Japanese society. Politicians, intellectuals, businessmen, and diplomats who refused to defer to them invited punishment or assassination.

The United States condemned and sought to contain Japanese expansion in Asia. In the wake of the Manchurian invasion, President Hoover's secretary of state issued the **Stimson Doctrine** in which the United States declared it would not recognize territory taken by aggression, specifically the puppet state of Manchukuo. Even though the United States was not a member of the League of Nations, an American participated on a League commission investigating the Japanese aggression in China. The **Lytton Commission** condemned the Manchurian invasion, prompting Japan to withdraw from the League as the Nazis had done.

Strongly influenced by Alfred Mahan's theories as well his longtime tenure as assistant secretary of the Navy under Wilson, Roosevelt entered office wary of Japan and determined to strengthen the Navy. The buildup included new cruisers, destroyers, and aircraft carriers. The Japanese launched a naval rearmament program in response to Roosevelt's buildup. These escalations effectively brought an end to the inclusion of Japan in naval arms control agreements.

In 1936 Japan and Germany (joined by Italy the next year) signed the Anti-Comintern Pact aimed squarely at the Soviet Union. In 1937 Japan invaded beyond Manchuria more deeply into China, opening an eight-year war. Beginning in December the Japanese perpetrated the **Nanking Massacre** in which tens if not hundreds of thousands (China claims 300,000) were killed by rampaging Japanese troops, who murdered, raped, burned, and terrorized the city and surrounding countryside. The next year Japan announced that it would construct a "new order" in Asia with Tokyo at the helm and the West eventually forced out.

The Roosevelt administration condemned all of these actions and opened secret discussions with British officials on the prospects of a naval blockade of Japan. In October 1937 Roosevelt delivered a major speech in Chicago, the heart of noninterventionist sentiment, declaring that aggressor states, like an outbreak of disease, needed to be "quarantined." Two months after the **quarantine speech** Japanese military aircraft bombed a US gunboat on China's Yangtze River, killing 2 and wounding 30 Americans. The Japanese government apologized for the ***Panay* Incident** and paid the United States indemnities, averting a potential break in relations.

Four years later Japanese aggression in China and Indochina, and the determination of the United States to confront them, would lead to war. Since the nineteenth century many Americans—traders, missionaries, naval strategists, politicians, and journalists—had developed strong attachments to China. The bestselling novel *The Good Earth* (1931) by Pearl Buck depicted the Chinese in a sympathetic light (the "good" Asians) while many viewed Japan conversely as the proverbial yellow peril (the "bad" Asians). After Pearl Harbor, *Life* ran an article entitled "How to Tell Japs from the Chinese." By the time of the Japanese invasion of China a full-blown **China Lobby** had political clout in the United States, promoting sympathy for the regime of **Generalissimo Chiang Kai-shek** and his English-speaking wife, Madame Chiang (Soong Mailing). Like her husband a Christian, she was invariably described as beautiful and charming in press accounts amid her frequent visits to the United States.

The Roosevelt administration stepped up its efforts to contain Japan through financial and strategic assistance to the Chinese nationalists while seeking to punish Japan by economic means. Contrary to its response to the Spanish Civil War, Washington did not invoke neutrality in the Sino-Japanese conflict, thus allowing for continued arms sales to China. After Japan announced its "new order" in Asia, the United States loaned $25 million to the Chinese government, which had removed to the western provinces to wage resistance against the invaders. Chiang distrusted US motives and his regime had no interest in democratic governance, but he gladly took in the weapons and financial assistance.

In 1940 the United States shocked Japan's leaders by abrogating a commercial treaty and virtually shutting off trade with Japan. That same year Japan entered into the "Axis" alliance with Germany and Italy, the **Tripartite Pact**, in which the signatories pronounced "a new order of things," recognized their respective spheres of influence, and pledged to aid one another in the event of attack by a country not currently at war, notably the United States.

Contemplating the possibility of a two-front war in Europe and Asia, the US military developed a **"Europe-first" strategy** that would be followed after US entry into World War II. Known as "Plan Dog" or "Plan D" in military jargon because it was the fourth in a series of options, the military designated liberation of Europe as the top priority and the Pacific theater as secondary.

By the fall of 1940 the Japanese, frustrated in their efforts to take control of China, embarked on a **southern advance** into Indochina (Vietnam, Laos, and Cambodia). The Japanese armies in China had employed indiscriminate warfare, including annihilation campaigns and use of chemical weapons, yet they could not subdue Chinese resistance. Japanese militarists decided that an invasion of the European-held colonies of Southeast Asia could provide a means to cut off Western assistance to the Chinese and thus enable them to take control of the situation. Japan had long resented and condemned European colonialism in Asia, including British possession of Hong Kong, India, Burma, and Malaya; French control of Indochina; the Dutch East Indies; Portuguese Timor; and the US possessions of Midway, Wake Island, Guam, Hawai'i, and the Philippines. Japan touted "Asia for the Asians," but conducted punitive occupations in Southeast Asia and thus failed to win over the local populations.

The Japanese southern advance incited fears that the United States would lose access to the abundant raw materials and natural resources of Southeast Asia. The United States imported rubber, tin, and more than a dozen other strategic resources as well as palm oil, coffee, spices, and other agricultural products and commodities through trade with the occupying European colonial powers. With the ongoing Depression still weighing over them, US officials feared that Japan would cut off Southeast Asia and deprive the Western nations of access to the vital resources of the region. In 1940 Stanley Hornbeck, the top Asian expert in the State Department, declared, "It is not an exaggeration to say that the United States would be compelled, for its existence is a major industrial state, to wage war against any power or powers that might threaten to sever our trade lines" with Southeast Asia.

In July 1941 the United States responded to the southern advance by freezing Japanese assets and cutting off access to oil. Roosevelt ordered the Filipino armed forces put under direct US command, pledged to send long-range bombers to Manila, and appointed General Douglas MacArthur to command US forces in East Asia. These actions spurred panic in Japanese ruling circles as a result of the country's dependence on oil. Undermined by Western economic sanctions and with nearly 1 million troops bogged down for a fourth year in China, Japan grew desperate.

Figure 8.6 Japan's ambassador to the United States, Nomura Kichisaburo, shown here
with Secretary of State Cordell Hull in February 1941, kept negotiations
open until days before the Pearl Harbor attack.

Source: Library of Congress, Prints and Photographs Division, LC-USZ62-52710.

As a result of an intelligence breakthrough, the United States by this time
had devised means to intercept and decode Japanese government messages in
a program known as **MAGIC**. The MAGIC intercepts left little doubt that
Japan would use military force to break what it perceived as encirclement
by the Western powers, but they also showed that Tokyo might be willing to
negotiate. Prime Minister Fumimaro Konoe had initiated unofficial conversations between Hull and Nomura Kichisaburo, but the talks went nowhere.
The United States proved unwilling to consider any proposal that would sanction Japan's aggression against Indochina, even for the short term, or which
would lead to a permanent "violation" of the Open Door in China. Seeking
to avoid war with the United States, Konoe proposed a direct summit with
Roosevelt, who rejected it. The United States at this time extended lend-lease
to the USSR, reflecting a growing determination to shape the course of the
world war.

In November 1941 the talks in Washington between Hull and Nomura, who
desperately sought to avoid war, offered a last-gasp opportunity. However, the
US ultimatum that Japan "withdraw all military, naval, and police forces from
China and from Indo-China" offered no face-saving formula for the militarists
in Tokyo. They thus called for a preemptive attack, as war with the United

States appeared inevitable and Japan was running short of oil. Emperor Hirohito approved the ill-fated plan for a quick and decisive series of strikes to try to win the war or at least gain concessions before Japan ran out of resources.

Contrary to popular conspiracy theories the United States did not know in advance, and sit by idly by, as the Japanese attacked Pearl Harbor as part of a devious plan to enter World War II through the "back door." US officials certainly knew war with Japan was a real possibility, did not shy away from it, and many perhaps including Roosevelt were eager for it. They did not, however, anticipate the audacious attack on Hawai'i—more than 4,000 miles from Japan—when other targets were much more accessible to Tokyo. In the first days of December MAGIC intercepts picked up the Japanese communications on the attack but by the time these messages were intercepted, decoded, and sent to Washington the attack had already occurred.

On the clear sunny morning of December 7 Japan pulled off the "sneak attack," as its air and naval forces slammed into the US base in Hawai'i, killing 2,323 Americans and crippling the Pacific fleet. Attacks on Singapore, Guam, the Philippines, and Wake Island followed. On December 8, with only one dissenting House vote, Congress declared war on Japan. On December 11 Hitler rashly declared war on the United States, which the Tripartite Pact did not obligate him to do because Japan had attacked rather than having been attacked. Italy followed blindly in Hitler's wake.

The direct attack on the US Pacific colony united Americans virtually overnight. "The war came as a great relief," *Time* acknowledged, as "Japanese bombs had finally brought national unity." The debate over involvement in the war ended, as noninterventionists disbanded their organizations, denounced Japan's aggression, and joined the war effort against the Axis powers. "Our principles were right," the AFC declared. "Had they been followed, war could have been avoided." Virtually all agreed, however, that the only course, now that Hawai'i had been attacked, was, as Senator Wheeler advised, "to lick hell out of them." The United States, in the "righteous might" invoked by Roosevelt in his stirring "day of infamy" war address, would proceed with its allies to do just that.

In addition to economic and strategic concerns, the cultural factors of race, gender, religion, and American exceptionalism played a significant role in the run up to involvement in the war. As in World War I Americans gradually came to the conclusion that the world's most economically advanced and providentially destined nation could not remain aloof from a war that would determine the fate of the world. In May 1940 Stimson went to the heart of the matter, observing, "Without real cooperation on our part toward securing victory we would have little influence at the end." If Americans were to fulfill their destiny to lead the world, the nation would have to intervene in the world war.

As in World War I the US affinity for the fellow Anglo-Saxon "mother" country, Great Britain, helped build support for war. Despite European imperialism in Asia, the United States had never considered intervention against "white"

Figure 8.7 In a desperate effort to keep his business alive an American of Japanese descent draped this large sign on the window of his grocery store in Oakland, California, but to no avail. The owner, a graduate of the University of California, was one of more than 100,000 first- and second-generation Japanese Americans to lose their homes and businesses and be forced to live in "War Relocation Authority Centers," essentially makeshift prisons, after the outbreak of war with Japan. In 1988 the US government offered an official apology and compensation to survivors of the Japanese internment and their relatives.

Source: Library of Congress, Prints and Photographs Division, LC-USZ62-23602.

colonialists, whereas racial perceptions fueled enmity over Japanese expansion. Following Pearl Harbor the United States orchestrated the **Japanese internment**, imprisoning and seizing the property of more than 100,000 first- and second-generation Japanese Americans in one of the more sweeping violations of civil liberties in American history. Long distrustful of Japanese Americans Roosevelt had anticipated as early as 1936 the possibility of confining them in "concentration camps" in the event of war. The US government also harassed and interned Italian and German Americans on a smaller scale.

Religious faith spurred support for war against the Japanese, the Nazis, and their "evil" designs for a militant new world order. American Jews and others had ample reason for revulsion against Hitler's anti-Semitism, though the full measure of its violence was not clear until the war got under way. Protestant fundamentalists supported the war but so did religious modernists. The influential theologian **Reinhold Niebuhr** championed "Christian realism" over religious pacifism, explaining that violence was sometimes necessary to achieve the greater good. In his Navy Day Address in 1941 Roosevelt, a devout Episcopalian, declared that Hitler and the Nazis "plan to abolish all existing religions—Catholic, Protestant, Muhammaden [sic], Hindu, Buddhist, and Jewish alike . . . The God of Blood and Iron will take the place of the God of Love and Mercy."

As in the past, in the United States as in other countries, war provided an outlet for masculine anxieties, especially in the wake of the debilitating Depression. With as much as one-third of the male workforce jobless during the economic collapse, men lost the ability to fulfill the role of family provider, causing an emasculating loss of confidence and rising rates of mental illness among men. Millions of American men literally lost strength during the Depression, as sickness and malnourishment became so pervasive that from 1940 to 1945 the armed forces rejected one-third of all men after physical examination following induction. A war waged against wicked foes offered the opportunity to reinvigorate American manhood.

The Grand Alliance

No one appeared more pleased by the news of US entry into the world war than Churchill. "At this very moment I knew," he wrote years later, "that the United States was in the war up to the neck and in to the death. So we had won after all." Churchill had no doubt that "Hitler's fate was sealed. Mussolini's fate was sealed. As for the Japanese, they would be ground to powder." As Churchill saw it, the Axis powers were no match for the combined might of his country, the United States, the Soviet Union, and the rest of the Allies. The outcome was only a matter of when, not if.

World War II played out much as Churchill expected, as the unlikely and thus "Grand" Alliance of the United States, Britain, and the Soviet Union defeated the Axis. The **Grand Alliance** was a marriage of convenience—only the Nazi aggression in Europe could have prompted the Western democracies to ally with Stalin's communist dictatorship. Nonetheless, with Roosevelt often acting as the glue, the alliance of the **Big Three**—Roosevelt, Churchill, and Stalin—prevailed throughout the war. Deft Alliance diplomacy overcame the extraordinary challenges of two-front war, disparate ideologies, and competing national interests to enable victory of the Allies over the Axis in both Europe and Asia.

World War II was truly a global conflict in which the United States was deeply engaged on every front: the Atlantic, the Pacific, Southeast Asia, the Middle East, North Africa, and peripherally in Latin America. In adherence to Plan Dog the European theater remained the top priority even after the Pearl Harbor attack, but the United States took a deliberate approach to direct conflict on the continent. While US factories engaged in around-the-clock production, American troops would not be plunged precipitously into the battle in the heart of Europe. With the Soviet Union suffering horrific losses, Stalin pleaded for his allies to open a **second front** on the European continent sooner rather than later. Roosevelt at first agreed to Stalin's request but backed off when he found that the United States would not be fully mobilized in time for an early European landing.

Deferring to Churchill, Roosevelt elected to begin direct US involvement not in Europe but in North Africa. In **Operation Torch** US and British forces attacked in Morocco, Algeria, and Tunis, which were under the authority of the Nazi puppet regime of occupied **Vichy France**. As 1942 came to an end the Allies won the campaign in North Africa while the Soviet Union continued to bear the brunt of the battle against German forces on the European continent. Meeting at Casablanca in January 1943, Churchill and Roosevelt attempted to reassure the absent Stalin by pledging that they would pursue the "**unconditional surrender**" of the Nazis. Neither wanted a repeat of World War I, from which Russia had withdrawn in the midst and Germany had sued for peace before being defeated, thus setting the stage for the rise of Hitler.

The turning point in the European theater of World War II came at the end of January 1943 when the Soviets defeated the Germans in the penultimate **Battle of Stalingrad** (Volgograd today). From that point forward the Nazi Armies would be put in reverse and eventually driven back to Berlin and total defeat. US war materiel and financial assistance had been critical but it was the Soviet Armies and populace that stopped the Nazis at a cost of massive death and destruction. US Army General George C. Marshall now pushed for the opening of the second front but Roosevelt again sided with Churchill, who called for a Mediterranean campaign instead of an invasion of occupied France. In the summer of 1943 the Allies successfully invaded Sicily and Italy, fighting north and forcing another Nazi retreat.

With the ultimate outcome of the European war increasingly clear, the Big Three held the first of a series of conferences to discuss final strategy and the fate of the postwar world. In November 1943 at the **Tehran Conference** in Iran, Roosevelt strove to reassure a wary Stalin of US and British support and commitment to ultimate victory. During the meetings Roosevelt jabbed and joked at Churchill's expense in the presence of Stalin in order to intimate that the two English-speaking allies were not teaming up against the USSR. Roosevelt, joined by Churchill, employed the affectionate term "Uncle Joe" for Stalin. The effort at inclusiveness was important, as the Soviets had been ostracized by the Western powers since the Bolshevik Revolution. Roosevelt, who had initiated diplomatic recognition of the USSR in 1933, was well positioned to win the cooperation of the Soviet dictator.

At Tehran the Big Three agreed that the United States and Britain would open the second front in 1944. Stalin pledged that the Soviets, formally still neutral in the Pacific War, would enter the war against Japan. The Allies persuaded Turkey to enter the war against the Nazis and agreed on the eventual joint occupation of Germany. The Big Three left Tehran with the Grand Alliance intact and on course to victory.

Figure 8.8 The Big Three—Joseph Stalin of the USSR, US President Franklin Roosevelt, and British Prime Minister Winston Churchill—were all smiles as they posed for photographs on the porch of the Russian embassy in Tehran, Iran, during the crucial wartime conference in November 1943. Following the death of Roosevelt and the end of the war in 1945 the Grand Alliance disintegrated.

Source: Library of Congress, Prints and Photographs Division, LC-USZ62-104520.

Roosevelt wanted Soviet help in the Pacific in order to keep US casualties as low as possible yet the United States was well on its way to victory over Japan. The crucial **Battle of Midway** marked the turning point in the Pacific War only six months after the Pearl Harbor attack. Fortunately not all of the US fleet had been docked at Pearl Harbor hence the United States had enough naval power to win the aircraft carrier battle at Midway. The Japanese had attacked China, the United States, Britain, and the Dutch East Indies, and now had all of them arrayed against Tokyo behind the formidable US Navy and American air power. Like Germany, Japan's days were numbered but no one knew what that number would be nor the extent of casualties that would be exacted to secure the unconditional surrender of Japan.

While the United States conducted an "island hopping" campaign in the Pacific, the Allies waged war to the north in the **China-Burma-India The-ater**. The Allies met with frustration, as Britain was more interested in retaining its colonial empire in India, Burma, and Malaya, and the Chinese leader Chiang Kai-shek was more interested in fighting the Chinese communists than

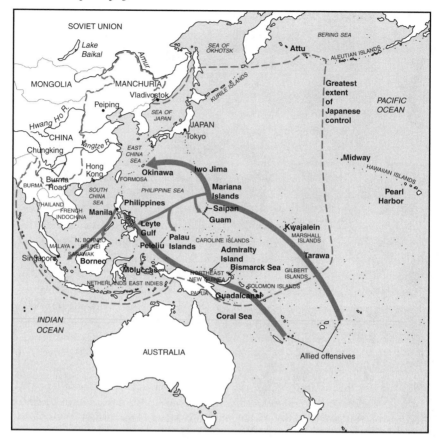

Map 8.2 World War II in the Pacific.

the Japanese aggressors. US General Joseph Stilwell clashed with Chiang, forcing Roosevelt to recall him at Chiang's request. As Japan receded, the communists continued to gain ground in China. Meanwhile, Churchill and the French government in exile in London chafed over Roosevelt's call for an end to European colonialism after the war.

In keeping with American tradition Roosevelt placed high hopes in China, which he expected to join the United States, Britain, and the USSR as one of the **"four policemen"** in the postwar world. In an effort to combine realism and idealism, Roosevelt wanted to achieve Wilson's dream of establishing a viable international organization to replace the League of Nations, but one that would be anchored by the four policemen. He was willing to recognize the reality of Soviet power in the postwar world while advocating for other nations' self-determination and the "four freedoms"—freedom of speech and of worship and freedom from want and from fear.

Figure 8.9 US diplomacy in East Asia rested on the ill-fated hopes that Generalissimo Chiang Kai-shek could establish China as the "fourth policeman" of the postwar world. Chiang is shown here with his wife Madame Chiang (Soong Mai-ling), who anchored the potent China Lobby in Congress.

Source: Library of Congress, Prints and Photographs Division, LC-USZ62-118807.

In October 1944 Churchill, concerned that the Soviets would put communist regimes in power in areas that they were liberating from the Nazis, particularly in Eastern Europe, entered into the **percentages agreement** at a meeting with Stalin in Moscow. Under the secret understanding they agreed that the Soviets would have predominant influence over the border states of

Romania and Bulgaria, the British would dominate liberated Greece, and the two powers would have equivalent influence over postwar Yugoslavia. A crucial stumbling block remained the borders and political orientation of postwar Poland.

As long as the war continued, and with Roosevelt as the fulcrum, the focus on the common enemy kept the Grand Alliance intact. In 1943 the Dumbarton Oaks Conference in Washington produced agreement on the new **United Nations (UN) Organization** to replace the League of Nations and to provide collective security in the postwar world. The next year the **Bretton Woods Conference** in New Hampshire launched two crucial international financial organizations, the **International Monetary Fund (IMF)** and the **World Bank**. The IMF would provide temporary relief to countries having trade and exchange problems in an effort to fend off protectionism or devaluation of currencies. Meanwhile wealthier countries would pool their resources in the World Bank in order to loan money to weaker economies, thus avoiding financial collapses and economic nationalism. The two new entities showed how much the shadow of the Depression and fear of its recurrence hung over the world. The two conferences held on US soil also reflected the rise of the United States to preponderant global economic and political power.

The high point of the Grand Alliance came with the long delayed but ultimately successful opening of the second front in the Normandy invasion. On June 6, 1944, the D-Day landings of **Operation Overlord** began under the direction of General Dwight D. Eisenhower. The successful landing led to the liberation of France and the Low Countries on the western coast of Europe. When in January 1945 the Allies repulsed a last-gasp Nazi offensive known as the **Battle of the Bulge**, the war in Europe was effectively over. Bitter fighting and a relentless Allied bombing campaign continued until Hitler committed suicide in his bunker and the Germans surrendered on May 8.

Three months previously, in February 1945 the **Yalta Conference**, held in the Soviet Crimea, reflected the arrival of the USSR to great power status as a result of the imminent victory in World War II. Though fatigued and long disabled by the polio virus Roosevelt nonetheless traveled to the Crimean Peninsula to shore up the Grand Alliance as the war wound down. The conference, the last meeting of the Big Three for Roosevelt, produced agreement on the structure of the UN, and the coming occupation of Germany. It also confirmed Soviet entry into the war against Japan and Stalin's willingness to recognize Chiang's nationalist regime rather than that of the communists amid what had become a full scale civil war in China.

The agreements at Yalta were substantial but the Allies diverged on the political composition of postwar Poland. They agreed that Poland's borders would be moved west, with areas in the east handed over to the USSR while new areas taken from Germany would become part of Poland to the west. But Stalin wanted the communist "Lublin Poles" to have predominant political influence whereas Churchill wanted to have the exiled "London Poles" compete for power. Britain had gone to war over Poland and the USSR had been invaded through the Polish Corridor so the fate of the country was important to both. Roosevelt worried about alienating Polish Catholic voters at home and did not want to see Poland become a Soviet sphere of influence. At Yalta the Big Three produced the **Declaration of Liberated Europe**, declaring there would be free elections, though Stalin had warned that he preferred the "math" of facts on the ground rather than the "algebra" of such grand declarations.

The death of Roosevelt on April 12 stunned everyone and left the Grand Alliance without its leading partner. The new president, Harry Truman, a senator from Missouri, had been put on the ticket for Roosevelt's fourth term in the 1944 campaign at the insistence of Democrats who believed Vice President Henry Wallace was too liberal and too tolerant of socialism and communism. Admitting that he had virtually no experience in foreign affairs, Truman turned for advice to the State Department, where staunch anti-communists had opposed collaboration with the Soviets and deeply resented Roosevelt's bypassing of the normal channels of diplomacy. The change was not immediate but over time Truman drew a harder line with the Soviets. Moreover, the victory in Europe removed the common enemy that had anchored the unlikely alliance in the first place.

In the summer of 1945 the Grand Alliance remained intact during the **Potsdam Conference** just outside Berlin, where Truman joined Stalin and Churchill for the first time. In the midst of the conference Clement Atlee replaced Churchill, whose government fell in London. Thus Stalin, who never faced anything as troublesome as a reelection campaign, was the only remaining member of the Big Three. More specific agreements on Germany emerged, but Stalin continued to insist on the primacy of the Lublin Poles. The Allies issued the Potsdam Declaration to the effect that Japan must surrender immediately and unconditionally or face "prompt and utter destruction."

Truman had learned by this time that the Trinity test blast in the New Mexico desert had been successful, confirming that the United States had developed an atomic bomb. At the outset of the war Roosevelt had authorized the **Manhattan Project**, an intensive scientific research program into the feasibility of creating a new weapon of unprecedented power by means of atomic fission. The British collaborated in the Manhattan Project but the Soviet Union had not been informed of its existence. The United States won the race to build the bomb and the subsequent decision to use it against Japan went virtually unquestioned. At Potsdam Truman casually informed Stalin that the United States had developed "a new weapon of unusual destructive force." The Soviet dictator feigned disinterest and told Truman he hoped they would use it on Japan. The successful atomic research program was no revelation to Stalin, who had been kept apprised all along by spies in Britain, Canada, and the United States.

Figure 8.10 The United States unleashed the atomic age with the bombing of the
Japanese cities of Hiroshima (shown here in the aftermath) and Nagasaki
on August 6 and 9, 1945, causing the deaths of more than 200,000 people.

Source: Library of Congress, Prints and Photographs Division, LC-USZ62-134192.

In Their Words

*Yoshitaka Kawamoto recalls the atomic bombing of Hiroshima on August 6, 1945.
Thirteen years old at the time, he was in his school classroom less than a mile from
the epicenter of the bombing*

One of my classmates, I think his name is Fujimoto, he muttered something and pointed outside the window, saying, "A B-29 is coming." He
pointed outside with his finger. So I began to get up from my chair and
asked him, "Where is it?" Looking in the direction that he was pointing
towards, I got up on my feet, but I was not yet in an upright position
when it happened. All I can remember was a pale lightning flash for two
or three seconds. Then, I collapsed. I don't know how much time passed
before I came to. It was awful, awful. The smoke was coming in from
somewhere above the debris. Sandy dust was flying around. I was trapped
under the debris and I was in terrible pain and that's probably why I
came to. I couldn't move, not even an inch. Then, I heard about ten of
my surviving classmates singing our school song. I remember that. I could
hear sobs. Someone was calling his mother. But those who were still alive
were singing the school song for as long as they could. I think I joined the

chorus. We thought that someone would come and help us out. That's why we were singing a school song so loud. But nobody came to help, and we stopped singing one by one. In the end, I was singing alone.

Source: Inicom, Inc., Voice of Hibakusha, Testimony of Yoshitaka Kawamoto

The decision had been made to drop two bombs on separate Japanese targets. On August 6 the United States dropped the first atomic weapon on Hiroshima and three days later bombed Nagasaki. The Japanese had not had time to fully understand and respond to the first attack, which killed some 100,000 people and leveled the city. The Soviet entry into the Pacific War on August 8 pushed Japan over the edge to surrender. On the day of the atomic bombing of Nagasaki, the Soviet Union invaded Manchuria, as stipulated by Allied war plans.

Interpreting the Past

The atomic bombings of Japan

The US decision to drop atomic bombs on Hiroshima and Nagasaki and the role of these new weapons in ending the war in August 1945 have generated considerable discussion and a stubborn mythology. In a carefully orchestrated official explanation, former Secretary of War Henry Stimson claimed in an article in *Harper's* magazine in February 1947 that the use of the bombs was "the least abhorrent choice," one that led to Japan's unconditional surrender and saved hundreds of thousands of Japanese and moreover American lives that would have been lost in a land invasion of the Japanese home islands. This explanation has enjoyed remarkable staying power in US society but historians have shown it to be deeply flawed.

By August 1945 Japan, surrounded by the US Navy, bereft of resources and war materials, and daily pounded by American air power, was on the brink of defeat. US planners did not believe it would be necessary to invade the home islands nor had they compiled studies projecting that hundreds of thousands of US soldiers would have to die to bring the war to an end. The atomic bombings made surprisingly little impact on Japanese war leaders, who had grown accustomed to massive US attacks such as the firebombing of Tokyo that killed about 100,000 people on March 9–10, 1945. Of more concern to the Japanese militarists was the massive, 1-million-man Soviet Red Army invasion of Japanese-occupied Manchuria, which began the day of the Nagasaki bombing and raised the specter of a brutal occupation and eventual communization of Japan. However, even after the atomic bombings and the Soviet invasion Japan still rejected the Allied demand of unconditional surrender. Only after the United States agreed to allow the emperor to remain on the throne albeit in a strictly ceremonial role did Japan's wartime leaders agree to end the conflict. The compromise on the status of the emperor rather than the atomic bombings thus ended the war.

Scholars have offered explanations for the use and impact of the bombs ranging from reiterations of Stimson's tendentious arguments of saving lives to claims that the United States used the bombs to defeat Japan before the Soviet invasion could improve Russia's position at the bargaining table. These scholars thus argued that use of the bombs was the opening salvo in the cold war. The best explanation for use of the bombs, however, is deceptively simple: the United States developed the new military technology with every intention of using it on the battlefield (as they believed their enemies would have done). The decision to drop the bombs reflected this technological imperative more than wartime strategy or humanitarian concerns.

On August 14, Japan surrendered aboard the USS *Missouri*, but only after General MacArthur pledged that Emperor Hirohito could remain enthroned purely as a figurehead. Previously the unconditional surrender policy held that the emperor must be deposed and thus potentially put on trial for war crimes. Japan would not surrender under such circumstances, hence the United States compromised on the status of the emperor after the atomic bombings.

Consequences of World War II

World War II was incomparably destructive and profoundly consequential. Precise figures will never be known but estimates are that more than 60 million people died in the war, with the USSR accounting for about 25 million of the total. Some 11 million Chinese died; about 7 million Germans and 7 million Poles; some 2 million Japanese; and about 400,000 Americans. The destruction of animals, crops, farms, homes, roads, vehicles, bridges, factories, and buildings in the belligerent countries of North Africa, Europe, and Asia was massive beyond measure. Looting, sexual assault, and other depredations occurred in all theaters of World War II and involved all the belligerent countries.

Although atomic weapons would change the nature and potential consequences of warfare, the Hiroshima and Nagasaki bombings complemented the overall Allied bombing campaign rather than diverged from it. War planners viewed air power as a transcendent force, opening the door to bombing campaigns that in the last months of the war became indiscriminate. Distinctions between military and civilian targets had eroded to such an extent that the military did not think twice about incinerating some 100,000 people in a single firebombing raid on Tokyo in March 1945. On the European front, Allied bombing killed more than 300,000 German *civilians* and left some 800,000

Germans wounded and 7.5 million homeless. The psychological impact of the war and the terror it unleashed, on soldiers as well as civilians of all theaters, was incalculable but profound.

Genocide was not new but the industrial style of the Nazi Holocaust targeting Jews and other minorities was unprecedented. Though most victims of Nazism died by conventional means—for example a gunshot to the head—the transporting, warehousing, and gassing primarily of Jews but also Romanies ("Gypsies"), homosexuals, and disabled people shocked the world. The Allies had known about the **Nazi genocide** since 1942 but had not taken direct action to stop the Holocaust so as not to deviate from what they viewed as the most efficient prosecution of the overall war effort.

The widespread death and destruction and the horrors of the Nazi genocide laid the groundwork for the emergence of the postwar peace and human rights movements. Eleanor Roosevelt, a longtime supporter of women's rights and of peaceful internationalism, played a major role. In 1945 Truman appointed the longtime first lady to the US delegation to the UN. Eleanor Roosevelt interviewed survivors of the Nazi genocide and insisted that the new UN take action in an effort to preclude such horrors in the future. In 1948 she played a key role in the drafting of the **Universal Declaration of Human Rights**, approved by the UN General Assembly on December 10 of that year. At the same time the UN also approved the **Convention on the Prevention and Punishment of the Crime of Genocide** defined as, "Any of a number of acts committed with the intent to destroy, in whole or part, a national, ethnic, racial or religious group."

The wartime emphasis on liberation from aggression and human rights fueled the postwar drive for **decolonization** in another highly significant consequence of World War II (Chapter 11). As in World War I the emphasis on self-determination combined with President Roosevelt's Four Freedoms resonated across the globe. The defeat of Germany and Japan and the weakening of Britain, France, Belgium, and the Netherlands left the colonized nations in a much stronger position to assert and achieve their independence than they were in the aftermath of the Great War. The gradual dissolution of the colonial empires would thus become one of the most consequential outcomes of World War II.

While the European powers suffered gravely and faced the dissolution of their colonial empires, other than the wartime casualties and the attack on colonial Hawai'i the United States escaped unscathed and emerged as the clear winner of World War II. The US economy, still mired in the seemingly endless depression before the war, roared to life under the demands of wartime production, creating full employment and unleashing a prolonged economic boom. The dollar reigned supreme, as New York emerged as the world's financial capital and Washington as the world's political capital. The United States dominated the new UN, headquartered in New York. With its economic and cultural influence soaring, American exceptionalism flourished as the United States strove to shape the direction of the world into the next century.

Figure 8.11 Eleanor Roosevelt redefined the role of "first lady" and became an important national and international figure perhaps most notably in helping to forge the Universal Declaration of Human Rights, approved by the UN General Assembly in 1948. Ten years earlier she had become the first woman ever to address the National Press Club luncheon (pictured above).

Source: Library of Congress, Prints and Photographs Division, LC-DIG-hec-47422.

Americans thus came to perceive World War II as a proud and just war waged against unambiguous enemies and culminating in the nation's providentially destined rise to global leadership. As two-thirds of American men aged 18 to 34 served, the war became a model of patriotic duty handed down to future generations. Iconic images from the "good war" endure, including the photograph from 1945 of US soldiers raising the American

Flag on Iwo Jima's Mount Suribachi; images of victory parades from Times Square to San Diego; and countless books and films in the ensuing years celebrating the wartime triumph of citizen soldiers, a veritable "band of brothers." World War II thus endured as the nation's preeminent reference point of pride, patriotism, a triumph of the "greatest generation." The "good war" imagery crowded out memories of unrestrained bombing, civilian deaths, and inaction in response to the Nazi genocide, among other less salutary legacies.

World War II profoundly affected American society. Women, African-Americans, and Hispanics moved around the country and entered the military and the workforce in unprecedented numbers. Their heightened sense of empowerment and rights' consciousness had sweeping consequences in the postwar era, giving rise to the civil rights and women's movements. The booming wartime and postwar economy spurred a boom of babies and the rapid growth of cities and suburbs, and the emergence of a highly mobile society albeit one increasingly dependent on crude oil and the automobile.

As in the Great War, persuasion gave way to propaganda during World War II, a trend that carried over into the postwar era. The Office of War Information dispensed reams of "public information" through print and radio, distributed evocative propaganda posters, and sponsored films and newsreels to ensure that Americans could distinguish their enemies from their allies and understand the nation's wartime goals and the sacrifices they needed to make to support them. Hollywood willingly accepted an unprecedented level of government censorship, as actors, writers, directors, and producers signed on to the government mandate to make films that would bolster the war effort and to refrain from making those that did not. The films reflected widespread American racial mores, as the "Japs" were routinely described in such terms as Nips, beasts, monkeys, and slant-eyed rats. The Italians and Germans fared somewhat better, as they were depicted as misguided European whites who had fallen victim of fanatic leaders who had to be subdued.

Finally, within a relatively short period of time the wartime Grand Alliance collapsed and gave way to a conflict that became known as the **cold war** (next chapter). No longer with a common enemy to unite them, and absent a figure of Roosevelt's towering stature to keep the Alliance intact, Soviet-American relations deteriorated. Ironically, the wartime propaganda set the stage for the cold war by depicting the Soviet Union and "Uncle Joe" Stalin as a willing partner in forging a pluralistic world order. When Stalin insisted on an expanded sphere of influence in light of the massive Soviet contribution to the Allied war effort, the public was quickly disillusioned and willing to embrace revived images of an implacably hostile, "godless communist," global adversary. Unable or unwilling to continue cooperation in establishing a new world order, the former Allies thus became bitter ideological and geopolitical antagonists, though they stopped short of engaging in a "hot" shooting war. Like World War II, the cold war would become global in scope and no less profound in its consequences.

Select Bibliography

Heinrichs, Waldo. *Threshold of War; Franklin D. Roosevelt and American Entry into World War II*. New York: Oxford University Press, 1988.

Dallek, Franklin D. *Roosevelt and American Foreign Policy*. New York: Oxford University Press, 1985.

Kimball, Warren F. *The Juggler: Franklin D. Roosevelt as Wartime Statesman*. Princeton, NJ: Princeton University Press, 1991.

Reynolds, David S. *The Creation of the Anglo American Alliance: A Study in Competitive Cooperation*. Chapel Hill: University of North Carolina Press, 1981.

Doenecke, Justus. *Storm on the Horizon: The Challenge to American Intervention, 1939–1941*. Lanham, MD: Rowan & Littlefield, 2000.

Sherry, Michael S. *The Rise of American Air Power: The Creation of Armageddon*. New Haven, CT: Yale University Press, 1987.

Rosenberg, Emily S. *A Date which Shall Live: Pearl Harbor in American Memory*. Durham, NC: Duke University Press, 2005.

Koistinen, Paul. *Arsenal of World War II: The Political Economy of American Warfare*. Lawrence: University of Kansas Press, 2012.

Schmitz, David. *Thank God They're on Our Side: The United States and Right-Wing Dictatorships, 1921–1965*. Chapel Hill: University of North Carolina Press, 1999.

Little, Douglas. *Malevolent Neutrality: The United States, Great Britain, and the Origins of the Spanish Civil War*. Ithaca, NY: Cornell University Press, 1985.

Carley, Michael J. *1939: The Alliance that Never Was and the Coming of World War II*. Chicago: Ivan Dee, 1999.

Cull, Nicolas. *Selling War: The British Propaganda Campaign Against American 'Neutrality' in World War II*. New York: Oxford University Press, 1995.

Dower, John. *War Without Mercy: Race and Power in the Pacific War*. New York: Pantheon Books, 1985.

Hitchcock, William I. *The Bitter Road to Freedom: A New History of the Liberation of Europe*. New York: The Free Press, 2008.

Jarvis, Christina S. *The Male Body at War: American Masculinity During World War II*. DeKalb: Northern Illinois University Press, 2004.

9 The Cold War

Overview

For the second time in a generation the United States had intervened and triumphed in a foreign war only to lose the peace. World War II, like World War I, failed to deliver on the American president's grand design of a world made safe for freedom and democracy. Having failed to produce either a fully "liberated Europe" or a "democratic China," the world war instead brought a perpetuation of hostility in the form of the global cold war. In the years immediately following World War II, the United States adopted a policy of global "**containment**" of communism, created a national security state, took the lead in escalating the nuclear arms race, and fought a "hot" shooting war on the Korean Peninsula.

The Division of Europe

In February 1941, months before US intervention in World War II, Henry Luce, born in China to missionary parents and the publisher of *Time-Life*, pronounced the arrival of the "**American Century**." Much as John O'Sullivan had trumpeted Manifest Destiny just prior to the Mexican War, Luce declared in an article followed by a bestselling book that the United States would dominate the twentieth century. Race, religion, and manliness underlay Luce's invocation of American exceptionalism. As a providentially chosen nation, the United States should assert its power, assume world leadership, and spread its way of life across the globe. The nation should "exert upon the world the full impact of our influence, for such purposes as we see fit and by such means as we see fit."

The Atlantic Charter complemented by the Four Freedoms had established the framework of war aims, including freedom of the seas, free trade, collective security, and other ideals reminiscent of President Wilson's Fourteen Points. On January 1, 1942, 26 nations signed the Declaration of the United Nations, committing themselves to the principles of the Atlantic Charter. Americans thus mobilized for war armed with the faith that their chosen nation was leading the world into a new era of liberal progress under God. Victory in the war would liberate Europe, as promised at the Yalta Conference, while China would emerge as the "fourth policeman" anchoring democratic values in Asia.

Figure 9.1 Claire Boothe Luce and her husband Henry Luce were both prominent internationalists. Henry Luce was the longtime publisher of *Time-Life*. In 1954, when this photograph was taken upon their arrival at New York's Idlewild Airport, Claire Boothe Luce was serving as the US ambassador to Italy.

Source: Library of Congress, Prints and Photographs Division, LC-USZ62-124600.

As President Harry Truman intoned after the war, "Now this great Republic— the greatest in history, the greatest the sun has ever shone upon—is charged with leadership in the world for the welfare of the whole world."

The United States emerged from the war as the most powerful nation in the world, but its values and leadership were not universally embraced. Europe was not fully liberated and China devolved first into civil war and then into a dictatorship under the Chinese Communist Party. Rather than a unified international order the world fell into a bitter ideological and geopolitical struggle fraught with violence and the threat of nuclear war.

Americans blamed the Soviet Union and the spread of communism for the onset of the cold war. The division of Europe, however, was also set up by the US strategy in the European theater of World War II. The United States had supplied the Russian war effort and sponsored the "unconditional surrender" policy that encouraged the Red Army to fight its way across Eastern Europe all the way to Berlin. By the time the Allies opened the second front in the Normandy invasion in June 1944, the Soviet Red Army occupied half of the European continent. The strategy had worked brilliantly in terms of winning the war while keeping US casualties to a minimum. Sixty-five Soviets died for every one American loss of life in World War II. But the strategy also provided the Soviets with considerable leverage in establishing the postwar order in Eastern Europe. Similarly the United States exploited its leverage and acted unilaterally in the occupations and postwar alignment of North Africa, Italy, Western Europe, and Japan while reinforcing the Monroe Doctrine in Latin America.

At Yalta Stalin acceded to his allies' request to sign the **Declaration of Liberated Europe** promising free elections after the war. At the same time, however, the Soviet dictator made it clear that Russia required "friendly" governments on its borders after being attacked twice within a generation by the Germans. Stalin had shown his intentions in the late summer of 1944 when the Red Army declined to come to the aid of the Poles in the **Warsaw Uprising** against the Nazis. Stalin despised the Polish nationalists who rose up precisely to try to take control of the capital city before the Red Army arrived. Ironically, however, without Soviet assistance they could not prevail. The Nazis crushed the uprising and destroyed the city, leaving Poland vulnerable to control by forces friendly to Moscow once the Soviets arrived and drove the Nazis out.

Roosevelt and especially Churchill had urged the "London Poles" to accept the new Soviet-dictated Polish borders and compromise with the Russian-backed "Lublin Poles." Churchill insisted, "The sacrifices made by the Soviet Union in the course of the war against Germany and its efforts toward liberating Poland entitle it" to acceptance of the new borders and political influence. The London Poles rejected the call to compromise. Unlike Roosevelt, who ignored them, State Department diplomats, especially those posted in Moscow, condemned the USSR. They decried the Soviet unwillingness to come to the aid of the rebels in Warsaw, inaction they viewed as a cynical means of ensuring the spread of Soviet influence over postwar Poland.

Well aware that in the previous war the Western powers had sought to isolate and destroy Bolshevism, Stalin pursued a buffer zone of "friendly" states around the USSR. "This war is not as in the past," he declared privately. "Whoever occupies a territory also imposes on it his own social system. It can be no other way." Similarly, Vyacheslav Molotov, Stalin's foreign minister, explained years later in his memoirs that Roosevelt had "miscalculated" in thinking that reconstruction aid after the war would restrain the USSR, and "they woke up only when half of Europe had passed from them . . . They certainly hardened against us but we had to consolidate our conquests."

While the Soviets sought a buffer zone and expanded spheres of influence, Stalin remained cautious, more traditional than ideological in his approach to diplomacy. He cared more about establishing a non-threatening Poland than necessarily a communist one. He restrained the ambitions of Bulgarian communists until the cold war began to solidify in 1947. Like the tsars Stalin held onto the Baltic Republics of Estonia, Latvia, and Lithuania, but in neighboring Finland he settled for a "soft" sphere of influence while showing little interest in the politics of Scandinavia. Stalin tried to hold back Yugoslavian communism and turned a deaf ear to continuing Greek communist pleas to support an armed takeover. The Soviets supported the non-communist coalition led by Charles de Gaulle in France, urged Italian comrades to compromise with the right wing, and initially held back the German Marxists who sought to push ahead with communization until the cold war led to the division of Germany.

Stalin proved willing to compromise and on occasion to back off but he could also harden the Soviet position in response to confrontational policies in the West. Seeking to exert control over the Black Sea, the Soviets applied pressure on neighboring Turkey. In 1946 they also failed to meet the agreed deadline to withdraw occupation troops from Iran. In both cases Western protests prompted Stalin to back off and avoid confrontation.

Conversely, when Stalin came to the conclusion that the United States and Britain were hardening against the Soviet Union, he responded angrily while carefully avoiding actions that might lead to war. Stalin had shown flexibility in 1946–47 but thereafter the Soviet sphere hardened commensurate with the breakdown of Allied diplomacy. Truman and Churchill—even though the latter was no longer in power—played a critical role in the coming of the cold war. Unlike Roosevelt, who kept his own counsel with the help of a handful of intimate advisers, the inexperienced Truman relied on the advice of diplomats, many of them inveterate anti-communists who had either never been in favor of allying with the USSR or no longer favored cooperation now that the war was over.

One such diplomat was George F. Kennan, fluent in Russian and the nation's preeminent Soviet expert. Posted on and off in Moscow since the opening of the US embassy in 1933, Kennan detested communism, considered Roosevelt naive, and opposed the Grand Alliance from the outset. In February 1946 Kennan sent the 8,000-word "long telegram" from Moscow warning that the USSR would continue to expand unless it was stopped. In the **long telegram** and an anonymously published article the following year in the establishment journal *Foreign Affairs*, Kennan urged adoption of a policy of long-term "containment" of communism. Containment, Kennan theorized, would curb Soviet influence, force the Russians to recede from East-Central Europe, and ultimately destabilize communism in Russia, which he asserted depended on expansion for survival. The ultimate goal of containment was thus the destruction of Soviet communism.

Figure 9.2 From 1944 to 1947 George F. Kennan, a veteran diplomat with extensive
experience in the USSR, articulated the US cold war strategy of anti-
communist "containment." By 1950 Kennan had concluded, ironically,
that the United States lacked the ability to carry out mature internationalist
diplomacy. He removed to Princeton and became a revered foreign policy
intellectual until his death in 2005 at the age of 101.

Source: Library of Congress, Prints and Photographs Division, LC-DIG-hec-12925.

In Their Words

*Excerpt from Winston Churchill's "Iron Curtain" speech in Fulton, Missouri,
March 5, 1946*

A shadow has fallen upon the scenes so lately lighted by the Allied victory. Nobody knows what Soviet Russia and its Communist international organization intends to do in the immediate future, or what are
the limits, if any, to their expansive and proselytizing tendencies. I have
a strong admiration and regard for the valiant Russian people and for
my wartime comrade, Marshal Stalin. There is sympathy and good will
in Britain – and I doubt not here also – toward the peoples of all the

Russias and a resolve to persevere through many differences and rebuffs in establishing lasting friendships. We understand the Russians need to be secure on her western frontiers from all renewal of German aggression. We welcome her to her rightful place among the leading nations of the world. Above all we welcome constant, frequent, and growing contacts between the Russian people and our own people on both sides of the Atlantic. It is my duty, however, to place before you certain facts about the present position in Europe – I am sure I do not wish to, but it is my duty, I feel, to present them to you.

From Stettin in the Baltic to Trieste in the Adriatic, an iron curtain has descended across the Continent. Behind that line lie all the capitals of the ancient states of central and eastern Europe. Warsaw, Berlin, Prague, Vienna, Budapest, Belgrade, Bucharest and Sofia, all these famous cities and the populations around them lie in the Soviet sphere and all are subject in one form or another, not only to Soviet influence but to a very high and increasing measure of control from Moscow. Athens alone, with its immortal glories, is free to decide its future at an election under British, American and French observation. The Russian dominated Polish government has been encouraged to make enormous and wrongful inroads upon Germany, and mass expulsions of millions of Germans on a scale grievous and undreamed of are now taking place. The Communist parties, which were very small in all these eastern states of Europe, have been raised to pre-eminence and power far beyond their numbers and are seeking everywhere to obtain totalitarian control. Police governments are prevailing in nearly every case . . . Whatever conclusion may be drawn from these facts – and facts they are – this is certainly not the liberated Europe we fought to build up. Nor is it one which contains the essentials of permanent peace.

Containment was a strategy that struck a chord with Truman and the foreign policy establishment in Washington. In January 1946 Truman declared that he was "tired of babying" the Soviets who were failing to abide by their wartime agreements. On March 5, speaking at Fulton, Missouri, with Truman beaming alongside, Churchill proclaimed that an "**iron curtain**" had descended across the European continent. Although he had entered into the percentages agreement seemingly acquiescing to a Soviet sphere of influence in 1944, Churchill now condemned Kremlin efforts to establish "totalitarian control." Stalin, who had given a speech of his own declaring the ultimate incompatibility of communism and capitalism, condemned Churchill's speech and called his former alliance partner a "firebrand of war."

Tensions accelerated in March 1947 with the pronouncement of the **Truman Doctrine**, a program of military aid to Greece and Turkey and a virtual US declaration of cold war. A homegrown communist insurgency was bidding for power in Greece while Russia put pressure on Turkey by calling for the revision of international agreements on control of the key straits of the Bosphorus and the Dardanelles. The British, weakened by the war, informed Washington they could no longer police their traditional sphere of influence in the Mediterranean. Truman stepped in, declaring that the United States was sending $400 million in economic and military aid to Greece and Turkey. With US aid the Greek monarchy eventually defeated the leftists while Turkey moved into the Western camp.

Truman's rhetoric went beyond the issue of military aid, however, as he declared that the world had become divided between "alternative ways of life" of freedom and totalitarianism. "It must be the policy of the United States to support free peoples who are resisting attempted subjugation by armed minorities or by outside pressures." The Truman Doctrine thus established a policy framework enabling a series of future US interventions against communist movements in countries all over the world. Despite the reference to supporting "free peoples," the United States, as in the case of Greece and Turkey, often armed and equipped undemocratic regimes, as long as they were anti-communist.

US officials sought military superiority in order to be able to intervene when and where such action was deemed essential to national security. While the USSR had the largest army in the world the United States had by far the dominant navy and air force and maintained a **global military base system**. Beginning with the destroyers for bases deal with Britain, the United States consolidated control of the Caribbean and asserted its preponderant influence on the Atlantic as well as the Pacific. World War II thus provided the foundation for the postwar global network of military bases, with profound implications not only for US security policy but for the host countries as well. With bases located in every major region of the world, US leaders would not shy away from assertions of power. "As long as we can out-produce the world, can control the sea and can strike inland with the atomic bomb we can assume certain risks otherwise unacceptable," Secretary of Defense James Forrestal advised in 1947.

As the cold war unfolded the United States reorganized the foreign policy and defense bureaucracy, developing a **national security state** in the process. The National Security Act (1947) made the Air Force, formerly part of the Army, into a separate branch of the military services, now overseen by a new entity, the **Joint Chiefs of Staff** (JCS), with the Army, Navy, Marines, and Air Force represented by a top general. While the State Department grew and remained at the center of American diplomacy, a new **National Security Council** (NSC) was set up to assess specific foreign policy situations and draw up recommendations, which became policy when approved by the president. Finally the National Security Act created the **Central Intelligence Agency** (CIA), primarily to gather information but also to spearhead "political warfare" and covert operations.

While the United States enhanced its capabilities to wage the cold war, diplomacy with the Soviets continued into 1947. The US, Soviet, and other

Allied foreign ministers discussed the ongoing joint occupation of Germany as well as plans for economic reconstruction. Still mindful of the delays in opening the second front and enormous losses in the war, the Soviet Union expected the United States to deliver on promises of major reconstruction aid. While the USSR lay in ruins, the United States emerged from the war unscathed and the economic powerhouse of the world. The Washington-dominated and -headquartered World Bank and IMF, established in 1944, provided the nation with unparalleled influence over postwar reconstruction efforts and the global economy.

The United States exercised its economic supremacy with the **Marshall Plan**, named after Secretary of State George Marshall and announced in June 1947. Formally the European Recovery Program (ERP), the Marshall Plan was a program of loans and reconstruction assistance designed to get the war-torn economies up and running. The United States and Britain were especially fearful that communist parties in France and Italy might exploit economic

Figure 9.3 President Harry Truman reaches out to shake the hand of General George C. Marshall, a World War II hero for his service as secretary of the Army. Months after becoming Truman's secretary of state in 1947, Marshall announced the European Recovery Program for postwar reconstruction of the continent. He later served as secretary of defense and in 1953 became the only career Army officer to receive the Nobel Peace Prize.

Source: Library of Congress, Prints and Photographs Division, LC-USZ62-103396.

weaknesses and come to power by legal means. If countries of Western Europe went communist, crucial economic linkages would be lost and the United States might lapse back into depression.

The ERP brought a needed infusion of money and optimism to the war-ravaged societies, thus linking Western Europe with the United States. The Marshall Plan closed the "dollar gap" by providing money needed by the Europeans to purchase goods. As many of these goods were manufactured in the United States, the Marshall Plan stimulated the US economy while spurring postwar reconstruction. The US financial assistance helped undermine the appeal of the Communist Parties in both France and Italy. The new CIA also covertly intervened with infusions of cash and political or psychological warfare to undermine the appeal of the Communist Parties. The CIA covertly funneled millions of dollars into the Italian Christian Democratic Party, thus helping to sway the national elections in 1948.

Beneficial for the United States and Western Europe, the Marshall Plan also cemented the division of Europe and thus fueled the cold war. US officials deliberately framed the Marshall Plan in such a way as to "make it quite impossible for the Soviet Union to accept [it]," as diplomat Charles Bohlen put it. Although devastated by the war, the USSR would have to contribute rather than receive aid and also divulge secret information about the Soviet economy. In July Molotov angrily walked out of the foreign ministers meeting in Paris. By this time the cold war can be said to have begun in earnest. The USSR forced Czechoslovakia out of the meeting, ousted its liberal leader Jan Masaryk (who was then either killed or committed suicide), and forcibly incorporated it into the Soviet sphere.

The Czech coup stirred bitter memories of Hitler and fueled a "**Munich syndrome**" in the halls of Western diplomacy. In 1938 at the Munich Conference the British and French had attempted to moderate Hitler with a policy of appeasement, but the Nazi dictator had instead seized control of Czechoslovakia and later invaded Poland thus bringing on the war. The lesson drawn from this history became known as the Munich syndrome, which held that appeasement of aggressors only encouraged further aggression and that it was thus necessary to draw a hard line. Foreign policy elites linked Nazi Germany and the USSR under the popular new framework of "**totalitarianism**," sometimes losing sight of important distinctions between Stalin and Hitler, the Soviet Union and Nazi Germany. Whereas Hitler was rash and gloried in war, Stalin though ruthless with his domestic enemies pursued a cautious foreign policy reflecting a determination to avoid war with the West.

In the wake of the Czech coup the Truman administration fomented an atmosphere of crisis emphasizing the threat of war with the USSR in an effort to ensure passage of the Marshall Plan and funding for the military, especially the new Air Force. Worried that the Republican Congress would not approve the Marshall Plan and its proposed military buildup, Truman administration officials, notably Marshall, Forrestal, and presidential adviser Clark Clifford, emphasized the threat of war and a Soviet master plan to

Figure 9.4 In 1948–49 the United States coordinated the Berlin Airlift in response to a Soviet ground blockade of the former Reich capital city.

Source: Library of Congress, Prints and Photographs Division, LC-USZ62-136389.

dominate the world. Soviet experts in Washington and Moscow privately rejected the war scare rhetoric as overwrought, but they were ignored. Administration officials including the president also emphasized an "internal security" threat of domestic communism, with Clifford later admitting it was "manufactured" in order to discredit left-wing opposition and especially presidential candidate Henry A. Wallace. The war scare helped gain congressional approval of the national security agenda, including a 30 percent increase in the Pentagon budget and a whopping 57 percent increase in aircraft procurement.

The Soviets sharply condemned the war scare rhetoric, which contributed to the Kremlin decision to clamp down in the eastern sphere of occupied Germany. While the Soviets sought reparations the US-led Western powers sought to reintegrate postwar Germany in a stable European economic order. Beginning in 1945 under **Operation Paperclip**, Washington also began secretly to bring German scientists and engineers including some former Nazis to the United States to tap their expertise in rocket science and other programs. In 1947 the United States and Britain, joined two years later by the French, merged their occupation zones, which became the eventual West Germany while the Soviets clung to their sphere, the eventual East Germany. In June 1948 the Soviets blocked Western access to Berlin, the former Reich capital located within the Soviet zone. The United States responded to the **Berlin**

Blockade with the Berlin Airlift, flying supplies over the obstructed roads and eventually prompting the USSR to abandon the blockade.

The war scare and the Berlin Blockade promoted worst-case scenarios and exaggerated Soviet capabilities while ignoring the adversary's intentions. The "Soviet threat" was primarily political and economic, that is countries "going" communist and closing off their markets to the capitalist system, not a direct military threat. The Soviet Union was in no position and had no intention of launching a military invasion of countries in Europe, as Hitler had done. World War II left the USSR devastated and in need of reconstruction and thus hardly eager for a renewal of warfare, as the American Soviet experts Kennan and Bohlen repeatedly pointed out. Moreover Stalin embraced an ideology in which capitalism was expected eventually to crumble from its own internal contradictions rather than from outside aggression.

Despite the absence of an actual military threat to Western Europe the United States sponsored a military alliance against the USSR. The **North Atlantic Treaty Organization (NATO)**, a collective security treaty in which an attack on one nation would be considered an attack on all, offered reassurance to anti-communist, western European nations scarred by war. Created in 1949, NATO complemented western European economic and political recovery under the Marshall Plan. NATO also reinforced strong US ties with Canada, an ally in both world wars and now in the cold war. The trans-Atlantic alliance forged a powerful anti-communist consensus among nations yet at the same time NATO, like the Marshall Plan, hardened the division of Europe.

With Congress approving the Marshall Plan, NATO, and the Pentagon budget by wide margins, both Democrats and Republicans trumpeted **bi-partisan foreign policy** in support of containing communism and vigorously waging the cold war. Partisan politics was said to stop at the water's edge during the cold war and it usually did. Gone were the acrimonious prewar debates over whether to intervene in Europe. Having approved military assistance under the Truman Doctrine, Congress stepped up military aid following the passage of NATO. By 1949 nothing remained of the Grand Alliance, as diplomacy had given way to confrontation and a military standoff in the heart of Europe. Hostile rhetoric, espionage, and psychological warfare emanated from both sides of the divide.

The image of the mushroom cloud and the threat of nuclear weapons cast a constant shadow over the world and helped to define the cold war era. Most Americans had celebrated the atomic bomb as the "winning weapon" that had brought an end to World War II. As long as the United States held a monopoly on "the bomb" there was little concern about international control of atomic weapons. Ignoring his scientific advisers, Truman naively believed other powers were years away from developing the bomb hence he had little interest in arms control. Under the **Baruch Plan**, offered in 1946 by the industrialist Bernard Baruch who had presided over the original military–industrial complex in the Great War, the United States proposed to retain the atomic monopoly while the USSR and other powers turned over all fissionable material and submitted to international inspections. As expected the USSR rejected both internal inspections as well as the proposal to give up their own research

Figure 9.5 Prominent internationalist Bernard Baruch, a New York financier shown here in the White House in 1938, chaired the War Industries Board in World War I and devised the ill-fated Baruch Plan on international control of atomic weapons in 1946.

Source: Library of Congress, Prints and Photographs Division, LC-DIG-hec-25185.

and materials while Washington retained its monopoly until the very last stage of the proposed control process. Soviet spies and scientists had already accessed atomic secrets and were hard at work on producing a bomb.

In 1949, much to the shock of the United States and the Western nations, the USSR successfully tested an atomic bomb much earlier than had been anticipated. In a world in which both antagonists were armed with weapons of mass destruction, a hot shooting war could have such devastating consequences that there would be no winners, only losers. Under **mutually assured destruction**—appropriately known as MAD—both sides recognized the potential suicidal consequences of a nuclear strike hence both were deterred from launching one. Accordingly, many argue that the existence of atomic weapons and MAD enabled the cold war to remain cold, as the primary antagonists would fight out the struggle through conventional means and typically by indirect conflict in other countries. In any case by 1949 international control had failed, as the nuclear arms race was under way and would spread to other countries. The JCS among others adamantly opposed attempting to negotiate arms limitation negotiations with Soviets. The next year the United States successfully tested an incomparably more destructive thermonuclear or **hydrogen bomb** and the Soviets followed suit.

The Cold War in Asia

Like World War II the cold war was a *global* phenomenon, with Asia proving to be a volatile theater of conflict. Ironically and in direct contrast to the world war, Japan became America's closest ally while China emerged as the nation's inveterate enemy. American images of the Japanese gradually shifted from the bloodthirsty, simian creatures of wartime to childlike depictions of a wayward Asian people in need of paternal direction from the United States. With China in turmoil amid a civil war involving nationalists, communists, warlords, and various ethnic groups the United States focused on the occupation of Japan. Under General Douglas MacArthur, the hero of the Pacific War, the United States had the power to shape events in postwar Japan that it sorely lacked in China. MacArthur pursued a program to reform Japan and to rein in its powerful, centralized economic structure, the Zaibatsu.

As the cold war unfolded in Europe, concerns mounted that punitive occupation policies and sweeping changes would destabilize Japan, weaken it economically, and make it vulnerable to communism. Under the **reverse course** in occupied Japan, the State Department reversed plans to break up the Zaibatsu, instead allowing men who had been central to the war effort and closely tied to the Japanese military to remain empowered. Under the reverse course, the United States thus emphasized internal security over democratic reform. Rather than conducting extensive war crimes trials, as with the Nuremberg Trials in postwar Germany, the Americans presided over the trial and execution of only a few Japanese wartime leaders. Thus Japanese society was not forced to confront its history of invasion, annihilation campaigns, POW (prisoner-of-war) slave camps, and sexual exploitation of Asian "comfort women." To establish security and fend off reform efforts occupation authorities employed tactics used in other imperial settings including the training of police forces, surveillance, harassment, incarceration, censorship, and intolerance of dissent.

The United States established Japan as the industrial center of the postwar global containment policy in Asia. Less developed countries of Southeast

Asia, including the newly independent Philippines, Malaya, Indonesia, and Indochina, would supply the vital raw materials and natural resources while becoming major trading partners with Japan and the United States. Under this framework, which proved successful, the postwar Asian economy would be robust and well positioned to contain the spread of communism.

In 1949 the "loss" of China to communism ruptured the containment policy in Asia, with far-reaching impacts on US diplomacy and on the home front as well. During World War II, with American traders, missionaries, and global strategists having held strong attachments to China for decades, Roosevelt groomed China to function as one of the "four policemen" in the postwar era (along with the United States, Britain, and the USSR). After nearly being destroyed by Chiang's forces in the 1930s, the Chinese Communist Party under the leadership of **Mao Zedong**, a former Beijing University librarian, took to the countryside and began to build popular support through land reform and mobilizing peasant resistance against the Japanese.

Figure 9.6 Americans responded with alarm to the shocking triumph of Chinese communism under Mao Zedong in 1949. The next year China and the USSR signed the "Sino-Soviet Treaty of Alliance, Friendship, and Mutual Assistance," making the world's most populous (China) and the geographically most extensive (USSR) countries united in the pursuit of global communism. In the above photograph a throng of Chinese celebrate the second anniversary of their revolution by hoisting portraits of the Soviet leader Joseph Stalin.

Source: Library of Congress, Prints and Photographs Division, LC-USZ62-70041.

Despite massive US financial assistance to Chiang's government as well as his security police, the regime could not defeat the communists. In 1945 Truman dispatched Marshall to China in an effort to mediate the civil war but the mission failed. In October 1949 the communists triumphed, and proclaimed the **People's Republic of China** (PRC) with Mao as the undisputed leader. Chiang retreated to Formosa (as the Japanese had named **Taiwan**) where his successors remain in power to this day. The advent of "Red China" stunned the American public, long influenced by the pro-nationalist China Lobby. Americans struggled to understand how the country could have "fallen" to communism. Secretary of State Dean Acheson issued a State Department report explaining that the civil war in China had transpired beyond the US ability to control it, but Republicans and some Democrats seized upon the issue of the "loss" of China, which would dog Truman and Acheson for the rest of the administration.

The Soviet Union had sent advisers to the Chinese communists since the 1920s, but under the Grand Alliance Stalin had acceded to Roosevelt's request to support Chiang and the nationalists rather than the Chinese communists. However, in February 1950, with the Grand Alliance a thing of the past and the cold war escalating, Stalin welcomed Mao to Moscow for the signing of the Sino-Soviet Treaty of Friendship, Alliance, and Mutual Assistance. The pact between the two communist giants radiated shock bordering on panic to the United States and other Western capitals. Despite fear of a monolithic global communist movement, the **Sino-Soviet Alliance**, much like the Grand Alliance, lacked deep roots. Mao felt forced to ally with the USSR even though Stalin had scarcely supported the Chinese revolution and Mao resented Stalin's contemptuous treatment of him. Stalin also rejected Mao's calls to turn Mongolia over to China and to help in reclaiming Taiwan from Chiang. Under the alliance Stalin did pledge to come to China's aid in the event of a direct US or Japanese attack on the mainland. Although the Western nations could not have known it at the time, the Sino-Soviet Alliance would not survive the decade of the 1950s.

Despite the remarkable success of the United States in reviving Western Europe and reorienting Japan, the perceived loss of China combined with the Soviet Union's atomic bomb test the same year unnerved the Truman administration and the US public. Americans had expected a "Free World" to evolve from World War II but instead communism, with its emphasis on a closed, top-down politics, a state-controlled economy, and atheism prevailed in arguably the two most important countries in the world outside of the United States. Moreover Marxist–Leninist ideology held that communism would spread inevitably across the globe. Now wedded more than ever to the containment policy, the United States would intervene directly with its own military if necessary to halt the spread of communism.

War in Korea

The Chinese communist triumph intensified the cold war and set the stage for direct US military intervention on the Korean Peninsula. Until the communist takeover in China and the Sino-Soviet Alliance, Korea had been considered relatively insignificant. No one could have expected that the United States would send its own military forces halfway around the world to fight a major war in the little known country. Only the fear of the spread of monolithic communism, and the determination to contain it on every front, can explain the US decision to intervene.

Like many other countries in the world—China, Greece, Vietnam, and Yugoslavia, for example—Korea was left divided and in political tumult in the wake of World War II. The onetime "hermit kingdom," forcibly "opened" by the United States in the 1850s (Chapter 6), long had been a bone of contention between the great powers of the region, China, Japan, and Russia. Japan won the contest for control over Korea, which it occupied and exploited for 35 years until its defeat by the United States in 1945. At that time the Allies agreed that the United States would occupy the southern half of Korea and the Soviet Union would replace the Japanese in the northern part until the country could be reunited.

In 1948 the United States recognized the Republic of Korea under the Princeton educated septuagenarian **Syngman Rhee**, who had been exiled from the country for almost 40 years. The CIA described him as "a demagogue bent on autocratic rule" on behalf of a small class of elites. Because of Rhee's intense anti-communism, the United States bolstered his regime, which it sought to integrate economically and politically with Japan as part of the containment strategy.

Violence wracked the country throughout the postwar period, as Rhee backed by police forces that formerly had collaborated with the Japanese occupation launched indiscriminate killing campaigns against reformers and alleged communists. Rhee received economic, political, and limited military support as well as police training from the United States, which helped hunt down political opponents and lodge them in concentration camps. In 1949, as Rhee conducted his campaign of repression, the United States withdrew its occupation forces and omitted Korea from the Asian "defense perimeter" in US military planning documents.

From his base in the northern part of the peninsula **Kim Il-sung** like Rhee aspired to unite Korea under his rule. Inheritor of Korea's "hermit kingdom" traditions, Kim sought to construct an independent and self-sufficient state under an ideology known as *Juche*, which then as now the Koreans distinguished from communism. Like Rhee, Kim liquidated his opposition but he also won followers to the intensely nationalistic ideology by carrying out a largely bloodless land reform empowering the peasantry. Kim received backing from the Kremlin, as he had fought with Soviet forces in Manchuria in the latter stages of the war against Japan.

Though neither Rhee nor Kim was a puppet of the United States or the USSR, both sought help from their great power benefactors in an effort to unite the country under their own rule. "The South Koreans wish to invade the North," US officials reported to Washington, adding that Rhee had an "inflated ego" and meant to proceed even if it "brought on a general war." While Rhee sought backing from Washington in the Korean civil war, Kim sent repeated messages to the Soviets asking for their approval of a military campaign to unite the peninsula. On June 25, 1950, after Stalin had finally given his assent, Kim launched an all-out attack on the southern forces. The assault progressed rapidly, as Kim's forces drove the southern resistance to the Pusan perimeter in the southeastern corner of the Korean Peninsula.

Meeting in a crisis atmosphere in Washington Truman and his advisers concluded that the United States should intervene directly with its own military forces to preclude Kim from taking over Korea. For most Americans, knowing little or nothing about Korea's divided postwar politics, the war appeared to be a sudden Sino-Soviet gambit on the global chessboard to claim another country for communism. Korea thus was viewed exclusively within a cold war prism as a struggle between the Free World and global communism. Unwilling to let another country "fall," the United States entered into the first but not the last hot war in Asia within the larger cold war.

The perception that "North Korea" invaded "South Korea" obscured the civil tumult that had roiled the peninsula for years prior to June 25, 1950.

Figure 9.7 US infantry troops take cover from incoming mortar fire near the Hantan River in central Korea. The ill-fated US decision to "liberate" the entire peninsula spurred a massive Chinese intervention, turning the Korean War into a bloody, three-year stalemate.

Source: Library of Congress, Prints and Photographs Division, LC-USZ62-72424.

Although the Soviets had given Kim their approval, until the United States intervened the conflict was a civil war being fought out exclusively among Koreans rather than an international conflict.

Truman called the US intervention a "**police action**," thus bypassing a congressional declaration of war and heightening the power of the executive branch in the process. Congress and the public overwhelmingly supported US military intervention in any case, as the cold war consensus to contain communism was deeply ensconced. The United States marshaled UN backing for the intervention, support that could have been vetoed by the Soviets had they not been boycotting the UN Security Council over its refusal to seat "Red" China. The UN had thus become thoroughly politicized by the cold war. Despite the UN vote the subsequent campaign was overwhelmingly a US war, planned and waged by American commanders and soldiers and with the United States taking 90 percent of the casualties on the "Allied" side.

The outbreak of a major war in Korea prompted Truman's approval of **National Security Council paper 68 (NSC 68)**, a policy paper that remained classified until 1975. NSC 68 defined the cold war as an existential crisis, "a real war" that would end in "the fulfillment or destruction not only of this Republic but of civilization itself." Communism was a "fanatic faith" that promoted "slavery" and sought "absolute authority over the rest of the world." NSC 68 framed the cold war in stark and simple terms, a battle of good versus evil with little room for complexity or gray areas. The policy paper urged dramatic increases in military spending to defeat the demonic foe. Following Truman's approval of NSC 68 on September 30, the defense budget soared from $13 billion in 1950 to $48.7 billion in 1953.

The momentum of fighting on the Korean Peninsula swung wildly in a matter of months. With MacArthur in command the United States pulled off a risky amphibious landing of troops at Inchon and within weeks reversed the course of the war and threatened to rout Kim's forces. At this point MacArthur's towering prestige led to disaster. MacArthur, who had made good on his vow to return to the Philippines in triumph during the Pacific War, insisted that the United States should seize control of the entire Korean Peninsula and ring up a decisive victory against communism. Anxious to silence their critics after being savaged for losing China, Acheson and Truman and the JCS followed MacArthur's lead.

In November 1950, as US forces drove Kim toward the Yalu River on the Chinese border, the PRC poured hundreds of thousands of troops across the border to attack US and South Korean forces. The Chinese intervention caught the Americans by surprise and changed the course of the war overnight. Though suffering massive losses, China's headlong assault sent the US and South Korean forces into retreat, and ultimately turned the war into a bloody stalemate, one that would leave Korea devastated and thus far permanently divided. Stunned once again by events on the far away peninsula Truman publicly contemplated using atomic weapons, which the JCS advised might blunt the Chinese attack. However, Truman decided not to use the ultimate weapon, which could kill masses of people but could not resolve what was ultimately a political contest for control in Korea.

MacArthur advocated use of the atomic bomb in an all-out war with China that would also require a "very great additional complement of ground troops." The JCS rejected this advice and received Truman's support. MacArthur publicly criticized Truman for "inhibitions" in the face of crisis. In

Figure 9.8 General Douglas MacArthur, hero of the Pacific theater of World War II, receives the Distinguished Service Medal from President Truman on Wake Island in October 1950. Five months later Truman sacked MacArthur for insubordination.

Source: Library of Congress, Prints and Photographs Division, LC-USZ62-59813.

April 1951 Truman, livid over the assault on his manhood and having decided not to expand the war, sacked MacArthur for insubordination. Despite being the architect of a disastrous escalation, and incorrectly predicting that China would not intervene, MacArthur returned home to a ticker-tape parade.

The military front stabilized under the leadership of General Matthew Ridgway, but fighting continued and Korea soon became an unpopular "limited war." Ridgway rebuilt military morale, devastated by the Chinese counterattack, halted the US retreat, and pushed the Chinese and North Koreans back, recapturing Seoul. Recalling "unconditional surrender" in World War II, many Americans argued that the United States was not doing enough to win the war, but there was no clear strategy for victory in Korea. Testifying before Congress in May 1951, General Omar Bradley, chairman of the JCS, declared that war with "Red China" would involve the nation in "the wrong war, at the wrong place, at the wrong time, and with the wrong enemy." With China willing to sacrifice hundreds of thousands of lives to defend its borderlands, the Korean War was destined to end in a stalemate. Unfortunately both sides were reluctant to face this fact hence fighting continued for two more years to little effect.

The United States had stopped Korea from "falling" completely to communism, but the war did not enhance US standing in the world. By contrast, China's international prestige soared in many "Third World" or developing countries (Chapter 11) for standing up to the "imperialist" Americans. The Soviets sent aid to North Korea but largely sat the war out, content to watch the United States struggle and bleed. The biggest losers of course were the Koreans, as for them the war was a virtual holocaust. While neither Kim nor Rhee succeeded in their reckless quests to unite the Korean Peninsula, more than 2 million Korean *civilians* died along with hundreds of thousands of combatants on all sides.

The Korean War featured savage fighting and abundant atrocities, both before and after the US and Chinese interventions. As a Korean truth and reconciliation commission later found Rhee's forces launched indiscriminate killing campaigns and carried out several massacres before June 25, 1950. After the outbreak of war US troops killed masses of refugees in sites such as No Gun Ri, actions that came as a revelation to Americans (but not Koreans) in 1999. US soldiers joined South Korean police in the "slaughter of hundreds of South Korean civilians, women as well as men," the *New York Times* reported. The United States liberally employed skin-shredding napalm and as in World War II bombed relentlessly, inflicting massive collateral damage. North Korean forces also slaughtered civilians, who were dumped into mass graves. Hundreds of POWs were summarily executed. Some 36,000 Americans died and more than 90,000 were injured. More than 100,000 South Korean soldiers, some 520,000 North Korean soldiers, and approximately 900,000 Chinese soldiers were killed in the war.

Sometimes called the "forgotten war," as it was sandwiched between victory in World War II and defeat in Vietnam, the Korean War had profound

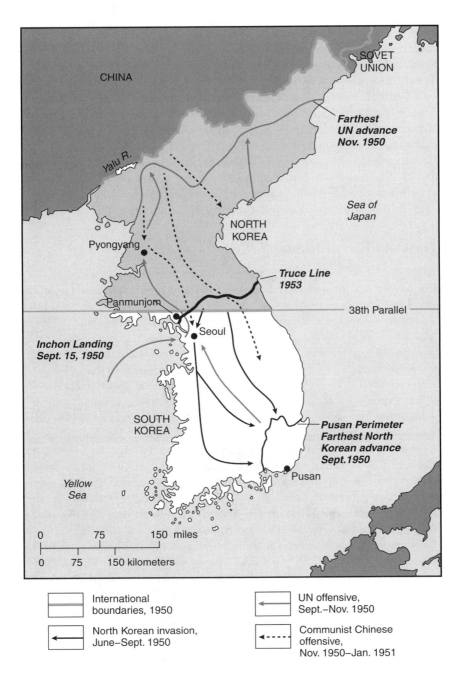

CHINA

SOVIET
UNION

*Farthest
UN advance
Nov. 1950*

Yalu R.

Sea of
Japan

NORTH
KOREA

Pyongyang

*Truce Line
1953*

Panmunjom

38th Parallel

*Inchon Landing
Sept. 15, 1950*

Seoul

SOUTH
KOREA

*Pusan Perimeter
Farthest North
Korean advance
Sept. 1950*

Yellow
Sea

Pusan

| 0 | 75 | 150 | miles |

| 0 | 75 | 150 | kilometers |

	International boundaries, 1950
	UN offensive, Sept.–Nov. 1950
	North Korean invasion, June–Sept. 1950
	Communist Chinese offensive, Nov. 1950–Jan. 1951

Map 9.1 The Korean War.

implications and consequences. The Korean conflict left a legacy of military confrontation and intensified cold war rivalry in Asia. In 1951 the United States bolstered its alliance with Japan by signing the **San Francisco Peace Treaty** formally ending the Pacific War. By that time the United States had established 132 military installations in Japan, 90 percent of them on Okinawa. The United States maintained bases and a close alliance in South Korea and has remained in the midst of perpetual hostilities on the Korean Peninsula ever since. At the outset of the Korean War the United States positioned the Navy's seventh fleet between the Chinese mainland and Taiwan, thus committing itself to a decades-long conflict between the "two Chinas." The hot war in Korea spurred fears of a wider war, prompting Washington to strengthen NATO, which added Greece and Turkey to the alliance in 1952.

The Cold War at Home

World War II, the cold war, and the national security state cast a long shadow over US politics and society. In December 1943 Roosevelt announced that "Dr. New Deal" and been replaced by "Dr. Win the War" hence the liberal reform era was over and would reappear only briefly in the 1960s. Truman's proposed "Fair Deal" program received little support from the Republican-dominated Congress elected in 1946. Nonetheless, Truman's cold war policies helped him to a surprise victory over Thomas Dewey in the election of 1948.

During the cold war Americans focused on perceived domestic enemies as well as foreign foes. Revelations of domestic spying and intolerance of the left characterized the return of **Red Scare politics** after World War II. The standard of strict protection of the First Amendment right to freedom of speech in the absence of a "clear and present danger" eroded during the war and the cold war. The targeting of perceived enemies within began under Roosevelt, who questioned the patriotism of noninterventionists and authorized spying and wiretaps against his critics. In 1938 the House of Representatives created a new **House Committee on Un-American Activities (HCUA)**, whose hearings encouraged the trend toward equating dissent with disloyalty.

Communism was contained at home as well as abroad with repression of the **Communist Party USA (CPUSA)**. During the Depression years CPUSA membership grew from 12,000 in 1932 to 80,000 in 1939. The CPUSA promoted unions, condemned racism, and advocated women's equality. Most American communists worked within the US political system even as they followed the "party line" emanating from Moscow. The cold war transformed communists from legitimate political activists into subversives by means of congressional legislation and sensational investigations ranging from New York to Hollywood. Aided by informants within the Screen Actors Guild (including future president Ronald Reagan), Congress investigated the alleged communist sympathies of hundreds of actors, directors, and screenwriters, calling many of them to Washington beginning in 1946 for televised hearings to answer whether they were now or ever had been members of the Communist Party.

Figure 9.9 Although typically associated with the 1950s, investigations of "un-American activities" actually began in the 1930s in the House committee chaired by Texas Democrat Martin Dies. On August 18, 1938, Homer Chaillaux (above), "Americanism director" for the American Legion averred, "Sinister forces are expending greater effort than ever before to wreck this nation."

Source: Library of Congress, Prints and Photographs Division, LC-DIG-hec-24962.

Some Hollywood figures declined to testify or "name names," for which they were jailed or, more typically, found themselves deprived of work after being placed on the **Hollywood blacklist**.

Red Scare politics blurred distinctions between communists and progressives, prompting the Democratic Party to move from the left toward the center. Abetted by the Truman administration, critics impugned the patriotism of former Vice President Wallace and the few other politicians who opposed confrontation with Russia while continuing to advocate progressive reform on the home front. The CPUSA supported Wallace, lending apparent credence to attempts to link his effort to revive domestic reform with communist subversion. Publicly discredited, Wallace received only 2.4 percent of the vote in the 1948 presidential election.

The "fall" of China and the Korean War dramatically escalated the revival of Red Scare politics. Americans had been promised a "Free World" but instead confronted a global "communist menace." In close association with the powerful China Lobby, Republicans charged that the Democrats and spies in the State Department had orchestrated the "Yalta sellout" of Eastern Europe followed by "selling China down the river." Foreign Service officers who had loyally served in China were drummed out of their jobs for alleged communist sympathies.

In Their Words

Senator Joseph McCarthy's Lincoln Day speech before the Republican Women's Club of Wheeling, West Virginia, February 9, 1950

Five years after a world war has been won, men's hearts should anticipate a long peace, and men's minds should be free from the heavy weight that comes with war. But this is not such a period—for this is not a period of peace. This is a time of the 'cold war.' This is a time when the world is split into two vast, increasingly hostile armed camps—a time of a great armaments race . . .

Today we are engaged in a final, all-out battle between communistic atheism and Christianity. The modern champions of communism have selected this as the time. And, ladies and gentlemen, the chips are down—they are truly down . . . This indicates the swiftness of the tempo of Communist victories and American defeats in the cold war. As one of our outstanding historical figures once said, "When a great democracy is destroyed, it will not be because of enemies from without, but rather because of enemies from within" . . .

The reason why we find ourselves in a position of impotency is not because our only powerful potential enemy has sent men to invade our shores, but rather because of the traitorous actions of those who have been treated so well by this nation . . .

This is glaringly true in the State Department. There the bright young men who are born with silver spoons in their mouths are the ones who have been the worst . . . In my opinion the State Department, which is one of the most important government departments, is thoroughly infested with Communists.

I have in my hand 57 cases of individuals who would appear to be either card carrying members or certainly loyal to the Communist Party, but who nevertheless are still helping to shape our foreign policy . . .

The loss of China followed by the Korean War dramatically accelerated Red Scare politics. Deprived of the White House for a generation, Republicans tarred Truman with the loss of China while demagogues led by Republican Senator Joseph McCarthy of Wisconsin floated the canard that the State

Department had deliberately sacrificed China to communism. McCarthy repeatedly made unsubstantiated charges about "known communists" in government and frequently engaged in character assassination. In 1954 the US Senate censured McCarthy, bringing an end to his reckless campaign. He drank himself to death three years later.

While McCarthy seized the headlines the most important individual in the counter-subversion campaign was J. Edgar Hoover, who had coordinated the Red Scare after World War I and then became director of the FBI at its creation in 1934. Hoover consolidated unprecedented power during World War II, as the FBI sprawled from a force of 898 to one of 4,886 persons. Hoover exercised virtually unchecked power for more than half a century, targeting progressives, communists, feminists, African-Americans, homosexuals, and other minorities with illegal wiretaps, infiltration, interference with the mails, and harassment.

Figure 9.10 FBI Director J. Edgar Hoover in 1948.

Source: Library of Congress, Prints and Photographs Division, LC-USZ62-117435.

Figure 9.11 In 1948 Progressive Party candidate Henry A. Wallace had to collect himself
after being pelted with eggs and tomatoes during a campaign appearance in
Greensboro, North Carolina.

Source: Library of Congress, Prints and Photographs Division, LC-USZ62-134509.

Hoover's FBI tracked down thousands of ongoing or former CPUSA members
and other alleged radicals, typically causing them to be summarily fired from
their jobs. FBI agents employed wiretaps, rifled trash, intercepted mail, broke
into homes and offices, leaked damaging information, supplied the Internal
Revenue Service with tips against alleged radicals, and committed other illegal
acts free of executive or congressional oversight.

Businesses, government at all levels, and educational institutions systematically rooted out the left. Universities sacrificed freedom of speech, thought, and
association through FBI informants and investigations leading to the dismissal

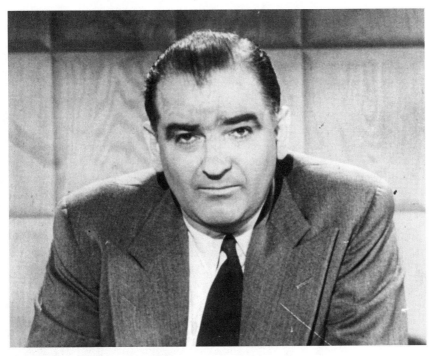

Figure 9.12 Senator Joseph McCarthy.
Source: Library of Congress, Prints and Photographs Division, LC-USZ62-71719.

of faculty members for alleged radicalism. Even though only 10 states, according to FBI estimates, counted more than 1,000 bona fide communists, investigative committees sprang up in state and local governments all over the country. Newly mandated loyalty oaths affected as much as 20 percent of the workforce from 1947–57, forcing thousands out of jobs and costing millions of dollars in state and federal loyalty investigations.

Ironically, though celebrated for its crime fighting successes against bank robbers and kidnappers, the FBI failed to combat Soviet espionage during World War II. Soviet spies infiltrated foreign embassies throughout the world. The HCUA and Hoover had been more focused on domestic radicals and minority dissent than on Soviet spies, who had infiltrated the United States as well as the governments of Britain and other Allies. Revelations of "atom spies" stunned the American public, most famously in the case of Julius and Ethel Rosenberg. In 1952 both were executed for espionage though only Julius Rosenberg had been a spy. In addition to passing on secret atomic research, spies advanced Soviet capabilities in radar, rocketry, and jet propulsion.

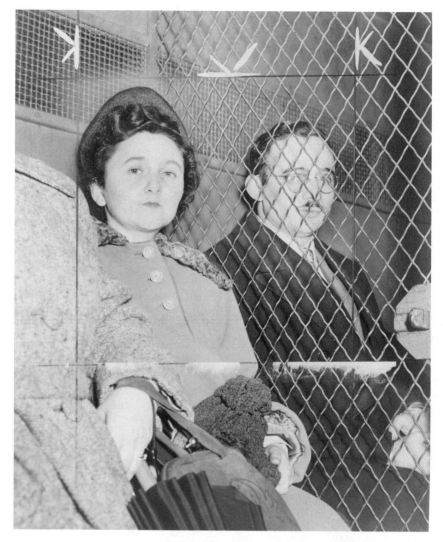

Figure 9.13 Julius and Ethel Rosenberg following the verdict guilty of treason.
Source: Library of Congress, Prints and Photographs Division, LC-USZ62-117772.

Interpreting the Past

The debate over the origins of the cold war

The causes and primary responsibility for the onset of the cold war
were intensely controversial throughout the duration of the conflict.
"Orthodox" scholars placed the blame for the cold war squarely upon
Stalin and the Soviet Union for violating wartime accords and ruthlessly

establishing "satellite" regimes in Poland and other border states while at the same time attempting to foment communist uprisings worldwide. They argued the United States stepped in to defend the Free World and that the US initiatives such as the Marshall Plan, Truman Doctrine, NATO, and the Korean War were necessary and justifiable steps to contain communism.

So-called revisionist scholars, emerging around the time of widespread disillusion over the Vietnam War (Chapter 12), argued conversely that the United States, the most powerful country in the postwar world, rejected compromise in an effort to enforce its universal values on every front. Truman and other cold warriors ignored the Soviet Union's massive sacrifices in the war, violated promises to provide reconstruction assistance, and chose confrontation rather than continuing Roosevelt's policy of diplomatic engagement of the USSR. Determined to maintain the Open Door of free trade and economic liberalization, the United States rearmed, flaunted its monopoly on atomic weapons, established the global base system, and went on the offensive in an effort to isolate and destroy the USSR.

Arguments that one side or the other was solely to blame have ebbed in recent years, not least because the cold war is now viewed as a transnational conflict involving far more than the interests and actions of the two primary antagonists, the United States and the Soviet Union. Often the actions within the smaller states, as in Korea, dictated the course of events. In geopolitical terms the cold war happened because massive power vacuums opened up in Europe and in Asia with the defeat of Germany and Japan, hence the world became an arena of highly charged competition for **spheres of influence** and geopolitical primacy.

The cold war was not inevitable but instead was created by the statements made and actions taken in the postwar era. The antagonistic ideologies of communism and capitalism certainly exacerbated the conflict but were not the only or even necessarily the primary causes of it. The world lacked order, stability, and balance in the wake of World War II. Confrontation and conflict, rather than peace and cooperation, ultimately emerged from the ashes of the world war.

The cultural forces of race, religion, and masculinity played an important role in the US cold war culture and in Red Scare politics. As the Russians were "white," race played less of a role than in attitudes toward "Red China." Nonetheless, in articulating the containment strategy Kennan exalted the superior "Anglo-Saxon" race while using such terms as "Oriental" and "neurotic" to depict the Soviets as less civilized than Western Europeans and Americans. In his Iron Curtain Address Churchill called on the "English-speaking world" to unite against Soviet expansion. Stalin responded that Churchill like Hitler was setting out "to unleash war with a race theory."

Figure 9.14 Diplomat and accused Soviet spy Alger Hiss.
Source: Library of Congress, Prints and Photographs Division, LC-USZ62-64417.

China was not merely "red" but also invoked deep-seated American fear of the "yellow peril" reminiscent of the Chinese Exclusion Act of 1882. Perceptions of racial inferiority contributed to underestimating China during the Korean War, with devastating consequences. The pejorative term "gook" circulated widely in the American lexicon during the Korean conflict, much as "Japs" and "Nips" and ape-like depictions of the Japanese dominated World War II representations.

Religion, perhaps more than race, animated the cold war conflict. As most Americans saw it, the cold war pitted the United States, providentially destined to lead the Free World, against the evil forces of "**godless communism**." In 1945 the first atomic test blast had been named for the Holy Trinity and many believed that God had provided the United States alone with the ability to harness the "very power of the Universe." The bomb was thus "sacred" and America was justified in retaining a monopoly and taking the lead in the nuclear arms race.

Truman like many Americans amid the euphoria of victory in World War II called the bomb "the greatest thing in history." He declared that God had provided the weapon to the United States. A Baptist and biblical fundamentalist, Truman framed the cold war in a religious context, as he spoke repeatedly of "the responsibility that I believe God intended this great Republic to assume." In 1948 in response to the coup in Czechoslovakia, Truman called on "moral God fearing peoples [to] save the world from Atheism and totalitarianism."

Truman's successor, the deeply reverent Dwight D. Eisenhower, launched a tradition of White House prayer breakfasts, added "one nation under God" to the Pledge of Allegiance, and made "In God We Trust" the nation's official motto. Referring to the cold war, Eisenhower declared, "The forces of good and evil are massed and armed and opposed as rarely before in history . . . freedom is pitted against slavery, lightness against the dark." Eisenhower chose as his secretary of state the prominent Presbyterian "Christian statesman" John Foster Dulles, who viewed the cold war as a moral struggle between good and evil. Dulles's religiosity predisposed him to rule out negotiations, oppose neutralism, or enter into "moral compromise" with godless communism. Religion prompted Dulles to back a series of leaders in predominately non-Christian Asian countries. These "Christian gentlemen who have suffered for their faith" were Chiang, Rhee, and Vietnam's Ngo Dinh Diem, all of whom eventually would be overthrown.

Theologians and evangelists rallied religious support for a tough-minded response to the communist menace. Reinhold Neibuhr's **Christian realism** transitioned seamlessly from World War II to the cold war, as he warned that turning the other cheek was no more an option against the communists than it had been against the Axis. Whereas Niebuhr was a Christian intellectual, populist appeals from the Catholic bishop Fulton J. Sheen and the southern Baptist evangelical Billy Graham reached audiences numbering in the tens of millions. By the 1950s both used the new medium of television to great effect. The popularity of these militant Christians overwhelmed the pacifism of A. J. Muste and other Christian peace internationalists.

From 1940 to 1959, membership in a church or synagogue rose from 49 to 69 percent of the population. In its Christmas issue in 1955, *Time* referred to the "unprecedented revival in religious belief and practice everywhere in the US," as faith in God, prayer, belief in the divinity of Jesus, and the Bible as the literal word of God soared throughout the cold war decade. Film provided a popular medium for representing biblical narratives through epic Hollywood productions such as Cecil B. DeMille's *The Ten Commandments*, released in 1956.

During the cold war **domestic containment** was as central on the home front as containment of communism abroad. Containment of feminism, homosexuality, and African-American and Hispanic civil rights at home was often framed in masculine terms. Kennan called for a "manly" containment

Figure 9.15 Released in 1956, the Hollywood epic *The Ten Commandments* grossed millions of dollars and received seven academy award nominations.

Source: Library of Congress, Prints and Photographs Division, LC-DIG-ppmsca-19347.

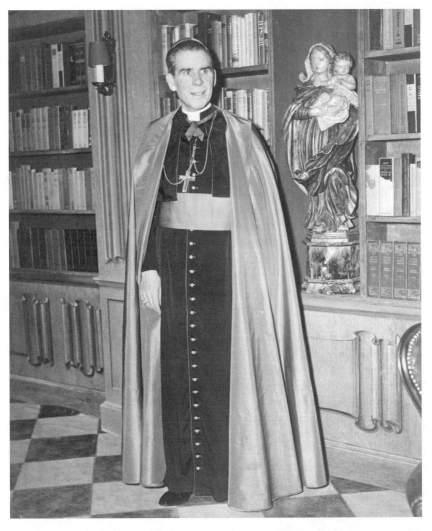

Figure 9.16 Roman Catholic Bishop Fulton J. Sheen captivated millions through radio
and television programs representing the cold war as a struggle between
good and evil.

Source: Library of Congress, Prints and Photographs Division, LC-USZ62-123461.

policy in which Soviet expansionism would meet with "superior strength" and
the application of "counterforce." Cold war rhetoric frequently juxtaposed
tough-minded realism with terms such as "sentimentality," "political steril-
ity," and "fatal weaknesses." Some Republicans criticized containment as a
defensive "pantywaist" diplomacy that eschewed a quest for victory in favor
of "limited war." The conservative *National Review* charged liberals with "defi-
nite antagonism toward all strenuous ideals of life." "Pink," a color typically

associated with femininity, became a pejorative label for persons perceived as pro-communist or too liberal in their political views.

Men were celebrated for victory in World War II reviving an American masculinity that had eroded during the Depression. While the New Deal faded away Congress passed the **GI Bill of Rights** in 1944 and allocated more than $7 billion a year to it from 1947–50, more than triple all other spending on social welfare, health, housing, and education. The GI Bill helped ensure that "America's fighting men" could anchor the nuclear family by resuming their patriarchal role as educated or trained and employed heads of households. Women, called into factories for wartime production, were encouraged to return to the domestic sphere.

Within the red scare, a **lavender scare** equated homosexuality with absence of masculinity and linked homosexuals with communists. As both homosexuals and communists remained closeted, "You can't hardly separate homosexuals from subversives," Senator Kenneth Wherry of Nebraska opined. In 1950 the sensational **Alger Hiss case** in which the State Department diplomat, who had been present at Yalta, was accused of being a Soviet spy, linked subversion with sexual deviance. Hiss's accuser, Whitaker Chambers, publicly "confessed" his homosexuality as well as his former communist sympathies. State Department diplomats, viewed as effete "striped pants boys," were tarred with being both communists and homosexuals. While the US Senate launched an investigation under the heading "Employment of Homosexuals and Other Sex Perverts in Government," Graham and other cold war clergymen praised the endeavors aimed at "exposing the pinks, the lavenders, and the reds that have sought refuge beneath the wings of the American eagle."

Tensions and anxiety over gender and sexuality surfaced repeatedly amid the cold war and the red scare. Despite her international prominence, including being referenced as the "first lady to the world," Eleanor Roosevelt came under attack for her liberalism. In 1954 even Eisenhower, who privately condemned McCarthy's tactics, approved of those "trying to save the US from Eleanor Roosevelt." Hoover gathered information on Eleanor Roosevelt in his "Sex Deviate" file. Relatively few women succeeded in American politics and those who did, such as Margaret Chase Smith, who served for decades in both the House and the Senate, often made their start by succeeding their deceased husbands. The Republican Smith favored women's rights and condemned McCarthyism, but ultimately won over her Maine constituents and the male-dominated Senate through a hawkish stance on communism and the cold war.

Red Scare politics undermined the career of Helen Gahagan Douglas, a three-term congresswoman from California who championed women's rights, civil liberties, and arms control. The former actress opposed US military aid to repressive regimes in Greece and Turkey under the Truman Doctrine. "In our opposition to communism" she explained, "we must not make the mistake of backing remnants of corrupt and decaying systems." In 1950 Douglas won the Democratic primary for the US Senate despite her opponent's sexually loaded charge that she was "pink right down to her underwear." In the general election

Figure 9.17 Congresswoman Helen Gahagan Douglas.
Source: Library of Congress, Prints and Photographs Division, LC-USZ62-111664.

the Republican, Nixon, picked up on the pink theme and defeated Douglas in a campaign dominated by Red Scare politics. Linking African-Americans with women as menacing forces, a mass mailing from the Nixon campaign featured "Vote for Our Helen for Senator," signed by the "Communist League of Negro Women."

Some political foes considered Eisenhower's opponent in the 1952 presidential campaign, Adlai Stevenson, as an effete, liberal "egg-head" and a homosexual (apparently because he had divorced and not remarried). Hoover (who never married) secretly launched a "whispering campaign" against Stevenson and kept a file on him labeled "Governor of Illinois—Sex Deviate." When Stevenson ran again in 1956, the popular journalist Walter Winchell declared, "A vote for Adlai Stevenson is a vote for Christine Jorgensen," referencing the first recipient of a sex change operation (from man to woman). Domestic containment, fueled by the cold war and Red Scare politics, largely succeeded in restraining the civil rights and women's movements and ensured that gays, lesbians, and transgendered remained closeted for decades.

Select Bibliography

Costigliola, Frank. *Roosevelt's Lost Alliances: How Personal Politics Helped Start the Cold War.* Princeton, NJ: Princeton University Press, 2012.
Campbell, Craig and Logevall, Fredrik. *America's Cold War: The Politics of Insecurity.* Cambridge, MA: Harvard University Press, 2009.

Gori, Francesca and Pons, Silvio. *The Soviet Union and Europe in the Cold War, 1943–1953*. New York: St. Martin's Press, 1996.

Kofsky, Frank. *Harry S. Truman and the War Scare of 1948: A Successful Campaign to Deceive the Nation*. New York: St. Martin's Press, 1993.

Hixson, Walter L. *George F. Kennan: Cold War Iconoclast*. New York: Columbia University Press, 1989.

Offner, Arnold A. *Another Such Victory: President Truman and the Cold War, 1945–1953*. Palo Alto, CA: Stanford University Press, 2002.

Leffler, Melvyn, ed. *The Cambridge History of the Cold War, Vol. I: Origins*. New York: Cambridge University Press, 2010.

Johnston, Andrew M. *Hegemony and Origins of NATO Nuclear First-Use, 1945–1955*. New York: Palgrave Macmillan, 2005.

Jespersen, Christopher T. *American Images of China, 1931–1949*. Palo Alto, CA: Stanford University Press, 1996.

Stueck, William, ed. *The Korean War in World History*. Lexington: University Press of Kentucky, 2004.

Cumings, Bruce. *The Korean War: A History*. New York: Modern Library, 2010.

Dower, John W. *Embracing Defeat: Japan in the Wake of World War II*. New York: W.W. Norton, 1999.

May, Elaine Tyler. *Homeward Bound: American Families in the Cold War Era*. New York: Basic Books, 1999.

Heale, M. J. *McCarthy's Americans: Red Scare Politics in State and Nation, 1935–1965*. Athens: University of Georgia Press, 1998.

Johnson, David K. *The Lavender Scare: The Cold War Persecution of Gays and Lesbians in the Federal Government*. Chicago: University of Chicago Press, 2004.

10 Evolution of the Cold War

Overview

The cold war dominated US foreign policy after World War II. The United States pursued a policy of "liberation" of countries from communism, but the Soviets and their eastern European allies quashed these efforts. A potential "thaw" in the cold war after the death of Joseph Stalin in 1953 proved short lived. The division of Europe, the nuclear arms race, militarization of foreign policy, and propaganda battles persisted. Absence of East–West diplomacy continued to characterize the cold war until the aftermath of the Cuban Missile Crisis, which took the world to the brink of nuclear war in 1962.

Pursuing "Liberation"

"Containment" was a misleading or at least incomplete term for describing US cold war strategy. The United States pursued not merely a defensive strategy of halting the expansion of communism, rather it pursued a policy of "**roll back**" or "liberation," destroying communism where it already existed. George F. Kennan's original strategy envisioned not merely containment but also driving the Soviet-backed regimes out of Eastern Europe. "We must get them out," he declared. "We cannot settle for them remaining there indefinitely." The "roll back" of communism from Eastern Europe, he added hopefully, could incite "a general crumbling of Russian influence and prestige" that would carry "into the heart of the Soviet Union itself."

Committed to rolling back communism the United States invested heavily in propaganda and **psychological warfare** to destabilize the Soviet Union and Eastern Europe. The Truman and Eisenhower administrations orchestrated a state–private network of civil society organizations to trumpet capitalism and democracy while calling for the overthrow of the communist regimes. Assisted by eastern European émigrés, they beamed propaganda through the Voice of America, the CIA-funded Radio Free Europe (RFE), Radio Liberation, Vatican Radio, and Radio in the American Sector (of Berlin). The Soviets responded to psychological warfare by jamming Western radio broadcasts and clamping down on dissidence. Organizations such as the Crusade for Freedom, covertly funded by the CIA, staged propaganda displays and sent leaflets behind the "iron curtain" in balloons, which burst at high altitudes and rained down calls for resistance. Spies infiltrated Eastern Europe but the vast majority, identified by Soviet "moles" within the Western governments, were captured and executed.

The Republican Party tapped into American frustration with the "limited war" in Korea by trumpeting a more aggressive policy of liberation. During the 1952 presidential campaign the hero General Dwight D. Eisenhower declared he would "go to Korea" and extricate the United States from the stalemated conflict. Eisenhower enjoyed tremendous prestige from his wartime leadership as architect of the Normandy invasion. After the war he served as NATO commander and president of Columbia University. John Foster Dulles, the new secretary of state, came from a long line of internationalists in his family (including two former secretaries of state) and had participated in the Paris peace conference after World War I. Following his overwhelming electoral victory, Eisenhower threatened to use atomic weapons if the Soviets and Chinese failed to pressure the North Koreans into coming to terms. The war had stalemated by this time in any case. On July 27, 1953, the United States, China, and the two Koreas signed the **Korean Armistice** (not a peace treaty) ending the fighting but not bringing an end to the cold war on the Korean Peninsula.

Figure 10.1 John Foster Dulles (left), the leading Republican internationalist of his era, anchored President Dwight D. Eisenhower's "New Look" foreign policy. Dulles appointed veteran diplomat Charles Bohlen (right) as the new ambassador to the Soviet Union.

Source: Library of Congress, Prints and Photographs Division, LC-USZ62-91783.

The threat to use "the bomb" reflected an effort to incorporate "massive retaliation" as part of the Eisenhower administration's "**New Look**" strategy. Massive retaliation complemented psychological warfare, as both Eisenhower and Dulles hoped to keep the communist powers on edge and uncertain as to US intentions and thus more restrained in efforts to spread communism. The greater reliance on nuclear weapons had another goal, however, providing "more bang for the buck," an important consideration for the fiscally conservative Eisenhower. Relying more on the threat of weapons of mass destruction than troops on the ground was cost effective.

Led by the United States, the nuclear weapons race, which pervaded the entire history of the cold war, escalated without restraint into the 1960s. In 1952 the United States developed the thermonuclear or **hydrogen bomb**—potentially hundreds of times more powerful than the atomic bomb—in a massive above ground test blast. In the **Castle BRAVO test**, radioactive fallout killed 23 Japanese fishermen and sickened scores of residents of the Marshall Islands, a US territory. Aided by spies, the Soviets successfully tested the hydrogen bomb in 1953. In a December speech at the UN Eisenhower called for US-Soviet cooperation in the peaceful uses of nuclear energy—"Atoms for Peace"—but he and, especially, Dulles actually had little interest in arms control. Dulles emphasized the "economic burden of the present arms race" in weakening the USSR, thus promoting escalation as a key component of US strategy. Similarly, in 1955 the Eisenhower administration proposed "Open Skies," a program of mutual aerial inspection of nuclear installations, knowing the Soviets would reject the plan after which Washington, as Dulles put it, "would make every effort to win the arms race."

The end of the Korean War and the threats posed by nuclear weapons prompted calls for a "thaw" in the cold war. In March 1952 Stalin issued a "Peace Note" advocating reunification of Germany, which would be demilitarized and kept out of any foreign military alliances. However, the United States, joined by Konrad Adenauer, chancellor of the Federal Republic of Germany, was already committed to West German integration into NATO. Dean Acheson summarily rejected Stalin's proposal as a propaganda move "intended solely to obstruct the building of the new Europe."

In April 1953 the newly elected Eisenhower delivered a largely conciliatory "Chance for Peace" speech but acquiesced to his advisers and excised from the original draft an offer of a summit meeting. Winston Churchill, serving once again as British prime minster, criticized Eisenhower's refusal to meet with the new leaders of the Soviet Union in the wake of Stalin's death in March 1953. Dulles, who opposed negotiations with communists, warned against the "illusions of peace" emanating from the Kremlin. The leading French newspaper *Le Monde* noted that "the conciliatory words and generosity of tone" in Eisenhower's speech had been contradicted by Dulles's "harangue" and "intransigence."

Whereas Stalin, increasingly paranoid as he neared death, had conducted a final purge to combat the so-called "Doctor's Plot," his successors showed signs of new thinking. They normalized relations with **Josip Broz Tito**, the communist leader of Yugoslavia, which had gone to the brink of war with the Soviets in 1948. The Kremlin allowed Finland to assume control of a Soviet base in that country. For the first time in years the USSR allowed Western journalists, artists, students, professors, and athletes to tour the country. In 1954 Soviet novelist Ilia Ehrenburg published *The Thaw* with implied criticism of Stalin, which became a metaphor for the possibility of liberalization in the USSR and improved relations with the West.

As pressure for a summit continued to mount, Eisenhower agreed to a meeting at Geneva in 1955. The meeting proceeded without acrimony, producing what some called "**the spirit of Geneva**." Privately the emerging Soviet leader **Nikita S. Khrushchev** dismissed "Open Skies" as a "bald espionage plot against the USSR," thus revealing to Eisenhower that he was "the real boss of the Soviet delegation." With the Soviets unwilling to abandon influence in Eastern Europe and the West unwilling to compromise on West German integration into the anti-Soviet NATO alliance, nothing concrete came from the meeting. The absence of meaningful diplomacy pleased Dulles, who had opposed the summit, fearing that any agreement would represent "appeasement" of Russia.

Dulles preferred to undermine the Soviets through militarization and psychological warfare rather than conduct diplomacy with the communists. He and other proponents of roll back and liberation had cause for optimism as Stalin's death had prompted mounting opposition to Soviet control over the eastern European "satellites." In 1953 in the German Democratic Republic (GDR), or East Germany, workers went on strike and demanded an end to the Communist Party dictatorship. Western and émigré propaganda encouraged the uprising, but Soviet forces crushed the **East German revolt** in June 1953, killing hundreds of protesters in the process.

In Their Words

Soviet Communist Party Leader Nikita S. Khrushchev denounces his predecessor, Joseph Stalin, at the Twentieth Party Congress, February 25, 1956

We have to consider seriously and analyze correctly [the crimes of the Stalin era] in order that we may preclude any possibility of a repetition in any form whatever of what took place during the life of Stalin, who absolutely did not tolerate collegiality in leadership and in work, and who practiced brutal violence, not only toward everything which opposed him, but also toward that which seemed to his capricious and despotic character, contrary to his concepts.

Stalin acted not through persuasion, explanation, and patient cooperation with people, but by imposing his concepts and demanding absolute submission to his opinion. Whoever opposed this concept or tried to prove his viewpoint, and the correctness of his position, was doomed to removal from the leading collective and to subsequent moral and physical annihilation. This was especially true during the period following the XVIIth Party Congress [1934], when many prominent Party leaders and rank-and-file Party workers, honest and dedicated to the cause of Communism, fell victim to Stalin's despotism . . .

Stalin originated the concept enemy of the people. This term automatically rendered it unnecessary that the ideological errors of a man or men engaged in a controversy be proven; this term made possible the usage of the most cruel repression, violating all norms of revolutionary legality, against anyone who in any way disagreed with Stalin . . . This led to the glaring violations of revolutionary legality, and to the fact that many entirely innocent persons, who in the past had defended the Party line, became victims . . . resulting in the death of innocent people. It became apparent that many Party, Soviet and economic activists who were branded in 1937–1938 as enemies were actually never enemies, spies, wreckers, etc., but were always honest Communists; they were only so stigmatized, and often, no longer able to bear barbaric tortures, they charged themselves with all kinds of grave and unlikely crimes . . .

Lenin used severe methods only in the most necessary cases, when the exploiting classes were still in existence and were vigorously opposing the revolution, when the struggle for survival was decidedly assuming the sharpest forms, even including a civil war.

Stalin, on the other hand, used extreme methods and mass repression at a time when the revolution was already victorious, when the Soviet state was strengthened, when the exploiting classes were already liquidated and Socialist relations were rooted solidly in all phases of national economy, when our Party was politically consolidated and had strengthened itself both numerically and ideologically. It is clear that here Stalin showed in a whole series of cases his intolerance, his brutality and his abuse of power. Instead of proving his political correctness and mobilizing the masses, he often chose the path of repression and physical annihilation, not only against actual enemies, but also against individuals who had not committed any crimes against the Party and the Soviet government.

In 1955 the Soviets tightened control over Eastern Europe with the **Warsaw Pact**, a political and military alliance in direct response to West German integration into NATO. However, at the same time the Soviets signed the Austrian State Treaty, making that country neutral in the cold war and a possible model for a loosening of great power domination at the center of the European continent. In February 1956 Khrushchev stunned the world with a supposedly **"secret speech"** before a meeting of the Soviet Communist Party Congress in which he denounced Stalin and his legacy. Khrushchev condemned Stalin for promoting a "cult of personality," for his "despotic character," and for violations of "socialist legality." Dulles's brother Allen Dulles, head of the CIA, viewed the speech as "a most serious mistake" providing "a great opportunity, both covertly and overtly, to exploit to our advantage."

Many people in Eastern Europe and especially in Poland and Hungary reasoned that if the Soviets could denounce Stalin and his legacy they would be justified in overthrowing their own regimes. Encouraged by Western anti-Soviet propaganda Poles and Hungarians walked off their jobs and took to the streets in protest. Khrushchev threatened to deploy military force before averting a bloodbath in Poland by compromising with the Polish communist reform leader Władysław Gomułka. The situation played out very differently in Hungary where the Soviets also tried to avoid direct intervention but ultimately concluded they had no other choice.

In the fall of 1956, with Western radio broadcasts encouraging the unrest, demonstrators filled the streets of Budapest, tore red star insignias off buildings, and brought in construction equipment to tear down a massive statue of Stalin. **Imre Nagy**, the reform prime minister in Hungary, freed from imprisonment the popular **Cardinal József Mindszenty**, who took refuge in the US embassy and called for Hungarian independence. Fearing, just as US psychological warriors had hoped, that the loss of Hungary would lead other countries to reject Communist Party authority in a roll back possibly extending to the USSR itself, Khrushchev ordered the **Hungarian intervention**. In November the Soviet tanks and troops quelled the rebellion following major street battles with the lightly armed Hungarians. Nagy and some 300 others were later executed and a pro-Soviet regime ensconced in power.

For Eisenhower the repression in Hungary was "indeed a bitter pill for us to swallow." When the events in Hungary first began Foster Dulles exulted, "The great monolith of communism is crumbling!" When repression rather than liberation ensued, the Dulles brothers and other architects of psychological warfare now had to contemplate the extent to which the West had encouraged the Hungarian uprising only to look on as the Soviets brutally crushed it.

The repression in Hungary suggested that rather than achieving liberation psychological warfare had served to harden Soviet hegemony over Eastern Europe. While some organs of Western propaganda had been straightforward and restrained in their coverage others such as the CIA-backed RFE had encouraged the Hungarian uprising. Disturbed that "our radio and balloon operations have led to belief that we would be prepared" to come to the aid of eastern European rebels, Eisenhower directed future propaganda efforts to offer straight news and information rather than inflammatory programming. The Eisenhower administration "came in with the idea that they could roll back communism by wishful thinking, or sending balloons over into Czechoslovakia, that sort of thing," veteran diplomat H. Freeman Matthews explained. "They had to learn and it took a while."

The Cold War and the Middle East

Eisenhower was incensed when the nation's closest allies—Britain, France, and Israel—launched a surprise invasion of Egypt just prior to the Soviet intervention in Hungary. The three US allies went behind Eisenhower's back to invade in response to the decision by Egyptian president **Gamal Abdel Nasser** to nationalize the Suez Canal, which had been built under French and British colonialism and completed in 1869. Eisenhower, who achieved fame by working closely with allies in the Normandy invasion and as NATO commander, was livid with the invaders for "double-crossing us." Moreover the attack on Egypt deflected world attention from the Soviet repression in Hungary.

The **Suez Crisis** underscored the rising importance of the oil-rich Middle East in the global cold war. The attack on Egypt was partly a reflection of the explosive **Arab-Israeli conflict**, which would become a central focus of global instability and US foreign policy for decades. The conflict had deep roots. Following British authorization under the **Balfour Declaration** in 1917, Jewish settlers had been flocking to the biblical holy land in hopes of establishing a Jewish homeland. Under the World War I mandate system Britain administered **Palestine**, a colony overwhelmingly inhabited by Muslim Arabs. Jews, Arabs, and the British occupiers clashed even before the Nazi Holocaust fueled the pace of Zionist emigration to Palestine. The Jewish influx sparked continuing conflict, as Britain lost control of the situation in Palestine after World War II.

Americans proved strong supporters of Zionism, which resonated powerfully with US racial and religious mores. Theodore Roosevelt had declared that it would be "entirely proper to start a Zionist State around Jerusalem." President Wilson endorsed the Balfour Declaration during the Great War. Although a longtime Zionist Franklin Roosevelt observed prophetically during World War II that as European Jews poured into the region "the millions of surrounding Arabs might easily proclaim a Holy War and there would be no end of trouble." Roosevelt's death left the matter in the hands of Truman and the newly established UN, neither of which succeeded in forging a peaceful settlement of the burgeoning conflict.

In 1947 a UN special committee called for termination of the British mandate and partition of Palestine into an Arab and a Jewish state. The Arabs including neighboring Egypt opposed the creation of the new Zionist state but lacked powerful allies, whereas both the United States and the Soviet Union endorsed partition. In 1948 Truman rejected the advice of Secretary George Marshall and the State Department by formally recognizing the new Jewish state of Israel. The diplomats warned of perpetual turmoil, threats to Middle East oil supplies, opportunities they feared the Soviets might exploit, but Truman embraced the Zionist cause. Motivated by his own biblical fundamentalism, sympathy for Jews in the wake of the Holocaust, and domestic political considerations, Truman overruled his advisers.

DESIGNED BY SAUL BASS

OTTO PREMINGER PRESENTS PAUL NEWMAN, EVA MARIE SAINT, RALPH RICHARDSON, PETER LAWFORD, LEE J. COBB, SAL MINEO, JOHN DEREK, HUGH GRIFFITH, GREGORY RATOFF, FELIX AYLMER, DAVID OPATOSHU, JILL HAWORTH IN "EXODUS." SCREENPLAY BY DALTON TRUMBO. BASED ON THE NOVEL BY LEON URIS. MUSIC BY ERNEST GOLD. PHOTOGRAPHED IN SUPER PANAVISION 70, TECHNICOLOR® BY SAM LEAVITT. TODD AO STEREOPHONIC SOUND. A UNITED ARTISTS RELEASE. PRODUCED AND DIRECTED BY OTTO PREMINGER.

Figure 10.2 The Truman administration, motivated by biblical fundamentalism, sympathy in the wake of the Nazi genocide, and political considerations, recognized Israel in 1948. *Exodus*, the 1958 Leon Uris novel followed by an epic film (1960), tapped into culturally rooted US support for Israel in an escalating conflict with the less popular Palestinians and Arabs.

Source: Library of Congress, Prints and Photographs Division, LC-DIG-ppmsca-05656.

Support for Israel reflected changing American attitudes about Jews, who had been classified as separate members of a "Hebrew race" under the 1924 immigration law and frequently subjected to stereotypes as moneylenders and killers of Christ whose loyalties did not lie first and foremost with the United States. Only after World War II did the change in immigration law and inclusive references to a US "Judeo-Christian" religious heritage become widespread. Support for Zionism also assuaged feelings of guilt over the US non-response to the Nazi Holocaust. "America could not stand by while the victims of Hitler's racial madness were denied the opportunity to build new lives," Truman declared.

Truman's decision was popular in the United States, which had the largest Jewish population in the world at the time, but Jews were not alone in embracing Zionism. Many fundamentalist Protestants supported the establishment of a Jewish homeland and other Americans perceived parallels between Israeli settler colonialism and the US history of frontier expansion. Americans thus viewed Israel as advancing the cause of "white" European modernity, redeeming the biblical Promised Land from the darker-skinned Arab Muslim inhabitants of the region, who were often stereotypically viewed as backward, treacherous, and decadent. Like Americans Israelis were a "chosen" people on a mission to implant civilization in the wilderness for the Kingdom of God. The emergence of the **US-Israeli "special relationship"** thus rested on powerful cultural ground, which trumped the concerns of oil companies and State Department diplomats.

Determined to resist what they perceived as a new wave of European colonialism, the Arabs fought back against the partition of Palestine. In 1948 in the first **Arab-Israeli War** Israel crushed the Palestinian opposition and repulsed regional Arab armies. The Jewish settlers perpetrated massacres and wiped out hundreds of towns and villages while driving some 750,000 Palestinian Arabs from their homes. By the time of the ceasefire in January 1949, Israel had increased in size from the 55 percent of the former British Mandate under the UN partition plan to 77 percent. In September 1948 Jewish extremists assassinated a Swedish diplomat appointed by the UN, who had condemned Israel's aggression and called for the repatriation of Palestinian refugees as well as international status for Jerusalem.

Israel's refusal to give up land beyond the boundaries of the UN partition conjoined with Arab vows to destroy the Jewish state to ensure that the conflict would continue. Raids, border clashes, and lethal Israeli reprisals prevailed between the 1949 armistice agreements and the Suez Crisis in 1956. In 1953 Israeli commandos led by **Ariel Sharon** carried out a massacre at the village of Qibya on the West Bank of the Jordan River, killing 69 people. The United States and the UN condemned the indiscriminate assault.

In 1952 Nasser ousted the Egyptian monarch and quickly emerged as a charismatic leader of the Arab world and critic of Israel and Zionism. The British and French decided to intervene over Nasser's nationalization of the canal, though he had pledged to keep it open and pay compensation. Nasser had also angered Eisenhower and Dulles by proclaiming neutralism in the cold war and offering diplomatic recognition of "Red" China. However, the Eisenhower administration sought to improve American standing with the Arab states as part of the cold war policy of containing communism by limiting Soviet influence in the region.

Eisenhower wanted to protect Western access to the vast Middle East oil supplies upon which the West was increasingly dependent in the postwar "hydrocarbon age." Following World War II the **Anglo-American Oil Company** secured access to the rich oil supplies of Saudi Arabia through collaboration with the monarchy of Ibn Saud. Washington cultivated close relations with the repressive Saudi regime well into the next century because it was staunchly anti-communist and kept the oil flowing. By contrast, **Mohammed Mossadeq**, the democratically elected prime minister of Iran, moved to nationalize the Anglo-Iranian Oil Company (today's BP). US officials described the septuagenarian Mossadeq as a "dizzy old wizard" plagued with an "oriental mind." They decried Mossadeq's socialist tendencies and feared Iran would drift into the "Soviet orbit," though the Kremlin had played no role in his

Figure 10.3 In 1953 the CIA's Operation Ajax led to the overthrow of Iranian Prime Minister Mohammed Mossadeq (above), who was replaced by Shah Reza Pahlavi. The Eisenhower administration orchestrated the coup after Mossadeq nationalized Iranian oil supplies.

Source: Library of Congress, Prints and Photographs Division, LC-USZ62-111608.

rise to power. If Mossadeq remained in power, Dulles averred, the "free world would be deprived of the enormous assets represented by Iranian oil." Moreover "if Iran succumbed to the communists there was little doubt that in short order the other areas of the Middle East, with some sixty percent of the world's oil reserves, would fall into communist control."

Keen on using covert operations as a vital component of the New Look strategy, Eisenhower went into collusion with the British and a select group of Iranians to overthrow Mossadeq. In 1953 the CIA initiated **Operation Ajax**, a program of destabilizing Iranian society leading to the ouster of Mossadeq. In 2013 the CIA acknowledged, "The military coup that overthrew Mossadeq and his National Front cabinet was carried out under CIA direction as an act of US foreign policy, conceived and approved at the highest levels of government." Coordinated by Kermit Roosevelt, Theodore Roosevelt's grandson, the secret operation fomented unrest, doled out bribes, and broadcast disinformation leading to the overthrow of Mossadeq. **Prince Reza Pahlavi**, although described by the CIA as "a dangerous megalomaniac," took over in Iran with US backing. Under the shah's rule Iran kept the oil supplies flowing, became a leading purchaser of US weapons and other goods, and a loyal ally until the shah's overthrow by Islamic fundamentalists in 1979.

By the time the Suez Crisis erupted the Eisenhower administration was thus committed to protecting access to oil supplies and excluding the Soviets from the Middle East. For these reasons and because the three invaders had gone behind his back, Eisenhower used US clout to force them to withdraw from Suez and Egypt's Sinai Desert. Under intense US and UN pressure, Britain and France withdrew but Israel defied the Americans and refused to withdraw without receiving guarantees pertaining to maritime access in the region. Eisenhower declared in a televised address that it was wrong "that a nation which invades another should be permitted to exact conditions for withdrawal," but assured Israel that its maritime access would be maintained. The Israelis grudgingly withdrew from the Sinai and the Gaza Strip but threatened to re-intervene if the access was cut off or if cross-border attacks on the Jewish state continued.

Deeply concerned about possible Soviet inroads in the region, Eisenhower and Dulles sharply increased US involvement in the Middle East in the wake of Suez. Just prior to the European-Israeli invasion a US offer to Nasser to fund construction of the **Aswan Dam** fell through. Though anti-communist, Nasser turned to the Soviets for assistance with the construction of the high dam and electric power project. The Eisenhower administration feared that instability in Iraq, where the monarchy fell to a coup in 1958, and in Lebanon, divided between Christians, Muslims, and various sects, could lead to communist expansion. In July 1958 Eisenhower dispatched some 14,000 US Marines to back the Christian government of Camille Chamoun in Lebanon. The president used the occasion to propound the **"Eisenhower Doctrine"** in which he declared the United States would intervene to stop the spread of communism in the Middle East. Dulles justified the unprecedented deployment of troops to the Middle East in masculine terms, explaining, "Turkey,

Iran and Pakistan would feel—if we do not act—that our inaction is because we are afraid of the Soviet Union." In 1959 the three nations cited by Dulles joined with Britain and Iraq to forge the Central Treaty Organization, an anticommunist alliance promoted and funded by the United States.

From Revolution to Evolution

Following the Soviet repression in Hungary Eisenhower deemphasized psychological warfare and the quest for liberation in favor of a more gradual approach to undermining communism. Created in 1953, the **United States Information Agency** (USIA) collaborated with the advertising industry to launch global campaigns such as "People's Capitalism," which emphasized the material prosperity and individual opportunity in market-driven societies. US propaganda emphasized that communism served to enslave workers rather than liberate them whereas in the West workers could live well and could unionize. Women could work, take care of their homes and families, and emerge happy and fulfilled. As "the partner and helpmate of her husband," one missive explained, "the working wife in the United States considers first the welfare of her family and then the contribution she makes to a better standard of living."

Interpreting the Past
Cultural exchange and "soft power"

While treaties, alliances, and wars have been the hallmarks of conventional diplomacy, scholars have also revealed the role of popular culture, exchange programs, and the exercise of "soft power" in foreign relations. Beginning in the late 1950s the United States began to invest more heavily in educational and cultural exchange and the opening of business and trade relations as a means to exert influence behind the "iron curtain." While aggressive anti-communist propaganda produced little in return, US officials discovered that American popular culture appealed to the "hearts and minds" of foreign audiences including those in Russia and Eastern Europe. With the USIA taking the lead, Americans began to coordinate the exchange of students, scholars, scientists, musicians, athletes, businesspeople, and films and television programs throughout the world.

While the United States "pushed" its culture abroad, people around the world including the Soviet bloc "pulled" in a desire to access Western culture. The USIA promoted sports, art, and Hollywood films, which found ready audiences abroad, and staged popular exhibitions focused on culture and consumer goods, fashions, and late model automobiles. Music, ranging from jazz to opera, played an important role. Proud of their own rich musical tradition, Russians eagerly accessed Western music. In 1955 enraptured Soviet audiences took in the American opera "Porgy and Bess," whose African-American cast members helped deflect criticism of US racism. In 1958 Soviet premier Khrushchev personally awarded the Tchaikovsky Prize to the brilliant young American pianist Van Cliburn who performed before rapt Soviet audiences. The jazz trumpeter Louis Armstrong attracted a wide audience in the USSR and Eastern Europe. In 1959 Leonard Bernstein took the New York Philharmonic on tour in the USSR, where audiences were more than enthusiastic. They lined up after the performances "to touch us, to embrace us, even to kiss my hand," Bernstein recounted.

By the end of Eisenhower's second term the United States had made a start in cultural diplomacy and exploitation of soft power, yet the overall investment was less than 1 percent of the $50 billion annual expenditure on national security. Recognition of the importance of soft power increased in subsequent years but remained dwarfed by the expenditures on weapons systems and conventional diplomacy.

The shift away from psychological warfare produced greater emphasis on cultural exchange and a breakthrough agreement with the Soviet Union in 1958. Under the **Cultural Agreement**—the first bilateral agreement between the two superpowers in the postwar era—the cold war adversaries agreed to exchanges of students, professors, artists, writers, athletes, agricultural and scientific experts, and films and television programs. They also laid the groundwork for staging national exhibitions on each other's soil. An executive agreement rather than a treaty, the Cultural Agreement did not require Senate approval.

The exchange of national exhibitions took place in 1959 with the opening that summer of the Soviet exhibition in New York City, which featured Russian accomplishments in space, agriculture, and industry as well as music and theatrical performances. The subsequent **American Exhibition in Moscow**, staged by the USIA, made more of an impact not least because it became the site of the famous finger wagging "**kitchen debate**" between Khrushchev and Vice President Richard M. Nixon. The US exhibition in Moscow's Sokolniki Park featured Detroit automobiles, Western fashion, IBM computers, modern art, home appliances, and above all consumerism. The displays as well as the youthful, Russian-speaking American guides made a positive impression on most of the 2.7 million Russians who attended the exhibition, more than three times the number of Americans who visited the Soviet display in New York. Sipping Pepsi-Cola, which he subsequently allowed to be marketed in the USSR, Khrushchev acknowledged the appeal of modern capitalist society, but vowed, "In another seven years we will be on the same level as America." The Nixon–Khrushchev exchange heated up in the model kitchen, as the two traded claims over the superiority of the rival social systems.

Figure 10.4 Soviet women survey a modern refrigerator and kitchen equipment at the 1959 American National Exhibition in Moscow's Sokolniki Park.

Source: Library of Congress, Prints and Photographs Division, LC-DIG-ds-02077.

Figure 10.5 Soviet Premier Nikita Khrushchev and Vice President Richard Nixon exchange views at the American National Exhibition in Moscow. In the famous "kitchen debate" both men claimed the superiority of their respective social systems.

Source: Library of Congress, Prints and Photographs Division, LC-DIG-ppmsca-19730.

While Khrushchev displayed anxiety over the advanced US economy and consumer culture, Americans reacted with virtual panic as the Soviets once again closed the gap in the nuclear weapons race more rapidly than expected. In October 1957 the launch into orbit of the satellite ***Sputnik*** underscored a new era of US vulnerability to Soviet rockets potentially armed with nuclear warheads. *Sputnik* created the illusion that Soviet scientists held a strategic advantage in the development of intercontinental ballistic missiles (ICBMs). When the Soviets followed up the *Sputnik* launch by hurtling a dog into space, *Newsweek* asserted, "For the first time in history the Western world finds itself mortally in danger from the East."

In the wake of *Sputnik* the Democrats, deprived of the White House for two terms, wielded the cold war as a political weapon, much as the Republicans had done after the "loss" of China and the stalemate in Korea. Democrats including the 1960 presidential nominee John F. Kennedy charged that *Sputnik* reflected a "**missile gap**" in which the United States had fallen dangerously behind the USSR in the nuclear arms race. This charge, like the claim that communist sympathizers had "sold China down the river" in 1949, had no basis in fact. The United States continued to maintain an advantage, especially through the air and sea, in the ability to deliver devastation to the USSR in the event of a nuclear war. However apocryphal, the missile gap proved a powerful political weapon for the Democrats and proponents of militarization and escalation of the arms race.

The *Sputnik*-inspired panic convinced many Americans that "Ivan" was progressing more swiftly in education than "Johnny," particularly in the realm of mathematics and science. As a result, in 1958 Eisenhower and Congress collaborated on the **National Defense Education Act** authorizing increased investment in education with emphasis on science and technology. The only other major domestic initiative of the Eisenhower years, the Interstate Highway Act (1956) also received impetus from national security considerations. During World War II Eisenhower had been concerned with the slow pace that troops and equipment moved across the continent on secondary roads. The limited access interstate highway system allowed for much swifter movement of people and goods in the event of war, as well as the betterment of commerce and public mobility.

Soviet boasts about Sputnik and the intercontinental ballistic missiles obscured their own concerns about the arms race, particularly as NATO moved to place **theater nuclear weapons** in Europe. Scholars such as Harvard professor Henry A. Kissinger, who published *Nuclear Weapons and Foreign Policy* in 1957, argued that nuclear weapons should be made usable in limited wars rather than adhering to the all or nothing approach of "massive retaliation." Kennan and other critics condemned the decision to expand the arms race onto European shores, arguing that the Soviets would reciprocate and tighten their grip over Eastern Europe. Khrushchev offered to negotiate over demilitarization and disengagement of the great powers from Europe. Dulles, former Secretary of State Acheson, and many US allies, especially Adenauer, remained adamantly opposed to such negotiations.

Khrushchev sought **peaceful coexistence** with the capitalist West in order to divert resources from the cold war to Soviet economic development, but the mercurial leader was also prone to emotional outbursts over Western imperialism and vows to "bury" capitalism. Khrushchev had denounced Stalin, abolished the communist international organization, and cut Soviet troop levels and defense spending, but he had generated little reciprocation from the West in toning down the cold war. Angered by the US rejection of diplomacy and the decision to place nuclear weapons in Europe, Khrushchev demanded resolution of the ambiguous status of Berlin. The former capital of the Third Reich lay inside East Germany but the West still had access rights. The city's access to the West undermined the authority of the East German government and opened the door to a "brain drain" of scientists and professionals. Hundreds of thousands of Germans migrated through Berlin in the expectation of greater opportunity in the capitalist West.

In November 1958, under pressure from hardliners inside the Kremlin and from Mao Zedong in China, Khrushchev issued the **Berlin ultimatum**. The Soviet leader announced plans to sign a treaty with East Germany and cut off Western access to Berlin. This second Berlin crisis carried the threat of war in the event that the Soviets blockaded the city and the West moved to retain access. The renewed Berlin crisis, coupled with *Sputnik* and the missile gap, empowered cold war hardliners in the major capitals, undermining the prospects of diplomacy and peaceful coexistence.

Khrushchev and Eisenhower persisted, however, and the Soviet leader made a historic visit to the United States for direct talks. Dulles had opposed the summit meeting, which Eisenhower scheduled only after Dulles's death from cancer in May 1959. In September Khrushchev arrived in Washington and soon embarked on a cross-country tour culminating in a visit to Los Angeles and San Francisco. Returning to Washington, the two leaders met at Eisenhower's retreat at Camp David, Maryland. They failed to resolve the Berlin issue, but continued the progress on a broad agenda of more open communications and cultural exchange. Despite clear evidence from past test blasts of the dangers of above ground nuclear tests, the United States had been reluctant to sign a **test ban treaty** with the Soviets. At Camp David the two leaders agreed to maintain a moratorium on above ground tests in anticipation of a formal treaty that would eliminate them.

With the "spirit of Camp David" the two powers appeared to be headed for a diplomatic breakthrough until the shoot down of an American spy plane over Soviet airspace shattered the prospects of accord. The CIA had been conducting secret aerial reconnaissance flights violating Soviet airspace for years, with Eisenhower personally approving of each mission. On May 1, 1960, the Soviets succeeded for the first time in shooting down the high-flying U-2 spy plane. Assuming the pilot had been killed, or taken the cyanide capsule he was supplied in event of capture, Eisenhower publicly denied Soviet charges of the spy mission whereupon Khrushchev embarrassed the administration by producing the pilot, Francis Gary Powers, who had parachuted to safety. The Soviet leader also put on display the plane's wreckage, including the sophisticated camera equipment.

Figure 10.6 The Soviets embarrassed the United States by putting on display in Moscow the remnants of a CIA U-2 spy plane, which secretly overflew Soviet airspace to photograph military installations until being shot down on May 1, 1960. The pilot, Francis Gary Powers, was put on trial but later exchanged for a Soviet spy. Powers died in 1977 when his television news helicopter crashed in southern California.

Source: Library of Congress, Prints and Photographs Division, LC-USZ62-87828.

The **U-2 incident**, compounded by its occurrence on the Soviet May Day holiday, undermined Khrushchev's standing with Soviet and Chinese hardliners, who insisted that the Americans could not be trusted as negotiating partners. Khrushchev, who would be ousted in 1964, wrote in his memoirs, "From the time Gary Powers was shot down in a U-2 over the Soviet Union I was no longer in full control." Less than two weeks after the U-2 incident Eisenhower and Khrushchev met as scheduled at the summit in Paris. Reflecting the new hard line, Khrushchev began the meeting by demanding an apology and renunciation of any future spy missions. The U-2 intelligence had been valuable, revealing that there was no missile gap hence Eisenhower refused to give it up or appear to be backing down to a Soviet ultimatum. Khrushchev responded by walking out of the summit. Eisenhower regretted that "the stupid U-2 mess" ended progress toward a test ban treaty and ruined the prospects of meaningful diplomacy for the rest of his term, including forfeiting his plans to visit the USSR.

The Military–Industrial Complex

In the wake of the U-2 incident Eisenhower lamented, "There was nothing left worthwhile for him to do until the end of his presidency," yet he would leave an important legacy by means of the most historic farewell address since George Washington's. Ironically, the military hero Eisenhower warned that the country had fallen into the grip of a militarized foreign policy in which an array of special interests dominated, skewed the allocation of national resources, and stood in the path of diplomacy. Eisenhower warned against "the acquisition of unwarranted influence, whether sought or unsought, by the **military– industrial complex**" (MIC). As public policy threatened to become "captive of a scientific–technological elite," the "potential for the disastrous rise of misplaced power exists and will persist." Eisenhower referred to an "almost insidious penetration of our own minds that the only thing this country is engaged in is weaponry and missiles." In sum, "a permanent armaments industry of vast proportions" menaced national life.

The MIC had deep roots but Eisenhower shared responsibility for the very problem he now condemned. In the eight years of his presidency the government had spent over $350 billion on defense, or 75 cents of every budget dollar for military-related purposes. The near hysterical response to *Sputnik* and the rise of the fictive "missile gap" had alerted him, however, to the problem that he now defined for the nation in the last act of his presidency. Eisenhower was not the first to issue such a warning. In the mid-1930s the Senate Nye Committee had called attention to the collusion between the military and private industry during World War I, but the phenomenon dramatically accelerated in World War II and became permanent with the creation of the cold war national security state. The MIC reflected the logic of NSC 68 (1950) that had called on the nation to spend whatever was deemed necessary regardless of cost to wage the cold war against the perceived existential threat of communism.

After World War II the Defense Department became the single largest patron of science. Perceived military needs determined what scientists and engineers studied, designed, and thought. Scholars understood that funding readily available for military research and development (R&D) would not be available for humanitarian research. In addition to the State and Defense Departments and the four armed service branches, the Atomic Energy Commission (AEC), CIA, FBI, NSC, the National Security Agency (NSA, created in 1953), the National Aeronautical and Space Administration (NASA, created in 1958), the Defense Intelligence Agency (DIA, created in 1961), and numerous other agencies sponsored university and scientific research. Interservice rivalry among the four armed service branches also fueled the MIC, as each sought funding for bases, weapons, and strategic priority in national security planning.

The Pentagon, the White House, Congress, corporations, universities, and foundations together fueled the MIC. During the cold war the defense establishment emphasized enemy capabilities, such as the virtually non-existent threat of a Soviet assault on Western Europe, at the expense of Soviet intentions, which were to defend the Soviet sphere of influence and homeland while avoiding war with the West. Intelligence agencies produced estimates of enemy capabilities that virtually ensured R&D of new weapons systems.

Generations of scientists, professors, and graduate students devoted their research to finding new ways to undermine communism. The Massachusetts Institute of Technology (MIT), Harvard, Caltech, and others received millions of dollars in federal funds. Federal appropriations approximately doubled after the Korean War, as Johns Hopkins, California-Berkeley, Stanford, Chicago, most of the Ivy League schools, and myriad state universities across the country received funding for military-related applied and classified research. The bulk of defense funding, however, went to a few elite institutions, led by Boston's MIT, which was dubbed "the Pentagon on the Charles [River]." The Ford Foundation, the Carnegie Fund, various Rockefeller groups, the Social Science Research Council, think tanks such as the RAND (for research and development) Corporation, and other foundations collaborated in the emergence of an "**academic security complex**."

With scientific research dictated by the national security establishment, academic programs and corporate products became skewed toward military technology and away from the civilian economy. Discoveries in nuclear physics, aerodynamics, and supercomputing produced a series of breathtaking advances in military technology. After development of the atomic and hydrogen bombs came ICBMs equipped with multiple warheads, silent and thus invulnerable nuclear submarines, warp-speed jet aircraft, massive bombers, sophisticated satellite, microwave, and laser technology, biological and chemical weapons, and myriad additional innovations.

Congress and private corporations worked hand-in-hand in fueling the MIC. Boeing, General Dynamics, Lockheed, and scores of other contractors joined more mainstream corporations, such as General Motors and General Electric, in the pursuit of the easy-to-come-by federal largesse for militarization. Congress became a compliant part of US militarization, as it routinely approved virtually every new weapons system that could be devised. With the cold war ethos firmly ensconced, and noninterventionists and peace internationalists politically moribund, the MIC flourished. The news media, overwhelmingly compliant during the cold war, rarely probed the rampant waste, fraud, and corruption built into the MIC.

By the time of Eisenhower's valedictory address, the MIC had created the most massive military machine in human history. The outgoing hero president's message was heard and remains historic but the message was not heeded. A series of cold war crises under incoming President Kennedy refueled the MIC, which has remained a powerful force in American life. By the early years of the twenty-first century the United States produced about half the world's armaments while its defense budget was roughly equivalent to those of the rest of the world combined.

Kennedy and Cold War Crises

The cold war was the major issue in the 1960 presidential campaign in which Kennedy narrowly defeated Nixon. The young Democrat blamed Eisenhower and Nixon for the Cuban Revolution leading to the triumph of **Fidel Castro** as well as other communist movements in the so-called "Third World" (Chapter 11). Kennedy made the most of the fictional "missile gap" and vowed to contain communism more effectively through a strategy of "**flexible response.**" In contrast to the New Look emphasis on "massive retaliation," the new administration's approach placed more emphasis on **counterinsurgency warfare** and other war-fighting strategies.

In Their Words

Excerpt from President Kennedy's Inaugural Address, January 20, 1961

We observe today not a victory of party but a celebration of freedom—symbolizing an end as well as a beginning—signifying renewal as well as change. For I have sworn before you and Almighty God the same solemn oath our forebears prescribed nearly a century and three-quarters ago.

The world is very different now. For man holds in his mortal hands the power to abolish all forms of human poverty and all forms of human life. And yet the same revolutionary beliefs for which our forebears fought are still at issue around the globe—the belief that the rights of man come not from the generosity of the state but from the hand of God.

We dare not forget today that we are the heirs of that first revolution. Let the word go forth from this time and place, to friend and foe alike, that the torch has been passed to a new generation of Americans—born in this century, tempered by war, disciplined by a hard and bitter peace, proud of our ancient heritage—and unwilling to witness or permit the slow undoing of those human rights to which this nation has always been committed, and to which we are committed today at home and around the world.

Let every nation know, whether it wishes us well or ill, that we shall pay any price, bear any burden, meet any hardship, support any friend, oppose any foe to assure the survival and the success of liberty.

This much we pledge—and more.

Committed to aggressive prosecution of the cold war, Kennedy vowed in his Inaugural Address that the United States would "pay any price, bear any burden" to defend its interests. By this time Khrushchev had joined Mao and other hardliners in trumpeting "**wars of national liberation**" against imperialist oppression in the developing world. With both sides drawing the line, the cold war was entering into its most dangerous phase since the revolution in China and the outbreak of the Korean War.

In June 1961 a meeting in Vienna between Khrushchev and the new American president went as badly as the last summit between Eisenhower and Khrushchev. The Soviet leader attempted to bully the young president, who was already reeling from the unsuccessful **Bay of Pigs invasion** of Cuba just two months earlier. After being briefed by Eisenhower, Kennedy had approved the CIA program to invade Cuba with an exile force in order to topple Castro. At the summit Khrushchev chided Kennedy for the failed invasion and reiterated the Berlin ultimatum. He informed Kennedy that the Soviets would sign a treaty with East Germany by the end of the year and if the West tried to infringe upon the closed air and ground access to Berlin it would mean war. "Force will be met with force," Khrushchev declared. "If the US wants war, that's its problem." Kennedy replied, "Then, Mr. Chairman, there will be a war. It will be a long, cold winter."

War was averted, however, by the East German and Soviet decision to build a wall through the heart of the city, cutting off East from West Berlin without restricting Western access to its half of the city. In August 1961 the erection of the wall began as military battalions faced off in Berlin. The **Berlin Wall**, which the East Germans called "an anti-fascist protective barrier," divided friends and families for generations but stemmed the "brain drain" and allowed the GDR to clamp down on the black market and strengthen its authority over the economy, which began to grow under a single currency. However, the Wall became a potent symbol of communist repression, especially as border guards began to shoot to kill would-be defectors. The United States and its allies declined to go to war over the division of the city but did not hesitate to call attention to the Wall as a propaganda weapon. In August Kennedy delivered a powerful speech in Berlin, declaring in German to a cheering crowd, "*Ich bin ein Berliner*" ("I am a Berliner.") The Berlin Wall marked the ultimate symbol of the cold war division of Europe but at the same time provided stability by removing the threat of war over the divided German capital.

With Europe divided but stabilized the cold war intensified in the "developing world," with Cuba by far the most acute point of contention as far as the United States was concerned. Castro's takeover and his conversion to communism were completely unacceptable to the United States, an embarrassing affront to US power in its "backyard," and a pernicious example for Latin America and the rest of the world. After the failure of the CIA's Bay of Pigs invasion, the agency launched a covert operation to assassinate the Cuban leader. All of the programs of **Operation Mongoose**, designed to overthrow or kill Castro, also failed hence the Cuban leader remained in power until 2008 when he turned the government over to his brother.

Figure 10.7 Cuba's revolutionary president Fidel Castro took center stage at the UN meeting in New York in September 1960. As Castro defied the United States and gravitated toward communism, the Eisenhower and Kennedy administrations put in motion ultimately unsuccessful plans to overthrow or assassinate him.

Source: Library of Congress, Prints and Photographs Division, LC-USZ62-134150.

The US efforts to overthrow or kill Castro prompted the Cuban leader to ally ever more closely with the USSR leading to the **Cuban Missile Crisis** of 1962. That summer the Soviets, seeking to confront the United States with a situation analogous to their own—having theater nuclear weapons aimed at them from Western Europe and adjacent Turkey—approached Castro about placing nuclear missiles in Cuba. Khrushchev and his comrades also wanted to provide Cuba with protection against invasion by the United States. Castro agreed and the top-secret construction project began.

The 13-day missile crisis unfolded in mid-October when US intelligence sources learned of the construction of the missile sites, confirmed by photographs taken on U-2 reconnaissance flights. Asked about the construction project the Soviets lied, denying any intentions to place nuclear missiles on the Caribbean island. Khrushchev underestimated Kennedy, anticipating that once the missiles were in place the US president would react with strong words but ultimately acquiesce to a *fait accompli*. Instead Kennedy and his advisers determined that the only acceptable outcome was removal of the intermediate range missiles from Cuba. The course of **brinksmanship** was thus set, as the crisis carried the palpable threat of nuclear war.

Figure 10.8 On October 22, 1962, President John F. Kennedy announced on national television that the United States was setting up a naval blockade to halt supply of nuclear missile parts to Cuba. The cold war adversaries went to the brink but averted nuclear war.

Source: Library of Congress, Prints and Photographs Division, LC-USZ62-129105.

On October 22 Kennedy went on national television to announce that the missiles would not be tolerated and that the United States was establishing a "quarantine" (in reality a blockade) of international waters through which Cuba could be supplied. Kennedy rejected the recommendation of some of the advisers on his Executive Committee to bomb the missile sites or launch a general invasion and takeover of Cuba. In addition to the blockade, Kennedy sent reinforcements to the US naval base at Guantánamo Bay, Cuba, and declared that a limited missile attack on the United States would precipitate a massive nuclear response. Khrushchev denounced the naval blockade, which was an act of war under international law, and said the US action was "propelling humankind into the abyss of a world-nuclear missile war." On October 27 the possibility of war spiked when an American U-2 was shot down over Cuban airspace by Soviet forces on the ground, killing the Air Force pilot. By that time, however, a diplomatic solution was in the offing, averting the most severe crisis in the history of the cold war.

The *modus vivendi* that brought an end to the missile crisis was Soviet agreement to withdraw the missiles in return for a US pledge not to invade Cuba and to dismantle some missiles of its own. Khrushchev first offered in a letter to Kennedy to dismantle the missiles in return for the pledge of nonintervention in Cuba. Under pressure from hardliners in the Kremlin, he quickly followed up with another letter demanding that the United States dismantle missiles aimed at the USSR from across the Black Sea in Turkey as well as from Italy. The president's brother and attorney general, Robert Kennedy, had opened a back-channel dialogue with Soviet ambassador Anatoly Dobrynin leading to resolution of the crisis. Publicly and through the UN the Soviets agreed to dismantle the Cuban missiles and the United States agreed to respect the sovereignty of Cuba. Secretly, Washington also promised to remove intermediate range nuclear missiles targeting the USSR from Italy and Turkey.

Keeping the latter part of the agreement secret facilitated Kennedy's claim to have forced the Soviets to back down on US terms. Masculinity played a role in the handling of the crisis and its aftermath, as Kennedy and other US leaders gloated that they had made the Soviets "blink first." Kennedy stated in graphic terms that he had de-masculinized Khrushchev. In the wake of a humiliating defeat in the Bay of Pigs, the Kennedy administration claimed a re-masculinizing triumph but only after going to the brink of nuclear war.

Revelations in subsequent years revealed how close the world came to nuclear conflict. The Soviets had nuclear warheads in place in Cuba and ready to use on artillery rockets and bombers. Had the United States attacked Cuba Castro later declared he would have demanded their use. During the crisis the US Navy surrounded and dropped depth charges on a Soviet submarine, prompting the captain to order a nuclear torpedo made ready to fire. After a heated argument on board the submarine the commander, Vasili Arkhipov, decided instead to comply with the demand to surface. Even after the crisis had apparently been resolved the Soviets decided to leave some 100 tactical nuclear weapons secretly emplaced in Cuba, as these had not been on the list for removal. However, Castro was so angry about the resolution of the crisis the Soviets feared he might act precipitously or that the crisis might be renewed, hence they abandoned the plan thus leaving Cuba where it began, bereft of nuclear weapons.

The Cuban Missile Crisis had many varied and significant consequences and repercussions. The crisis spurred progress in diplomacy, as the United States and the USSR agreed to establish a "**hotline**" for emergency telephone communications between the governments in the event of future crises. Secondly, a year after the missile crisis the United States, the USSR, and Britain signed the **Limited Test Ban Treaty (LTBT)**, which the US Senate confirmed, finally bringing an end to above ground nuclear tests. The LTBT established the groundwork for future and more far-reaching nuclear arms control agreements.

For Khrushchev the Cuban Missile Crisis was another blow to his prestige, setting the stage for his ouster in 1964. The Soviets felt humiliated and forced to back down in the crisis, which Khrushchev had instigated with reckless disregard for the potential consequences. Castro and, especially, Mao condemned the Soviets for weakly backing down. On the other hand, the US guarantee of Cuban sovereignty confirmed Castro's control over the island, enabling the Cuban leader to continue to defy the United States for decades.

Allies backed Washington during the missile crisis but played no role in the decision making of the Kennedy administration. Washington kept Harold Macmillan, the prime minister of Britain, which was the only other country in the world with nuclear weapons at the time, well informed about the Cuban crisis. Although the British had not supported US efforts to isolate Castro, and also viewed the Caribbean blockade as illegal under international law, Macmillan and opposition Labor Party leaders nonetheless backed the American play. As with the British, US allies in Ottawa, Paris, and Bonn, among other capitals, were shown photographs of the missile sites and supported the US decision to force them out. Although French President Charles de Gaulle backed the United States, the Caribbean crisis showed how easily Europe might be brought indirectly into a nuclear war, influencing his later decision to withdraw France from NATO's integrated military command. The Kennedy administration received crucial backing from the Organization of American States (OAS). On October 23 the OAS endorsed the "quarantine," which Washington promptly cited as legal justification for the blockade.

In the weeks following the missile crisis, as the initial glow of triumph wore off, Kennedy reflected on the sobering event. He concluded that the cold war should not continue to be conducted in such a way as to take the world to the brink of nuclear war. On June 10, 1963, in his **American University Address** in Washington Kennedy called for "Genuine peace . . . not merely in our time but peace in all time." He urged progress toward a comprehensive test ban treaty and set the stage for signing the LTBT a few months later. Finally, the president called for a "reexamination" of Western attitudes toward the USSR, noting that Americans frequently overlooked the fact that no nation "suffered more than the Soviet Union in the Second World War." Khrushchev commended the speech, which the Soviet press reprinted uncensored and unabridged.

The Cuban Missile Crisis heightened fears of reckless actions or military coups that might culminate in nuclear war. In 1964 the films *Failsafe* and *Dr. Strangelove*, the former a drama and the latter a dark comedy, were widely viewed and critically acclaimed, as the cold war continued to impact American popular culture. Thousands of Americans as well as people in other countries constructed backyard **fallout shelters** stocked with medicine, water, and canned goods, where families could retreat in the event of nuclear war. Contingency plans for possible nuclear war entered into urban planning and renewal projects as "disaster relief" facilities.

Grassroots activist groups gained momentum in the wake of the missile crisis and played a key role in lobbying for the eventual test ban treaty and future arms control agreements. In 1957 arms control advocates created **SANE**— National Committee for a Sane Nuclear Policy—which garnered the support of Eleanor Roosevelt, African-American leaders A. Philip Randolph and Martin Luther King, and labor leader Walter Reuther. Another influential group was **Women Strike for Peace** (WSP), formed in 1961 after more than 50,000 women across the country marched for peace and in opposition to above ground nuclear tests. The mostly white, educated, and middle-class women of WSP self-consciously adopted a successful strategy of using the primary postwar cultural role of women as housewives and mothers to advocate for peace for the sake of children and families.

Sino-Soviet Split

The Cuban Missile Crisis exposed a growing rift in the communist world that Americans had once perceived as monolithic. Despite the 1950 alliance, the divisions between the Soviets and the Chinese were deep seated. Mao resented Stalin's support for Chiang Kai-shek and the nationalists during World War II and for what he considered Stalin's rude and contemptuous treatment of him personally. In addition to tensions in the Sino-Soviet relationship, in 1948 Tito rejected Stalin's authority, which brought Yugoslavia and the USSR to the brink of war. "Titoism" became a model that American diplomats urged eastern European nations to adopt as part of the overall strategy to promote fissures in the communist world.

Khrushchev's thoroughgoing denunciation of Stalin in 1956 alarmed Mao, who never embraced the new Soviet leader as steward of the communist world. The USSR aided many development programs in China only to have Mao adopt his own radical road to communism. Mao rejected the gradualism of Soviet style five-year plans for utopian initiatives centered on the concept of "continuous revolution." In 1958 Mao launched the **Great Leap Forward**, a radical political and economic reform program. By 1960 the great leap had been backward into economic disaster and famine, necessitating additional Soviet economic assistance.

Mao often reminded the Soviets that the Chinese rather than they were the true communists willing to battle US imperialism head on even at the risk of nuclear attack. They had undertaken that risk in Korea and did so again in the **Taiwan Strait conflict**. The Chinese nationalist regime, having fled to Taiwan in 1949, held onto the islands of Jinmen and Mazu, located 2 and 10 miles, respectively, in the Taiwan Strait off the coast of the mainland. Both the nationalists and the communists viewed the islands as a possible staging ground for an invasion, which never occurred despite sporadic clashes.

The United States, which had interposed the seventh fleet between Taiwan and the mainland with the outbreak of the Korean War, maintained its support for Taiwan, or the Republic of China (ROC). The Chinese viewed with hostility the US-led **Southeast Asia Treaty Organization** (SEATO), a NATO clone signed in Manila in 1954, and designed to contain communism in Asia. In September of that year the cold war in Asia escalated when the PRC began bombardment from the mainland of Jinmen, followed by similar assaults on Mazu and the Dachen Islands, also held by the nationalists. Determined to back Taiwan's possession of the islands, the United States signed a mutual defense treaty, pledging to back the ROC in the event of attack by the PRC. Congress got in on the act in 1955, passing the **Formosa Resolution** authorizing the president to take whatever action deemed necessary to defend Taiwan and the offshore islands. The PRC deeply resented US interference in what it considered an internal Chinese conflict whereas Taiwan continued its effective cultivation of the China Lobby and generous US military assistance.

In both this instance and in the **Second Taiwan Strait Crisis** in 1958 the Eisenhower administration invoked the threat of "massive retaliation" with nuclear weapons to preclude the repatriation of the small islands with the mainland. When the PRC resumed bombing of the offshore islands in the second crisis, the administration dispatched a virtual naval armada including seven carriers and threatened to use the bomb. The Eisenhower administration resupplied Taiwan, Chiang's Air Force held off the attack, and the second crisis soon ebbed. A strange stability emerged and lasted for 20 years in which the PRC and the ROC symbolically shelled each other's military positions along the strait on alternate days.

The resumption of bombardment of the offshore islands in 1958 came as an unwelcome surprise to Khrushchev, who called on the PRC to moderate its behavior, fearing it could lead to superpower conflict. Embarking on the radical Great Leap at this time, Mao criticized not only the Soviet path to socialism but also Khrushchev's emphasis on peaceful coexistence, which Mao opposed. Mao viewed Marxism–Leninism and capitalism as inveterate oppositions and trumpeted "wars of national liberation" in the developing world. He criticized the Soviets for lack of aggressive support for Third World revolutions. For Mao the Soviets backing down in Cuba was an example of craven appeasement of the US-led imperialist forces.

Figure 10.9 Mao's growing radicalism, embodied by the concept of "permanent revolution," contributed to the full-blown Sino-Soviet rift. In 1966 the "great helmsman"—"the reddest, reddest sun in our heart"—instituted the decade-long Great Proletarian Cultural Revolution, which convulsed Chinese society killing and displacing millions of people.

Source: Library of Congress, Prints and Photographs Division, LC-USZC4-3376.

The Sino-Soviet rift, emerging full-blown in 1963, opened up genuine possibilities for American diplomacy to exploit, a process that unfolded in the 1960s and 1970s. The cleavage grew wider during this time, as Mao denounced Khrushchev's successor, **Leonid Brezhnev**, for taking the USSR down the "capitalist road." In 1966 Mao launched his most radical program, the **Great Proletarian Cultural Revolution**, underscoring his commitment to "permanent revolution." The disastrous campaign lasted 10 years and further strained Mao's relations with the USSR and the United States as well as his own people. The Sino-Soviet rift peaked in 1969, as the two communist powers fought a border war along the Ussuri River. China had become a nuclear power in 1964 but remained militarily inferior to the USSR, which threatened a wider war. Washington, ironically, called for restraint in the conflict between the two communist powers.

Japan and the two Koreas remained key players in the cold war in Asia. In 1951 the United States, Japan, and 46 other countries signed the **San Francisco Peace Treaty** resolving issues of the Pacific War. Czechoslovakia, Poland, and the USSR attended the summit but refused to sign the treaty. Japan gave up claims to its former colony of Korea as well as various islands including Formosa (Taiwan), Sakhalin, and the Kurile Islands. Japan turned over control of **Okinawa** as a US military base, which it remained well into the twenty-first century. With the United States providing for its defense Japan focused on economic growth, which took off with the Korean War and remained robust for decades.

Many Japanese resented neo-colonial subjugation to the United States and thus demanded revision of the San Francisco Treaty. The **revised security treaty of 1960** curbed the US ability to act unilaterally in Japan but maintained the military occupation. The revised treaty spurred massive protests in Japan and forced cancellation of a planned visit to the country by Eisenhower. Prime Minister Kishi Nobusuke resorted to high-handed maneuvers to get the revised treaty ratified by the Japanese parliament.

The Soviets under Khrushchev normalized relations with Japan in 1956 but Dulles essentially vetoed a compromise over the disputed status of the Kurile Islands. The Japanese were set to agree to the return of two islands while the Soviets would retain control of the other two, but Dulles told the Japanese the United States would never leave Okinawa if Japan signed the accord with the USSR. Dulles succeeded in keeping Soviet-Japanese relations unsettled, which reinforced Japan's military dependence on the United States in the event of conflict with the USSR. In subsequent years Japanese officials began referring to all four of the Kurile Islands as the "Northern Territories," ensuring continued disputation with the Soviets over the status of the islands.

The divided Korean Peninsula remained at the center of the power struggle in Asia. Kim Il-sung viewed Khrushchev's ascendancy and denunciation of Stalin as destabilizing, but the North Korean leader fended off Soviet efforts to force reforms or oust him from leadership. From that point forward Kim skillfully played the Soviets and the Chinese off amid the growing Sino-Soviet split. He threatened to enter into alliance with one or the other as a means of gaining resources and military backing from both while maintaining his own ironclad dictatorship.

The Korean War vaulted South Korea to the center of the US containment strategy throughout Asia. The heavy US troop presence and dramatically increased involvement in Korea's economy and society made the state a virtual colony of the United States. As in Japan resentment of US domination emerged. Student protests in 1960 drove Rhee from power, but the United States backed as his successor a military dictatorship under **Park Chung-hee**, which lasted until his assassination in 1979. In 1965 Park signed a peace treaty with Japan, whose loans and economic assistance accelerated South Korea's rapid economic growth in sharp contrast to lagging development in North Korea.

Select Bibliography

Hixson, Walter L. *Parting the Curtain: Propaganda, Culture, and the Cold War, 1945–1961.* New York: St. Martin's Press, 1997.

Sherry, Michael S. *In the Shadow of War: The United States Since the 1930s*. New Haven, CT: Yale University Press, 1995.

Leffler, Melvyn, ed. *The Cambridge History of the Cold War, Vol. I: Origins*. New York: Cambridge University Press, 2010.

Harrison, Hope M. *Driving the Soviets Up the Wall: Soviet-East German Relations, 1953–1961*. Princeton, NJ: Princeton University Press, 2003.

Larres, Klaus and Osgood, Kenneth. *The Cold War After Stalin's Death: A Missed Opportunity for Peace?* Lanham, MD: Rowan & Littlefield, 2006.

Hasegawa, Tsuyoshi. *The Cold War in East Asia, 1945–1991*. Washington: Woodrow Wilson Center Press, 2011.

Tucker, Nancy. *Dangerous Strait: The US-China-Taiwan Crisis*. New York: Columbia University Press, 2005.

Jacobs, Matthew F. *Imagining the Middle East: The Building of an American Foreign Policy, 1918–1967*. Chapel Hill: University of North Carolina Press, 2011.

Yaqub, Salim. *Containing Arab Nationalism: The Eisenhower Doctrine and the Middle East*. Chapel Hill: University of North Carolina Press, 2004.

Schoultz, Lars. *That Infernal Little Cuban Republic: The United States and the Cuban Revolution*. Chapel Hill: University of North Carolina Press, 2009.

Fursenko, Aleksandr and Naftali, Timothy. *One Hell of a Gamble: Khrushchev, Castro, and Kennedy, 1958–1964*. New York: W.W. Norton, 1997.

Roman, Peter J. *Eisenhower and the Missile Gap*. Ithaca, NY: Cornell University Press, 1995.

Koistinen, Paul A. *The Political Economy of American Warfare, 1945–2011*. Lawrence: University Press of Kansas, 2012.

Robin, Ron. *The Making of the Cold War Enemy: Culture and Politics in the Military-Intellectual Complex*. Princeton, NJ: Princeton University Press, 2001.

Chatfield, Charles. *The American Peace Movement: Ideals and Activism*. New York: Twayne Publishers, 1992.

11 Diplomacy in the "Third World"

Overview

The postwar period was not only the era of the cold war it was also the era of decolonization and the rise of the "**Third World**." In the wake of World War II millions of people in Asia, Africa, and Latin America sought to throw off Western colonialism and its legacies. The combination of the cold war and decolonization proved volatile. Both the "first" and "second" worlds of capitalism and communism contended for allies, markets, and influence in the decolonizing world. As Koreans could attest, the cold war was not always cold in the Third World, where the conflict was often fought with devastating consequences for developing nations.

Decolonization

Around 1900, at the height of the colonial era, more than half of Asia, more than 90 percent of Africa, and much of Central America and the Caribbean were under colonial rule. Motivated by economic exploitation and imperial rivalry, and justified by racism and technological superiority, Europeans and Americans colonized vulnerable peoples. Violent repression was intrinsic to colonialism, as the occupying powers typically policed rebellions, imprisoned resistance leaders, cultivated collaboration, and often used extreme measures to control the population. In the late nineteenth century colonial policies in Asia and Africa produced famines.

World War I dealt a body blow to colonialism as a result of the emphasis on "self-determination" and a world made "safe for democracy." This was music to the ears of colonial resistance leaders such as **Jawaharlal Nehru** in India and **Ho Chi Minh** in Vietnam. However, Wilson had meant self-determination for white Europeans, as the US president and his European allies did not believe the dark-skinned residents of the developing world were ready for independence. Secretary of State Robert Lansing warned Wilson that the rhetoric of self-determination was "loaded with dynamite" as it posed "the danger of putting such ideas into the minds of certain races." Rather than liberating the non-Western world the United States defended its primacy over the Americas while collaborating with the European powers in the **mandate system**, a perpetuation of colonial rule in Asia and Africa.

World War II shook the foundations of colonialism and spurred renewed hopes of liberation for millions of people in the developing world, or the "global South" as it is sometimes referenced. President Franklin D. Roosevelt criticized European colonialism and declared that the occupying powers should make plans to transition their colonies to independence after the war. Britain, France, Belgium, and the Netherlands had been badly damaged by German and Japanese triumphs over them and had lost credibility and prestige in the developing world. The colonial powers nonetheless vowed to resist decolonization. British Prime Minister Winston Churchill led the resistance, rejecting any "suggestion that the British Empire is to be put in the dock and examined by everyone to see if it is up to standard."

Toward the end of the war Roosevelt gave ground to the Allies' resistance to rapid decolonization. A trusteeship system that differed little from the post-World War I mandates emerged. The West promised gradual emancipation of the colonies while the United States and its European allies maintained control of their commerce and used them as strategic assets and sites for military bases. This approach bitterly disappointed the people of the developing world who had invested considerable hope in Roosevelt's leadership and the idealism of the **Atlantic Charter** and the **Four Freedoms**.

While US power and influence expanded around the globe following World War II the British Empire was under siege. In 1947 **Indian independence**, fired by the inspirational leadership of Mohandas Gandhi, dealt a crippling blow to British colonialism. Faced with resistance throughout the Empire, the British soon acquiesced to the independence of Burma, Ceylon, Egypt, Malaya, Palestine, and Singapore. Belgium, France, the Netherlands, and Portugal would try in vain to hold onto their colonial empires. In the two decades after World War II some 40 new nation states emerged in the formerly colonized global South. From 1945 to 1968 membership in the new United Nations spiraled from 51 to 126 nations.

As the cold war evolved and intensified the United States prioritized anti-communist **containment** over decolonization. The combination of the cold war and decolonization converted the newly independent nations into battle-grounds, as their ideological orientation became a vital issue to the great powers. Determined to prevent countries from "going communist," the United States intervened indirectly by economic and political means, or directly if deemed necessary by military means, as in Korea and Vietnam. With the cold war struggle between good and evil serving as the primary foreign policy framework, the United States backed states that accepted US ideological leadership and development strategy and opposed those that did not.

As under colonialism and throughout the history of US diplomacy, cultural perceptions shaped the US approach to the decolonizing world. Americans

Figure 11.1 Jawaharlal Nehru, the first prime minister of post-colonial India, became a leader of the so-called Third World. Here Nehru meets with President Eisenhower at the White House in 1956. To the left are Mamie Eisenhower and Indira Gandhi, who would become prime minister of India a decade later. Patricia Nixon, wife of the vice president, appears in the background.

Source: Library of Congress, Prints and Photographs Division, LC-USZ62-106330.

tended to view the Third World countries as lands of plentiful resources and natural beauty but occupied by racially inferior, primitive, and backward peoples. Third World leaders were derided as weak and irrational while their religions such as Buddhism, Hinduism, or Islam were delegitimized. Overall, the peoples of the Third World were, as George Kennan once put it, "neurotic products of exotic backgrounds and tentative Western educational experiences."

While the United States tried to distance itself from the legacy of European colonialism, the condescension, interventions, and exploitation of Third World resources alienated many peoples. Washington frequently collaborated with oligarchs and militarists who often attacked their own peasant populations in order to suppress reformist or radical liberation struggles. As "the leader of the Free World," the United States would intervene to prevent virtually any country from going communist out of fear that if it stood by the world would disintegrate "like apples in a barrel infected by one rotten one," as Secretary of State Dean Acheson put it.

Interpreting the Past

Third World agency

Although the cold war created a bipolar world of fierce competition between the Soviet-led communist and US-led capitalist blocs, in recent years scholars have paid much more attention to the ways in which "Third World" countries exerted influence and sometimes dictated the course of events. Developing nations and their leaders were not mere pawns in the larger geopolitical struggle, rather they exerted influence and often proved adept at manipulating the superpowers. That influence while real should not be exaggerated, however: smaller states could shape the course of events, but many were also devastated by cold war foreign interventions and proxy wars that were beyond their ability to control.

Third World nations often exercised agency through their decisions on whether to collaborate or resist foreign powers. Developing nations frequently provided or withheld political support or military assistance in return for economic incentives. They sometimes, as with Third World oil-producing nations, wielded raw materials and natural resources as potent weapons of their own. Developing countries did not simply receive culture, rather they exchanged culture as their art, fashion, and music filtered into the developed nations.

Figure 11.2 Achmed Sukarno, the popular leader of post-colonial Indonesia, hosted the Bandung Conference of neutral or non-aligned nations in 1955. He visited Washington (above) the following year.

Source: Library of Congress, Prints and Photographs Division, LC-USZ62-134160.

In Their Words

Declarations of the Bandung Conference, April 18–24, 1955

Human rights and self-determination

The Asian-African Conference deplored the policies and practices of racial segregation and discrimination which form the basis of government and human relations in large regions of Africa and in other parts of the world. Such conduct is not only a gross violation of human rights, but also a denial of the fundamental values of civilisation and the dignity of man . . .

Problems of dependent peoples

The Asian-African Conference discussed the problems of dependent peoples and colonialism and the evils arising from the subjection of peoples to alien subjugation, domination and exploitation.

The Conference is agreed:

a. in declaring that colonialism in all its manifestations is an evil which should speedily be brought to an end;
b. in affirming that the subjection of peoples to alien subjugation, domination and exploitation constitutes a denial of fundamental human rights, is contrary to the Charter of the United Nations and is an impediment to the promotion of world peace and cooperation;
c. in declaring its support of the cause of freedom and independence for all such peoples; and
d. in calling upon the powers concerned to grant freedom and independence to such peoples . . .

Declaration on the promotion of world peace and cooperation

The Asian-African Conference gave anxious thought to the question of world peace and cooperation. It viewed with deep concern the present state of international tension with its danger of an atomic world war. The problem of peace is correlative with the problem of international security. In this connection, all States should cooperate, especially through the United Nations, in bringing about the reduction of armaments and the elimination of nuclear weapons under effective international control . . . all nations should have the right freely to choose their own political and economic systems and their own way of life, in conformity with the purposes and principles of the Charter of the United Nations.

Free from mistrust and fear, and with confidence and goodwill towards each other, nations should practice tolerance and live together in peace with one another as good neighbors and develop friendly

> cooperation . . . The Asian and African Conference declares its convic-
> tion that friendly cooperation . . . would effectively contribute to the
> maintenance and promotion of international peace and security, while
> cooperation in the economic, social and cultural fields would help bring
> about the common prosperity and well-being of all.

In 1955 US anxiety about the decolonizing world deepened amid the **Bandung Conference**, a meeting in Indonesia of 29 neutral and "non-aligned"
nations. Led by Indonesian President **Achmed Sukarno** as well as Nehru,
Egypt's Gamal Abdel Nasser, and other prominent leaders of former colonies,
the participants rejected the bipolar worldview in which they must become either
communist or capitalist states. To distinguish themselves they popularized the
French term *tiers monde*, or Third World. The Eisenhower administration condemned the gathering, in part because "Red China" participated as a developing
country, but also out of conviction there should be no neutrality in the cold war
battle between good and evil. "Non-alignment is immoral," declared Secretary
of State John Foster Dulles. In 1961, undeterred by US opposition, Third World
leaders proclaimed the **Non-Aligned Movement** to focus on development and
political cooperation beyond the confines of the bipolar cold war.

Figure 11.3 In 1960 Kwame Nkrumah (standing on stool) was sworn in as the first
president of the newly independent Republic of Ghana. The continent was
changing so rapidly that 1960 was dubbed "the year of Africa."

Source: Library of Congress, Prints and Photographs Division, LC-USZ62-112312.

Despite exerting their influence Third World nations ultimately could not escape the cold war. The effort to create an enduring bloc of neutral or non-aligned countries that began in the 1950s had dissipated by the 1970s. Charismatic leaders from the early years of decolonization—Nehru, Sukarno, and **Kwame Nkrumah** of Ghana—had passed from the scene. Many Third World nations had succumbed to authoritarian or direct military rule or had been devastated by superpower conflict. The structural conditions of the US-dominated global economy led most Third World countries into indebtedness and dependence. Under this system the global South nations suffered from low prices for their raw materials while having to pay high prices for the finished products and technologies that they needed to develop.

The Soviet Union also intervened in the Third World in the context of the global cold war. The post-Stalin Soviet leadership under Georgi Malenkov and Nikita Khrushchev viewed the developing world as ripe for communist expansion. Unlike Stalin, Khrushchev toured beyond Soviet borders including a highly publicized Asian trip in 1954, in an effort to improve the image and standing of the USSR. The Soviet Union offered development consistent with its models of central planning, promotion of heavy industry, and collectivization of agriculture.

In the postwar era **modernization theory** guided the US effort to integrate Third World countries into the capitalist world. Under this theory the application of scientific and technical rationalism could transform developing countries, igniting a "take off" of their economies. Academics played an important role in the cold war as they studied Third World nations and devised development, technical assistance, and military and security programs. The Ford and Rockefeller foundations pumped millions of dollars into modernization schemes targeting the global South.

The United States promoted modernization and sharply opposed land reform initiatives that threatened economic elites or restricted corporate access to raw materials and natural resources. The US-led effort to transform predominately rural agricultural societies into modern industrial societies brought dramatic and often destructive change to the traditional societies. In Asia the so-called **green revolution**, an effort to transform societies from subsistence farming to commercial agribusiness, shattered bonds of village and family. Assaults on the peasant way of life spurred mass migration into urban slums thus perpetuating cycles of poverty rather than igniting economic growth and modernization. While people in the developed world moved into apartments and into suburbs, impoverished and unsanitary conditions characterized urban sprawl of Third World cities such as Bangkok, Bombay, Cairo, Calcutta, Lagos, Manila, Mexico City, Saigon, and São Paulo.

When modernization efforts alone could not curtail communism the Pentagon offered **counterinsurgency** programs and military intervention. By 1958 the United States had agreed to train and equip military and police forces in more than 70 countries, had formal security commitments with 43 of them, and about a million and a half troops posted in 35 nations. Throughout the cold war the United States intervened in a range of Third World countries from Latin America to Southeast Asia. Washington often succeeded in containing communism but other times failed and suffered debilitating consequences most sensationally in the Second Indochina (Vietnam) War.

Many decolonized states had been forced precipitously into modernity and locked into borders drawn during the era of colonial occupation. These arbitrary borders were often inappropriate for the ethnic composition of the countries, thus exacerbating conflict and impeding political stability and economic development. While some scholars have argued that the stalemate during the early cold war led to a "long peace" in Europe, conditions in the Third World during this era were usually anything but peaceful.

South of the Rio Grande

The United States did not dictate events in Latin America yet it possessed considerable economic and political leverage. As he moved toward US intervention in World War II, Roosevelt built popular support by exaggerating the Nazi threat to Latin America. US propaganda warned that the Nazis would foment rebellion or launch a surprise attack or invasion and possessed elaborate plans to rule the region. Both the US and much of the Latin American publics rallied behind the **Good Neighbor Policy**, the Atlantic Charter, the Four Freedoms, and the inspirational leadership of Roosevelt. Washington doled out some $400 million in lend-lease aid, further solidifying its military influence over the region. With the notable exception of **Juan Perón** in Argentina the United States received widespread support for the anti-Axis coalition.

If Latin Americans expected US economic assistance as a reward for hemispheric loyalty they were disappointed. As the world war ended and the cold war unfolded the Truman administration left little doubt that Europe was its top priority, with Asia a secondary concern, leaving Latin America just ahead of Africa on the list of US global priorities. Latin Americans expressed frustration as the United States initiated the Marshall Plan of European economic recovery while nothing of the sort materialized south of the Rio Grande. "There has always been a Marshall Plan in effect for the Western Hemisphere," Truman responded, " . . . known as the Monroe Doctrine." The analogy made little sense to Latin Americans whose per capita income at the time hovered around $250 annually while the average lifespan was 43 years. Between 1945 and 1952 Belgium and Luxembourg received more US economic aid than all of Latin America.

As with Africa and Asia cultural factors and notably racial stereotypes of the mixed race and supposedly "hot-blooded" Latin Americans underlay US policy. Truman, who like most Americans knew little about the region, compared Latin Americans with Jews and the Irish, all being "very emotional." Acheson averred that "Hispano-Indian culture—or lack of it" accounted for Latin America "piling up its problems for centuries." Dulles reflected US condescension, noting "You have to pat them on the back and make them think you are fond of them." In a notoriously contemptuous report following a tour of the region in 1950 Kennan asserted that despite the "inordinate splendor and pretense" of the Latin American capitals, there was "no other region of the earth" in which "nature and human behavior could have combined to produce a more unhappy and hopeless background for the conduct of human life." As Latin Americans lacked the maturity to be reliable anti-communist allies in the cold war, the United States "must concede that harsh governmental measures of repression may be the only answer."

Washington emphasized military security rather than economic assistance while demanding from the Latin American states loyalty in the global struggle against communism. In 1947 the United States took the lead in the **Treaty of Rio de Janeiro**, an anti-communist collective security accord. "We have preserved the Monroe Doctrine and the inter-American system," the Republican Senator Arthur S. Vandenberg declared, adding that the United States now had in effect "a complete veto" over any changes in the hemisphere. While Roosevelt had nudged the Latin American states toward embracing democracy, the cold war encouraged close relations with Latin American militarists, including Perón who was forgiven for his neutrality in World War II.

As the cold war intensified in Europe and Asia Washington strengthened its commitment to military security, alliances with economic oligarchies, and containment of reformers and radicals. Most US economic assistance went into the Latin American military forces under the **Mutual Security Program**. Other investments went into extractive industries and thus did little to provide for long-term growth and stability. Latin American militarists often received backing from the Roman Catholic Church in defense of social conservatism. US support for militarism and conservatism contained the left but worked against democratic reform and social change in postwar Latin America.

While exerting influence politically, economically, and through military assistance, US leaders sought to preserve the Good Neighbor Policy by avoiding direct military intervention. In 1948 the United States affirmed the policy of nonintervention by joining in the creation of the Organization of American States (OAS). The **OAS Charter** renounced intervention "directly or indirectly, for any reason, whatever, in the internal or external affairs of another state." The Rio Treaty and the OAS offered the appearance of collective decision making but the Latin Americans found that US power and influence remained predominant. While it would avoid direct intervention until 1965, the United States repeatedly intervened covertly and indirectly in the affairs of Latin American states.

World War II had deepened the US commitment to oversight of the Caribbean, which continued throughout the cold war. The United States fought off Puerto Rican nationalist demands for independence, particularly after two of them attempted unsuccessfully to assassinate Truman in November 1950. In 1952 Puerto Rico became a "commonwealth" and thereafter repeatedly rejected both independence and statehood in periodic referenda. Puerto Rico remained subject to the dictates of Congress while the US Navy used Vieques, an island located eight miles east of the main island and inhabited by some 10,000 people, as a bombing range. Critics pointed out that Puerto Rico received no compensation for use of the island to test weapons and carry out war games, which had deleterious environmental impacts. In 2003, after years of protests, the Navy terminated the bomb tests.

Washington closely monitored the Caribbean and Central America from military outposts in the region, from Florida to Guantánamo Bay to Panama. In 1954 the United States intervened covertly but decisively in Guatemala, establishing a precedent for cold war diplomacy in the region. Planning for the **Guatemalan intervention** began under Truman but came to fruition under Eisenhower, who had made CIA covert operations, as demonstrated in the Iranian coup of 1953, a central component of his New Look strategy. Guatemala was a desperately poor and racially polarized Central American state, about evenly divided between indigenous people and descendants of the Spanish. More than 70 percent of the population was illiterate and the per capita income was less than $200 a year. Social conditions were even worse for the indigenous people living mostly in the highlands and exploited for plantation labor and sex.

The political power of landed elites, the military, and the Catholic Church, the dominant forces in Guatemala, came under challenge from reformers. **Jacobo Árbenz**, who had risen through the military and was elected president, spearheaded the reforms from 1951 until his overthrow in 1954. Árbenz implemented a broad range of progressive reforms including redistributing land to peasant farmers, expanding voting rights, establishing a minimum wage, and promoting literacy and health care programs. US national security elites saw conspiracy behind the key initiative of agrarian reform. The redistribution "makes land available to all Guatemalans in the communist pattern," a CIA officer explained. Moreover the land distribution program threatened the unchecked power of the dominant landholder in Guatemala, the Boston-based banana importer, the United Fruit Company.

Amid the intense anti-communism of the 1950s, Eisenhower and Dulles viewed the Guatemalan reforms as part of the global communist conspiracy. "The Kremlin was exploiting" economic conditions in Latin America and the "communist infection" threatened to take root and spread from Guatemala, CIA Director Allen Dulles asserted. Determined to "roll back" communism, the administration authorized a coup against Árbenz even though he was not a Soviet puppet and the USSR had no involvement in his rise to power. An arms purchase by the Árbenz government for the Guatemalan military from Soviet-allied Czechoslovakia was the last straw as far as Eisenhower and the Dulles brothers were concerned.

The CIA covert operation, codenamed **PBSUCCESS** and initially funded at $3 million, encompassed a campaign of psychological warfare backed by naval and air support and incitement of the Guatemalan military to drive Árbenz from power. From a base in Florida the CIA orchestrated the "black propaganda" campaign and effectively infiltrated student, labor, church, business,

Figure 11.4 In 1954 the CIA orchestrated a coup in Guatemala ousting the reformist
government of Jacobo Árbenz in favor of a military junta. Colonel Castillo
Armas (above) became the new president until his assassination in 1957.

Source: Library of Congress, Prints and Photographs Division, LC-USZ62-121329.

and women's groups to promote denunciations, strikes, and resistance to the Árbenz government. With the coup under way, Senate Majority Leader Lyndon Johnson condemned the "flagrant" effort by "the Soviet Communists" to "penetrate the Western Hemisphere." With only one dissenting vote in the entire Congress a concurrent House and Senate resolution supported the overthrow of the legitimately elected government of Guatemala. The US press proved compliant, describing Árbenz as a Soviet-backed radical and ignoring evidence of US support for the coup.

A US-backed military government took power led by Colonel Carlos Castillo Armas, who had received training at the US Army base at Fort Leavenworth, Kansas. Armas revoked the land reform, returned the oligarchy to power, and launched a reign of terror. Peasants and reformers who had supported Árbenz were arbitrarily arrested and executed, establishing a pattern for the future. In 1999 a 3,500-page UN-sponsored "truth commission" report detailed the two generations of indiscriminate violence carried out by the Guatemalan regime. The report condemned the United States for training, covert assistance, and overall complicity in the slaughters and "disappearing" of some 200,000 Guatemalans.

At the time the Eisenhower administration celebrated the coup in Guatemala and backed other dictatorial regimes in Latin America to ward off reform and instability. Secretary Dulles was "very tolerant" of dictators "as long as they took a firm stand against communism" while Vice President Richard Nixon declared, "Latinos had shown preference for a dictatorial form of government rather than a democracy." Whereas the Democrats had "lost" China and fought an unpopular and inconclusive war in Korea, the Republicans were on the offensive. After successful coups in Iran and Guatemala, the CIA and the Eisenhower administration had faith that covert operations could deliver low-cost victories in the struggle against communism. Events in Cuba would shatter those perceptions.

Castro and the Bay of Pigs

While the Eisenhower administration celebrated the Guatemalan operation the Latin American left redoubled its efforts to overthrow US-backed repressive regimes. The Argentine revolutionary **Che Guevara**, who had witnessed the Guatemalan repression, called for revolution across the continent. Many Latin Americans resented the United States for its support of right-wing regimes, as Nixon discovered when an angry crowd rocked his limousine during a visit to Caracas, Venezuela, in 1958. Nixon escaped the mob and the incident made only a fleeting impression, but the same would not be true of the **Cuban Revolution** the following year.

The United States had renounced intervention in Cuba under the Good Neighbor Policy, but had maintained economic and political control through the pro-American military dictatorship of **Fulgencio Batista**. Sugar-producing corporations, Cuban oligarchs, and the Mafia, which operated profitable casinos and brothels in Havana, bolstered the regime until its collapse in 1959. Led by **Fidel Castro**, the son of a prosperous family who had earned a law degree before becoming a rebel, Cuban revolutionaries drove Batista out of power in 1959. Castro was not a Marxist–Leninist when he came to power, but he condemned the United States for repressing Cuban nationalism following the Spanish–American War. Recalling US neo-colonialism under the **Platt Amendment**, Castro viewed the United States as "the sworn enemy of our nation."

Like Árbenz, Castro carried out agrarian reform targeting wealthy elites in order to improve the plight of the peasantry. Castro expropriated US investments in Cuba, shut down the Mafia rackets in Havana, and demanded racial equality for Afro-Cubans, the targets of discrimination under the Batista regime. Tens of thousands of Cuban elites, bitter over the level of compensation offered for their expropriated property, fled to Miami where they became a potent political force against Castro for generations to come. By the time Castro legalized the Communist Party, ousted moderates, summarily tried and killed some 500 opponents of the Revolution, outlawed foreign ownership, denounced US imperialism in a speech at the UN in September 1959, and signed a commercial agreement with the Soviet Union, the Eisenhower administration had decided to remove him from power.

Although Castro had not yet pronounced himself a communist, the Eisenhower administration concluded that the Cuban example would lead other Latin American leftists to overthrow the US-backed regimes, seize private property, and make the continent more vulnerable to communism. "This kind of change, when it brings communism in its wake," Eisenhower explained to the British prime minister in 1960, "is intolerable from the standpoint of our national interests and of the liberal democratic Christian tradition that we all share." Racial stereotypes proliferated, as US officials variously described Castro as "emotional," "like a child," "wild," and, *Time* magazine averred, a reflection of "the Latin capacity for brooding revenge and blood purges."

President John F. Kennedy concurred with Eisenhower that Castro had to go, hence he gave the green light when informed of the CIA's plans for the Bay of Pigs invasion. In mid-April 1961 some 1,400 Cuban exiles, trained and equipped in Florida, landed on Cuba's southwestern coast hoping to form a beachhead leading to a wider uprising and the overthrow of the Castro regime. The operation failed miserably, as Castro's forces defeated the invaders. Critics later blamed Kennedy for lack of air support (though there had been some) but the CIA's own postmortem analysis concluded the operation had been doomed to failure. Cuba was not Guatemala, Castro's forces were well trained and experienced from years of guerrilla resistance, moreover there was no evidence "that Cubans in significant numbers could or would join the invaders or that there was any kind of effective and cohesive resistance movement under anybody's control." Kennedy regretted approving the CIA operation, wondering, "How could I have been so stupid, to let them go ahead?"

Figure 11.5 The Cuban exile community centered in Miami backed US efforts to overthrow or kill Castro in the wake of the failed Bay of Pigs invasion and the Cuban Missile Crisis. The Cuban exiles became a potent political force in domestic politics, ensuring that US policies of economic sanctions and non-recognition of the communist government in Cuba would continue for decades.

Source: Library of Congress, Prints and Photographs Division, LC-USZ62-92297.

Livid over the embarrassing defeat just three months into his presidency, Kennedy and his brother and attorney general Robert Kennedy proceeded, "absolutely like demons," with a variety of "nutty schemes," as CIA director Richard Helms put it, to overthrow or kill Castro. Eisenhower acknowledged authorizing actions "approximating gangsterism" against Castro, including working directly with the Mafia in plots to kill the Cuban leader. In November 1961 the CIA launched **Operation Mongoose**, a covert program to overthrow or kill Castro. Armed with $50 million, 400 CIA employees and thousands of Cuban exiles headquartered on the University of Miami campus devised a campaign of sabotage, terrorism, and assassination. The plots ranged from another amphibious landing to killing Castro with poisoned darts or cigars, or contaminating his skin-diving snorkel, but none of them could be carried out. As the Americans strove to overthrow or kill him, Castro turned increasingly to the USSR for support, leading to the **Cuban Missile Crisis** and a close brush with nuclear war.

Despite its pledge to respect Cuban sovereignty as a means of ending the missile crisis, the Kennedy administration continued covert raids and sabotage operations against Cuban targets. Some months after the Kennedy assassination (November 22, 1963), President Johnson canceled the covert war on Cuba, later explaining, "We were running a damn Murder Incorporated in the Caribbean." Johnson, however, maintained pressure on the OAS and western European allies to support a US-led economic embargo against Cuba as well as diplomatic non-recognition of the Castro regime. Mexico defied the United States and kept up relations with Cuba yet also sometimes shared information on Cuban activities with Washington. Despite the dictatorial nature of Castro's regime, many Latin Americans admired him for successfully resisting US domination.

With the exception of Cuba, cooperation prevailed over conflict in the Caribbean. The British, Dutch, and French, all with island possessions in the West Indies, worked with Washington and the islanders on various forms of quasi-independent commonwealth arrangements. The United States failed in an effort to promote a **West Indian Federation** uniting the former British colonies of Trinidad and Jamaica in an anti-communist alliance. The Jamaicans rejected the plan and opened relations with the Castro regime, yet through moderation and British mediation a blowup with the United States was avoided. Washington also vacated a military base in Trinidad that it had held since World War II.

Kennedy had entered office with grandiose plans for Latin America embodied in the **Alliance for Progress**. Rooted in the cold war quest for modernization to win over the "hearts and minds" of the developing world, the Alliance was a 10-year program to raise economic growth rates, education, and promote community development and health care. The United States sought to improve the lives of Latin Americans thus winning their backing and precluding the rise of communism. The Alliance for Progress was never funded at a high enough level to make a dramatic impact and many of the Latin American regimes squandered the funds through corruption. The Alliance did not come close to meeting its targets for economic growth, thus the threat of revolution remained in Latin America. Particularly after the Cuban crises, the administration focused on counterinsurgency and political support for military regimes, which seized control of six Latin American countries during Kennedy's 1,000-day presidency.

The failure to oust Castro combined with the heating up of the cold war in Asia and Africa encouraged US alignment with the repressive military regimes. The Cuban Revolution along with rampant economic inequality inspired left-wing activism in Latin America. Actions included agitation, propaganda, protests, and sporadic violent resistance, but these would be dwarfed by the overwhelming power of state violence. Most Latin American countries were conservative, prepared to use force against left-wing reformers, and eager for US military training and assistance to accomplish these aims.

Fears of Cuban-inspired, left-wing revolts lay behind a series of US interventions in Latin America during the Johnson years. Johnson, like Kennedy, invested heavily in masculinity and was determined to show his toughness and credibility in the wake of the "loss" of Cuba. In 1964 the administration blamed "left-wing agitators" for riots that erupted against US occupation of the **Panama Canal Zone**. Three days of rioting left more than 20 Panamanians dead, $2 million in property damage, but moreover damage to the American image throughout the region. Also in 1964 a persistent CIA campaign of destabilization in the former British colony of Guyana ousted Cheddi Jagan, the elected prime minister and socialist reformer. As Jagan's successor the CIA backed Forbes Burnham, a bigoted dictator.

Much more significant than tiny Guyana was Brazil, the colossus of South America, which if allowed to "fall" to communism would have precipitated domestic political fallout perhaps more severe than the loss of China. In the early 1960s the reformist government of **João Goulart** expropriated corporate holdings, limited the repatriation of funds taken from foreign-owned industries such as the US-based International Telephone and Telegraph (ITT) Corporation, and broadened ties with labor and communist governments. Goulart refused to support the campaign against Castro and tolerated the left, including the Brazilian Communist Party. The US ambassador warned Washington that Goulart intended to "take Brazil into the communist camp." In March 1963 Kennedy declared, "We've got to do something about Brazil."

The United States launched a covert destabilization campaign and conspired with the Brazilian military to overthrow the Goulart government and force him into exile in April 1964. A US carrier task force appeared offshore but did not have to take a direct role to bring off the coup, which the Brazilian right wing carried out on its own. Johnson proffered immediate diplomatic recognition, sent his "warmest regards," and lavished funding and security training on the military regime. Johnson declared that "constitutional democracy" had been upheld in Brazil but in actuality the coup set up more than 20 years of military dictatorship, repression, and human rights violations. Other South American nations such as Argentina and Uruguay followed Brazil's lead into military dictatorship and police state repression, including the practice of "disappearing" regime critics. Beginning in the late 1960s the Brazilian economy grew rapidly but relatively little trickled down to the masses of people who remained mired in rural and slum-ridden poverty.

Determined not to appear weak by allowing "another Cuba," Johnson poured 24,000 US Marines into the Dominican Republic in 1965 thus bringing to an end the 30-year Good Neighbor tradition of avoiding direct US military intervention. The **Dominican intervention** came in the wake of CIA collusion in the assassination of **Rafael Trujillo**, formerly a compliant dictator. When the social democrat Juan Bosch came to power in a free election, the United States backed a military coup led by a pro-US leader. When Bosch attempted to retake the government Johnson dispatched the Marines to oust him and empower light-skinned militarists and oligarchs to ensure anticommunism and bring an end to reform.

Figure 11.6 In 1962 João Goulart, the president of Brazil received a ticker-tape parade
on a visit to New York. Two years later the United States conspired with the
Brazilian military to overthrow Goulart's reform government and replace it
with a right-wing regime.

Source: Library of Congress, Prints and Photographs Division, LC-USZ62-128919,

By the late 1960s the much-feared threat of left-wing revolution had been
substantially contained by conservative Latin American states aided by Washington. In October 1967 the romantic revolutionary Guevara was captured and
summarily executed as he attempted to foment revolution in Bolivia. Hindered
by the US-led economic embargo, Cuba depended increasingly on the USSR

for financial support. The conservative Soviet leaders, moving toward détente with the United States, pressured Castro to rein in *foco* activities whereby a small cadre of guerrillas would seek to incite uprisings and the overthrow of regimes.

Latin America was peripheral to the vision of President Nixon and his national security adviser Henry A. Kissinger. In Kissinger's "realist" perspective, Europe and East Asia mattered whereas "What happens in the South has no importance." Despite such statements Nixon and Kissinger invested heavily in a tough-minded realism and meant to contain communism on every front, especially in the American "backyard."

In Chile in 1970 the election of socialist reformer **Salvador Allende**, a physician who had been active in the Pacific nation's parliamentary democracy since the 1930s, incited perennial fears of another Cuba. The United States first targeted Allende in the 1964 Chilean election in which the CIA spent millions of dollars on a propaganda campaign that depicted a future with Soviet tanks in the streets and Cuban firing squads. Allende lost the election but continued to build support. In 1970 the CIA again funneled millions into the electoral campaign, but this time Allende won by a plurality. In October 1970 the CIA recruited and funded the assassins of General René Schneider, the Army commander who was determined to stand by the Chilean constitution regardless of which candidate was elected.

Once in office Allende launched a program of land redistribution and nationalization of resources, especially of abundant copper. Determined not to follow Soviet and Cuban models of Marxist dictatorship, Allende accomplished the reforms through legal and constitutional means while urging workers and leftists to avoid violence. Conversely, the Chilean right wing, encouraged by the military government in Brazil as well as the United States, would embrace violence to topple the regime and crush the left. "That son of a bitch Allende," Nixon thundered. "We're going to smash him." Kissinger added, "I don't see why we have to let a country go Marxist just because its people are irresponsible."

US national security elites, not just Nixon and Kissinger, broadly shared the desire to topple Allende because he was a socialist, friendly with Castro, and critical of US intervention in Latin America as well as in Vietnam. Allende, however, sought normal relations with Washington and pursued an independent foreign policy that included criticism of past Soviet interventions in Hungary and Czechoslovakia. Castro was a friend and adviser of Allende but the Chilean president rejected Castro's advice to use armed force to bolster the government and ward off the threat of a coup. While the United States mounted a campaign to "make the economy scream," Chilean conservatives impeded reforms, spread chaos and disorder, and exaggerated the threat of Cuban influence. Washington continued to pump millions into an anti-Allende propaganda fund and tripled direct assistance to the Chilean military. Kissinger later acknowledged that the United States "created the conditions as great as possible" for a coup but was uncertain about the prospects of success and would not initiate it directly.

Knowing that they had the backing of the United States as well as Brazil and other militarist regimes in the southern cone of South America, the Chilean military launched the coup. On September 11, 1973, the military used tanks and warplanes in an assault on the national palace in Santiago. Determined not to turn his country into a bloody battleground, Allende delivered a final radio address from inside the palace, declaring he had ultimate faith in the Chilean people, and then committed suicide. Two days later the White House instructed the US ambassador to convey the US "desire to cooperate with the military junta." On September 24 the United States proffered diplomatic recognition of the military regime. Many of its members had received military training in the United States. US economic assistance, denied to Allende, now poured into Chile.

Assured of US support General **Augusto Pinochet** presided over a "Caravan of Death" as the Chilean military rounded up, tortured, and murdered more than 3,000 alleged leftists (including three US citizens) and imprisoned and tortured tens of thousands more. Continually encouraged by the Chilean right wing, the Brazilian regime, and the United States, which had provided the names of suspected Chilean leftists, the military carried out the bloody purge in an effort to destroy the Chilean left once and for all. Before his death in 2006 Pinochet would be charged under international law with committing "crimes against humanity." In June 1976, after three years of state violence and dictatorship, Kissinger reassured Pinochet, "We are sympathetic with what you are trying to do here . . . We want to help, not undermine you." Three months later Michael Townley, the son of a US corporate executive with ties to Chile, carried out a terrorist car bombing in Washington, DC, in collusion with the Chilean secret police. The **Embassy Row bombing** killed Orlando Letelier, a Chilean diplomat who had backed Allende, as well as a US citizen riding with him. The United States downplayed the terrorist act that occurred a half mile from the State Department and leaked disinformation that the Chilean junta was not responsible. *Time, Newsweek,* the *New York Times,* and the *Washington Post* quoted unnamed "intelligence officials" as having "virtually ruled out" the responsibility of the Pinochet regime for the murders.

The United States worked proactively with other Latin American military dictatorships in **Operation Condor**, a campaign of repression of the left encompassing terror, torture, and assassination. Operation Condor sought to stamp out left-wing dissent in Argentina, Bolivia, Brazil, Paraguay, and Uruguay. General Alfredo Stroessner, who came to power in 1954 and ruled Paraguay for 35 years, disappeared thousands of reformers and political opponents. The United States backed the Paraguayan, Uruguayan, Peruvian, and Bolivian regimes through ongoing training in counterinsurgency and police state techniques at the School of the Americas. Washington encouraged and supported the Argentine military, which seized power in 1976, and launched a "dirty war" campaign of disappearing thousands of reformers. Kissinger understood the generals' need to "establish authority" and advised, "If there are things to be done you should do them quickly." The regime proceeded to kill perhaps 30,000 Argentinians. In subsequent years the generals would be charged with crimes against humanity and some were imprisoned. Americans coordinated repression from a headquarters in the Canal Zone and often employed Cuban exiles as extra-national forces in the counterinsurgency dirty wars.

The brutal military regimes that took power in Latin America acted on their own and with considerable backing from anti-communist forces within their own societies. While the United States was thus not a puppet master pulling all the strings in Latin America, US political, economic, and military support relieved the regimes of concerns that the great power in the hemisphere would stand in the way of their assault on democracy and political pluralism. The United States supported brutal right-wing dictatorships because they were anti-communist, resonated manly militancy, represented light-skinned elites, stood for oligarchy and corporate power, and usually received backing from the Catholic Church because of their cultural conservatism. Determined to prevent "another Cuba" the United States bolstered brutal dictatorships to achieve that aim.

Mexico did not experience the cold war convulsions of the other Latin American states because the Mexican Revolution and the clash with the United States over nationalization of resources had already unfolded prior to World War II. An authoritarian one-party state rather than a pluralist democracy, Mexico conducted campaigns against left-wing reformers on its own and largely independent of US involvement. The Mexican Communist Party was legal in theory but subject to constant surveillance, harassment, and control by the Mexican government. Unlike most other Latin American states, the United States did not have a major military assistance program with Mexico because it was not needed. Mexico City frequently irritated Washington, for example by recognizing Cuba and conducting a modest trade with China, but it also often voted with the United States against the communist powers in the UN. In sum, while Mexico followed its own path it was for the most part a cooperative conservative partner to the United States in the cold war.

Tensions often flared on the US–Mexican border but more often they were managed cooperatively. From 1942–64 the Mexican Farm Labor Program, known as the **Bracero Program**, enabled some 4.5 million Mexican migrant workers to cross the border for agricultural labor in the United States. The migrants helped meet US demands for cheap labor and enabled the Mexican workers to send money back to their families. Many of the migrants secured green cards for US residency, whereas others remained illegally, hence millions of Mexican-Americans today trace their roots to the arrival of their fathers or grandfathers into the country under the US-Mexican agreement. Following the demise of the Bracero Program, migrant workers organized in the **United Farm Workers** union founded by Cesar Chavez.

African Decolonization

As the cold war was a global conflict, the United States closely monitored events in Africa and stood ready to intervene to contain communism throughout the vast continent. White Americans tended to share the same views that underlay decades of European colonialism perceiving "black Africa" as primitive and backward. As decolonization movements stirred, US officials viewed Africans as unready for independence. They feared that newly independent African states would be unstable and thus vulnerable to communism. "Without the discipline and control of Western nations ancient antagonisms would burst their present bounds and numerous races or tribes would attack traditional enemies in primitive savagery," a State Department diplomat posted in Africa observed. "To endow these African groups prematurely with independence and sovereignty would only result in creating political entities which almost immediately become pawns of the Kremlin."

African decolonization coincided with the burgeoning postwar civil rights movement inside the United States, thus compounding the anxieties of American decision makers. The prospects were liberating for the peoples of Africa and of the **African diaspora** (peoples of African origin dating back to the international slave trade). For the architects of US foreign policy, however, both movements appeared threatening. US officials feared the decolonizing states would use the UN's **Universal Declaration of Human Rights** (1948) to challenge racial inequality in the United States.

During World War II African-Americans supported and participated in the war effort out of patriotism and to seize new opportunities for economic and social advancement. Black men entered the armed forces in segregated units while African-American leaders promoted the **"Double V" campaign** of victory over the Axis abroad and at the same time victory in the quest for jobs and civil rights on the home front. As African-Americans moved around the country and into war industries, violent resistance erupted. In 1943 alone more than 200 racial clashes broke out in 45 cities. The brutal Detroit riot that year forced Roosevelt to divert 6,000 troops to the industrial heartland while fighting a war in Europe and Asia. While rigid segregation and disfranchisement prevailed in the southern states, economic and social inequality was a nationwide reality for black Americans. Most African-Americans lived below the poverty line, millions lacked electricity and indoor plumbing, suffered from an infant mortality rate twice that of whites, were the last hired and first fired, and remained subject to various campaigns of discrimination, incarceration, and violent repression; hence a UN forum on US race relations would be unwelcome and divert attention from Soviet domination of Eastern Europe.

Despite deeply rooted racism, Americans including even white supremacists realized that World War II had permanently altered race relations. The war had not only fueled the drive for decolonization, but also discredited theoretical justifications for white supremacy through its association with the genocidal Nazi regime. "The Huns have wrecked the theory of the master race," an

Alabama politician lamented. The loyalty shown in the Double V campaign conjoined with the wartime emphasis on freedom and democracy created rising expectations on the home front.

During the cold war the United States sought to contain the black left both at home and abroad. With the help of the FBI, led by segregationist director J. Edgar Hoover, the United States reined in black radicals while taking grudging steps toward accommodating the more restrained agenda of mainstream organizations such as the National Association for the Advancement of Colored People (NAACP). Left-wing organizations that denounced colonialism and linked the United States with the African diaspora, notably the **Council on African Affairs**, were spied upon, harassed, contained, and eventually forced to disband. The NAACP and other groups that supported the Truman Doctrine, Marshall Plan, and the anti-communist agenda abroad remained in position to advocate civil rights on the home front. Left-wing critics such as the longtime black leader W. E. B. Du Bois, who denounced the "reactionary, warmongering colonial imperialism of the [Truman] administration," were isolated and undermined. The Marxist actor and singer Paul Robeson had his passport revoked, was called to a loyalty hearing in before Congress, and in 1949 nearly succumbed to mob violence in a racial backlash in Peekskill, New York.

Figure 11.7 The backlash against court-ordered desegregation of Central High School in Little Rock, Arkansas, captured on television and distributed worldwide, threatened US claims to represent freedom and democracy in contrast to communist oppression.

Source: Library of Congress, Prints and Photographs Division, LC-DIG-ppmsca-19754.

The United States ultimately accommodated progress in *civil rights* while warding off a focus on *human rights* linking US race relations with colonialism and African decolonization. After the *Brown v. Board of Education* Supreme Court decision (1954) mandating school desegregation, the issue of civil rights could no longer be avoided. Moreover, the ensuing **Little Rock Crisis** (1957) had profound foreign policy as well as domestic implications. The angry white supremacist response to school integration in the Arkansas capital, replete with spitting, hurling of epithets, and violence, all captured on television and circulated abroad, undermined the US position as leader of the "free world." Secretary Dulles was "sick at heart" because "this situation was ruining our foreign policy." The Eisenhower administration launched an emergency propaganda campaign in which the USIA circulated propaganda and photographs of "smiling Negroes," trumpeted the accomplishments of African-American athletes and artists, and called attention to benevolent US policies toward Hawai'i, Puerto Rico, and the Philippines.

As the civil rights movement unfolded at home, African decolonization took off abroad. Fears of communist expansion in Africa had been acute from 1948–50 as mass protests erupted in key states such as the Gold Coast (later Ghana), Kenya, and Nigeria. As African states decolonized, entered the UN, and began to exert themselves in forums such as the Bandung Conference, US officials became anxious. The Soviet Union had little influence in Africa and the emerging nationalist leaders there had little interest in communism. They were much more interested in Western assistance for economic development while insisting, however, on an end to colonization.

The United States offered trade and aid to the new African states but only under certain conditions, namely anti-communism and corporate access to raw materials and natural resources. US officials thus exerted economic and political influence in an effort to manage decolonization in sub-Saharan Africa while containing radicals and reformers. In 1957 Ghana under the charismatic leadership of former political prisoner Kwame Nkrumah became the first African state to declare anti-colonial independence. The British and Americans cautiously backed Nkrumah as well as other patriarchs of new sub-Saharan African states including Jomo Kenyatta in Kenya, Nnamdi Azikiwe in Nigeria, and Julius Nyerere in Tanzania.

With some success officials in London and Washington contained the threat of radicalism while integrating the new states into the postwar international system. US officials were not overly optimistic about the prospects of modernization in Africa and often viewed reformers as potential radicals or communists. Even though "some of the people of Africa have been out of the trees for only about fifty years," Nixon advised that the United States could not afford to alienate them and drive them into the communist camp. After criticizing the Eisenhower administration during the 1960 campaign for alienating Third World peoples, Kennedy made an effort to offer assistance and cultivate the support of African leaders in the cold war.

Unlike his predecessors Kennedy openly condemned European colonialism notably a blood soaked effort by the French to stifle an independence movement in Algeria. Long a dominant colonial power in Africa, France clung tenaciously to Algeria where thousands of French and other Europeans had built permanent settlements. France acquiesced to independence in Tunisia and also in Morocco, where the United States had established permanent air bases since the North African campaign of 1942. Having lost the First Indochina War, France fought bitterly to retain its empire in North Africa.

The ultimately victorious **Algerian independence** struggle inspired anticolonial resistance throughout Africa and the world. Fighting raged in Algeria from 1956–62 killing about a million people, the vast majority African. The Algerians wore down the French and with the acquiescence of the French president Charles de Gaulle voted overwhelmingly for independence in a plebiscite in 1962.

The United States intervened in the Congo following its independence in 1960 after decades of notoriously brutal Belgian colonization during the late nineteenth century reign of King Leopold II. Much like Árbenz in Guatemala, **Patrice Lumumba**, the democratically elected prime minster of the Congo, was a left-leaning reformer and thus a target for removal. Depicted in the West as "erratically irresponsible," a "sorcerer," and a "red weed," Lumumba insisted that he was an African nationalist not a communist. A proponent of non-alignment, Lumumba favored "positive neutrality" in the cold war but he demanded the immediate departure of Belgian troops from the Congo. Although Belgium had acquiesced to formal independence, Brussels set up a neo-colonial framework through which it would maintain control of the resource-rich Katanga region. Lumumba sought assistance from the UN and the United States in securing genuine independence for the Congo, but when these requests were rejected he turned to the USSR, which sent supplies and a small contingent of advisers.

In August 1960 Allen Dulles informed the CIA in Kinshasa that Lumumba's "removal must be an urgent and prime objective" and provided a deadly poison to be administered to the prime minister. Belgian troops allied with Congolese opponents preempted the CIA assassination, however, as they captured Lumumba and turned him over to his enemies in Katanga. In January 1961 Lumumba was tortured for five hours and then executed by firing squad. As in Guatemala, a military regime took over under **General Joseph Mobutu**. In 1963 Kennedy received Mobutu at the White House and declared, "Nobody in the world had done more than the General to maintain freedom against the communists."

Embracing Acheson's advice not "to pander to the dark and delirious continent of Africa," Kennedy maintained US alliances with the **apartheid regimes** of South Africa and Rhodesia (later Zimbabwe), where legally mandated racial separation prevailed. South Africa was the world's leading gold supplier and offered Americans strategic cooperation by allowing a satellite tracking station in the country. Eisenhower had offered uncritical support for the regime whereas Kennedy criticized South African apartheid yet took no direct action to challenge it. Adopting a realist stance, Secretary of State Dean Rusk avowed that the cold war was a "total confrontation" and "a matter of life and death of our own nation" hence "moral issues" such as apartheid could not be allowed to outweigh strategic alliances.

Like Lumumba, **Nelson Mandela**, the founder of the African National Congress (ANC), was not a communist but he demanded social progress and an end to apartheid. US diplomats charged that the ANC was "dominated by the Communist Party at the leadership level" hence the CIA helped the South African government capture Mandela. Tried and convicted for subversion in 1964, Mandela began serving a prison sentence that was to last almost three decades. Washington also backed Pretoria in efforts to rein in the Southwest African People's Organization (SWAPO), a national independence movement in the former German colony on the southwest African coast.

In the mid-1960s, as the civil rights movement culminated with desegregation and voting rights on the home front, the United States seemed poised to confront white supremacy in Africa as well. Later in the decade racial unrest and the conjunction of the black power and Vietnam anti-war movements prompted the Johnson administration to turn away from the transnational anti-apartheid movement. Beginning in 1969 the Nixon administration brought an end to racial activism on the home front and reinforced the US alliance with South Africa and Rhodesia. In 1971 the US Congress passed the **Byrd Amendment**, which specifically exempted Rhodesia, which was 95 percent black yet ruled by a white minority, from trade sanctions with respect to strategic materials, mainly chrome.

Deepening Conflict in the Middle East

A perennial tinderbox throughout the postwar era, the Middle East exploded in 1967. Palestinians and other Arabs had continued to oppose Israel, which had expanded its borders in the 1948 war and had joined with Britain and France in the Suez assault against Egypt in 1956. The situation remained unstable after Suez, as *Fedayeen* ("redeemers") continued to launch episodic attacks on Israeli border settlements and the Israelis continued to respond aggressively. Israel rejected calls for repatriation of hundreds of thousands of Arab refugees driven from their homes in the 1948 war.

The **Palestine Liberation Organization (PLO)**, proclaimed in 1964, condemned Zionism and agitated worldwide for the creation of a Palestinian state. Democratic presidents Kennedy and especially Johnson closed ties with Israel, increasingly viewed as an outpost of modernity and a bulwark of anti-communism in the Middle East. They urged Israel to compromise with the Arabs, but refrained from pressuring Tel Aviv on the matter. The United States began to send more military aid to Israel than it provided to any other country in the world, including tanks, missiles, and fighter aircraft. The US leaders accepted Israel's oft-repeated but ultimately mendacious pledge that it would not develop a nuclear weapons program.

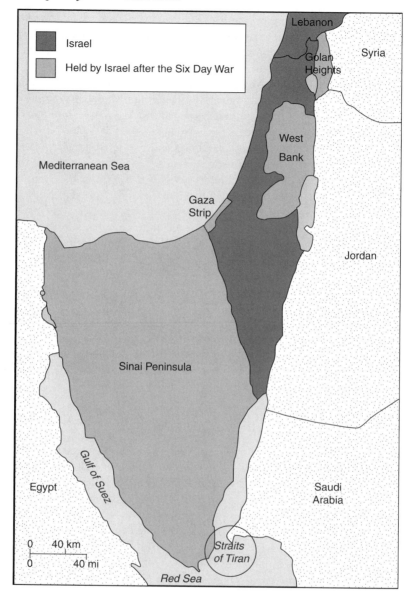

Map 11.1 This map shows the area taken by Israel in the 1967 Six Day War. In a 1979
treaty Israel returned the Sinai Peninsula to Egypt. Israel formally withdrew
from the Gaza Strip in 2005. The West Bank and Golan Heights remain
under Israeli control.

Widely accepted as the leader of the Arab world, Nasser came under increasing pressure to confront Israel and lead the way toward the establishment of a
Palestinian state. With encouragement from the USSR, Egypt entered into an
alliance with Syria, a former French colony. A few days later Israel responded to
a *Fedayeen* attack with a large-scale assault into neighboring Jordan, which killed

18 people and destroyed hundreds of buildings. In clashes with Syria Israel shot down six Soviet-made MIG fighter jets and buzzed the capital Damascus. At this point Nasser moved troops into the demilitarized Sinai Peninsula and entered into a military alliance with Jordan. When Nasser closed the Gulf of Aqaba to Israeli shipping, Israeli leaders decided to go to war.

By the time of the 1967 War or **Six Day War** Israel had developed an aggressive military strategy emphasizing preemptive strikes and rapid deployments to quickly subdue its enemies. Beginning on June 5 Israel implemented the strategy with a massive assault on Egyptian airfields, taking Cairo out of the war from the outset. The Israelis then crushed Syria and Jordan. The United States, the Soviet Union, and the UN called for an immediate ceasefire but the Israelis pushed ahead. On June 8 Israeli fighter aircraft and torpedo boats carried out successive assaults on the *Liberty*, a US intelligence vessel anchored in international waters and flying a large American flag. Thirty-four sailors were killed and 174 injured in the attacks, which the United States sharply condemned. Israel claimed the attacks were accidental and eventually paid a $3.3 million indemnity, but the CIA and most US officials rejected the explanation. "I didn't believe them then, and I don't believe them to this day," Rusk wrote in his memoirs. "The attack was outrageous." The best evidence suggests the Israelis deliberately attacked the ship to prevent it from reporting on preparations to seize the Golan Heights from Syria in the last phase of the six-day conflict, an operation that was duly carried out.

In Their Words

United Nations General Assembly Resolution 242, November 22, 1967

The Security Council,

Expressing its continuing concern with the grave situation in the Middle East,

Emphasizing the inadmissibility of the acquisition of territory by war and the need to work for a just and lasting peace in which every State in the area can live in security,

Emphasizing further that all Member States in their acceptance of the Charter of the United Nations have undertaken a commitment to act in accordance with Article 2 of the Charter,

1. Affirms that the fulfillment of Charter principles requires the establishment of a just and lasting peace in the Middle East which should include the application of both the following principles:

    (i)   Withdrawal of Israel armed forces from territories occupied in the recent conflict;

    (ii) Termination of all claims or states of belligerency and respect for and acknowledgment of the sovereignty, territorial integrity and political independence of every State in the area and their right to live in peace within secure and recognized boundaries free from threats or acts of force;

2. Affirms further the necessity

   (a) For guaranteeing freedom of navigation through international waterways in the area;
   (b) For achieving a just settlement of the refugee problem;
   (c) For guaranteeing the territorial inviolability and political independence of every State in the area, through measures including the establishment of demilitarized zones;

3. Requests the Secretary-General to designate a Special Representative to proceed to the Middle East to establish and maintain contacts with the States concerned in order to promote agreement and assist efforts to achieve a peaceful and accepted settlement in accordance with the provisions and principles in this resolution;

4. Requests the Secretary-General to report to the Security Council on the progress of the efforts of the Special Representative as soon as possible.

The swift and stunning victory in June 1967 electrified Israeli public opinion while devastating the Arabs. The United States backed UN Security Council **Resolution 242**, a "land for peace" formula under which Israel would withdraw from the newly seized territories—the West Bank, the Sinai and Gaza Strip, and the Golan or Syrian Heights—in return for Arab recognition. Egypt, Jordan, and Israel endorsed Resolution 242, but the Israelis soon claimed the resolution's reference to "the inadmissibility of the acquisition of territory by war" did not mean specifically "the" territories it had just seized. The leaders in Tel Aviv stonewalled the Johnson administration and the UN and soon began to authorize settlements in the newly occupied territories. While the Israelis pursued the dream of *Eretz Yisrael,* or the greater biblical Israel, the Arabs vowed to drive the Israelis from Palestine. Meeting at a summit in Khartoum, Sudan, eight Arab states issued the "Three No's": no peace with Israel, no recognition, and no negotiations.

Overwhelming public support for Israel precluded US officials from pressuring Tel Aviv to pursue a "land for peace" agreement encompassing withdrawal from the territories occupied in the 1967 war. Opinion polls showed an almost 20–1 ratio of pro-Israel sentiment in the midst of the Six Day War. Race and religion anchored American perceptions of Arabs as backward, untrustworthy, and prone to violence whereas the Israelis, mostly Europeans, were credited with taking civilization to an unruly land, much as the Americans had done on their own frontier. Millions of American Protestants joined Jews in support of Israel's claim to the biblical holy land. US media and public opinion emphasized Arab terrorism and refusal to recognize Israel, downplaying Palestinian statelessness and often-disproportionate Israeli state violence.

In the wake of the 1967 war, the **American Israel Public Affairs Committee** (AIPAC), founded in 1951, emerged as one of the most powerful lobbies in Congress.

While Israel fended off the Johnson administration's gentle persuasion, Nixon and Kissinger were preoccupied with the Vietnam War and lacked enthusiasm for a Middle East peace accord. Kissinger, a German-born Jew whose family had been victimized by the Nazi genocide, undermined Secretary of State William Rogers's peace plan based on Resolution 242. The Six Day War shattered the leadership of Nasser, who died in 1970, but the Arabs remained determined to strike back against Israel. In October 1973 they did just that.

Egypt, now led by **Anwar Sadat**, allied with Syria and attacked Israel on Yom Kippur, the holiest day under Judaism, which also fell during the Muslim holy month of Ramadan. The Egyptians drove back the Israelis in the surprise assault at the outset of the **1973 Arab-Israeli War**, but the Israeli forces quickly regrouped and went on the offensive. As in 1967 Israel dispatched the Syrians in short order and—aided by a resupply of US arms—prepared for a punishing assault on Egypt. At this point the Soviet Union, which had clashed with the Israelis at sea, threatened to intervene on behalf of its Arab allies. When this threat arrived in Washington, in the midst of the Watergate crisis, the Nixon administration went to **DEFCON 3**, or defense condition three, a state of readiness for all-out war.

Figure 11.8 Twice during the 1970s decreased world oil supplies prompted by political instability underscored growing Western dependence on Middle East crude. Here drivers are shown in 1979 maneuvering their cars in a long line at the fuel pumps.

Source: Library of Congress, Prints and Photographs Division, LC-DIG-ppmsca-03433.

As in the Cuban Missile Crisis, the only previous time the United States had gone to DEFCON 3, the possibility of a superpower conflict was apparent. While the Pentagon mobilized in the event of war, Kissinger and Soviet officials worked toward a cessation of hostilities in the Middle East. On October 25 all the parties agreed to a ceasefire, bringing an end to the war after nearly three weeks of intense conflict. The Egyptians claimed some measure of restored pride for their early success in the war but the Israelis remained fully ensconced in the occupied territories (OT) and embittered by the surprise attack. The Arab members of the Organization of Petroleum Exporting Countries (OPEC) punished the United States for its support for Israel early in the war by embargoing oil supplies. Oil prices rocketed as a result of the **1973 OPEC oil embargo**, leading to long lines at US gas pumps, an economic downturn, and underscoring US and western European oil dependence. In March 1974 OPEC lifted the embargo, but a second oil crisis erupted five years later in the wake of the Iranian Revolution.

In July 1974 the United States helped mediate a military conflict between two of its NATO allies, Greece and Turkey, over the political status of Cyprus, an island nation strategically located adjacent to Europe and the Middle East. Following a Greek supported coup on the island Turkish forces invaded and all-out war seemed imminent. Since the Truman Doctrine the United States had overseen developments in the strategically important Mediterranean Sea. Washington had heavily armed and bolstered dictatorships in Turkey, which had joined in the Korean War and hosted US missile sites. As the cold war dawned the United States had intervened in the Greek civil war on behalf of the right wing, which it continued to support. In 1967 Washington backed the seizure of power in Athens by a brutally repressive military regime, which killed and tortured political opponents.

The **1974 Cyprus crisis** ended with Kissinger joining the British in backing a negotiated partition of the island between Greek and Turkish Cypriots. US relations with Turkey had been damaged, however, by an arms embargo put in place as a result of Greek-American pressure groups in Washington. In 1978 the arms embargo ended, US bases in Turkey were secured, and Turkey became the third largest recipient of US military assistance behind Israel and Egypt. The Cyprus conflict helped bring an end to the brutal Greek dictatorship, which had aroused widespread opposition thus fueling the emerging global human rights movement. Greece restored parliamentary democracy but anti-American sentiment endured in the islands as a result of US support for the military regime.

South Asian Diplomacy

In 1947 the decolonization and independence of India, once the jewel of the British Crown, transformed South Asia and the world. The cost was high, as millions died in the struggle for independence and in the ethnic and religious conflict that followed. The tumult ended with partition and the creation of

Figure 11.9 President Kennedy attempted to improve thorny US relations with India, appointing the respected economist John K. Galbraith as ambassador and dispatching Jacqueline Kennedy on a goodwill tour in 1962. Here the first lady receives a ceremonial *bindi* on her forehead in Jaipur, India. The Nixon administration later carried out the US "tilt" in favor of India's bitter rival Pakistan.

Source: Library of Congress, Prints and Photographs Division, LC-USZ62-106288.

separate states of India and Pakistan. The two countries would remain inveterate enemies well into the next century.

US relations with India were rocky from the start, as Nehru charted a non-aligned course in foreign policy. The Indian nationalist leader had little respect for Truman, referring to the US president as a "mediocre man." By contrast, Pakistan responded enthusiastically to the United States and proved willing to act as a US ally in return for economic and military aid to enhance its security against India. As Secretary Dulles promoted collective security treaties to enhance anti-communist containment, Pakistan willingly entered both the CENTO (Central Treaty Organization) and SEATO (Southeast Asia Treaty Organization) alliances, for the Middle East and Southeast Asia, respectively. Pakistan also provided the United States with a key air base facilitating the U-2 flights over Soviet airspace.

While sending millions of dollars to Pakistan the United States monitored the uneasy relations between India and China, which erupted in the **Sino-Indian War**. In 1962 China prevailed in the brief conflict. Committed to containing China the United States sent military aid to India. Kennedy made a special effort to reach out to India but US support and assistance to Delhi angered the Pakistanis. Islamabad demanded more money and weapons from Washington, which complied. Thus in 1965 when India and Pakistan resumed a conflict that began in 1947 over the disputed region of Kashmir, US-supplied armies were at war with one another.

Both India and the United States, acting covertly through the CIA, fomented **unrest in Tibet**, the Buddhist province inside the PRC. In 1959 the Chinese Red Army brutally repressed an uprising, killing tens of thousands of protesters and reinforcing PRC suzerainty. The teenage **Dalai Lama**, the spiritual leader of Tibetan Buddhism, fled to India where he could freely condemn China, further undermining Sino-Indian relations.

Operating from a base in neighboring Nepal, the Eisenhower administration sought unsuccessfully to destabilize Chinese authority in Tibet. The CIA trained Tibetan resistance fighters at a base in Colorado and funneled millions of tons of weapons over the Himalayas. US propaganda denounced Chinese rule and the CIA put the exiled Dalai Lama on its payroll. Washington had little expectation that Tibet could secure independence but worked with India and Taiwan to undermine Chinese communist authority in every way possible. In 1974, with tens of thousands of Tibetans dead or made into refugees, the Dalai Lama called off the futile resistance. Tibet remained a Chinese province, though Buddhist-led eruptions against Han Chinese authority continued episodically into the twenty-first century.

US-Indian relations deteriorated sharply under Nixon and Kissinger, as the duo forged new relationships with both Pakistan and China. In 1971 Pakistan acted as the go-between in Kissinger's secret visit to China, which paved the way for Nixon's highly publicized summit with Mao Zedong in Peking (Beijing) the following year. Nixon and Kissinger simultaneously carried out the **tilt toward Pakistan** causing relations with India to deteriorate sharply. In 1971 the United States backed a military government in Islamabad as it carried out a genocidal campaign against the Bengali population of East Pakistan, killing as many as 800,000 people. Despite a warning from a State Department diplomat on the scene that Pakistan was engaged in "indiscriminate killing," the Nixon administration armed and encouraged the Pakistani militarists. Nixon and Kissinger expressed contempt for India, the world's largest democracy, which turned to the Soviet Union for military assistance.

The United States backed the loser, as India led by Prime Minister **Indira Gandhi** intervened and crushed Pakistan. The crisis on the Indian subcontinent had carried the threat of a wider and potentially nuclear war, one in which China and the United States might side with Pakistan against India and the USSR. The great powers avoided direct involvement, however, as Pakistani military forces crumbled at the hands of their archrival. As India withdrew the new nation of **Bangladesh** was created in place of East Pakistan. India bitterly resented US support for Pakistan while the latter criticized Nixon and Kissinger for failing to bail them out. Indian-Pakistani relations remained embittered and both nations strove successfully to become nuclear powers.

Select Bibliography

McMahon, Robert, ed. *The Cold War in the Third World*. New York: Oxford University Press, 2013.

Westad, Odd A. *The Global Cold War*. New York: Cambridge University Press, 2005.

Ekbladh, David. *The Great American Mission: Modernization and the Construction of an American World Order*. Princeton, NJ: Princeton University Press, 2010.

Kwon, Heonik. *The Other Cold War*. New York: Columbia University Press, 2010.

Rabe, Steven G. *The Killing Zone: The United States Wages Cold War in Latin America*. New York: Oxford University Press, 2012.

Schoultz, Laars. *That Infernal Little Cuban Republic: The US and the Cuban Revolution*. Chapel Hill: University of North Carolina Press, 2009.

Harmer, Tanya. *Allende's Chile and the Inter-American Cold War*. Chapel Hill: University of North Carolina Press, 2011.

Anderson, Carol. *Eyes Off the Prize: The United Nations and the African-American Struggle for Human Rights, 1944–1955*. Cambridge: Cambridge University Press, 2003.

Borstelmann, Thomas. *The Cold War and the Color Line: American Race Relations in the Global Arena*. Cambridge, MA: Harvard University Press, 2003.

Kuzmarov, J. *Modernizing Repression: Police Training and Nation-Building in the American Century*. Amherst: University of Massachusetts Press, 2012.

Namikas, Lise. *Battleground Africa: Cold War in the Congo, 1960–1965*. Washington: Woodrow Wilson Center Press, 2013.

Little, Douglas. *American Orientalism: The United States and the Middle East Since 1945*. Chapel Hill: University of North Carolina Press, 2002.

Raz, Avi. *The Bride and the Dowry: Israel, Jordan, and the Palestinians in the Aftermath of the June 1967 War*. New Haven, CT: Yale University Press, 2012.

Rotter, Andrew J. *Comrades at Odds: The United States and India, 1947–1964*. Ithaca, NY: Cornell University Press, 2000.

McMahon, Robert. *The Cold War on the Periphery: The United States, India, and Pakistan*. New York: Columbia University Press, 1994.

12 Ordeal in Southeast Asia

Overview

The vast region of Southeast Asia became a contentious battleground in the postwar era of decolonization and cold war. Though far from American shores, US national security elites viewed Southeast Asia as a vital proving ground in the global campaign against communism. US foreign policy affected every country in the region, notably Vietnam where the United States entered into a long and ultimately futile war to prevent unification of the country under the communist banner. US strategies delivered massive destruction but could not prevent Indochina from "falling" to communism. By the time it finally came to an end in 1975 the Second Indochina War left Americans divided at home and the nation's reputation damaged abroad.

From Colonialism to Cold War

Major US involvement in Southeast Asia began with the Spanish–American War (1898) and the decision to annex the Philippine archipelago. After prevailing in a lethal counterinsurgency war in the early years of the twentieth century the United States established military bases and coaling stations in the Philippines, Hawai'i, and across the Pacific, deepening relations with Japan, China, and Korea. Despite its rhetorical support for liberty and democracy the United States bolstered European colonialism, as Asian peasants were not deemed fit for self-determination. These racially and culturally driven perceptions prevailed through the interwar period, but World War II shook the foundations of colonialism. By driving the Europeans out of French Indochina, British Malaya, and the Dutch East Indies, the Japanese had shown the people of Southeast Asia that the Europeans were not infallible or inherently superior to Asians. As the United States and its allies defeated the Japanese in World War II, European powers sought to regain their colonial empires while millions of people in Southeast Asia demanded national independence.

Victory over Japan and the establishment of military bases and colonies made the United States the preeminent Pacific power after World War II. In addition to major air and naval bases in Okinawa and the Philippines, the United States maintained political and military outposts across the Pacific, including Guam and Samoa as well as Alaska and Hawai'i, both of which transitioned to statehood in 1959. In 1947, a year after the atomic bomb test on Bikini Atoll in the Marshall Islands, Washington took control of the former Japanese mandate islands generally known as Micronesia under a UN trusteeship. In the 1990s the US–UN trusteeship formally ended with the establishment of three independent but still heavily US-influenced states of Micronesia, the Marshall Islands, and Palau, as well as a US territory, the Commonwealth of the Northern Mariana Islands.

By the late 1940s the cold war affected every country in Southeast Asia. As the new governments strove to suppress radical and reform movements, communist parties mounted insurgencies and violent resistance. These communist movements acted on their own initiative and received almost no direction from Moscow, which had little involvement in the region in the years immediately following World War II. However, local communist parties followed the growing East–West confrontation in Europe and adapted the Soviet political line to their own local needs. Likewise, even before the triumph of Chinese communism local parties and military regimes paid close attention to US policy and tapped the Americans for military and security assistance.

In 1946 Washington followed up on a previous congressional pledge by granting **Philippine independence**. Throughout the twentieth century the US and Filipino elites collaborated on a repressive security regime rife with bossism, corruption, and ruthless police forces throughout the archipelago. While an oligarchy dominated the Filipino economy, containing leftists and reformers, the United States solidified the Philippines as a strategic outpost in the Pacific. The US military established Clark Air Base and Subic Bay Naval Base, the two largest overseas US military bases in the world, on the Philippine island of Luzon.

As the cold war unfolded the United States joined with the Filipino elite to contain the **Hukbalahap Rebellion**, named after the People's Army Against the Japanese, which had led the resistance during World War II. Comprised largely of rural peasants and farmers, the Huks pursued land reform and sought to work within the political system for social and economic change. Filipino and US national security elites viewed the Huks as radicals and communists and sought to annihilate them. By the mid-1950s, the counterinsurgency campaign led by a shrewd, US-backed Filipino president, **Ramon Magsaysay**, had defeated the Huks. Magsaysay reorganized the Philippine armed forces, offered economic incentive programs, and implemented psychological warfare operations devised by his close adviser, the CIA agent Edward Lansdale. The United States provided economic and political support to the crony capitalist regime of President **Ferdinand Marcos**, who came to office in 1965. Backed by the US trained Filipino security forces, the staunchly anticommunist Marcos jailed reformers and sometimes killed political opponents. In 1969 Marcos rigged his reelection before dispensing with any pretense of democracy and ruling from 1972 to 1986 by martial law. Despite blatant corruption and human rights abuses, the United States bolstered the Marcos regime with military and security assistance because he left the country open to

Figure 12.1 Ramon Magsaysay took over as president of the Philippines in 1953 and defeated the Hukbalahap Rebellion with the help of his CIA adviser Edward Lansdale. Magsaysay died in a plane crash in 1957.

Source: Library of Congress, Prints and Photographs Division, LC-USZ62-107085.

foreign investment, facilitated the US air and naval bases, and backed American intervention in Vietnam.

Containment of communism and protection of foreign investment also animated US foreign policy on the Malay Peninsula following World War II. Rich in valuable tin and rubber, the peninsula had been colonized by the British, whose power receded after the war. The Malayan Communist Party, comprised mostly of ethnic Chinese, led the resistance against Japan during the war and against Britain in its aftermath. During **The Emergency** (1948–60) the United States backed the British in a counterinsurgency war against the guerrillas. The campaign included resettlement of villagers to control the insurgents, who unlike the later struggle in Vietnam were identifiable because of their Chinese ethnicity. After quelling the insurgency the former British colony transitioned into the new Federation of Malaysia in 1963.

The United States and the British paid special attention to **Singapore**, the island city state located at the tip of the peninsula and with a sprawling port at the access point to a critical waterway, the Strait of Malacca. While ethnic Chinese were a minority in Malaya they made up 80 percent of the population of Singapore, heightening Western fears in the years after the "fall" of China. The United States bolstered anti-communist forces on the island but the CIA's effort to infiltrate the dominant political party was exposed. Nonetheless, US economic, cultural, and propaganda efforts paralleled the ambitions of the man who became Singapore's longtime authoritarian ruler, **Lee Kwan Yew**. After first joining with Malaysia, Singapore became independent in 1965 and rapidly developed as a strongly anti-communist and thriving center of Southeast Asian commerce.

The allied British Commonwealth countries of Australia and New Zealand anchored liberal capitalism in the South Pacific. Indonesia became pivotal in the era of decolonization and cold war. As the United States retreated from Roosevelt's anti-colonial stance in deference to anti-communist containment, Washington backed the Netherlands with funds and arms in 1947 as it dispatched a mass army in an ultimately futile effort to reassert colonialism. The Dutch proved unable to defeat the guerrillas hence the **Republic of Indonesia** achieved independence in 1949. Like India under Nehru and Vietnam under Ho Chi Minh, the Indonesians embraced a popular nationalist hero in **Achmed Sukarno**, who led the drive for independence from the Netherlands.

Indonesia under Sukarno expropriated Dutch and other Western properties, recognized "Red China," and allowed political participation by the Indonesia Communist Party (**PKI**), all of which appeared threatening to the Americans. A key leader of the non-aligned movement, Sukarno hosted the Bandung Conference in 1955. President Eisenhower and, especially, Secretary of State John Foster Dulles denounced "neutralism" in the cold war and created SEATO, based on the NATO model, to promote anti-communist containment in the region. The Eisenhower administration exercised its penchant for covert operations in an effort to topple Sukarno. Mobilized from the outlying islands Sumatra and Sulawesi in 1958, the operation was a complete failure.

In the mid-1960s US frustration with Sukarno mounted, as the Indonesian leader criticized the escalating war in Vietnam, continued to tolerate the PKI, and turned to China for advice on land reform. In 1965, a failed coup by disaffected military officers provided a pretext for the overthrow of Sukarno followed by a genocidal assault on leftists and reformers. The Indonesian military forced Sukarno out of power and proceeded to slaughter at least 500,000 and perhaps a million people. Thugs and youth gangs summarily executed PKI members, reformers, students, teachers, professionals, and ethnic Chinese.

Time reported a "serious sanitation problem," as "the humid air bears the reek of decaying flesh" while streams were "literally clogged with bodies."

US officials advised General **Suharto**, the military dictator who would rule the country until 1998, that Washington was "generally sympathetic with and admiring of what the army was doing." Britain and Australia joined the United States in supporting the murderous campaign. "The anti-PKI massacres in Indonesia rank as one of the worst mass murders of the twentieth century," a CIA analysis concluded in 1968. Nonetheless, the State Department exulted, "Indonesian political development has been drastically altered in a direction favorable to United States interests." The staunchly anti-communist military dictatorship restored expropriated property, opened Indonesia to foreign investment, and replaced Sukarno's "guided democracy" with military dictatorship. Washington hailed the new Indonesia as a model of anti-communist modernization and lavished the regime with military advising, modern weaponry, and police training.

A decade later the United States once again backed indiscriminate killing by the Indonesian military dictatorship, with the campaign focused this time on the former Portuguese colony of **East Timor**. Indonesia held West Timor, but Suharto's claim to a "common brotherhood" with the East Timorese belied distinctions of language, religion, and culture between predominantly Islamic Indonesia and the Catholic and Animist eastern islanders. The bloodbath against the leftist **Fretilin guerrillas**, explicitly approved by Henry Kissinger, began the day after President Gerald Ford departed from a state visit in Jakarta. Suharto's forces swept into East Timor from air and sea to conduct massacres, torture, and rape followed by famine. Between 110,000 to 200,000 people died from a population of some 600,000. The Carter administration, despite its promotion of human rights, maintained the policy of backing Suharto. At the time US arms sales to Suharto had eclipsed more than a billion dollars. In 1999, after decades of resistance, East Timor finally gained independence following the fall of Suharto.

The most intense US involvement in Southeast Asia came on the Indochinese Peninsula and especially in Vietnam, Laos, and Cambodia. Thailand—formerly Siam, the only country in Southeast Asia to escape European colonization—became a military regime and a close US ally in the Southeast Asian cold war. Myanmar, known as Burma at the time, like Thailand and the rest of Southeast Asia had suffered from Japanese occupation during the war and experienced many divisions thereafter. In 1948 the British terminated their colonization of Myanmar on the heels of decolonization of the Indian subcontinent. The newly independent government put down a communist insurgency and banned the Communist Party in 1953, though some insurgents remained active near the Chinese border.

The so-called "Vietnam War" was one of most wrenching and pivotal conflicts in the entire history of American diplomacy. Called the "American War" by the ultimately victorious North Vietnamese, the conflict is best understood as the **Second Indochina War**, as direct fighting involved not only the United States and Vietnam but also Laos, Cambodia, and to a lesser extent Thailand. Beyond Indochina, the war affected all of Southeast Asia, as well as the Soviet Union, China, US allies in Europe, and the decolonizing world. The "Second Indochina War" was thus an international conflict. In the hills and rice paddies of Indochina the cold war and decolonization clashed most violently. By the time the war ended in 1975 the United States had suffered a humiliating defeat but it was Indochina that suffered the direct effects of the most destructive conflict in the entire history of the cold war.

The First Indochina War

Beginning in World War I, Vietnamese nationalist leader **Ho Chi Minh** responded enthusiastically to American pledges to support self-determination. Ho, an educated elite, and other Vietnamese nationalists opposed French colonialism, which had been established in the last half of the nineteenth century to exploit Indochinese natural resources, mainly rubber, and to enhance French prestige. Racially driven French colonialism had been ruthless, bolstered by violence and imprisonment. The French exploited laborers on rubber plantations, as tens of thousands of Vietnamese died of overwork, disease, and malnutrition. The French, however, imported their culture, architecture, and, ironically, knowledge of their own revolutionary tradition that would inspire educated Vietnamese, including Ho.

Hoping for support from the seemingly anti-colonial Americans, Ho returned to Vietnam after a long exile overseas and collaborated with the United States during the war against Japan. In 1941 Ho and his followers created the **Vietminh** (Vietnamese Independence League), which aided the covert US Office of Strategic Services, precursor to the CIA, fighting the Japanese. At the Potsdam Conference in 1945, with Japan on the brink of defeat, the Allies decided that China (not yet communist) would secure the Japanese surrender in the northern half of Vietnam and the British would occupy the southern part when the Japanese were driven out. Both occupations were problematic for Vietnamese nationalists: China was a historic enemy that had once occupied Vietnam for a thousand years while the British were closely allied with the French and shared their desire to revivify the colonial empires after the war.

In Their Words

Excerpts from Ho Chi Minh's Declaration of Vietnamese Independence in Hanoi, September 2, 1945

"All men are created equal. They are endowed by their Creator with certain inalienable rights, among these are Life, Liberty, and the pursuit of Happiness."

This immortal statement was made in the Declaration of Independence of the United States of America in 1776. In a broader sense, this means: All the peoples on the earth are equal from birth, all the peoples have a right to live, to be happy and free.

The Declaration of the French Revolution made in 1791 on the Rights of Man and the Citizen also states: "All men are born free and with equal rights, and must always remain free and have equal rights." Those are undeniable truths.

Nevertheless, for more than eighty years, the French imperialists, abusing the standard of Liberty, Equality, and Fraternity, have violated our Fatherland and oppressed our fellow-citizens. They have acted contrary to the ideals of humanity and justice. In the field of politics, they have deprived our people of every democratic liberty.

They have enforced inhuman laws; they have set up three distinct political regimes in the North, the Center and the South of Vietnam in order to wreck our national unity and prevent our people from being united.

They have built more prisons than schools. They have mercilessly slain our patriots—they have drowned our uprisings in rivers of blood . . . To weaken our race they have forced us to use opium and alcohol.

In the fields of economics, they have fleeced us to the backbone, impoverished our people, and devastated our land. They have robbed us of our rice fields, our mines, our forests, and our raw materials . . .

After the Japanese had surrendered to the Allies, our whole people rose to regain our national sovereignty and to found the Democratic Republic of Vietnam . . . We, members of the Provisional Government, representing the whole Vietnamese people, declare that from now on we break off all relations of a colonial character with France; we repeal all the international obligation that France has so far subscribed to on behalf of Vietnam and we abolish all the special rights the French have unlawfully acquired in our Fatherland . . .

We are convinced that the Allied nations which at Tehran and San Francisco have acknowledged the principles of self-determination and equality of nations, will not refuse to acknowledge the independence of Vietnam.

A people who have courageously opposed French domination for more than eighty years, a people who have fought side by side with the Allies against the Fascists during these last years, such a people must be free and independent.

For these reasons, we, members of the Provisional Government of the Democratic Republic of Vietnam, solemnly declare to the world that Vietnam has the right to be a free and independent country, and in fact it is so already. The entire Vietnamese people are determined to mobilize all their physical and mental strength, to sacrifice their lives and property in order to safeguard their independence and liberty.

In September 1945, with Japan having surrendered, Ho quoted from the Declaration of Independence as he proclaimed the new **Democratic Republic of Vietnam** (DRV). He failed to get recognition from the United States or the Allied powers. President Truman did not share Roosevelt's anti-colonial sentiments, which had been waning in any case under pressure from the colonialist Allies, and thus ignored Ho's call for recognition. By the end of the year French military forces returned to Vietnam and soon replaced the Chinese in the north of the country. Ho traveled to Paris for prolonged and ultimately futile negotiations aimed at securing Vietnamese independence. In 1946 Ho returned to Vietnam and the Vietminh took up direct resistance against the French.

Figure 12.2 Before the United States intervened in Vietnam the French fought an eight-year conflict (1946–54) to retain their colony in Indochina. In 1954 the French suffered a devastating defeat to the Vietminh at Dien Bien Phu, forcing them to withdraw and bringing an end to the First Indochina War.

Source: Library of Congress, Prints and Photographs Division, LC-USZ62-95420.

The **First Indochina War** (1946–54) evolved in concert with the outbreak and intensification of the cold war in Europe and Asia. Because Ho was a communist as well as a Vietnamese nationalist, the struggle transcended colonialism and Vietnamese independence. The First Indochina War became a pivotal event in the global conflict between Soviet-led communism and US-led liberal capitalism. As in Africa, Latin America, South Asia, and the Middle East, the convergence of decolonization and the cold war spurred violent conflict.

In the late 1940s, as the global containment policy emerged, policy planners deemed Southeast Asia vital to US national security. The loss of Indochina, they believed, would lead to the spread of communism to Malaya, the Dutch East Indies (Indonesia), and ultimately to the Philippines, leaving Japan vulnerable. In this worst case scenario—and such scenarios often provided the basis of US cold war policies—all of Asia might be lost to communism.

In 1949 and 1950, respectively, the "fall" of China and the outbreak of the Korean War dramatically accelerated the US fear of global communism. China and the USSR recognized the DRV, ensconced in northern Vietnam, and China began to send military and other equipment across the border. The United States recognized the French puppet government in the southern half of Vietnam, led by the former emperor **Bao Dai**, and began to send direct military aid to help the French wage the Indochina War. By the end of 1950 the United States had already invested some $100 million in the containment of communism in Indochina.

Under the exigencies of the cold war the United States thus abandoned all vestiges of anti-colonialism and began to bolster and finance the French war effort. The renewal of Red Scare politics on the home front reinforced this determination to contain communism virtually everywhere in the world, rendering doubters susceptible to the charge of appeasement if not treason. Eisenhower and Dulles came to office determined to find a way out of stalemate in Korea while redoubling the commitment not to "lose" Vietnam to communism. Eisenhower publicly invoked the **domino theory** (one country after another falling to the momentum of communism) to explain why support for the French in the obscure country of Vietnam was deemed vital to national security.

The DRV military forces, led by **General Vo Nguyen Giap**, suffered heavy losses in the First Indochina War but so did the French. Vietnam, Laos, and Cambodia, which together had comprised the Indochinese Union under French colonialism, began slipping away. The denouement came at the isolated base of **Dien Bien Phu** in northwest Vietnam where the French had dug in around an air base for what they hoped would be a victorious decisive battle with the Vietminh. Showing the kind of tenacity that characterized the entire history of the Indochina wars, the Vietnamese forces hauled artillery inch by inch up a mountainside to besiege the French base. While their howitzers pounded the French positions, the Vietminh inexorably tunneled their way into the base and eventually overran it. On the eve of defeat the French pleaded with the United States to intervene. Eisenhower considered both conventional bombing and a nuclear strike but neither option seemed viable nor did they win endorsement from the British. On May 7, 1954, some 10,000 French troops surrendered at Dien Bien Phu, effectively bringing an end to the First Indochina War. The French would leave Vietnam in total defeat.

The DRV won the war on the battlefield but lost the peace at the **Geneva Conference of 1954**. Once again Ho proved willing to compromise in an effort to win international support for Vietnamese independence and reunification. The death of Stalin and the Korean armistice created the possibility of a thaw in the cold war. Both China and the USSR urged the DRV to compromise in order to get the French out of the country and to avoid antagonizing the United States, which they feared might intervene directly to prevent Vietnam from "going communist." At Geneva, where representatives of Britain, Cambodia, China, France, Laos, the United States, the USSR, and Vietnam convened, an attempted diplomatic settlement of the Indochina conflict emerged.

"Nation Building" in "South Vietnam"

Dulles opposed negotiations with communists and the United States subsequently did not sign the **Geneva Accords** that brought a formal end to the First Indochina War. The accords drew a temporary division of Vietnam at the seventeenth parallel to be followed by reunifying elections in 1956. Everyone knew that Ho, the longtime champion of Vietnamese independence, would win any such election, hence neither the United States nor Bao Dai's representatives would sign the accords. In fact both the Americans and the South Vietnamese set about to ignore the agreement and attempt to create an independent, non-communist "South Vietnam."

Ever the international lawyer, Dulles sought a legal framework for US intervention through SEATO, but lack of participation by Southeast Asian countries called into question the legitimacy of the new alliance. SEATO members included Australia, Britain, France, New Zealand, Pakistan, the Philippines, Thailand, and the United States. The Philippines and Thailand, both of which Washington paid handsomely for backing its policies in Indochina, were the only nations located in Southeast Asia to join the new alliance.

The United States sought to subvert democratic elections in Vietnam and ensconce an anti-communist alternative to Ho, with SEATO providing a quasi-legal justification for the intervention. Bao Dai, who was widely discredited for now having collaborated with both the Japanese and the French, turned over power to **Ngo Dinh Diem**, named prime minister of the new Republic of Vietnam (RVN) or South Vietnam. From a prominent family, Diem was a Catholic in a predominately Buddhist country. He had served three years as a monk in a Maryknoll mission in New Jersey, where he became familiar with the US way of life. Once ensconced at the helm in South Vietnam, the staunchly anti-communist Diem established an authoritarian Confucian-style government. He demanded loyalty from the people yet appeared oblivious to the diversity and everyday challenges of ordinary Vietnamese. In his memoirs

Bao Dai wrote that he had been aware of Diem's "fanaticism and messianic tendencies" but there were few other viable prospective leaders.

In Washington Eisenhower and Dulles fully supported Diem, while the CIA operative Lansdale provided assistance in Saigon. As a morally upright Christian, Diem was the right man to try to establish a non-communist alternative in Vietnam, Dulles declared. The United States thus embarked on an ambitious program of "**nation building**"—a protean effort to help Diem establish a viable South Vietnam that could stand on its own. From 1955 to 1961 Diem's government received more than $2 billion in military and economic assistance, making the RVN one of the largest recipients of US aid in the world. The Americans helped Diem build a police force, a uniformed military, a legislative assembly, a civil service, monetary reforms, state-supported industries, and a variety of modernization initiatives.

Establishing unity in the "wild south" of Vietnam was a major challenge. Factions, warlords, organized crime, and religious sects competed for power in South Vietnam. Some 800,000 people, mostly Catholics eager to support Diem, migrated from North Vietnam to the South in the wake of the Geneva Accords. Landlords and wealthy elites, many with direct ties to Diem's extended family, supported the regime. Diem and a younger brother, **Ngo Dinh Nhu**, who took charge of internal security in the RVN, expanded and reorganized the **Army of the Republic of Vietnam** (ARVN).

Diem stubbornly refused to broaden his government or accommodate the interests of powerful religious sects and crime bosses, instead launching a war against them in an effort to consolidate power. Not for the last time US officials criticized Diem for failing to heed their advice, which had been to reach out to the opposition. In 1955 the Cao Dai and the Hoa Hao sects joined with the crime lords of the Saigon-based Binh Xuyen in a battle against the "Diem dictatorship." The Americans were on the verge of concluding that Diem was unfit to carry out the project of nation building in South Vietnam. Thousands died in pitched street battles but Diem surprised the Americans by prevailing in the end. US observers began to describe Diem as a non-communist beacon, a "miracle man," even "the Winston Churchill of Asia," according to Senator Lyndon Johnson. From this point until 1963 the United States lavished aid on South Vietnam out of a commitment to "sink or swim with Ngo Dinh Diem." In 1957 Eisenhower accorded Diem a rare honor for a Third World leader by personally greeting his aircraft upon its landing in Washington for a much-publicized meeting of "free world" allies.

Although he appeared to have conquered the sects and the crime lords, Diem embittered these and other opponents of the regime rather than broadening his political base. The absence of popular support eventually would doom Diem, but not for several years. In the meantime Diem consolidated his dictatorship, "winning" 98 percent of the vote in an obviously fraudulent US-backed election, instituting press censorship, and continuing to crack down through arbitrary arrests of regime opponents. Thousands of DRV supporters remained in the South and began to mobilize the many constituencies—the sects, small farmers, students, artists and intellectuals, democrats, and Buddhist monks—in opposition to the Diem clan rule.

While the United States poured money into the RVN the Soviets and the Chinese aided the DRV. In 1955 a land reform initiative went badly in the North, precipitating opposition and repression in which thousands were killed. Ho acknowledged the errors but by this time the venerable leader had been displaced at the helm of the communist party. The new leadership under **Le Duan** criticized Ho and Giap for compromising with the "imperialists" in both 1946 and 1954 and for continuing to counsel a gradual approach to "liberating" the South and reuniting all of Vietnam under the communist banner. The regime became less tolerant, establishing the apparatuses of a police state and cracking down on internal party debate and external dissent.

In 1959, under increasing pressure from a growing opposition in the South, Diem and Nhu stepped up their own repression, including a new law forbidding virtually any criticism of the regime. That same year Le Duan and his colleagues in the North concluded the time was ripe to begin offering more support to their revolutionary brethren opposing the "My-Diem" regime (US–Diem) in the South. The North Vietnamese dismissed Diem as a US puppet, a depiction affirmed by Diem's dependence on the Americans for funding of his fledgling government, but belied by Diem's penchant for ignoring directives from Washington. The North did not create the opposition or the growing insurgency in the South, but began to work directly with it through the formation of the **National Liberation Front** (NLF) in 1960. At the outset the NLF was a true coalition, blending both communist and non-communist forces in opposition to Diem, but over time the communists became dominant. Diem charged from the start that the NLF was nothing but a communist front organization. He dubbed the insurgents the **Viet Cong**, a slur meaning Vietnamese communists.

By the early 1960s Diem's government was under siege from a growing internal opposition, a widespread revolt in the countryside increasingly backed by the DRV. Diem continued to demand rather than earn loyalty, but only a minority of well connected elites profited from the politics of South Vietnam. Most of Diem's initiatives failed to win popular support. An **Agroville** initiative, for example, failed to improve the plight of the peasantry and alienated many by forcing them to live further from their rice fields or to abandon their ancestral lands. Meanwhile, the NLF engaged in community organizing that often proved effective in mobilizing opposition to the regime.

President John F. Kennedy was no less committed to containment of communism in Indochina than his predecessors or successors, especially after the Bay of Pigs debacle in Cuba. Kennedy had first feared for the fall of Laos, where the communist forces the **Pathet Lao** were bidding for power. Kennedy sought to avoid a showdown in Laos, as he and other US officials embraced stereotypes of the Lao as too timid and childlike to be reliable allies in fighting the communists, whereas the South Vietnamese appeared to offer better prospects for success. At another great power summit in Geneva in 1961, China, the United States, and the USSR agreed on "neutralization" of Laos, thus paving the way for a decisive struggle in South Vietnam. The CIA, however, would in subsequent years wage a secret war in Laos facilitated by a fake commercial airline company, Air America. The covert operation adopted a classic colonial strategy of arming a minority ethnic group, the **Hmong**, who lived primarily in mountainous regions and were a traditional foe of the Lao majority.

Enamored with covert operations and **counterinsurgency warfare**, Kennedy championed special forces such as the Green Beret and other irregular warfare initiatives designed to contain guerrilla insurgencies. In 1963 the administration launched the **Strategic Hamlet Program** to isolate the rural villagers from the NLF guerrillas by forcing them into fortified villages. Those not living in the hamlets could be presumed insurgents, hunted down and killed. The program of removing people from their homes and villages alienated the bulk of the peasantry, thus failing to win their "hearts and minds." The NLF exploited the growing discontent and continued to expand its base through political mobilization and guerrilla warfare in the countryside.

In 1963, with power already slipping out of his hands, Diem sealed his fate by launching an ill-advised crackdown in the **Buddhist crisis**. Buddhist monks had mobilized demonstrations against the Catholic regime, which had discriminated against them. In a famous incident captured on film, the 76-year-old monk **Thich Quang Duc** burned himself alive in protest against the regime. Nhu's wife, Tran Le Xuan, who served as first lady of the regime, as Diem was unmarried, ridiculed the protest as a Vietnamese "barbeque," further inciting the Buddhists and their sympathizers. US advisers had warned Diem not to make a bad situation worse by cracking down on dissent, but as was often the case he ignored his benefactors and unleashed the Army against the Buddhist pagodas. What began as a Buddhist protest accelerated into a general revolt, as students and other opponents mobilized against Diem and the RVN.

Accustomed to ignoring advice on the assumption that he would gain US support by winning in the end, Diem believed he would put down the revolt just as he had overcome the domestic opposition in 1955. In Washington, however, the Kennedy administration concluded Diem was losing the country to communism. Reluctantly, Kennedy signed off on a military coup against his fellow Catholic leader, one that South Vietnamese generals had been anxious to carry out in any event. In November 1963, just three weeks before Kennedy's own death, Diem and Nhu were captured in a Catholic church, thrown into the back of a military van, and executed. The United States had advocated Diem's overthrow but not his assassination, which left Kennedy unnerved. Vietnam's "miracle man" was no more and the entire containment project in "South Vietnam" was under serious threat of dissolution.

The American War Begins

By the time of Diem's overthrow Kennedy had sent some 16,000 advisers to help contain the insurgency in South Vietnam and the United States had begun to take casualties. Kennedy's keen interest in counterinsurgency, his sending of advisers, and endorsement of the coup against Diem underscore his commitment to containing communism in South Vietnam. Although Truman laid the foundation, Eisenhower deepened the commitment, and Kennedy got the United States directly involved, it was Johnson who dramatically escalated the Indochina conflict into an *American* war.

Johnson's considerable political skills lay mainly in the domestic arena, beginning with his service as a New Deal Democrat in Texas through his tenure as majority leader of the Senate. His primary focus as president was the **Great Society** liberal reform program, which marked a series of accomplishments including civil rights, job training, and health care reform. Johnson made limited efforts to internationalize the Great Society, including a famous offer to Ho, summarily rejected, to call off the NLF resistance in return for a US-financed Mekong River Valley dam and economic development project. During his presidency Johnson also pursued population control and famine relief for India, but the results were mixed. Johnson feared the Great Society would be lost if Vietnam were lost to communism, but he and his advisers were confident that the United States could manage the situation in Vietnam.

Johnson maintained continuity with the fallen president by retaining Kennedy's foreign policy team, notably Secretary of Defense Robert McNamara, Secretary of State Dean Rusk, and National Security Adviser McGeorge

Figure 12.3 Lyndon Johnson meets with South Vietnamese soldiers and US advisers while serving as vice president in 1962. The Kennedy administration sent thousands of advisers to Vietnam, but Johnson dramatically escalated US involvement after assuming the presidency in November 1963.

Source: Library of Congress, Prints and Photographs Division, LC-DIG-ds-01314.

Bundy. As the 1964 presidential campaign approached Johnson sought to deflect criticism he was receiving from the Republican Party nominee, Arizona Senator Barry Goldwater, who charged the administration was weak on communism in the face of Hanoi's renewed push to win the revolution in the South. Goldwater declared that if elected he would consider using tactical nuclear weapons and threatened to turn Vietnam into "a parking lot" if the communists refused to back off.

Johnson confronted a deepening crisis. Rather than improving the political situation the overthrow and murder of Diem precipitated a series of destabilizing military coups. Johnson wanted a free hand to use US military power to avoid defeat in South Vietnam. While political turmoil reigned in Saigon the NLF guerrillas were gaining ground and winning over adherents. The North Vietnamese, backed by the USSR and China, were stepping up infiltration and material support to the South.

In August 1964 Johnson deliberately misrepresented an incident in the Gulf of Tonkin off the coast of North Vietnam to reassure the public that he would not back down to communism. The **Tonkin Gulf incident** stemmed from covert US operations assisting the South Vietnamese naval forces conducting intelligence gathering and hit and run raids against North Vietnamese coastal installations. One US destroyer was struck with a torpedo in international waters by a North Vietnamese vessel, suffering insubstantial damage and no casualties, while another claimed to have been hit as well, a report later shown to be false. Johnson told the public that the US ships had been attacked for no reason as they navigated the high seas. He received with only two dissenting votes from the entire Congress a "blank check" to take whatever military action he believed advisable in the face of North Vietnamese "aggression." The **Tonkin Gulf Resolution** provided the president with a legal framework and unfettered authority to escalate US involvement in Vietnam while simultaneously stealing Goldwater's thunder.

Within months the campaign of reprisal bombing Johnson initiated in the wake of the Tonkin Gulf incident became a sustained operation known as **Rolling Thunder**. The United States bombed rebel strongholds in South Vietnam, select targets in North Vietnam, and all along the so-called **Ho Chi Minh Trail** (HCMT). The HCMT was a labyrinthine route of paths, roads, and bridges linking North and South Vietnam but also going through neighboring Laos and dipping into Cambodia. Often using heavily laden bicycles the communists sent men and equipment down the HCMT to resupply and equip the southern insurgency. The United States hoped to interdict this resupply through bombing, but the Vietnamese proved extraordinarily adept at redirecting the trail and quickly reconstructing roads and bridges in the wake of bombing raids.

Despite its unprecedented scope, US bombing for the most part failed to achieve its aims throughout the war. As in the Battle of Britain in World War II, bombing tended to unite the Vietnamese in their determination to oust the foreign foe despite its overwhelming destructive power. Johnson took a carrot

Figure 12.4 Robert McNamara, secretary of defense under Kennedy and Johnson, shown here at a press conference in 1965, was a proponent of escalation and architect of the US bombing campaign in the Vietnam War. McNamara resigned in 1967 after concluding that both the war and the bombing were ill conceived and would fail. In a 1995 memoir he wrote, "We were wrong, terribly wrong."

Source: Library of Congress, Prints and Photographs Division, LC-USZ62-134155.

and stick approach to the bombing, calling periodic halts that he pledged to perpetuate if North Vietnam put a stop to infiltration. The North Vietnamese leaders ignored these offers and exploited the pauses to rebuild damaged roads and facilities and to resupply the southern forces.

The United States could blunt DRV offensives with bombing and superior firepower but Johnson was careful not to unleash the full destructive power of the United States on the North out of justifiable concern that, as in Korea, China might enter the war. Neither Johnson nor US allies, nor the Soviets and the Chinese for that matter, wanted a superpower conflict in Indochina. But Vietnam like Korea shared a border with China hence Mao assured the North Vietnamese that China *would* enter the war if the Americans pushed too far. Much like MacArthur in the Korean War era, advocates of a more aggressive US assault on the North ignored the warning that the action would mean another war with China. From 1965 to 1968 China stationed more than 320,000 troops inside Vietnam, greatly enhancing Hanoi's security and enabling the government to send more of its own forces into the South.

In February 1965 the United States made the fateful transition from an advisory to a direct US combat role in the wake of a "Viet Cong" attack on a US air base at **Pleiku** in the Central Highlands. The "sapper attack" by elite assault forces killed 8 Americans and injured more than 100 at Pleiku. Johnson promptly authorized Flaming Dart, reprisal bombing of North Vietnamese bases, to which the enemy immediately retaliated with an attack on a US base at Qui Nonh, 75 miles east of Pleiku, killing 23 more Americans. Johnson authorized another retaliatory air assault, but by this time US Army General William Westmoreland, a veteran of World War II and Korea and commander of US forces in Vietnam, recommended a direct combat role. The troops would bolster defense around the vulnerable US bases and could also undertake offensive operations.

From this point forward US Army and Marine units embarked on "**search and destroy**" operations to root out and crush the Vietnamese guerrilla insurgency. In 1963 ARVN had failed in its first major military confrontation, the **Battle of Ap Bac**, won handily by the NLF, but Westmoreland and the JCS were confident that US forces could prevail in the field. Exploiting its unprecedented helicopter mobility, artillery, skin-peeling napalm, strafing, and bombing, the Americans would wage a relentless **war of attrition** against the enemy. In addition to direct military force, the United States unleashed ecological warfare in **Operation Ranchand**, a campaign of aerial spraying of defoliants in order to denude the Vietnamese countryside and thus remove the enemy's potential to take cover in the tropical rainforests. The principal defoliant was "**Agent Orange**," which contained the deadly chemical dioxin and poisoned thousands of US military personnel, untold millions of Vietnamese men, women, and children, and more than 5 million acres of flora and fauna. Not fully grasped at the time, dioxin causes cancer, produces birth defects in children, and renders arable land unusable for generations.

US strategy supposed that the NLF and the North Vietnamese, when confronted with superior US technology and firepower backed by lethal search and destroy operations, would perceive that resistance was futile and thus would abandon the insurgency against South Vietnam. Having never lost a war (despite the bloody stalemate in Korea), Americans were vastly overconfident and at the same time dramatically underestimated their enemy. Racial and cultural perceptions continued to shape US foreign policy, as the "pajama" clad Vietnamese rebels were depicted as backward, small in stature, and easily outmanned as a fighting force. Diplomats, missionaries, tourists, and academics had long applied such terms as "primitive," "lazy," "cowardly, "unclean," "childlike," and "dishonest" to describe the "Annamites" (a derisive term popularized by the French), but little actual historical or cultural analysis lay behind US perceptions of Vietnam. To the extent that they acknowledged the Vietnamese victory over the French, Americans tended to ascribe the outcome to "Old World" French weakness rather than Vietnamese success. Virtually no one believed that a "fourth-rate piss-ant country" like Vietnam could hold its own against the United States, the preeminent military power in the world.

In November 1965 the **Battle of Ia Drang** (Drang River) in the Central Highlands seemed to affirm the American strategy. Helicopter-borne US air cavalry units landed in the area unaware that it was heavily occupied by PAVN

(**People's Army of Vietnam**) forces. In the subsequent bloody fight more than 300 Americans died before driving out the PAVN, which retreated into neutral Cambodia. Although the battle made November the bloodiest month in the war for Americans up to that time, US commanders knew that they had killed more than ten times as many Vietnamese and inflicted thousands more casualties. The lesson seemed to be that the war of attrition would prevail, as no enemy could sustain a more than ten-to-one disparity of casualties and maintain the will to fight. That was a miscalculation, as the PAVN and the leadership in Hanoi took from the battle a different lesson: that despite the advanced weaponry and helicopter mobility of the Americans the Vietnamese forces could inflict severe damage, regroup, and fight another day. Eventually the Americans like the French would tire from the effort and the suffering of their forces and conclude that the war was not worth the losses. This calculation would prove in time to be the correct one.

The United States sent increasing numbers of troops to Vietnam in an effort to control the situation on the ground but in some important respects Americanization backfired. US troop presence grew steadily, from 184,000 at the end of 1965 to 537,000 US troops in Vietnam at the end of 1968. The Americanization of the conflict retarded the development of ARVN, already plagued by desertion and other weaknesses. While myriad counterinsurgency and civic action programs sought to win the "hearts and minds" of the Vietnamese people, the destructiveness of the wider war undermined these efforts. The bombing and counterinsurgency war drove masses of Vietnamese into the cities and towns as refugees.

The vast majority of US military personnel in Vietnam did not play a direct combat role, but they were a visible presence. The Americans took their modern conveniences overseas and in so doing made a sweeping impact on Vietnamese society. Saigon and other cities increasingly catered to the Americans, thus transforming Vietnamese culture. Street vendors, bars, cafes, drug dealers, and prostitutes serviced the Americans. The dollar overshadowed Vietnamese currency. A black market and corrupt businesses often linked with the RVN flourished.

As in future wars private contractors profited from the war business and turned South Vietnam into a construction zone. The Americans imported millions of board feet of lumber, 11 million pounds of nails, 750,000 sheets of plywood, and 98 million pounds of asphalt. A construction consortium removed earth, dredged canals, built pipelines, and paved roads and airfields. Imported trucks and tractors moved an average of more than 500,000 tons of goods every month. The American soldiers, support personnel, money, war materiel, and manufactured goods had social consequences, transforming the landscape, customs, and culture of Vietnam.

Turning Point: The Tet Offensive

At the end of January 1968 the Tet Offensive shook the foundations of the US war effort. From 1965 to 1968 the United States had Americanized the war while ringing up body counts purporting to show steady progress toward certain victory. While rife with corruption and essentially a military grafted onto a government, the RVN leadership under **Nguyen Van Thieu** established a measure of stability in the wake of the series of coups. Many Americans had profound doubts about the intervention, but Westmoreland assured Johnson that the US and RVN forces were in the process of taking command in South Vietnam.

Violating a ceasefire marking the Lunar New Year holiday, the NLF caught the Americans and the RVN by surprise in the Tet Offensive. Coming out into the open, the guerrillas struck in 36 of 44 provincial capitals and unleashed warfare in cities throughout South Vietnam in hopes of spurring a general uprising. "The enemy struck hard and with superb attention to organization, supply, and secrecy," a US diplomat acknowledged. However, the United States used its superior firepower to beat back the offensive, retaking all of the cities and towns often through extended combat as in the imperial city of Hue. The fighting was intense and the destruction massive. Some 3,000–6,000 civilians died, including an unknown (and highly disputed) number of South Vietnamese executed by the communists in the "**Hue Massacre**."

The Tet Offensive further destabilized South Vietnam and moreover sharply eroded support for the war back in the United States. Militarily, however, Tet was disastrous for the NLF. Hanoi's wishful thinking came up empty, as the US and RVN forces not only retook all of the cities but devastated the NLF in the process, and no general uprising occurred. "We had somewhat underestimated the capabilities and reactions of the enemy and had set our goals too high," Vietnam's official history of the war would later acknowledge. "Our plan for military attacks was too simplistic and . . . We did not reassess the situation in a timely fashion."

Fortunately for Hanoi the Tet Offensive stunned the American public, which had been led to believe the enemy was virtually subdued and the war would soon be winding down. Tet suggested that the public had been misled, that the war might continue for a very long time, and was perhaps destined, like Korea, to end in stalemate. Many Americans and people worldwide cringed at the destructiveness of the war, vividly displayed as Vietnam was the first "television war." To many it seemed incongruous for the United States to employ its massive military power including B-52 bombers, napalm, and artillery against a peasant society characterized by dirt roads, straw huts, ox carts, and rice fields. The draft of young Americans into Vietnam military service was becoming unpopular and openly resisted, particularly as the number of men returning home in body bags increased in 1968–69, the bloodiest years of the war. Opposition promptly mobilized after Tet to an announcement that Westmoreland had requested more than 200,000 new troops.

Nations throughout the world criticized US militarism in Indochina. A steady drumbeat of condemnation of American imperialism from China, Russia, and other communist states could be expected, but criticism from allies was another matter. US intervention in Vietnam challenged the "special

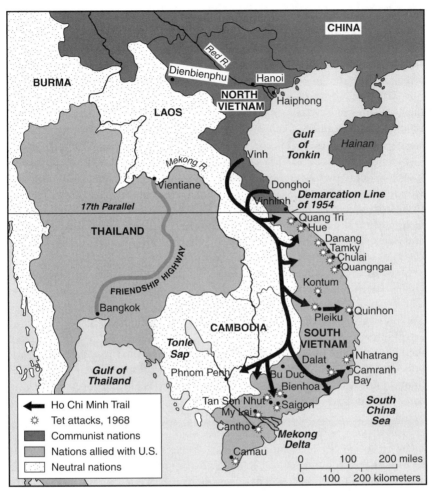

Map 12.1 The Vietnam War.

relationship" with Britain and fellow Anglophone nations of Canada, Australia, and New Zealand. The latter two nations were closer to the conflict and thus in 1951 had entered into the Australia, New Zealand, United States Security Treaty (**ANZUS**), an anti-communist alliance. Australia sent advisers and several thousand air, ground, and naval forces. With anti-war protests heating up down under in the wake of the Tet Offensive, Australian forces began to withdraw and were gone by the end of 1972. Australia suffered 520 dead and some 2,400 wounded in the conflict. New Zealand responded modestly, dispatching military forces that peaked at 548 and ended with 39 deaths and 187 wounded. Despite its minimal involvement, the Indochina War proved highly controversial in New Zealand as in Australia. In both countries critics condemned the government for its perceived subservience to Washington.

The closest US ally, Great Britain, refused to put "boots on the ground" in Indochina, but otherwise offered economic and security cooperation to the Saigon government while condemning Hanoi and the NLF as aggressors. As the US bombing campaign intensified, Prime Minister **Harold Wilson** drew criticism from the press, anti-war leaders, and within his own Labor Party over the "cruel war" and his perceived subservience as "President Johnson's poodle." Wilson tried to dampen criticism through British efforts at mediation, but to little effect. Similarly, Canada avoided direct intervention but sided with the United States and offered myriad forms of security assistance. A few thousand Canadian men joined the US armed forces to serve in Vietnam while tens of thousands of Americans took refuge in Canada to avoid the draft. Anti-war sentiment flourished in Canada. In 1965 Canadian Prime Minster **Lester Pearson** criticized the war during a US visit, prompting an angry Johnson to collar him the next evening and declare, "You pissed on my rug!" Johnson and especially Nixon resented Pearson's successor, Pierre Trudeau, for opening Canada to the American draft resisters and criticizing the bombing.

Drawing on France's direct colonial experience and the First Indochina War, French President **Charles de Gaulle** advised both Kennedy and Johnson that the war would drag on, the US would not win, and that the escalation was a threat to world peace. African, Asian, European, and Latin American leaders as well as UN General Secretary U Thant from Myanmar criticized the US escalation and especially the bombing. Thus American allies in no way pressured the United States to escalate its involvement in Vietnam. Neither did Johnson nor his successor Richard Nixon allow international condemnation to deter them from carrying out their wartime policies.

On the home front prior to the Tet Offensive the cold war consensus anchored overwhelming support for anti-communist containment. Outside of a few critical reports media coverage had been largely favorable to the war effort and the global cold war. In the wake of Tet, however, media reporting became much more critical. The most popular American broadcaster, Walter Cronkite of CBS, returned from weeks in the field in Vietnam and pronounced the war a stalemate.

Inside the Johnson administration adviser George Ball offered an early warning about escalation and the lack of an exit strategy. "Once on the tiger's back," he averred in 1964, "we can't pick the time to dismount." Senate Majority Leader Mike Mansfield privately expressed his doubts to Johnson as did Senator William Fulbright, also a fellow Democrat and chairman of the influential Foreign Relations Committee. In 1966–67 Fulbright held highly publicized hearings on the war, which included doubts expressed by prominent foreign policy experts such as World War II hero and Army General James Gavin and George Kennan, the "father" of containment. Angered by doubters, Johnson dubbed Fulbright, a Rhodes scholar and creator of the famous international program of scholarly exchange, "Senator Half-bright."

By the time of Tet, Defense Secretary McNamara, architect of the bombing, concluded that his own strategy would fail and advised Johnson of his grave doubts. McNamara left office, replaced by Clark Clifford, who called for a general review of Vietnam policy and of expectations for victory. A skilled attorney, Clifford grilled the JCS and found they could not predict when or precisely how the United States might win the war. As more and more advisers, pundits, and the public turned against the war, Johnson made the stunning announcement that he would open peace talks with Hanoi and would not run for another term as president.

Figure 12.5 Civil rights leader Rev. Martin Luther King, shown speaking at an antiwar demonstration in New York City in 1967, declared that the promise of President Johnson's Great Society had been "shot down on the battlefield of Vietnam."

Source: Library of Congress, Prints and Photographs Division, LC-USZ62-111165.

The **anti-war movement** had become visible and vocal well before the Tet Offensive. The convergence of the anti-poverty, civil rights, black power, and anti-war movements divided US society by the mid-1960s. The civil rights reforms, peaking in 1964 and 1965, did not arrest the problems of poverty, urban decay, racism, and police profiling that plagued African-American communities. Violent racial unrest erupted in American inner cities or ghettoes from Newark to Los Angeles, prompting a government commission to conclude in 1968 that American society was "moving toward two societies, one black and one white—separate and unequal." Middle and upper class white youth, many college students, and members of SDS—**Students for a Democratic Society**, formed in 1962—condemned poverty, racism, and the Indochina War. Some charged that a "generation gap" existed between baby boomers and their "uptight" and conformist parents' generation. Some young people became hippies, smoked marijuana and sampled other drugs, defied conventional modes of dress, grew long hair, practiced "free love," and urged others to "turn on, tune in, drop out." The alternative lifestyle, in which rock music played a major role, helped forge a "**counter-culture**," which rejected mainstream US society, including the Vietnam War. The counter-culture was an international rather than a US phenomenon, however, as youthful protests erupted not only in Chicago and other American cities, but also in West Berlin, Paris, Prague, Mexico City, and other venues. The Vietnam War figured prominently in the global protests, which often linked the violence against Asian villagers with racial repression within Western societies.

The domestic unrest, building gradually throughout the1960s, intensified in the wake of the Tet Offensive. Only months after Tet the assassinations of Martin Luther King in April and Robert Kennedy in June 1968 further destabilized society. In communities all over the country **"hawks" and "doves"** vigorously debated Vietnam policy. Students occupied buildings in an effort to shut down business as usual on college campuses and in a few cases rebellious youth bombed and burned Reserve Officer Training Centers and other defense-related buildings on campuses. Churches and clergymen divided over the war, some insisting on the need to contain "godless communism," others charging that the war was immoral. Challenging traditional gender roles, women became increasingly politicized, as the civil rights and anti-war movements spurred the rise of the women's liberation movement. Women Strike for Peace, the group that organized in opposition to the arms race and above-ground nuclear tests, turned its focus to opposition to the Vietnam War and became one of many groups to march on Washington in protest.

In August 1968 the tensions roiling American society exploded at the **Democratic National Convention in Chicago**. Charging that the Democratic Party "has blood on its hands," youthful protesters converged on the city, defying Chicago Mayor Richard Daley, who authorized the police force to attack protesters in the streets. While the Democrats nominated Johnson's vice president Hubert Humphrey inside the convention hall, a "police riot" took place on the streets outside. Hundreds of people were arrested and scores were injured in the melee. The tumult played into the hands of Nixon, the Republican presidential nominee, who declared not only that he would restore law and order but also that he had a plan to bring an honorable end to the Vietnam War. He won a narrow victory the following November.

Nixon's War

While many came to doubt him Nixon did have a plan, one that proved simultaneously ingenious and fundamentally flawed, and required the duration of his entire first term to implement. Nixon's plan centered on **Vietnamization**, strengthening and equipping the RVN to fight the war on its own while gradually withdrawing US combat forces. Nixon proclaimed as his "doctrine" that in the future the United States would continue to contain communism by supporting non-communists in other nations while eschewing direct intervention. The United States would no longer "pay any price, bear any burden," as Kennedy had pledged in his inaugural address.

The more original aspects of Nixon's Vietnam exit strategy included what he privately called the "**madman theory**." A combative personality, Nixon was not only willing but eager to use more force than his predecessors, to keep the North Vietnamese and their benefactors off balance and fearful of what he might do next. Yet Nixon and national security adviser Kissinger meant to blend brute force with diplomatic finesse. Together they transformed the relationship between the United States and the two communist giants, the USSR and China, in hopes that an honorable exit from Vietnam could be brokered through Moscow and Beijing.

Working closely together and in secrecy, "Nixinger" exploited the by now full-blown Sino-Soviet split to make both China and the USSR fearful that Washington would favor or ally with one to the detriment of the other communist power. This "**triangular diplomacy**" fundamentally changed world politics, as the United States entered into trade and arms control agreements with the USSR and forged a new relationship with Mao's China. In February 1972 Nixon visited China and the two powers issued the **Shanghai Communiqué** in which they pledged to work toward normalizing relations while containing "hegemony" in East Asia, a euphemism for the Soviet Union. Not to be outdone the Soviets hosted Nixon on a state visit to Moscow three months later.

Nixon and Kissinger implemented **détente** (relaxation of tensions) with great fanfare and to broad international acclaim. However, the effort to condition or "link" détente and triangular diplomacy with getting help from the communist powers to enable the United States to leave Vietnam "with honor" ultimately failed. Neither China nor the Soviet Union could convince or compel the leadership in Hanoi to give up its quest to reunite Vietnam under communism. Thus despite his promise to end the war, Nixon ended up escalating the conflict instead.

Nixon moved to replace the draft with a lottery but meanwhile the body bags continued to be flown home, stirring anti-war sentiment. Many Americans were angered with the continuation of the war, which seemed increasingly senseless and destructive. For example, in May 1969 in the battle of "**Hamburger Hill**" (Dong Ap Bia) in the Ashau Valley, US soldiers suffered heavy casualties (hence the "hamburger" metaphor) while taking the hill from the entrenched PAVN. A few North Vietnamese soldiers showed their resolve by roping themselves into a tree at the top of the hill ensuring that they would die defending the position. Yet the hill itself mattered nothing in strategic terms, hence the United States departed after the battle and the enemy forces promptly reclaimed the hilltop.

By the late stages of the war military discipline began to break down, as troops began disobeying orders, and in some cases fired on their commanders ("fragging") rather than risking their lives by marching into the "boonies." As the anti-war movement picked up, US soldiers nervously awaited the end of their one-year rotation "in-country" and asked, "Who wants to be the last man to die for a mistake?" Discipline had been sound in the earlier years of the conflict but by 1970 disobedience, occasional racial strife within the ranks, and growing drug use undermined the US military in Vietnam. Some returning veterans, who organized as Vietnam Veterans Against War, became a potent force in the anti-war movement, especially as some testified in graphic detail to US atrocities.

Revelations of the atrocities spurred the anti-war movement as well as international condemnation of the "immoral" American war. News of the **My Lai Massacre** in which US forces had slaughtered as many as 500 (the precise number is disputed) unarmed women, children, and elderly men in the aftermath of the Tet Offensive led to prosecution followed by Nixon's presidential pardon of an Army lieutenant (he publicly expressed remorse 40 years later). Under extreme psychological stress from snipers, booby traps, the deaths of their comrades, and uncertainty as to friend and foe, other young American soldiers (the average age was 20) committed murders of noncombatants, wantonly destroyed property, and raped women, all violations of their training as well as international law. While these events were not the norm and were rarely punished they occurred more often than the military liked to admit.

In 1968 the United States instituted the **Phoenix Program**, often described as an assassination program, in which special forces went into villages in a quest to identify and eliminate NLF cadres. CIA Director William Colby later acknowledged to Congress that many "unjustifiable abuses" occurred under the program. An estimated 20,000 to 40,000 Vietnamese, many of them innocent civilians, were killed under the program which nonetheless failed in its goal to undermine the NLF infrastructure.

The "madman" aspects of Nixon's strategy prompted the greatest condemnation, beginning with his provocative expansion of the war into neighboring Cambodia. In response to PAVN and NLF exploitation of Cambodian neutrality, Nixon secretly began to bomb communist sanctuaries. In May 1970 he went a step further, announcing an "incursion" of US forces to attack a supposed communist headquarters inside Cambodia. The latter was never found, though weapons caches were seized, but the main impact of the US assault was to further destabilize Cambodia undermining the nation's leader **Norodom Sihanouk**, a longtime critic of US intervention in Indochina. The United States backed the military dictator who replaced Sihanouk, Lon Nol, who eventually would be driven out by the genocidal **Khmer Rouge**.

In Their Words

President Nixon's Speech on Cambodia, April 30, 1970

Good evening my fellow Americans:

Ten days ago, in my report to the Nation on Vietnam, I announced a decision to withdraw an additional 150,000 Americans from Vietnam over the next year. I said then that I was making that decision despite our concern over increased enemy activity in Laos, Cambodia, and in South Vietnam.

At that time, I warned that if I concluded that increased enemy activity in any of these areas endangered lives of Americans remaining in Vietnam, I would not hesitate to take strong and effective measures.

Despite that warning, North Vietnam has increased its military aggression in all these areas, and particularly in Cambodia . . . To protect our men who are in Vietnam and to guarantee the continued success of our withdrawal and Vietnamization programs, I have concluded that the time has come for action. Tonight, I shall describe the actions of the enemy, the actions I have ordered to deal with that situation, and the reasons for my decision. Cambodia, a small country of 7 million people, has been a neutral nation since the Geneva agreement of 1954—an agreement, incidentally, which was signed by the Government of North Vietnam.

American policy since then has been to scrupulously respect the neutrality of the Cambodian people . . . North Vietnam, however, has not respected that neutrality . . .

Tonight, American and South Vietnamese units will attack the headquarters for the entire Communist military operation in South Vietnam. This key control center has been occupied by the North Vietnamese and Vietcong for 5 years in blatant violation of Cambodia's neutrality. This is not an invasion of Cambodia. The areas in which these attacks will be launched are completely occupied and controlled by North Vietnamese forces. Our purpose is not to occupy the areas. Once enemy forces are driven out of these sanctuaries and once their military supplies are destroyed, we will withdraw. . . .

We take this action not for the purpose of expanding the war into Cambodia but for the purpose of ending the war in Vietnam and winning the just peace we all desire. We have made and we will continue to make every possible effort to end this war through negotiation at the conference table rather than through more fighting on the battlefield . . .

The action that I have announced tonight puts the leaders of North Vietnam on notice that we will be patient in working for peace; we will be conciliatory at the conference table, but we will not be humiliated. We will not be defeated . . . If, when the chips are down, the world's most powerful nation, the United States of America, acts like a pitiful, helpless giant, the forces of totalitarianism and anarchy will threaten free nations and free institutions throughout the world.

Nixon's **Cambodian incursion** reignited the anti-war movement, as college campuses, relatively quiet since the election, exploded anew with protest. At Kent State University in Ohio the National Guard, armed with live ammunition, fired randomly into protesters, killing four students, three of them more than 100 meters away, and wounding nine others. The **Kent State shootings** shocked the nation and contributed to the growing radicalization of a minority faction of the SDS, the **Weathermen**, who took up bank robbery, bomb making, and exploding of the devices (including one in a Pentagon restroom) in an effort to "bring the war home." A minority of youths called for "revolution" to topple the "Establishment," which depended on the "pigs" (police) to remain in power.

Unsympathetic and unfazed by anti-war protesters, Nixon once let it be known that he was enjoying a college football game on television in the White House as more than 500,000 people converged on Washington to protest the war. Nixon worked with FBI director J. Edgar Hoover to spy upon individuals, infiltrate groups, and deny the civil liberties of a variety of civil rights and anti-war protesters in an operation known as **COINTELPRO**. The National Security Agency secretly read the communications of civil rights and anti-war activists as well as journalists and politicians. Revelations of these and other actions became part of the **Watergate scandal**, which eventually forced Nixon's resignation.

In 1971 Nixon, who kept an updated "enemies list" in his desk drawer in the Oval Office, attempted to discredit Daniel Ellsberg, a former Marine and government military analyst who had turned against the war. Ellsberg began to illegally smuggle out of his office a classified internal US government history of the war that revealed among other things a pattern of government deceit dating to the 1950s. He then "leaked" a copy of the **Pentagon Papers** to the *New York Times*. When the *Times* began publishing the smuggled documents, the Nixon administration received an injunction to halt publication. However, the Supreme Court overturned the ruling in favor of press freedom. The courts later dismissed the charges against Ellsberg. Nixon, who had begun to take illegal action against his "enemies," ordered the burglary of the office of the psychiatrist who had treated Ellsberg. Kissinger, who was secretly wiretapping his own national security staff, dubbed Ellsberg "the most dangerous man in America."

Attempting to capitalize on US internal divisions, the Hanoi government under Le Duan launched a new offensive. Not only were the Americans divided over the war, ARVN had flunked the first big test of Vietnamization, **Lam Son 719**, an invasion into Laos, which was repulsed in 1971. In April 1972 the North Vietnamese leaders concluded the time was right to initiate what became known as the **Easter Offensive**, a massive assault designed to take as much ground in the northern part of South Vietnam as possible before being stopped. They succeeded in this aim but incurred the wrath of Nixon who unleashed the madman strategy, as he put it, "in spades." Nixon ordered **Linebacker**, a massive bombing campaign intended to "bring the enemy to his knees . . . We will do what is necessary, believe me if we have to level the goddamned place, we will do it." Nixon added, "We won't aim for civilians, but if a few bombs slop over, that's just too bad." Ordering the military to "bomb those bastards like they've never been bombed before," Nixon simultaneously risked cancellation of his planned summit in Moscow by **mining Haiphong Harbor**. Although a few mines struck Soviet ships delivering supplies to the North, the Kremlin went ahead with the summit anyway, underscoring Soviet fears that the United States and China would ally against them.

Up to this point all sides had preferred to fight rather than negotiate but the situation had changed by the end of 1972. In the past Johnson's peace talks had gone nowhere. In 1966 a Polish diplomat stationed in Saigon proposed to mediate a settlement based on neutralization of South Vietnam and *eventual* unification of the divided country under communist rule. A proposed secret meeting, code named **Marigold**, collapsed at the last minute as Johnson resumed bombing after a brief halt. The talks initiated by Johnson in Paris after Tet went badly from the outset, as the participants argued for weeks about who would get a seat at the table and moreover what shape of table would be utilized (some Vietnamese did not want to sit across from or next to each other). By the time the talks got underway they were quickly stymied, as the world awaited the unfolding of Nixon's plan.

In the wake of the Easter Offensive, the North Vietnamese had been bludgeoned by Linebacker and did not know how much longer they could count on their communist allies, who were trying to sell them out to the Americans through détente, as they saw it. Nixon, meanwhile, wanted to deliver at the last minute on his 1968 campaign promise to bring an honorable end to the war. Kissinger, who had begun secret talks with **Le Duc Tho**, Le Duan's closest associate, began to negotiate in earnest. In October Kissinger announced "Peace is at hand." However, South Vietnamese President Thieu sharply opposed the proposed agreement because it would allow North Vietnamese forces to remain in place inside South Vietnam. Kissinger urged Nixon not to go ahead without Thieu's support hence the agreement collapsed. Le Duc Tho was irate because he gave in on the North's long-held position that Thieu was a puppet and would not be acknowledged in any peace accord, only to see the Americans renege on the deal.

Safely reelected by a landslide yet no less determined to get a peace accord, Nixon once again reverted to his madman persona, darkening the skies over Hanoi with B-52 bombers in an unprecedented campaign in the midst of the holiday season. Dubbed the **Christmas bombing**, or Linebacker II, the United States carpet bombed Hanoi and other sites. The DRV fought back, as Soviet-supplied surface to air missiles shot down 15 of the massive bombers, killing at least 30 US airmen. More than 1,000 North Vietnamese died, thousands more were injured, and countless structures in Hanoi (including Bach Mai Hospital) were destroyed in the devastating campaign. The bombing brought the North back to the table but Hanoi did not relent on keeping its troops ensconced in the South. Thieu protested but the United States lavished military aid and new equipment on the regime (**Operation Enhance Plus**) and Nixon promised to re-intervene if the North Vietnamese mounted aggression. Given little choice, Thieu relented and in January 1973 the **Paris Accords** were signed, the US prisoners-of-war came home, and the United States finally withdrew from Vietnam. The nation had suffered more than 58,000 deaths and tens of thousands of wounded, both physically and psychologically. Obsessed with upholding a manly "**credibility**" by staying the course, Nixon and Kissinger had kept the United States at war in Vietnam for four additional years with little to show for it.

All of the participants understood that the Paris Accords were a way for the United States to get out and little else. It was not a real peace agreement, as both the DRV and RVN immediately began to violate the terms. As Nixon succumbed to his own undoing in the Watergate scandal, resigning as president in August 1974, the Hanoi government launched yet another offensive, which they again hoped would improve their positioning for a future reunification drive. Much to their own surprise, RVN and ARVN ineptitude was such that South Vietnam this time melted away in the face of the northern offensive. The rapidity with which South Vietnam disintegrated speaks volumes about the ultimate failure of the US–RVN nation building effort upon which the entire Vietnam War ultimately depended.

The unelected President Ford, advised by Kissinger, had called for re-intervention, but the US Congress, reflecting consensus public opinion, had long since had enough of Vietnam. Congress had cut off funding for the bombing, revoked the Tonkin Gulf Resolution, and passed the **War Powers Act** trying to rein in an "imperial presidency." In April 1975, as the remaining US personnel scurried onto their helicopters, ships, and aircraft, Americans witnessed the depressing scenes on their televisions as US forces had to beat back mobs of South Vietnamese attempting to flee the new order. Hundreds of thousands of former South Vietnamese became "**boat people**," taking to the seas to escape communism only to be victimized by pirates if not drowned in their rickety craft. Most who made it to other ports were promptly turned away upon arrival. Many eventually went back to Vietnam, although from the

1970s into the twenty-first century hundreds of thousands of Vietnamese and other Indochina refugees settled in the United States.

The DRV exulted in the ultimate victory, proclaimed the country reunified as the new Socialist Republic of Vietnam, and allied with the Soviet Union. The regime took no responsibility for the devastation wrought by the war, though its strategies and military decisions often heightened the level of death and destruction. Clearly the United States bore primary responsibility for the Second Indochina War as a result of its decision to intervene, but that hardly meant that the North Vietnamese were beyond reproach. The Hanoi regime ousted the more moderate Ho, ran roughshod over the NLF and other non-communist advocates of national independence, and established dictatorial rule in the wake of the conflict. The United States responded to the newly reunified communist Vietnam with contempt, non-recognition, and used its vast international economic influence to isolate Vietnam and undermine its economy. The communists carried out some executions, but not an oft-predicted "bloodbath," instead subjecting tens of thousands of former South Vietnamese to reeducation camps.

In Laos the US effort to contain communism failed as the Pathet Lao took power in concert with Vietnamese unification. US saturation bombing had devastated entire regions such as the Plain of Jars in a futile effort to interdict supplies on the Ho Chi Minh Trail and defeat the Laotian communists. The Pathet Lao overcame the US-created Hmong Army, which had been partly financed with illegal yet CIA-authorized opium exports. Tens of thousands of Hmong were executed or sent to reeducations camps but tens of thousands more made their way to the United States and other countries of refuge.

The Khmer Rouge seized power in Cambodia, where the United States engaged in its final military clash of the Indochina wars. In the **Mayaguez incident** of May 1975 Ford and Kissinger ordered a precipitous military rescue assault after the Khmer Rouge captured a US container ship, the *Mayaguez*, and detained its crew. By the time the attack to retake the ship got underway, unbeknownst to the assault force the Khmer Rouge had released the hostages who returned home safely. US forces suffered 18 dead, 50 wounded, with another 23 dying in a related helicopter crash in Thailand. Three Marines inadvertently left behind on the Cambodian island of Koh Tang were rounded up and executed by the Khmer Rouge thus becoming the last US casualties in the Indochina war.

From 1975 to 1979 the Khmer Rouge carried out a genocide in which some 1.7 million people were killed or died from disease, starvation, or lack of health care. Debate raged over the extent to which the United States was responsible for paving the way for the Khmer Rouge by undermining Sihanouk and bombing and invading the country. The NLF and North Vietnam had also blatantly violated Cambodian neutrality and thus shared some of the responsibility for what occurred, though the victorious Vietnamese and the Khmer Rouge were bitter enemies. In December 1978 Vietnam invaded Cambodia to oust the Khmer Rouge and bring a halt to the genocide, which included the mass killing of ethnic Vietnamese. This Vietnamese invasion prompted China, allied with the Khmer Rouge, to "punish" Vietnam with a cross-border attack. China suffered the heavier losses, however, before pulling back.

This **Third Indochina War**, pitting Vietnam and the Soviet Union against China and Cambodia, made a mockery of a once deeply held US fear of "monolithic communism" and falling dominoes. In the UN, the United States and China recognized the genocidal Khmer Rouge as the legitimate government of Cambodia over the Vietnamese-backed Cambodian government. The Vietnamese eventually pulled out of Cambodia, the Khmer Rouge were driven from power, and Cambodia regained its independence. By the late 1980s Vietnam followed the lead of the new Soviet leader, Mikhail Gorbachev, and initiated economic reforms, a program known as **doi moi**.

Indochina suffered massive destruction in the series of brutal wars. While genocide ravaged Cambodia, the United States made tiny, land-locked Laos the most heavily bombed country in human history before pulling out and leaving the Hmong allies to fend for themselves. Overall, the United States dumped far more tonnage of bombs on Indochina than all the belligerents in all the theaters of World War II. Vietnam as a whole suffered some 3 million deaths, 14 million wounded, and some 300,000 missing in action (MIA). The war continued to kill long after it was over by such means as unexploded ordinance (more than 40,000 deaths since 1975) as well as cancer, other diseases, and birth defects attributable to the American ecocide. The United States also left behind a devastated infrastructure and millions of unemployed, orphaned, and destitute people. Accomplished at war but not at social reconstruction, the new socialist republic proved unimaginative and slow to rectify these problems and rebuild the economy.

Aside from Laos and Cambodia no other countries in Southeast Asia "fell" to communism. In fact the Second Indochina War, in concert with the Association of Southeast Asian Nations (ASEAN), created in 1967, spurred capitalism in the region, as the United States sent billions of dollars to Indonesia, Malaysia, the Philippines, and Thailand to bolster the war effort and strengthen their economies. The conflict had been unquestionably an American war, but other Asian states led by South Korea contributed. South Korea sent some 50,000 troops, who earned a reputation as vicious fighters, while Australia, New Zealand, the Philippines, South Korea, and Thailand sent 20,000 combined. The US backed military regime in Thailand played a crucial role as the primary base for the US air war and a popular destination for troops on R&R. The United States paid Thailand $50 million, the Philippines $39 million, and South Korea $1 billion for their military assistance. SEATO member Pakistan refused a request to supply troops.

As throughout the history of US foreign policy, the cultural factors of race, gender, and religion played a role in the US intervention in Indochina. Some Americans viewed the Vietnamese as racially inferior, subject to childlike manipulation and control, and mere "gooks" who could be killed in large numbers because Asians, as Westmoreland once notoriously opined, did not value life as Westerners did. Part of the larger cold war campaign against "godless

Figure 12.6 The Vietnam Memorial Wall, like the war itself, proved controversial at the outset, as some veteran groups and President Ronald Reagan initially opposed the Asian-American artist Maya Lin's simple design of a granite reflecting wall with the names of American servicemen who died in the war. A combat bronze was added to the memorial site on the Washington Mall, which soon became one of the most popular tourist attractions in the nation's capital.

Source: Library of Congress, Prints and Photographs Division, HABS DC,WASH, 643–11.

communism," religion also came directly into play through US support for both Diem and Thieu, Roman Catholic leaders in a predominately Buddhist–Confucian cultural tradition. Gendered notions of masculinity manifested in the determination not to withdraw or appear weak or undergo the loss of manly credibility through defeat. "If I let the Communists take over South Vietnam, then I would be seen as a coward and my nation would be seen as an appeaser," Johnson explained. The American people, he added, will "forgive you for anything except being weak."

Figure 12.7 The POW/MIA flag, which has been called "the second American flag," emerged during the Vietnam War.

Source: US POW/MIA flags, in front of the Lincoln Memorial, Milwaukee Wisconsin, 31 May, 2008.

Interpreting the Past

Myths and Lessons of the Vietnam War

The Vietnam War produced no shortage of controversy as well as widely embraced national mythologies. Most but not all Americans concluded that "Vietnam" was a tragic mistake, a war that should never have been fought, and one that cost the United States economically, politically, and in damage to international reputation as well as to the nation's collective psyche. During the 1980 presidential campaign Ronald Reagan sounded a different note and played a key role in revising the lessons of the Vietnam War. Reagan described the war as a "noble cause," one the US government had been "afraid to let [the US military] win." Such statements belied the massive and multi-faceted US military commitment and invariably ignored the threat of a wider war with China, but the pronouncement, echoed in films such as *Rambo: First Blood: Part II* ("Do we get to win this time?"), was no less popular.

While most analysts agreed that the US military strategy of incremental escalation and the war of attrition were badly flawed, there was no clear-cut strategy for victory in Vietnam. Winning the war ultimately required creation of a viable South Vietnam that could stand on its own, a reality that never materialized despite billions of dollars and a determined US and South Vietnamese effort at "nation building." Some analysts argued that Washington should have continued to support South Vietnamese President Ngo Dinh Diem rather than approving his overthrow, but by 1963 Diem had shown he could not generate popular support or quell the insurgency.

Perhaps the most sensational myth to emerge out of the Vietnam War, though utterly baseless, was that the US government deliberately left behind prisoners of war and men missing in action, and then covered up its craven behavior. The POW/MIA myth was fueled once again by B movies such as *Missing in Action*, bogus photographs of supposed US prisoners, and widespread rhetorical support from politicians and public figures. In 1993, after years of proliferating mythology, a bipartisan congressional committee put the canard to rest after extensive investigations produced no evidence that even a single American had been deliberately left behind. Like the myth that scores if not hundreds of US veterans had been spat upon by war protesters on their return home (there is no verified evidence that such incidents occurred), the POW/MIA myth lacked factual basis.

Despite can-do American optimism and a prolonged and massive war effort, the United States simply could not control the situation on the ground (or through the air) in Indochina. Even though a "decent interval" had passed from the US withdrawal to the fall of Saigon, the United States had clearly now lost a war and would in the ensuing years have to grapple with the legacy of defeat, dubbed the "**Vietnam syndrome**."

Select Bibliography

Foster, Anne L. *Projections of Power: The United States and Europe in Colonial Southeast Asia, 1919–1941*. Durham, NC: Duke University Press, 2010.

McCoy, Alfred. *Policing America's Empire: The United States, the Philippines, and the Rise of the Surveillance State*. Madison: University of Wisconsin Press, 2009.

Simpson, Bradley R. *Economists with Guns: Authoritarian Development and U.S.-Indonesian Relations, 1960–1968*. Stanford, CA: Stanford University Press, 2008.

Lawrence, Mark A. *The Vietnam War: A Concise International History*. New York: Oxford University Press, 2008.

Prados, John. *Vietnam: The History of an Unwinnable War, 1945–1975*. Lawrence: University Press of Kansas, 2009.

Herring, George C. *America's Longest War: The United States in Vietnam, 1950–1975*. Boston: McGraw Hill, 2002.

Bradley, Mark P. *Imagining Vietnam and America: The Making of Postcolonial Vietnam, 1919–1950*. Chapel Hill: University of North Carolina Press, 2000.

Miller, Edward. *Misalliance: Ngo Dinh Diem, the United States, and the Fate of South Vietnam*. Cambridge, MA: Harvard University Press, 2013.

Chapman, Jessica. *Caldron of Resistance: Ngo Dinh Diem, the United States, and 1950s Southern Vietnam*. Ithaca, NY: Cornell University Press, 2013.

Randolph, Stephen P. *Powerful and Brutal Weapons: Nixon, Kissinger and the Easter Offensive*. Cambridge, MA: Harvard University Press, 2004.

Nguyen, Lien-hang. *Hanoi's War: An International History of the War for Peace in Vietnam*. Chapel Hill: University of North Carolina Press, 2012.

Asselin, Pierre. *A Bitter Peace: Washington, Hanoi, and the Making of the Paris Agreement*. Chapel Hill: University of North Carolina Press, 2002.

Hess, Gary R. *Explaining America's Lost War*. Malden, MA: Blackwell, 2009.

Schulzinger, Robert. *A Time for Peace: The Legacy of the Vietnam War*. New York: Oxford University Press, 2008.

Laderman, Scott and Martini, Edwin. *Four Decades On: Vietnam, the United States, and the Legacies of the Second Indochina War*. Durham, NC: Duke University Press, 2013.

13 End of the Cold War

Overview

At the end of the 1970s diplomacy gave way to renewed confrontation and a revival of the cold war. The Soviet invasion of Afghanistan, coupled with the Iran hostage crisis and US economic woes, facilitated the landslide election of Ronald Reagan in 1980. Branding the USSR an "evil empire," Reagan escalated the cold war, expanded the nuclear arms race, and vigorously opposed communism from Central America to southern Africa.

In the midst of these efforts the Soviet Union, suffering from grave economic weaknesses and the exhaustion of its worldwide ideological appeal, chose a new leader. Beginning in 1985 **Mikhail Gorbachev** enacted sweeping reforms, including a dramatic de-escalation of the cold war. Gorbachev hoped his reforms would reinvigorate the USSR and the world socialist movement, but instead and in stunning fashion, the Soviet Empire disintegrated.

Détente

Relative stability albeit within the context of the East–West cold war paved the way for the emergence of **détente**, or a relaxation of tensions. In Western Europe the Allies had forged a successful program of economic and military integration. The United States clearly took the lead, a process that began with the Marshall Plan in 1947. In the ensuing years the United States represented an "irresistible empire" or "empire by invitation" in Western Europe. While Europeans had their own rich cultural traditions and did not simply adopt the American way of life, the United States led the way in promoting liberal democracy, free trade, consumerism, popular culture, and cultural exchange.

While "soft power" solidified the Western alliance, propaganda and covert operations reinforced an uncompromising anti-communism. Beginning in 1948 the CIA intervened in the Italian and French elections and thereafter worked with other agencies to clamp down on perceived radical threats. NATO cultivated a clandestine program (code named **Gladio**, "sword" in Italian) to repress left-wing political movements, going so far on occasion as to carry out terrorist assaults replete with deaths and civilian casualties which were then blamed on left-wing terrorists in order to justify crackdowns. Various covert operations designed to undermine the left unfolded in virtually every NATO country, including the United States, most of which remained secret until the 1990s.

As the events in East Germany (1953) and Hungary (1956) had shown, the Soviets and their East European allies would repress uprisings against Communist Party authority. Suppression of the revolts underscored that the US-led efforts to destabilize or "roll back" communism had failed and thus gave way to a more gradualist strategy by the end of the Eisenhower years. The soft power approach emphasizing trade and cultural exchange increased East–West contacts and enhanced the prospects of tapping into the latent desire within the Soviet Empire for political liberalization, free speech, and access to Western-style consumerism. Over time the transformation of the "iron curtain" into a "nylon curtain" underlay the end of the cold war.

The Cuban Missile Crisis had been sobering and paved the way for détente, as the Soviets and Americans created the "hotline" and came to terms on the Limited Test Ban Treaty (LTBT) in 1963. However, the prospects for relaxation of East–West tensions did not appear promising later in the 1960s, as the American war against communism raged in Vietnam and the Soviet Union clamped down in Czechoslovakia. In August 1968 Soviet tanks and troops shattered the **Prague Spring** reform movement in Czechoslovakia. Calling for "socialism with a human face," the Czech Communist Party leader Alexander Dubcek proposed market reforms and loosening restrictions on travel, the media, and freedom of expression, prompting the Soviets to crack down. More than 70 protesters were killed and hundreds injured in the intervention. The Soviets deposed Dubcek and took him into custody (he eventually returned to Czechoslovakia and would be honored in the 1980s). In the wake of the unrest the Kremlin pronounced the **Brezhnev Doctrine**, which essentially held that communist states would not be allowed to enact reforms that would lead them to turn capitalist. Both the United States and the Chinese, as well as myriad other nations, condemned the intervention and the hegemonic Brezhnev Doctrine.

Despite the Czech intervention cleavages within the Warsaw Pact alliance belied the Western oversimplification of regimented Soviet "satellite" states. Although an orthodox and brutally repressive Communist Party leader, Romania's **Nicolae Ceauşescu** pursued a foreign policy independent of the Kremlin. In 1967 Ceauşescu recognized West Germany and the next year refused to take part in the Soviet repression of the Prague Spring. Yugoslavia under the Communist leader Josip Broz Tito had defied the Kremlin since 1948. Albania's longtime Communist Party dictator Enver Hoxha denounced the USSR and allied with the Chinese communists.

With the Americans waging war in Indochina and the Soviets clamping down in Prague, Europeans took the lead in promoting détente. In 1966 President Charles de Gaulle withdrew France from NATO, criticized US intervention in Vietnam, and called for a more mature and less dangerous approach to the communist world. West German Chancellor Willy Brandt, the former mayor of West Berlin and leader of the German Social Democrats, took a critical step in 1969 with a new policy of ***Ostpolitik*** (Eastern policy) aimed at improving relations with the USSR and the eastern European regimes. He achieved agreement over the status of Berlin, signed a non-aggression treaty with the USSR, and normalized West German relations with East Germany, Czechoslovakia, and Poland. Brandt received often-intense criticism for his policies but the West German leader perceived that soft power embodied in relaxation of tensions, increased contacts, trade, and cultural exchange ultimately would do more to destabilize the Communist Party regimes than a foreign policy of confrontation.

While détente thus originated in Europe, President Richard M. Nixon belied his long history of fervid anti-communism by seizing upon détente and pursuing it with maximum fanfare. Nixon and Henry Kissinger embraced détente in part out of the realization that the USSR had achieved strategic parity (caught up with the United States) in the nuclear arms race. Building on the precedent of the LTBT, Soviet and US negotiators came to agreement in Strategic Arms Limitation Talks (SALT), culminating in the **SALT I** accord (1972). Rather than actually cutting the stockpiles of nuclear weapons and warheads, the superpowers established ceilings on the future size of their nuclear arsenals. The USSR retained more intercontinental ballistic missiles (ICBMs) while the United States enjoyed an advantage in multiple independently targeted reentry vehicles (MIRVs). Significantly, the Americans and the Soviets also signed an **ABM** (anti-ballistic missile) **agreement** allowing each power only two sites for defensive systems, one around the capital city the other around a military base. The ABM agreement reflected deterrence theory based on MAD whereby both powers accepted their vulnerability to a nuclear weapons attack precisely because this made such an attack less likely to occur.

By the time the United States and the Soviet Union took these halting steps it was too late to stop the spread of nuclear weapons to other nations. Britain (1952), France (1960), and China (1964) acquired "the bomb." In 1968 the United States and the USSR sponsored the **Non-Proliferation Treaty** (NPT), which forbade transfer of nuclear technology to other countries. The nuclear powers thus sought to retain their arsenals while precluding expansion of nuclear weapons, especially into Third World countries. Sixty-two nations signed the treaty, which the US Senate ratified by a vote of 83–15. However, India, Israel, Pakistan, and South Africa, all of which would successfully test nuclear weapons, refused to sign. The United States lavished Israel with conventional weapons in an effort to ward off the ongoing nuclear program at the Dimona nuclear reactor site. Despite pledges to the contrary Israel took the conventional weapons but developed the bomb anyway.

Washington and Moscow thus achieved minimal progress in arms control under détente but they were more successful at freeing up trade and cultural exchange. The Soviets belatedly agreed to pay their World War II lend-lease debt and in return the United States granted MFN trade status (trade on the best available terms). In 1972 the United States sold a massive amount of wheat at a favorable price to the USSR, but the "great grain robbery" raised prices at home, angering some US consumers. Although the implications were not fully recognized at the time, the USSR's need to purchase wheat from the United States reflected the failure of agricultural production and evidence of a broader decline of the Soviet economic system.

Normalization of trade relations with the USSR proved highly controversial because of the issue of Jewish emigration. In 1974 Congress unanimously passed the **Jackson–Vanik Amendment**, signed into law the next year, which denied MFN status to "nonmarket economy countries" that engaged in emigration restrictions. The clear target of this amendment was the USSR, which levied a tax on Jews who wanted to leave the country and sometimes denied them exit visas. Angered by the US intrusion into their domestic policies, the Soviets responded to the Jackson–Vanik Amendment with dramatic cuts to Jewish emigration. In this respect the amendment backfired but to the extent its purpose was to undermine détente the amendment succeeded.

Other divisive issues surfaced throughout the 1970s, as détente encountered persistent roadblocks and eventually collapsed. In 1973 when Brezhnev visited Washington Nixon was under siege over the expanding Watergate scandal. The same year the renewal of warfare in the Middle East heightened US–Soviet anxieties and created a broader war scare. By the time Nixon's successor, Gerald Ford, met Brezhnev at Vladivostok the next year, agreeing on a framework for **SALT II**, détente was under serious challenge.

Continuing violent conflict in the global South or Third World undermined détente. Nixon and Kissinger pursued a policy of **linkage** in which they expected certain behavior from the USSR in return for relaxation of cold war tensions. Washington wanted the Kremlin to pressure the North Vietnamese to offer favorable terms for US withdrawal from Vietnam. The inability to achieve that aim was a failure of linkage. US leaders also sought to link continuation of détente with Soviet restraint in the developing world. However, the Soviets did not perceive détente as precluding continuing ideological competition in the global South and notably in Africa. The Russians pointed out that the United States continued to arm and equip Third World regimes hence they would continue to support revolutionary movements.

The **Helsinki Final Act** (1975) marked the crowning achievement of détente. The summit in Helsinki, Finland, produced a series of agreements, including recognition of the current cold war boundaries in Europe as "inviolable." This accord underscored détente's emphasis on stability and cooperation in Europe. The Soviets welcomed the agreement to legitimize their own and the eastern European communist regimes in the eyes of the World, but this aspect angered conservatives and eastern European ethnic groups in the

Figure 13.1 Soviet leader Leonid Brezhnev and President Richard M. Nixon consult
under a portrait of George Washington, June 18, 1973.

Source: Library of Congress, Prints and Photographs Division, LC-DIG-ds-04421.

United States. Critics charged that the West was "appeasing" the Soviet Union and condemning the people of Eastern Europe to permanent oppression. Reagan, who made an unsuccessful bid to wrest the Republican nomination from Ford in 1976, called détente a "one-way street" and declared that "all Americans should be against" the Helsinki Accords.

A triumph of soft power diplomacy, the Helsinki Accords elevated the status of **human rights** in global diplomacy. At the end of World War II, amid realization of the shocking scope of the Nazi Holocaust, the international community focused attention on war crimes and the term "human rights" entered the international lexicon. On successive days in 1948 the UN passed the Convention on the Prevention and Punishment of the Crime of Genocide and the Universal Declaration of Human Rights (Chapter 8). These watershed events spurred discussion of human rights and demands for international standards and efforts to publicize and punish offending states.

The definition of what constituted human rights was contested. The rise of the Third World, symbolized by the Bandung Conference in 1955, called attention to the massive human rights abuses under colonialism and spurred demands for rectification. This perspective encompassed economic rights and social change to address basic human needs for jobs, food, housing, and health care rather than a more restrictive view of human rights focused on political and civil rights. The United States emphasized the latter perspective and often opposed countries and mass movements that pursued reforms emphasizing the economic dimension of human rights.

The 35 signatory nations to the Helsinki Final Act pledged their "respect of human rights" as well as "equal rights and self-determination of peoples." Kissinger paid little attention to such paper pledges as opposed to the "realities" of national interests and balance of power diplomacy. The Soviets held the same view and had shown in Czechoslovakia that they had no intention of granting "self-determination" to Eastern Europe. Neither would the Kremlin show "respect for human rights" to dissidents and critics of the regime. Both the Soviets and Western critics of détente failed to realize, however, that such paper pronouncements were in fact highly significant, as they provided reformers with a platform to criticize the USSR, a campaign that would eventually contribute to undermining the Soviet Empire.

Following his narrow election victory over Ford in 1976, Jimmy Carter made human rights the rhetorical centerpiece of his diplomacy. While conservative Democrats and Republicans targeted restrictions on Jewish emigration and other Soviet transgressions in their invocation of human rights, Carter applied the term more broadly. The president chided US allies such as South Africa, South Korea, and the repressive, US-backed military regimes in Central and South America. At the same time international non-governmental organizations (NGOs) such as Amnesty International and Human Rights Watch sharpened the focus on human rights around the world.

The emphasis on human rights appealed to Americans in the wake of the brutal legacies of the US war in Indochina replete with bombing, napalm, and widely publicized atrocities such as the My Lai Massacre. Americans could regain their sense of moral leadership of the world by calling attention to the human rights deficiencies of other nations. Human rights discourse thus affirmed American exceptionalism.

The Camp David Accords

Carter, a devout Christian who viewed the creation of Israel as the fulfillment of biblical prophesy, labored tirelessly to promote a peaceful settlement of the Middle East conflict. He faced a formidable challenge given the bitter legacies of the 1967 and 1973 Arab-Israeli Wars, including the continuing Israeli occupation of the West Bank, the Gaza Strip, the Sinai Peninsula, and the Golan Heights. US public support for Israel remained overwhelming, particularly as some Palestinian factions employed terrorism. In 1972 millions of Americans followed on television as Palestinian militants took 11 Israeli athletes hostage during the Olympics in Munich, all of them dying in a German police assault on the terrorists. Four years later Americans, coming off their own de-masculinizing defeat in Indochina, cheered as Israeli commandos pulled off a daring raid at Entebbe, Uganda, in which they reclaimed a commercial airliner that Palestinian hijackers had diverted from Tel Aviv.

Widespread US support for Israel bolstered by AIPAC, the influential **Israel Lobby**, complicated Carter's task of urging Tel Aviv to make concessions in order to achieve a comprehensive settlement of the Middle East conflict. Israeli Prime Minister **Menachem Begin**, who himself had led a terrorist organization during the era of the British mandate over Palestine, authorized new Jewish settlements in the OT. Begin viewed the OT as part of the greater biblical Israel and had no intention of returning it to the Palestinians.

The impetus for achievement of the **Camp David Accords**, over which Carter presided in 1978, came from Egyptian President **Anwar Sadat**. After declaring he would "go to the ends of the earth for peace, even to the Knesset itself," Sadat accepted an invitation and indeed appeared before the Israeli Parliament, where he was received with prolonged applause. Carter then hosted the summit at the presidential retreat in Maryland to forge an agreement between the longtime adversaries who had fought major albeit brief wars in 1967 and 1973. Following nearly two weeks of intensive negotiations Begin and Sadat agreed to a "framework for peace in the Middle East," including "Palestinian autonomy" and "the legitimate rights of the Palestinian people." This portion of the Camp David Accords was immediately contested and failed to materialize, but the talks did lead to an Israeli-Egyptian peace agreement the following year. Israel agreed to vacate the Sinai in return for Egyptian recognition and normalization of diplomatic relations between the two states.

The Sinai was not part of the biblical Israel hence Begin had been willing to relinquish it but not the West Bank, the Golan Heights, or the Gaza Strip. In its 1977 platform Begin's right-wing Likud Party declared, "The right of

Figure 13.2 President Jimmy Carter (center), Egyptian President Anwar Sadat (left), and Israeli Prime Minister Menachem Begin shown here reviewing US Marines, achieved a breakthrough in the Camp David Accords (1978). While the summit paved the way for an Egyptian-Israeli peace accord, Carter clashed with Begin over his unwillingness to move on the issue of Palestinian statehood in territories occupied by Israel since the 1967 war.

Source: Library of Congress, Prints and Photographs Division, LC-DIG-ppmsca-09788.

the Jewish people to the land of Israel is eternal and is an integral part of its right to security and peace." The "land of Israel" included the West Bank, which some Israelis referenced by the biblical names "Judea" and "Samaria" rather than as UN-demarcated Arab territory. Other Israelis, including a newly formed activist group called Peace Now, favored returning the OT in order to achieve a comprehensive peace with the Palestinians and other Arabs. Many Arabs viewed Sadat's willingness to make peace with Israel as a betrayal, especially to the cause of the Palestinians who remained without a homeland. In 1981 Islamic fundamentalists assassinated Sadat in the midst of a military parade in Cairo.

During his successful presidential campaign in 1980, Reagan criticized Carter for putting pressure on Israel and subsequently showed little interest in pursuing a broader Middle East accord. Reagan branded the PLO an illegitimate terrorist organization and contravened the UN and international law by declaring that he did not view the rapidly accelerating Israeli settlements in the OT as illegal. Following his landslide victory, Reagan stepped up aid to Israel and initially backed an effort by Tel Aviv to destroy the PLO infrastructure through an attack on neighboring Lebanon. Israel viewed

Lebanon, the small former French colony plagued by sectarian strife, as a breeding ground for terrorism emanating from its sprawling Palestinian refugee camps. In 1978 Israel had killed some 2,000 Palestinians in a retaliatory cross-border attack in Lebanon in the wake of a terror attack in Tel Aviv that killed 37 Israelis.

In 1982 the militant Israeli Defense Minister **Ariel Sharon** authorized an invasion, airstrikes, and indiscriminate bombardment of Beirut, the Lebanese capital, with heavy loss of civilian life, including many non-Palestinians. Under international pressure Reagan dispatched diplomat Philip Habib to pursue ceasefire talks, which were opposed by Sharon and the Likud government. Sharon ordered Israeli troops into West Beirut in violation of a truce negotiated by Habib. Sharon then urged and transported Lebanese Christian militias to carry out the **Sabra and Shatila Massacre**, the slaughter of between 800 to 3,500 people (the precise figure is unknown). The victims at the two Palestinian refugee camps were overwhelmingly innocent civilians including women and children. In the invasion as a whole some 20,000 Lebanese died compared with 657 Israeli recorded dead by 1985.

In 1983 Secretary of State George Shultz secured an Israeli withdrawal from Lebanon, but the United States paid a steep price for its involvement in the conflict. In April a suicide bombing on the US embassy in Beirut killed 63 people, 17 American. Working closely with Israel, US warships shelled targets in Lebanon and Syria, which was embroiled in the Lebanese sectarian conflict. In October Islamic militants carried out a massive suicide bombing on the US Marine compound in Beirut. The **Beirut barracks bombing** killed 241 US Marines as well as scores of French soldiers, part of a multi-national occupation force in Lebanon.

The Israeli invasion drove the PLO out of Lebanon but ultimately backfired by spurring the rise of **Hezbollah** in its place. The Iranian and Syrian backed Islamic guerrilla force would plague Israel from its base in southern Lebanon for decades. Violence and unrest in Israel-Palestine continued throughout the 1980s. In 1985, after three Israelis were killed in a terror attack in Cyprus, Israel attempted unsuccessfully to kill PLO Chairman Yasser Arafat by bombing the PLO headquarters, which had been removed to Tunisia. In 1988 the Mossad, Israel's secret service, assassinated Abu Jihad, one of the founders of the PLO, at his home in Tunis.

In 1987, as Israel continued to establish "facts on the ground" by constructing new settlements in the OT, the Palestinians launched a mostly non-violent resistance known as the **Intifada**, or "shaking off" of the occupation. The Israelis responded to public demonstrations and stone throwing with mass arrests, snipers, and destruction of Palestinian homes and villages. By the end of 1989 the Palestinian death toll in the Intifada reached 626 as compared with 43 Israeli dead. Some 38,000 Arabs were wounded and as many as 40,000 were arrested. In February and again in April 1988 the United States vetoed UN Security Council resolutions condemning violations of Palestinian human rights and calling on Israel to pursue a peace agreement under UN auspices. On both occasions the vote was 14–1 with only the US vote preventing passage of the resolutions.

While Israel and the United States branded the PLO a terrorist organization, more militant groups had arisen in the wake of the Iranian revolution and amidst the Israeli occupation. Hezbollah, Islamic Jihad, the Muslim Brotherhood, and Hamas ("Enthusiasm"), created in 1988, all took a more militant stance than the PLO. Indeed in 1988 Arafat made a historic offer to accept the 1947 UN borders and to recognize the state of Israel. The Israeli government under **Yitzhak Shamir** refused to recognize or negotiate with the PLO and continued to authorize new settlements in the OT.

Intensification of the Cold War in Africa

US anxiety about communist expansion during the era of détente spiked as decolonization, the cold war, and racial oppression produced a series of violent conflicts. In 1974 the collapse of the Portuguese dictatorship provoked grave concern, as the US airbase in the Azores Islands provided a major artery for the projection of American power into Africa, Europe, and the Middle East. The overthrow of the dictatorship in Lisbon came in the midst of violent anti-colonial revolts in Portugal's African colonies of Angola, Guinea, and Mozambique. For decades Washington backed Portuguese dictator Antonio Salazar, who used US-made napalm and chemical defoliants to wage a counterinsurgency war against independence fighters in Angola. In 1975 the rebels triumphed, creating a newly independent Angola and dramatically altering the balance of power in southern Africa.

Staunchly anti-communist and thus a close US strategic ally, South Africa viewed neighboring black liberation struggles as an existential threat to its own security. A former British possession, independent since 1961, South Africa faced growing internal and international resistance to its **apartheid policy** of racial separation. Angola, rich in oil and diamonds, became a cold war battleground as the communist Popular Movement for the Liberation of Angola (**MPLA**) bid for power. The United States continued to oppose communism worldwide, but in this case the US commitment intensified as a result of direct Cuban intervention on behalf of the MPLA. The Cubans sent troops to Angola on their own initiative, though US officials assumed and charged that Castro's forces were acting as Soviet proxies. In fact Cuba had long been committed to African independence struggles where the Kremlin lacked the motivation to get involved. In the early 1960s Cuban forces and the charismatic Argentine Che Guevara had arrived too late to help Patrice Lumumba in the Congo. By 1974, however, Cuban support enabled the rebel victory in the small West African country of Guinea, forcing Portugal to abandon the colony.

In Angola Cuban intervention facilitated the triumph of the MPLA guerrillas. In 1975 South Africa received backing from Washington for an invasion

Figure 13.3 President Gerald R. Ford (left) conversing with Secretary of State Henry
A. Kissinger a few days after President Nixon's resignation in August 1974.

Source: Library of Congress, Prints and Photographs Division, LC-DIG-ppmsca-08443.

of Angola but some 36,000 Cuban troops aided the MPLA in repelling the assault. The United States sent arms and mercenaries until the renascent US Congress, determined to avoid any hint of another Vietnam, cut off funding for intervention in Angola, an action condemned by Ford and Kissinger, among others. In the end, as a CIA report privately acknowledged, "Havana's African policy," a reflection of its "activist revolutionary ethos," had won a major victory in southern Africa.

Following the election of Reagan in 1980, the United States reversed the Carter administration's emphasis on human rights in favor of "**constructive engagement**" with South Africa. By this time the United States was the leading trade partner of South Africa, which remained the "key policeman," as Kissinger once put it, in anti-communist containment throughout southern Africa. Reagan's tolerant approach, including casting UN votes backing the apartheid regime, angered human rights activists worldwide but allowed the United States to maintain trade, investments, and military security collaboration with South Africa.

Strategically located near the Red Sea and Indian Ocean and in close proximity to Mideast oil supplies, the **Horn of Africa** also became a focal point of superpower conflict. The United States suffered another setback, as Ethiopia, a longtime US ally, changed sides in the cold war. With the Soviet Union directly involved this time, the Horn of Africa conflict contributed directly to the collapse of détente. The Soviets sold arms to their new communist ally

Figure 13.4 Zbigniew Brzezinski, President Carter's national security adviser, sharply
opposed détente in the wake of the Soviet intervention in the Horn of
Africa.

Source: Library of Congress, Prints and Photographs Division, LC-DIG-ds-00589.

in Ethiopia, Mengistu Haile Mariam, who simultaneously expelled Americans from the country. In the ensuing war in the Ogaden Desert, the Soviets sent massive arms shipments to Ethiopia to use against neighboring Somalia, a former Kremlin ally, now backed by the United States. In 1978 the Soviet aid, assisted by another infusion of Cuban troops, proved decisive in forcing Somalia back to its borders. The United States remained allied with Somalia, establishing a US military base there, while the USSR consolidated its position in Ethiopia.

Already angered by Carter's emphasis on human rights inside the USSR, the Soviets willingly jeopardized détente by intervening in the Horn. The Brezhnev regime preferred Nixon, Ford, and Kissinger to Carter, who embraced the cause of Soviet exiles and dissidents, notably novelist Alexander Solzhenitsyn and physicist Andrei Sakharov. Carter's top foreign policy advisers, Secretary of State Cyrus Vance and National Security Adviser Zbigniew Brzezinski, a Polish émigré, frequently diverged over cold war strategy. For Brzezinski détente was for all practical purposes finished with the Soviet intervention in Ethiopia, but the more moderate Vance still wanted to pursue SALT II and other diplomatic initiatives. Carter further irritated the Soviets by calling for changes in the SALT II framework agreed to at the Ford–Brezhnev summit in Vladivostok in 1974. Finally, Carter successfully froze the Soviets out of the Middle East peace talks by sponsoring the ultimately successful peace treaty between Egypt and Israel in 1979.

The collapse of détente intensified conflict in southern Africa. South Africa and its neighboring white supremacist regime in Rhodesia feared with good reason that they were being surrounded and undermined by black radicalism. Both Zambia and Mozambique sponsored guerrilla forces against Rhodesia and South Africa. After gaining independence from Portugal in 1974–75, Mozambique like Angola became a communist revolutionary government backed by Cuba and the USSR. The **Mozambique Civil War** erupted, as Rhodesia and South Africa sponsored rival factions against the communist-led government. Before the UN could broker a peace agreement in 1992, an estimated 1 million people died and millions more were injured or displaced. In 1980 the British Commonwealth supervised negotiations terminating the white supremacist regime in Rhodesia, which became the new state of Zimbabwe.

Aided by the CIA and an Angolan faction, South African troops fought against the Angolan MPLA, Cuba, and the USSR in a war in the former German colony of Southwest Africa. The Cubans again played a key role by aiding the Southwest Africa People's Organization (**SWAPO**) in resistance against South African occupation and neo-colonialism. Although the UN recognized SWAPO as the legitimate representative of the people striving for **Namibian independence**, the Reagan administration labeled SWAPO a terrorist organization and backed South Africa. In 1990 Namibia became an independent nation after years of bitter fighting and negotiations involving Angola, Cuba, SWAPO, the United States, and the USSR .

Figure 13.5 F. W. de Klerk (left), the last president of apartheid South Africa and his successor, the former political prisoner Nelson Mandela, wait to speak in Philadelphia in 1993. The two leaders received the Liberty Medal for achieving the transition to majority rule in South Africa.

Source: Library of Congress, Prints and Photographs Division, LC-DIG-highsm-16040.

In Their Words

Excerpt from Nelson Mandela's Inaugural Address as he assumed the presidency of South Africa after the end of Apartheid, May 10, 1994

Today, all of us do, by our presence here, and by our celebrations in other parts of our country and the world, confer glory and hope to new-born liberty.

Out of the experience of an extraordinary human disaster that lasted too long, must be born a society of which all humanity will be proud.

Our daily deeds as ordinary South Africans must produce an actual South African reality that will reinforce humanity's belief in justice, strengthen its confidence in the nobility of the human soul and sustain all our hopes for a glorious life for all.

All this we owe both to ourselves and to the peoples of the world who are so well represented here today . . . We, the people of South Africa, feel fulfilled that humanity has taken us back into its bosom, that we, who were outlaws not so long ago, have today been given the rare privilege to be host to the nations of the world on our own soil.

We thank all our distinguished international guests for having come to take possession with the people of our country of what is, after all, a common victory for justice, for peace, for human dignity.

The time for the healing of the wounds has come.

The moment to bridge the chasms that divide us has come.

The time to build is upon us.

We have, at last, achieved our political emancipation. We pledge ourselves to liberate all our people from the continuing bondage of poverty, deprivation, suffering, gender and other discrimination . . . We are both humbled and elevated by the honour and privilege that you, the people of South Africa, have bestowed on us, as the first President of a united, democratic, non-racial and non-sexist South Africa, to lead our country out of the valley of darkness.

We understand it still that there is no easy road to freedom.

We know it well that none of us acting alone can achieve success.

We must therefore act together as a united people, for national reconciliation, for nation building, for the birth of a new world.

Let there be justice for all.

Let there be peace for all.

Let there be work, bread, water and salt for all.

Let each know that for each the body, the mind and the soul have been freed to fulfill themselves.

Never, never and never again shall it be that this beautiful land will again experience the oppression of one by another and suffer the indignity of being the skunk of the world.

Let freedom reign.

Having lost its white supremacist ally, Rhodesia, and surrounded by black majority states, South Africa's apartheid regime was teetering. Moreover "constructive engagement" ended with Reagan and South Africa now confronted intensified grassroots international condemnation and economic boycotts. Between 1990 and 1993 South Africa transitioned to democracy. In 1994 the **ANC**, the longtime revolutionary opposition to apartheid South Africa, won 62 percent of the vote in national elections. ANC leader **Nelson Mandela**, who spent 27 years as a political prisoner, became president in a triumph for racial equality and majority rule. UN sponsored truth and reconciliation commissions facilitated the transition.

Iran and Afghanistan

Ironically, even as détente gave way to a cold war revival, both the Soviets and the Americans confronted a common enemy in Islamic fundamentalism. In November 1979 the takeover of the US embassy in Tehran by radical Islamists gutted the Carter presidency through the national humiliation that followed in the 444-day **Iran hostage crisis**. The crisis came in the wake of the **Iranian Revolution**, which overthrew the longtime US strategic ally Shah Reza Pahlavi. Carter had described the shah as a "rock of stability" in the Middle East, this despite the Iranian monarch's egregious human rights record. The shah created a massive backlash against his modernization of Iranian society, paving the way for the triumph of Islamic fundamentalism.

While Iran underwent social and political convulsions, Carter attempted to negotiate the hostages' freedom. Failing that he opted in April 1980 for a high-risk rescue mission to extricate the 66 Americans. When three US helicopters malfunctioned in the Iranian desert, Carter accepted a military recommendation to abort the rescue mission. Compounding the failure upon departure from the staging area a helicopter crashed into a transport jet, killing eight US servicemen and an Iranian. The debacle contributed to the landslide electoral triumph of Reagan. On January 20, 1981, as the new president arrived at the White House, the Iranians finally released the hostages unharmed.

Fundamentalist Islam also plagued the USSR, as the Iranian Revolution inspired Islamists along the Soviet borders. The vast region of **Soviet Central Asia** encompassed the socialist republics of Kazakhstan, Kyrgyzstan, Tajikistan, Turkmenistan, and Uzbekistan. Since the 1920s the USSR had cultivated the Afghan government in Kabul as a buffer state on the Soviet southern border. A communist coup in 1978 briefly reassured the Soviets but in the wake of the revolution in Iran, which borders Afghanistan, Islamists began to rise against the regime. In 1979 in the western city of Herat, Islamists and locals fought off the Afghan Army in a major clash in which some 5,000 people died. A civil war between the Afghan government and Islamists followed.

A Soviet Politburo report blamed "religious fanaticism" stemming from "the actions and events in Iran" for the uprising, which they meant to contain. The Soviets were far from eager to intervene in Afghanistan yet they feared falling dominos of their own if the Islamist movement spread into Soviet Central Asia. "Under no circumstances may we lose Afghanistan," Foreign Minister **Andrei Gromyko** declared. The murder of the Soviet-backed Afghan president prompted the final decision to intervene. Kremlin analysts feared the man who carried out the murder and took over the Afghan government, Hafizullah Amin, would ally with the United States and establish a hostile regime on the Soviet border. Before the Soviet intervention the CIA had set up a program to funnel covert aid to the Afghan rebels through neighboring Pakistan, a US ally.

The Soviet intervention in Afghanistan, and Carter's feverish reaction to it, brought a definitive end to what little was left of détente. On Christmas Eve 1979 the Soviets poured troops eventually numbering 85,000 into Afghanistan in the only Soviet intervention outside of Eastern Europe during the entire history of the cold war. Soviet Special Forces assassinated Amin, set up a puppet government, and set out to contain the Islamist uprising.

Already plagued by the hostage crisis and economic "stagflation" at home, Carter reacted vehemently, as the cold war was suddenly running red hot. Declaring that Brezhnev had lied to him and would now "suffer the political consequences," Carter recalled the US ambassador to Moscow, curbed trade and cultural exchange, announced a boycott of the upcoming Summer Olympic Games in Moscow, increased aid to Pakistan and the Islamist resistance forces in Afghanistan, and shelved SALT II. In his January 1980 State of the Union Address, Carter declared that the Afghan intervention "could pose the most serious threat to the peace since the Second World War." Carter, Brzezinski, and other officials suggested that the Soviet intervention might be the first step in a "grand strategy" to expand across Pakistan in order to access a warm water port and cut off Western oil supplies from the Persian Gulf. The exaggerated threat had no basis in fact, as Soviet ambitions did not extend past warding off Islamists and bolstering an allied regime in Kabul.

The Kremlin leaders were surprised by the magnitude of the US reaction—they had not expected the intervention to lead to a heightening of cold war tensions to levels not experienced since the Korean conflict. The Soviet intervention in Afghanistan along with much else fueled the Reagan presidential campaign theme of growing US weakness in the world and alleged vulnerability to Soviet nuclear attack. Reagan was a successful former Hollywood actor, a skilled communicator, and a longtime dedicated conservative anti-communist. He pledged that if elected he would restore American power, and confront Soviet ambitions worldwide.

"Evil Empire" Diplomacy

Bolstered by cold war lobbies such as the Committee on the Present Danger, Reagan eschewed détente in favor of a dramatic conventional and nuclear military buildup. He declared the United States had fallen behind in the arms race and said the nation faced a "window of vulnerability" to a nuclear first strike. Reagan terminated SALT II, declared his opposition to a comprehensive test ban treaty, and ordered a modernized theater nuclear missile force targeting the Soviet Union placed in Western Europe. The "window of vulnerability" was as fictitious in 1980 as was the charge made by the Democrats in 1960 that President Eisenhower had allowed the emergence of a "missile gap" in which the United States had fallen dangerously behind the USSR. In 1980 the United States possessed thousands of nuclear warheads, poised for delivery by air, land, and sea. US and Soviet nuclear forces remained roughly equivalent and deterrence through MAD was firmly intact. The Reagan buildup of both nuclear and conventional weapons reignited the military–industrial complex, as weapons manufacturers and defense contractors lined up for an unprecedented spurt of federal government largesse.

In Their Words

Excerpts from President's Reagan's speech at the Annual Convention of the National Association of Evangelicals, Orlando, Florida, March 8, 1983

There is sin and evil in the world, and we're enjoined by Scripture and the Lord Jesus to oppose it with all our might . . . As good Marxist–Leninists, the Soviet leaders have openly and publicly declared that the only morality they recognize is that which will further their cause, which is world revolution. I think I should point out I was only quoting Lenin, their guiding spirit, who said in 1920 that they repudiate all morality that proceeds from supernatural ideas—that's their name for religion—or ideas that are outside class conceptions. Morality is entirely subordinate to the interests of class war. And everything is moral that is necessary for the annihilation of the old, exploiting social order and for uniting the proletariat. Well, I think the refusal of many influential people to accept this elementary fact of Soviet doctrine illustrates an historical reluctance to see totalitarian powers for what they are. We saw this phenomenon in the 1930's. We see it too often today.

This doesn't mean we should isolate ourselves and refuse to seek an understanding with them. I intend to do everything I can to persuade them of our peaceful intent . . . At the same time, however, they must be made to understand we will never compromise our principles and standards. We will never give away our freedom. We will never abandon our belief in God. And we will never stop searching for a genuine peace . . .

Yes, let us pray for the salvation of all of those who live in that totalitarian darkness—pray they will discover the joy of knowing God. But until they do, let us be aware that while they preach the supremacy of the state, declare its omnipotence over individual man, and predict its eventual domination of all peoples on the Earth, they are the focus of evil in the modern world . . .

I ask you to resist the attempts of those who would have you withhold your support for our efforts, this administration's efforts, to keep America strong and free, while we negotiate real and verifiable reductions in the world's nuclear arsenals and one day, with God's help, their total elimination.

While America's military strength is important, let me add here that I've always maintained that the struggle now going on for the world will never be decided by bombs or rockets, by armies or military might. The real crisis we face today is a spiritual one; at root, it is a test of moral will and faith.

I believe we shall rise to the challenge. I believe that communism is another sad, bizarre chapter in human history whose last pages even now are being written. I believe this because the source of our strength in the quest for human freedom is not material, but spiritual. And because it knows no limitation, it must terrify and ultimately triumph over those who would enslave their fellow man . . .

God bless you, and thank you very much.

In March 1983, speaking before a group of evangelicals, a core constituency, Reagan denounced the Soviet Union as an "**evil empire**" and "the focus of evil in the modern world." He rejected growing calls for a **nuclear freeze** on development and deployment of new weapons. The previous year a massive peace march in New York's Central Park rallied behind the freeze movement. Many Western Europeans protested the arms race, asserting that Reagan's policies were reckless and would leave them vulnerable on the front line in the event of a superpower war.

Just two weeks after the "evil empire" speech Reagan announced the **Strategic Defense Initiative** (SDI), which he declared would someday render nuclear weapons "impotent and obsolete." A long-term, multi-billion-dollar research program, immediately dubbed by critics "Star Wars" in honor of the popular movie fantasy, SDI reopened competition on defensive weapons systems and took the arms race into space while providing government contracts for scientists as well as windfall profits for defense industries. SDI violated the 1972 ABM agreement limiting defensive weapons systems in deference to MAD and deterrence theory. The announcement of SDI stunned the Soviets and much of the Western public and heightened fears of a never-ending arms race with a growing threat of nuclear war. In 1983 a record audience of more than 100 million people viewed the made-for-television film *The Day After*, which depicted the grisly aftermath of nuclear war. Scientists suggested that atomic warfare would have a severe impact on climate, blocking sunlight, dramatically lowering temperatures on earth, and in effect unleashing a devastating **nuclear winter**.

On the other hand popular culture also responded favorably to Reagan, picking up on his heavily gendered assertion that America would once again "stand tall" in world affairs. Reagan thus revived American masculinity, which had been damaged by defeat in Vietnam and 444 days of humiliation in the Iran hostage crisis. While Reagan revised the history of the Vietnam War as a "noble cause," John Rambo flexed his bulging muscles before massive movie audiences in scripts that blamed the government for not letting the troops win the Second Indochina War. Other popular Reagan-era films included *Red Dawn*, depicting resistance to a Soviet invasion of the United States, and *Top Gun*, which glorified military aviation and led to sharp increases in naval recruitment. *Soldier of Fortune* magazine catered to mercenaries and the popular action figure GI Joe received a new, more muscular makeover. While Reagan promoted a new frontier of space-based nuclear weaponry, author Tom Clancy's super patriotic "techno-thrillers" topped the bestseller lists.

Amid the Reagan-inspired revival of national patriotism, the US-Soviet confrontation peaked in the fall of 1983 with the shooting down of a Korean

Airlines jet. **KAL Flight 007** inexplicably took the wrong flight pattern and flew deep into Soviet airspace. On September 1 the Soviets shot down the plane mistaking it in the darkness for a similarly shaped though smaller US RC-135 reconnaissance jet. RC-135s frequently flew missions darting in and out of Soviet airspace, part of ongoing gamesmanship and intelligence gathering carried out by both sides during the cold war. The destruction of KAL 007 killed all 269 passengers and brought international condemnation upon the USSR, which made a bad situation worse by initially remaining mute about the incident. The Reagan administration charged without evidence that the Soviets had identified the plane as a civilian aircraft and shot it down anyway, an "act of unprecedented barbarism" affirming the "evil" character of the regime.

Two months later amid the heightened tensions of the renewed cold war the Soviets initially mistook **Able Archer 83**, a NATO exercise simulating the transition from conventional to nuclear war with the USSR, as genuine preparation for a US first strike. Unlike the USSR, the United States and NATO had refused to rule out "first use" of nuclear weapons in the event of war. Soviet leader **Yuri Andropov** had warned that the deployment of the new theater missiles in Europe, which could strike the USSR within 10 minutes, increased the risk of miscalculation and inadvertent nuclear war. What US intelligence officials described as an "unprecedented Soviet reaction" to Able Archer 83, the details of which remain classified, apparently included rapid mobilization for a preemptive strike on the West. Fortunately the Soviets determined before it was too late that the NATO exercises were indeed hypothetical rather than genuine preparations for a first strike. The world remained (and largely remains) unaware of the most serious nuclear war scare since the Cuban Missile Crisis.

Under political pressure Reagan had replaced SALT with **START** (Strategic Arms Reduction Talks) but this effort failed to progress amid the tense cold war atmosphere. Less than three weeks after the war scare, and amid the continuing deployment of the new missiles in Europe, the Soviets walked out of arms control talks in Geneva. The Kremlin went ahead with plans to deploy a new series of the missiles of their own targeting Western Europe. Criticized for refusing to negotiate with the Soviet leaders, Reagan quipped, "They keep dying on me." Andropov, the former Soviet secret police director who had assumed power with the death of Brezhnev in 1982, had died in February after an illness. His replacement, the elderly apparatchik Konstantin Chernenko was already in poor health and lasted only a year, dying in March 1985. The resumption of meaningful nuclear arms negotiations would await the arrival of a vigorous, new Soviet leader.

The Cold War in Central America

Long committed to retaining US authority in the "backyard" of the Caribbean and Central America, Reagan had excoriated Carter for the "giveaway" of the Panama Canal. The **Panama Canal Treaties**, the centerpiece of Carter's Central American policy, turned the canal over to Panama beginning in 1999 but with provisions for US military intervention in the event of any effort to close off the waterway. In 1979 the treaties barely achieved the required two-thirds support in the Senate, passing by identical votes of 68–32. Carter sacrificed much of his waning political capital in the vociferous debate over the canal. In its aftermath cold war lobbyists trumped up the "discovery" of a **"Soviet combat brigade"** in Cuba, which in actuality was a small contingent that had been on the island with US acquiescence since 1962.

In 1979 concerns about communist expansion in the Americas spiked when rebels in Nicaragua ousted the decadent Somoza family dictatorship. After decades of US support, the Carter administration had cut off aid to Somoza as a result of blatant corruption and human rights violations. The new government of the Sandinista National Liberation Front (FSLN), named after a rebel hero who had been assassinated in 1934 (Chapter 5), was socialist in orientation. Cuba supported the **Sandinistas** but the Soviet Union had not played a role in their rise to power.

Before he left office Carter had undertaken an effort to undermine the Sandinistas and to fend off a left-wing rebellion in tiny El Salvador led by the **Farabundo Martí National Liberation Front** (also named after a rebel leader murdered in 1932). A right-wing military government replete with **death squads** sought to exterminate the Salvadoran rebels. Critics of the regime included Archbishop **Óscar Romero**, a proponent of liberation theology, which emphasized that the Catholic Church should use its influence to promote social justice. Romero appealed to Carter "as a Christian" and proponent of human rights not to back the Salvadoran government. In March 1980 a death squad assassin murdered Romero as he lifted the chalice while delivering mass in a Catholic Church in San Salvador. In another notorious incident in December, a death squad raped, murdered, and buried in shallow graves four American churchwomen on a mission in El Salvador.

Carter suspended US aid after the rapes and murders of the churchwomen, but Reagan's intense anti-communism and his opposition to putting human rights at the center of diplomacy bolstered the right-wing government in San Salvador. The Sandinistas provided assistance to the Salvadoran rebels in the hopes of improving their chances of staying in power by establishing a neighboring allied government in Central America. In nearby Guatemala peasants and indigenous people mounted a resistance against the dominant oligarchy backed by the armed forces. As the United States intervened against the left, the Soviet Union and its allies began to arm the rebels.

Declaring that Soviet- and Cuban-sponsored communism threatened to take over Central America, Reagan embarked on a concerted campaign of counterinsurgency warfare. The administration strove to overthrow the Sandinistas while supporting right-wing military governments in the neighboring states of El Salvador, Guatemala, and Honduras. Only Costa Rica remained a functioning democracy largely free of the violence that ravaged the isthmus.

Jeane Kirkpatrick, Reagan's UN ambassador, provided the intellectual justification for backing right-wing regimes. The former college professor argued that "traditional authoritarian regimes" were "less repressive" than revolutionary governments in part because they left capitalist economic systems intact. The United States thus bolstered the authoritarian regimes that dominated South America while at the same time arming and equipping counter-revolutionary forces in Central America. Washington stepped up counterinsurgency training, CIA covert operations, and backed paramilitary operations targeting popular resistance forces.

Reagan described Nicaragua as a "totalitarian dungeon" but this was an exaggeration. Sandinista reforms markedly improved the lives of masses of people through literacy, education, anti-poverty, and health care programs. Some of the Sandinistas were communists with close ties to Castro whereas others were moderate reformers. The Sandinistas initiated compulsory military service, made arbitrary arrests, and forced unwanted changes on the indigenous Mosquito Indians. The new constitution called for free elections (which the Sandinistas won in 1984) and they pledged not to host a Soviet or Cuban base. The Managua government did receive aid from both Moscow and Havana, but the amounts were less than they received from US-allied governments in Western Europe, most of which opposed the US intervention.

Committed to toppling the Sandinistas before they could establish Nicaragua as "another Cuba," the Reagan administration simultaneously assisted local forces in brutal repression of the leftist insurgencies in El Salvador and Guatemala. The United States pumped millions of dollars into Guatemala for tanks, helicopters, grenade launchers, and other weapons and spare parts. Human rights reformers and other critics called attention to indiscriminate violence, rape, and repression under **General Efraín Ríos Montt**, but Reagan visited Guatemala City in 1982 and declared that the military ruler had received a "bum rap."

By dispensing with human rights concerns, the Reagan administration gave a green light to death squads in El Salvador and Guatemala. The Ríos Montt regime destroyed hundreds of villages, killing 50,000 to 75,000 people and forcing some 800,000 more out of their communities. A similar scenario unfolded in El Salvador. In December 1981, in the most notorious of many incidents, the army carried out the **El Mozote Massacre**, slaughtering an entire Salvadoran village of some 800 residents.

Argentinian, Israeli, and South African military advisers joined the Americans in training and equipping Central American counterinsurgency forces. The Argentinian military regime, although engaged in a campaign of "disappearing" thousands of its own domestic critics, was eager to crush leftist insurgencies throughout the Americas. However, in 1982 the Argentinian generals made the mistake of attempting to seize disputed South Atlantic islands from Britain thus igniting the **Falklands War**. The Reagan administration disappointed the Argentinians by failing to invoke the Monroe Doctrine and instead tilting toward Britain in the conflict. Argentina suffered a humiliating defeat that led to the overthrow of the military regime.

In October 1983, in the midst of its counterinsurgency campaign in Central America the United States invaded and easily toppled the revolutionary government on the tiny Caribbean island of Grenada. In 1979 radical reformers

known as the New Jewel Movement took over the island and received support
from Cuba, including construction of a new airfield. An extreme leftist rebel
overthrew and executed the popular leader of the New Jewel Movement, Mau-
rice Bishop, providing an opportunity for the US **invasion of Grenada**.
Britain, Canada, and the UN condemned the unauthorized US attack on the
former British possession but some of the island's Caribbean neighbors welcomed it. The timing of the operation raised questions, as it deflected attention
from the disastrous US intervention in Lebanon in which two days earlier 241
US Marines had been killed in an attack on their barracks at the Beirut Airport.

The Iran–Contra Affair

Overthrowing the Sandinistas remained the top priority in the region, with the
campaign centered on US funding and the equipping of the so-called **Contras**, the opponents of the Sandinistas. The Contras proved controversial, as
most were former members of Somoza's repressive National Guard. Human
rights organizations and other critics condemned the Contras as terrorists
because of their regular resort to intimidation, kidnapping, rape, torture, and
murder. Their victims included Sandinista government officials but also teachers, students, doctors, lawyers, priests, and anyone perceived as supporting the
left-wing regime. As human rights groups reported, the Contras "systematically
engage in violent abuses . . . as their principal means of waging war." The CIA
under Director William Casey not only knew of the Contra tactics, it sponsored and encouraged them.

Reagan offered no apology for supporting the "freedom fighters" to overthrow
what he called a "communist reign of terror" in Nicaragua. By the late 1980s
the Contra force numbered about 15,000. The Contra operation turned the
Honduran border into a paramilitary staging ground for intrusions into Nicaragua. Contra forces also attacked Nicaragua by sea, leading to revelations of the
CIA's **illegal mining of Nicaragua's harbors** in which some of the mines
damaged neutral shipping. In June 1986 the **International Criminal Court**
in the Netherlands convicted the United States in response to a suit brought by
the Nicaraguan government. Reagan belittled the ruling, but other revelations
came to light the same year delivering a severe blow to the administration.

The revelations, known as the **Iran–Contra Affair**, showed that the Reagan administration had violated congressional restrictions on funding of the
Contras. Funding for the Contras had been intermittent as Reagan and the
Congress battled over the propriety of the US intervention in Nicaragua. In
1984 the second **Boland Amendment**, named after Massachusetts Rep.
Edward Boland, renewed the cutoff of funding for the Contras, but Casey
and other administration officials subverted the law through secret fundrais-
ing operations. The operations included taking money from Central American drug lords, some of it funneled through Panamanian dictator **Manuel
Noriega**, a longtime CIA "asset" who cooperated in the US-led Contra war
in return for direct payments and drug profits.

In a stunning revelation the public learned that the NSC had secretly generated funding through arms sales to Iran. The operation was illegal, as Iran was subject to an arms embargo and had been labeled a terrorist state since the hostage crisis. Reagan had vowed never to do business with terrorist states. In the complex secret operation, the United States sold weapons at inflated prices to Iran via Israel. Iran, embroiled in a vicious eight-year war with neighboring Iraq, paid inflated prices for the badly needed weaponry including Hawk missiles and spare parts. In return for the sale of the weapons the Iranians agreed to seek the release of US hostages who had been seized in Lebanon, but little came of this promise. As details of the unseemly affair unfolded it was learned that private US and international armsdealers skimmed profits off the top and that at one point the United States had attempted to win over the Iranian mullahs with gifts of a chocolate birthday cake and a Bible.

Congress convened nationally televised hearings that featured a former Marine officer, Oliver North, unapologetically defending the illegal operation that he had coordinated for the NSC. North received immunity but he and other witnesses implicated the highest officials of the Reagan administration. While the popular president, emphasizing his humanitarian desire to free the hostages in Lebanon, received a pass, a special prosecutor indicted dozens of others. They included Casey (who died amid the scandal), Defense Secretary Caspar Weinberger, and NSC Adviser Robert McFarlane, who unsuccessfully attempted suicide. Vice President George H. W. Bush claimed he was "out of the loop" and unaware of the dealings, which others disputed. Bush subsequently won election to the presidency in 1988. After being defeated in his reelection bid in 1992, Bush issued executive pardons before he left office for six convicted felons, including Weinberger and McFarlane.

The counterinsurgency wars in Central America ended with negotiated settlements, elections, and truth commissions. In the wake of the unseemly Iran–Contra revelations and with the cold war coming to an end, a ceasefire and elections took place in Nicaragua. The United States poured money into the campaign of Violeta Chamorro, who defeated Daniel Ortega, the leader of the Sandinistas. Ortega would recapture the presidency in the 2006 election. More than 30,000 people died in the Nicaraguan conflict, most killed by the Contras. More than 200,000 died in the long Guatemalan civil war, also overwhelmingly at the hands of the US-backed and equipped government forces. In 1996 a UN-brokered peace agreement finally ended the deadly struggle. Death squad activity continued in El Salvador until the signing of a peace agreement in Mexico City in 1992 brought an end to the conflict. More than 70,000 died in the tiny country of 5.3 million, most of them killed by the US-backed death squads. More than a quarter of the population was displaced. UN-sponsored truth and reconciliation commissions condemned the Guatemalan and Salvadoran military and security forces as well as the United States for the high levels of death and destruction in the Central American conflicts.

Collapse of the Soviet Empire

Preoccupied with the fear of losing ground to communism in places like southern Africa and Central America, US national security elites overlooked the growing weaknesses inside the Soviet Empire. Ironically, in the early 1980s, in the wake of the Vietnam War, Watergate, economic "stagflation," and the Iran hostage crisis, many argued that it was the United States and not the USSR that was in decline. History would show that the opposite was true. As events unfolded it became evident that the Soviet Union was in such an advanced state of deterioration—political, economic, and social—that it could not be saved. The sudden collapse of the Soviet Empire brought a rapid and unpredictable end to the cold war.

The Soviet and eastern European economies had grown steadily from the 1950s to the 1970s. As people's lives improved genuine faith in socialism flourished. However, by the early 1970s corruption, inefficiency, lack of incentives, declining agriculture, and overinvestment in military research and development retarded these economies. They especially failed to provide abundant and affordable consumer goods, which stocked the store shelves in the West. Political corruption, cynicism, elitism, and cronyism undermined Soviet communism. The ruling elite (*nomenklatura*) increasingly enriched themselves while the bulk of the population fell behind. The political leadership—Brezhnev, Andropov, Chernenko—was decrepit, both physically and in terms of ability to govern. With the death of Chernenko in 1985, the Soviet Politburo turned to a new generation of leaders under **Mikhail Gorbachev**. At age 54, Gorbachev was a significantly younger and far bolder leader than the previous Soviet rulers.

Calling for "new thinking" Gorbachev moved swiftly instituting sweeping reforms in an effort to revive Soviet socialism. Domestically, he instituted *perestroika* (economic restructuring) and *glasnost* (openness). Gorbachev proved equally bold in his diplomacy, denouncing the arms race and the failed Soviet intervention in Afghanistan. He called for a new relationship with China and the United States and demanded nothing less than the end of the cold war. US officials responded with skepticism leaving British Prime Minister **Margaret Thatcher**, highly popular in the wake of the victorious Falklands War, to take the lead. When Thatcher, a fellow conservative and Reagan's closest foreign ally, declared after meeting the Soviet leader, "I like Mr. Gorbachev. We can do business together," the Reagan administration followed her lead.

After a preliminary meeting in Geneva in the fall of 1985, Reagan and Gorbachev conducted intensive arms control negotiations the following year at the **Reykjavik Summit** in Iceland. The two leaders considered the "zero option"—eliminating all nuclear weapons within a decade—but Reagan refused Gorbachev's demand to prohibit testing of defensive systems under SDI as a condition of abolishing nuclear weapons. The summit collapsed without agreement but paved the way for a substantive arms control accord the following year, the Intermediate Nuclear Force or **INF Treaty**. Signed by

Reagan and Gorbachev at a summit in Washington in December 1987, the INF Treaty eliminated all nuclear-armed, ground-launched ballistic and cruise missiles with ranges between 300 and 3,400 miles. It was the first nuclear arms control agreement actually reducing the number of weapons, as some 2,700 nuclear systems were eliminated. Gorbachev agreed to verification through on-site inspection of nuclear facilities, something the USSR had previously rejected. The INF Treaty helped Reagan to soften his image as an uncompromising cold warrior and to rebuild his leadership, which had been badly damaged by the Iran–Contra Affair as well as financial scandals following sweeping deregulation of Wall Street.

The INF agreement came in the aftermath of the **Chernobyl disaster**, a catastrophic nuclear accident in the Soviet republic of Ukraine in April 1986. As a nuclear reactor malfunctioned, shutdown efforts failed, causing radiation to be released into the atmosphere, killing 31 people and forcing massive evacuations and leaving behind a monumental cleanup effort. The accident underscored the dangers of nuclear power and raised questions as to the reliability of other Soviet nuclear and chemical and biological weapons facilities. The Chernobyl disaster also served as something of a metaphor for the general failure of the Soviet system.

The ongoing war in Afghanistan, which Gorbachev called a "bleeding wound," also underscored the decline of Soviet power. Following the Soviet invasion under Brezhnev in December 1979, Carter increased aid to Pakistan and began supporting a resistance to the Soviets. Upon entering office Reagan ramped up funding for Pakistan and the **Mujahedin**, a resistance movement led by Islamic fundamentalists. Egypt, Israel, and China joined the United States and Pakistan in undermining the Soviet position in Afghanistan. The CIA played a key role by equipping the Mujahedin with shoulder-fired Stinger and Blowpipe missiles, which eroded Soviet air superiority and made the conflict longer and more costly, both financially as well as in casualties. The USSR pulled out of Afghanistan in 1988–89.

From 1989–91 the Soviet Empire collapsed from the outside in—from Eastern Europe to Moscow's Red Square. Poland, the largest and most populous of the Soviet "satellites," set the process of dissolution in motion. Beginning in the early 1980s workers in the **Solidarity** trade union led by Lech Wałęsa went on strike in the shipyards of Gdansk. They demanded that unions should be independent of the Communist Party and the state. Dissent quickly spread to the Soviet Baltic Republics (Estonia, Latvia, and Lithuania) and to Belarus and Ukraine. In December 1981, under pressure from the Kremlin the Polish leader declared martial law to rein in the unrest, which never fully abated. By the end of the decade all of the eastern European communist regimes confronted popular revolt.

One by one the Eastern Europeans threw off the Soviet-backed communist regimes and transitioned to more pluralist societies. A poet and novelist, Václav Havel, who would become the first president of the independent Czech Republic, called it a **"velvet revolution"** in that the dramatic changes in

Eastern Europe occurred for the most part through non-violent means. The major exception was Romania wherein the Ceauşescu dictatorship instituted repression killing more than 1,000 people. Ceauşescu lost in the end, however, as he and his wife Elena were arrested and summarily executed by firing squad as they sang the communist "Internationale."

Nothing symbolized the cold war more than the **Berlin Wall**. Speaking at the Brandenburg Gate in 1987, Reagan famously declaimed, "Mr. Gorbachev, tear down this wall!" However, on November 9, 1989, it was the Germans themselves who performed the hard labor of bringing down the historic blockade. When East Germans voted to join with the West, **German reunification** became one of the most significant consequences of the end of the cold war.

Events radiated back to the USSR, where the economy had collapsed. Empty food store shelves angered consumers and underscored the failure of *perestroika* to deliver a successful economic restructuring. Moreover, *glasnost* backfired on Gorbachev. He had sought to revivify socialism through criticism and reform, but freedom of expression instead led to critical assessments of Soviet history and widespread denunciation of the communist ideology. In August 1991 an elite cabal of veteran communists detained Gorbachev and attempted to reassert Party control but it was too late. The coup was defeated, but at the same time Gorbachev's bubble had also burst. The Soviet Union collapsed as various republics broke off into a reconstituted Commonwealth of Independent States. With the ouster of Gorbachev and the collapse of the USSR the cold war effectively came to an end.

Interpreting the Past

Soft power and the end of the cold war

The soft power embodied in trade, cultural exchange, and exposure to pluralist societies played a dramatic role in bringing down the Soviet Empire. The increased trade and cultural exchange exposed more and more Soviets and East Europeans to the allure of Western culture, press freedom, consumer goods, technologies, and individual opportunity. Increased travel and circulation of foreign currencies began to transform the economies and societies of the eastern European regimes. Eastern Europeans and Russians eagerly consumed US soft drinks, fast food, movies, and more. In terms of entertainment and consumer culture, the West increasingly was perceived as best.

In retrospect, though condemned at the time by cold war conservatives in the West, the policy of détente culminating in the Helsinki Accords played an important role in bringing down the Soviet Empire. Critics had condemned détente for recognizing Europe's cold war borders as permanent, but the elevation of human rights and relaxation of restrictions on travel and cultural contacts propelled soft power and helped undermine the Communist Party dictatorships. East German Foreign Minister Otto Winzer was close to the mark when he dubbed détente, "aggression in slippers."

Americans claimed victory in the cold war though its end did not inspire victory parades. Some credited the popular Reagan with implementing a mythical grand strategy that delivered victory in the cold war, but in truth the rapid disintegration of Soviet power had taken almost everyone by surprise. The individual most responsible for the dramatic dissolution of communism was not Reagan but Gorbachev, even though events hardly transpired as he had hoped. To be sure, Western containment policies and military spending contributed to the weakening of the Soviet Empire, which in the end could not keep pace with the West. Critics of US militarization argued that the conflict had carried on much longer than necessary, entailed great waste of resources and destructiveness, and could have been ameliorated or ended sooner in the absence of confrontational polices. As with the origins of the cold war, its end thus stimulated debate.

To some extent the dissolution of the Soviet Empire reflected broader trends in European and in world politics. In the mid-1970s the Greek dictatorship, which came to power in a US-backed coup in 1967, fell and Greek democracy was restored. Spain and Portugal had also transitioned to democracy after longtime dictatorships. Leftists could participate in European politics, hence "Euro-communism" had provided a model for Gorbachev and Eastern Europeans, one that suggested that socialism could still be pursued within a reformed political context. During the 1980s democracies also replaced military regimes in key South American countries such as Argentina and Brazil. In the late 1980s, on the eve of the eastern European revolts, the Philippines and South Korea ousted dictatorships through popular uprisings.

Developments in East Asia

Dramatic changes occurred in East Asia as well as Eastern Europe but they stopped short of undermining the authority of the Chinese Communist Party. The transformation of US East Asian policy began with the Nixon–Kissinger détente and "triangular diplomacy." Following the death of Mao Zedong in 1976, **Deng Xiaoping** gradually overcame opposition from the "Gang of Four," which included Mao's wife, and became the unquestioned leader of China. Domestically, Deng instituted sweeping economic changes that ultimately transformed the Chinese economy. In foreign affairs, Deng made it clear that the USSR rather than the United States was now China's primary adversary in the world. The Sino-American rapprochement angered the Soviets, especially when Beijing joined Washington in denouncing the Soviet invasion of Afghanistan. In February 1979 China also attacked Vietnam, Russia's ally, and the next year joined in the boycott of the 1980 Moscow Olympics.

Figure 13.6 China's new leader Deng Xiaoping applauds President Jimmy Carter during
a historic visit to Washington in 1979. Carter completed the normalization
of US relations with China while Deng initiated market reforms igniting
rapid economic growth.

Source: Library of Congress, Prints and Photographs Division, LC-DIG-ppmsca-09795.

To Japan, the closest US ally in the region, the announcement of the new
US relationship with China was just one of the so-called "**Nixon shocks**"
that Tokyo received in the summer of 1971. In an effort to combat inflation
and other economic concerns, Nixon de-linked the US dollar from the price
of gold and also instituted import tariffs that strongly impacted Japan. By this
time Japan, benefiting from postwar rebuilding of new industries as well as
its remarkably productive workforce, had begun to outcompete the United
States in key industries such as electronics and fuel-efficient automobiles. The
US rapprochement with rival China and the economic changes were not only
shocking, they were also insulting to Japan, as Nixon had taken the actions without either consulting or informing Tokyo. Japan, however, remained largely
dependent on the United States for its security, hence relations recovered.

Japan was not the only nation concerned in 1978, as the Carter administration completed what Nixon had started by establishing full normalization of
relations with China. Taiwan especially feared abandonment because normalization of relations with Beijing entailed US recognition of the mainland as
the "real" China. The Chinese had offered a conciliatory approach of "one
country, two systems," meaning there was only one China but Taiwan would
have a degree of autonomy. Since the "fall" of China to communism in 1949
Taiwan had had a powerful lobby and strong support in the US Congress.

That remained the case in 1979, as Congress rejected proposals from the State Department and passed the **Taiwan Relations Act**, which Carter signed into law. Under its provisions the United States pledged to arm and defend Taiwan in the event of attack by China. Thereafter the United States maintained a policy of selling sophisticated weapons to Taiwan, often over strenuous objections from Beijing.

Through its strong military base presence in Japan, the Philippines, and South Korea, the United States played a pivotal role in Asian security matters. In 1978, at the urging of the United States Japan and China signed a treaty of peace and friendship. The two entered into a long-term trade agreement in which Japan contributed technology and profited from an economic takeoff in China that sprang from Deng's economic reforms. In the 1980s Americans seemed to revert back to their longing for a special relationship with China while sometimes adopting a critical stance toward Japan. As the Japanese auto industry made inroads in the US market, cities such as Akron, Cleveland, Detroit, and Pittsburgh, which had prospered with the automobile, glass, rubber, and steel industries, now underwent a painful deindustrialization.

In addition to China and Japan, the "**four tigers**" of Taiwan, South Korea, Singapore, and the former British colony of Hong Kong spurred economic growth throughout the region. These economies fostered a robust trade in raw materials and finished goods between East and Southeast Asian nations, which closed economic and political ties through the ASEAN, formed in 1967. The Philippines, rife with unrest and corruption under the US-backed dictator **Ferdinand Marcos**, lagged behind. Hosting the US bases at Subic Bay and Clark Field, the Philippines was an important security asset. In 1972 Nixon and Kissinger backed Marcos when he instituted martial law, jailed and exiled his pro-democracy opponents, and enabled domination of the sugar and coconut industries by his family and friends. Most Filipinos lived in poverty while the greed displayed by Marcos and his clique seemed to have no limits, as was exemplified by his wife Imelda's notorious collection of thousands of pairs of shoes.

In 1983 political tumult accelerated in the Philippines when the Marcos regime assassinated exiled senator **Benigno Aquino** when he stepped off the plane in a return to Manila. Marcos tried to shore up his backing from the United States, where Aquino had lived in exile, by contributing $10 million to Reagan's 1984 reelection campaign, but it was too late. In 1986, following mass demonstrations known as **People Power**, Marcos was forced into exile under US auspices in Hawai'i. Benigno's widow, Corazon Aquino, assumed the presidency. Rather than emphasize economic and social reform Aquino called for "police and military action" to combat the New People's Army (NPA), the armed wing of the Communist Party that had grown dramatically in the barrios and in the countryside during Marcos's reign. Backed by the United States Aquino launched a counterinsurgency war against the NPA as well as social activists, labor organizers, and church and human rights groups. International human rights monitors cited "a widespread pattern of extra-judicial execution, torture and illegal arrest throughout the Philippines."

Like Marcos the South Korean dictatorship became the target of protest culminating in the overthrow of the regime. In 1979 massive demonstrations followed the assassination of **Park Chung-hee**, the longtime US-backed dictator who cooperated closely with Washington, including sending troops to Vietnam. The new regime declared martial law and cracked down on pro-democracy dissent, including the **Gwangju Massacre** in which some 200 protesters were slaughtered and more than 800 injured. Carter had begun troop withdrawals from South Korea and criticized the human rights record of the regime, which eventually succumbed to domestic pressure on the eve of hosting the 1988 Summer Olympics in Seoul. In 1987 South Korea transitioned to a constitutional democracy and began to conduct regular democratic elections.

US relations with North Korea remained deeply strained, as underscored by the ***Pueblo* incident** in 1968. Just two days after a stunning but unsuccessful commando raid intended to assassinate President Park in Seoul, the North Koreans seized the *Pueblo*, a US naval intelligence vessel. Pyongyang claimed the *Pueblo* had invaded their territorial waters while the United States, insisting that the ship was patrolling in international waters, demanded its return and the immediate release of the crew. The North Koreans refused, charged the Americans with "imperialist aggression," and declared they were "fully prepared to deal a crushing blow to the United States" in the event of any military reprisals. Already deeply embroiled in Vietnam, President Johnson dispatched an aircraft carrier to South Korea but otherwise exercised restraint and eventually negotiated the release of the crew of 82 men (1 had died of injuries incurred during the assault) after 11 months of captivity replete with interrogation and torture. North Korea kept the *Pueblo* and in 2013 put it on display.

While the wave of reform and regime change movements could not penetrate the tightly policed borders of North Korea, they did have a dramatic impact on China. As the communist regimes began to fall in Eastern Europe, Chinese leaders grew increasingly apprehensive about a potential threat to their monopoly on political power. In 1989 a budding pro-democracy movement gained momentum following the death of Hu Yaobang, a revered reformer and advocate of political liberalization. Students and reformers encamped in peaceful protests in the historic Tiananmen Square in the heart of Beijing. Deng initially tolerated the tent encampments but as protests erupted in other cities he clamped down. On June 3 and 4 tanks and troops carried out the **Tiananmen Massacre**, driving out the protesters and killing hundreds of them (the precise number is unknown).

The bloom was off of the new US-China relationship but President George H. W. Bush, who had served as ambassador to China in the mid-1970s, responded with moderation. Rejecting calls to sever relations with China, Bush's main priorities were, as he wrote in his diary, to "preserve this relationship" and "cool the rhetoric." Bush, who knew Deng personally, wrote the Chinese leader a letter "straight from my heart" urging him to moderate the regime. While the Chinese economy continued to grow at an amazing rate under Deng's economic reforms, Tiananmen showed that the Chinese leadership drew a hard line on political reform.

Select Bibliography

De Grazia, Victoria. *Irresistible Empire: America's Advance Through Twentieth-Century Europe.* Cambridge, MA: Harvard University Press, 2005.

Keys, Barbara J. *Reclaiming American Virtue: The Human Rights Revolution of the 1970s.* Cambridge, MA: Harvard University Press, 2014.

Snyder, Sarah B. *Human Rights Activism and the End of the Cold War: A Transnational History of the Helsinki Network.* New York: Cambridge University Press, 2011.

Quandt, William P. *Camp David: Peacemaking and Politics.* Washington: Brookings Institution, 1986.

Kramer, Mark and Smetana, Vit. *Opposing, Maintaining, and Tearing Open the Iron Curtain.* Lanham, MD: Lexington Books, 2014.

Leffler, Melvyn and Westad, Odd. *The Cambridge History of the Cold War.* New York: Cambridge University Press, 2010.

Garthoff, Raymond L. *The Great Transition: American-Soviet Relations and the End of the Cold War.* Washington: Brookings Institution, 1994.

Zubok, Vladislav M. *A Failed Empire: The Soviet Union in the Cold War from Stalin to Gorbachev.* Chapel Hill: University of North Carolina Press, 2007.

Wilson, James G. *The Triumph of Improvisation: Gorbachev's Adaptability, Reagan's Engagement, and the End of the Cold War.* Ithaca, NY: Cornell University Press, 2014.

Pons, Silvio and Romero, Federico. *Reinterpreting the End of the Cold War: Issues, Interpretations, Periodizations.* New York: Frank Cass, 2005.

Carothers, Thomas. *In the Name of Democracy: US Policy toward Latin America in the Reagan Years.* Berkeley: University of California Press, 1991.

Rabe, Stephen G. *The Killing Zone: The United States Wages Cold War in Latin America.* New York: Oxford University Press, 2012.

Grandin, Greg and Joseph, Gilbert. *A Century of Revolution: Insurgent and Counterinsurgent Violence During Latin America's Long Cold War.* Durham, NC: Duke University Press, 2010.

Byrne, Malcolm. *Reagan's Scandal and the Unchecked Abuse of Presidential Power.* Lawrence: University Press of Kansas, 2014.

Hasegawa, Tsuyoshi. *The Cold War in East Asia, 1945–1991.* Washington: Woodrow Wilson Center Press, 2011.

14 A New World Order

Overview

Globalization flourished in the generation from the end of the cold war to September 11, 2001. Presidents George H. W. Bush and William J. Clinton presided over this era, one in which the United States possessed unprecedented influence over world affairs as a result of the collapse of the Soviet Empire. The United States asserted its economic and geopolitical supremacy, as its leaders trumpeted the dawning of a "**new world order**" in the wake of the fall of communism and victory in the Persian Gulf War.

Despite the resurgence of ebullient American exceptionalism in the wake of the collapse of communism, other countries pursued their own agendas—notably a rapidly rising China—and many global issues remained intractable. Ethnic cleansing and genocide erupted from the Balkans to Central Africa while the crisis in the Middle East deepened. Advances in communications technology fostered global interconnections of economy, human rights, arms control, and the growing influence of a broad array of NGOs. By the twenty-first century the world was increasingly recognized as an intertwined "global village."

Bush and the Soviet Collapse

George H. W. Bush brought to the White House extensive experience in foreign policy. Prior to his two terms as President Reagan's vice president, Bush had been ambassador to the United Nations and to China as well as former director of the CIA. Although limited to one term, Bush's eventful presidency coincided with the end of the cold war and the dawning of a new era of international relations. He carried out an invasion in Central America, a major war in the Middle East, and left office with the United States embroiled in conflict in the Horn of Africa.

In contrast to the divisions over foreign policy under Jimmy Carter, and the turmoil under Reagan in the wake of the Iran–Contra Affair, Bush put together a unified foreign policy team. Secretary of State James Baker, Secretary of Defense Dick Cheney, National Security Adviser Brent Scowcroft, and Chairman of the Joint Chiefs of Staff Colin Powell concurred on most major foreign policy issues and assessments. Determined to hew out his own path, Bush took a cautious approach to the ongoing disintegration of the Soviet Empire. Whereas Reagan ultimately embraced the reform leader Mikhail Gorbachev, Bush initiated a "pause" in relations in order to carry out a thoroughgoing policy review. History did not pause, however, as the Soviet Empire continued its rapid disintegration.

Bush and European leaders resolved uncertainty over the future of the newly united Germany through diplomacy. In 1990 former World War II Allies—Britain, France, the United States, and the USSR—agreed on a framework for **German reunification**. The Soviets reluctantly acceded to German membership in the US-led NATO alliance with the understanding that no NATO troops would be stationed in the former East Germany. Under the agreement Soviet troops had three to four years to withdraw from East Germany while Germany agreed to provide economic assistance to the Soviet Union.

At the end of his first year in office Bush finally met with Gorbachev at a summit in Malta. Meeting in Washington several months later, the two leaders regained the momentum for nuclear arms control that had been achieved under the INF Treaty (1987). In a July 1991 meeting in Moscow, Bush and Gorbachev signed START I slashing the size of their respective nuclear arsenals. Meanwhile the momentum of the unraveling of the cold war continued beyond the ability of either Bush or Gorbachev to control the situation.

In Their Words

Excerpt from Mikhail Gorbachev's speech marking the end of his presidency and the dissolution of the USSR, December 25, 1991

Dear compatriots, fellow citizens, as a result of the newly formed situation, creation of the Commonwealth of Independent States, I cease my activities in the post of the USSR president. I am taking this decision out of considerations based on principle. I have firmly stood for independence, self-rule of nations, for the sovereignty of the republics, but at the same time for preservation of the union state, the unity of the country.

Events went a different way. The policy prevailed of dismembering this country and disuniting the state, with which I cannot agree.

Fate had it that when I found myself at the head of the state it was already clear that all was not well in the country. There is plenty of everything: land, oil and gas, other natural riches, and God gave us lots of intelligence and talent, yet we lived much worse than developed countries and keep falling behind them more and more.

The reason could already be seen: The society was suffocating in the vice of the command-bureaucratic system, doomed to serve ideology and bear the terrible burden of the arms race. It had reached the limit of its possibilities. All attempts at partial reform, and there had been many, had suffered defeat, one after another. The country was losing perspective. We could not go on living like that. Everything had to be changed radically.

The process of renovating the country and radical changes in the world turned out to be far more complicated than could be expected. However, what has been done ought to be given its due. This society acquired freedom, liberated itself politically and spiritually . . . The totalitarian system which deprived the country of an opportunity to become successful and prosperous long ago has been eliminated. A breakthrough has been achieved on the way to democratic changes. Free elections, freedom of the press, religious freedoms, representative organs of power, a multiparty (system) became a reality; human rights are recognized as the supreme principle . . .

We live in a new world. The Cold War has ended, the arms race has stopped, as has the insane militarization which mutilated our economy, public psyche and morals. The threat of a world war has been removed. Once again I want to stress that on my part everything was done during the transition period to preserve reliable control of the nuclear weapons.

We opened ourselves to the world, gave up interference into other people's affairs, the use of troops beyond the borders of the country, and trust, solidarity and respect came in response . . .

I am leaving my post with apprehension, but also with hope, with faith in you, your wisdom and force of spirit. We are the heirs of a great civilization, and its rebirth into a new, modern and dignified life now depends on one and all.

Some mistakes could surely have been avoided, many things could have been done better, but I am convinced that sooner or later our common efforts will bear fruit, our nations will live in a prosperous and democratic society.

I wish all the best to all of you.

In August 1991 an attempted coup by Kremlin hardliners failed but left Gorbachev, his policies of *perestroika* and *glasnost* already in disarray, fatally weakened. Throughout the fall, the various Soviet Republics declared their independence from the now defunct USSR. In December, Belarus, Russia, and Ukraine announced they were forming a new confederation of states. On December 25, 1991, Gorbachev had no choice but to resign as the president of the Soviet Union.

Invading Panama

The end of the cold war precipitated discussion of a possible "peace dividend" and demilitarization of world affairs, but the United States instead carried out two wars under Bush. The smaller of the two conflicts targeted the Panamanian dictator **Manuel Noriega**, who had been a CIA "asset" in the wars against the Central American left but had begun to thumb his nose at his powerful neighbor to the north. Reagan and then Bush urged Noriega to relinquish his grip on Panamanian politics after the CIA payoffs and drug dealing had been exposed during the Iran–Contra investigation. In 1988 a federal grand jury indicted Noriega on drug trafficking charges, spurring demands by members of Congress for the United States to oust the Panamanian military ruler. In May 1989 Noriega nullified the results of the Panamanian presidential election, which his handpicked candidate had lost. Noriega's political opponents were brutally beaten on the streets of Panama City. An internal coup attempt failed, prompting renewed calls for US intervention. When in December 1989 the Bush administration learned that Noriega's military forces had killed a US serviceman and attacked two other Americans, Bush decided to act.

On December 20 Bush launched the **invasion of Panama** (Operation Just Cause) by more than 27,000 US troops. It was the largest US troop deployment since the Vietnam War. The US forces quickly took charge and eventually tracked down and arrested Noriega, who was sentenced to a long prison term in Miami. While the precise number of casualties is disputed, hundreds if not thousands of Panamanians died compared with a disproportionate 23 US combat deaths. Property valued in the millions of dollars was destroyed and thousands of Panamanians were made homeless. The UN General Assembly and the OAS condemned the invasion, which was illegal under international law yet popular in the United States. Panamanian reaction was mixed: few lamented the fall of Noriega yet many resented the destructiveness of the US invasion.

The Persian Gulf War

In 1991 the Bush administration entered into and decisively triumphed over Iraq in the **Persian Gulf War**. The conflict stemmed from an Iraqi invasion of the neighboring emirate of Kuwait in August 1990. Iraqi dictator **Saddam Hussein** sought to seize Kuwaiti oil and also to provide Iraq, whose illogical borders had been drawn under British colonialism, with greater maritime access. Throughout the 1980s the United States had backed Iraq in a long and bloody war with neighboring Iran. Saddam met with the US ambassador April Glaspie, whom critics later charged sent mixed signals over US policy on the Iraq-Kuwait dispute. In the meeting, however, Glaspie told the Iraqi leader that the United States would "never excuse settlement of disputes by other than peaceful means." Saddam launched the invasion anyway in hopes of presenting the international community with a *fait accompli*. The takeover of Kuwait was blatantly illegal under international law and promptly condemned by the UN, which demanded an unconditional Iraqi withdrawal.

Bush also condemned the invasion but his initial response, freezing Iraqi assets and dispatching US warships to the Persian Gulf, was restrained. However, Bush's advisers, notably Scowcroft, as well as British Prime Minister Margaret Thatcher argued forcefully that Saddam's aggression should be punished.

Bush concurred and thereafter pursued a path to war. "This will not stand," he declared, demanding an Iraqi pullout from Kuwait, adding in manly fashion that the United States was "drawing a line in the sand." Bush stepped up his rhetoric, depicting the war as a moral crusade between "good and evil."

Bush repeatedly invoked the time honored term "appeasement," a reference to the 1930s when the Western nations failed to stand in the way as Nazi Germany embarked on a path of aggression. The history lesson postulated that if left unchecked aggressors would be emboldened to escalate their aggression. In Saddam's case the United States, its allies, and the US-backed Saudi monarchy feared that Saudi Arabia might be the next target for the power hungry Iraqi dictator unless he could be forced to withdraw from Kuwait. Bush reinforced the oil rich kingdom, dispatching US forces to the Saudi holy land, an action that enraged many devout Muslims. Among them was a little known, wealthy Saudi elite **Osama bin Laden**.

While preparing for a massive US military assault against Iraq, Bush gave diplomacy a final chance. In early January Baker met for several hours with Iraqi Foreign Minister Tarik Aziz in Geneva, Switzerland, but Iraq would not back down. On January 12 Bush asked for and received authorization for war through a congressional resolution (as opposed to a formal declaration of war), which narrowly passed the Senate by a vote of 52 to 47 after a favorable vote of 250–183 in the House of Representatives.

A broad coalition of US allies, Arab states, and the UN Security Council backed and financed the US-dominated war effort. The cold war could truly be said to be over, as Gorbachev and the Soviet Union (not yet out of existence) endorsed the US-led invasion. China, which sought US support in its bid for MFN trade status, also did not oppose the assault on Iraq. Finally, Bush's diplomacy dissuaded Israel from involvement in the war so as not to play into Saddam's hand by putting Arab states in the untenable position of allying with Israel amid its ongoing occupation of Arab territories. When the war erupted Saddam promptly fired Scud missiles at Israel, which did relatively little damage. The United States provided the Israelis as well as Saudi Arabia with defensive Patriot missiles and Israel kept its pledge to refrain from direct involvement in the war.

On January 17 (Iraqi time) **Operation Desert Storm** began with a massive aerial assault that quickly established dominance. The US-led coalition pounded Iraq, paving the way for the ground invasion in late February. Of the some 800,000 troops more than 500,000 were American. Saddam blew up Kuwaiti oil wells and dumped millions of gallons of crude in the Persian Gulf but was powerless against the invasion forces. The much-vaunted Iraqi Republican Guard lost a series of tank battles and proved to be a shell of an army that lacked motivation to fight for a dictator against the most powerful military in the world. On February 27 coalition troops arrived in Kuwait City. On March 3 Iraq, having been thoroughly defeated, capitulated to the US commander, General Norman Schwarzkopf. Only 148 Americans died in the conflict compared with many tens of thousands of Iraqi deaths (the overall Iraqi

Figure 14.1 President George H. W. Bush and Canadian Prime Minister Brian Mulroney dedicating a new Canadian embassy in Washington in 1989. Experienced in diplomacy, Bush put together a broad allied coalition, strongly supported by Britain and Canada, behind the Persian Gulf War.

Source: Library of Congress, Prints and Photographs Division, LC-DIG-highsm-14717.

casualty figure is disputed). Reflecting controversies over the "body count" in Vietnam, Schwarzkopf declared, "I have absolutely no idea what the Iraqi casualties are and if I have anything to say about it, we're never going to get into the body-count business."

Across the United States the unambiguous military victory ignited a wave of patriotic fervor and reinvigorated American exceptionalism, which had yet to fully recover from defeat in Vietnam. "By God, we finally kicked the Vietnam syndrome once and for all," Bush gushed. "We had given America a clear win at low casualties in a noble cause," Powell explained, "and the American people fell in love again with their armed forces."

Celebratory mainstream media coverage offered additional evidence that the Persian Gulf War was the antidote to the Vietnam War, the latter stages of which had produced critical news reports. Television, where most Americans got their news, embraced the Bush administration and Pentagon versions of events in the run-up to the war, including broadcasts of lurid, albeit untrue stories of Iraqi invaders storming into hospitals to rip Kuwaiti babies out of incubation. The evils of Saddam Hussein were well chronicled but the repressive, anti-Semitic nature of the "liberated" Kuwaiti regime went unmentioned. The war reinvigorated the military–industrial complex and national security state, generated profits for defense industries, produced contracts to rebuild Kuwait, and closed ties with the Saudi kingdom. Millions of

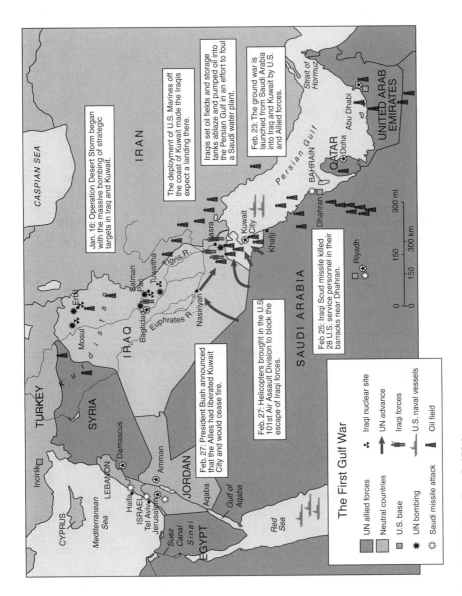

The First Gulf War

Jan. 16: Operation Desert Storm began with the massive bombing of strategic targets in Iraq and Kuwait.

The deployment of U.S. Marines off the coast of Kuwait made the Iraqis expect a landing there.

Iraqis set oil fields and storage tanks ablaze and pumped oil into the Persian Gulf in an effort to foul a Saudi water plant.

Feb. 23: The ground war is launched from Saudi Arabia into Iraq and Kuwait by U.S. and Allied forces.

Feb. 25: Iraqi Scud missile killed 28 U.S. service personnel in their barracks near Dhahran.

Feb. 27: President Bush announced that the Allies had liberated Kuwait City and would cease fire.

Feb. 27: Helicopters brought in the U.S. 101st Air Assault Division to block the escape of Iraqi forces.

Legend:
- UN allied forces
- Neutral countries
- U.S. base
- UN bombing
- Saudi missile attack
- Iraqi nuclear site
- UN advance
- Iraqi forces
- U.S. naval vessels
- Oil field

Map 14.1 The First Gulf War.

Americans cheered in front of their television screens as they watched high tech "smart bombs" pulverize Iraqi targets, with little attention focused on the death and destruction within Iraqi civil society. The US military largely excluded reporters from the battlefield, thus increasing their reliance on Pentagon briefings. Anti-war protests occurred but were downplayed by the media and thus most of the public. In sum, Americans were hungry for an easy and decisive victory that would give them cause to celebrate and the Persian Gulf War delivered.

In Their Words

President George H. W. Bush on the "New World Order," January 21, 1991 State of the Union Address

Mr. President and Mr. Speaker and Members of the United States Congress:

I come to this House of the people to speak to you and all Americans, certain that we stand at a defining hour. Halfway around the world, we are engaged in a great struggle in the skies and on the seas and sands. We know why we're there: We are Americans, part of something larger than ourselves. For two centuries, we've done the hard work of freedom. And tonight, we lead the world in facing down a threat to decency and humanity.

What is at stake is more than one small country; it is a big idea: a new world order, where diverse nations are drawn together in common cause to achieve the universal aspirations of mankind—peace and security, freedom, and the rule of law. Such is a world worthy of our struggle and worthy of our children's future . . .

Saddam Hussein's unprovoked invasion—his ruthless, systematic rape of a peaceful neighbor—violated everything the community of nations holds dear. The world has said this aggression would not stand, and it will not stand. Together, we have resisted the trap of appeasement, cynicism, and isolation that gives temptation to tyrants . . .

The end of the cold war has been a victory for all humanity . . . and America's leadership was instrumental in making it possible . . . The world can, therefore, seize this opportunity to fulfill the long-held promise of a new world order, where brutality will go unrewarded and aggression will meet collective resistance.

During the buildup to the war Bush proclaimed that the conflict would usher in a new world order of collective security under US leadership. The name stuck, as to many observers the Persian Gulf War marked the end of the bilateral cold war and the dawning of a new era of US supremacy as the world's sole remaining superpower. One theorist declared that the collapse of the Soviet Empire and the US military victory in the Persian Gulf signaled nothing less than the "end of history." He explained that with communism in disrepute and an aggressive dictator defeated the world was moving into a final phase of history dominated by US-led, liberal capitalist internationalism. Critics charged that the new world order was vague and idealistic rather than a realistic framework or policy prescription.

No new order or liberal regime emerged in Kuwait or Saudi Arabia, much less postwar Iraq. The Bush administration had gone to war to force Iraq out of Kuwait and not explicitly to overthrow the regime even though Bush had repeatedly compared Saddam with Hitler. Despite the rhetoric of a new world order the Bush administration viewed Iraq under Saddam as a counterweight to Iran. Moreover, Bush and his advisers concluded that ousting Saddam would require a longer and wider war that could produce a failed state and spread instability throughout the oil rich region. Years later, with George W. Bush in the White House, the father would be proven wiser than the son on this point.

In 1991 Bush openly called on the Iraqi people to topple Saddam, yet the United States and its allies did not back the rhetoric with action. A secular Sunni Muslim, Saddam slaughtered with impunity tens of thousands of Shia Muslims as enemies of the state. Similarly, Saddam used chemical weapons to kill some 20,000 ethnic Kurds amid calls for creation of a Kurdish state in northern Iraq. The United States and the international community provided some food and shelter and established a "no fly zone" to restrict Iraqi military action against the domestic foes. A broad array of international economic sanctions remained in place but these victimized the Iraqi people more than the regime. In the ensuing years the International Red Cross reported that "hundreds of thousands" of Iraqis died from disease and privation.

Gender and Sexuality Issues

Prior to the Panama intervention and the Persian Gulf War many Americans, especially men, displayed doubts about Bush's masculinity in contrast to the perceived boldness of his ever-popular predecessor Reagan. The juxtaposition was odd, given that Reagan had chosen to serve in Hollywood during World War II whereas Bush was a decorated naval veteran who flew 58 combat missions and had bailed out of his aircraft after it went down over the Pacific. However, whereas Reagan had vowed upon taking office that America would once again "stand tall," Bush had sounded a different note, calling for a "kinder, gentler nation." The intervention in Panama and, especially, the Persian Gulf War relieved Bush of the "wimp factor" referenced by critics and pundits prior to the conflicts.

Despite his display of manliness and the overwhelming triumph in Iraq, Bush lost his reelection bid amid an economic downturn. Bill Clinton, the former governor of Arkansas who had little foreign policy experience, won the 1992 presidential election by a plurality. Like Bush, Clinton faced doubts about his manliness at the helm of US global leadership. Like Cheney and hundreds of thousands of other young American males, Clinton had taken steps to avoid the Vietnam draft. Moreover Clinton made it clear that his wife and political confidant, Hillary Clinton would play a key role as an adviser in his administration. An attorney and embodiment of newly empowered women after the "second wave" of the women's movement, Hillary Clinton appeared threatening to critics who rallied around popular, right-wing radio talk show hosts in the 1990s who referenced the threats posed by "Femi-Nazis."

Assaults on Bill Clinton's manliness accelerated during the presidential campaign when he declared that gays and lesbians should be allowed to serve in the US military just like other Americans. Cultural conservatives and leaders of the armed forces sharply opposed the move citing threats to "unit cohesion" and the "morale" of the troops. Clinton bowed to the opposition and backed off on his campaign pledge. The policy that emerged was "**don't ask, don't tell**," enabling gays and lesbians to serve in the military as long as they remained closeted, or silent about their sexual preference. Inherently discriminatory, the policy was discarded in 2011 under President Barack Obama (and Secretary of State Hillary Clinton) with the support of a new generation of military leaders.

During his second term Clinton embroiled himself in scandal as a result of a tryst with a White House intern. The opposition party-dominated Congress deemed lying about a sex act sufficient cause to impeach Clinton, though he

Figure 14.2 President Bill Clinton, shown here with the Joint Chiefs of Staff, including future Secretary of State Colin Powell (third from left), clashed with the military and rival politicians over the proposal to allow gays and lesbians in the US military.

Source: Library of Congress, Prints and Photographs Division, LC-USZ62-113157.

was not convicted. In 1999, as Clinton prepared to go to war in the Balkans, some questioned whether the intervention was an effort to deflect attention away from the presidential scandal, the theme of a popular dark comedy film of the era (*Wag the Dog*).

Both Clinton and his successor George W. Bush advanced participation by women in the traditionally male field of diplomacy. In 1997 the Senate confirmed Madeleine Albright, who had been Clinton's ambassador to the UN, as the first-ever female secretary of state. In 2001 Bush chose as his national security adviser the academic and Russian specialist Condoleeza Rice, who went on to become secretary of state in Bush's second term. She was the second woman and the second African-American—after Bush made Powell secretary of state—to hold the Cabinet position. By the twenty-first century women from both political parties were serving in Congress in unprecedented numbers, though still a distinct minority. Prominent female senators, the Maine Republican Olympia Snowe and the California Democrat Barbara Boxer among them, were recognized for their expertise on defense and foreign policy issues. Although the **Foreign Service Act of 1980** mandated making the diplomatic service more "representative of the American people," progress had been halting until the 1990s and relatively few women held significant diplomatic posts. From that point forward the Foreign Service and other agencies

Figure 14.3 President Clinton appointed Madeleine Albright, shown here addressing the Democratic Convention in 2008, as the first female secretary of state in US history. The Senate confirmed her nomination by a vote of 99–0, a reflection of the growing acceptance of an expanded role for women in the traditionally male-dominated field of diplomacy.

Source: Library of Congress, Prints and Photographs Division, LC-DIG-highsm-03820.

within the national security bureaucracy substantially increased representation of women, African-Americans, and Hispanics.

The Arab-Israeli "Peace Process"

The George H. W. Bush administration avowed that victory in the Persian Gulf War created a climate conducive to the pursuit of a general Middle East peace accord as part of the new world order. As usual such efforts ran headlong into formidable opposition. PLO Chairman Yasser Arafat lost prestige with Arabs, Israelis, and the United States for backing Saddam in the Persian Gulf War. More militant groups such as Hamas, Islamic Jihad, and Hezbollah in southern Lebanon continued to gain ground and sponsor attacks on Israel. They refused to recognize Israel, which continued its refusal to allow for a Palestinian state.

US public opinion remained solidly behind Israel, which had kept its pledge to stay out of the Persian Gulf War despite the Iraqi Scud missile attacks. Bush, however, emphasized that the proliferation of Israeli settlements in the OT impeded the creation of a Palestinian state and thus stymied his efforts to forge a general Mideast peace accord. The US president pressured Israel to halt settlements and in an unprecedented move withheld a $10 billion loan guarantee promised to Tel Aviv for its cooperation in Persian Gulf War strategy. Speaking at the annual meeting of the AIPAC, Baker boldly told the Israel Lobby to halt new settlements and come to terms with the Palestinians and other Arabs.

From 1991 to 1993 the Bush administration sponsored the **Madrid Conference** in Spain, but the peace talks between the Arabs and Israelis failed. Israeli Prime Minister Yitzhak Shamir pursued a rejectionist path and continued to authorize new settlements in defiance of the US president. Shamir later acknowledged Tel Aviv's strategy over the years had been to "drag out talks on Palestinian self-rule . . . while attempting to settle hundreds of thousands of Jews in the occupied territories." Yitzhak Rabin replaced Shamir in 1992, the same year that Bush lost his reelection bid to Clinton, who had criticized him for pressuring the Israelis. From the 1988 to the 1992 election Bush's support among US Jews dropped from 35 to 11 percent.

Despite the failure to achieve accord the Madrid talks had at least brought the Arabs and Israelis together, leading to a broader agreement in the **Oslo Accords**. In 1993, with Washington uninvolved in the negotiations in Norway, Arafat and the PLO affirmed "the right of the state of Israel to exist in peace and security" and pledged to end resistance in return for Palestinian statehood. Israel officially recognized the PLO as representative of the Palestinian people and pledged to begin negotiating a settlement. Tel Aviv did not, however, recognize a Palestinian state nor agree to withdraw from the OT. Clinton, meanwhile, did not pressure Israel on new settlements and defied the UN and the vast majority of governments and world opinion by refusing to condemn the ongoing Israeli occupation of territory beyond its recognized international borders. As Albright put it, "We simply do not support the description of territories occupied by Israel in the 1967 war as 'occupied Palestinian territory.'"

The Oslo Accord thus allowed the occupation and settlements to continue alongside the establishment of a weak new **Palestinian Authority**—a quasi government and police force with a headquarters but no state. In 1994 Israel and Jordan came to peace terms but Israeli-Syrian talks over the occupation of the Golan Heights broke down. Oslo produced no agreement on the right of Palestinian refugees to return or on the status of Jerusalem. Palestinians continued to suffer from increasingly high unemployment and deprivations, including lack of reliable access to basic services such as water and power. The conditions were especially dire in the refugee camps and in the densely populated Gaza Strip. Terror assaults by both Arabs and Jews continued. In 1994 Hamas killed 22 Israelis in a suicide bombing in Tel Aviv. That same year a Jewish immigrant from New York killed 29 Arabs in an assault on a Muslim holy site in the occupied West Bank city of Hebron.

The Arab suicide bombing attacks traumatized Israelis and fueled the right-wing Likud Party. The militant Ariel Sharon and rising Likud politicians such as the US-educated **Benjamin Netanyahu** condemned the Labor Party for recognizing the PLO and Rabin and for shaking hands with Arafat. In November 1995 a zealot assassinated Rabin at a peace rally in Tel Aviv. Netanyahu was elected prime minister the following year. Meanwhile the Oslo process began to break down in disputes over the occupation, as Israel continued to settle and divide the territories with new bypass roads, roadblocks, and checkpoints cutting off and isolating the Arab population. Arab terror attacks accelerated in 1996 and brought swift and brutal Israeli reprisals, including a 16-day bombardment of southern Lebanon in which a UN compound at Qana was deliberately targeted, killing 106 civilians.

In July 2000 Clinton sponsored a last-gasp effort to save the Oslo "peace process" in the **Camp David Summit** at the presidential retreat. Israeli Prime Minister Ehud Barak refused to negotiate directly with Arafat, thus requiring Clinton to act as a go-between. While Clinton and Barak later blamed Arafat for rejecting an Israeli "generous offer," the terms would have required a rump and disjointed Palestinian state to attempt to function amid the rapidly proliferating roadblocks and checkpoints. The number of Jewish settlements in the West Bank had doubled since the Oslo talks began in 1993 creating "facts on the ground" that undermined the prospects of a viable Palestinian state connecting the West Bank, Jerusalem, and Gaza. The breakdown of the Camp David Summit would lead to yet another wave of violence and destruction as the new century unfolded.

Ethnic Cleansing in the Balkans

The violent breakup of the former Yugoslavia quickly dashed hopes that the end of the cold war would usher in an idyllic new world order under US stewardship. Created in 1918, after World War II Yugoslavia became a communist state, though not an ally of the Soviet Union. In the 1990s the collapse of the Soviet Empire foreshadowed the dissolution of the multi-ethnic Slavic state, which was also divided religiously between Orthodox Christians, Catholics, and Muslims, among others. As the crisis escalated the former Yugoslavia became the site of vicious campaigns of **ethnic cleansing**—killing and driving off the land rival ethnic groups.

In contrast to drawing "a line in the sand" against Iraqi aggression in the Middle East, the Bush administration initially avoided involvement in the exploding conflict in the Balkans. The United States, Baker famously said, had "no dog in this fight." Some argued that with the collapse of the Soviet Empire Yugoslavia was no longer as important to the United States as it had been as a bulwark between East and West in the cold war. Despite the claims that the United States was the unquestioned leader of the new world order the Bush administration preferred that Europeans handle the problem in the Balkans. The new Germany, however, flunked its first test of renewed leadership in Central Europe by encouraging Slovenia and Croatia in their efforts to secede from the Yugoslav federation. Their secession in 1991 opened the floodgates, sparking ethnic tensions, other secession movements, and, ultimately, the violent cleansing campaigns.

The United States and the Europeans might have prevented the conflict by drawing a hard line against secessionist movements but instead they encouraged them. In 1992, the Bush administration asserted itself into the conflict, shooting down a proposal at the Lisbon Conference for regional autonomy that might have averted the crisis. Washington instead backed Bosnian Muslim secession. The Bush administration and most European allies badly misjudged Serbian President **Slobodan Milošević** and his followers, who attacked on behalf of Bosnian Serbs while at the same time seeking to forge a powerful Serbian state out of the ruins of the Yugoslav federation. While depicting Serbia as the protector of the Slavic federation Milošević actually sought to destroy the legacy of interethnic cooperation in favor of Serbian dominance. The Serbian Army and paramilitaries embarked on campaigns of mass rape and murder. While the United States and other Europeans remained disengaged, Croats, Muslims, Slovenes, and other ethnic and religious groups joined the Serbs in waging wars of ethnic cleansing.

During the 1992 presidential campaign Clinton criticized Bush for inaction, but after becoming president Clinton was also initially wary of intervention in the ethnic conflict. Clinton's first secretary of state, Warren Christopher, a veteran diplomat, called it "a problem from hell" and saw little to be gained from direct US involvement in a place where "ancient enmities" prevailed. However, as the ugly cleansing campaigns accelerated, a US-led NATO coalition intervened. In 1994 NATO airstrikes attacked Serbian positions in the wake of the Serbs' brutal shelling of Sarajevo. More airstrikes followed in 1995 as public criticism of Western inaction mounted amid televised scenes of ethnic slaughter and revelations of rape houses set up to service the invading paramilitaries. Many Muslims around the world rallied behind the plight of the Bosnian Muslims and condemned the West for allowing the rapes and killings. Two of the future September 11, 2001, hijackers fought in the Bosnian wars.

In 1995 after three years of ethnic warfare Washington and the NATO allies forged a ceasefire and a settlement in the **Dayton Accords**. Meeting outside a US air base in southwestern Ohio, the presidents of Bosnia, Croatia, and Serbia recognized the independence of Bosnia-Herzegovina. However, Serb aggression had been rewarded with the carving out of a separate Serbian republic within the federation. Croats and Muslims also forged their own republics within the federation. The Dayton Accords ended much of the violence but long-term stability of the Bosnian federation remained problematic.

Before the Dayton Accords could be fully implemented the United States moved unilaterally to rein in Serbian aggression in Kosovo, a small region located between Serbia and Albania. Secretary of State Albright, a Czech emigrant whose family had been victimized by the Nazis, called for a more active US role in Europe. As Serbia conducted ethnic cleansing campaigns against the majority Albanians in Kosovo the Kosovo Liberation Army mounted a guerrilla opposition. An inflexible, US-NATO-brokered proposed settlement left the Serbs no face-saving formula to deescalate the crisis over Kosovo, which they viewed in any case as sacred to their ethnic identity.

By 1999 Milošević and Serbia had been fully ensconced in Western perceptions as the progenitor of the Balkan conflict, an oversimplified version of events that obscured the fact that other states and leaders, such as Croatia's **Franjo Tudjman**, were equally racist and eager to mount ethnic cleansing campaigns. While Serbs were compared with Nazis and the numbers put to death in their "extermination camps" exaggerated, the Croatian slaughter of Serbs in a 1995 assault on Krajina elicited little condemnation from Washington. Albright publicly drew the parallel between Hitler and Milošević, invoked the time-honored warning against "appeasement" of aggressors, and urged Clinton to go to war.

In 1999 the United States led a massive NATO bombing campaign orchestrated by General Wesley Clark to force the Serbs out of Kosovo. The 78-day bombing campaign sought to "demolish, destroy, devastate, degrade, and ultimately eliminate the essential infrastructure of Yugoslavia." The carpet-bombing killed and wounded thousands of people and created more than a million displaced persons. The punishing campaign forced the Yugoslav Serbs to pull back and accept an accord placing Kosovo under an interim UN command. The US-led bombing campaign was illegal under international law, as the UN Security Council had not approved it, and was sharply opposed by China, India, and the new Russia, among others. Domestic critics charged that Clinton was attempting to deflect attention from the sex scandal with his intern through the bombing campaign. In fact, however, momentum for intervention had been growing under Albright and amid rising outrage over Serb transgressions. Most of the US public rallied behind the American Flag in wartime.

The Balkan conflict reinforced US primacy over NATO as well as the European Union (EU), which had aroused concerns by floating its own currency (the euro) in 1999 to compete with the US dollar. Like the Persian Gulf War the US-NATO intervention served to justify maintenance of a large defense budget in the post-cold war years and established a new US military base in Kosovo. Intervention in the Balkan conflict thus enabled the United States to reassert its dominance in Europe, underscored a new mission as well as an expansionist agenda for NATO, and reinvigorated the MIC.

Intervention and Genocide in Africa

Criticized for inaction as the violence unfolded in Yugoslavia, Bush near the end of his term sent US forces on a humanitarian relief mission to Somalia in the Horn of Africa. Civil society in Somalia had collapsed into clan-based warfare. By the early 1990s tens of thousands of civilians were dead and hundreds of thousands were starving as mass famine gripped the East African country. In 1992 the UN intervened in an effort to force warlords to distribute food supplies that they sought to control, often to trade for weapons to enhance their power. UN General Secretary **Boutros Boutros-Ghali**, an Egyptian, urged US support for the program to demonstrate that Americans were concerned about starvation in the impoverished African country.

Initially **Operation Restore Hope** succeeded in improving distribution of food and medical supplies, but UN and US forces soon clashed with Somali warlords amid a nascent civil war in the country. Innocent civilians died as UN troops fired into crowds and carried out airborne assaults against clans and religious leaders. Many Somalis grew resentful of the foreign intervention, which began to seem more like an occupation than a humanitarian relief mission. Longstanding Western racial and religious prejudices surfaced in the description of Somalis, as they often did with Arabs. Intent on punishing the Somali "bandits," and "thugs," the Army launched an ill-fated assault into "Indian country" to take on the local "skinnies."

In October 1993 the famous **"Black Hawk down" incident** occurred amid a series of US assaults targeting warlords and militias in the Somali capital of Mogadishu. After shooting down a US Blackhawk helicopter, Somalis killed 18 American soldiers and paraded their bodies through the streets. The Army Rangers had gone in "like Rambo," as the Eritrean president put it, and were unprepared for the scope and ferocity of the counterattack. "We just didn't expect to meet the kind of resistance that we did," a Pentagon official acknowledged. US forces lashed out in response, killing some 500 Somali men, women, and children. Clinton, who had inherited the operation from Bush, announced a US pullout from Somalia. In 1994 the UN terminated the relief operation and Somalia remained in the grip of civil conflict and famine.

As the United States pulled out of Somalia, genocide sparked by political and ethnic turmoil erupted in Rwanda and eventually spread through the Great Lakes region of Central Africa. The **Rwandan genocide**, in which some 800,000 to 1 million people were slaughtered, resulted from deep-seated divisions rooted in draconian Belgian colonial rule over the region. The Belgians had empowered a Tutsi minority, comprising less than 15 percent of the country's population, over the Hutu majority, who took power when Rwanda became independent in 1962. The genocide erupted on April 7, 1994, the day after the presidents of Rwanda and neighboring Burundi, both Hutus, were assassinated when a missile shot down their aircraft on its descent into Kigali. Evidence overwhelmingly suggests that the Rwandan Patriotic Front (RPF) under **Paul Kagame** ordered the assassination of the two Hutu presidents.

The United States and Britain supported Kagame and the RPF, a Tutsi exile movement based in Uganda. Kagame, who had received military training at Fort Leavenworth, Kansas, in the early 1990s, precluded left-wing reform and backed US economic and security policies in the region. Washington and London thus opposed UN intervention when the violence began in hopes that the RPF could quickly triumph over the Hutu majority. The RPF thus invaded Rwanda and ultimately drove the Hutus out of Kigali, but not before Hutu bands carried out an ethnic slaughter of hundreds of thousands of Tutsis. Hutus were also victimized, however, as the genocide was not, as widely believed, one-sided nor purely an ethnic conflict but fundamentally a political one flowing from the ultimately successful RPF–Kagame effort to seize power in Rwanda. The killings in Rwanda comprised the worst incident of genocide since the Khmer Rouge rampaged through the Cambodian countryside following the Vietnam War.

By precluding UN intervention the United States facilitated the mass killing in Rwanda, most of which had been carried out within 100 days. Boutros-Ghali blamed the United States for the genocide, explaining, "The US effort to prevent the effective deployment of a UN force for Rwanda succeeded with the strong support of Britain." In 1996 the United States forced out Boutros-Ghali from his post as UN secretary-general. In 1998 Clinton formally apologized during a visit to Rwanda, declaring the United States and the global community should have intervened to stop the genocide. The apology notwithstanding, Washington continued to support Kagame and the RPF, which had instigated the conflict with the assassinations and orchestrated the mass killing of Hutus. Washington stifled a UN investigation when it threatened to implicate Kagame by gathering evidence of RPF–Tutsi perpetration of massacres.

Backed by Clinton and British Prime Minister Tony Blair, Kagame depicted himself as a hero who had brought an end to an exclusively Hutu genocide. He followed up the takeover of Rwanda by invading the Congo and slaughtering thousands more Hutus, including some who had taken part in mass killings and later fled to refugee camps. Kagame's invasion of Congo drove a broader Great Lakes conflict with Rwandan and Ugandan rebels on one side and the Congo government backed by Angola, Namibia, and Zimbabwe on the other. Some 5 million people died in the high-stakes conflict in which control over Congo's rich mineral deposits including gold, diamonds, and copper was at stake. Kagame remained in power in Rwanda through blatantly fraudulent elections, the assassinations of exiled critics, and long prison terms for anyone who questioned the official version of the genocide. Washington, which credited Kagame with resurrecting the Rwandan economy, continued to supply the regime with foreign assistance and political support.

Sensitive to charges that the United States had been disinterested in the deaths of hundreds of thousands of black Africans, Clinton stepped up

AIDS relief to Africa and also intervened in Haiti to return to power a reform government. The UN Security Council authorized the Haitian intervention (Operation Uphold Democracy) after a military coup overthrew the popular and legally elected government of **Jean-Bertrand Aristide**, a Roman Catholic and left-leaning reformer. US forces oversaw Aristide's return to power and remained in Haiti to promote political stability and a humanitarian relief and reform effort. In 1995 the UN assumed authority over the mission and US forces withdrew. Haiti remained impoverished and politically troubled but the US intervention had prevented a bloodbath and fended off a possible mass exodus of Haitian refugees to US shores. Aristide, however, was a dedicated reformer who defied US economic prescriptions for Haiti. As a result the US-led international financial institutions cut off loans and assistance and colluded in overthrowing his elected government in 2004.

Human Rights and Foreign Policy

Human rights diplomacy, evolving since World War II, achieved unprecedented prominence in the 1990s in the wake of the disturbing events in Africa, the Balkans, and elsewhere. Under traditional "realist" approaches to diplomacy, basing foreign policy on issues such as human rights was considered idealistic and likely to do more harm than good. That view had changed substantially by the 1990s. The outbreaks of genocide in Africa and the Balkans fueled the growing influence of international human rights organizations. Amnesty International, created in 1961, and Human Rights Watch (1978) were among the more influential of a growing number of NGOs that focused international attention on a variety of issues, human rights among them.

Human rights gained momentum toward the end of the cold war and during the presidency of Jimmy Carter, who made human rights the rhetorical centerpiece of his approach to foreign relations. Patricia Derian, a State Department diplomat, aggressively pursued human rights-based diplomacy under Carter, though other advisers contested her efforts. To some it appeared that criticism of Derian as with April Glaspie reflected prejudicial, gendered doubts about female diplomats. Carter displayed his realist credentials with frequent compromises on human rights in order to back repressive allied regimes in, among other nations, Indonesia, Iran, the Philippines, and South Korea. Nonetheless, Carter's rhetorical emphasis on human rights spurred the growth of the international movement.

During the era of détente the Helsinki Conference (1975) fueled momentum, as the US-Soviet accord included the pledge to "respect human rights and fundamental freedoms including the freedom of thought, conscience, religion or belief for all without distinction as to race, sex, language or religion." Thereafter "Helsinki watch" organizations monitored compliance not only in the Soviet Empire, but also among military dictatorships in Africa, Asia, and Latin America. Pressure to conform to human rights norms thus increased across the globe. Gorbachev responded to international pressure by freeing political prisoners from the Soviet gulag, but China and many other nations condemned international pressure on such matters as interference with their domestic affairs.

When the end of the cold war produced a wave of genocide rather than a new world order of peace and progress, human rights organizations demanded action. In 1993 the UN Security Council responded to the ethnic cleansing in the Balkans by establishing an international criminal tribunal, which eventually tried and convicted Milošević and other offenders. The UN created a similar tribunal for the Rwandan perpetrators of genocide. These ad hoc tribunals provided the impetus for the **International Criminal Court (ICC)**. By 2011 more than 100 nations had signed on in support of the ICC, but among the most notable exceptions were the United States and Israel. Despite its rhetorical support for human rights the United States refused to accept the jurisdiction of an international court with the power to sit in judgment of its actions in foreign affairs.

The international human rights agenda extended beyond war crimes and political repression to include women's rights, treatment of children, economic and social rights, and the rights of indigenous people. Eleanor Roosevelt, who had played a key role in the drafting of the Universal Declaration on Human Rights in 1948, was among the first to call for international action to address the unequal treatment of women, yet meaningful change had been slow to evolve. By 1975 the UN had become more active, sponsoring International Women's Year and holding the first World Conference on Women in Mexico City. Many societies, however, remained opposed to equal treatment of women and also engaged in discrimination based on sexual orientation. Sexual trafficking of women was a growing and little policed international problem. Revelations of widespread sexual trafficking of children spurred a more robust response, as many countries including the United States wrote new laws and stepped up enforcement and punishment for sexual exploitation and trafficking of minors, but nonetheless could not eliminate the problem.

On September 13, 2007, Australia, Canada, New Zealand, and the United States cast the 4 negative votes—compared with 143 in favor—against the UN General Assembly's **Declaration on the Rights of Indigenous Peoples**. All four were settler colonial societies built on the dispossession of indigenous people. The United States later offered a qualified endorsement of the declaration with a "finalizing disclaimer" reasserting its ultimate sovereignty over Native Americans. In December 2010 the United States offered "official apologies for the past ill-conceived policies by the US government toward native peoples of this land and reaffirm our commitment toward healing our nation's wounds and working toward establishing better relationships rooted in reconciliation." Like the apology in 1993 to indigenous Hawaiians for the US takeover of their islands, the apology to Native Americans was scarcely noticed as it was squirreled away, ironically, within a military appropriations bill and entailed no legal responsibility or offer of relief or compensation.

Interpreting the Past

The Washington consensus

From the Reagan years into the post-cold war era the United States took the lead in enforcing the "**Washington consensus**," a set of economic principles emphasizing privatization, free trade, fiscal discipline, and financial deregulation. With the collapse of global communism the United States and its European allies were empowered to enforce this economic agenda, which facilitated resource extraction and enhanced the power of corporations, financial institutions, and wealthy elites. Critics argued the global financial regime aided multi-national corporations by exporting US jobs abroad and repressing wages and job growth at home.

Overseas, nations in search of loans and assistance for development had to comply with the Washington consensus or face economic and political isolation if not the overthrow of their governments. The terms typically included "structural adjustment," enforced austerity programs, cuts in public services to reduce government spending and indebtedness. This form of "shock therapy" opened nations to private sector investment and profit taking on terms favorable to foreign investors, but often threw people out of work and deprived them of a broad array of social services. Unrepresentative regimes spurred social unrest by removing farm subsidies, unemployment assistance, and cutting health and education. As the gap between rich and poor nations and peoples widened, and Asia suffered a severe financial crisis, opposition to the Washington consensus spread across the globe.

Globalization

The rise of human rights diplomacy and the heightened role of NGOs were inextricably linked with the broader phenomenon of **globalization**. The term referred to sweeping changes in technology, especially communications and transportation, that made the world increasingly integrated and interconnected. At its essence globalization transcended the nation-state in deference to transnational forces underscoring the interconnectedness of the "global village." The personal computer and the Internet were the calling cards of the increasingly interconnected globalized environment. Globalization reflected other flows as well, notably the dissemination of popular culture, the spread of disease including the global AIDS crisis, energy interdependence, global climate change, and ultimately a "global war on terror."

Although the term became popularized in the 1990s globalization was not new, rather its pace was accelerating. As the United States and the Soviets waged the cultural cold war in the Third World, the importance of transnational flows grew accordingly. NGOs such as the Carnegie, Ford, and Rockefeller Foundations promoted international education, development, and cultural exchange.

The Fulbright exchange program, created in 1946, over time sent hundreds of thousands of teachers, students, professors, and citizens around the globe to disseminate education and exchange culture. US high schools and colleges incorporated area studies programs to teach more about the world. Air travel and tourism grew exponentially in the postwar period.

Globalization enhanced the availability and demand for consumer goods and popular culture, creating opportunities for soft power to flourish. During the postwar decades music, fashion, and consumer goods—an endless array of items: Coca-Cola, fried chicken, sushi, Marlboro cigarettes, designer jeans, Barbie dolls, records, disks, and Play Stations—traversed the world. So did sex, drugs, gambling, and organized crime. The ubiquity of television and the Internet made sport global, as millions followed World Cup football matches, the Olympics, and the US-led world of professional sports. US television programs and Hollywood films circulated into the most remote regions of the world.

Globalization spurred economic growth, innovation, and productivity, but also delivered economic crises and ultimately widened the gap between rich and poor. In the 1990s the rapid unfolding of the computer industry and "dot.com revolution," centered in California's Silicon Valley, fueled economic growth, lower interest rates, declining unemployment, and an economic boom that re-fired US global economic supremacy. Whereas Japan and Europe had outpaced the United States during the "stagflation" of the 1970s, the US economy reigned in the 1990s. The export driven US Gross National Product grew sharply in the decade. However, other countries, notably China and India, were on the rise as well, while Russia entered into a period of rampant corruption, inequality, and relative decline.

President Clinton championed the Washington consensus including the removal of international trade barriers and global economic integration under capitalism in the wake of the collapse of communism. "It's the economy, stupid," Democrats quipped in explaining Clinton's victory over Bush, as a mild recession carried more weight with the voting public than the military triumphs in Panama and the Persian Gulf. A third party candidate, business tycoon Ross Perot, also emphasized economic issues. Once ensconced in the White House Clinton, sometimes referred to as the "globalization President," secured passage of the **North American Free Trade Act** (NAFTA), previously negotiated by the preceding Bush administration. The agreement provided a 15-year phasing out of tariffs and trade barriers among Canada, Mexico, and the United States. Perot had warned that passage of NAFTA would produce "a big sucking sound" of US jobs going south of the border. In November 1993 the House passed NAFTA 234–200 while the Senate approved it by a vote of 61–38.

NAFTA promoted free trade but not free labor flows. Critics of illegal immigration demanded greater US border security while the Republican-led Congress considered restrictive legislation. In 1994 Clinton preempted congressional and state level action with **"Operation Gatekeeper"** whose aim was to control the San Diego–Tijuana border. Clinton doubled the budget for law enforcement along the border and ordered construction of miles of new

fencing. The policy failed to make significant reductions in unauthorized border crossings, as the illegals migrated through the less populated deserts and
mountains to the east. Illegal immigration continued, as did efforts to combat
it, into the next century.

NATFA, like ASEAN and the EU, reflected the growth of regional integration in concert with implementation of the Washington consensus. In addition
to the World Bank and the IMF, both created at the end of World War II
and headquartered in Washington, the **World Trade Organization** (WTO)
anchored the consensus. Created in 1995, the WTO emphasized free trade and
deregulation, and championed the private sector. By 2007 it had 151 member
states worldwide. Under the Washington consensus countries received loans
and development assistance, but only if they complied with the demands of
"structural adjustment" bolstering the private sector while forcing reductions in
government spending and indebtedness. Meanwhile illicit economic activities
such as the burgeoning global market for drugs, weapons, and sex flourished in
the "free trade" environment.

The Washington consensus often fueled economic growth, created jobs,
and encouraged education and literacy, but it also spread low wages, inequality, a profusion of sweatshops, environmental degradation, and lack of access
to health care. The Washington consensus thus ultimately helped the United
States and other advanced economies while often retarding economic growth
in developing countries. Joseph Stiglitz, who served for three years as chief
economist of the World Bank, resigned in disgust over the "hypocrisy of pre-
tending to help developing countries by forcing them to open up their markets
to the goods of the advanced industrial countries while keeping their own markets protected." The Nobel Prize winning economist found that globalization
fueled "policies that make the rich richer and the poor more impoverished—
and increasingly angry."

The dark side of globalization became apparent with the outbreak of the
Asian financial crisis of 1997–98. The ensuing economic collapse radiated
from Indonesia and Thailand to Russia to Africa and Latin America while the
United States and Western Europe remained relatively unscathed. The IMF
worsened the deepest economic crisis since the Great Depression by forcing
afflicted states to raise interest rates. Nations such as Indonesia, which held to
the IMF regime, suffered the most, while those such as China, Malaysia, and
South Korea, which rejected economic orthodoxy for state intervention and
recovery policies, emerged with less damage.

Growing economic inequality produced resistance to the Washington consensus. Although total world income increased under globalization, uneven
distribution found corporations and executives ringing up record profits and
cashing in massive bonuses while the number of people living in rural and
urban poverty increased by nearly 100 million. Multi-national corporations
located their factories abroad in order to exploit cheap labor and avoid taxes
and environmental regulation while ringing up record profits. Nike, internationally recognized for its swoosh logo and brilliant marketing of sports figures

such as basketball star Michael Jordan, paid pennies on the hour to Asian "sweatshop" laborers, but the Oregon-based shoe manufacturer was hardly alone.

International resentment over global inequality erupted with protests, hunger riots, and violent resistance. In 1999 the unrest came home to Americans in the "**Battle of Seattle**," as protesters fought in the streets at the site of a global WTO forum. An ugly scene materialized as police beat and gassed nonviolent, civil disobedience demonstrators protesting inequality, sweatshops, and global environmental degradation.

Resistance to the Washington consensus spread into the US "backyard" of Latin America. While Clinton orchestrated NAFTA and other free trade agreements, and bailed the Mexican peso out of crisis in 1994, other Latin American nations bolted from the orthodox economic regimen. Most notable was Venezuela, which elected and repeatedly reelected **Hugo Chávez**, a left-wing reformer allied with Cuba's Fidel Castro. Chávez built popular support through policies of racial equality and income redistribution from rich to poor. In 2002 a US-backed coup attempted to topple Chávez over his defiance but it failed. Similar democratic electoral revolts followed in Bolivia, Ecuador, Nicaragua, Paraguay, and Peru. Chile, long considered the laboratory of neo-liberal structural adjustment under the US-backed dictatorship of General Augusto Pinochet, also revolted against the US-led economic orthodoxy.

The United States closed ties with the right-wing government and paramilitaries in Colombia to reinforce the Washington consensus. Beginning in the 1990s under **Plan Colombia**, the United States spent billions of dollars ostensibly to combat drug traffickers but actually to contain the left. Wracked by internecine violence for decades, Colombia was divided between the elite-dominated, right-wing government in the cities and left-wing control of most of the countryside by **FARC** (Revolutionary Armed Forces of Colombia). Beginning in the 1980s, as American drug consumers indulged a nearly insatiable appetite for cocaine, the United States launched a "war on drugs" that included collusion with the Bogotá government and the right-wing paramilitaries against FARC and an urban-based rebel group.

The United States justified Plan Colombia as part of the drug war against "narco-terrorists" but in actuality both the Colombian government and the rebels were implicated in the cocaine trade. The government worked with the Cali and Medellín cartels while FARC defended the peasant farmers who cultivated the coca leaves. In 2000, as Albright made Plan Colombia the centerpiece of her Latin American policy, the United States poured more than a billion dollars into Colombia, most of it destined for the military and with little oversight. In return for massive US funding and military assistance the Colombian government remained true to the Washington consensus, which deepened the gulf between rich and poor in the country, which in turn generated continuing support for the rebels. Despite the largesse Plan Colombia failed to halt the drug trade or destroy the FARC, which continued its rural-based guerrilla opposition into the next century.

Relations with Post-Communist Russia

Among the countries faring worst under globalization was post-communist Russia. The Soviet economy had collapsed under Gorbachev, who was under increasing pressure to sign on to the Washington consensus at the time of his ouster. **Boris Yeltsin**, a maverick former Communist Party elite, assumed the Russian presidency and received backing from the United States. In August 1991 Yeltsin had stood atop a tank and vowed to face down the leaders of the attempted pro-communist coup. Many Americans thus viewed Yeltsin as a hero of democracy and reform, but in fact he often ruled by decree and in 1993 bypassed the constitution and ordered the shelling of the Russian parliament building, killing hundreds of people.

Yeltsin was an unstable leader plagued by alcoholism but he uncritically accepted the Washington consensus and allied with the United States on most issues. "Yeltsin drunk is better than most of the alternatives sober," Clinton decided. By embracing "shock therapy" and neo-liberalism at a breakneck pace and with virtually no safeguards, Russia sent its economy into a tailspin and its society into an orgy of corruption. Economic growth declined while inequality soared in the former communist state.

With Yeltsin disengaged or putty in their hands, speculators and corrupt Russian Mafiosi laid claim to state property and enterprises, converting them into their private economic fiefdoms. Trumpeting the gospel of privatization, oligarchs plundered the country. The once drab Soviet cities sparkled with new stores and enterprises and ostentatious displays of wealth, but few Russians could afford to purchase much beyond the bare necessities of bread, sausage, and vodka. Poverty and unemployment rose sharply, health declined, and already high rates of alcoholism and suicide spiked even further. Critics were cast aside or worse, as in the case of journalists and opposition figures investigating corruption, assassinated on the streets of Moscow. "For a long time we lived under the dictatorship of the Communists," Russian writer Grigory Gorin observed, "but now we have found out that life under the dictatorship of the business people is no better."

The United States avoided direct involvement in the last half of the 1990s as Russia fought two brutal wars with **Chechnya**, a partly Muslim province in the mountainous Caucasian region between the Black and Caspian Seas. More than 100,000 people died in the wars and terror attacks. In 2000, amid the Second Chechen War, the former Soviet secret police chief **Vladimir Putin** replaced Yeltsin as president. Putin, who was deeply implicated in the corruption and plundering of state resources, would dominate the Russian Federation over the next generation. As the Russian economy gradually picked up with rising revenues from oil and gas sales, Putin tried to reassert Russia's status as a major power, which brought him into increasing conflict with Washington.

Despite the economic disarray in post-Soviet Russia, the United States successfully negotiated pivotal nuclear arms control agreements. Negotiations produced a crucial agreement on **denuclearization of the former Soviet republics** except Russia. Belarus, Kazakhstan, and Ukraine, site of the Chernobyl disaster, all agreed to turn over their nuclear arsenals and sign

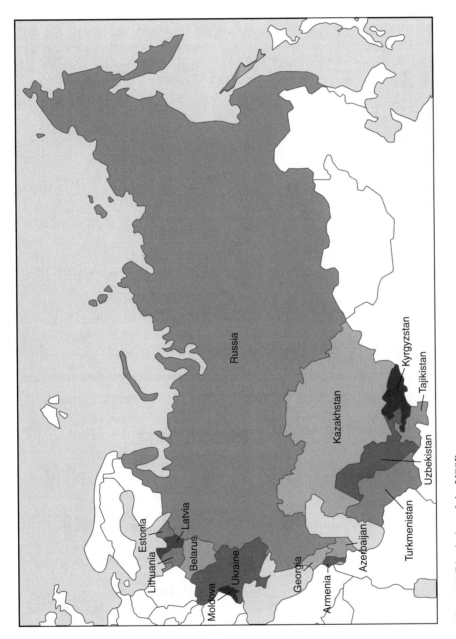

Map 14.2 Dissolution of the USSR.

the non-proliferation treaty. This accord facilitated keeping track of the number and location of the former Soviet nuclear arsenals, a prerequisite for arms control and essential in efforts to prevent the spread of weapons or fissionable material to other states or terror groups.

Building on the START I agreement signed by Bush and Gorbachev in 1991, Clinton and Yeltsin agreed on further reductions in each side's arsenal of nuclear warheads under **START II**. In 1996 Congress ratified the agreement, with some conditions, and the Russian Duma followed suit in 2000. First signed under Bush, a chemical weapons convention finally achieved congressional approval in 1997. Under the convention the two powers agreed to eliminate stockpiles of chemical weapons and outlawed development and production of such weapons in the future.

Russia and the United States remained divided into the twenty-first century over the issue of **nuclear missile defense** (NMD) and especially the US quest to establish NMD sites in former Soviet allied states of Eastern Europe. Under pressure from the Republicans, who took over the Congress in 1994, Clinton reversed his former position and committed to pursuit of NMD technology and testing. To counter opposition charges that he was "soft" on defense, Clinton signed the **National Missile Defense Act** of 1999, a decision denounced by China, Russia, and several US allies but welcomed by the MIC. Putin declared that the $10.5 billion appropriation for testing interceptor defenses would "destroy the strategic balance in the world." The Republican-led Congress also shot down the **Comprehensive Test Ban Treaty** (CTBT), approved by the Russian parliament, which would have strengthened arms control by ending nuclear weapons tests. In 2000 the Senate defeated the CTBT by a vote of 51–48, prompting Clinton to complain, "Even the Russia Duma was more progressive on arms control than the US Senate."

More alarming still to the Russians was US-sponsored **NATO expansion** into the former Soviet Empire. The end of the cold war brought an existential crisis for NATO, as the alliance had been designed to contain the Soviet Union, which had ceased to exist. However, the Balkan conflict culminating in the NATO bombing campaign in Kosovo had reinvigorated the Washington-dominated alliance, which subsequently expanded into former Soviet allied states. NATO expansion offered an opportunity to strengthen the Pentagon and fuel the MIC. As the *New York Times* pointed out in 1998, "American arms manufacturers who stand to gain billions of dollars in sales of weapons, communications equipment, and other military equipment if the Senate approves NATO expansion have made enormous investments in lobbyists and campaign contributions to promote their cause in Washington."

NATO expansion aroused Russian fears of Western encirclement particularly as the alliance had been designed to contain Russia. The United States responded that NATO expansion did not target Russia but rather was meant to enhance European security. Western officials insisted that a strengthened NATO would facilitate European economic and political cooperation and serve to bring an end to conflict, as had occurred in the Balkans.

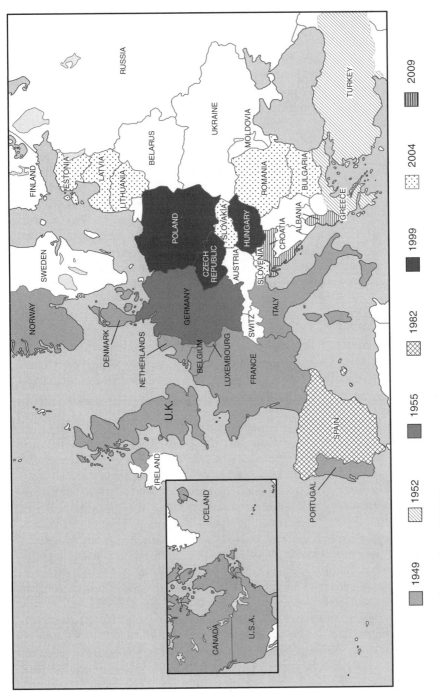

Map 14.3 Eastward expansion of NATO.

■ 1949   ▨ 1952   ■ 1955   ■ 1982   ■ 1999   ⬚ 2004   ▦ 2009

NATO expansion had bipartisan support from both Clinton and the Republican majority, which had made NATO enlargement a key part of its "Contract with America." In a 1997 graduation address before Army cadets at West Point, Clinton declared NATO expansion would "help secure the historic gains of democracy." In 1999 Albright oversaw NATO expansion into her Czech homeland as well as into Hungary and Poland. Both Yeltsin and Putin and the majority of Russians sharply opposed the entry of the formerly Russian allied countries into NATO, but the expansion was popular in Europe as well as the United States and thus proceeded despite bitter Russian objections. American and NATO officials established limitations on the number of tanks and troops that would be lodged in the former Soviet allied states and also pledged not to deploy offensive nuclear weapons in Eastern Europe. These concessions did little to reassure the Russians, especially as Clinton declared he would work toward the day when the Baltic states of Estonia, Latvia, and Lithuania, part of the tsarist Russian Empire, could "walk through" the door to NATO membership. The Russians also criticized the establishment of a US air base in the former Soviet republic of Uzbekistan. As the issue of NATO expansion and an eventual clash in Ukraine demonstrated, the US-Russian geopolitical rivalry had not been relegated to the past.

Rising China and East Asian Diplomacy

During the era of globalization China became a rising world power, a development that carried important implications for East Asia, the United States, and the world. In the 1990s China and the United States clashed over economic and security issues as well as human rights. While the relationship was frequently strained, diplomacy prevailed as the two superpowers managed to find an uneasy accommodation with one another.

Following his ascension to power in 1978, **Deng Xiaoping** instituted dramatic economic reforms that integrated China into the market-driven, global capitalist system. One of the more pivotal economic reforms was the creation of special economic zones on China's southern coast in a move that broadened ties with the dynamic Asian economies of Hong Kong, Singapore, South Korea, and Taiwan. In relatively little time China transitioned from a closed, often-xenophobic regime under Mao Zedong to a rising, globally integrated economic powerhouse. With abundant natural resources and endless supplies of cheap labor, China's productivity and exports soared.

As its economy grew China became more assertive as an East Asian and world power, though Beijing typically sought to avoid direct conflict. In 1997 following years of negotiations China assumed sovereignty over Hong Kong while making pledges not to impose its socialist system on the former British colony or on the former Portuguese colony of Macau, which it also absorbed in 1999. The PRC still considered Taiwan part of China, though the island had gone its own way since the communist takeover of the mainland in 1949. Taiwan continued to receive heavy military backing from the United States. Under the **Taiwan Relations Act**, passed in 1979 as Washington accepted the "one China" policy and normalized relations with Beijing, the United States declared that aggression against Taiwan would be viewed as a "threat to peace and security" and would require the president to consult with Congress on a response.

In 1995 Sino-American relations approached a crisis point when Clinton bowed to political pressure from the Republican Congress to grant a visa to Taiwan President Lee Teng-hui, an advocate of independence, who attended a class reunion at Cornell University. Beijing's reaction was severe, including terminating talks and cutting back various ties with Taiwan and the United States; carrying out provocative ballistic missile tests; and threatening to go to war in the event of a formal declaration of independence by Taiwan. Lee and his followers refrained from such a declaration. The angry response reflected powerful nationalist sentiment in China. Most Han Chinese viewed Taiwan as part of China that had been wrongfully taken away by Western imperialism.

The United States sent two carrier battle groups in response to the threats over Taiwan, but diplomacy prevailed. Meeting in a summit with China's leader Jiang Zemin in New York in 1997, Clinton affirmed the one China policy, though the United States would continue to supply Taiwan with advance weaponry. The PRC did not renounce the possibility of using force in the event of a formal declaration of independence by Taiwan. The two leaders pledged to pursue "constructive strategic partnership," including crucial US support for eventual Chinese membership in the WTO.

In 1999 nationalist sentiment erupted once again in response to the accidental **US bombing of the Chinese embassy** in Belgrade as part of the NATO campaign against Serbia in Kosovo. Five guided bombs struck the embassy, which had been wrongly identified as a Yugoslav military office building, killing 3 Chinese and wounding 20. Angry protesters, including many college students and other youths, poured into the streets in cities all over China. They threw stones, burned a US diplomatic residence, and forced the closure of American fast food outlets that had begun to proliferate throughout the PRC. Clinton swiftly apologized and shared with Jiang Zemin and the PRC military evidence of the accidental nature of the attack, but the regime made little effort to convince the Chinese public. Most Chinese doubted that the United States, with its sophisticated military technology, could make an error of such magnitude, yet Washington had no reason for such an attack and evidence is overwhelming that the embassy bombing was a reckless error.

Once again tensions gradually abated, in part because Clinton overcame Republican opposition and backed Chinese entry into the WTO. Clinton also affirmed China's MFN trade status. With the repression in Tiananmen still in mind, Republicans and some Democrats had opposed these moves and condemned China for political and religious restrictions among other human rights issues. Just weeks before the embassy bombing the US media heavily publicized a Chinese crackdown on a fringe religious sect, the Falun Gong, who mounted public protests outside the government complex in Beijing. China bitterly resented Western interference with its internal political policies, but at the same time craved international acceptance, hence WTO membership was a key issue. For the same reason China bid to host the Olympic Games. Beijing lost its initial bid but in 2002 won the right to host the 2008 Games, which set off a joyous celebration throughout the country, were carried off successfully, and duly enhanced China's international prestige.

The PRC strove for broader integration into the international community as its export-driven economy continued to grow at a rapid pace. China proved to be a reliable partner on nuclear arms control, though as with the United States this required little sacrifice, as the PRC already possessed nuclear weapons of its own. Nevertheless Beijing supported the NPT and signed the chemical weapons convention as well as the CTBT, which the US Senate ultimately rejected. China joined the Clinton administration and much of the world community in condemning India and Pakistan, the two bitter rivals that both conducted nuclear tests in 1998 in violation of the arms limitation treaties. India and Pakistan cited threats from each other but India also cited longstanding tensions with China as justification for becoming a nuclear power.

The West increasingly sought China's assistance in reining in North Korea's nuclear ambitions in the wake of a war scare in 1994. Under Soviet pressure North Korea had accepted the NPT in 1985 but renounced that position in 1993 and began work on nuclear weapons development. The Clinton administration made plans for a preemptive strike on North Korean nuclear facilities, a plan that would have alarmed China but moreover South Korea, which wanted to contain the North but believed that an airstrike might result in a resumption of the Korean civil war on the ground. At this point former President Carter intervened, traveling to Pyongyang as a private citizen and convincing the regime to allow international inspectors into the Yongbyong nuclear site. In a subsequent agreement North Korea agreed to cease plutonium production and in return Japan, South Korea, and the United States agreed to assist North Korea in building reactors for peaceful nuclear power with appropriate international safeguards.

Clinton maintained close relations with Japan, the cornerstone of the large US military presence in East Asia and a major trading partner. Japan depended on the United States for defense, especially in the event of conflict with China, as relations between the two Asian countries had remained strained for the most part since World War II. In 1994 the US-Japanese security arrangements came under strain as a result of a highly publicized gang rape by US soldiers of a Japanese girl on Okinawa, where some 47,000 US troops were stationed. After sometimes-tense negotiations the United States and Japan affirmed their security arrangements in April 1995, hence Japan remained the centerpiece of US East Asian military strategy.

The Clinton administration transformed US relations with its former bitter adversary Vietnam. In 1994 Clinton unilaterally ended the punitive trade embargo, which the United States had placed on Vietnam since the end of the war in 1975. The next year Clinton announced **normalization of US-Vietnam relations** and plans to build a new US embassy in Hanoi. For the first US ambassador Clinton sent Pete Peterson, a partially disabled Vietnam War veteran. By that time bank and finance corporations and shoe and soft drink companies, among many others, were eager to tap into the Indochina market. In November 2000 Clinton became the first president to visit Vietnam since the US withdrawal in 1973.

With his final term winding down Clinton made concerted efforts to forge peace agreements in Northern Ireland and the Middle East. In Northern Ireland Clinton marked a foreign policy success whereas his efforts to forge peace in the Middle East failed. The breakdown of the Clinton-sponsored Camp David Summit precipitated a new and violent phase of the conflict between Palestinian Arabs and Israel.

The conflict over British possession of Northern Island dated back for decades, including sometimes-violent resistance by the **Irish Republican Army** (IRA). In 1994 the IRA declared a ceasefire and Clinton, visiting Belfast the next year, sought to broker a solution to the conflict, which had interested him since his days as a Rhodes scholar in Oxford. In 1998 with US encouragement the British and the Irish governments signed the **Good Friday Agreement**, which granted legitimacy to differing viewpoints about the political status of Northern Ireland while establishing several confidence building measures relating to civil and cultural rights, use of force, and issues of justice and policing. Irish Catholic and British Protestant relations remained problematic in Northern Ireland but were more stable as a result of the accord.

Select Bibliography

Iriye, Akira. *Global Interdependence: The World After 1945*. Cambridge, MA: Harvard University Press, 2014.

Iriye, Akira, Goode, Petra, and Hitchcock, William. *The Human Rights Revolution and International History*. New York: Oxford University Press, 2012.

Naftali, Timothy. *George H. W. Bush*. New York: Times Books, 2007.

Sarotte, Mary E. *1989: The Struggle to Create Post-Cold War Europe*. Princeton, NJ: Princeton University Press, 2009.

Dumbrell, John. *Clinton's Foreign Policy: Between the Bushes, 1992–2000*. New York: Routledge, 2009.

Schraeder, John. *Intervention into the 1990s: US Foreign Policy in the Third World*. Boulder, CO: Lynne Rienner, 1992.

Glaurdic, Josip. *The Hour of Europe: The Western Powers and the Breakup of Yugoslavia*. New Haven, CT: Yale University Press, 2011.

Gibbs, David N. *First Do No Harm: Humanitarian Intervention and the Destruction of Yugoslavia*. Nashville, TN: Vanderbilt University Press, 2009.

Hirsch, John L. and Oakley, Robert. *Somalia and Operation Restore Hope: Reflections on Peacemaking and Peacekeeping*. Washington: Institute of Peace Press, 1995.

Eckes, Alfred and Zeiler, Tom. *Globalization and the American Century*. New York: Cambridge University Press, 2003.

Conroy, John. *Rwanda's Untold Story*, BBC Documentary, 2014.

Philpot, Robin. *Rwanda and the New Scramble for Africa: From Tragedy to Useful Imperial Fiction*. Montreal: Baraka Books, 2013.

Stiglitz, Joseph E. *Globalization and Its Discontents*. New York: W.W. Norton, 2003.

Klein, Naomi. *The Shock Doctrine: The Rise of Disaster Capitalism*. New York: Picador, 2008.

Shirk, Susan L. *China: Fragile Superpower*. New York: Oxford University Press, 2007.

15 Global War on Terror

Overview

The terror attacks of September 11, 2001, transformed US foreign relations virtually overnight. President George W. Bush proclaimed a "global war on terror" (**GWOT**) and launched US military invasions of Afghanistan and Iraq. Both wars proved costly and inconclusive. President Barack Obama continued the GWOT with a lighter US "footprint" on the ground as he pursued a graduated withdrawal of American combat forces from Iraq and Afghanistan. However, Obama continued US bombing and expanded the scope of the terror wars through increased drone attacks and targeted assassinations.

While the United States remained deeply embroiled in the GWOT, Obama attempted to "pivot" US relations toward Asia and Africa. Both initiatives reflected concern over China's steady rise and expanded ties with the non-Western world. US relations with post-communist Russia deteriorated sharply under both Bush and Obama. Several Latin American countries moved to the left in rejection of the Washington consensus. As Obama's presidency wound down the United States remained the most powerful nation in the world, but the limits of that power were apparent.

Response to the September 11 Attacks

Like the attack on Pearl Harbor 60 years earlier the September 11, 2001, assaults seemed to the public to be a "bolt from the blue." In actuality the threat of international terror strikes against American targets had been escalating for several years. On February 26, 1993, Islamic terrorists carried out the first attack on the World Trade Center by igniting a truck bomb in the basement-parking garage. Six people died and thousands were injured but the bomb failed to bring down the North Tower, as intended. On August 7, 1998, **al-Qaeda**, a Sunni Muslim terrorist group, carried out virtually simultaneous bombings of the US East African embassies in Kenya and Tanzania. The United States responded with cruise missile strikes in Afghanistan and Sudan, the latter destroying the country's major pharmaceutical factory after misidentifying it as a chemical weapons manufacturing plant. On October 12, 2000, al-Qaeda struck again with a bomb attack on the US destroyer *Cole*, harbored in Aden, Yemen, killing 17 sailors and injuring 39.

Figure 15.1 The September 11, 2001, airborne, hijacking attacks on the twin towers of the World Trade Center in New York City (above) as well as the Pentagon stunned the American public.

Source: Library of Congress, Prints and Photographs Division, LC-DIG-ppmsca-02121-0011

In Their Words

Statement by Osama bin Laden, issued on October 7, 2001, justifying the September 11 attacks on the United States

I bear witness that there is no God but Allah and that Mohammed is his messenger. There is America, hit by God in one of its softest spots. Its greatest buildings were destroyed, thank God for that.

There is America, full of fear from its north to its south, from its west to its east. Thank God for that. What America is tasting now, is something insignificant compared to what we have tasted for scores of years. Our nation (the Islamic world) has been tasting this humiliation and this degradation for more than 80 years. Its sons are killed, its blood is shed, its sanctuaries are attacked, and no one hears and no one heeds.

When God blessed one of the groups of Islam, vanguards of Islam, they destroyed America. I pray to God to elevate their status and bless them. Millions of innocent children are being killed as I speak. They are being killed in Iraq without committing any sins and we don't hear condemnation or a fatwa from the rulers.

In these days, Israeli tanks infest Palestine – in Jenin, Ramallah, Rafah, Beit Jalla, and other places in the land of Islam, and we don't hear anyone raising his voice or moving a limb. When the sword comes down (on America), after 80 years, hypocrisy rears its ugly head. They deplore and they lament for those killers, who have abused the blood, honor, and sanctuaries of Muslims. The least that can be said about those people is that they are debauched. They have followed injustice. They supported the butcher over the victim, the oppressor over the innocent child. May God show them His wrath and give them what they deserve.

I say that the situation is clear and obvious. After this event, after the senior officials have spoken in America, starting with the head of infidels worldwide, Bush, and those with him. They have come out in force with their men and have turned even the countries that belong to Islam to this treachery, and they want to wag their tail at God, to fight Islam, to suppress people in the name of terrorism.

When people at the ends of the earth, Japan, were killed by their hundreds of thousands, young and old, it was not considered a war crime, it is something that has justification. Millions of children in Iraq, is something that has justification. But when they lose dozens of people in Nairobi and Dar es Salaam [capitals of Kenya and Tanzania, where US embassies were bombed in 1998], Iraq was struck and Afghanistan was struck. Hypocrisy stood in force behind the head of infidels worldwide, behind the cowards of this age, America and those who are with it.

These events have divided the whole world into two sides. The side of believers and the side of infidels, may God keep you away from them. Every Muslim has to rush to make his religion victorious. The winds of faith have come. The winds of change have come to eradicate oppression from the island of Muhammad, peace be upon him.

To America, I say only a few words to it and its people. I swear by God, who has elevated the skies without pillars, neither America nor the people who live in it will dream of security before we live it in Palestine, and not before all the infidel armies leave the land of Muhammad, peace be upon him. God is great, may pride be with Islam. May peace and God's mercy be upon you.

The attacks by al-Qaeda and other Islamic terrorist groups constituted **"blowback"** against the United States as a result of a variety of actions and perceived offenses to the Islamic world. The Iranian Revolution of 1979, overthrowing the US-backed Shah of Iran, fueled Islamic fundamentalism and calls for holy war against the United States (the "Great Satan") and its allies. Anger and resentment gained momentum in the 1980s and 1990s over unstinting US support for Israel at the expense of stateless Palestinian Arabs. The al-Qaeda leader **Osama bin Laden**, from a wealthy Saudi family, was among millions of Muslims outraged by the establishment during the Persian Gulf War of a US military base in Saudi Arabia, home to the two holiest sites in Islam, the

cities of Mecca and Medina. Millions of Muslims viewed as a double standard US support for Israeli settlements in occupied Arab territories whereas
the United States had crushed Iraq over its invasion of Kuwait. Opinion polls
would show that Muslims also resented apparent US indifference to the deaths
of hundreds of thousands of Iraqis through war and the regime of economic
sanctions.

Efforts by the Clinton administration to brief the incoming Bush administration on the threat of terror attacks, including specifically bin Laden's determination to strike directly in the United States, had little effect. Thus the Bush
administration and the US pubic were stunned by the spectacular September 11
airborne hijacking assaults in which 19 militants armed only with box cutters
brought down both towers of the World Trade Center as well as the west wall of
the Pentagon. The response, however, was immediate, emotional, and sweeping.

Within hours the Bush administration lurched from disinterest in terrorism and pledges to carry out a "humble" foreign policy to proclaiming the no
holds barred war of unlimited scope and duration against a borderless, stateless enemy. Appearing before Congress, which subsequently authorized him to
"use all necessary and appropriate force" against any and all "nations, organizations or persons he determines" were implicated in the terrorist attacks,
Bush depicted a world divided between good and evil. "The advance of human
freedom . . . now depends on us," the president intoned. "Every nation, in
every region now has a decision to make. Either you are with us, or you are
with the terrorists."

The global scope and open-ended means employed in the GWOT thus
extended well beyond a campaign focused on the September 11 attacks. Within
a context of combating terror the Bush administration formalized a strategy of
"full-spectrum dominance" over air, land, sea, and space. The strategy sought
to ensure US military supremacy while safeguarding access to oil, gas, and
other resources and facilitating their exploitation by multi-national corporations. The strategy emphasized unilateral action, as the UN, regional, and multilateral institutions were considered hindrances to the assertion of US power.
The United States reserved the option of using overwhelming military force at
the places and timing of its choosing, including **preemptive war**. Under the
GWOT incarceration without trial and targeted assassination of alleged terrorists also became routine components of US foreign policy.

The blank check from Congress enabled key Bush advisers, notably Secretary of Defense Donald Rumsfeld and Vice President Dick Cheney, to promote
a second US war with Iraq. On September 11, with Bush taking to the air for
security reasons aboard Air Force One, Rumsfeld called a meeting in which
he emphasized plans to "hit S.H. [Saddam Hussein] at same time. Not only
U.B.L. [Osama bin Laden]." The terrorist attacks created an opportunity to
"go massive . . . Sweep it all up. Things related, and not." Rumsfeld, Cheney,
and several lower-level officials viewed the removal of Saddam Hussein as the
first step toward a transformation of the Middle East. Iraq, the second largest
oil producer in the world, could be modernized and oriented toward the West

Figure 15.2 Unlike his father George W. Bush had little experience in foreign affairs, which dominated his presidency in the wake of the September 11 attacks.

Source: Library of Congress, Prints and Photographs Division, LC-DIG-ppbd-00371.

while simultaneously removing one of Israel's inveterate enemies from power. The United States would continue to arm and befriend oil-soaked Kuwait, Saudi Arabia, and the United Arab Emirates as well as the authoritarian regimes of **Hosni Mubarak** in Egypt and **Pervez Musharraf** in Pakistan, thus isolating Iran, Syria, and Hezbollah in southern Lebanon.

Figure 15.3 Bush sought advice on foreign affairs from Vice President Richard Cheney, who had served the first president Bush as secretary of defense.

Source: Library of Congress, Prints and Photographs Division, LC-DIG-ppbd-00367.

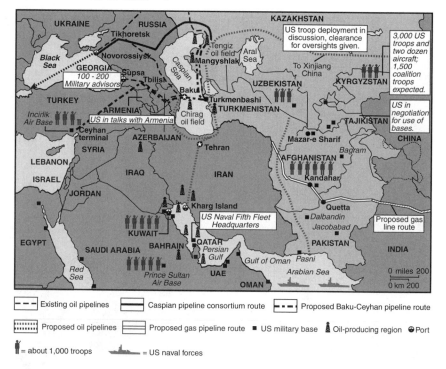

Map 15.1 Oil and military presence in Caspian and Middle East region.

Most of the world sympathized with the United States in the wake of the 9/11 attacks, which killed nearly 3,000 people and left scenes of horror and devastation. The United States thus enjoyed broad international as well as domestic support for a military assault against the **Taliban**, the Sunni militants who had no direct role in the attacks but had taken over Afghanistan and made it a safe haven for bin Laden and al-Qaeda. Ironically, throughout the 1980s Washington had armed and encouraged the Islamic holy warriors in Afghanistan in support of their long and ultimately successful war of resistance against the invading Soviet forces. Bin Laden had been instrumental in funding the war of resistance against the Soviets in the 1980s.

The anti-Soviet Afghan War, coming on the heels of the Islamic revolution in Iran, created broad international support for Islamic fundamentalism and spurred seemingly endless waves of jihadist volunteers. The Reagan administration pumped more than $3 billion into the Afghan resistance in the largest paramilitary operation in US history. The CIA supplied the Mujahedin with some 2,500 shoulder-fired Stinger missiles, which proved devastating to Soviet helicopters and aircraft. Following the Soviet withdrawal from Afghanistan in 1988–89, the CIA attempted to buy back the missiles at inflated prices but some 600 remained at large. In 1992 the Taliban capped their rise to power in Afghanistan by torturing, castrating, and executing the Afghan president and his brother and hanging their bodies in the street. Intolerant religious zealots, the Taliban had alienated many Afghans with repressive measures, including beatings, executions, subjugation of women, destruction of pre-Islamic culture and artifacts, outlawing of kite flying and

Figure 15.4 "Taliban, do you think you are safe?" This double-sided pictorial issued by the Department of Defense in the wake of the September 11 attacks depicts Taliban fighters struck by US missiles in their cave encampment. Two men are buried in the rubble and the other three sealed in their cave. In actuality, however, bin Laden escaped from Tora Bora into Pakistan. The Bush administration prioritized Iraq, allowing the Taliban to revive in Afghanistan after initially being driven from power by US-backed forces.

Source: Library of Congress, Prints and Photographs Division, LC-DIG-ppmsca-02031/LC-DIG-ppmsca-02032.

chess playing, and mandating that women cover their bodies and that men wear full beards.

Within weeks of the September 11 attacks the Bush administration inserted CIA officers and Special Forces into Afghanistan. Capitalizing on the unpopularity of the regime, and adding to the incentive with millions of dollars in payoffs, Washington recruited warlords to oppose the Taliban. Bolstered by sustained US and British air power, a coalition known as the Northern Alliance drove the Taliban from power in March 2002. Washington backed a new Afghan government under **Hamid Karzai**, but warlords, some fully as oppressive as the Taliban, actually controlled most of the rugged south central Asian nation. Having campaigned against "nation building," Bush sought to withdraw from Afghanistan as quickly as possible, leaving Karzai and the warlords in charge.

Aided by the indigenous population US Special Forces located al-Qaeda, including bin Laden, hunkered down in the caves of Tora Bora on the border with Pakistan. The limitations of the US alliance with Pakistan became readily apparent, however, as the Pakistani forces failed to block escape routes through the mountain passes as they had pledged to do. US Army and Marine forces could have been summoned to capture or hunt down and kill bin Laden but the Bush administration ruled out a direct US combat role in Afghanistan. Bin Laden thus escaped and defied the United States for 10 more years before US forces located and killed him at his secret compound in northeastern Pakistan in 2011.

The Bush administration, with the support of the UN, NATO, and other allies, withdrew from Afghanistan without providing an adequate security framework. Reconstruction funds proved inadequate and various reform efforts, divided up between Britain, Germany, Italy, Japan, the United States, and other allies, private corporations, and NGOs, failed to rekindle the Afghan economy, build up civil society, or rein in corruption and drug trafficking. The Taliban quickly regrouped and launched insurgent attacks from tribal regions along the Afghan–Pakistan border. By that time the Bush administration had already set its sights on an invasion of Iraq and thus paid increasingly less attention to events in Afghanistan.

The War in Iraq

Despite the unambiguous US triumph in the Persian Gulf War Saddam Hussein had been left in power in Iraq, which thus remained a foreign policy sore spot for the United States. Washington and its allies had been forced to police Iraqi airspace to prevent Saddam from attacking his own people notably opposition Shia Muslims as well as the ethnic Kurds in northern Iraq. International economic sanctions on Saddam's regime had turned Iraq into a humanitarian nightmare. While the dictator, his equally sadistic sons, and scores of Ba'ath Party insiders continued to live well, hundreds of thousands of people suffered and died from disease and deprivation. Moreover US intelligence services suspected Saddam of cultivating weapons of mass destruction (**WMD**), a category encompassing nuclear, chemical, biological, and other weapons capable of broad and indiscriminate killing.

During his two terms Clinton maintained the George H. W. Bush policy of containing Iraq. In 1993 Clinton ordered Tomahawk missile attacks on the headquarters of the Iraqi Intelligence Service over a foiled plot to assassinate former President Bush during a celebratory trip to Kuwait. Again in December 1998 the United States, joined by the British, carried out an intensive, four-day bombing campaign to "degrade" Saddam's potential to manufacture or stockpile WMD in the wake of his refusal to cooperate fully with UN-sanctioned international inspections of Iraqi weapons facilities. Earlier that year Congress passed the **Iraq Liberation Act**, which sent aid to opposition groups while calling for the overthrow of Saddam's regime. George W. Bush naturally resented the foiled plot to kill his father while several of his advisers wanted to remove Saddam in order to establish a pro-American government in Baghdad that would anchor perceived economic and security interests in the Middle East. Other advisers, notably Secretary of State Colin Powell, opposed such a plan. So apparently did President Bush until the September 11 attacks changed his mindset, precipitating the GWOT, with another invasion of Iraq as the centerpiece.

The trauma of the September 11 attacks, followed by a terrorist mailing of letters containing deadly anthrax spores, killing five people, galvanized the GWOT. Bush and some of his advisers realized that they had paid insufficient attention to the outgoing Clinton administration's warnings of the probability of attacks by al-Qaeda and other terrorists groups. Fearful that additional attacks might be imminent Bush went on the offensive. The Bush administration rejected CIA and other intelligence reports emphasizing the absence of any connection between Saddam and the al-Qaeda perpetrators of the 9/11 attacks. Far from being allies, Saddam and bin Laden detested one another. Led by Cheney, the administration strove to link Saddam with the September 11 attacks. With urging from the Bush administration Congress demanded strengthening of UN WMD inspections and authorized the use of force against the "continuing threat posed by Iraq." Rumsfeld pushed for war, not only to topple Saddam but also to showcase his plans to transform the military into a cost efficient, high speed, high tech force that could achieve military goals with limited use of ground forces.

As the Bush administration mobilized public support for war, the overwhelming majority of the international community urged reliance on the UN inspections of Iraqi facilities to contain the threat of WMD. Administration officials insisted that intelligence sources confirmed Iraqi possession of WMD but this assertion was false. Saddam stalled the UN inspectors and refused to admit that he did not in fact possess WMD, apparently because he feared such an admission would make him appear weak to his enemies in Iran and elsewhere. **Hans**

Blix, the UN chief inspector, insisted that the UN inspections were achieving their aims albeit slowly and should be allowed to stay the course. The UN and most world leaders believed war should be the last resort when all other diplomatic initiatives had been exhausted. The Bush administration, however, had made the decision for preemptive war, which Congress authorized with an enabling resolution.

On March 20, 2003, amid patriotic bunting and with a majority of Americans behind them, the Bush team launched **Shock and Awe**, a massive military assault on Iraq. The nearly 30,000 air strikes and some 20,000 guided missile attacks encompassed conventional bombs, indiscriminate cluster bombs, napalm, depleted uranium bombs, and chemical agents in the form of white-phosphorous bombs. The campaign of "asymmetrical warfare" devastated Iraq while minimizing US casualties. The US military used gendered language to define the goal of "rendering the adversary completely impotent."

As in the Persian Gulf War the US public, craving revenge for the September 11 attacks, reveled in the assertion of power and the revival of American exceptionalism that inhered in decisive military victory. Achieved in about three weeks, the military triumph appeared to vindicate Rumsfeld's strategy of high tech warfare requiring only minimal ground operations. As US officials had anticipated, the Iraqi people initially welcomed the American troops and delighted in the overthrow of Saddam, who was captured and in 2006 executed on the orders of an Iraqi court. On May 1, 2003, Bush, appearing in an aviation jumpsuit on the flight deck of the aircraft carrier *Abraham Lincoln*, declared that "major combat operations" had ended in a US victory in Operation Iraqi Freedom. A large banner in the background read, "Mission Accomplished."

The Failed Occupation

Within a month of the toppling of a statue of Saddam and the welcoming of US forces into Baghdad the illusion of victory gave way to a long and bitter occupation. Contrary to Rumsfeld's prescriptions the United States lacked sufficient ground forces to secure key Iraqi facilities and borders, to prevent looting, and ultimately to preclude the formation of a large-scale "insurgent" opposition. Troublesome signs first materialized with the looting, including most sensationally the historic National Museum of Iraq, famous for its rare collections from ancient Mesopotamian civilization. Absent orders to stop the looting or establish martial law, US forces stood by as looters reduced to rubble the museum along with other offices and businesses in Baghdad and other cities. Already reeling from the massive US military onslaught, most Iraqis were appalled at the ongoing destruction of their country and the theft of its most valued cultural artifacts.

Ignoring a substantive State Department study on how to approach the challenges of maintaining order and restoring public services in Iraq, the Bush administration left the occupation in the hands of Rumsfeld and the Defense Department. The results were disastrous. Presiding over the occupation, retired Army General Jay Garner sought to establish order by creating a new security force drawn from the Iraqi armed forces and backed by civil servants from the Ba'ath Party. Rumsfeld rejected this plan and joined Cheney in urging Bush to replace Garner with conservative diplomat L. Paul Bremer at the head of a new Coalition Provisional Authority (**CPA**).

While the Bush administration focused its attention on an increasingly futile search for Iraqi WMD, civil authority rapidly deteriorated throughout the country. Rather than attempt to reform or work with existing Iraqi institutions Bremer dissolved the Iraqi government, the Ministry of Defense, and all military, security, and intelligence operations. With US forces insufficient to secure weapons and munitions facilities, hundreds of thousands of unemployed, angry, and well-armed Iraqis mobilized against the US occupation. Over the opposition of some military leaders, Bremer received the backing of Bush, Cheney, and Rumsfeld for his decision to liquidate the Ba'ath Party, whose members included hundreds of thousands of largely non-political civil servants, teachers, engineers, bureaucrats, and technocrats who might have anchored a return to stability. Many instead joined the insurgency.

The Bush administration had anticipated a spontaneous rising of democracy in Iraq but instead its actions spurred violent sectarian conflict and the disintegration of the nation. Operating from the security of the fortified Green Zone in central Baghdad, the CPA divorced itself from the grim realities of life outside the secure foreign compound. Politically connected American appointees, mostly young, inexperienced, and devoid of Arabic, devised occupation policies ranging from economic reform to judicial procedures. Washington doled out billions of dollars in reconstruction and military contracts to private US contractors rather employing Iraqi businesses and workers. Iraqis lined up outside the Green Zone seeking jobs and assistance but rarely was their patience rewarded.

As the Bush administration shifted focus from the nonexistent WMD to democracy promotion, it sponsored the drafting of a constitution and supervised national elections with hopes of producing a government capable of establishing order and facilitating exploitation of the abundant Iraqi oil supplies. Majority Shiites joined by Kurds dominated the new government, as Iraqi Sunnis boycotted the elections. Virtually from the outset of the occupation Sunnis had battled US forces in Fallujah, the famed "city of mosques" located on the Euphrates River 40 miles west of Baghdad. In a sensational incident in 2004, four US contractors with the private security firm **Blackwater** were killed and two of them hanged from a bridge in the city after precipitating a clash with local forces. Livid, Bush ordered the Marines to strike back. Before the year was out the United States had conducted two major operations pounding Fallujah with airstrikes and artillery that killed hundreds and left the city in ruins.

While the Sunni forces resisted the US occupation, impoverished Shiites rallied behind **Muqtada al-Sadr**, son of a beloved cleric, who controlled an enclave of Baghdad known as Sadr City. The Mahdi Army, Sadr's paramilitary force, battled Americans in Sadr City as well as Karbala, Najaf, and cities and towns mostly in southern Iraq. A growing number of non-Iraqi jihadists, some affiliated with al-Qaeda, poured into the country through its unsecured borders. The Bush administration, which had failed to find the desired link between Iraq and al-Qaeda, had now created one. A multi-faceted conflict thus evolved featuring sectarian violence between Shias and Sunnis as well as an insurgency targeting US forces.

As the military situation deteriorated with a massive increase in insurgent attacks in 2006, US casualties mounted and increasing numbers of Iraqi civilians became victims and refugees. The Americans encountered hit and run attacks and suffered the effects of low tech but no less devastating homemade roadside bombs, or improvised explosive devices (**IEDs**). The United States fought back with night raids, house-to-house fighting, and aerial assaults. As US casualties mounted, the Bush administration summoned reserve forces and extended the tours of duty of US soldiers. Because the administration had anticipated a quick and painless victory with a light combat footprint, many of the US men and women lacked state of the art combat vests and other equipment.

The US public, largely enthusiastic during the Shock and Awe phase, turned critical, and Bush's approval rating plummeted. At the end of 2006 Bush expanded the American military presence by 30,000 in what was called "**The Surge**." The expanded forces would also pursue a different strategy of counterinsurgency warfare emphasizing protection of the civilian population in an attempt to win them over while building up the capabilities of the Iraqi government and military. Under General David Petraeus US forces focused on securing Iraqi homes, neighborhoods, towns, and cities rather than destroying them, but at the same time stepped up covert operations including assassinations of suspected insurgent leaders. The United States also paid off insurgents who had been fighting against it. According to one estimate some 100,000 Iraqis were put on the US payroll from 2007 to 2009. In Anbar province the United States spurred the "Sunni awakening" in which tribal leaders and former insurgents took US payments and agreed to fight al-Qaeda in Iraq, which had spurred opposition through bombings and coercion of the local population. Al-Qaeda in Iraq suffered a blow in June 2006 when a US targeted assassination killed its leader, Musab al-Zarqawi, a Jordanian and close ally of bin Laden. Meanwhile Sadr pulled back his Mahdi Army as the United States paid Shiite militiamen for work in public sector jobs.

By the summer of 2008, when the number of US forces returned to the pre-Surge level, the sectarian violence and the insurgency waned leaving Baghdad and other cities more secure. That same year, Democrat Barack Obama, a persistent critic of the war, pledged to withdraw US forces from Iraq. Following his election Obama undertook the gradual troop withdrawal, which culminated in December 2011. Washington had hoped to leave a stable Iraqi government in its wake but the country remained physically devastated and politically divided, as the sectarian violence continued.

The US-backed Iraqi president, **Nouri al-Maliki**, a Shiite partisan devoid of leadership skills, widened the sectarian rift. A US assessment noted, Shiite police units "cannot control crime and . . . routinely engage in sectarian violence including the unnecessary detention, torture, and targeted execution of Sunni Arab civilians." Iraq essentially devolved into a civil and sectarian war, with neighboring Iran backing the Shiites, Saudi Arabia backing the Sunnis, and the Kurds holding fast in the north of the country. As the conflict spilled over into neighboring Syria, which devolved into a crushing civil war, the Iraq War became increasingly intractable.

Costs and Consequences of the Iraq War

Iraq suffered more than a million deaths and millions of others were wounded and displaced. No one knows how many Iraqis died from attacks by US forces. Like General Schwarzkopf in the Persian Gulf War General Tommy Franks, the hero of Shock and Awe reiterated early on, "We don't do body counts." High rates of birth defects, cancer, malnutrition, and infant mortality plagued Iraq. Water supplies, sewage treatment plants, hospitals, bridges, and electricity supplies remained devastated. Illiteracy rates accelerated and many educated Iraqis, whose expertise would have aided the rebuilding effort, fled the country.

The Iraq War damaged the international reputation of the United States. Most of the world opposed the US invasion. The UN Security Council did not approve the US assault, making it illegal under international law. The Bush administration went to war backed only by a "coalition of the willing." While several countries formally joined the coalition, only Australia and Great Britain, an enthusiastic US ally under Prime Minister **Tony Blair**, provided substantive military assistance. Canada had supported the Afghan War but pointedly opposed US intervention in Iraq. The decision strained relations between the neighbors, which were salved when Ottawa announced that it would contribute to the postwar reconstruction of Iraq. While several small countries joined the "coalition of the willing" major powers such as China, France, Germany, and Russia opposed the US-led war. Especially resentful of French criticism, Americans in 2003 briefly renamed one of their favorite fast foods "freedom fries."

Beginning in 2003 revelations of torture and "extraordinary rendition"— capturing and removing prisoners to another country known to practice torture—further undermined the US international image. Leaks of information and disgraceful photographs led to investigations that unveiled the

Figure 15.5 In the early stages of the global war on terror the United States adopted a no holds barred approach encompassing torture of detainees in facilities ranging from Abu Ghraib in Iraq to Guantánamo Bay, Cuba. The myriad "enhanced interrogation techniques" employed by US forces included hooding, posing, and electric shock, as shown in this iconic photograph of a prisoner at Abu Ghraib.

existence of detention camps, including Abu Ghraib in Baghdad, the US military base in Guantánamo Bay, Cuba, as well as the outsourcing of detainees and torture to allied authoritarian regimes. The "enhanced interrogation techniques" employed by the United States included blindfolding, hooding, roping, beating, prolonged squatting and arm lifting, stripping, exposing to extreme weather, starving, near drowning, isolating, humiliating, simulating sex, sodomizing, sleep depriving, loud music playing, and threatening with menstrual blood, attack dogs, and even a lion. Amid the widespread outrage, both domestic and foreign, Bush condemned the "disgraceful conduct by a few American troops, who dishonored our country," yet the abuse had been widespread and authorized by the administration's policies in violation of international law.

Bush administration attorneys dismissed the Geneva and other international conventions that prohibited "cruel, inhuman or degrading treatment or punishment." A military intelligence email summed up the no holds barred approach, declaring, "The gloves are coming off gentlemen regarding these detainees." Under the US occupation, the prisoners lodged and tortured at Abu Ghraib, Guantánamo, and secret detention camps in countries including Egypt, Jordan, Lithuania, Pakistan, Poland, Romania, and Thailand, were "enemy combatants" rather than prisoners of war hence they had no rights under either US or international law. The United States thus claimed the right to detain and torture prisoners at will under an ad hoc legal rendering.

Compounding the problem a clear majority of those who were arrested and tortured were neither insurgents nor lawbreakers, but rather turned out to be innocent civilians. Their abuse fueled the Iraqi insurgency and spurred jihadist volunteers worldwide. Some of the minority of actual terrorists or combatants disgorged "actionable intelligence" under the pressures of waterboarding and other tortures, yet it was difficult to rely on information received under torture as people often confess to virtually anything to get the mistreatment to stop. For example, in the lead-up to the Iraq War a detainee under torture duly provided the false but nonetheless "actionable intelligence" that Saddam was allied with al-Qaeda.

The Iraq War proved costly to the United States, with some 4,500 combat deaths and tens of thousands of men and women suffering from the physical and emotional wounds of war. Overwhelmed, the Veteran's Administration failed to keep pace with the needs of the physically and psychologically wounded. The Iraq War monopolized resources and attention, allowing domestic problems to pile up while limiting the ability to carry out an effective foreign policy in other parts of the world. The war had cost the United States as much as $3 trillion, contributing to the yawning budget deficit that opened up during the Bush years and helped precipitate the Great Recession beginning in 2008.

During the Bush administration US military spending eclipsed the total spent by the rest of the countries in the world combined and included unprecedented reliance on private military firms (**PMF**s). "Without public debate or formal policy decision, contractors have become a virtual fourth branch of government," the *New York Times* pointed out. Blackwater and other PMFs received massive defense contracts absent competitive bidding and took a direct role in combat and covert operations. US casualties included more than 1,000 PMF employees. During the GWOT the national security industry far surpassed Hollywood and the music industries in size and scope. Military and government officials moved in and out of private defense industries, which became heavy political contributors especially but far from exclusively to the Republican Party.

The venerable military–industrial complex thus sprang to life under the GWOT. While the overall economy went into a tailspin defense industries and PMFs recorded record profits. Houston-based Halliburton, directed by Cheney before he became vice president, led the way with more than $20 billion in government contracts during the Iraq War, about three times what the US government paid to fight the entire Persian Gulf War. Major corporations—a veritable "coalition of the billing"—queued up for government contracts. They included Apple, Bechtel, Boeing, the Carlyle Group, Dell, the Fluor Corporation, General Dynamics, ITT, Lockheed Martin, and Northrup Grumman. DynCorp received more than a billion dollars to train the Afghan police and stem the drug trade, but neither was close to being a success story. Universities led by Johns Hopkins and MIT received millions in government grants. Outback shipped shrimp and steak dinners to the troops and then paid the retired General Franks to sit on its board of directors. Starbucks opened three stores at the Guantánamo detention center alone. Oakley provided state of the art desert boots and fashionable sunglasses. Taxpayers funded pro-military Hollywood films, NASCAR auto racing sponsorships, bowling alleys, and at least 172 military-owned golf courses. Pentagon and PMF personnel often flew first class, stayed in posh hotels, and sat in on elaborate conference proceedings. Notoriously resistant to audits, no one knows precisely how much the Pentagon spent on government contracts or the cost of the Iraq War as a whole.

In addition to profligate spending the GWOT also undermined American civil liberties. At the start of the Iraq conflict anti-war protesters took to the streets (as well as the Internet) where they were harassed and some arrested while receiving scant media attention. Meanwhile journalists, "embedded" within military units under a shrewd new Pentagon media policy, reported uncritically on the early phases of the "allied" war effort. On the home front the profusion of flags, yellow ribbons, and calls to "support our troops" tarred anti-war protesters with lack of patriotism. As the ubiquitous cliché averred, the troops were "fighting for our freedoms" hence the US military was virtually beyond reproach, even in the later years with the war efforts clearly foundering in Iraq and Afghanistan.

The **USA Patriot Act**, passed by Congress with virtually no investigation and signed into law by Bush six weeks after the 9/11 attacks, undermined privacy rights and civil liberties. The unsubtly named legislation authorized data mining of banking, medical, library, and other records and activities, including telephone conversations, email messaging, and Internet activity by millions of citizens. The communications giants AT&T, MCI, Sprint, and others willingly provided the US government with details on consumer telephone numbers and email addresses.

While investigating alleged links with broadly defined terrorist groups, the NSA and the FBI worked with local law enforcement to identify, bug, infiltrate, and harass Muslims and left-wing groups and individuals. Mosques and Muslim homes were invaded and searched despite having no connections with foreign jihadists. Angered by such infringements as well as attacks on Muslims worldwide, some American and European Muslims turned against their home countries and joined the jihadist movement. On two occasions Muslim terrorists tried but failed to blow up US airliners on which they were passengers. More successful in his attack was a Muslim-American Army psychiatrist, Nidal Hasan, who opened fire on the US military base in Fort Hood, Texas, killing 13 men and wounding 143 others.

In addition to the Patriot Acts—the original act was extended and renewed by both Bush and Obama—secret executive orders authorized spying on citizens while bypassing provisions for public oversight. The US government was "dangerously targeting Americans who are engaged in nothing more than lawful protest and dissent," the American Civil Liberties Union charged. In 2002 the Bush administration and Congress combined agencies and departments to create a massive new Cabinet-level **Department of Homeland Security** (DHS), which eventually employed nearly a quarter of a million people. The federal government became more secretive than ever, reclassifying government documents, blocking access to public information, even (until reversed by Obama) prohibiting photographs of the flag-draped coffins of US soldiers returning from the nation's battlefields.

As the GWOT evolved leaks revealed the massive and unprecedented extent of US government secrecy and data mining. In 2006 a new online organization **WikiLeaks** began publishing volumes of secretly leaked documents including top-secret information and "war logs" from the Iraq and Afghan Wars. The material included the *Collateral Murder* video of a US Apache helicopter strike that killed Iraqi journalists. US officials responded with alarm, identifying, trying, and imprisoning under the Espionage Act one of the leakers, Army Private Bradley (Chelsea) Manning. The WikiLeaks founder Julian Assange went into exile to avoid prosecution as did **Edward Snowden**, a US intelligence contractor and computer expert who in 2013 leaked thousands of documents exposing massive domestic and government surveillance operations including the private communications of US citizens. Snowden's leaks also revealed US phone tapping of close allies, including German president **Angela Merkel**, actions that sowed distrust and strained US alliances. Described variously as a traitor or alternatively a champion of freedom of information, Snowden received asylum in Russia while Americans began to debate the issues of government secrecy and the decline of privacy rights in the "age of terror."

Race, Religion, and Gender in the Terror Wars

The cultural factors of race, religion, and gender influenced American depictions and actions in the GWOT. Direct expressions of racial prejudice materialized but more often racial stereotypes blended with those of religion and gender in the cultural process of defining the terrorist enemy. Ignoring the sources of blowback, Bush depicted the terrorists as mindless fanatics devoid of any political purpose and simply out to destroy the American way of life. "They hate our freedoms—our freedom of religion, our freedom of speech, our freedom to vote and assemble and disagree with each other," he explained.

Taken by surprise in the stunning 9/11 attacks, Americans responded with masculine resolve in the aftermath of the wrenching assaults. While some European critics expressed concern about a warlike "cowboy" mentality as the United States went to war, most Americans, especially men, embraced the war and the expressions of strength and power that accompanied it. Bush frequently displayed masculine rhetoric and posturing, with one columnist referring to the Texan president's "gunslinger pose, his squinty-eyed gaze, his dead or alive one liners." As the Iraqi insurgency stepped up in 2006, Bush proclaimed, "Bring 'em on!" a remark he later regretted. As the conflict deepened Bush and others vowed to stay the course rather than "cut and run" in unmanly retreat. Bremer pledged not to pursue the past "limp-wristed" policies in Iraq. Once in office Obama, condemned by Cheney among others for being a "soft" liberal more interested in health care reform than national security, combated such charges with bellicose rhetoric and military assaults.

Gender fused with race and religion in depictions of Muslims, especially in popular discussion of the treatment of Muslim women. Taliban regimentation and subjugation of women helped justify driving them out of Kabul even though many of the warlords backed by the United States pursued the same repressive cultural policies. Americans and Europeans publicized the *burka*, an Islamic garment covering the full female body including the head and face. The Taliban and other ultra orthodox Muslim groups forced women to cover their bodies fully in public, yet most Muslim women across the globe wore only a headscarf leaving their faces uncovered. The Western obsession with the *burka* encouraged notions of Islamic societies as backward and uniquely and universally oppressive of women.

The ordeal of **Jessica Lynch**, an innocent looking, 19-year-old, blonde haired and blue eyed Army private from West Virginia, revived the captivity narrative, which had been deeply entrenched in American culture since the pre-Revolutionary conflict with Indians. In March 2003 Lynch suffered severe injuries after her company took a wrong turn and came under fire from Iraqi soldiers, who killed several of her comrades. The Pentagon and a compliant media claimed that Army Rangers then freed Lynch from captivity in a "daring mission" by fighting their way into the hospital in which she was being held. In fact she was not a captive but rather being cared for in the Iraqi hospital. There was no resistance requiring a "daring" rescue. In 2007 Lynch denounced the manipulation of her traumatic experience, but at the time she had been celebrated as the proverbial damsel in distress and an icon of Operation Iraqi Freedom. She appeared on the cover of *People*, made talk show appearances, and received a showering of cards and gifts.

Perhaps more than race and gender religion surfaced as an underlying cultural component of the American war effort. The Taliban, al-Qaeda, and Iraqi insurgents were invariably depicted as religious fanatics, an accurate description for many but not all of the Muslim resistance. The depiction obscured the deep-seated political grievances that lay behind the terrorist blowback assaults. Bush, like his staunch British ally Blair, was a "born-again" Christian who referenced the war as a "crusade" and like some previous presidents came to believe he had been chosen by God to lead the fight for freedom. Three days after the hijacking assaults, Bush asserted that the nation's "responsibility to history is already clear: to answer these attacks and rid the world of evil." There could be "no neutral ground between good and evil, freedom and slavery, and life and death." Popular evangelists condemned Islam and the Prophet Muhammad while lauding the righteousness and superiority of Christianity and Judaism. Franklin Graham, son of famed evangelist Billy Graham, declaimed in a Good Friday service held at the Pentagon that Christianity and Islam were "as different as lightness and darkness"; that Islam was "a very wicked and evil religion"; and that "there's no way to God except through Christ."

Obama Embraces the GWOT

Although his presidential campaign emphasized change and sharply criticized the Bush administration for its extra-legal policies of detention and torture, Obama continued and in some important respects accelerated the GWOT. During the campaign Obama condemned the war in Iraq while calling for more aggressive war against al-Qaeda and in Afghanistan. Early in his presidency Obama tried to assure Muslims throughout the world that the United States was not an enemy of their faith, rather only sought to capture or destroy those groups or individuals who had or would launch terror attacks. In 2009 this effort to reach out won Obama the Nobel Peace Prize, but his acceptance speech was surprisingly militant, emphasizing that "evil" existed in the world and war was sometimes necessary to eliminate it.

Under Obama the focus shifted back to Afghanistan, where ground had been lost to both the Taliban and al-Qaeda while the Bush administration was preoccupied with the war in Iraq. Although provided with reconstruction assistance by the United States, NATO, various NGOs, the UN and other agencies, the Afghan government remained economically and politically unstable. The reconstruction program was chaotic and ineffectual while Karzai proved corrupt, mercurial, and lacked authority over much of the country. In 2009 massive vote rigging allowed Karzai to claim reelection following a political campaign funded by drug lords, underscoring the inability to establish a viable government in Kabul, as in Baghdad.

Once in office Obama weighed hawkish advice from the Pentagon against the doubts of various advisers before authorizing a "surge" of his own sending some 30,000 troops to bolster the Karzai regime and to combat the Taliban. Obama insisted the surge was temporary and that he meant to terminate the direct US combat role in both the Iraq and Afghan Wars. In 2011 Obama completed the pullout of combat forces from Iraq, though he sent back advisers and reinstituted bombing three years later. He remained committed to pulling out of Afghanistan while extending the projected withdrawal date from 2014 to 2016.

Despite his pledge to end the wars, terminate torture, and shut down the US prison at Guantánamo Bay, Obama continued aggressively to wage the GWOT. Significantly, Obama thus institutionalized the GWOT as bipartisan, infinite in duration, and limitless as to fronts. The new president retained key military architects of both the covert and counterinsurgency war efforts and sharply expanded supposedly surgical strikes and targeted assassinations. He also backed off his pledge to shut down Guantánamo and other terrorist retention sites.

Surgical assaults and targeted assassinations carried out by unmanned aerial vehicles, popularly known as **drones**, fit Obama's style. Guided by a joystick from remote locations across the globe, the high-altitude, precision-guided drones unleashed deadly missile strikes before the victims had time to react. Moreover being unmanned there was no direct risk to American lives through the drone strikes. Both the Pentagon and the CIA cultivated drone programs and competed for primacy, which encouraged the growing reliance on them. Obama sought to centralize command over the drone program while expanding it.

Figure 15.6 Despite his quest to withdraw US troops from Iraq and Afghanistan, President Barack Obama's two-term presidency gradually became dominated by the ongoing global war on terror. Vice President Joe Biden (left), a longtime US senator with extensive foreign policy experience, urged Obama to reduce the US combat "footprint," propelling a reliance on bombing and targeted drone assaults.

Source: Library of Congress, Prints and Photographs Division, LC-DIG-highsm-03832.

The Bush administration had initiated drone strikes in 2002 but Obama dramatically accelerated their use on the rugged Afghan–Pakistan border and in Iraq, Somalia, and Yemen. In his first 10 months in office Obama authorized as many drone assaults as Bush had done in eight years. Sensational incidents of mistaken targets and high numbers of civilian casualties aroused opposition in all of the affected countries spurring new recruits for jihad against the United States and the regimes it supported. On several occasions Karzai condemned the drone attacks for the deaths of innocent Afghan citizens. The Pakistani government likewise demanded an end to drone attacks on its territory, some of which prompted anti-American demonstrations replete with flag burning.

Drone attacks became especially controversial in Yemen, contributing to the triumph of a Shia rebel sect, which in January 2015 stunned national security elites by toppling the US-backed government in Sana'a. The United States had invested millions in nation building in Yemen while at the same time targeting al-Qaeda affiliated terrorists. US assaults, backed by the pro-American Yemeni president, had killed hundreds of people, some terrorists but others innocent civilians. In 2009 a Tomahawk missile unleashed by a drone killed 40 Yemenis, including 12 women and 22 children. In December 2013 a drone mistakenly struck a wedding party for which the Yemeni government, financed by the United States, paid an indemnity of more than $1 million.

In 2014 Obama vigorously defended use of drones as the best means to eliminate individual terrorists and terrorist cells while avoiding direct intervention and a heavy American "footprint" that would be resisted and resented in foreign countries. The president acknowledged that innocent civilians sometimes died in the drone attacks as well as conventional bombing, though he contested studies suggesting that far more civilians than terrorists had been killed in drone assaults. Obama also defended the legality of drone use under domestic and international law, which many legal experts disputed, and insisted that Congress had been informed in every instance of drone attack. Obama additionally defended the targeted drone killing of a US citizen, Anwar al-Awlaki, a former Muslim imam in Virginia who had advocated jihad but was not, as Obama publicly claimed, "a leader of al-Qaeda in the Arabian Peninsula." Two weeks after the killing of al-Awlaki in September 2011, another drone attack in Yemen killed his US-born, 16-year-old son in the midst of an outdoor barbeque with his cousins. He had no known involvement with terror groups.

With Obama, the national security establishment, and, according to opinion polls, most Americans firmly behind the drone attacks, they became entrenched as the signature new technology in the evolving GWOT. The attacks were notably less popular inside the countries where they actually occurred and thus served as effective recruiting tools for al-Qaeda and other jihadist groups. Drone attacks took out individual terrorists, some of them key leaders, but assassinations, mistaken targeting, and the terror inspired by the drones undermined the quest to create stable and supportive governments.

The drone assaults rather served along with bombing, detention, and torture as rallying points for resistance.

Mounting Instability in Afghanistan and Pakistan

The counterinsurgency war in Afghanistan languished in the face of effective recruiting by the militants, Karzai's weak leadership, endemic corruption, civilian casualties, and dwindling international commitment, as some of the NATO partners withdrew their forces. The scores of billions of dollars in US military aid to Afghanistan dwarfed the amount devoted to civilian development. Much of the money went into profits for US contractors or bribes to Afghan elites. Washington pumped millions of dollars into the Afghan national police and Army but they remained largely ineffectual, rife with corruption, and infiltrated by terrorists, who periodically turned their weapons onto their American and NATO trainers. The Allies sought to win Afghan hearts and minds through food drops, vaccinations, opening schools, hospitals, and sponsoring elections, but poverty, more than 50 percent unemployment, growing numbers of refugees, a massive and deeply entrenched opium trade, and other social problems undermined the effort. Episodic sensational lapses of military discipline, including film of US soldiers carrying out mass burnings of the Koran and urinating on dead Taliban fighters, widened the opposition to US-backed rulers.

At the heart of the problem, Afghanistan was not so much a country as a grouping of tribes and clans ruled by warlords. Most of the Afghan Taliban were Pashtuns, the largest and most powerful ethnic group, whereas the Northern Alliance backed by the United States in the wake of 9/11 was comprised mostly of minority Tajiks and Uzbeks. The rugged Pashtun lands on the Pakistan–Afghan border provided an ideal haven for the Taliban, al-Qaeda, and other jihadists. The Pashtun clans and tribes, notoriously xenophobic, were not only hostile to foreigners they also had never been loyal to the central government. Thus the coalition efforts to bring Pashtun lands of the south and east under the control of Kabul spurred resistance.

Equally problematic was the supposed US ally Pakistan, which pursued its own agenda in Afghanistan, including collaboration with the Taliban, warlords, and other militants. Throughout its history the transcendent enemy of the Pakistani state was India, which had humbled it repeatedly in war. After collaborating in the ouster of the Soviet Union from Afghanistan the Pakistanis' main goal was to prevent the establishment of an Afghan government friendly with India. The Islamist Taliban fit this requirement, hence Pakistan was far less eager than the Americans to drive them out. Moreover, India supported the Northern Alliance that had initially replaced the Taliban in 2002. The Pakistani intelligence service, the **ISS**, or Inter-service Intelligence Agency, had deep ties with the Taliban, warlords, and clans, especially in the tribal areas along the Afghan–Pakistan border. The United States provided Pakistan billions of dollars but received limited cooperation in return.

Washington repeatedly pressured the government in Islamabad and it just as repeatedly defied the United States, backed by large segments of Pakistani public opinion. Pakistanis bitterly resented unilateral US military assaults on their soil, including the raid on bin Laden's compound, carried out in May 2011 without warning to the Pakistani government. Pakistanis were already livid over the shooting deaths of two Pakistanis by Raymond Davis, a US covert operative formerly with Blackwater. The Obama administration falsely insisted Davis was a diplomat and therefore had immunity from prosecution. The United States eventually paid the dead men's families $2.4 million in "blood money" to gain Davis's release from prison.

While relations with Pakistan verged on collapse, the Obama surge and revivified counterinsurgency efforts in Afghanistan sputtered in failure. The US and Afghan forces engaged in "**mowing the lawn**"—clearing an area of Taliban only to have "the grass" grow back a few weeks later, a persistent problem in counterinsurgency warfare. The Pentagon and Obama's civilian advisers remained divided over strategy in Afghanistan as well as other fronts in the terror wars. In 2010 Obama withdrew one commander for publicly criticizing the administration while his successor, General Petraeus, resigned amid a sex scandal with his biographer, with whom he shared state secrets. The effort to save Afghanistan further destabilized Pakistan, a nation equipped with nuclear weapons but increasingly torn by political unrest and ethnic and geographical divisions.

Committed to covert and counterinsurgency warfare, the United States made little effort to pursue negotiations with Taliban moderates. Some US officials urged negotiations to exploit factionalism among the Taliban, al-Qaeda, and other groups including the Haqqani network, named after a veteran Mujahedin fighter. In 2014 the Obama administration offered millions of dollars in bounties to rein in the Haqqani militants, who had close ties with the Pakistani ISS in the tribal borderland regions. The United States rejected the option of reaching out to Shiite Iran, inveterate foes of al-Qaeda and the Sunni militants, as relations with Tehran remained hostile.

The "Arab Spring"

As the GWOT unfolded the "**Arab Spring**" reform movement spread across North Africa and the Middle East. The movement encompassed growing demands throughout the Arab world for democracy, civil rights, curbs on state power and corruption, economic opportunities, and ultimately transformation of Arab identities. Demonstrations, facilitated by cellphones and social media, erupted throughout the Arab world, much to the consternation of entrenched monarchies and regimes, many backed by the United States. In 2009 popular protests advocating reform of the Islamic government in Iran were quickly snuffed out, but the Arab Spring gained momentum in other countries the following year.

The North African country of Tunisia sparked the Arab Spring, as reformers mounted street demonstrations against corruption and political repression to overthrow authoritarian rule in 2011. The same year in Libya the dicta-tor **Muammar Gaddafi**, a onetime supporter of terrorism who changed his spots and allied his brutal secret police with the United States in the GWOT, was overthrown and executed. Protesters forced out the president of Yemen and put pressure on myriad other governments across the Middle East and North Africa. Perhaps most significantly, a revolution toppled the longtime dic-tatorship of the US allied Mubarak regime in Egypt.

The United States responded to the Arab Spring with public rhetorical sup-port for democratic reform combined with private concern that the unrest would undermine the GWOT, access to oil, and other economic and cor-porate interests. In 2013 the United States and the Persian Gulf monarchies supported the return of military rule in Egypt following the overthrow of the elected government, which had spurred widespread opposition by attempting to implement Islamic laws. The United States allied with Saudi Arabia and the monarchies to repress Arab Spring demonstrations in Bahrain.

By 2015 the once hopeful Arab Spring had become an Arab winter. In addi-tion to the return of military rule in Egypt, Islamic fundamentalists overthrew the reform government of Yemen. Post-Gaddafi Libya fell into civil tumult, exacerbated by the arrival of foreign fighters. On September 11, 2012, ter-rorists attacked the US consulate in Benghazi, Libya, killing the ambassador and three other Americans. The worst violence erupted in the **Syrian civil war** in which the dictator Bashar al-Assad conducted a remorseless military campaign, including the use of chemical weapons. Under US pressure, with assistance from Russia, a longtime Syrian ally, Syria ceased the use of chemical weapons but continued conventional attacks against civilian targets amid the ongoing civil tumult. Hawks pressured Obama to do more to support the Syr-ian resistance, but the United States urged a negotiated settlement and offered only limited aid to the disparate rebel groups. The civil war continued, devas-tating Syria, killing more than 200,000 people, and spilling over into Lebanon, which remained plagued by violent sectarian divisions.

The GWOT escalated midway through Obama's second term as a new ter-ror group, **ISIS** (the Islamic State in Iraq and Syria) lashed out on behalf of Sunnis who had been targeted and victimized by Maliki's Shiite-dominated government in Baghdad. ISIS rapidly gained control of key cities and ulti-mately more than one third of the territory in Syria as well as Iraq, where the Maliki government fell. In September 2014, in the wake of a series of sen-sational ISIS beheadings of captives, Obama pledged that the United States would "degrade and destroy" the group without resuming direct US ground combat operations. The United States reintroduced some 3,000 US "advisers," however, while securing the participation of both European and Middle East-ern allies such as Britain, France, Jordan, Saudi Arabia, and Turkey.

Operating out of its massive air base in Qatar, the United States launched a punishing bombing campaign against ISIS, including for the first time direct strikes in Syrian territory. Obama emphasized the need for economic as well as military measures, including humanitarian assistance and a public information campaign to appeal to moderate and reform Muslims. Paradoxically, the campaign against ISIS Sunnis pleased US foes in the Shiite-dominated states Iran and Syria, in effect helping Assad to remain in power in Damascus and benefiting Hezbollah as well. As Obama's second term wound down, Iran was gaining influence by defeating ISIS on the ground. The GWOT thus carried on with ambiguous results at best and moreover with no end in sight.

Collapse of the "Peace Process"

Following the failure of the Camp David Summit in 2000, the Arab-Israeli conflict became increasingly violent, with the Arabs paying by far the heaviest price. In October 2000 the right-wing Likud Party leader **Ariel Sharon** sabotaged plans for the resumption of peace talks with a carefully orchestrated visit to the al-Aqsa Mosque, a Muslim holy site in Jerusalem. The provocative visit, underscoring Israeli claims to control of the holy spaces in Jerusalem, triggered the **Second Intifada**, mass demonstrations that became much more violent than the original Intifada. Over the next two years Arabs carried out suicide bombings while Israel carried out disproportionate military reprisals. A total of 325 Palestinians died along with 36 Israelis and 4 others. More than 10,600 Palestinians were injured compared with 362 Israelis.

The Palestinian uprising paved Sharon's path to power, as he won election as prime minister in 2001 and became a close ally of Bush in the GWOT. Bush fully backed Sharon, who was hostile to the so-called peace process, which thus broke down completely. Traumatized by Arab suicide bombings of civilian targets, Israel attacked Palestinian communities with lethal force, expanded settlements in the territories occupied since the 1967 War, and constructed a "security wall" as well as new roads and checkpoints isolating Arab communities and neighborhoods. In August 2002 a UN General Assembly resolution demanding an immediate end to new settlements and to the violence passed by a vote of 114–4 with only Israel, the United States, and the US Pacific outposts of Micronesia and the Marshall Islands opposed.

Under international pressure Bush announced a "road map" for peace and the creation of a Palestinian state, but the road came to a familiar dead end. In 2004 Sharon uprooted settlements and withdrew Israel from the Gaza Strip, a 140-square-mile territory packed with a population of nearly 2 million people, including hundreds of thousands of refugees from the previous wars. Bush lauded the Israeli withdrawal from Gaza, which paved the way, however, for an expansion of Jewish settlements aimed at permanent occupation of the West Bank and Arab East Jerusalem. Bush, backed by the powerful Israel Lobby as well as fundamentalist Christians, among others, declared that the recognized international boundaries should no longer constrain Israel. In 2006 Washington backed another Israeli military assault into Lebanon, including massive bombing of civilian targets, but Hezbollah held fast, forcing a UN-brokered Israeli withdrawal.

In 2006 the people of Gaza chose the more radical group **Hamas** over Fatah, the only Palestinian entity recognized by Israel and the United States.

Viewing Hamas purely as a terrorist organization, the United States and Israel refused to recognize the outcome of the free election and closed off the borders of Gaza, undermining its ability to function economically. In 2008–09 and again in 2014 Israel reduced the vulnerable strip of land to rubble, killing thousands of civilians while also carrying out targeted assassinations. Hamas lobbed rockets across the border into Israel, but these weapons paled in comparison with the state of the art Israeli military forces and did comparatively little damage. On both occasions the United States called for a ceasefire while fully backing Israel amid a chorus of international condemnation of Tel Aviv's often-indiscriminate use of force.

Upon entering office Obama called for an end to Israeli settlements in the occupied territories and urged a viable two-state solution, but these proposals fell on deaf ears. The US-educated Likud leader **Benjamin Netanyahu** disliked Obama, ignored his call for a two-state solution, and won support from the majority of the US public. By the time of the second assault on Gaza in 2014, the peace process was dead and the Israelis continued to build settlements aimed at absorbing the West Bank and East Jerusalem while relegating Palestinians to enclaves enclosed by roadblocks, checkpoints, and the separation wall. In 2004 the wall isolating the Palestinian enclaves had been ruled illegal by an advisory opinion of the International Court of Justice.

Republicans shared Netanyahu's dislike of Obama and they thus invited the Israeli leader to address US Congress in March 2015 to decry ongoing negotiations over Iran's nuclear development, which Netanyahu condemned as appeasement. In his first year in office Obama had reached out to Iran, making a deliberate reference to "the Islamic Republic of Iran" and offering the prospect of improved relations if Iran would comply with UN restrictions pertaining to the possible use of fissionable material in nuclear weapons development. Support for Netanyahu remained strong both in Israel, where he won reelection, and in the United States. From its creation after World War II to 2015 Israel received more than $121 billion in US foreign assistance, far more than any other country in the world.

The Terror Wars in Africa

The GWOT was truly global, with Africa emerging as a major battleground. Seeking to avoid a large troop presence in Africa, Washington relied on antiterror alliances, training, economic and military assistance, and covert operations including drone strikes. Much of the US counter-terrorism initiative centered on East Africa, where al-Qaeda had carried out the synchronized US embassy bombings in 1998. In the wake of 9/11 Washington opened a new military base in Djibouti, a tiny republic strategically located on the coast at the Horn of Africa. The base became the staging ground for drone assaults in Africa and the Middle East.

Foreign intervention turned Somalia, of which US officials had remained resentful since the Black Hawk Down disaster in 1993, into a battleground in the war on terror. Al-Qaeda and other militants were few in number in Somalia until Washington sent money and arms to the country's warlords, viewed as reliable partners in the GWOT. The US Navy and Special Forces also clashed with Somali pirates who preyed on merchant ships in the Indian Ocean. In 2006 Washington denied being behind a proxy invasion of Somalia by its hated enemy, neighboring Ethiopia, which in truth had been encouraged, funded, and equipped for the attack by the United States.

The foreign assaults took a heavy toll on Somali civilians, undermined the Mogadishu government, and spurred what the intervention had been initiated to avoid, the growth of al-Qaeda and Islamic militancy in Somalia. The US-Ethiopian attacks killed scores of citizens as a result of flawed intelligence and targeting, an all too frequent occurrence in the GWOT. On the ground the Ethiopian assault turned into a brutal occupation. As in Iraq and Afghanistan, the foreign intervention facilitated recruitment of Islamic militants from other countries to come to Somalia to wage holy war against the Christian Ethiopian invaders backed by the Christian Americans.

In the wake of the Black Hawk Down intervention the United States established a military base in neighboring Kenya, site of the bombing of the Nairobi embassy in 1998. The Kenyan government lined up for US military aid and other largesse being handed out to allies in the GWOT in the wake of 9/11. Kenya allied with Washington and bolstered the assault on Somalia, but paid a heavy price in return. Islamic militants carried out a series of attacks, which undermined a thriving tourist industry, and included a four-day siege of a shopping mall in Nairobi in 2012, killing some 80 people.

Special Forces worked to stymie the expanding terrorist network throughout Africa, including efforts by Islamic militants to take control of Libya after the fall of Gaddafi. Sudan remained deeply impoverished and bitterly divided over oil revenues and between Christians and Muslims, eventually leading to a split and the creation of a new nation of South Sudan after a referendum endorsed by Washington. US diplomats worked with the African Union and France, which had longstanding ties to northern and central Africa, to combat terrorism and promote economic and political stability. In 2014, with Americans back to eating *French* fries, Obama authorized $10 million in military aid to help French military forces combat Islamic militants in the northwestern African countries of Chad, Mali, and Niger. US covert operations also assisted in an effort to hunt down Islamic militants in Uganda while Washington remained allied with the Rwandan regime despite its continuing intervention in the Congo. In West Africa the United States sent security assistance to Nigeria, one of the more prosperous countries in Africa primarily as a result of oil revenue. In 2014 Islamic militants based in northeastern Nigeria carried out sensational terror assaults notably by attacking schools for women, taking some 200 as hostages and holding them for ransom.

In 2014 Obama, whose father was Kenyan, focused attention on Africa by hosting a historic summit in Washington. With the exception of a few pariah regimes, notably Zimbabwe under dictator for life Robert Mugabe, the leaders of all the African nations, more than 40 in all, attended the three-day gathering. The **African Summit** brought productive talks and a US pledge of $34 million in trade and investments in Africa. Funding for security remained paramount, however, with Obama pledging more than $100 million in such assistance to Ethiopia, Ghana, Rwanda, and other states. Some activists and Africa specialists criticized the military and security emphasis, arguing that more should be done to combat authoritarian leadership, violations of basic human rights, inequalities of wealth, and a US economic relationship with Africa still rooted in the extraction of resources.

Washington stepped up involvement in Africa not only to combat Islamic militants but also to contain China, which in 2009 replaced the United States as the leading trade partner with the continent. Keen on tapping into natural resources, especially oil and minerals, China went on a diplomatic "smile offensive" in Africa as well as in Asia and Latin America. The United States sought to shore up its position in Africa through increased aid, trade, investment, humanitarian relief, and disease control. The outgoing Bush administration made a major contribution with a $15 billion initiative to combat the AIDS epidemic, which remained at its most virulent in Africa, especially in South Africa.

Sino-American Relations in the New Century

Preoccupation with the GWOT deflected attention away from East Asia, where China was a rapidly rising world power. The Chinese economy continued to boom behind dynamic manufacturing and exports, with the United States the top purchaser of Chinese goods. China facilitated exports by keeping the prices of its products low by suppressing the price of the renminbi rather than allowing it to fluctuate in the world currency markets. As the US defense and military budget vaulted to unprecedented levels during the GWOT, a huge budget deficit opened with most of the American Treasury notes held by the Chinese. US officials criticized China for devaluing its currency, which facilitated a trade imbalance and the accumulation of debt. At the same time, however, China remained dependent on the United States as the leading market for its exports. Thus economic interdependence forged a tenuous equilibrium between the two world powers.

Several other issues complicated the Sino-American relationship in the new century, including human rights, disputes over espionage and intellectual property, relations with Japan, denuclearization of the Korean Peninsula, and China's sharply rising defense spending and muscle flexing, especially on the South China Sea. Rapidly increasing economic ties between China and Taiwan led to smoother relations and a diminution of the Taiwanese independence movement. Chinese relations with Japan remained tense even as economic ties continued to grow between the two traditional East Asian powers.

Human rights was a sore spot, as the United States continued to criticize China for its authoritarian Communist Party dictatorship and confinement of political prisoners, among other issues. US public figures, many from the entertainment industry, condemned Chinese repression in Tibet, but the US government recognized Chinese authority over the far western, predominately Buddhist province. Since taking over the province and driving the Dalai Lama into exile, Beijing incentivized Han Chinese migration and development in the region, provoking resentment from devout Buddhists and their followers. In 2008 China cracked down with tanks and combat troops on protesting Buddhist monks in the Tibetan capital city of Lhasa, killing, injuring, and jailing unknown hundreds. Sporadic clashes continued there as well as the vast northwestern province of Xinjiang, also the site of extensive in-migration by Han Chinese. Opposition to Chinese authority spiked in the twenty-first century amid the worldwide revival of fundamentalist Islam, which attracted increasing numbers of the Islamic Uyghur population in Xinjiang. As in Tibet China responded to unrest, demonstrations, and riots with arrests and military repression, which were stepped up in 2014 after a Uyghur suicide bombing in central Beijing.

The United States did not make a major issue of China's policing of its own provinces in deference to broader concerns, including nuclear weapons development in North Korea. After the war scare abated in the Clinton years, Bush ramped up the rhetoric with his provocative inclusion of North Korea as part of an "**axis of evil**." In his 2002 State of the Union Address, amid the feverish atmosphere spawned by 9/11, Bush linked North Korea with Iran and Iraq and invoked the World War II metaphor of an "axis" even though none of the three states were aligned and indeed Iran and Iraq were bitter enemies. In 2003 the North Korean dictator **Kim Jong-Il** responded by renouncing non-proliferation and moving to develop nuclear weapons. In 2006 the regime fired a missile near the coast of Japan followed by a successful test of a small nuclear weapon. China joined the international community in condemning North Korea for violating the non-proliferation regime and helped restart arms control talks.

While China often acted as a go-between, US relations with Pyongyang remained deeply problematic. Near the end of his presidency Bush removed North Korea from the list of terrorist states and Kim responded by destroying the cooling tower at the Yongbyon nuclear facility. Relations deteriorated once again under Obama, however, as the North Korean regime, which is economically isolated and dramatically underdeveloped compared with South Korea, responded with bellicosity to perceptions of encirclement by Japan, South Korea, and the United States. Military exercises carried out by the three powers invariably produced a menacing response including the firing of rockets, threats of war, and a termination of diplomatic engagement on the nuclear issue culminating in another North Korean nuclear test in 2009. International tensions thus remained high and potentially explosive on the Korean Peninsula.

Increasing assertiveness in the South China Sea, which China sought to dominate, brought conflict with its neighbors and posed a challenge to US military supremacy in the Asia-Pacific region. Fast rising as a military power, China built its first aircraft carrier, announced plans for expanded patrols of a blue-water navy, and attempted to strong-arm its neighbors out of the South China Sea by initiating conflict over islands scattered throughout the region. These actions precipitated a violent clash with Vietnam replete with casualties. China's drive for hegemony angered virtually all of its maritime neighbors including Japan, Malaysia, the Philippines, Singapore, and Vietnam, all of which thus welcomed a larger US naval presence.

Washington condemned the increased Chinese defense spending and stepped up its air and naval patrols in the South China Sea, which Beijing viewed as a provocation. The South China Sea became the scene of tense and sometimes deadly encounters. In April 2001 a Chinese fighter jet tracking a US reconnaissance aircraft just 70 miles off the coast of China's Hainan Island came too close and crashed, killing the Chinese pilot. The Chinese government detained the US air crew for 11 days until Washington, while declining to confess any wrongdoing, declared it was "very sorry" that the event had occurred. The incident, coming only two years after the inadvertent bombing of the Chinese embassy in Belgrade, angered the Chinese public as well as the government.

In 2011 concern about China's rising military power and assertiveness spurred the Obama administration's "**Asian pivot**" announced by Secretary of State Hillary Clinton. The pivot, according to the administration, was an effort to "rebalance" US strategy after an over-commitment of forces to Afghanistan and the Middle East, but was widely viewed as an initiative to contain China, protect access to the resources of Southeast Asia, and shore up alliances with Australia, Japan, New Zealand, and South Korea. The pivot repositioned Australia toward the center of US Asia-Pacific strategy, a point Obama emphasized in a speech before the Australian parliament in 2011. The two governments announced an increased US troop, naval, and air presence to complement beefed up Australian military forces and close cooperation in intelligence gathering. Under the rebalancing the United States bolstered offensive capabilities as well as installation of missile defense systems, all of which would be in play in the event of conflict with China.

Sino-American tensions periodically flared over mutual allegations of espionage and US charges of widespread Chinese theft of intellectual property. Despite these issues and the trade imbalance economic relationships remained extensive and the two governments engaged in regular dialogue. American and Chinese cultural exchange continued to expand as well, as tens of thousands of Chinese and American students studied in each other's country and tourists went back and forth in record numbers. At a surprisingly productive November 2014 meeting in Beijing, Obama and Chinese President Xi Jinping set goals for combating climate change and agreed on exchanges of

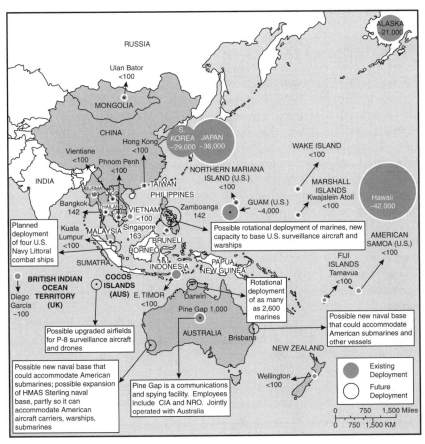

Map 15.2 US "pivot" in Asia. This map shows the current and planned deployment of American military personnel in Asia and the Pacific.

anti-terrorist intelligence and information technology. Though complex and fraught with potential stumbling blocks, Sino-American relations appeared manageable.

Southeast Asia

Despite lingering resentment over the US role in the 1997–98 Asian financial crisis, Southeast Asian nations largely welcomed an expanded American presence in the region to balance China's steady rise. As in much of the world the United States competed with China for access to markets, natural resources, and military bases in Southeast Asia. By 1999 Indonesia, Malaysia, the Philippines, Singapore, and Thailand had signed military access arrangements with the Pentagon. US relations with Cambodia, Laos, and Vietnam remained primarily trade-orientated. Washington joined other international groups in condemning human rights violations in Myanmar, where the rigid military regime kept pro-democracy Nobel Prize winner **Aung San Suu Kyi** under house arrest. In 2011 the effort began to pay off with her release and other reforms, prompting a state visit from Obama in 2014.

The onset of the GWOT expanded US military relationships spreading from the major US bases in Japan south to the Philippines and throughout maritime Southeast Asia. The Bush administration received mostly cooperative responses from Indonesia, Malaysia, the Philippines, Singapore, and Thailand, and in efforts to root out al-Qaeda linked jihadist groups. In October 2002 one such group, Jemmah Islamiyah, orchestrated a terrorist bombing of a nightclub in Bali, Indonesia, killing 202 people. Additional attacks followed, highlighting the jihadist threat to the region.

The GWOT forged closer ties between the United States and the Philippines, which confronted a guerrilla insurgency in the predominately Islamic southern island of Mindanao. After expelling US forces from the major naval and air bases in a surge of nationalism in the early 1990s, the Philippines had restored military ties (though not bases), joint training, and exercises, as both nations cast a wary eye on China. After September 11, 2001, Philippine President Gloria Macapagal-Arroyo offered unqualified support in the GWOT, which brought in hundreds of millions of dollars of security assistance to the Philippines. The United States sent elite troops into the southern Philippines where they joined the Philippine security forces in tracking down the Muslim insurgent group Abu Sayyaf and assassinating its leaders. Meanwhile Arroyo exploited the climate of suppression amid the GWOT to unleash death squads against the Philippine left.

The predominately Islamic nations of Southeast Asia, notably Indonesia and Malaysia, encountered higher levels of public opposition to their cooperation in the GWOT. The Bush administration's penchant for unilateralism in the Iraq War, the branding of Islamic states as "evil," and the revelations of torture sparked anti-American protests and limited the cooperation from Indonesia and Malaysia, though Singapore, concerned about the security of the Straits of Malacca, remained stalwart. Although accorded "major non-NATO ally" status, the Philippines and Thailand under public pressure withdrew their direct participation as part of the "coalition of the willing" in Iraq. Washington remained closely allied with both, however, and in 2015 carried out military maneuvers with the Thai military dictatorship after it overthrew the elected government and instituted press censorship and political repression.

Failure of the Russian "Reset"

Relations with Russia, which had appeared promising at the end of the cold war, deteriorated at first gradually and then precipitously in the twenty-first century. The Russians had long criticized growing US unilateralism in the wake of the demise of the Soviet Union. They had opposed the US war in Kosovo, were alarmed by NATO expansion, condemned the invasion of Iraq, and protested the US pursuit of a defensive weapons shield and refusal to approve a comprehensive test ban treaty, which Russia had ratified.

In 2002 **Vladimir Putin**, the former KGB director who took over as Russian president in 2000 condemned Bush for his decision to abrogate the 1972 anti-ballistic missile treaty in deference to aggressive pursuit of missile defense. However, with Russia having fought its own "terror wars" in Chechnya and other breakaway provinces, Putin largely cooperated with the GWOT. Diplomacy thus continued and culminated in 2002 with the signing of the Strategic Offensive Reductions Treaty (**SORT**) further reducing the two powers' nuclear arsenals. Relations quickly deteriorated, however, over Bush's decision to place defensive missile interceptors in the formerly Soviet allied states of Czechoslovakia and Poland.

Consistent with its general condemnation of the Bush administration's policies, Obama entered office advocating a "**Russian reset**" to improve diplomatic relations. Obama deferred the planned deployments in Poland and the Czech Republic while securing Russian support for the effort to head off nuclear weapons development in Iran. Obama and Dmitry Medvedev, Putin's successor, signed an interim arms control agreement and then in 2009 a major accord, the **New START Treaty**, further reducing the number of deployed warheads, weapons launchers, and nuclear weapons equipped heavy bombers. Obama won broad support from Congress for what he called "the most significant arms control agreement in nearly two decades." Russia also ratified the treaty, which took effect in 2011.

Russian-American relations deteriorated rapidly in Obama's second term, culminating in the **Ukraine border crisis**. Relations were already deeply strained before the crisis erupted in the former Soviet Republic. The Russians charged the US-led NATO alliance with carrying out a strategy of economic and geopolitical encirclement as if the cold war remained in force. Washington did little to assuage Russian concerns, as NATO commander General James Jones, later Obama's national security adviser, acknowledged in 2006, "NATO is developing a special plan to safeguard oil and gas fields in the [Caspian Sea] region . . . Our strategic goal is to expand to Eastern Europe and Africa." Russia remained deeply concerned about the expansion of US missile defense systems, which the Obama administration deployed in Poland, Romania, Turkey, and on Navy destroyers entering the Black Sea.

The Russians thus determined to act forcefully to retain influence over Ukraine. In 2013, with Ukraine's economy deteriorating President Viktor Yanukovych turned to Moscow for financial support, an action that spurred violent street protests by proponents of Ukraine joining the EU and thus orienting West rather than East. An interim agreement to restore order broke down, the protesters forced Yanukovych to flee the country, and Washington promptly recognized the unelected government. This action, in the wake of the decades of NATO expansion as well as previous efforts to "fast-track" Ukraine into the Western camp angered Putin, who had reassumed the presidency. A hostile

Ukraine aligned with NATO could close off Russian access to the country's most important naval base in the Crimea Peninsula on the Black Sea. Accordingly in March 2014 Putin annexed Crimea, sparking condemnation in the West and charges of "Russian aggression" reminiscent of the cold war. Most ethnic Russians backed Putin in the conflict with Ukraine.

The conflict escalated as fighting broke out in the Donbass region of eastern Ukraine, heavily populated by Russians as well as Ukrainians. The casualties of the war included 298 passengers on a Malaysian civilian airliner, shot down in the airspace over the conflict in July. Washington and the Ukrainians blamed the shoot down on the Russian separatists, who denied the charge. An investigation was ongoing in 2015. As the conflict accelerated the United States entered into informal military collaboration with the Ukrainian government in Kiev and successfully urged the EU to implement a broad range of sanctions against Russia for violating Ukrainian territorial integrity. By 2015 efforts continued to forge a lasting ceasefire in a conflict that had killed thousands and ushered in a revival of cold war hostility, threatening the future of nuclear arms control and myriad other global security issues requiring American, EU, and Russian cooperation.

US-Latin American Relations in the New Century

While the United States waged the GWOT Latin America moved to the left in the new century. In Brazil the election in 2002 of Labor Party leader **Luiz Lula da Silva** spurred a burst of social and economic reforms aimed at raising living standards in defiance of the Washington consensus. The new president cut the national poverty rate in half, down to 11 percent, but Brazilians continued to struggle and demand health, education, and social reform. In 2013 US-Brazilian relations deteriorated sharply over revelations from the Snowden leaks that the NSA had tapped the phone calls and emails of the new Brazilian president Dilma Rousseff. She condemned the United States for the spying and canceled a scheduled state dinner at the White House.

Washington remained hostile to Venezuela's **Hugo Chávez**, who in 2012 easily won his fourth term as president, but died the following year from cancer. In the constitutionally mandated presidential election of 2013, the Chávez ally Nicolás Maduro won a narrow victory. In 2014–15 hoarding produced shortages of food products and other essential goods while declining oil prices cut into Venezuela's substantial export revenues. Barricades and street protests materialized in the wealthier neighborhoods of Caracas, as elites sought to overthrow the *Chavista* government now that Chávez was gone. The protesters received overt as well as covert support from Washington, which in 2015 applied new sanctions against the constitutional government.

The left remained ensconced in defiance of the Washington consensus in Argentina, Bolivia, Chile, Ecuador, and Uruguay. In Chile **Michelle Bachelet**, a physician and a socialist whose father, an Air Force general, had been tortured to death following the 1973 US-backed military coup, became the first Chilean president since 1932 to win reelection. In Argentina as in Chile a left-leaning woman, Cristina Fernández, won a second term as president in 2011. In Bolivia Evo Morales, first elected in 2006, won a third term as president in 2014, bolstering his agenda of constitutional reform, poverty reduction, education and literacy, and health reform while condemning the legacies of the Washington consensus. Like Morales, Rafael Correa of Ecuador won the presidency in 2006, embraced Chávez-style social reform, opposed corporate influence, and twice won reelection. Ollanta Humala, the center-left president of Peru in 2014, pursued modest redistribution of wealth but was more open to US investments.

The United States continued to fund and support the right-wing government in Colombia, which provided a base to monitor and try to contain the left in the neighboring states Bolivia, Ecuador, Peru, and Venezuela. The corporate friendly Bogotá government adhered to the Washington consensus, enabling resource extraction including oil in return for massive US financial and military assistance. From 2000 to 2011 Washington pumped more than $8 billion into **Plan Colombia** under which the left-wing FARC rebels were branded "narco-terrorists" for their support of the peasant coca farmers. Unstated was the Colombian government's collusion with the drug cartels and right-wing paramilitaries, responsible for the deaths and disappearance of masses of people. FARC also employed violence as well as kidnapping and ransom, as the Colombian people continued to bear the brunt of the internecine conflict. Finally, in 2012 President Juan Santos called for a negotiated settlement with the FARC rebels in an effort to bring an end to a decades-long guerrilla war that had killed an estimated 220,000 Colombians and displaced millions more. Cuba took the lead hosting negotiations in Havana, which produced some interim agreements but as of 2015 had not led to a comprehensive settlement or an end to the violence.

US relations with Mexico remained stable despite seemingly insoluble drug trafficking and immigration issues. As in Colombia Washington pumped millions of dollars into the war on drugs in Mexico without making a substantial dent in the supply. Under the Obama administration a botched US government initiative, **Operation Fast and Furious**, sponsored illegal gun sales to the Mexican drug cartels in an effort to identify the buyers and sellers of guns and drugs. Drug sales and related killings only increased, leading to a promised crackdown by Mexican president Enrique Nieto following his election in 2012. Nieto and Washington pursued cooperation on economic growth and energy supplies but immigration remained a thorny issue, as the Republican dominated US Congress refused Obama's call to pass immigration reform.

In 2006 Congress did pass the **Secure Fence Act**, authorizing the construction of additional border fencing by the DHS. The increasingly formidable walls and fences, made of reinforced steel topped with cyclone barbwire, underscored the desire for a permanent barrier as the solution to illegal immigration. However, about half of the illegal immigrants living in the United States overstayed their visas rather than crossing the border illegally, an issue that fortifying the border did not address. Moreover seemingly no amount of walls and fences could bring a halt to the infiltration by tunneling, circumventing, and other forms of access. As then Arizona Governor and later Secretary of DHS Janet Napolitano advised in 2006, "Show me a 50-foot wall and I'll show you a 51-foot ladder."

Concerns about border infiltration heightened in 2013 when tens of thousands of unaccompanied minors, refugees from gang violence in Central America, gained entry into the United States. The Obama administration voiced sympathy but moved to deport the children who had little means to prove they had "credible fear" of violence if they returned home, the standard for gaining asylum. In 2014 Obama summoned the presidents of El Salvador, Guatemala, and Honduras to the White House in an effort to halt the flow of the migrant children to the unwelcoming US southern border. The crisis over the child victims underscored the deprivation, drug trafficking, and violence that wracked Central America. A US-backed coup overthrew the Honduran government in 2009 while left-wing governments clung to power in El Salvador and Nicaragua. Panama and Costa Rica were more stable but the entire isthmus faced severe economic challenges and the potential for political unrest.

The United States continued to police the Caribbean and in the case of Haiti supported the overthrow of the elected government of **Jean-Bertrand Aristide** in 2004. The popular Catholic priest, Haiti's first democratically elected president, defied the vested interests of the island elite and the Washington consensus. Aristide instead instituted a variety of reforms including health care, literacy, land reform, low-cost housing, food distribution, and curbs on Haitian military abuses of its own people. As a result of his defiance of the US-mandated market driven economic program the Bush administration backed the extra-legal coup that forced Aristide into exile in Africa. Haitian elites backed by Washington precluded Aristide's party from participating in national elections in 2010, the same year an earthquake heaped more devastation on Haiti. The next year Aristide returned to Haiti but the Obama administrations maintained support for the one-man rule of US-friendly businessman Michel Martelly.

Puerto Rico and the Virgin Islands remained relatively stable US colonial possessions, although Puerto Rico inched closer to conducting another referendum on statehood backed by funding from the Obama administration. The governor in San Juan opposed statehood, however, a position backed by the Republican Party on the mainland, which feared the Hispanic island would become a Democratic stronghold. The United States conducted robust trade, aid, and tourism with the Dominican Republic, which also proved a reliable partner on security issues in the Caribbean Basin. The Dominican Republic backed the right wing in neighboring Haiti, which mirrored its own penchant for jailing and killing Haitian refugees and political opponents.

In 2015 Obama announced a major policy shift, affording **diplomatic recognition of Cuba**. Obama argued that recognition and expanded travel and cultural ties between Cuba and the United States was a more productive policy than the decades long and failed efforts to isolate and destroy the Marxist regime. President **Raúl Castro**, Fidel's brother and successor, enacted reforms creating independent space between the Communist Party and the Cuban government, but the island continued to grapple with severe economic challenges. Virtually all Latin American states, long opposed to the US effort to undermine the Cuban government, applauded Obama's initiative. Conversely, many Republicans and the Miami-based Cuban exile community sharply opposed any efforts to improve US-Cuban relations unless they entailed overthrowing the regime.

US proximity, economic influence, cultural exchange, tourism, human rights, and other forms of soft power assured lasting influence in Latin America. On the other hand the series of leftist victories, with many of the campaigns centered on criticism of US intervention and the Washington consensus, underscored deep-seated strains in hemispheric relations.

Select Bibliography

Coll, Steve. *Ghost Wars: The Secret History of the CIA, Afghanistan, and bin Laden, from the Soviet Invasion to September 10, 2001*. New York: Penguin Press, 2004.

Bamford, James. *A Pretext for War: 9/11, Iraq, and the Abuse of America's Intelligence Agencies*. New York: Anchor Books, 2005.

Mamdani, Mahmood. *Good Muslim, Bad Muslim: America, the Cold War, and the Roots of Terror*. New York: Pantheon, 2004.

Bird, Tim and Marshall, Alex. *Afghanistan: How the West Lost Its Way*. New Haven, CT: Yale University Press, 2011.

Filkins, Dexter. *The Forever War*. New York: Vintage Books, 2009.

Caldwell, Dan. *Vortex of Conflict: U.S. Policy toward Afghanistan, Pakistan, and Iraq*. Stanford, CA: Stanford University Press, 2011.

Scahill, Jeremy. *Dirty Wars: The World Is a Battlefield*. New York: Nation Books, 2013.

Amar, Paul and Prashad, Vijay. *Dispatches from the Arab Spring: Understanding the New Middle East*. Minneapolis: University of Minnesota Press, 2013.

Johnson, Chalmers. *Blowback: The Costs and Consequences of American Empire*. New York: Metropolitan Books, 2000.

Smith, Charles D. *Palestine and the Arab-Israeli Conflict: A History with Documents*. New York: St. Martin's Press, 2010.

Cole, Juan. *Engaging the Muslim World*. New York: Palgrave Macmillan, 2009.

Singer, P. W. *Corporate Warriors: The Rise of the Privatized Military Industry*. Ithaca, NY: Cornell University Press, rev. ed., 2008.

Cohen, Warren I. *America's Response to China: A History of Sino-American Relations*. New York: Columbia University Press, 2013.

Stent, Angele. *The Limits of Partnership: US-Russian Relations in the Twenty-First Century*. Princeton, NJ: Princeton University Press, 2014.

Grandin, Greg. *Empire's Workshop: Latin America, the United States, and the Rise of the New Imperialism*. New York: Henry Holt, 2007.

16 Diplomacy of the Future

Overview

Historians can analyze the past but they cannot with any certainty predict the future. What is certain, however, is that the world has become increasingly interconnected and interdependent. Nationalism remains powerful, but global and transnational forces are increasingly prominent. Moreover the critical foreign policy challenges of the present and future—militarization and terror, WMD, population growth, poverty and disease, human rights, environmental degradation and climate change—all transcend national boundaries. More than ever before, diplomacy and seeking out of global solutions are essential.

The Future of US Global Leadership

The GWOT, the spread of advanced weaponry, and WMD all pose major challenges for US foreign policy and the global future. Religious fanaticism, growing global inequalities, and unresolved ethnic and geopolitical conflicts were among the factors that continued to fuel terrorism. The prospects of early resolution of the GWOT appeared remote, raising the questions of how long it will last and how it can be brought to an end.

Also uncertain is the future of US global leadership as the twenty-first century evolves. A combination of economic and military might as well as the soft power appeal of American democracy and consumerism vaulted the United States to global leadership and kept it there for decades. As of 2015 US economic, political, and diplomatic relations with Canada, Europe, and Japan remained deeply intertwined and a source of strength despite periodic disagreement. The United States enjoyed strong trade and diplomatic relationships with many African, Asian, and Latin American countries, though influence over the latter had diminished.

The so-called **BRIC countries** (Brazil, Russia, India, and China) can be expected to play increasingly prominent roles in world affairs and possibly challenge US global leadership. BRIC were in no position to displace the United States but at least some of them, notably China, had the potential to do so. However, despite its enormous economic growth, China faced equally enormous challenges of meeting the demands of a teeming population, widespread corruption, absence of representative government, environmental degradation, and tensions with its neighbors. Although functioning democracies, India and Brazil faced similar domestic challenges even as their economies grew dramatically albeit unevenly. The weakest of the four was Russia, plagued by political reaction, corruption, ethnic divisions, and reduced international support in the wake of the heavy hand it played in Ukraine. However, the possibility of a renewed alliance between Russia and China—both subject to criticism from Europe, Japan, and the United States—bore watching as the twenty-first century evolved.

Clearly the economic and political clout of the United States, which constituted less than 5 percent of the world's population, far exceeded its size, a disparity that could be expected to narrow in the coming years. It also remains to be seen how long the United States can maintain a defense budget roughly equal to the rest of the world combined. US military spending and arms sales (about 44 percent of the world total in 2014) dwarfed that of its closest competitors. Throughout the nuclear age the United States placed more emphasis on researching, developing, and deploying new military technology than control of nuclear weapons and other WMD. The United States, its allies, and the UN now labor to halt the spread of WMD through diplomacy and possibly force. Countries such as North Korea, which has nuclear weapons, and Iran, which does not but may seek to develop them, are potential sites of conflict. The same can be said for bitter and nuclear-armed adversaries, India and Pakistan.

World population growth promises to put enormous strain on global resources and environments with profound implications for US foreign policy and international relations generally. World population doubled from 3 billion in 1950 to 6 billion in 2000 and may double again by mid-century or soon thereafter. Rising population and diminishing resources create economic challenges and heighten ethnic and religious differences, producing violent conflict and outbursts of genocide. A densely crowded world exacerbates problems pertaining to food, water, shelter, and disease. As the AIDS crisis, influenza epidemics, and the threat of the spread of the Ebola virus showed, disease is a global threat that requires the cooperation of nations working in concert with the UN World Health Organization.

The massive growth of NGOs and the rise of international norms pertaining to health and human rights offer hope for the global future. An increasingly united international community has condemned and sought to curb genocide, abuse of women and children, political imprisonment, torture, and internal police repression. The UN, most of its member governments, and NGOs promote free elections as well as political pressure and sanctions against violators. As the world's preeminent power, the United States will play a critical role in determining whether enforcement of human rights will be selective, as often has been the case, or universal.

US Environmental Diplomacy and Climate Change

Arguably the greatest threat to the global future is **climate change**, which will exacerbate all of the problems discussed above. On the other hand, effective action to combat climate change could become a source of strength in encouraging higher levels of international cooperation. Thus far, however, such efforts have been halting and ineffective. Climate change has not been a high priority of US foreign policy hence the nation has displayed little global leadership on the issue.

Effective environmental diplomacy requires scientific research demonstrating the need for protection or preservation and the will to act accordingly. Since the early twentieth century environmental protection frequently has been sacrificed to economic self-interest. Early twentieth century efforts to control fisheries, for example, largely failed because nations and fishermen prioritized economic self-interest over concern about the depletion of the resource. On the other hand, the Migratory Bird Treaty Act of 1918 between Britain, Canada, and the United States successfully protected eagles and other threatened bird species. The birds were more popular than fish and protective measures caused little economic sacrifice hence the protective treaty was secured.

Energy and environmental concerns evolved in tandem and grew especially pronounced in World War II and the cold war. Both global conflicts

Figure 16.1 The remnants of a miniature golf course on the Gulf Coast in Biloxi, Mississippi in the wake of Hurricane Katrina in 2005. The massive Category One storm killed nearly 2,000 people and caused billions of dollars in damages.

Source: Library of Congress, Prints and Photographs Division, LC-DIG-highsm-04858.

underscored the relationship between resources, especially oil, and national security. The advent of nuclear weapons called attention to the potential for human destruction of the planet. As biological and ecological sciences produced more knowledge, environmental consciousness grew. Rachel Carson's remarkable campaign against spraying of the toxic herbicide DDT, culminating in her pivotal book *Silent Spring* (1962), brought new energy to environmental protection. In the United States the inauguration of **Earth Day** and the creation of the Environmental Protection Agency, both in 1970, heightened environmental consciousness.

The environmental movement was a generation ahead of its time, anticipating the globalization of the 1990s by urging people to "think globally." In 1972 growing global environmental awareness led to the **Stockholm Conference**, formally the UN Conference on the Human Environment. The Stockholm summit emphasized environmental protection while still pursuing economic growth through "sustainable development" policies. While worldwide environmental consciousness expanded so did global population, Third World development, consumerism, and dependence on fossil fuels, all of which took a toll on the natural environment including wildlife. By the end of the 1970s a series of pressing environmental issues demanded attention including ozone depletion, acid rain, massive clear cutting of rain forests, and the rapid destruction of flora and fauna.

By the time of the UN "Earth Summit" in Rio de Janeiro, Brazil, in 1992, climate change had been added to the list of pressing environmental concerns. The **Rio Summit** focused attention on global environmental deterioration but failed to enact measures that would actually limit deforestation, reduce emission of greenhouse gases, and preserve biodiversity. The United States, the world's greatest consumer of energy and leading emitter of greenhouse gases at the time, opposed binding agreements. Likewise representatives of developing nations argued that their economies should not be limited and in effect punished because of the environmental damage already done by developed nations. The Rio Summit underscored the main challenge of the global environmental movement: convincing nations to compromise their perceived national economic interests for the betterment of the planet as a whole.

In 1997 growing awareness of global warming and climate change led to negotiation of the UN sponsored **Kyoto Protocol** in which industrialized nations agreed on specific, legally binding limitations on emissions of greenhouse gases. In 1998 President Bill Clinton signed the Kyoto Protocol but did not submit it to a hostile, Republican-led Senate. In March 2001 the George W. Bush administration rejected the Kyoto Protocol, citing perceived threats to economic growth and exemptions on emissions provided to India and China. Although the overwhelming majority of nations in the world signed the Kyoto Protocol, the absence of US support was a damaging blow to global cooperation on climate change.

Polling data showed that more Americans consistently ranked climate change as a lower priority than many other global issues. Beginning decades ago with defense of the tobacco industry, a small group of credentialed hired guns, supported by corporations and private foundations, lobbied with remarkable success to discredit verified scientific evidence on a series of health and environmental issues. After long denying the relationship between smoking and cancer, these debunkers of peer reviewed scientific knowledge also denied the discovery of a hole in the ozone layer as well as pollution from acid rain. Finally, they long asserted that global warming and climate change were natural rather than human caused phenomena and in any case did not pose much of a threat. The US media, including top newspaper and television networks, members of Congress, and corporate lobbyists promoted the junk science of denial despite a broad and today overwhelming scientific consensus on human causation of climate change.

The Obama administration showed leadership on climate change, as the United States reduced its greenhouse gas emissions and urged other countries to follow its example. Despite these efforts by 2014—officially the hottest year ever recorded on the planet—global greenhouse emissions were still increasing, though by this time polls showed about three-fourths of the US public had accepted the scientific consensus on climate change. US environmental planners meanwhile sought to address the concerns of developing countries through financial incentives and assistance in an effort to promote clean energy development. Speaking at the UN-sponsored "Climate Summit" in New York in September 2014 Obama called for immediate action—"not next year, or the year after, but right now, because no nation can meet this global threat alone."

Progress toward shifting from fossil fuels to cleaner sources of energy remained halting and problematic despite Obama's efforts to encourage wind, solar, and other alternatives. Development of alternative energy sources could not keep up with global demand, which was expected to increase by as much as a third from 2010 to 2030. By that year forecasters still expected about three-fourths of the world's energy to come from carbon-based fossil fuels. Like the shift from coal to oil in the industrial era, the transition to cleaner energy was expected to be slow and halting. Putting aside accidents at Three Mile Island in Pennsylvania (1973) and Chernobyl (1986), proponents called for renewed emphasis on nuclear energy, but the meltdown in March 2011 of the Fukushima Daiichi complex in Japan as a result of a massive tsunami served as a reminder of the risks of reliance on nuclear energy, and of the growing intensity of storms in the era of climate change.

Thus for the foreseeable future temperatures will continue to rise with sweeping consequences including volatile weather, erosion of coastlines, depletion of plant and animal species, and declining conditions of life for millions of people. After failures at Rio and Copenhagen (2009), and with another UN-sponsored climate summit scheduled in Paris in 2015, the need for US global leadership and action on climate change had never been greater. The Obama administration was ready to go forward but continued to face stiff opposition from deniers, energy lobbyists, and their myriad backers in the US Congress. Meaningful efforts to address climate change also required the cooperation of other nations especially China, which had displaced the United States as the world's leading consumer of energy and greatest contributor to greenhouse gas emissions, as well the other three BRIC countries.

Successful efforts to combat ozone depletion and to promote cleaner air and purer water showed that effective environmental action was possible when political will could be mobilized. Whether the world with the United States still in the lead could summon that will remained to be seen.

Conclusions

US foreign policy is a vast and complex subject posing significant challenges for any effort at overarching conclusions. Nonetheless some major themes stand out over the history of US diplomacy and should be addressed. The United States has a long history of intervention in other nations' affairs, including a willingness to arm and finance repressive regimes. The nation regularly resorts to war. Interventionist foreign policy often leads to resentment and blowback, as in the September 11 attacks and the global terror wars. It also leads to the growth of secrecy and the erosion of civil liberties.

The United States needs to show more global leadership in seeking non-violent solutions to international problems. Given the interconnectedness of the planet and the inevitability of future challenges to US global supremacy Americans must make greater efforts to work with other countries as well as the UN, NGOs, and business entities in seeking out multilateral solutions to global problems. The shift away from unilateralism requires understanding that while American exceptionalism serves as a force of national unity on the home front, it can become destructive when carried abroad. While adopting greater humility in foreign affairs Americans should also reexamine perceptions of other peoples, avoiding racial, religious, gendered, and other stereotypes that can serve to promote conflict.

Interventionist foreign policy invariably flows from the highly subjective justification that "national interests" require it. There are other ways to pursue national interests, however, notably through the powerful appeal of American democratic traditions and the allure of the nation's consumer and popular culture. The United States has dramatically underestimated the appeal of soft power, which arguably has done far more to win "hearts and minds" than foreign intervention. The United States has fought long destructive military conflict in Vietnam, waged an aggressive cold war for decades, and as of 2015 remained mired in the inconclusive global terror wars. None of these interventions succeeded. The end of the cold war came not from decades of military interventions all over the world, but rather because the peoples of the former Soviet Empire chose the model of representative government and US-led Western consumer culture over the Kremlin-backed communist system. In sum, Americans should have much more faith in soft power and much less faith in foreign interventions.

Perhaps the most severe challenge the United States confronts in any effort to reform its external relations is to rein in vested interests and the sprawling national security bureaucracy. Today's military–industrial complex dwarfs in power and influence the one that so concerned President Eisenhower in 1961. The military and national security industry is highly profitable and thus garners the support of corporations, powerful lobbies, generals and politicians who migrate between government service, political think tanks, and defense industries. Unless profound regulatory changes are made, the United States may well continue down the path of a warfare state.

Ironically, the US penchant for intervention and warfare undermines the very exceptionalism that is often invoked to justify it. Americans would do well to remember the advice of John Quincy Adams, who in his address on July 4, 1821 warned against the nation seeking out "monsters to destroy." America should, he advised, be "the well-wisher to the freedom and independence of all [but] the champion and vindicator only of her own." The United States should lead through "the benignant sympathy of her example" rather than becoming embroiled "beyond the power of extrication, in all the wars of interest and intrigue, of individual avarice, envy, and ambition." Through such interventions US foreign policy would "insensibly change from *liberty* to *force*." In such circumstances the nation would risk becoming "the dictatress of the world" and "no longer the ruler of her own spirit."

Select Bibliography

Nadkarni, Vidya and Noonan, Norma. *Emerging Powers in Comparative Perspective: The Political and Economic Rise of the BRIC Countries*. New York: Bloomsbury, 2013.

Dorsey, Kurkpatrick. *The Dawn of Conservation Diplomacy: U.S.-Canadian Wildlife Protection Treaties in the Progressive Era*. Seattle: University of Washington Press, 1998.

Oreskes, Naomi and Conway, Erik M. *Merchants of Doubt: How a Handful of Scientists Obscured the Truth on Issues from Tobacco Smoke to Global Warming*. New York: Bloomsbury Press, 2010.

Yergin, Daniel. *The Quest: Energy, Security, and the Remaking of the Modern World*. New York: Penguin Books, 2012.

McKibben, Bill. *Eaarth: Making a Life on a Tough New Planet*. New York: Times Books, 2010.

Johnson, Chalmers. *The Sorrow of Empire: Militarism, Secrecy, and the End of the Republic*. New York: Henry Holt, 2005.

Acronyms

ABM—anti-ballistic missile
AEC—Atomic Energy Commission
AEF—American Expeditionary Force
AFC—America First Committee
AIPAC—American Israel Public Affairs Committee
ANC—African National Congress
ANZUS—Australia, New Zealand, United States Security Treaty
ARVN—Army of the Republic of Vietnam
ASEAN—Association of Southeast Asian Nations
BRIC—Brazil, Russia, India, and China
CENTO—Central Treaty Organization
CIA—Central Intelligence Agency
CPA—Coalition Provisional Authority (Iraq)
CPUSA—Communist Party of the United States of America
CSA—Confederate States of America
DEFCON 3—Defense Condition 3
DHS—Department of Homeland Security
DIA—Defense Intelligence Agency
DRV—Democratic Republic of Vietnam
ERP—European Recovery Program
EU—European Union
FARC—Revolutionary Armed Forces of Colombia
FBI—Federal Bureau of Investigation
FSLN—Sandinista National Liberation Front
GDR—German Democratic Republic
GNP—Gross National Product
GWOT—global war on terror
HCMT—Ho Chi Minh Trail
HCUA—House Committee on Un-American Activities
ICBM—intercontinental ballistic missile
ICC—International Criminal Court
IED—improvised explosive device
IMF—International Monetary Fund

INF—Intermediate Nuclear Force
IRA—Indian Removal Act
IRA—Irish Republican Army
ISIS—Islamic State in Iraq and Syria
ISS—Inter-service Intelligence Agency (Pakistan)
ITT—International Telephone and Telegraph
JCS—Joint Chiefs of Staff
LTBT—Limited Test Ban Treaty
MAD—mutually assured destruction
MFN—most favored nation (trade status)
MIA—missing in action
MIC—military–industrial complex
MIRV—multiple independently targeted reentry vehicle
MIT—Massachusetts Institute of Technology
MPLA—Popular Movement for the Liberation of Angola
NAACP—National Association for the Advancement of Colored People
NAFTA—North American Free Trade Act
NASA—National Aeronautical and Space Administration
NATO—North Atlantic Treaty Organization
NGO—non-governmental organization
NLF—National Liberation Front
NMD—nuclear missile defense
NPA—New People's Army
NPT—Non-Proliferation Treaty
NSA—National Security Agency
NSC—National Security Council
OAS—Organization of American States
OPEC—Organization of Petroleum Exporting Countries
OT—occupied territories
PAVN—People's Army of Vietnam
PKI—Communist Party of Indonesia
PLO—Palestine Liberation Organization
PMF—private military firm
POW—prisoner-of-war
PRC—People's Republic of China
R&D—research and development
R&R—rest and recuperation
RFE—Radio Free Europe
ROC—Republic of China
ROK—Republic of Korea
RPF—Rwandan Patriotic Front
RVN—Republic of Vietnam
SALT—Strategic Arms Limitation Talks
SANE—National Committee for a Sane Nuclear Policy
SDI—Strategic Defense Initiative

SDS—Students for a Democratic Society
SEATO—Southeast Asia Treaty Organization
SFRC—Senate Foreign Relations Committee
SORT—Strategic Offensive Reductions Treaty
START—Strategic Arms Reduction Talks
SWAPO—Southwest African People's Organization
UN—United Nations
USIA—United States Information Agency
USSR—Union of Soviet Socialist Republics
WIB—War Industries Board
WILPF—Women's International League for Peace and Freedom
WMD—weapons of mass destruction
WSP—Women Strike for Peace
WTO—World Trade Organization
YMCA—Young Men's Christian Association

Index